Contents

Tables

NORTH AMERICA

The Historical Geography of

a Changing Continent

Second Edition

EDITED BY

THOMAS F. MCILWRAITH AND **EDWARD K. MULLER**

ROWMAN & LITTLEFIELD PUBLISHERS, INC.
Lanham • Boulder • New York • Oxford

ROWMAN & LITTLEFIELD PUBLISHERS, INC.

Published in the United States of America
by Rowman & Littlefield Publishers, Inc.
4720 Boston Way, Lanham, Maryland 20706
www.rowmanlittlefield.com

12 Hid's Copse Road
Cumnor Hill, Oxford OX2 9JJ, England

Copyright © 2001 by Rowman & Littlefield Publishers, Inc.

Distributed by NATIONAL BOOK NETWORK

British Library Cataloguing in Publication Information Available

Library of Congress Cataloging-in-Publication Data

North America : the historical geography of a changing continent / [edited by] Thomas F. McIlwraith and Edward K. Muller.—2nd ed.
    p. cm.
   Includes bibliographical references and index.
   ISBN 0-7425-0018-7 (alk. paper). — ISBN 0-7425-0019-5 (pbk. : alk. paper)
   1. North America—Historical geography.   I. McIlwraith, Thomas F.   II. Muller, Edward K.

  E40.5.N69   2001
  911'.7—dc21   2001019876

Printed in the United States of America

Figures

Preface

The publication of *North America: The Historical Geography of a Changing Continent* in 1987 responded, in the words of the original editors, Robert D. Mitchell and Paul A. Groves, "to a felt need in the discipline for an up-to-date, comprehensive treatment of the evolving geography of North America during the past four centuries." Although the first edition of *North America* admirably fulfilled its editors' goals, suggestions for improvement led to the planning in 1996 of a second edition. However, just as a few new and revised chapters began to arrive in the mail, events conspired to derail the project. Paul Groves died unexpectedly in January 1997, and Bob Mitchell retired a year later. At Bob's suggestion, Susan McEachern of Rowman & Littlefield asked us to assume the editing of the second edition. After encountering some difficulty in recovering and assembling extant materials, and with the generous patience of authors who doubted if their chapters would ever be published, we have completed a second edition that retains the strengths of the original volume and addresses many of its shortcomings.

Readers of the first edition of *North America* will recognize the chronological structure and emphasis on the formation and growth of North American regions, as well as many of the chapters. Most of the familiar chapters have been revised, some thoroughly. Jeanne Kay Guelke, for example, so extensively revised chapter 12, "The Far West, 1840–1920," that she now shares authorship with the original author, David Hornbeck. Kenneth C. Martis wrote a new chapter, "The Geographical Dimensions of a New Nation, 1780s–1820s," to replace the original one on the topic. Six new chapters have been added. Those by John C. Hudson, Richard S. Harris, and Edward K. Muller bolster examination of the 20th century through discussion of rural and urban topics. Two other chapters at the end of the second edition have been crafted to address specifically the student audience of this book. Along with these new chapters, new maps have been added and original ones redrawn.

The book has been written primarily for upper-division undergraduate and beginning graduate students. Some members of the general public will find much of interest as well. Scholars often find it difficult to write for such an audience, for they know colleagues will read their essays, too. This apprehension can lead to more scholarly expression than is desirable. We asked authors to revise their chapters with the goal of making them more accessible to the target audience. In addition, Ronald E. Grim, Thomas A. Rumney, and Thomas F. McIlwraith fashioned a chapter to guide students to the basic sources, including websites, for starting research into the historical geography of North America.

The more than 20 chapters of this new edition display a variety of approaches and sources for inquiry into past geographies. Despite the enormous scope of this volume, some important themes are not the subject of any individual chapter. Historic preservation of the landscape, for example, is regrettably not covered. More importantly, perhaps, the tremendous temporal expanse and cultural diversity of Native settlement before the arrival of Europeans to the continent proved difficult to capture adequately in one chapter; students will find discussions of native peoples, mostly after European contact, in several chapters. A similar comment can be made for the issues of race and gender in the historical geography of North America. Further, new trends in scholarship since 1987 are enriching our understanding of the past. We asked Anne Kelly Knowles to close the second edition with a brief chapter that describes for students these challenging directions.

The completion of this second edition of *North America* involved the assistance of many people. Our first acknowledgment must be to the original editors, Paul and Bob, who conceived of the first edition, brought it to fruition, and set into motion the process for a second edition. Then, we must thank our authors for kindly interrupting their work without complaint, at least that we heard, in order to revisit manuscripts that had sat unattended while the project was in limbo. Byron Moldofsky at the University of Toronto has done an excellent job of revising maps on a limited budget. We also appreciate the efforts of readers of chapters, including Van Beck Hall, University of Pittsburgh; Conrad Heidenreich, York University; Steven Hoelscher, University of Texas; Adrienne Hood, University of Toronto; David Meyer, Brown University; Don Mitchell, Syracuse University; Arthur Ray, University of British Columbia; Randy Widdis, University of Regina; and Graeme Wynn, University of British Columbia. We are most appreciative of the excellent editorial support from Cheryl Hoffman, Lynn Weber, and Matt Hammon down the home stretch. Finally, we express our gratitude to Susan McEachern for sticking with this project when all must surely have seemed doomed, then helping us revive it, and answering question after question and working out new arrangements. In our view, the profession owes her a great deal of thanks for seeing that the new *North America: The Historical Geography of a Changing Continent* is available to another generation of students.

Thomas F. McIlwraith
Edward K. Muller
Toronto and Pittsburgh
April 2001

PART I

INTRODUCTION

The Muses care so little for geography.

Oscar Wilde, *Sententiae*

We shall not get far if we limit ourselves in any way as to human time in our studies. Either we must admit the whole span of man's existence or abandon the expectation of major results from human geography. Either we must produce or warm over what others have prepared. I see no alternative. From all the earth in all the time of human existence, we build a retrospective science, which out of this experience acquires an ability to look ahead.

Carl O. Sauer, foreword to *Historical Geography*

The old past is dying, its force weakening, and so it should. Indeed [we] should speed it on its way, for it was compounded by bigotry, of national vanity, of class domination. . . . May history step into its shoes, help to sustain man's confidence in his destiny, and create for us a new past, as exact as we can make it, that will help us achieve our identity.

J. H. Plumb, *The Death of the Past*

The North American Past:
Retrospect and Prospect

ROBERT D. MITCHELL

This book is about a place that was not supposed to exist. Fifteenth-century European views of the world had inherited from Ptolemy and the ancient geographers the idea that the earth as the home of humankind comprised the three continents of Europe, Africa, and Asia; that the world was latitudinally symmetrical (comprising a torrid zone bordered successively by temperate and frigid zones); and that it was occupied by many strange peoples (mostly uncivilized because they lacked Christianity and urban life). The landscapes and societies Columbus encountered in the Caribbean in October 1492 hardly matched previously recorded descriptions of Japan and eastern China. Yet it is doubtful that Columbus fully appreciated his discovery of a world that was not simply another appendage of Asia.

It did become clear, however, as the delineation of a new continental mass took shape during the 16th century, that the Spaniards who followed Columbus had identified the central and southern parts of their newly claimed territory as being of most interest to them. The area that has become known as North America was considered to be of little consequence. It presented the appearance of a sparsely populated territory occupied by Native societies that had created none of the grandeur and offered none of the resource potential of the Aztec-Maya and the Incas. Yet during the last 400 years this least promising part of the New World has been transformed, in the culture-bound terms of the development specialist, from one of the world's most backward areas into its most advanced: a dynamic world comprising two vast political units, Canada and the United States, that have created the earth's most materially successful postindustrial societies of over 300 million inhabitants. The task of the historical geographers in this book is to explore and to understand this remarkable creation.

THE NORTH AMERICAN PAST: RETROSPECT

"Past" and "present" are simplified notions of our conceptions of time. If the past is indeed prologue to the present, the present is continually reshaping the past as new ideas, approaches, and information allow us to produce an improved retrieval of previous human conditions. Time, therefore, is the exclusive domain of no single set of practitioners, although in the Western world historians generally have been viewed as the special guardians of the human past. Earth-space, similarly, is a concept fundamental to many organized branches of endeavor. The geographer's principal claim to this domain rests on elucidating the relationships that exist between people and place as they are reflected in locational, environmental, distributional, and regional expressions. The primary concern of the historical geographer is to study how and why these expressions persist and change in place and over space through time. The hope is to create a more historically informed human geography, a more accurate context against which to gauge the complex content of the present.

Retrieving the past, however, is an exceedingly difficult task and one that, even in its most detailed form, can hope to reconstruct only a small fraction of human actions and events.

What was "prospect" in 1987, when this chapter first appeared, has become the most recent part of "prospect" by the time of publication of this second edition in 2001. Rather than change the text and compromise Mitchell's particular writing style, the editors have chosen to let his observations stand as originally written. For an overview of developments in historical geography since 1987, readers may turn to chapter 21; there Anne Knowles presents the prospects for historical geography into the 21st century.

Retrieving the past geographically has been the task of a mere handful of geographers at any given time, and they have always been greatly outnumbered by historians. Historical geography until very recently, therefore, was influenced enormously by a few unusually creative individuals who have had distinctive ideas about the uses of the past.

Early Uses of the Past

The professionalization of knowledge in a North American context began during the last third of the 19th century as the academic world reorganized its structure and its curricula. This reorganization occurred within the framework of a post-Darwinian world dominated by the perspective of the natural sciences and by the presumed closing of the American settlement frontier. In history, the first generation of American professional historians began to replace 19th-century views of the past as the exemplification of Western ideas of progress with approaches that rested on more empirical and systematic foundations. Shortly thereafter, a group of Canadian historians, known as the Laurentian school because of their interests in the impact of the Canadian (or Laurentian) Shield land and landscape on human settlement, began to redefine the Canadian past.

Geographers, trained almost exclusively in the natural sciences, had a different use for the past. Their principal concern was to elucidate what they believed to be the immutable relationship between humanity and the biophysical environment. The relationship for them was primarily one of the direct, or almost direct, control of this environment over human actions and human distributions, and the limitations thus placed upon human behavior. It seemed logical to them to look for these environmental forces in the past as well as in the present. The American past became the vehicle for testing their ideas rather than a subject of study in its own right. Despite some common concerns in the everyday affairs of society, the association between geographers and historians remained superficial. Such ideas as the presumed causal connection between the siting of major Atlantic seaboard cities (Philadelphia, Baltimore, Washington, and Richmond, for example) and the location of falls and rapids on major eastward-flowing rivers and the theory that the seemingly impenetrable barrier of the Appalachians "forced" late-colonial settlements to remain east of the mountains were promulgated in works, such as Ellen C. Semple's *American History and Its Geographic Conditions* (1903), that were influenced by current geographical thought in Europe. Not only did these so-called environmental determinists base their work on assumptions that were highly questionable from a scientific point of view, but they also approached the past in terms of the physical setting of human activities rather than from the viewpoint of the human participants themselves, and they used as evidence the secondary sources of historians and others rather than the primary sources generated by past societies. It is understandable, therefore, that most historians dismissed their conclusions as being simplistic, extreme, and ultimately ahistorical.

Neither Semple (1863–1932) nor her contemporaries were determinists in the strictest sense. That such a label can prove somewhat misleading over time may be observed in the research and teaching of Harlan H. Barrows at the University of Chicago, in one of the first geography departments in North America. Barrows (1877–1960) began in the early Semple mold, gradually toned down environmental "controls" to "influences," and by the early 1920s was advocating geography as human ecology. Nevertheless, the basic assumptions of such an approach increasingly were called into question by the first generation of geographers not trained solely in the natural sciences.

Alternative Uses of the Past

The most direct challenge to the deterministic perspective came during the early 1920s from the young Carl Sauer at the University of California at Berkeley. He excited his colleagues with the suggestion that human geography should focus not on the presumed effects of the natural setting but on the processes whereby human beings had altered patterns of land use and distributions of living forms on the earth's surface (an approach to which he had been introduced in Germany). Sauer's particular contribution was to present the subject as the impact of culture on nature and to examine how "natural landscapes" were transformed into "cultural landscapes." Culture, in Sauer's view, was as much a genetic or historical concept as a functional one. Human geography was thus historical geography writ large, because one needed to understand how societies had created different cultural patterns from place to place in terms of their origins, evolution, and spread.

Sauer (1889–1975) influenced many of his 37 doctoral students and other contemporaries, during a period of more than 50 years of teaching and research, to approach the past as a fertile field for studying culture history. He introduced new concepts to the geographer's repertoire—culture traits and complexes, diffusion, cultural landscape, and culture area, for example—and traced many genetic themes (such as the origins and spread of cultures, the introduction of plants and animals to new environments, and the destruction of natural habitats) over long periods of time. Sauer encouraged studies grounded in fieldwork and in prehistory: fire as a tool in landscape change, the origins of agriculture in the New World, and the diffusion of Native American traits. The breadth of Sauer's own interests can be appreciated in two collections of essays, *Land and Life* (1963) and *Selected Essays 1963–1975* (1981). Some of his hypotheses were almost impossible to verify, and he and his students often had more in common with the anthropologist and the archeologist than with the historian. Their work was distinctively genetic, empirical, diffusionist, materialist (concentrating on tangible culture traits), and diachronic (viewing time "vertically" rather than as "horizontal" cross sections) and in many respects ran counter to what was later to become a more accepted historical geography firmly based on the written historical record.

Despite Sauer's enormous influence, and indeed the modifications he made in his own interests and ideas during the last 15 years of his life, the culture history approach came in for increasing criticism after the 1950s. It was based on historicism (phenomena to be comprehended only through tracing their origins and development); it was nontheoretical and noncomparative; it was overly diffusionist (to the relative exclusion of other processes); and it was focused on preindustrial societies (to the neglect of urban-industrial processes and phenomena). But the most penetrating criticism has been that it was overly materialist and neglected "the inner workings of culture," the formation of the habits, beliefs, attitudes, values, and institutions behind the practices, actions, and phenomena themselves. The concept of the cultural landscape, for example, was ambiguous because it involved not only the content in the landscape but also the perception of that content. In the past few years, however, as historians in particular have penetrated deeper into the North American past, there has been renewed interest in Sauer's ideas about European exploration and colonization, culture contact, and habitat modification, as he articulated them in his later studies.

At least three other approaches to the past that were contemporaneous with Sauer's views also influenced how geographers dealt with time and place: Derwent Whittlesey's refinement of the concept of sequent occupance; John K. Wright's mapping interests and advocacy of historical geosophy; and Ralph H. Brown's concern with reconstructing past geographies.

The notion of occupance, or settlement, of an area has been a long-standing theme in human geography. Derwent Whittlesey (1890–1956), who was trained in history and geography and taught for most of his career at Harvard University, had interests in regional and political geography as well as in historical studies. What intrigued him most by the late 1920s and early 1930s was the study of "chronology in place" rather than the geography of past times; that is, the idea of the sequential stages of occupance that he believed had occurred in all places over time. American geography had entered a period dominated by economic and regional studies, and Whittlesey's refinement of the sequent occupance concept by emphasizing place, land use, and economic activities made it acceptable to many geographers interested in regional description and classification. Geographers added a "historical" dimension to what were primarily regional studies. Every settled area in North America, it was assumed, had undergone a series of sequential landscape changes as different groups of people at progressively more complex stages of development had occupied it. The geographer's task was to identify, describe, and reconstruct these stages by the landscape features that typified each stage at particular cross sections in time. California, for example, could be examined in terms of its Native American, Spanish Mexican, or early and later American stages of occupance, each with its own distinctive human patterns.

When such general ideas were put into practice, however, several problems arose. Most damaging was the fact that neither the concept of areal or regional variation nor that of change through time was dealt with adequately. It became apparent that the sequent occupance concept was best suited to areas where the basic settlement features had persisted over substantial periods of time. Where change was rapid, problems of transition between, and overlapping of, stages occurred, and little allowance was made for differential rates of change of specific phenomena such as population, land use, and settlement. Few studies, moreover, paid much attention to making connections between stages; process was believed to be implicit in stage; and factors producing change between cross-sectional reconstructions were generally inferred rather than analyzed. Internal regional differences were also slighted because the concept emphasized the dominant landscape elements that gave character to an area rather than how phenomena varied from place to place within the area. Each area delimited was viewed discretely without reference to other areas, and changes induced from outside the area tended to be regarded as aberrations.

Despite further experimentation and modification during the 1930s and early 1940s, the concept of sequent occupance proved to be an oversimplification of both temporal change and areal variation. Yet it continued to appear in unpublished theses well into the 1960s. One modification that did have short-term significance was the idea of "relict features" of previous occupance stages surviving in later landscapes. The method employed here was retrospective—that is, it worked backward in time and traced these elements to their historical contexts. It was seldom easy to identify specific phenomena with specific contexts, and it was also clear that the past influenced its future in more important ways than by leaving material residues. Further experimentation with the whole idea ended in the 1950s.

John K. Wright's contributions were of a more diffuse character. Trained in both geography and history, Wright (1891–1969) spent most of his career on the staff of the American Geographical Society in New York and thus had few opportunities to train students. He made three enduring contributions to the understanding of the North American past. First, he became involved in editing the society's publications, one of which was the historian C. O. Paullin's massive *Atlas of the Historical Geography of the United States* (1932), a collection of maps depicting the history of the United States and arranged in episodic cross sections. Although the work is now much dated, the sections dealing with the 19th century have yet to be superseded. Wright's three-year involvement with this project has been acknowledged in the profession by the work's being referred to simply as "the Paullin and Wright" atlas. Second, Wright was one of the first geographers to advocate the importance of studying the perceptions and worldviews that societies entertained about peoples and places in the past—"human nature in geography," as it came to be identified. His views of geography as a subjective, humanistic discipline were not much heeded at the time and were overshadowed by the views of Sauer and his students. Not until the more sympathetic environment of the 1960s was the prescience of Wright's suggestions appreciated. Third, Wright made a plea for a fusion of historical geography and the history of geography, a kind of historical "geosophy," as he termed it. For Wright the link between the two endeavors was exploration and the growth of geographical knowledge and ideas through time, because they again involved "terrae incognitae: the place of imagination in geography"—the context within which all geographical study should be undertaken.

Between the early 1930s and the 1950s geography in North America became identified increasingly with regional, functional, and morphological studies that had a distinct predilection for field-oriented and applied techniques grounded firmly in the present. The distinction between geography and history was clear. Geography was a discipline concerned with identifying the areal association and differentiation of phenomena distributed over the earth's surface (chorology). History was a discipline that dealt exclusively with the past (chronology). Studying a past period as geography was a permissible if rather odd practice, despite the historical tradition within the discipline, but one that had little substantive contribution to make to geography as a whole. It was in this atmosphere that Ralph H. Brown worked to put the study of the North American past on a sounder historiographic basis.

Trained as an economic and regional geographer, Brown (1898–1948) began his historical research at the University of Minnesota, where, because of the absence of an organized graduate program during his tenure, he had no students to continue his work directly. His early studies, during the late 1920s and early 1930s, were characterized by the use of the sequent occupance concept and the employment of historical maps in conducting regional studies of Colorado and adjacent areas of the Great Plains. By the mid-1930s, however, he had shifted his interests to the eastern seaboard and to the use of early maps in clarifying the area's settlement history. Yet a visit to a variety of libraries and repositories along the East Coast convinced him that insufficient primary data were available to reconstruct the geography of early America until after 1790. (Herman Friis was to prove him wrong by publishing his meticulously constructed monograph, *A Series of Population Maps of the Colonies and the United States, 1625–1790,* in 1940.) Instead, Brown examined the materials available for the 1790–1810 period and decided to write a geographical description of the seaboard as it might have appeared to a Philadelphia geographer in 1810. He published the study in 1943 as *Mirror for Americans: Likeness of the Eastern Seaboard, 1810.* Methodologically, the work represented something of a dead end: it dealt with only a brief cross section in time; it was highly imaginary; and it used only sources available before 1810. Literally, however, it has become a geographical classic. Independently Brown had taken Wright's suggestion for the use of imagination in geography to its logical conclusion; he made extensive use of primary source materials, and he has given us a vivid portrait of a place in time.

The problem remained, however, for geographers to deal adequately with examining, in a dynamic manner, changes within and between places through time. Brown addressed this issue directly in his last major work, *Historical Geography of the United States,* published in 1948 shortly after his death. It was the first attempt to provide a comprehensive reconstruction of the geography of the United States in past times using both secondary and primary sources. Brown divided his text into six parts: the colonization period; the Atlantic seaboard at the opening of the 19th century; the Ohio River and the lower Great Lakes region to 1830; the new Northwest, 1820–70; the Great Plains and bordering regions to 1870; and the area from the Rocky Mountains to the Pacific Coast to 1870. He began by reminding the reader, as he had done in *Mirror for Americans,* that people have always been "influenced as much by beliefs as by facts." By using contemporary eyewitness accounts and early maps within the context of more general narrative description, Brown believed, such past perceptions could be identified. He created an elaborate series of regional geographies, paying close attention to diversity within and between areas as he progressed westward across the country. The work was clearly more selective than comprehensive; more than one-third of the space is devoted to the early eastern seaboard, and there is little reference to the seaboard, the South, or the Middle West after the early 19th century. The study, moreover, ends in the last quarter of that century, perhaps reflecting less the possibility that Brown ran out of time than his apparent conviction that there were two "pasts"—past geographies that could be reconstructed by the methods of historical geography and a more recent antecedent past that could be incorporated in the geography of the present.

Revised Uses of the Past

Ralph Brown's contributions to the understanding of the North American past on its own terms might have been pushed aside eventually by the increasing ahistorical bias of the discipline if one of his younger contemporaries, a Canadian named Andrew H. Clark, had not taken the reins and proceeded aggressively during the 1950s and 1960s to make a powerful case for historical studies in geography. Exposed to training in mathematics, economic history, and geography at the University of Toronto before completing his doctorate under Sauer at Berkeley in 1944, Clark (1911–75) established at the University of Wisconsin the foundations of a historical geography in North America not only as a perspective in geography but also as a recognizable subfield with its own distinctive procedures and scholarly contributions.

In 1954 Clark authored a committee report on historical geography as part of a larger inventory of geography during the first half of the 20th century. The report was more of a plea for a historical geography to be than a survey of a proud lineage of past achievements. Clark could point only to the work of Brown, Wright, himself, a few others, and, with some ambivalence, Sauer and his students as elements on which to build a revised and improved use of the past. Thirteen years later, in 1967, Cole Harris, one of Clark's students, made a similar plea for Canada. Asked to survey the Canadian scene, Harris bemoaned the fact that little substantive research had been done since the 1930s and that most of it was hidden in unpublished theses. With few achievements to discuss, he suggested the outlines of a research program that could rejuvenate historical geography in the future. When Clark again reviewed the progress in historical geography throughout North America five years later, in 1972, the tone of his presentation was more confident. Not only could he point to a proliferation of new studies of the past, but he could also present the published achievements of many of his 19 doctoral students.

The transformation that occurred in the renewed interest in the North American past between the early 1950s and the early 1970s can be attributed in part to Clark's leadership in teaching and research. His enduring contribution was to build upon Brown's historiographic predilections and to impart an appreciation of high-quality scholarship, thorough empirical research, the importance of both archival and field methods, current historiographic issues, and, above all, the value of geography. Clark had already been well trained in historical methods before going to Berkeley and was thus less influenced by some of Sauer's cultural history ideas than were his contemporaries. He proceeded to create one of the first coherent programs of publishable work in historical geography. He was to devote most of his own research to elucidating the geographical outcomes of European colonization in maritime Canada. In 1960 he argued before an audience of economic historians for greater cooperation between the two subdisciplines and for historians to recognize the importance of "geographical change through time," a concept he defined generally as the study of continually changing geographies revealed through changing patterns and relationships between phenomena in and through areas. He made a more explicit statement on how this was to be achieved than had been done earlier: by examining the locational aspects of change itself (the mapping of change); by measuring

rates of change; by identifying the distribution of individually significant phenomena; by appreciating the multiple functions of phenomena; and by identifying the important interactive processes involved. This statement of his approach to the past was designed to go beyond previously stated views of historical geography as the reconstruction of past geographies, whether as the tracing of genetic cultural themes, temporal cross sections, or the geography of a past period. The emphasis needed to be placed on a more analytical approach to geographical change itself.

This was an ambitious program indeed and one that Clark himself could not always live up to, because it forced him out of the regional historical-geographical framework that continued to be his basic approach to the past. This tension can be seen in his two books on Canada. In *Three Centuries and the Island* (1959), Clark chose Prince Edward Island as the laboratory for a very intensive study of geographical change, one that traced patterns of rural settlement and land use through five successive eras by means of a series of temporal cross sections and the use of 155 maps of distributions and areal characteristics. He thus had addressed already his suggestions of identifying the locational aspects of change and the distribution of individual phenomena, and trying to measure change. His *Acadia: The Geography of Nova Scotia to 1760* (1968) also was an intensive case study, but its intent was to provide a sequential presentation of development over a 125-year period and to integrate a systematic treatment of relevant topics into the time frame. The focus was again on colonization and the formation of rural localities in new environments, with considerable attention to the statistical presentation of change but with much less attention this time to measuring change through the comparative mapping of distributions at selected time periods. In a concluding section Clark attempted to view Nova Scotia within the larger historiography of Canada by evaluating the region with reference to the well-established frontier and metropolitan-dominance interpretations of Canadian development. The published result was recognized by Canadian historians as a prizewinning performance.

Yet major changes had occurred in geography in North America during the 1960s, making the *Acadia* study quite controversial. The basically empiricist world of pre-1960 geography had come under mounting criticism as the discipline was influenced increasingly by the emerging social sciences. A distinct shift was in progress toward the formation of a more analytical and systematic geography more concerned with the formulation of hypotheses, generalization, and the testing of theories. Historical geography was not immune to such changes, and Clark's work came in for criticism because it did not demonstrate these desired qualities. A younger generation of geographers, less exposed to the regional and cultural traditions of human geography but interested in historical problems, argued that Clark's work had avoided explicit generalization and had remained essentially inductive. For Clark, generalization was an end in itself and not to be indulged in lightly; rather, synthesis was the highest goal to which a geographer could aspire after careful compilation of conclusions derived from a number of case studies. More pointed was the argument that Clark had been unable to fill his prescription for confronting geographical change. What he had done was to quantify changes and modifications in certain features through maps and, by means of sequential comparisons, to identify the periodic results of change. But he had not really addressed the dynamics of change through time, because he had placed little emphasis on the processes themselves. As Donald Meinig has put it, Clark tended to be more interested in area than in process, in changing geographies than in geographical change. But he had helped to create a vigorous historical geography in North America and to provide a framework for the debate that was to ensue among young historical geographers, many of whom were of Canadian or British origin.

THE NORTH AMERICAN PAST: PROSPECT

The magnitude of change that occurred in historical geography in North America during the 1970s and 1980s was such that one might have difficulty relating its genealogy to its current status and practice. Some observers labeled the results a "new" historical geography fundamentally different in philosophy and practice from previous efforts. The trends, however, are often unclear, frequently contradictory, and subject to various interpretations. The aggregate changes,

for example, were confusing. The number of professional geographers with avowed interests in the subject increased substantially, especially in Canada; the number of publications grew, and in 1975 the first international journal devoted solely to the subject, the *Journal of Historical Geography,* appeared as a forum for scholarly communication. Yet the broader context within which geographical studies of the past were undertaken challenged this progress. Geography and history experienced considerable philosophical and methodological changes in the 1970s and emerged in the 1980s as more analytical and pluralistic disciplines. Trends in geography in the 1980s, for example, were toward increasing specialization, increased cross-disciplinary communication, and greater emphasis on technical applications and policy implications.

Historical geographers have derived much from these trends: trading ideas, concepts, and comparative themes with other disciplines; making wider use of statistical methods; developing, applying, and testing generalizations; and exploiting more explicit behavioral approaches to the past. But at the same time, they acquired a status that is marginal to the contemporary scientific and ahistorical character of geography, and they have been confronted with a larger cadre of historians who have assimilated geographical ideas and techniques and applied them to a broad range of problems, such as human-environment relations and landscape interpretation, long assumed to be the geographer's domain.

Approaches and Objectives

Historical geographers in North America rarely have devoted as much time as their western European (especially British) counterparts to philosophical discourse. Assumptions about objectives generally have been implicit rather than explicit, and most of the "founding fathers" avoided making overt philosophical or methodological statements. But trends in history and the social sciences in the 1970s and 1980s have forced a greater awareness of the need to examine basic assumptions underlying historical research in geography. Philosophy is important because it guides inquiry. How we approach the past will help us to determine whether and how we choose significant topics, frame insightful questions, identify current research problems or issues, formulate sound methodological procedures, identify relevant sources, and choose appropriate techniques. In general, most historical geographers would agree that the history of a place or of a population is embedded in its geography; that spatial structures and patterns are both a condition and a result of social and biophysical situations; and that the geography of change needs to be viewed in terms of both processes and effects. These assumptions underlie the geographical synthesis of North America that the essays in this book represent.

Yet the debate that ensued in North America during the 1970s over alternative approaches to the past originally was framed within the context of the opposing goals of synthesis and theory. Concepts rather than specific personnel became the driving force for progress in the discipline. Synthesis involved a humanistic, even particularistic, perspective that focused on comprehending the special character of places, regions, and landscapes as they persisted and changed in past periods. Theory involved the application of deductive models of geographical patterns to the past to identify process laws that provided explanations of the changing distribution of phenomena that were still present in the contemporary world. Regional historical geography, with its long lineage, seemed to contrast with a retrospective, theoretical geography that used the past for more current objectives. Later participants tended to exaggerate these distinctions and to identify a dichotomy between the particular interests of more "traditional" historical geographers, with their references to the distinctiveness and differentiation of places that were not capable of scientific testing, and the insights to be gained from "new" generic approaches, which involved the application of current principles and generalizations to examining everything from past geographical regularities to the perceptions of past landscapes. In this latter view, a genealogy of geographical uses of the past as traced earlier in this chapter was irrelevant or, if addressed, was employed as a purgative to indicate a habit of mind that should no longer exist.

The intellectual tension created was tempered by two factors that resulted in a reframing of positions by the early 1980s. First, it had become clear that geographical theory could not be separated from social theory. Attempts to comprehend spatial patterns as attributes of place proved inadequate because spatial arrangement and areal variation were not independent variables; they could not be explained in terms of their own formation independent of a cultural and social context. Second, contemporary theories of social behavior produced far-from-satisfactory explanations of current societies, thus making moot their wholesale application to past circumstances. If there were indeed historical regularities in patterns of behavior, there had also been fundamental changes. Defining the specific locational and environmental dimensions of this behavior and explaining long-term, secular changes in society and economy remained in their infancy. Distinctions between the range of perspectives on the past tended to be overdrawn, even while generalization had become a widely accepted goal throughout all branches of the discipline. Geographers interested in the past tend to generate historiographic generalities that are associated with interpreting and comparing studies within an increasing pool of knowledge about related places. Geographers more concerned with the contemporary world use concepts and principles from modern human geography and apply them to past situations to determine their general applicability. And those who profess interest in long-run developmental perspectives often employ reconstructions of past geographies as part of their analysis. The distinctions between "old" and "new" approaches to the past appeared less and less clear; all studies that involved a historical dimension could benefit from these philosophical and methodological exchanges.

Nevertheless, a contrast does remain between studies that use the past as the distinctive focus to be examined on its own terms and those that use the past selectively to explore the historical validity of current theories of human behavior. The former position maintains that one cannot comprehend the present without comprehending the past and that the applicability of current ideas needs to be evaluated for particular historical contexts. The latter position is more concerned with evaluating the universality of current processes in the past without necessary reference to the contextual framework within which the processes operate. The "historical" position is likely to produce a discussion of urban growth, for example, that takes note of current social and economic theory and adapts it discriminately to illuminate and explain the growth of a place or set of places during a particular period. The more "contemporary" approach to urban growth in the past would be to view it as a general process fully comprehensible in terms of current social and economic theory and needing few adjustments for particular places or periods.

Methodological Trends

Philosophy and methodology scarcely can be separated. The debates of the 1970s and 1980s have both created and been shaped by the increasing range and variety of our questions about the past. Among historical geographers in North America, methodological issues continue to generate more discussion than ideological issues. We operate differently today than we did before the early 1970s. First, we pay more attention to measuring and generalizing the geography of change itself. Second, we have humanized the past by incorporating social processes of behavior more firmly into our work. And third, we have redressed the topical imbalance in earlier studies by paying more attention to urban and industrial patterns. These trends, in turn, have forced us to rethink our ideas of time and periodicity, the scales at which we operate, the techniques we can use, and the sources we deem important.

Analyzing the Geography of Change

The fact that we can now approach the past more systematically and more analytically is the result primarily of expanding and reframing the line of questioning about change that Sauer and Clark began before 1960. First, we ask about origins—when and where a particular process or set of events began. We can then define the start of an occurrence and locate the appearance of phenomena. Second, we ask about sequence —what followed what in time and how this is related to the distribution of the phenomena. Third is the question of temporal and spatial structure—the order of the occurrence and distribution, and why the change happened in the sequence that it did. Fourth is the matter of timing—why things happened when and where they did and not at some other time or place. The last question is particularly important because it helps us not only to identify the fac-

tors producing change (the necessary conditions) but also to determine the minimum combination of these factors that might account for change (the sufficient conditions). Fifth, we must ask about duration and rate—how long the sequence lasted, how extensive the distribution became, and whether different elements changed at different rates. And, finally, we may need to address the question of magnitude or scope—whether the change occurred within a temporal and spatial system as a matter of degree (evolutionary or developmental) or instead involved a change in the entire system as a matter of kind (transformational or revolutionary). The initial colonization of North America by Europeans fits into the latter category, while later changes generally are interpreted within the former.

Historical geographers prior to the late 1960s, insofar as they studied processes in the past, largely focused on what they regarded as factors that would account for spatial patterns or regional distinctiveness without direct reference to behavioral considerations. We saw earlier how cultural geographers were being taken to task by the mid-1960s for failing to incorporate into their studies the deeper, mental aspects of culturally informed behavior. But when the change came in historical geography, it was less influenced by culture theory, which remains weakly developed, than by social and economic theory. We can demonstrate this with two examples: the revised synthesis of American cultural and social origins, and the rise of urban historical geography.

American Origins

The study of American origins and American regionalism is epitomized by the research contributions of Donald Meinig. Although Meinig, who received his graduate training at the University of Washington and who has spent most of his career at Syracuse University, has cut an independent path through the North American past, his approach effectively integrates the traditions of Sauer, Brown, and Clark. Meinig's interest in origins began, after a brief examination in the 1950s of the colonial era, with a study of the trans-Mississippi West. His research focused on processes of settlement and regional formation on a broad scale. His interpretations are characterized by a special interest in the creation of cultural regions and cultural landscapes, portrayed with a felicity of style and cartographic exposition seldom matched by his peers.

His study of the Mormon cultural region (1965) attempted to elucidate the origins and spread of one of America's most distinctive cultural groups from their hearth area of the Great Salt Lake basin in Utah. This was followed by *The Great Columbia Plain* (1968), a historical regional geography of the Palouse area of the Pacific Northwest between 1805 and 1910, which remained until the mid-1980s his most substantive contribution to understanding the shaping of North America. This rich and massive study of the settlement and resource development of what was to become one of the continent's principal wheat-producing areas combined Sauer's emphasis on cultural origins and diffusion with the regional historical concerns of both Brown and Clark, the field orientation of Sauer, and the primary source concerns of Clark. "The distinguishing mark of historical geography," Meinig wrote, "is its emphasis upon places rather than persons"—a position that he has maintained ever since. Meinig also turned his attention to the Southwest, which resulted in *Imperial Texas* (1969), an extended essay on the evolution of the state's cultural distinctiveness, and *Southwest: Three Peoples in Geographical Change 1600–1970* (1971), which he described as "a coherent picture of regional change" from the beginning of Spanish contact until the present. He later synthesized his ideas on the geographical emergence of the trans-Mississippi West in an essay entitled "American Wests: Preface to a Geographical Interpretation" (1972). Employing themes of population, culture, political organization, and interregional integration, Meinig considered his perspective and methodology applicable, with modification, to other areas of colonization.

When other geographers applied this approach to the origins and development of the American East, however, they found, as Wilbur Zelinsky did, that "the cultural gradients tend to be much steeper and the boundaries between regions more distinct than is true for the remainder of the continent. There is greater variety within a narrower range of space." Meinig himself was no stranger to America's colonial origins. He had contributed a sketch of the early American colonies in 1958 and chapters on the

historical geography of New York State in a book on regional geography in 1966. And, in 1978, he restated his research philosophy before the American Historical Association. Geographers needed to focus on two issues: culture hearths, which deal with why and where major cultural patterns and movements originate; and spatial diffusion, which is concerned with how these patterns and movements spread to other peoples and places. Some scholars continued the tradition of viewing American colonial origins in terms of culture hearths, spatial diffusion, and enduring cultural pluralism. But this approach came under increasing criticism by 1980 on the grounds that the scale of analysis is too broad, the attention to primary documentation too limited, the evidence from surviving cultural traits and landscape relicts too inconclusive, and the treatment of economic processes too simplistic.

When migration and dispersion are viewed in a more analytical fashion as a series of "creative interactions" in which settlers were faced with a number of functional alternatives, an alternative approach can be followed. The point of departure for exploring colonial origins need not be western Europe, but rather the Atlantic seaboard, where the initial encounters with a new world took place. What settlement and social characteristics actually emerged there can then provide clues for further inquiry. Who actually came, and precisely how and where did they settle?

Evidence from shipping records, as well as from county and parish records, has revealed that transatlantic migration was a more selective process than formerly recognized. Many settlers had been mobile geographically in their home territories prior to migration to America, making it difficult to determine their local cultural "source areas." Cultural transfer was associated also with the social context of settlement. Early New England, for example, was distinctive not only because most early settlers were "Puritans" but also because it was settled predominantly by families who had been formed long before emigration. Thus the creation of new, cohesive communities was more regular and continuous in New England than in the Chesapeake tidewater, where settlement and societal characteristics were dominated by commercial interests; high immigration rates of single, male indentured servants; and a slower process of societal formation. Moreover, the institution of slavery was not integrated into this Chesapeake system until 70 years after initial settlement, which contradicts the notion of some simultaneously forming "hearth" process.

An examination of the pioneering process at local county and township levels has revealed a more drastic cultural simplification than previous scholars had imagined. Institutional settings were pared initially to their bare essentials in the New World. Land was abundant and relatively easily acquired, resulting in widespread landownership, regardless of regional location. Both labor and capital were in short supply. While fixed capital emerged from the creation of productive farms and liquid capital appeared (theoretically) as surplus commodities were sold, labor shortages were endemic. The high costs of labor helped to create a variety of labor institutions to complement family labor: indentured servitude, periodic contractual wage labor, and eventual hereditary slavery. The complex interdigitation of free and slave labor revealed intricate patterns of internal differentiation within as well as between the so-called hearth regions. Rather than three initial regional divisions, basically there were two, a northern region of free labor with minor slave concentrations, and a southern region of substantial slave populations with significant proportions of alternative labor systems.

It has been suggested that the thesis of liberal individualism seems to fit best the particular actions of the early colonists. Settlers, regardless of cultural heritage, were almost everywhere motivated by values of property ownership, the overwhelming importance of individual and family interests, participation in a market-oriented economy, and social stability guaranteed by limited but benevolent governmental intrusions into private life. The most dramatic landscape effect was the virtual ubiquity of dispersed settlement based on the individual family farm. Moreover, an examination of land records to determine where and how settlers actually took up land has demonstrated that, although there was some group settlement, the dominant pattern was one of great intermixing of national and cultural groups. This provided a social environment within which a widespread sharing of commonly held goals and values led to a distinctive American worldview probably by the early 18th century.

Urban Historical Geography

Historical geographers prior to about 1970 operated within a narrow range of topical interests. Most studies dealt with three major topics: rural settlement and agriculture, regional distinctiveness and identity, and cultural origins and diffusion. The most dramatic growth in research and publication in the 1970s and 1980s, however, has been in urban and industrial topics and especially in exploring the relationships between large-scale immigration, urbanization, and industrialization during the 19th and early 20th centuries. The focus on such topics remains somewhat uneven, but urban historical geographers have developed two principal orientations: the evolution of cities in terms of internal spatial and social structure, and the emergence of city systems and the external relations of cities. These topical concerns also presented new methodological problems, because the processes of urban change and their spatial consequences seem less explicit and less enduring than those associated with rural and preindustrial North America. Change has been more rapid, more massive, and thus more dramatic.

Internal Evolution. The study of the internal geography of the city proceeded within the context of understanding the urban past from empirical studies, especially by social historians, and from the application of spatial concepts from contemporary human geography. Studies of population turnover in large northeastern cities during the second half of the 19th century have revealed rates of geographical mobility that were higher than those experienced during the 20th century. If this was indeed true, how had the formation of European immigrant and African American ghettos been made possible? Linked with this theme of transiency, therefore, has been the theme of inequality, as revealed in evolving urban class structures, the residential movements of the upper classes, and the residential persistence of the poor. The framework for analyzing this pattern-process relationship is still the subject of debate. Older environmentalist perspectives that were common until the 1940s have been replaced with a model of laissez-faire "privatism." Urban development occurred under the decision-making conditions associated with mercantile and, later, industrial capitalism that reversed the social and spatial gradients of the early-19th-century city. European immigrants and southern African Americans moved into the central areas of cities after 1850, and intraurban transport innovations after 1870 allowed the upper classes and, later, the skilled and professional middle classes to move to the suburbs.

Much of the early work done on American mobility was based on record linkages of individuals at ten-year census dates and at the level of census enumeration districts and city blocks. But as the exploration of residential patterning proceeded, scholars faced scale problems of how best to organize the manuscript census data in terms of units of analysis (single blocks, block faces, and household addresses) and of appropriate sampling techniques for handling the sheer mass of material. A second problem was how to interpolate information between census-year data. The available censuses between 1850 and 1910 provided detailed information only at ten-year intervals. Thus a major concern has been to construct computerized files on individuals and families between census years from sources ranging from tax and occupational records to church records and family papers. This data collection revealed considerable discrepancies in the availability of source materials from one city to another. Hence it has proved difficult to make interurban comparisons of residential and occupational patterns at similar levels of discrimination.

Another research thrust in the 1980s has been to try to delineate the functional and spatial links between urbanization and industrialization. This has been explored in two ways: the distinctive characteristics of mercantile cities, and the processes of urban growth during periods of industrialization. Research into urban evolution has led scholars to conclude that the appropriate model of early American urbanism is the mercantile city, rather than the classical preindustrial city. American postcolonial cities, in the Northeast in particular, were dominated not by landed elites but by business elites who organized factors of production not only in wholesale and overseas trade but also in manufacturing. The onset of large-scale industrialization during the third quarter of the 19th century, therefore, was more of an elaboration of existing trends than a revolution in economic activities, even though the scale and pace of industrial change were unprecedented. But there has been little empirical underpinning to this research through the 1980s. The study of the larger cities has focused on three elements: expansion of the central business district, the emergence of factories and large-scale industrial employment, and intraurban transportation. There has been little discussion yet on what happened with these elements in smaller cities and towns.

City Systems. The study of the emergence of city systems, on the other hand, has been of much more interest to historical geographers than to urban historians. Consequently, geographers have monopolized research into the evolution of urban networks, using theoretical constructs from modern human geography. The use of descriptive models has been especially noteworthy.

What appears to fit best the evolution of a North American urban system is an imperial model of the colonial cities along the Atlantic seaboard. They created their own internal hinterlands and were linked with a mercantilist transatlantic trading world dominated by London and the demand and supply needs of the mother country. A mercantile model of wholesale trading patterns suggests that these colonial cities became the key unraveling points of trade with the expanding interior—that is, the final destination of a sufficient number of supply lines—to assure the profitability of long-distance trade to the traders. As settlement and trade spread farther westward, new cities emerged along major trade routes at highly accessible localities, where frontier merchants concentrated to organize and conduct wholesale trade. These cities became interior unraveling points with forward linkages to the seaboard metropolises and backward linkages into the expanding settlement frontier, thus pulling the entire system together into a functioning whole. These wholesaling cities also became the points of origin for the creation of more regional and localized retailing trading systems. The application of central-place theory is more appropriate for this level of activity. The arrangement of retailing at this scale was more hierarchical and the spacing of towns more regular. The larger the urban center, the greater was its array of central functions (the number and kind of retail and service businesses), the more extensive its hinterland, and the farther it was located from other cities of equal size.

Mercantile and central-place theories provide some valuable clues to the emergence of national patterns of city systems, but they create demand-generated models that fail to account for differential rates of development of regional urban systems, the unusual size and regional concentration of the largest cities, and the impact of industrial localization, among others. The first problem has been addressed by regional growth theory, which seeks to address the core-periphery dynamics that occur within urban regions. This combines examining the selective results of interregional trade impacts (between the Northeast, the Middle West, and the South) and their varying control, in particular by the northeastern cities. It also involves examining interregional growth through the intensification of commercial activities in the largest cities, which influences the growth and distribution of agricultural and processing activities in local hinterlands. The concept of metropolitan dominance has been refined to help resolve the second problem. In a continent that has undergone such recent settlement, it is an easier matter to unravel the processes of urban evolution than it would be in a longer-settled continent such as Europe. Thus, areas in proximity or easily accessible to newly emerging towns will have their economies influenced by these towns. The towns, in turn, achieve an "initial advantage" in influencing economic development over centers founded later, which explains the initial and continued importance of the northeastern seaport cities (especially New York) and Montreal and Toronto.

The onset of industrialization during the second quarter of the 19th century superimposed industrial factors of location on the preexisting pattern of commercial city systems. This development has forced researchers to focus on two issues: the concentration of high manufacturing capacity in the major cities of the Northeast, and the emergence of specialized regional-industrial systems. A model of circular and cumulative growth has been used to explain how the mercantile city benefits from establishing industries by means of a "multiplier effect." The growing urban workforce creates a demand for consumer goods and industrial raw materials that, through time, produces new local or regional thresholds of demand, which then stimulate further industrial expansion and, by encouraging innovations, may also create new industries. This model says

little, however, about the forces that encouraged industrial activities in medium- and small-sized towns and, consequently, about the timing, regional arrangement, and interregional spread of entire urban-industrial complexes. Only recently has there been an attempt to explain the coalescing of these complexes into the world's greatest industrial region during the late 19th century. This research has focused on the expansion of demand for processed and consumer goods in the major cities and their hinterlands and the critical importance of producer durable goods (for example, machinery, iron foundries, and transport equipment) to supply not only local and regional demand but also, ultimately, interregional and national markets for such products. This, in turn, led to the emergence of specialized regional manufacturing districts that, through regional spread, had coalesced and consolidated in the Northeast and eastern Middle West before the end of the 19th century to form the American Manufacturing Belt.

Enduring Themes

From this survey of interpreting the past, a number of principal themes can be identified around which this synthesis of the North American experience can be organized. The choice of themes must necessarily be arbitrary, but the seven chosen here appear to capture much of the dynamic element of change that has shaped the geography of the continent during the past 400 years and continues to shape it today.

Acquisition of Geographical Knowledge

As a "new world," what came to be known as North America had to be discovered and eventually uncovered through exploration, description, mapping, and subsequent place-naming in a continuous process of growth, repetition, and revelation. This was a complex process involving mental as well as physical negotiation of a vast new continent. To the educated European a direct relationship existed between the appearance of the landscape and the cultural quality of its inhabitants. The wild landscapes of North America suggested a need for taming and transformation into semblances of the subdued landscapes of western Europe; the seeming wildness of the natives suggested a lowly status for them in the great chain of civilization and cast doubts on their capacity to become Christians.

Geographic knowledge of the continent continued to increase during the interior penetrations of the 18th and 19th centuries, largely following major river courses, and built up a vast storehouse of information about a seemingly inexhaustible territory. This information was collected and described by a variety of observer-explorers, traders, missionaries, travelers, naturalists, and occasionally artists (who were indispensable before the beginnings of photography in the 1840s). It was not until the great railroad and scientific surveys of the trans-Mississippi West after 1860 that we began systematically to record the continent as a whole. Vast areas of northern and western Canada remained only partially explored at the beginning of the 20th century.

The accumulation of geographic knowledge had important effects on later settlement. Prior discovery was used by England, France, and the Netherlands to justify territorial acquisition and colonization. Early maps and descriptions of particular areas therefore need to be viewed with caution, because they were often designed to please royal patrons or investors and to promote settlement. As well as accurate information, the cartographic record is replete with exaggeration, misconception, and geographical fantasies. If sound geographical knowledge could guide pioneer settlers to new agricultural lands, geographical misinformation could retard settlement in other areas. Early visitors to the western High Plains reported the area as barren and unsuitable for farming. The image of a "Great American Desert" portrayed in eastern newspapers and in official government reports probably retarded large-scale settlement of the area until the last quarter of the 19th century.

Cultural Transfer and Acculturation

No other landmass, except perhaps Australia, has undergone such a dramatic cultural replacement and transformation in such a short time as has North America. The Europeanization of the continent in the later 16th and 17th centuries, though rapid, was a highly selective process. Only a few western European countries controlled colonization, and settlers who came (except for African slaves) were more geographically and socially mobile than those who remained in Europe. They brought with them only a sample of their national cultures, which, through hybridization with native and imported traits, eventually created distinct colonial cultures and societies.

A process of Americanization set in during the 18th century as colonial-born generations had increasingly weaker ties with the mother country. The ethos of this American society lay in liberal individualism, capitalism, and geographical expansion. The dramatic break with Britain left the continent with a robust new nation, dominated by Anglo-American institutions and the presence of slavery, and a Canadian colony in which both French- and English-speaking settlers remained under direct British control.

The principal cultural configurations of the two territories were well established by the time of the massive European immigration that occurred after 1830. The 50 million immigrants who arrived in the United States before 1920 had to adjust to an already existing framework of the English language and other American institutions. They, in turn, enriched the continent's cultural heritage. Instead of a continental "melting pot," a widespread sharing of common values occurred while ethnic diversity increased. These processes of cultural and social intermixing have left a distinctive imprint on modern North America. The persistence of older cultural forms remains evident, for example, among French Canadians, among Hispanics in the Southwest, and on some Indian reservations. The more varied cultural heritage of the United States is reflected in the presence of large African American and Hispanic populations that do not exist in Canada. Both countries continue to be, in reduced ways, "nations of immigrants," and the 19th- and early-20th-century urban concentrations of European and Asian immigrant groups have given way to massive 20th-century suburbanization and renewed migration, whose long-term cultural results are as yet uncertain.

Frontier Expansion

There is little need to dwell here on the historiographic and symbolic importance of an interior-moving settlement frontier in North America. Both Frederick Jackson Turner in the United States and the Laurentian school in Canada have etched in the national psyche the significance of settling the land. In the United States this was especially significant because of the continuity of the frontier experience across a vast, midlatitude territory that encountered few obstacles to settlement until the Great Plains were reached in the middle of the 19th century. In Canada, on the other hand, westward settlement expansion was interrupted in the 19th century by the immense extent of the heavily glaciated, generally infertile, and extensively forested Canadian Shield that separated Ontario from the prairies. Thus many immigrants to Canada during the 19th century who wished to acquire farmland did so in the northern Middle West of the United States.

Frontier expansion was a process of both continual reappraisal and increasing geographical divergence. The so-called westward movement was a process of sustained geographical mobility that has always characterized American life, an experience that was cumulative and undertaken under different temporal and locational contexts. Successive pioneer generations swept across the country, bringing with them knowledge accumulated through earlier encounters with modifying new areas for settlement. The pace of this development was speeded up further by the American government's desire, after 1790, to dispose of the public domain to the private sector as rapidly as possible and by the impact, after 1850, of the railroads; these reoriented both the direction and the pace of frontier expansion and reduced the traditional isolation of pioneering. In the Far West a slight reversal of this westward process occurred as settlement expanded discontinuously eastward from the Pacific coast or from isolated interior centers. The end result of this frontier process was the creation of an elaborate system of rural-agrarian regions and subregions latitudinally across the continent (until the Rockies), each defined by its own settlement experiences and regional economic development.

In 1890, the director of the U.S. census declared, somewhat inaccurately, that the American frontier was officially "closed." No new agricultural areas remained to be occupied; the filling of the vast national ecumene was complete. America was now a "closed space" entity of finite resources that would have to be used more carefully; further dynamism for American life would have to be sought in urban and industrial opportunities. Such ideas influenced the New Deal measures employed by Franklin Roosevelt's administrations to alleviate the stresses of national economic depression and the Dust Bowl disaster. The opening up of Alaska since 1945 has, in a small way, kept open the idea of the American frontier, while for some Canadians settlement of "the North" remains an unfulfilled dream.

Spatial Organization of Society

The processes whereby a society arranges its members, its institutions, and its materials on the ground provide a fundamental geographical expression of its goals and achievements. What is remarkable about the social initiation of the new continent was the way in which the diversity of pioneer societies was integrated by the early 18th century within a social framework characterized by liberalism, individualism, Protestantism, and capitalism. The overwhelming concern for material well-being, social stability, and continuity within the vast spaces of North America provided ample opportunities for the acquisition of land and the pursuit of commercial interest or, conversely, for the right to be left alone on the social or geographic margins of society. Most settlers saw little conflict between religious and material ends; the work ethic was believed to provide access to the spiritual world through success in the material world. North American society soon deviated from its European counterparts: it was less hierarchical and more egalitarian; there was no hereditary aristocracy and, at least in the American system, no imposed state church. The options for creating a new life were greater than in Europe, although this was often at the expense of the native Indian or the imported African.

In the new American nation two forms of society emerged: a largely free-labor, mixed-farming system in the North and a more stratified, slave-labor, and staple-farming system in the South. The reduction of differences between the two societies was to remain unresolved until the Civil War, and the continued social distinctiveness and economic dependency of the South remained well into the 20th century. But the expression of these two early societies on the ground was broadly similar in the form of dispersed farmsteads. Attempts to recreate European-style settlements failed almost everywhere, even in French Canada where the social nexus was tighter, and the ubiquity of dispersed settlement was guaranteed by the reassignment of the public domain under the design of cheap land policies and rectangular survey systems initiated in the United States and Canada during the 1790s.

Early North American urban life had demonstrated a more complex differentiation of wealth and social status than in the countryside. While rural tenancy was present, in the burgeoning 18th-century cities were collected those who had found or made few opportunities in the new land, the urban poor and the unskilled laborer. Problems of residential congestion, traffic, sanitation, and crime were apparent long before the large-scale immigration, urbanization, and industrialization of the mid-19th century. If the expression of social segregation in rural life became symbolized in southern slave quarters and in western Native reservations, it was represented in the urban centers of the Northeast and Middle West by the inner-city immigrant ghettos and slum quarters that formed in the late 19th century. This segregation was enhanced enormously by the transportation developments of the late 19th and early 20th centuries that allowed the wealthy to move to emerging suburbs. The most dominant social expression of the past 60 years has been the increasing suburbanization of skilled and professional middle classes that now comprise more than half the total population of North America.

Resource Exploitation

The concept of resources, like that of hazards, involves continuous reappraisal of nature and society. The future of North American economic development was founded on European ideas about natural resource exploitation played out on a vast 7.5-million-square-mile canvas. After initial searches for gold, silver, and quick riches, the continent settled down to gradual extraction of its immense animal, agricultural, forest, and mineral wealth with few concerns for the rate and magnitude of exploiting finite resources. The process was to be also distinctly territorially unbalanced. The more southerly, midlatitude United States was to prove far more amenable to resource development than its northern neighbor; more than 65 percent of the total area of the United States, for example, has been used for agricultural purposes, while only 16 percent has been so used in Canada.

Early Americans were thus a people of plenty. Their successful transformation of nature was predicated on a rich resource base; a liberal, free-market economy; overseas trade; and a growing internal demand that led to increasing regional specialization. Eastern Canada was to remain largely a raw-material supplier of fish and furs, and later of timber and wheat; the northern colonies produced small grains, livestock products, and small crafts; and the southern settlements focused on tobacco, rice, indigo, and, after 1790, on cotton. The urbanization and industrialization of the northeastern United States during the mid-19th century oriented economic development in new directions: the cities produced the manufactured goods and the financial and marketing organization, while their peripheries produced the food supply and the industrial raw materials. The settlement of the western periphery presented new problems and possibilities: the near extinction of the buffalo, competition for the Plains grasslands, problems of water supply in the Southwest, the timber resources of the Pacific Northwest, and the oil discoveries of the turn of the century. By the end of the 19th century the United States had surpassed Germany and Britain as the world's most productive industrial nation. At the same time, this immense growth fostered increasing sensitivity toward the conservation of resources and the creation of preserved natural places in the 20th century.

The resource legacy has been staggering. Probably between one-quarter and one-third of all the wheat, coal, iron ore, and petroleum extraction from the earth's surface during the past 200 years has occurred in North America. But continued change remains uneven. Regionally, maritime Canada and Appalachia prove the effects of differential resource fortunes. On a continental scale, the economic dependency of Canada on American investment and markets remains high. And Americans continue to generate a 30 percent greater demand for electrical energy than their Canadian neighbors. On a global scale, the increasing decline of older smokestack industries within the Manufacturing Belt, and the global competition from both advanced economies, such as Japan, and low-cost, developing economies guarantees new challenges to North American resource strategies into the 21st century.

Regional and National Integration

One of the most remarkable characteristics of North America is that it came to be divided not into a series of little Europes but into only two national-political units of approximately equal size. To be sure, the northern territory proved to be less attractive for settlement, so that Americans continue to outnumber Canadians by almost ten to one. But the sheer challenge of conquering the vast spaces and distances of the continent by technological means and within similar cultural traditions meant that both countries had much to share.

In the American colonies, a range of institutional units was created to organize local affairs: counties, townships, and parishes. Patterns of political behavior varied enormously within a colonial system that, nevertheless, allowed for a relatively wide participation in the political process. The provision for a new nation was a remarkable experience: a democratic republic formed as a federal union, with a central government of limited power, and its idealism patently recorded in a series of written documents. Threats to the unity of the United States might have come from the settlement of the West, where factors of distance and isolation, sparsely settled populations, and discrete urban cores created a potentially fragmented situation (as in Mormon Utah) until the development of the railroads and the telegraph. The greatest threat was to come during the Civil War, which, if its outcome had been different, might have resulted in an American experience that paralleled rather than diverged from that in South Africa. Since the 1920s, however, the increasing redistribution of population to the West and South and the increasing movement of African Americans from the South have created a regional balance of economic and political power throughout the United States. Today, the integration of unwieldy metropolitan regions, where deep political and social cleavages exist between inner-city and suburban populations, remains a major problem.

Canada's political evolution and efforts at national integration have taken a somewhat different direction. The late acquisition of independence from Britain (in 1867), the deep geographical divisions between French and Anglo Canada, and the slow growth of population relative to the United States left Canadians with a less unified legacy. The division between French and English Canada had been institutionalized first in the recognition of Lower Canada (French Quebec) and Upper Canada (English Ontario) in 1791 and then into the provinces of Quebec and Ontario in 1867. The Canadian provincial system was thus well established before independence so that the allocation of powers between governing units resulted in a relatively weak central government, strong provinces, and continued constitutional ties with Britain. A confident American nation negotiated the boundary between the two territories west of the Great Lakes in its favor, thus leaving Canada as the "true country of the North." The delayed westward movement in Canada produced an additional problem of integrating the Prairies and British Columbia into a seemingly distant eastern Canada by means of a transcontinental railroad. The American presence exerts considerable influence on Canadian affairs, although the reverse is less true, and this continues to raise questions both about Canadian identity and about North American unity in the early 21st century.

Landscape Change

Landscape has been an unending theme in the geography of the North American past. But it is not simply a collection of observable objects on the continent's surface, nor does it reflect equally all the forces and processes that have occurred during the past 400 years. It is a receptacle for continuity and change, a palimpsest that can be read for what it contains as well as for what it represents symbolically.

The most important attribute of landscape is its capacity to synthesize the formative ideas that have shaped the continent. Control over nature is expressed dramatically in the selective removal of much of the forested wilderness to create more familiar, more domesticated environments; these have come to be identified with the rural and small town "middle" landscapes between the less desired forested and urban wildernesses at the extremes. The idea of individualism is reflected in a range of landscape expressions from the colonial dispersed farmstead to the modern low-density residential suburb. Private property meant a multitude of fragmented, small private territories that continue to dominate most of the settlement landscapes of North America.

The emergence of a new nation encouraged regularity and symmetry that resulted in perhaps the most extensive geographical expression of values on the landscape. The creation of national rectangular survey systems produced a sequence of designed rural landscapes of grid-pattern roads, fields, and settlements that stretch almost uninterrupted from southern Ontario and the Alleghenies westward to the Pacific. In urban North America, the rectangular street and block patterns and regular naming and numbering of streets are a more widespread expression of urbanism than the late-appearing skyscraper. Design can also be observed in the continued pattern of regionally diverse folk housing styles, as well as in a myriad of borrowed urban architectural styles. Regional landscapes, therefore, continue to survive despite the homogenizing influences of historic national survey systems and contemporary urban life, as any trip to Quebec, the Appalachians, Louisiana, or New Mexico will attest.

Ideas of separation and segregation are also well expressed in the landscape. We can observe the dismal results of Native American removal to western reservations, while we appreciate their potential for fostering cultural survival. If the slave plantation is a thing of the past, we can interpret the continued segregation of African Americans in inner cities and whites in the suburbs as a reflection of the enduring racial divisions of American society that compound the urban-suburban tensions of modern metropolitan life. We can appreciate also the idea of conservation on a continent that has experienced more rapid and extensive resource exploitation than any other. The creation of wilderness and recreation areas, national parks, national forests, national seashores, and wildlife management areas reflects abiding concern in the management, if not always the preservation, of landscape and nature. And ultimately, on a continent that is seemingly notorious for lack of a sense of place or a sense of past, we can acknowledge the survival of landscape relics from previous settlement eras, from historic structures to "living farms," from factories and foundries to sanitized colonial townscapes, that still reflect on the landscape the forces of change, paradox, and contradiction that continue to reshape North America.

ADDITIONAL READING

Baker, A. R. H. 1972. *Progress in Historical Geography.* New York: Wiley.

Baker, A. R. H., and M. Billinge, eds. 1982. *Period and Place: Research Methods in Historical Geography.* Cambridge: Cambridge University Press.

Baker, A. R. H., and D. Gregory, eds. 1984. *Explorations in Historical Geography: Interpretive Essays.* Cambridge: Cambridge University Press.

Barrows, H. H. 1962. *Lectures on the Historical Geography of the United States as Given in 1933.* Edited by W. A. Koelsch. Chicago: University of Chicago, Department of Geography.

Brown, R. H. 1943. *Mirror for Americans: Likeness of the Eastern Seaboard, 1810.* New York: American Geographical Society.

———. 1948. *Historical Geography of the United States.* New York: Harcourt, Brace & World.

Clark, A. H. 1959. *Three Centuries and the Island: A Historical Geography of Settlement and Agriculture in Prince Edward Island, Canada.* Toronto: University of Toronto Press.

———. 1960. "Geographical Change: A Theme for Economic History." *Journal of Economic History* 20: 607–13.

———. 1968. *Acadia: The Geography of Early Nova Scotia to 1760.* Madison: University of Wisconsin Press.

Ehrenberg, R. E., ed. 1975. *Pattern and Process: Research in Historical Geography.* Washington: Howard University Press.

Friis, H. R. 1968. *A Series of Population Maps of the Colonies and the United States, 1625–1790.* Rev. ed. New York: American Geographical Society.

Gibson, J. R., ed. 1978. *European Settlement and Development in North America: Essays on Geographical Change in Honour and Memory of Andrew Hill Clark.* Toronto: University of Toronto Press. See chapters by Meinig, Mitchell, Ward, and Lemon.

Grim, R. E. 1982. *Historical Geography of the United States: A Guide to Information Sources.* Detroit: Gale.

Guelke, L. 1982. *Historical Understanding in Geography: An Idealist Approach.* Cambridge: Cambridge University Press.

Harris, R. C. 1967. "Historical Geography in Canada." *Canadian Geographer* 11: 235–50.

———. 1970. *Reflections on the Fertility of the Historical Geographic Mule.* Toronto: University of Toronto, Department of Geography.

———. 1971. "Theory and Synthesis in Historical Geography." *Canadian Geographer* 15: 157–72.

———. 1977. "The Simplification of Europe Overseas." *Annals of the Association of American Geographers* 67: 469–83.

———. 1978. "The Historical Geography of North

American Regions." *American Behavioral Scientist* 22: 115–32.

Herbert, D. T., and R. J. Johnston, eds. 1981. *Geography and the Urban Environment: Progress in Research and Applications*. Vol. 4. New York: Wiley. See chapters by Conzen and Radford.

Lemon, J. T. 1980. "Early Americans and Their Social Environment." *Journal of Historical Geography* 6: 115–32.

Lowenthal, D., and M. J. Bowden, eds. 1976. *Geographies of the Mind: Essays in Historical Geosophy in Honor of John Kirtland Wright*. New York: Oxford University Press.

Meinig, D. W. 1965. "The Mormon Culture Region: Strategies and Patterns in the Geography of the American West, 1847–1964." *Annals of the Association of American Geographers* 55: 191–220.

———. 1968. *The Great Columbia Plain: A Historical Geography, 1805–1910*. Seattle: University of Washington Press.

———. 1969. *Imperial Texas: An Interpretive Essay in Cultural Geography*. Austin: University of Texas Press.

———. 1971. *Southwest: Three Peoples in Geographical Change, 1600–1970*. New York: Oxford University Press.

———. 1978. "The Continuous Shaping of America: A Prospectus for Geographers." *American Historical Review* 83: 1186–217.

Meyer, D. R. 1983. "Emergence of the American Manufacturing Belt: An Interpretation." *Journal of Historical Geography* 9: 145–74.

Mitchell, R. D. 1983. "American Origins and Regional Institutions: The 17th-Century Chesapeake." *Annals of the Association of American Geographers* 73: 404–20.

Norton, W. 1984. *Historical Analysis in Geography*. London: Longman.

Sauer, C. O. 1963. *Land and Life: A Selection from the Writings of Carl Ortwin Sauer*. Edited by J. Leighly. Berkeley and Los Angeles: University of California Press.

———. 1966. *The Early Spanish Main*. Berkeley and Los Angeles: University of California Press.

———. 1971. *16th-Century North America: The Land and the People as Seen by the Europeans*. Berkeley and Los Angeles: University of California Press.

———. 1981. *Selected Essays 1963–1975*. Berkeley: Turtle Island Foundation.

Semple, E. C. 1903. *American History and Its Geographic Conditions*. Boston: Houghton Mifflin.

Thompson, J. H., ed. *A Geography of New York State*. 2d ed. Syracuse: Syracuse University Press, 1977. See chapters by Meinig.

Vance, J. E., Jr. 1970. *The Merchant's World: The Geography of Wholesaling*. Englewood Cliffs, N.J.: Prentice Hall.

———. 1977. *This Scene of Man: The Role and Structure of the City in the Geography of Western Civilization*. New York: Harper & Row.

Ward, D. 1971. *Cities and Immigrants: A Geography of Change in Nineteenth-Century America*. New York: Oxford University Press.

———, ed. 1979. *Geographic Perspectives on America's Past: Readings on the Historical Geography of the United States*. New York: Oxford University Press.

Warkentin, J., ed. 1968. *Canada: A Geographical Interpretation*. Toronto: Methuen.

Whittlesey, D. 1929. "Sequent Occupance." *Annals of the Association of American Geographers* 19: 162–65.

Wright, J. K. 1966. *Human Nature in Geography: Fourteen Papers, 1925–1965*. Cambridge: Harvard University Press.

Zelinsky, W. 1973. *The Cultural Geography of the United States*. Englewood Cliffs, N.J.: Prentice Hall.

———. 1978. "Introduction, Human Geography: Coming of Age." *American Behavioral Scientist* 22: 5–13.

PART II

COLONIZATION

1490s–1770s

If the soil were as good as the harbours, it would be a blessing; but the land should not be called the New Land, being composed of stones and horrible rugged rocks; for along the whole of the north shore [of the Gulf of St. Lawrence], I did not see one cart-load of earth and yet I landed in many places. . . . In fine, I am rather inclined to believe that this is the land God gave to Cain.

Jacques Cartier, *Journal,* 1535

Thus I have given a succinct account of the Indians; happy, I think, in their simple State of Nature, and in their enjoyment of Plenty, without the Curse of Labour. They have on several accounts reason to lament the arrival of the Europeans, by whose means they seem to have lost their Felicity, as well as their Innocence. The English have taken away a great part of their Country, and consequently made everything less plenty amongst them. They have introduc'd Drunkenness and Luxury amongst them, which have multiply'd their Wants, and put them upon desiring a thousand things, they never dreamt of before.

Robert Beverley, *The History and
Present State of Virginia,* 1705

Why should we, in the Sight of Superior Beings, darken its People? Why increase the sons of Africa, by planting them in America, where we have so fair an Opportunity, by excluding all Blacks and Tawneys, of increasing the lovely White and Red? But perhaps I am partial to the Complexion of my Country, for such kind of Partiality is natural to Mankind.

Benjamin Franklin, *Observations Concerning
the Increase of Mankind,* 1751

2

European Encounters:
Discovery and Exploration

LOUIS DE VORSEY

One of the most colorful and exciting stories in humankind's history describes the discovery and exploration of North America by Europeans. The Age of Discovery and Exploration is almost universally acknowledged as a major temporal division, employed to help organize and focus understanding of humanity's march through time. Its significance to historical geography derives from what it can reveal about areas discovered, the cultural groups responsible for the modification of those areas, and the resultant cultural landscapes. As Carl Sauer put it, in 1925:

> Historical geography may be considered as the series of changes which the cultural landscapes have undergone and therefore involves the reconstruction of past cultural landscapes. Of special concern is the catalytic relation of civilized man to area and the effects of the replacement of cultures. From this difficult and little-touched field alone may be gained a full realization of the development of the present cultural landscape out of earlier cultures and the natural landscape. (*Land and Life,* 344)

The North American cultural landscape, in all its incredible richness of diverse patterns, forms a document. Reading it is challenging because it is not like a modern printed document that reveals its message easily. Rather, today's landscape is similar to ancient parchments, ordinarily goat- or sheepskins, called palimpsests. Parchment, being expensive and durable, was seldom thrown away and was used over and over again. Scholars and monks merely scraped the ink off portions they wanted to change ("palimpsest" comes from the Greek for "scraped again") or crossed out errors or old ideas and introduced their changes and corrections between the lines of written text. The phrase "to read between the lines" is commonly used to indicate the search for hidden or deeper meaning. Because the scraped erasures and cor-

rections were imperfectly done, it became the fascinating task of scholars not only to translate the later records but also to reconstruct the original writings by deciphering the dim fragments of letters partly erased and partly covered by subsequent texts. The patterns of trails, streets, power-line grids, railways, highways, fields, and farmsteads contributing to today's urban and rural landscapes can be viewed as modern interlinings and glosses on a centuries-old landscape palimpsest.

CREATION OF THE ABORIGINAL LANDSCAPE

The first bands of Old World hunters spreading across the broad, low-lying belt of tundra, inadequately described as the Bering Land Bridge, found North America in a truly natural state. As they moved south to exploit the continent some 20,000 to 30,000 years ago, they began to alter their surroundings and permanently change ecological relationships. Their numbers were small, but they possessed and made wide use of fire for major landscape modification.

The people who erroneously came to be called Indians by the first Europeans who met them—"Native Americans" today, or, in Canada, "First Nations"—continued to add their cultural signatures and messages to North America's landscape palimpsest. During the centuries that followed, majestic earthworks, massive effigies, and mounds were raised; palisaded villages were built; fields and trails were hewn from the forest; fish traps were constructed in rivers, lakes, and coastal lagoons; and everywhere fire was deliberately loosed on the land to drive game, clear undergrowth, and achieve other desired alterations. Giovanni da Verrazano, whose first landing near Cape Fear, North Carolina, was guided by Native fires, was only one of the early 16th-century visitors to North

America who drew attention to their recurrent use of fire as a tool in landscape modification and management.

As their cultures evolved and their numbers grew, the Native Americans altered their habitat in major ways. The sum total of these alterations to the natural state of the continent by the time of the first European contacts is still to be determined accurately. One thing is clear, however: eastern North America was far from being a primeval forest when Europeans reached it in the 16th century. On the contrary, what the European explorers found and reported is best described as an aboriginal landscape—a palimpsest already inscribed with patterns and forms reflecting its cultural use by Natives for whom it had been a home for centuries. North America was a "New Land" only to the Europeans. In the words, in 1964, of John Collier, longtime U.S. Commissioner of Indian Affairs, "At the time of white arrival there was no square mile unoccupied or unused. . . . The million Indians of the United States and Alaska were formed within more than six hundred distinct societies, in geographical situations ranging from temperate oceansides to arctic ice, from humid swamps to frozen tundras, from eastern woodlands to western deserts" (101–2).

It is through the eyes and accounts of the early explorers that we can gain glimpses of the landscapes created by native North Americans before Europeans began to exploit the continent's resources. Great care must be taken in interpreting their texts and maps, however, for we must be aware of the motives and aspirations of the individual explorers who wrote and drew them. Furthermore, nuances of meaning may be lost in translation, and changes take place in all languages, including those of cartography, over long periods of time. Giovanni da Verrazano, for example, was obviously trying to create a favorable impression in the mind of his sponsor, the king of France, when he penned the earliest detailed description of "the Country of Refugio"—around modern Newport, Rhode Island—which he visited for more than two weeks in 1524.

Many times we were from five to six leagues inland, which we found as pleasing as it can be to narrate, adapted to every kind of cultivation: grain, wine, oil. Because in that place the fields are from 25 to 30 leagues wide, open and de-void of every impediment of trees, of such fertility that any seed in them would produce the best crops. Entering then into the woods, all of which are penetrable by any numerous army in any way whatsoever, and where trees, oaks, cypresses, and others are unknown in our Europe. . . . Animals there are in very great number, stags, deer, lynx, and other species. (cited in Hoffman 1961, 111)

But when due allowance is made for his hyperbole and obviously favorable spin, one can gain a considerable amount of insight concerning the landscape that had been shaped by the Natives in one of the most densely inhabited parts of the continent:

We saw their habitations, circular in form, of 14 to 15 paces compass, made from semi-circles of wood separated one from the other . . . covered with mats of straw ingeniously worked, which protect them from rain and wind. . . . They change said houses from one place to another according to the season. . . . There live in each a father and family to a very large number, so that we saw 25 and 30 souls. Their food is like the others; of pulse [succotash] (which they produce with more system of culture than the others, observing the full moon, the rising of the Pleiades, and many customs derived from the ancients), also of the chase and fish. (Hoffman 1961, 111)

At a landfall near Casco Bay in present-day southern Maine, Verrazano reported a rather different landscape:

We found a high land and full of very thick forests, the trees of which were pines, cypresses [red cedar] and such as grow in cold regions. The people . . . were full of uncouthness and vices, so barbarous that we were never able, with howsoever many signs we made them, to have any intercourse with them. . . . If, trading at any time with them, we desired their things, they came to the shore of the sea upon some rock where it was very steep and we remaining in the small boat—with a cord let down to us what they wished to give, continually crying on land that we should not approach, giving quickly the barter, nor taking in exchange for it except knives, hooks for fishing, and sharp metal. They had no regard for courtesy, and when they had nothing more to exchange, at their departing the men made at us all the signs of contempt and shame which any brute creature could make. (Hoffman 1961, 111)

Verrazano named the area Land of the Bad People in his report to the king.

These extracts from Verrazano's report suggest a number of hypotheses concerning the true nature of the geography of aboriginal North America. The landscape of southern New England was greatly altered by its Native occupants armed with fire. "Fields . . . from 25 to 30 leagues wide" sounds exaggerated but is clear evidence of their achievement. It is probable that many areas inhabited by Native Americans exhibited a relatively open, parklike appearance, although forests still constituted the dominant land cover of most of the Atlantic seaboard. The behavior of the Natives—Verrazano's "bad people"—suggests further hypotheses. Could it be that these hunter-gatherers were wary because they had already encountered Europeans and had been mistreated? Although not universally accepted, there is evidence that points to the presence of European vessels on the fishing banks off northeastern North America as much as a century before Verrazano's voyage. Perhaps John Cabot's 1497 landfall was not the first for modern Europeans on these coasts.

THE TRAGEDY OF THE COLUMBIAN EXCHANGE

One of the great disappointments of the historical record is that few, if any, of the early European explorers possessed either the time or the training to record the subtle cultural differences and nonmaterial nuances of Native social and political life. As a consequence, we must view the period of original contact between the people of the Old and New Worlds through a dark and often distorted lens. By the time that more careful and complete records of their beliefs, lifestyles, and landscapes were being compiled, the Native Americans had already begun to suffer the catastrophic fatal shocks introduced by Old World epidemic diseases such as smallpox, measles, and influenza.

Thomas Hariot, a member of Sir Walter Raleigh's abortive Virginia settlement in the 1580s, described his visits to the Native villages on the coastal plain of North Carolina. He mentioned that he and his English companions "sought by all means possible to win them by gentleness" but that, "within the few days after our departure from every such town, the people began to die very fast, and many in short space, in some towns about twenty, in some forty, and in one six score, which in truth was very many in respect of their numbers" (Corbett 1953, 97). Any doubt that this postcontact decimation of the Natives was caused by some infectious disease being carried by members of Hariot's party is dispelled by his further observation that "this happened in no place that we could learn, but where we had been. . . . The disease also was so strange, that they neither knew what it was, nor how to cure it, the like by report of the oldest men in the country never happened before, time out of mind" (Corbett 1953, 97).

This example of the impact of disease typifies an important aspect of what historian Alfred Crosby investigated in his study *The Columbian Exchange*. Thanks to the acceptance of Crosby's work, the term "Columbian exchange" is now widely used to describe the complex and many-faceted chain of ecological exchanges and impacts that began with Columbus. As Crosby points out regarding Columbus's 1492 landfall, "The two worlds which God had cast asunder, were reunited, and the two worlds which were so very different, began on that day to become alike. That trend toward biological homogeneity is one of the most important aspects of the history of life on this planet since the retreat of the continental glaciers" (Crosby 1972, 3).

Native Americans, like the aborigines of Australia, had enjoyed the ultimately perilous, long-term isolation from the people inhabiting the Old World of Afro-Eurasia and its fringing islands. As a consequence, they had not inherited the resistance to disease that had evolved in Old World populations. Even commonplace diseases, such as whooping cough, scarlet fever, and chicken pox, proved to be devastating scourges when introduced to vulnerable populations for the first time.

It is tempting to hypothesize that the "bad people" of Verrazano's account were aware of the doleful consequences of close-up, hand-to-hand exchange with Europeans. Perhaps they possessed the sort of awareness described by French Jesuit missionaries almost a century later. They wrote that the Natives

are astonished and often complain that, since the French mingle with and carry on trade with them, they are dying fast and the population is thinning out. For they assert that, before this association and intercourse, all their countries were very populous and they tell how one by one, the different coasts according as they have begun to traffic with us, have been more reduced by disease. (Crosby 1972, 41)

Once begun, the Columbian exchange could not be reversed; the New World and the Old World were launched on an inexorable course toward today's global village.

PRE-COLUMBIAN CONTACTS BETWEEN THE OLD AND THE NEW WORLDS

Hardly a month goes by that the news media do not report some new evidence or theory concerning a pre-Columbian "discovery" of the New World. Many verge on the bizarre and fail to bear up under even mild scientific scrutiny. Some, however, spawn fascinating and often long-lived debates that add spice to the history of discovery.

The Kensington stone, found in the small Minnesota farming community of that name in 1898, bore Scandinavian markings reporting that 8 Swedes and 22 Norwegians from Vinland had been there in the year 1362, a full 130 years prior to Columbus's first landfall in the Bahamas. Careful linguistic analysis showed that the Kensington stone was fraudulent, very probably inscribed in 1898, the year of its alleged discovery. Exactly why this elaborate hoax was prepared and perpetrated remains unclear. Still, the debate waxed and waned for a half-century, and the episode can still enliven discussions and stir Nordic pride among many residents of the upper Midwest.

The Vinland map, owned by Yale University, has likewise stirred debate. Amid fanfare and the widest possible news media attention, the Yale University Press chose Columbus's birthday in 1965 to present publicly their scholarly study entitled *The Vinland Map and the Tartar Relation*. In this handsome and well-illustrated volume, three internationally respected scholars discussed the map that was being presented to the world as "the earliest known and indisputable cartographic representation of any part of the Americas." The Vinland map is an elliptically shaped world image that includes the western ocean (Atlantic) with delineations of Iceland, Greenland, and a large island or landmass identified as "Island of Vinland, discovered by Bjarni and Leif in company." The analysis of the map and the document with which it had once been bound—the "Tartar Relation"—led to the conclusion that both map and text had been copied in about 1440 from earlier originals.

That Norsemen had visited North America as much as 500 years before Columbus's voyage was not a new idea. The Icelandic sagas and the archeological finds at L'Anse aux Meadows on the north coast of Newfoundland about 1970 had provided convincing evidence. What was new was the fact that a map dating from before 1492 showed a land called Vinland in the position of North America. In the words of Yale University Press releases, the Vinland map was "the most important cartographic discovery of the century." Not all scholars were convinced of the map's authenticity, however. The provenance of the map was shadowy, if not suspect. It had been bought from an unidentified owner in Europe then resold to a wealthy anonymous buyer, who gave it to Yale. Seaver, writing in 1997, argued that a German Jesuit priest and map scholar drew the Vinland map in the 1930s. If she is correct, Yale is custodian of one of the greatest scholarly hoaxes of all time.

What can be determined and generally accepted with respect to the Norse contacts with North America in the period around A.D. 1000? First, the historical record makes clear that the peoples of northern Europe in the early Middle Ages were an extremely energetic and venturesome group. The progenitors of the peoples we now know as Swedes, Norwegians, and Danes appear to have poured forth from their northern homelands in a number of waves from the 8th to the 11th centuries. What triggered these movements is not entirely clear. Some suggest that overpopulation may have been the stimulus for sea roving and migration; others hold that political unrest, stirred by unpopular and repressive rulers, provided the impetus.

The western wing of this Norse expansion surged beyond continental Europe to reach and colonize the remote shores of Iceland in the 9th century. From Iceland, the next step was to the largely ice-covered island that the outlawed Eric the Red named Greenland to encourage

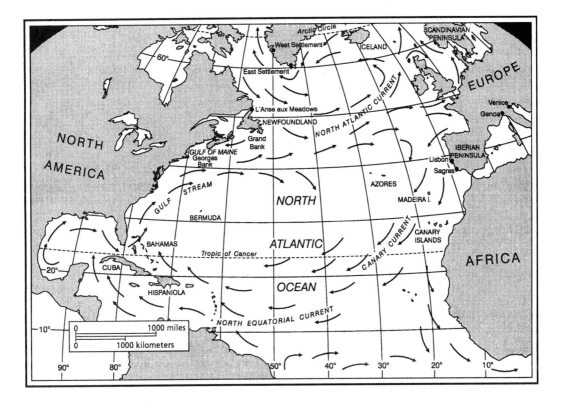

Figure 2.1 The North Atlantic, a New Mediterranean

others to follow and join in the settlement he pioneered. In time, two Norse communities—East Settlement and West Settlement—were founded on the coast of southern Greenland (fig. 2.1).

Like their relatives in northern Europe, the settlers of Iceland and Greenland were pagans who worshipped the old Norse gods Odin, Freya, and Thor. According to many experts, Leif Ericson brought Christianity to Greenland from Norway in the same year he is believed to have sighted Vinland. According to interpretations of the Icelandic sagas, Norway's King Olaf converted Leif and sent him to spread Christianity to Greenland. In the words of the saga:

> The king provided him with a priest and various other holy men to baptize folk there and instruct them in the true faith. Leif set sail for Greenland that summer [A.D. 1000], and while at sea picked up a ship's crew of men who lay helpless there on a wreck. On this same journey he found Vinland the Good. He reached

Greenland at the end of the summer and went to the lodge of Brattahild with Eric his father. From this time forward men called him Leif the Lucky, but his father contended that one thing cancelled out the other, in that Leif had rescued a ship's company and saved the men's lives, but had also introduced a man of mischief [as Eric styled the priest] into Greenland. (Quinn 1979, 1: 33)

In spite of reactionaries like Eric, the pagan status quo gave way to the zeal of the early Christian missionaries. Churches were built, and by 1126 an ecclesiastical jurisdiction was established in the East Settlement to provide for the spiritual needs of the almost 10,000 Greenland colonists.

Whatever the specific dates and details concerned with the Norse discovery of North America may be, one thing appears reasonably clear: the Greenland colonists, and not the Viking kingdoms in Europe, provided the manpower and equipment that made New World contacts a reality. Further, the small numbers of

Greenlanders and their limited resource base soon came under stress, which eventually led to their loss of contact with Europe and ultimate extinction. Carl Sauer is only one of many scholars who have speculated on the reasons for the decline of the Greenland colonies. The mystery of Vinland and its Norse colonists will be understood only when the larger mystery of the decline and extinction of the Greenland settlements is solved.

It is best to keep an open mind on the whole subject of pre-Columbian contacts with America. That such contacts took place seems certain. Exactly who made them and when and where they occurred represent challenges to researchers in a number of historical disciplines. Most scholars would agree that impacts of those early contacts were probably very limited compared with the revolutionary character of the impacts that flowed from the European rediscovery of the New World spearheaded by Columbus.

A THEORY OF EXPLORATION

J. D. Overton, writing in the *Journal of Historical Geography,* correctly criticized the traditional narrative approach that has characterized most writing on the history of exploration. He urged that geographical exploration be studied in its widest context with greater emphasis placed on its causes and effects, rather than simply on the colorful personalities and dramatic events that have dominated most literature in the field.

In developing a theoretical model of a more process-oriented approach to exploration, Overton was careful to distinguish between geographical discovery and exploration. Discoverers, he argued, merely find or uncover places; it remains for explorers to begin the continuing assessment and evaluation. He wrote that "whether an area is 'known' or 'unknown' depends on how much knowledge and what type of knowledge is required." Reassessments and reevaluations of areas for newly determined purposes or needs are thus just as legitimate for study as are the reports of the first explorers or surveyors who provided the earliest descriptions or maps of those areas. Exploration, in Overton's scheme, implies an intention that results in "a conscious search for knowledge within and about imperfectly known areas." Thus, Colum-

bus should be considered as an explorer consciously searching for a western sea route to Asia, who unwittingly encountered two continents that had been absent from the worldview of the Europeans and the Old World from which they came.

Exploration seen as a process involves six main elements (fig. 2.2). The first, demand for exploration, represents push factors that encourage a society or individual to extend interest to unexplored or little-known areas. Overton suggested economic conditions, such as scarcity of land or natural resources, restricted fields of trade, or isolation from markets, as typical factors that have prompted exploration. Religious zeal and scientific curiosity have also operated to create demand. At the individual level, the desire for wealth and status has been a potent force leading many to leave the security of homelands to blaze new trails in distant areas. The second element is the choice of area to be explored. Just when journeys of exploration occur is largely determined by demand factors, but the choice of where these journeys go is related to the assessment and evaluation of prospective unexplored or underexplored areas before exploration is undertaken.

The next step is the actual journey of exploration, on which, as Overton noted, writers have concentrated. The product of that journey is the explorer's report. This vital component, in written form or related orally, and either official or private, includes the descriptions and assessments of the newly explored area. The explorer's report is then evaluated by decision makers, who judge the adventure to be either successful or unsuccessful. If it is less than successful, the demand factors remain unfulfilled and the process may be repeated in a newly selected area. A judgment of success, whether partial or full, could trigger development of fisheries, trading posts, mines, plantations, missions, or permanent settlements in the newly explored territory. In due course, if the area becomes fully developed, the pioneer occupants themselves enter into the exploration process.

A further important component of Overton's model is the concept of perception. He emphasized the fact that, as Ralph Brown wrote, "men at all times have been influenced quite as much by beliefs as by facts." Explorers, like most human beings, view, assess, and describe environments they encounter from the perspective of

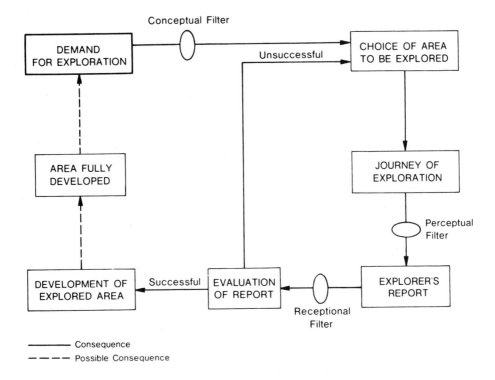

Figure 2.2 Main Elements of the Process of Exploration (after Overton)

the culture group and age to which they belong, as well as from their personal backgrounds, beliefs, aspirations, and values. These can be thought of as forming selective filters or lenses through which passes the information gleaned from the exploratory process. Overton's model forms, he wrote, "a more holistic perspective, stressing the links between the different facets of the exploration process and placing exploration in its broader economic and social context."

EUROPE'S ATLANTIC OUTLOOK RESUMES

The many original impulses leading Europeans to the discovery and exploration of North America can be compared with the roots of a large tree, which can be followed in any number of directions. The Age of Discovery had complex and interlocking origins that touched almost every facet of European life and existence. Only a few of the many rich themes elucidating the causes and effects of the European New World

exploration can be considered here. Important among these themes is the emergence of the Atlantic outlook and orientation that came to characterize and eventually dominate the lives of western Europeans. By the middle of the 17th century, the Atlantic Ocean ceased to be the limit of the known world and became another Mediterranean—a sea within the lands—to those Europeans now occupying or exploiting practically its whole littoral (fig. 2.1).

To understand how this came about, it is necessary to appreciate that the orientation of Europe toward the Mediterranean Sea and the East did not end with the decline of Roman control and the onset of the so-called Dark Ages. Crusaders from the far corners of Christian Europe and merchant travelers, such as Marco Polo, were familiar with Middle Eastern caravansaries, where luxuries and indispensable spices from the East Indies and Cathay (as eastern Asia was known) were traded. European demand for these commodities grew, if for no other reason than increasing population. It is estimated that, between the beginning of the Christian era and A.D. 1500, the world's population doubled from 250 million to 500 million. The increases appear to have been greatest in the areas of the old Roman Empire, with western and central Europe showing the largest gains.

Shortly after Marco Polo's return from China in 1295, the power balance in the Mediterranean basin tipped sharply against the interests of the Europeans and Christendom. The capture of Acre in northern Palestine by the sultan of Egypt eliminated the last of the many Christian strongholds won during the Crusades. An awareness of the strength of Islam was thrust on the Europeans, as first Egypt and then the Ottoman Empire gained control of the trade routes to sources of the commodities, particularly spices, on which the Europeans had come to rely. Food preservation and preparation in that unrefrigerated age demanded that spices be acknowledged as essentials and not luxuries for the favored few. Indeed, a whole range of commodities known today as pharmaceuticals and dyestuffs are usually included under the term "spices" as used in historical discussions of this sort. Italian merchant republics, dominated by Venice and Genoa, entered into trading alliances with the Muslim powers and became profiteering middlemen in commercial links with the East.

As these pressures developed in the trading system connecting Europe, the Mediterranean, and the Middle East, important events were transpiring on the Atlantic front of Europe. Technological advances pioneered by Mediterranean navigators made safe oceanic sailing a reality. The compass, astrolabe, and portolan sea charts aboard ships rigged so that they could sail almost into the wind were the basic tools needed for exploring the far reaches of the globe. All had been perfected in the Mediterranean and were at hand when the Spanish and Portuguese led the way into the Atlantic during the 15th century.

Portugal and Henry the Navigator

Portugal was particularly well suited to adopt programs of Atlantic exploration. A long Atlantic coastline provided numerous ports vital in the sea link between northwestern Europe and the Mediterranean. Genoese merchants and navigators formed important and influential communities in those ports and contributed to the growth of the Portuguese merchant fleet. Aided by their Genoese guests, the Portuguese began to probe the Atlantic off their shores and northern Africa. Prince Henry (1394–1460), immortalized with the title "Navigator," played a truly extraordinary role in these developments. As the third son of his royal father, Henry had little hope of ever assuming the throne and seemed destined for an army career. He led the military campaign that drove the Moors from Ceuta in north Africa in 1415 and planted the first seed of what was to become a vast Portuguese empire in Africa.

Henry's encounters with the Moors probably gave him good opportunities to absorb their geographical lore and add it to his own body of European knowledge. He was instrumental in mounting expeditions that discovered and colonized the islands of the Madeiras and the Azores (fig. 2.1). Oceanic discovery and exploration were not hit-or-miss undertakings to Henry. On the contrary, he is believed to have set up a highly organized center at Sagres in southern Portugal for gathering geographical intelligence and training navigators (fig. 2.3). From this "think tank" command center at Europe's southwestern tip, he conducted a national program of discovery and exploration that culminated, after his death, in the rounding of Africa and regular trade between Portugal and India and beyond. Reflecting on the Portuguese accomplishment, Carl Sauer argued that Portugal could have gained control of the Atlantic had not wars with the kingdom of Castile, which invaded Portugal repeatedly, and the Black Death impeded her.

By the time Columbus sailed under the banner of Portugal's enemy neighbor, Spain, Madeira had become integrated into the economies of Europe and Africa. T. Bently Duncan wrote, "The island was the prototype of that momentous and tragic social and economic system of sugar and slavery that was to be repeated, on a far larger scale, in the West Indies and Brazil." Only 75 years after first settlement, Madeira was the world's greatest sugar producer and an important center of commerce and navigation.

Spain and Columbus's Western Sea Route Hypothesis

Christopher Columbus (ca. 1451–1506) was one of the many Genoese navigators familiar with the Iberian coast and Atlantic sea routes to northern Europe. Experts believe that he voyaged aboard ships bound as far as Iceland, an important source of salt fish for Iberia's Roman Catholics. If this is true, he may well have gained a knowledge of the lore surrounding the early Norse voyages west of Greenland. It is certain that he shipped aboard Portuguese vessels to the coast of western Africa, where trading contacts followed Prince Henry's exploratory expeditions.

Columbus married the daughter of a wealthy Madeira landowner, but after her death he and his brother took up residence in Lisbon and entered the nautical chart and instrument trade. There he put his experiences and acquired knowledge to work in formulating a well-thought-out hypothesis and proposal concerning a western sea route across the Atlantic to the islands and coasts of easternmost Asia. When one considers his background, it is not difficult to imagine that Columbus was able to structure a convincing and persuasive proposal.

The widespread European belief in legends of islands and lands in the Atlantic to the west doubtless aided such a scheme. The story of Antilia—a rich, luxurious island far west off the coast of Africa peopled by Christians who had migrated there from Europe—was typical of these legends (fig. 2.4). Some scholars believe that Antilia may have been based on misunderstood or garbled reports of the early Greenland settlements. Whatever its inspiration, Antilia, in one form or another, was a fixture on pre-Columbian maps and did nothing to detract from Columbus's hypothesis and bold scheme for discovery.

In 1484 Columbus petitioned the king of Portugal to send him on a voyage of discovery to the west. But Portugal was deeply committed to a southern approach to the Orient and refused. Over the next several years he vainly attempted to gain royal backing for his venture. At last, in 1492, following the Spanish expulsion of the Moors from Granada (their last Iberian stronghold), Columbus was granted his long-sought support. Spain, now at peace and eager to enter the exploratory race with its neighbor Portugal, decided that Columbus's scheme was worth a modest investment.

Figure 2.3 Monument of the Discoveries, near Lisbon (author)

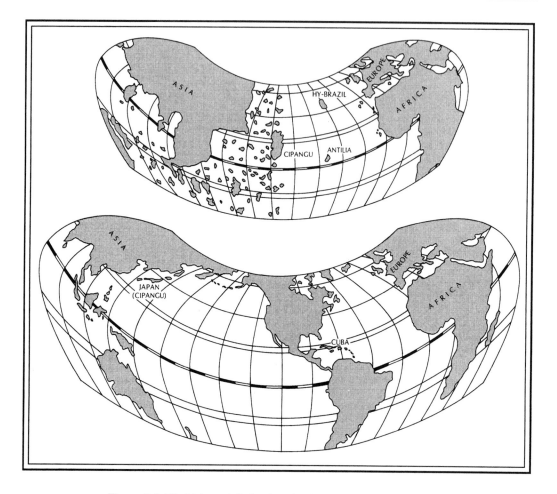

Figure 2.4 Worldview of Columbus (top) and Real World (bottom)l

COLUMBUS'S WORLDVIEW AND THE BEHAVIORAL ENVIRONMENT

The world was a sphere, as Columbus and every other educated European of his day well knew. What he did not share was the prevailing estimate of the earth's circumference and the width of the Atlantic Ocean. He was convinced that the value of a degree of longitude at the equator was about 45 nautical miles in length, rather than the actual length, 60 nautical miles. In other words, he underestimated the earth's size by 25 percent. On his small world, the three continents of Europe, Asia, and Africa were surrounded by an all-embracing ocean (fig. 2.4). Asia, in his mind, stretched far beyond its true east-west width to face Europe across a sailable

Atlantic. The Canary Islands, by his calculations, were only 2,400 nautical miles from Japan, less than one-quarter of the actual distance of 10,600 nautical miles. Columbus had assiduously gathered sources and authorities to support his hypothesis that the earth was small and Asia wide.

Columbus's worldview was largely in keeping with what geographer William Kirk would recognize as the "behavioral environment" of his day, a view generally shared by his informed western European contemporaries in the late 15th century. Kirk urges that we try to put ourselves into the minds of people like Columbus and other past decision makers to understand why and how they undertook actions that profoundly affected world history and geography.

In the view of Spanish royal advisers, Columbus was promoting a reasonable scheme worth a modest gamble in terms of demand factors current at the time.

What Columbus accomplished has been termed by his biographer, Samuel Eliot Morison, "the most spectacular and most far-reaching geographical discovery in recorded human history." But it was not immediately perceived as such. Many experts believe that Columbus may never have realized the true nature of his great discovery and died still assuming that the Caribbean islands and shores were parts of eastern Asia, rather than portions of two new continents. He reported Cuba as the eastern-most cape of Asia and stated that Honduras, Nicaragua, and Costa Rica were provinces of Cathay. This misrepresentation did not, however, prevent Spain from beginning to colonize the new discoveries almost as soon as he had found them.

King Ferdinand and Queen Isabella endorsed Columbus's proposal to return to the West Indies (as we would call them today) and establish a trading colony on Hispaniola (fig. 2.1). In their instructions, issued on May 29, 1493, they set the conversion of the Natives to Christianity as the first object for Columbus's second expedition. Six priests were assigned to the fleet, and Columbus was ordered to see that the Natives were "treated very well and lovingly." Despite the pride of place given these lofty religious aims, the expedition's commercial motive is amply revealed in the fact that most of the 1,500 other people recruited were aboard for the second declared motive, the creation of a trading colony. A third charge to Columbus, now an admiral, was to explore Cuba and establish whether it was a part of the Asian mainland and a potential route to the riches of Cathay.

THE DISCLOSURE OF A NEW WORLD

John Cabot (1450–98), like Columbus, appears to have been born in or near Genoa. Some time after assuming Venetian citizenship, he found his way to Bristol, England's second-largest port. In the early 1490s, Bristol was a large fishing port as well as an important center in the trading network that linked Iceland, northwestern Europe, the Iberian Peninsula, and the Mediterranean. Leaders in both the merchant and the fishing communities of Bristol were responding to demand factors and sponsoring occasional exploratory voyages during the 1480s and 1490s. From two to four ships a year went in search of the legendary island of Hy-Brazil and the Seven Cities of Antilia. Exploration for new fisheries and trade routes was a recognized undertaking.

Cabot's scheme of discovery, in broad outline, shared much with the one Columbus had promoted successfully. Cabot proposed sailing west to the Indies by a route farther poleward and thus shorter than the admiral's. On his route, Hy-Brazil took the place of Antilia as a way station (fig. 2.4). King Henry VII of England would not invest directly in the expedition but did issue a patent allowing Cabot to sail to any part of the world unknown to Christians. This device, by which England did not appear to be in direct competition with the Iberians, asserted England's right to sail in search of unknown lands. This declaration meant little at the time but later served as a significant argument when England actively began to compete for overseas trade and possessions. Prior discovery was frequently used to justify colonization.

Cabot first undertook a single-ship reconnaissance voyage in 1497 to test his thesis. His navigation was good, and wind conditions allowed him to make a swift crossing from Bristol to Newfoundland in just over a month. If Samuel Eliot Morison's reconstruction of that voyage is correct, Cabot made his first North American landing only a few miles from the L'Anse aux Meadows site that is believed to be the location of Leif Ericson's Norse settlement—a remarkable coincidence. Cabot's first voyage appears to have caused a brief sensation when he rushed to London to inform the king, and Henry rewarded him with a gift of £10 "to hym that founde the new Isle." Unfortunately, little is known of where Cabot explored and what he reported. What evidence exists must be inferred from the letters and reports of others. Unlike those of Columbus, no journals or reports by Cabot have survived.

In February 1498, Henry VII issued letters patent giving John Cabot permission to organize a large expedition to explore the coast he had discovered. According to one contemporary report, Cabot planned to sail along the coast to the island of Cipangu (as Japan was known), where

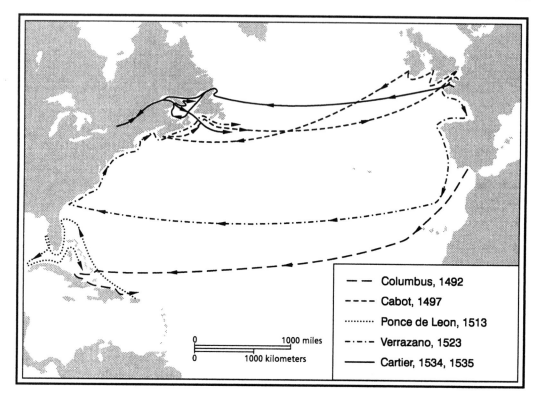

Figure 2.5 Early Transatlantic Voyages to 1535

he felt the jewels and spices of the world originated (fig. 2.4). Once there he intended, it was reported, to set up a trading factory and make London "a more important mart than Alexandria." In the late spring of 1498 four ships sailed past Ireland on a westward course; they vanished, never to be heard from again. What befell Cabot's second expedition remains unknown. His son, Sebastian, had not been with the flotilla and continued in his father's footsteps with a later expedition. After failing to find a northwest passage to Asia, Sebastian shifted his service to Spain and became the pilot major for that country, responsible for recording discoveries and making corrections to charts and sailing distances.

Transatlantic probes like those of Columbus and Cabot were contributing to a growing but still disconnected fund of geographical intelligence bearing on the western rim of the Atlantic (fig. 2.5). The description of coasts and islands forming that rim failed to match what was known to exist in eastern Asia. Where were the rich and teeming cities? What about the wealthy potentates and their palaces? None could be found in these "Indies" of the explorers, and nothing that even remotely began to approach the inherited "reality" that formed the behavioral environment of the Europeans with respect to Asia.

Many innovative hypotheses were formulated to accommodate the emerging new geography (fig. 2.6). Several involved the concept of a projection or peninsula of Asia that jutted far to the east. Others were based on the belief that explorers had found remote peninsulas and islands off the Asian coasts and not the known lands of Cathay, Japan, and India. When studying maps drawn during the Age of Exploration, it is a good idea to think of them in this abstracted, graphic form, for what may appear to modern eyes to be bizarre distortions of the continents and oceans were, for their time, entirely reasonable geographical ideas.

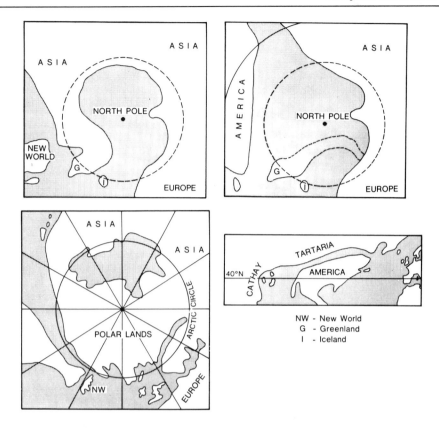

Figure 2.6 Diagrammatic Models of Several New World Hypotheses

THE NAMING OF AMERICA

In the early 1500s, a circle of scholars in the small Vosges mountain town of St.-Dié, in what is today Alsace-Lorraine, was working on a project to publish an atlas that would incorporate the new discoveries being reported. The Gymnase Vosgien, as the group was known, was equipped with a printing press on which their material could be copied rapidly. One member of the small group was a German-born priest named Martin Waldseemüller, who, in addition to having a knowledge of geography, was a skilled draftsman and cartographer. When word of Amerigo Vespucci's discoveries along the South American coast reached Waldseemüller and his colleagues, they were quick to realize that Vespucci had been skirting more than a mere peninsula of Asia. In *Cosmographiae Introductio,* their printed treatise of 1507, the St.-Dié scholars explained that

Vespucci had in truth found "another fourth part of the world." In *Keys to the Encounter* I quote the paragraph that gives the rationale for its name:

> Now, really these parts of the earth [Europe, Africa, and Asia] have been more extensively explored and another fourth part has been discovered by Americus Vespucci. . . . Inasmuch as both Europe and Asia received their names from women, I see no reason why anyone should object to calling this part Amerige, i.e. the land of Amerigo, or America, after Amerigo, its discoverer, a man of great ability. (De Vorsey 1992, 154)

The *Cosmographiae* was accompanied by Waldseemüller's maps, showing a separate landmass in the sea between Europe and Asia. They are the first maps to use the name America to designate a major portion of the New World. The fundamental concept of a tripartite world, tracing its roots back to the ancient Greeks and emerging as a theological truism when Christianity flowered, was extremely hard for the Europeans to abandon. The accumulating evidence of the existence of a New World became overwhelming in time, however, and they were forced to wrestle with the countless spiritual and material ramifications that this realization brought to their lives.

EXPLORATION OF THE
EASTERN SEABOARD

Perhaps the most surprising aspect of the exploration of North America is how slow the process was in getting under way. For most of the century following its discovery by the Europeans, North America represented a hazily defined barrier rather than an attractive field for exploration. Only slowly did the New World enter the minds of Europeans as an arena in which exploratory effort should be expended. This attitude accounts for the unusually long period during which, as historical geographer Ralph H. Brown put it, "beliefs about America were dominant over facts." As he further noted, "the long years intervening between the arrival of the adventurous explorers and the no less courageous colonists had been curiously unproductive of new geographical knowledge." The remainder of this chapter will provide a brief review of those long years to illustrate the process by which the European colonial powers followed initial discovery with exploration, resource appraisal, and territorial acquisition along the eastern seaboard of North America.

The 15th century closed with the discoveries by Columbus in the south and Cabot in the north, still considered essentially disconnected events. Europeans believed that Columbus and Cabot each had reached islands lying east of a vast Asian continent (figs. 2.5 and 2.6). Not until the 16th-century voyages of Juan Ponce de León and Hernando de Soto, sponsored by Spain, and those by Giovanni da Verrazano and Jacques Cartier, under the French royal banner, did the continuity of North America from Florida to Labrador begin to become an accepted fact. Only then can true exploration of North America be said to have started.

Juan Ponce de León

In 1513, Juan Ponce de León (ca. 1460–1521), already rich from successful gold mining ventures in Puerto Rico, received a royal license "to discover and settle the island of Bimini," which was rumored to lie to the north. His voyage passed along the Atlantic side of the Bahamas to the coast of northern Florida (fig. 2.5). The party clashed with local Natives, probably in the vicinity of St. Augustine, and another battle ensued when a landing was made on the west coast of Florida, probably near San Carlos Bay. Although nothing of exceptional value was found and the Natives were notably inhospitable, Ponce proceeded with an attempt at settlement in 1521. Possibly encouraged by reports of the fabulous wealth being found in Mexico, he equipped a party of 200 colonists with livestock, seed, and supplies for a settlement on the southwest coast of Florida. Here, Ponce probably reasoned, all ships leaving or entering the Gulf of Mexico would find it convenient to trade and take on stores and water. Unfortunately, he had not improved his negotiating skills, and shortly after landing, the Spaniards were driven out by vigorous Native attacks; Ponce de León was mortally wounded.

Ponce's unsuccessful excursion to the Florida mainland was soon followed by the equally ill-fated adventures of Lucas Vasquez de Ayllon on the coast of South Carolina and Georgia and those of Pánfilo de Narváez and Álvar Núñez Cabeza de Vaca on the Gulf Coast. By the end of 1528, Spain had experienced a series of failed adventures and had acquired only the sketchiest knowledge of the outline of North America from Texas to South Carolina. The failure to find gold or other great wealth, coupled with the presence of warlike Natives, discouraged further Spanish interest in Florida for several decades.

The most significant discovery by Ponce de León was the powerful Gulf Stream—the *carrera de las Indias*—flowing northward along Florida's Atlantic coast. He reported that, "although we had a great wind, we could not proceed forward [in those waters], but backward and it seemed that we were proceeding well, but in the end it was known that it was in such wise the current which was more powerful than the wind." Off Cape Canaveral the Gulf Stream had a daily summer flow of 70 miles. It was not long before Spanish navigators were regularly returning from Caribbean and Central American waters on the Gulf Stream to the latitude of the Carolina Outer Banks, and thence eastward to Iberia on the prevailing westerlies (fig. 2.1). When Spain finally did establish St. Augustine as an enduring outpost on the eastern seaboard of North America in 1565, a key motivation was to protect this maritime jugular vein of her New World empire.

Giovanni da Verrazano

The coastal region to the north of Florida was first described by Giovanni da Verrazano (ca. 1485–ca. 1528). He and others firmly believed that somewhere between the latitude of Florida and the codfish-rich coasts first sighted by John Cabot might be found a sea passage to Cathay and the Spice Islands. Verrazano persuaded Francis I of France to support a westward voyage in 1523–24, partly on the basis of reports from the survivors of Magellan's circumnavigation of the world. He crossed the Atlantic at approximately 32° N, using the tried-and-true technique of latitude sailing (fig 2.5). Fearing contact with Spaniards, who he felt might be in the Florida area, Verrazano turned his attention to the unknown latitudes to the north.

The chief outcome of Verrazano's reconnaissance of what we know as the eastern seaboard of the United States was the widespread realization that North America was a great independent landmass, important in its own right. Thanks to his detailed descriptions of the land and its aboriginal inhabitants, Europeans began to perceive North America as a verdant and potentially rich land. A typical description follows, made the day Verrazano left his ship, lying offshore just outside the inlet now spanned by the Verrazano Narrows Bridge between Staten Island and Brooklyn, and entered lower New York Bay with the ship's boat. Carl Sauer's transcription of what Verrazano wrote appears in *16th-Century North America:*

> We entered the river into the land for about half a league, where we saw that it formed a very beautiful lake about three leagues [ten miles] in circuit, on which about thirty of their [the Natives'] barks were going from one side to the other, carrying an infinite number of people coming from different parts to see us. Suddenly, as befalls in navigating, there rose a strong contrary wind from the sea which forced us to return to the ship and, greatly to our regret, to leave that land, so hospitable and attractive, and we think, not without things of value, all the hills showing minerals. (Sauer 1971, 55)

The description of the Native landscape Verrazano might have provided would have to await a future chronicler.

Another product of Verrazano's voyage had a major influence on the cartography of North America throughout much of the 16th century. It grew from observations made while he was cautiously sounding his ship, the *Dauphine,* through the hazardous shallows that extend seaward from North Carolina's range of narrow barrier islands now known as the Outer Banks. Perhaps because of poor visibility, Verrazano did not observe that there were narrow inlets between the islands making up the banks. In his report to the king, he wrote of finding, in place of long, narrow islands and inlets, "an isthmus one mile wide and about two hundred miles long, in which we could see the eastern sea from the ship. . . . This is, doubtless, the one which goes round the tip of India, China and Cathay." To his eager eye, the broad expanse of Pamlico Sound was the Pacific Ocean. Numerous maps drawn in the century following his report prominently showed the "Sea of Verrazano" separated from the Atlantic Ocean by a narrow isthmus in the general area now occupied by North Carolina and Virginia.

Some authorities believe that Verrazano may have elaborated somewhat on his actual observations in an effort to improve his stature in the king's eyes and ensure support for follow-up expeditions. His hopes were not realized, however, because Francis I embroiled France in a disastrous war in Italy, and Verrazano lost his life on an expedition to Central America in about 1528. Although he did not live to know about it, the concept of a New France on the western rim of the Atlantic had taken root.

Jacques Cartier

Ten years passed before the French king once again was ready to back a voyage to North America, but during that time French fishermen were active on the rich grounds and banks around Newfoundland. Despite their caution about sharing geographical information, they appear to have drawn attention to the Strait of Belle Isle, the long, narrow arm of sea separating the Labrador coast from the northern part of Newfoundland. So it was that in 1534 Francis I commissioned Jacques Cartier (1491–1557) "to voyage and go to the New Lands and to pass the Strait of the Bay of Castles." Another contemporaneous document revealed that he was expected to "discover certain islands and lands where it is said he should find great quantities of gold and other rich things." It appears that Cartier's expedition was to discover a route to Asia and find treasure-bearing lands along the way. This was a prophetic vision in view of the fabulous wealth the French fur trade in the St. Lawrence Valley and Great Lakes basin ultimately yielded.

Cartier sailed from St.-Malo in northern France in late April 1534 and arrived off eastern Newfoundland in an amazingly brief 27 days (fig. 2.5). He explored the coast of today's eastern New Brunswick and the Gaspé Peninsula and named the large bay separating the two areas Chaleur in recognition of the early summer heat. For a short time he believed that Baie de Chaleur might even be the passage to the Pacific. During a detailed survey of the bay, Cartier encountered a large number of Natives who showed a lively interest in trading with the crew. We pick up his story through Sauer:

> We likewise made signs to them that we wished them no harm and sent two men ashore to give them some knives and other iron goods and a red cap to give to their chief. Seeing this they sent to the shore a party with some of their furs; and the two groups traded together. The savages showed marvelous great pleasure in possessing and obtaining these iron wares and other commodities, dancing and going through many ceremonies and throwing salt water over their heads with their hands. They bartered everything they had to the extent that all went back naked without a thing on them; and they made signs that they would be back on the morrow with more furs. [Cartier and his men explored Chaleur Bay to its head] whereat we were grieved and disappointed. At the head of the bay, beyond its low shore were very high mountains. And seeing that there was no passage we proceeded to turn back. (Sauer 1971, 80)

Such was the beginning of the fur trade, a chief source of wealth for early Canada.

At least one more large Native group—some 300 Mi'kmaq—engaged in an active session of bartering in the days that followed and further demonstrated the commercial potential of the region. Cartier never found the entrance to the St. Lawrence valley, but the voyage nevertheless was judged a success. He returned to St. Malo with furs and local Natives to be tutored in French and serve as guides on his next expedition.

The following year (1535), Cartier entered the St. Lawrence River and proceeded to explore it, doubtless aided by the geographical intelligence the Natives were able to provide. Near the site of present-day Quebec City, where the St. Charles River joins the St. Lawrence, Cartier decided in September to establish a base for the winter. His description of the area near the important Native town of Stadacona painted a most attractive picture:

> This is as good land as can be found and is highly productive, with many fine trees of the nature and kinds of France, such as oaks, elms, ash, nut trees, plum trees, yews, cedars, vines, hawthorns with fruits as large as damson plums, and other trees, beneath which there grows as good hemp as that of France, and it grows without sowing or labor. (Sauer 1971, 86)

Cartier continued upriver with his smallest vessel and two longboats, through a valley he described in similarly glowing terms. On October 2, 1535, more than 1,000 Natives at the site of present-day Montreal met his party "with as good a welcome as ever a father gave to his son." Their town, Hochelaga, was an impressive settlement surrounded by a strong, well-engineered defensive palisade. Cartier found, within the enclosed space,

> some fifty houses . . . each fifty or more paces long and twelve to fifteen wide, made of timbers and covered, roof and sides, by large pieces of bark and rind of trees, some as wide as a table and artfully tied according to their manner. And inside are a number of rooms and chambers and in the center of the house is a large room or space upon the ground, where they make their fire and live together, the men thereafter retiring with wives and children to their private rooms. Also houses have lofts on

high in which they store their corn. (Sauer, 1971, 88)

At the fortified winter camp downriver, the Canadian winter closed in with a ferocity that amazed the Frenchmen. Their position was almost two full degrees of latitude south of St.-Malo and was presumed to have been similar in climate, if not even milder. All might have gone well if an infectious disease had not been spread to the local Stadacona Natives. Cartier, fearing that his party might contract the scourge decimating their neighbors, forbade them from entering the fort or having any contact with the French. It is ironic that this reaction to the Natives' plight was to prove fatal to the Europeans. Cut off from contact with those who supplied fresh fish and game, the French party was forced to subsist on ship's biscuit and salt meat they had brought from France. Predictably, a virulent attack of scurvy hit the snowbound and vitamin-deficient French, and by mid-February almost all were seriously ill. Twenty-five died and 40 more were near death before one of the Natives, who had been to France with Cartier, taught them a local remedy, made by boiling the needles and bark of evergreen trees. As the party returned to health, contact with the Natives resumed, and fresh fish and game became available once again.

In May 1536 the survivors returned to St.-Malo after completing the longest and most revealing reconnaissance yet of the heart of the region that would become, in the following century, New France. No route to Asia was found, and instead Cartier, together with Jean-François de la Rocque de Roberval (ca. 1500–1560), undertook ill-fated attempts to establish settlements in the 1540s. Once again the unbridled ferocity of the Canadian winter proved too great a hardship, and the alleged gold and precious stones that turned out to be iron pyrites and worthless rock broke the spirit of the entrepreneurs. Attempts at permanent settlement in New France were abandoned for more than 60 years, until Samuel de Champlain came along early in the 17th century (fig. 2.7).

Hernando de Soto

At about the same time that Cartier and Roberval were facing difficulties in the St. Lawrence, far to the south Hernando de Soto (ca. 1499–1542) was undertaking one of the most incredible exploratory adventures in the annals of history. De Soto, already wealthy and influential after 15 years of gathering treasure in Central America and Peru, turned his eyes to the mainland of what is now the American South. After receiving the necessary royal permissions and privileges, the successful conquistador had little trouble in recruiting an expedition of more than 700 treasure seekers in Spain. A convoy of ten ships was required to move the party, so large that it resembled an invasion force. Some 600 soldiers and more than 100 servants and camp followers, along with 200 horses, 300 pigs, and an impressive baggage train, were finally landed on the southwest coast of Florida on May 25, 1539 (fig. 2.7).

Unlike the other Spanish adventurers who had preceded him, de Soto had no interest in coastal settlement. Rather, he followed the procedure of the conquistadors in Central and South America, where gold and precious objects had been found in the interior. De Soto proceeded to lead his unwieldy expedition along a rambling route that ultimately touched portions of the present states of Florida, Georgia, South Carolina, North Carolina, Tennessee, Alabama, Mississippi, Arkansas, Louisiana, and Texas. The typical plan would be to capture a local Native chief and force his tribe to ransom him for food and bearers to carry the camp equipment and baggage to the next major tribal center, where the process would be repeated. As might be expected, the Natives suffered drastically, particularly as they fell prey to the European diseases.

The expedition crossed the Appalachian Mountains and the Mississippi River and encountered Plains dwellers. From these people de Soto, apparently still indefatigable, attempted to learn of the route "to the other sea," as the Pacific was termed. But by 1542, nearly four years after his landing in Florida, he appears to have given up the quest and decided to return to civilization. On the trail to the coast, however, he took a fever and died. His body was committed to a watery grave in the Mississippi River for fear that it might be mutilated by vengeful Natives. About 300 Spaniards managed to survive the ordeal and reach the Mexican town of Panuco in the autumn of 1543, empty-handed and dressed in patches of hides taken from the Natives. Perhaps the best summary of de Soto's

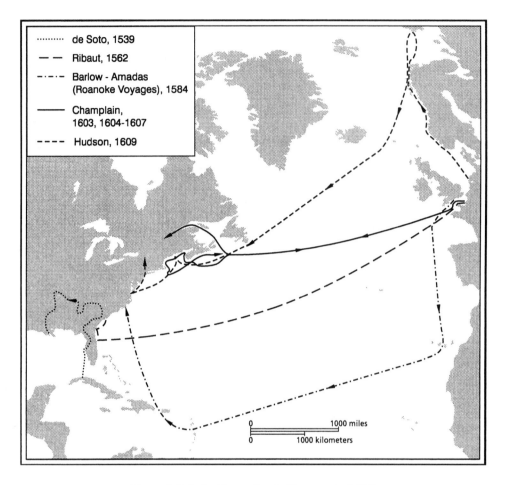

Figure 2.7 Later Transatlantic Voyages to 1609

incredible enterprise was provided by the Spanish historian Lopez de Gomara, who wrote:

> He went about for five years hunting mines, thinking it would be like Peru. He made no settlement and thus he died and destroyed those who went with him. Never will conquerers do well unless they settle before they undertake anything else, especially here where the Indians are valiant bowmen and strong. (Sauer 1971, 78)

In the years that followed de Soto's adventure, Florida remained an uninhabited coast vaguely visible in the west to the hundreds of treasure-laden Spanish galleons that sailed along it in the strong north-flowing Gulf Stream.

Jean Ribaut

Settlement in the St. Lawrence region may have been problematic in the 16th century, but France did not ignore the possibility of settlement in Florida. French Protestants, known as Huguenots, were a nonconforming minority increasingly under stress in the predominantly Catholic monarchy of the mid-16th century. The Huguenot protector was also the admiral of France and held authority over merchant as well as naval shipping. The idea of establishing overseas colonial refuges for the Huguenots was thus supported at the highest level. If such a colony could be established along the Florida coast, it could be expected to serve as a valuable base for French attacks on the antagonistic rival Spaniards. Spanish official policy excluded all other European powers from North America, as had been the case since the papal decree of 1494. In addition, a Florida colony would enjoy a more genial climate than the bitter one experienced by Cartier.

In February 1562, two French ships under the command of Jean Ribaut (ca. 1520–65) and Goulaine de Laudonnière made a fast passage from Le Havre, in heavily Protestant Normandy, to the St. Johns River in northern Florida (fig. 2.7). The local Natives stood in awe as the French explorers erected a large stone column bearing the royal arms and announced France's annexation of Florida. Ribaut continued north to explore the coast of Georgia and South Carolina, where he found that "many other rivers and arms of the sea divide and make many other great islands by which we may travel from one island to another between land and land. And it seemeth that we may go and sail without danger through all the country and enter into the great seas, which were a wonderful advantage." This fine description of the Sea Islands, sounds, and estuaries along this coast presaged the development of the Gulf Intracoastal Waterway of the modern era.

The French built an outpost, Charlesfort, on Port Royal Sound (in present day South Carolina) and garrisoned it with volunteers. The main party then sailed for France to raise additional support for a colony. They arrived to find that the long-feared religious war had broken out, and the planned relief for the volunteers on Port Royal Sound had to be abandoned. Not until the spring of 1564 was the Huguenot leadership able to send out another expedition to Florida under the command of Ribaut's lieutenant, Laudonnière. He found the St. Johns River after a quick passage and received an enthusiastic welcome from the Natives. With their advice and assistance, Laudonnière began construction of Fort Caroline a few miles upstream from the river's mouth and not far from present-day Jacksonville. The fort was to serve as the French base for further exploration designed to follow up Native stories of precious metals and other wealth in the interior.

It is fortunate that Laudonnière's party included a gifted artist who was assigned the task of keeping a visual record of the expedition's discoveries. Jacques Le Moyne's many sketches and drawings of Florida's landscape and Natives were published as engravings later in the centu-ry and constitute the first widely circulated visual account of North American aboriginal life and landscape. Little is known about Le Moyne's training or background except that he was from Dieppe, an important center of artistic cartographic development in the early 16th century. The Dieppe school is famed for its richly embellished maps that showed details of the flora and fauna of newly discovered lands in addition to their location and configuration.

The Spanish were aware of the French activities in Florida and resolved to remove the French from the region. In the late summer of 1565, Fort Caroline was attacked and taken by a force under the command of Pedro Menéndez de Avilés. About 132 French lives were lost in the attack, and a short while later a reinforcing fleet under the command of Jean Ribaut was wrecked by a hurricane along the coast to the south. Making its way north toward Fort Caroline, the French party was intercepted and brutally massacred by Menéndez, who spared only a few Catholics from the sword in an orgy of killing near the waterway still known as Matanzas Inlet (the place of slaughter), close to modern St. Augustine. The Spanish once again controlled the vital Gulf Stream sea route. St. Augustine boasts that its date of founding, 1565, makes it the oldest city settled by Europeans in North America. For the next two centuries Florida would form a bastion of the Spanish empire on the Atlantic seaboard of the new continent.

Walter Raleigh

Just as religion played a role in encouraging the French to explore Florida, it had a fundamental influence in the English exploration of the Carolinas and Virginia. Once Queen Elizabeth, a Protestant, was securely on the throne in England in 1558, the country's latent sentiment against Spanish Catholics surged to the surface. The Spanish monopoly over all trade with the New World was a major annoyance to seafaring English Protestants sailing from west-of-England ports. Attacks on Spanish fleets and towns by mariners like John Hawkins and Francis Drake signaled the rise of English sea power and inexorably drew the two nations toward war. It is not surprising that the line between New World exploration and privateer attacks against the Spanish was often blurred in the latter 1500s. Sir Humphrey Gilbert published a tract in 1577 in which he described "how Her Majesty might annoy the King of Spain by fitting out a fleet of war-ships under pretense of a voyage of discovery, and so fall upon the enemy's shipping and destroy his trade in Newfoundland and the West Indies."

After Gilbert's death, his half-brother Walter Raleigh (1552–1618), a particular favorite of Queen Elizabeth, received a patent "to discover, search, find out, and view such remote heathen and barbarous lands, countries, and territories, not actually possessed of any Christian prince, nor inhabited by Christian people, as to him . . . shall seem good, and the same to have, hold, occupy and enjoy to him, his heirs and assigns forever." The English view was that if the Spanish were not already occupying and developing New World areas, those regions would be fair game for England's subjects to exploit. In 1584 Raleigh sent a two-ship reconnaissance party under the command of Philip Amadas, a well-qualified navigator, and Arthur Barlowe, a capable soldier (fig. 2.7).

The historical record is not entirely clear as to Raleigh's precise ambitions, but we may conclude that any place he undertook to colonize had the potential to be a good base for attacks on the Spanish. Raleigh's thinking also may have been influenced by a growing desire for alternative sources for products traditionally imported from Spain. Because contemporary climatic theories held that regions occupying similar latitudinal positions were similar climatically and would produce the same range of crops, many observers reasoned that such products as olive oil, wine, leather, and sugar could be procured from a colony in the Carolinas or Virginia. Furthermore, they felt that the depressed economic conditions prevalent in England could be expected to produce willing colonists.

Barlowe prepared a report—"The First Voyage Made to the Coasts of America with Two Barks . . ."—for Raleigh at the conclusion of the 1584 voyage. He told of approaching the coast near 36° N, "where we smelled so sweet and so strong a smell as if we had been in the midst of some delicate garden abounding with all kinds of odoriferous flowers, by which we were assured that the land could not be far distant." The report described how the small fleet anchored near an inlet through the Outer Banks, entered Pamlico Sound in boats, and formally took possession of the land in the name of

Queen Elizabeth. Arriving at Roanoke Island, Barlowe found many "goodly woods full of deer, conies [rabbits], hares and fowl, even in the midst of summer in incredible abundance." He found the local Natives friendly and hospitable, and not much time was lost before "we fell to trading with them, exchanging some things that we had for chamois, buff and deer skins." Barlowe emphasized the profitability of the trade, describing how a bright tin plate was exchanged for "twenty skins worth twenty crowns or twenty nobles."

Barlowe's report was clearly designed to serve Raleigh as a promotion tract and was well larded with favorable adjectives. Nevertheless, Carl Sauer correctly categorized it as a balanced and perceptive observation of the flora, fauna, and Native culture of the Carolina and Virginia region on the eve of its colonization by the English. Like Cartier, Amadas and Barlowe "brought home also two of the savages, being lusty men, whose names were Wanchese and Manteo." It is no coincidence that North Carolina's capital city today is named Raleigh and that the two towns on Roanoke Island are named Manteo and Wanchese. Raleigh, with Barlowe's favorable report in hand and the Roanoke Natives on show around London, lost no time in organizing a follow-up venture. His fortunes were greatly enhanced by the favor he won from England's queen, in honor of whom he named the newly explored lands Virginia.

Roanoke Island proved lacking as a haven from which attacks could be mounted on treasure-laden Spanish galleons. But it did appeal to a group associated with John White, an artist-cartographer who may have been on the Amadas-Barlowe expedition of 1584. White's maps and drawings form an absolutely invaluable record of the land that attracted England's first colonists in North America. With help from Raleigh, White, appointed governor "of the Cittie of Raleigh in Virginia" in 1587, led a group of 110 settlers to reoccupy Roanoke Island; it included his daughter, who gave birth to Virginia Dare, the first English child born in America. White returned home for reinforcements, only to be caught up in the long-anticipated war with Spain—the Armada—early in 1588. By the time a relief expedition reached Roanoke Island, it was August 1590, and the colonists were nowhere to be found. At the time, the only evidence of the existence of the settlement, known ever since as the Lost Colony, was the enigmatic word "Croatoan" carved in a tree.

CONCLUSION

As the end of the 16th century drew in sight, both the French and the English had successfully challenged Spain's claim to a monopoly over the North American continent, and the Dutch were soon to follow. Along the Atlantic shoreline adventurers had planted a fragile colonial presence. The perception of North America was rapidly changing from that of a barrier, to be bypassed on the way to Asian riches, to that of a field for exploration and potentially profitable resource exploitation.

Events up to the start of the 17th century amply demonstrate the strength of Overton's expression of the process of exploration (fig. 2.2).

The demands—for empire and power—remain unchanged, but the scene (and attitude) has shifted from craving Asia to experiencing America. Hundreds of expeditions occurred, yielding reports in every sort of textual and visual form and generating opinions that invariably mixed incredulity with greed. More expeditions followed, feeding on what was already known and so much more that people now wanted to discover. Passage through the steps in the Overton diagram was intensifying. For the next two centuries Native Americans, African Americans, and European Americans would interact in an elaborate exercise to bring North America under control. Those readers who might think of this process as essentially "Europeanization" should contemplate the simplicity of sweeping historical generalizations. Chapters throughout this book will address the complex sequence of events in the development of modern North America.

ADDITIONAL READING

Allen, J. L. 1997. *North American Exploration*, vol. 1. Lincoln: University of Nebraska Press.

Brown, R. H. 1948. *Historical Geography of the United States*. New York: Harcourt, Brace & World.

Butzer, K. W., et al. 1992a. "The Americas before and after 1492: An Introduction to Current Geographical Research." *Annals of the Association of American Geographers* 82, no. 3 (September): 345–68.

———, ed. 1992b. "The Americas before and after 1492: Current Geographical Research." Special issue of *Annals of the Association of American Geographers* 82, no. 3 (September).

Collier, J. 1964. *Indians of the Americas: The Long Hope*. New York: New American Library.

Corbett, D. L. 1953. *Explorations, Descriptions, and Attempted Settlements of Carolina, 1584–1590*. Raleigh: University of North Carolina Department of Archives and History. Hariot report, p. 97. Barlowe report, pp. 14–26.

Crosby, A. W. 1972. *The Columbian Exchange: Biological and Cultural Consequences of 1492*. Westport, Conn.: Greenwood Press.

———. 1986. *Ecological Imperialism: The Biological Expansion of Europe, 900–1900*. New York: Cambridge University Press.

Cumming, W. P., and L. De Vorsey. 1998. *The Southeast in Early Maps*. Chapel Hill: University of North Carolina Press.

Cumming, W. P., R. A. Skelton, and D. B. Quinn. 1971. *The Discovery of North America*. New York: American Heritage Press.

De Vorsey, L. 1976. "Pioneer Charting of the Gulf Stream: The Contributions of Benjamin Franklin and William Gerhard de Brahm." *Imago Mundi* 28: 105–20.

———. 1978. "Amerindian Contributions to the Mapping of North America: A Preliminary View." *Imago Mundi* 30: 71–78.

———. 1992. *Keys to the Encounter: A Library of Congress Resource Guide for the Study of the Age of Discovery*. Washington: Library of Congress.

De Vorsey, L., and J. Parker, eds. 1985. *In the Wake of Columbus: Islands and Controversy*. Detroit: Wayne State University Press.

Driver, H. E. 1961. *Indians of North America*. Chicago: University of Chicago Press.

Duncan, T. B. 1972. *Atlantic Islands: Madeira, the Azores, and the Cape Verdes in 17th-Century Commerce and Navigation*. Chicago: University of Chicago Press.

Fernandez-Armesto, F. 1991. *The Times Atlas of World Exploration*. London: Times Books.

Fuson, R. H. 1999. *Juan Ponce de León and the Spanish Discovery of Puerto Rico and Florida*. New York: McDonald & Woodward.

Hébert, J. R. 1992. *1492, an Ongoing Voyage*. Washington: Library of Congress.

Hoffman, B. G. 1961. *Cabot to Cartier: Sources for a Historical Ethnography of Northeastern North America, 1497–1550*. Toronto: University of Toronto Press. Verrazano report, p. 111.

Juricek, J. T. 1975. "English Territorial Claims in

North America under Elizabeth and the Early Stuarts." *Terrae Incognitae* 7: 7–22.

Kelley, J. E., Jr. 1979. "Non-Mediterranean Influences That Shaped the Atlantic on the Early Portolan Charts." *Imago Mundi* 31: 18–35.

Macpherson, A., and B. Wallace. 1987. "Norse Voyages and Settlement." In *Historical Atlas of Canada: From the Beginning to 1800,* ed. R. Cole Harris. Toronto: University of Toronto Press, plate 16.

McManis, D. R. 1972. *European Impressions of the New England Coast, 1497–1620.* Chicago: University of Chicago Department of Geography.

Meinig, D. W. 1986. *The Shaping of America: Atlantic America, 1492–1800.* New Haven: Yale University Press.

Morison, S. E. 1971. *The European Discovery of America: The Northern Voyages* A.D. *500–1600.* New York: Oxford University Press.

———. 1974. *The European Discovery of America: The Southern Voyages* A.D. *1492–1616.* New York: Oxford University Press.

Overton, J. D. 1981. "A Theory of Exploration." *Journal of Historical Geography* 7: 53–70.

Quinn, D. B. 1976. "The English Contribution to Early Overseas Discovery." *Terrae Incognitae* 8: 91–97.

———. 1977. *North America from Earliest Discovery to First Settlements: The Norse Voyages to 1612.* New York: Harper & Row.

———, ed. 1979. *New American World: A Documentary History of North America to 1612.* 5 vols. New York: Arno Press. Icelandic saga, 1: 33.

Sauer, C. O. 1925. "The Morphology of Landscape." *University of California Publications in Geography* 2, no. 2: 19–54. Reprinted in *Land and Life: A Selection from the Writings of Carl Ortwin Sauer.* Edited by J. Leighly. Berkeley and Los Angeles: University of California Press, 1963, 315–50.

———. 1968. *Northern Mists.* Berkeley and Los Angeles: University of California Press.

———. 1971. *16th-Century North America: The Land and the People as Seen by the Europeans.* Berkeley and Los Angeles: University of California Press.

Skelton, R. A., T. E. Marston, and G. D. Painter. 1965. *The Vinland Map and the Tartar Relation.* New Haven: Yale University Press.

Taylor, E. G. R. 1958. *The Haven Finding Art: A History of Navigation from Odysseus to Captain Cook.* London: Hollis & Carter.

Thrower, N. J. W. 1979. "New Light on the 1524 Voyage of Verrazzano." *Terrae Incognitae* 11: 59–65.

Vachon, A. 1982. *Dreams of Empire: Canada before 1700.* Ottawa: Public Archives of Canada.

Vigneras, L. A. 1979. "The Projected Voyage of Juan de Agramonte to the Carolinas, 1511." *Terrae Incognitae* 11: 67–70.

Viola, H. J., and C. Margolis. 1991. *Seeds of Change.* Washington: Smithsonian Institution Press.

Washburn, W., ed. 1966. *Proceedings of the Vinland Map Conference.* Chicago: University of Chicago Press.

Wroth, L. C. 1970. *The Voyages of Giovanni da Verrazano, 1524–1528.* New Haven: Yale University Press.

3

The Spanish Borderlands

RICHARD L. NOSTRAND

In 1992 people on both sides of the Atlantic Ocean celebrated the quincentenary of Christopher Columbus's encounter with the New World. All knew that in 1492 the intrepid mariner sailing for Spain brought the Eastern Hemisphere into permanent contact with the Western Hemisphere. But for many, perhaps especially in the United States, the event was tempered by some reinterpretations of history. Whereas in 1792 Columbus symbolized for Americans a newly won independence from England, and in 1892 he stood for American progress and potential, in 1992 he was viewed by Native Americans as having despoiled their cultures and decimated their numbers, by African Americans as the harbinger of a forced migration and slavery, and by environmentalists as having initiated much ecological destruction. In the eyes of these people Columbus had slipped from hero to villain. Whatever one's view of Columbus in 1992, the quincentenary did renew interest in Spain's role in the Americas and more particularly in the area under discussion here, the Spanish Borderlands.

THE BORDERLANDS CONTEXT

The term "Spanish Borderlands" refers to the once remote and sparsely populated Spanish frontier in North America, that stretch of the subtropics that spans from California on the Pacific to Florida on the Atlantic (fig. 3.1). The Borderlands term was popularized by Herbert Eugene Bolton and his entourage of student-historians at the University of California at Berkeley, although it was not Bolton but an unknown editor at Yale University Press who suggested it as the title for Bolton's seminal book. The Borderlands label has one major drawback: it is anachronistic, at least when applied to Spain's vast northern frontier before political borders existed. Its plural use ("Borderlands"), on the other hand, does underscore the area's environmental and cultural diversity, and it re-

minds us of the difficulties of defining clearly the border between today's Republic of Mexico and the United States. Although entrenched in the literature, the Borderlands label is on the decline, as suggested by the titles of the three major books that synthesize its history: Bolton's *Spanish Borderlands* (1921), Bannon's *Spanish Borderlands Frontier* (1970), and Weber's *Spanish Frontier in North America* (1992).

Christopher Columbus apparently never set foot in the Borderlands. On October 12, 1492, he landed on an island in the Bahamas that he named San Salvador, apparently either today's Watling Island or Samana Cay (fig. 3.1). After exploring the coast of Cuba, he established his headquarters on Española (Hispaniola), an island base to which he would return on three subsequent voyages over the next 12 years. Columbus was significant because he and the many other Spaniards who soon arrived initiated the two-way transfer of plants, animals, and diseases that has so profoundly altered both hemispheres. From Europe came wheat, oats, and barley; horses, oxen, and cattle; and pathogens including malaria, measles, and smallpox; these did indeed decimate Native Americans, including the unfortunate Caribs after whom the Caribbean Sea was named. To Europe and Africa went maize (corn), cacao (chocolate), the "Irish" potato, tobacco, a virulent form of syphilis, and even Native Americans themselves; Columbus returned from his first voyage with seven of them captives. In the 30 years after 1492 the Caribbean became something of a Spanish lake, administered by a captain general whose seat of power after 1515 was Havana, Cuba.

From Cuba, Hernán Cortés led a major expedition to conquer the Aztecs of New Spain (fig. 3.1). Landing near Veracruz in 1519, Cortés moved inland, and aided by horses, firearms, and Tlascalan Indians, who were enemies of the Aztecs, he toppled Moctezuma II, the Aztec emperor, in 1521. Tenochtitlán, the Aztec capital

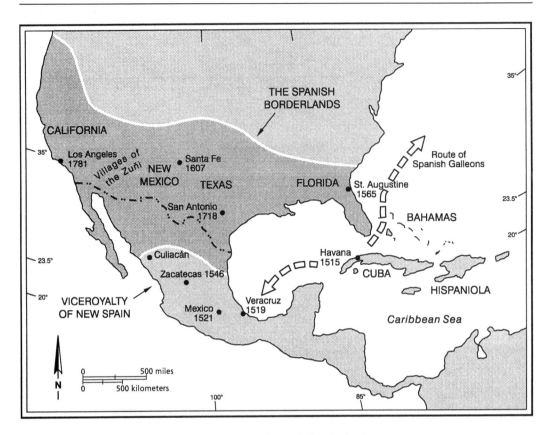

Figure 3.1 The Spanish Borderlands

on an island in Lake Texcoco, was destroyed, and rising from its ruins was Mexico City, made the seat of the Viceroyalty of New Spain in 1535. Meanwhile, an unusual series of events had prompted the newly appointed viceroy, Antonio de Mendoza, to send a second expedition, in size the likes of that of Cortés, north to the Borderlands. Álvar Núñez Cabeza de Vaca, second in command of the ill-fated Pánfilo de Narváez expedition to Florida, was shipwrecked on the Gulf coast of Texas in 1528. Enslaved by Native Americans for six years, he and three other survivors, one of whom was a black Moorish slave named Esteban, escaped, and for nearly two years between 1534 and 1536 the four walked across present-day Texas and northern Mexico, where finally they encountered fellow Spaniards at newly founded Culiacán. Ushered to Mexico City, Cabeza de Vaca excited Mendoza with stories of unbounded wealth to the north that on appearances promised to rival Tenochtitlán. Although Cabeza de Vaca had not

seen them, the fabled Seven Cities of Cíbola (or "bison"), which apparently were the villages of the Zuñi, were part of the lure. In 1540 Mendoza sent Francisco Vásquez de Coronado to find the cities, and although Coronado traveled for two years and saw the Zuñi villages and explored as far east as today's central Kansas, he found neither gold nor silver. Interest in the north quickly waned.

In traveling from Florida to Culiacán, Cabeza de Vaca experienced two fundamentally different environments. The Borderlands region is subtropical, so temperatures vary according to altitude. In the lowlands, summers are long and hot and winters are mild; this is the case with St. Augustine, San Antonio, and Los Angeles. In contrast, the summers in Santa Fe, located in a high part of New Mexico, are merely warm and the winters long and cold. But the more fundamental environmental contrast concerns precipitation. From eastern Texas to Florida average annual precipitation everywhere exceeds 30 inches; at St. Augustine, for instance, it is more than 50 inches. Heat and high humidity, the Spaniards quickly learned, combined to make seven months of the year quite oppressive. Climate, together with sandy soils and a pine forest, handicapped Spanish colonization in the southeastern Borderlands. By contrast, between central Texas and California the average annual precipitation is generally less than 20 inches. Native vegetation is sparse and shrublike, and crops have to be irrigated, even at San Antonio which, with 29.6 inches of precipitation, is classified as subhumid. The Spanish adapted more readily to these dryland conditions of the southwestern Borderlands.

THE INSTITUTIONAL CONTEXT

Much of what Spaniards did in the Americas was prescribed in the Laws of the Indies (1573) and its recodifications—decrees guiding Spanish activity in the New World. Because of this, a remarkable degree of uniformity characterized Spanish settlements, even in the remote and sparsely populated Borderlands. In the vanguard of frontier occupance were the presidio and mission. Presidios—institutions of conquest—were garrisoned fortresses built in the form of rectangles with ramparts (thick walls) surmounted by parapets (small walls) and flanked in opposite corners by bastions (projecting towers). Soldiers were charged with maintaining order among neighboring Indians and with protecting missionaries and colonists. Missions—institutions of Christianization—often were located within a few miles of the presidios. Missions in Florida and New Mexico consisted of churches and *conventos* (friaries) built right at, or next to, the Native American villages, but elsewhere in the Borderlands they were large rectangular compounds to which Native Americans were attracted for purposes of conversion and acculturation.

As prescribed in the Laws of the Indies, all presidios and missions were eventually to be converted to civil communities; that is, institutions for farmers and artisans that would form the backbone of Spain's colonial efforts throughout the Americas. These civil communities—called *pueblos* (places), *villas* (villages), or *ciudades* (cities) according to their projected size—consisted each of a grant of land of 4 square leagues, or approximately 27 square

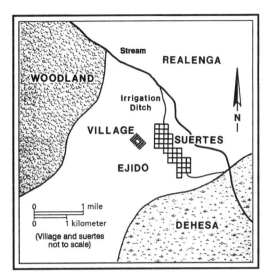

Figure 3.2 An Ideal Civil Community after the Laws of the Indies

miles (fig. 3.2). A gridiron village was located near the center of these grants, with the corners of the grid positioned in the four cardinal compass directions—explicitly to divert the "four principal winds" but undoubtedly also so that shade would be cast into the streets. A central plaza was to take up four blocks of the grid. Around the plaza were the Roman Catholic church, which was to be elevated and thus more venerated, a palace of the governors if the settlement was the seat of government, a customhouse, a granary, and house lots *(solares)*. The most prestigious citizens owned houses fronting the plaza. Beyond the village, community land was apportioned to arable fields *(suertes)*, common land *(ejido)*, pasture *(dehesa)*, woodland, and lands reserved for the Crown *(realenga)*.

In addition to presidios, missions, and civil communities, Spanish officials awarded land grants of several kinds in newly occupied areas. In 17th-century New Mexico, officials issued *encomiendas,* literally "entrustments," of Pueblo Indians and the land they occupied to an *encomendero.* Such awards entitled an encomendero to draw upon the labor of Natives, which often degenerated to Indian exploitation. Pressure from the Roman Catholic Church forced political authorities to discontinue issuing encomiendas in the 18th century; encomiendas seem to have existed only in New Mexico in the Borderlands. Private land grants for stock raising and farming (called *estancias* or *haciendas* early in the colonial period) were also issued in New Mexico; California and Texas grants for stock raising were called *ranchos*. After 1821, in the Mexican era, a flurry of rancho grants occurred in California, while in Texas individuals *(empresarios)* were awarded tracts of land into which they were to introduce a specified minimum number of colonists within a limited time.

FLORIDA (1565–1819)

Before Spaniards introduced any of these institutions to the Borderlands, New Spain developed as a rich silver-mining frontier. Zacatecas, discovered in 1546, became the richest strike of all (fig. 3.1). And through the Straits of Florida sailed the biannual convoys of silver-carrying galleons, headed north along the Florida coast to catch the prevailing westerlies for Spain (fig. 3.3). The Spanish needed a port community where these galleons could seek protection from storms and pirates. Yet Spain delayed this decision, and no lasting settlement was established before St. Augustine in 1565. News that the French, who also claimed the area, had established a fort near the mouth of the St. Johns River in 1564 triggered St. Augustine's founding. To counter the French, Pedro Menéndez de Avilés sailed from Spain, paused briefly in Puerto Rico, and then went to Florida, where he established St. Augustine on the coast south of the mouth of the St. Johns River. Menéndez thus initiated permanent colonization of the Borderlands. He also cruelly disposed of the unwelcome French.

The permanent site for St. Augustine, selected in 1570, was on the mainland behind a break in the offshore barrier beach islands. A fort, Castillo de San Marcos, was positioned to guard the narrow entrance to the harbor, and south of the fort stretched the wall-enclosed village (fig. 3.3). Although founded before Spaniards codified the Laws of the Indies in 1573, St. Augustine nevertheless embodied the attributes prescribed for civil communities: a plaza, which in coastal communities faced the water; a Roman Catholic church and a palace of the governors; and beyond the plaza a gridiron street pattern, which in St. Augustine contained the monastery headquarters of the Franciscans, who replaced

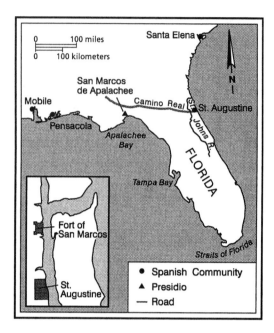

Figure 3.3 Florida, 1565–1819

the Jesuits in 1573. This key settlement became the source area for further Spanish expansion and the point of dissemination for crops, including wheat, olives, grapes, and peaches, and for cattle, sheep, pigs, and chickens.

Outward from the St. Augustine mission-presidio, Spaniards founded settlements in three directions (fig 3.3). First, settlements were established along the coast from Tampa Bay to modern South Carolina, a "saltwater" mission field that stretched along the barrier beach islands. The site of one of these communities, Santa Elena (1566–1587), the onetime principal settlement of Menéndez, was discovered in 1979 under a Marine Corps golf course on Parris Island. The second direction of expansion was behind St. Augustine along the St. Johns River, a relatively unsuccessful "freshwater" mission field. The third and most successful direction of expansion followed the Camino Real (Royal Highway) across the Florida peninsula beyond Apalachee Bay (present-day Tallahassee), and to today's central Alabama. Franciscan missionaries built their churches and conventos at a number of Native American villages in Florida. These Natives spoke a number of mutually unintelligble Muskhogean languages. They cultivated corn, beans, and squash, and they lived in villages that had circular public plazas and round houses with dome-shaped, palm-thatched roofs.

Despite this energetic expansion, between 1680 and 1706 the Florida missions collapsed at the hands of Englishmen now located in Carolina and their Native American allies. In Florida, Spaniards failed in their raising of wheat, olives, and grapes, turning instead to indigenous corn, beans, and squash. Oranges, peaches, melons, and watermelons from the Old World adapted in the new environment, but sheep did not. So the Spaniards replaced their preferred meat—lamb and mutton—with pork, beef, and chicken, supplemented by fish, venison, birds, and turtle. By 1763 Florida was little more than an impoverished military outpost, which, in the absence of riches, tractable Natives, and a familiar environment, had attracted barely 3,000 or 4,000 Spaniards. Florida had been a significant drain on the Spanish treasury.

In 1763 Florida became a British colony, and the new owners created two districts, East Florida and West Florida. Britain returned these to Spain in 1783. The Spanish retained the British divisions and reoccupied St. Augustine (in the east) and San Marcos de Apalachee, Pensacola, and Mobile (in the west). In 1819 Spain transferred all of Florida to the United States under the terms of the Adams-Onís Treaty as payment for debts. When compared with the northern frontier of New Spain to the west, Spain left only a modest lasting impress on Florida.

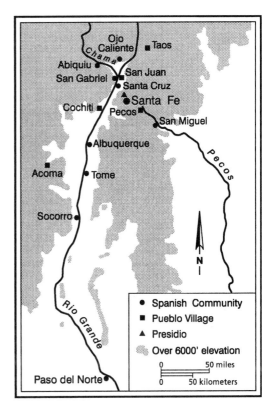

Figure 3.4 New Mexico, 1598–1821

NEW SPAIN'S NORTHERN FRONTIER (1598–1821)

New Mexico

Colonization of the present-day American Southwest began in New Mexico (fig. 3.4). Wealthy Juan de Oñate of Zacatecas, attracted by the peaceful sedentary Pueblo Indians and convinced that gold and silver could be found, petitioned the viceroy for permission to colonize New Mexico as a private venture. Permission was granted in 1598. How many soldier-settlers accompanied Oñate up the Rio Grande valley that year is not known, yet the majority of the 210 documented colonists, most of whom had been recruited in the Mexico (City) and Zacatecas areas, had been born in southern and central Spain, especially in Andalusia and Castile. At the confluence of the Rio Chama and the Rio Grande in the northern reaches of the Pueblo Indian realm, Oñate made his headquarters at the Pueblo village of Ohke, which he renamed San Juan. By Christmas of 1600 he had shifted his small settlement across the Rio Grande to Yúngé, an abandoned part of the same Pueblo village, which he renamed San Gabriel. Authorities promptly placed Franciscan missionaries at several Pueblo villages. Meanwhile, Oñate explored the area from what is central Kansas today west to the Gulf of California, but, like Coronado, he found no gold or silver. Accused of misdeeds including cruel treatment of the Pueblo people, Oñate was recalled in 1607.

Spanish authorities in Mexico City, persuaded that New Mexico should be retained as a missionary province, sent Pedro de Peralta to replace Oñate as governor. In 1610 Peralta made Santa Fe, a community now thought to have been founded in 1607, his headquarters. Spaniards laid out Santa Fe, like St. Augustine,

Figure 3.5 The Franciscan Church at Zuñi in Ruins. Photographed by
Timothy H. O'Sullivan in 1873. (Courtesy Maxwell Museum of Anthropology,
University of New Mexico, Albuquerque)

with a plaza, a palace of the governors, and a Roman Catholic church, although it lacked a gridiron street pattern. Designated a villa, Santa Fe became the region's largest community and its hub of activity. Here officials carried out Oñate's policy of awarding Pueblo villages as encomiendas to soldier-settlers and granted estancias or haciendas for stock raising and farming. Spaniards began to distinguish between two environments located north and south of the Cochiti Pueblo: Rio Arriba (upriver country), which was higher and therefore wetter and more wooded, and Rio Abajo (downriver country), which was lower and therefore drier but favored by a longer growing season (fig. 3.4). In 1629 the 46 local Franciscan friars (apparently the maximum number for the century) extended their missionary activities to include the Acoma, Zuñi (fig. 3.5), and Hopi villages, and in 1659 they founded a mission at Paso del Norte.

Spaniards fled to the Paso del Norte district in the Pueblo Revolt of 1680. For seven decades they had forced the Pueblo Indians to serve as laborers, grow maize, and weave cotton textiles called *mantas*. Finally, the numerically superior Pueblos, in an unprecedented show of unity, joined forces, notably in the Rio Arriba, and in 1680 attacked the 2,500 Spaniards, many of whom lived in Santa Fe. Some were taken captive, several hundred were killed, and about 2,000 survivors took refuge in the Paso del Norte district, accompanied by several hundred loyal Pueblo Indians from the Rio Abajo. A second villa, Paso del Norte, became New Mexico's new headquarters.

Diego de Vargas led the reconquest of the northern reaches of New Mexico beginning in 1692, and late the next year he reoccupied Santa Fe by force. To secure the capital, a presidio was established. (The adobe fortress attached to the palace of the governors had been manned only by volunteers, not soldiers, before the revolt and technically did not qualify as a presidio; see fig. 3.6.) Spaniards founded additional plaza-centered villas at Santa Cruz in 1695 and at Albuquerque in 1706 (fig. 3.4). Loosely agglomerated farmsteads known as ranchos came to exist along irrigation ditches that paralleled rivers. These communities had to be consolidated as wall-enclosed "plazas" in the later 18th century, owing to raids by nomadic Indians. The Spaniards had also expanded east to places near San Miguel (founded in 1794) in the upper Pecos River valley. By the close of the Spanish era in 1821, perhaps 30,000 Spaniards effectively occupied the area enclosed by Taos, San Miguel, Socorro, and Acoma.

After the reconquest Franciscans rebuilt many of their missions at the Pueblo villages. The Spanish-born friars, however, were now less intent about forcing Roman Catholicism on their charges. Indeed, they and the other Spaniards with whom the Pueblos came in contact began to grow apart from the Pueblo population. The supply of friars, which seems never to have exceeded 40 in the 1700s, was too small to staff all the Pueblo villages, and as the Spanish population increased relative to that of the Pueblos, the friars ministered more and more to

the Spaniards. By 1821, Franciscans staffed only 5 of the 20 remaining Pueblo villages.

As Spaniards and Pueblo Indians went their separate ways, a new relationship developed between the Spaniards and nomadic Indians— Apaches, Comanches, Navajos, and Utes— whose lands completely surrounded the Pueblo village region. During much of the Spanish era, nomadic peoples had sporadically raided the villages of the Pueblos and the Spaniards, carrying off children to be used as servants or slaves. The Spaniards had retaliated by capturing the nomads' children, whom they used as domestic servants or sold for much profit in Chihuahua in northern Mexico. Known as *genízaros* to New Mexico's Spaniards, these captives were eventually Hispanicized. Authorities allowed some to colonize communities of their own, provided these were at frontier locations. Ojo Caliente (by 1735), Tome (in 1739), Abiquiu (in 1744), and San Miguel all began in this way. Other genízaros intermarried with Spaniards and were assimilated into the Spanish population. The precise significance of this nomadic Indian strain in the *mestizaje* process that created New Mexico's modern-day Spanish Americans (or

Figure 3.6 The Palace of the Governors, Facing the Plaza, Santa Fe, New Mexico, about 1885
(Dana B. Chase; courtesy Western History Department, Denver Public Library)

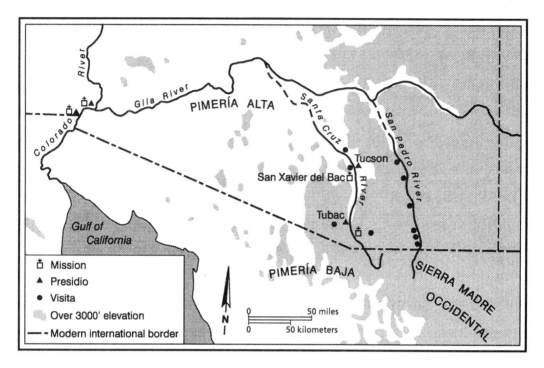

Figure 3.7 Pimería Alta, 1700–1821

"Hispanos") is not known, yet its existence differentiates Hispanos from Mexican Americans and Mexicans today.

Pimería Alta

Pimería Alta was the name for the northern realm of the Pima Indians in present-day northern Sonora and southern Arizona (fig. 3.7). During the 17th century, Jesuits had gradually advanced their missionary frontier north along the Pacific-facing slopes of the Sierra Madre Occidental to Pimería Baja. Then, in 1700, the celebrated Jesuit Eusebio Francisco Kino founded Mission San Zavier del Bac in Pimería Alta. During the next decade Kino supervised the founding of additional missions and small outlying chapels *(visitas)* in the upper Santa Cruz and San Pedro River valleys.

After Kino died in 1711, Jesuit activity languished because of the constant raids of Apaches, who were formidable foes of Spaniards and Pima Indians in Pimería Alta. The Jesuits renewed their missionary efforts, but by then the Pimas, like the Pueblo peoples, were no longer willing to accept Spanish subjugation, and in 1751 they revolted. This event resulted in the construction of a presidio at Tubac in 1752 and then a second presidio at Tucson in 1776 (fig. 3.7). By this time King Carlos III had expelled the Jesuits from Spain and its New World colonies and had replaced them with members of the Franciscan order. Two Franciscan mission-presidio compounds briefly existed near the confluence of the Gila and Colorado Rivers about 1780, and Spaniards issued a dozen stock-raising rancho grants in the vicinity of the Santa Cruz and San Pedro valleys. For more than half a century life in Pimería Alta cycled back and forth as Spanish and Apache took turns being in control of the area. Signs of Apache-induced abandonment of Spanish settlement were common, and by 1821 the area's several hundred Spanish inhabitants appear to have been clustered rather precariously within or near Tucson and Tubac.

Texas

The third thrust into this northern frontier went to Texas (fig. 3.8). Once again Frenchmen triggered the Spaniards into action. In the 1680s, under the sieur de La Salle, the French, who like the Spaniards were jockeying for territory, established themselves briefly at Matagorda Bay on the Gulf of Mexico. This initiative prompted the Spaniards in the early 1690s to build several missions and presidios in east Texas among the Caddo-speaking Tejas ("Texas") Indians, efforts that also proved to be ephemeral. The French then advanced up the Red River in present-day Louisiana, where they established a fort at Natchitoches in 1714. To stifle this thrust, Spaniards responded in 1716 by establishing a mission and later a presidio some 15 miles to the west at Los Adaes (Robeline, Louisiana, today). Between these French and Spanish outposts the small Arroyo Hondo became the international boundary, and Spaniards made Los Adaes the capital of Texas. A century later, in 1819, the Sabine River became the boundary between Spanish Texas and the state of Louisiana.

Three lasting mission-presidio complexes then emerged in present-day Texas (fig. 3.8). One was at Nacogdoches, founded in 1716. Another was built at San Antonio in 1718, where there was also a villa called Béjar. This complex grew to include four new missions down the San Antonio River by 1731, the year 55 Canary Island colonists arrived to revive Béjar, which they renamed San Fernando. The third mission was La Bahía, established on Matagorda Bay in 1722 and relocated to Goliad on the lower San Antonio River in 1749. On the lower Rio Grande, colonists occupied land grants in the area of Laredo, a community founded in 1755 and elevated to the status of villa in 1767. During Spanish times the Nueces River, not the Rio Grande, marked the southern boundary of Texas, so this activity was in the province of Nuevo Santander.

The Texas capital moved from Los Adaes to San Antonio in 1768 (and was officially recognized in 1773). Like St. Augustine and Santa Fe, San Antonio became the local seat of Spanish political power and the provincial focus. But political and military upheaval in the decade before 1821 saw the Tejano population fall from 4,000 to 2,000 Spaniards, living along the upper San Antonio River and at Nacogdoches and Goliad.

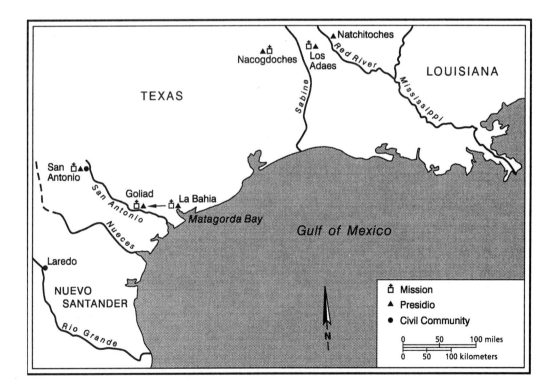

Figure 3.8 Texas, 1716–1821

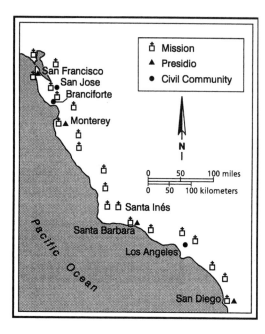

Figure 3.9 Alta California, 1769–1821

Alta California

Spaniards directed the final Borderlands entrada to Alta California, where southward-moving Russian fur traders posed a threat in the 18th century (fig. 3.9). In 1769 the Spaniards converged by land and sea on San Diego, where they built a mission-presidio pair. They founded three more such pairs: at Monterey, designated the provincial capital in 1770; at San Francisco, in 1776; and at Santa Barbara, where the presidio was built in 1782 and the mission in 1786. Eventually, a chain of missions 20 strong linked San Diego with San Francisco in a pattern that primarily reflected the distribution of Chumash and other smaller Native American groups. (In 1823, a 21st link was added at Sonoma.)

Felipe de Neve, California's governor from 1777 to 1782, implemented a geographical strategy in locating two new civil communities. In 1777 he established San Jose in the fertile Santa Clara valley between San Francisco and Monterey and, in 1781, Los Angeles in the fertile Los Angeles basin between San Diego and Santa Barbara (fig. 3.9). The plan, which worked, was for San Jose and Los Angeles to supply soldiers at the four presidios with grain and vegetables. California's third civil commu-

nity, a villa named Branciforte founded near modern Santa Cruz in 1797, was not successful.

Meanwhile, the Franciscans' missions prospered under the able leadership of Fray Junipero Serra. Mission complexes were built in well-chosen valleys along California's coast, and near them Native Americans drawn from California's relatively dense population were gathered together in *reducciones,* or villages. The Natives produced such large surpluses of grains and foodstuffs that the friars could afford to have supply ships bring tools, clothing, chocolate, snuff, and goods that they used to recruit more Natives (or replace those killed by European diseases) and to build additional missions. To monopolize the Indian labor, Serra and other Franciscans worked successfully to stifle the growth of the civilian population in the civil communities and to limit the granting of ranchos. By 1821 California had become primarily a mission field, and the number of Spaniards was only 3,200.

Four Outpost Clusters

In colonizing their northern frontier between California and Texas, Spaniards introduced fruits, grains, and livestock, and because this environment was similar to that of Spain and Mexico, adjustment went easily. Lacking sufficient precipitation during the summer growing season, Spaniards readily irrigated their crops. Lacking adequate timber at all but the higher elevations in New Mexico or humid eastern Texas, they built with sun-dried adobe, as they had done in Spain and Mexico. They introduced tomatoes, chilis, and new varieties of corn and squash from central Mexico to New Mexico, as well as foods with Nahuatl (the Aztec language) names, including tortillas, tamales, and posole. These supplemented their Old World wheat, wine grapes, deciduous fruits, cantaloupes, and watermelons. Sheep adapted especially well in New Mexico, in part because of the highland terrain but also because sheep are slow and resisted being stampeded by Indian raiders. Because California Indians did not farm, Spaniards had no agricultural example to follow. Yet it seems clear that they quickly found California to be much like Spain and Mexico, the mild winters even allowing them to grow frost-sensitive oranges.

Thus, at the time of Mexico's successful revolt from Spanish rule in 1821, four outpost clusters—Alta California, Pimería Alta, New

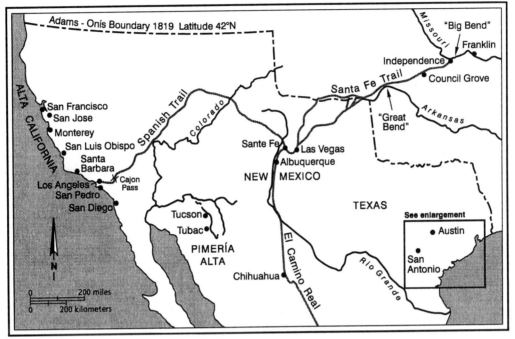

Figure 3.10a Mexico and the Southwest, 1821–1846

Mexico, and Texas—stretched from the Pacific to the Gulf of Mexico (fig. 3.10). All were similar in their tenuous connections with remote Mexico City and in their isolation from the others. Each was different, however, in its time of initial colonization and in its size of population, factors that gave rise in the American period to several colonial-derived subcultures. In the Adams-Onís Treaty signed in 1819, the boundary between New Spain and the United States was drawn generously north of these four outpost clusters. This boundary defined the limits of what the United States had acquired from France in the Louisiana Purchase of 1803. It also marked Mexico's northern limits during the coming era, which intruding Anglos ensured would be tumultuous.

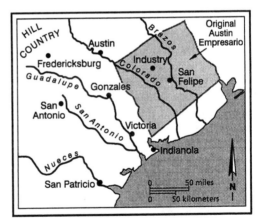

Figure 3.10b Texas,. 1821–1846
(enlarged area)

THE ANGLO INTRUSION INTO NORTHERN MEXICO (1821–1846)

New Mexico

In 1821 the new Republic of Mexico opened its northern frontier to non-Mexican traders and colonists. This was a significant departure from previous Spanish policy, and late that year William Becknell and a small party of Americans traveled from (Old) Franklin, Missouri, to New Mexico with goods to trade. Near the site of Las Vegas, which would not be founded until 1835 (fig. 3.11), Becknell encountered a Captain Gallegos, who invited the Americans into Santa Fe. Becknell returned to Missouri early in 1822 with New Mexico merchandise, which he

Figure 3.11 Las Vegas, New Mexico, in the Late 1860s. Plaza in center.
(Photographer unknown; courtesy Western History Department,
Denver Public Library)

sold for a substantial profit. News of this venture spread quickly and resulted in the Santa Fe trade. Each spring, beginning in 1822, wagons left the Big Bend of the Missouri River (where Independence would be founded in 1827), formed caravans at Council Grove, took one of two diverging wagon trails beyond the Great Bend of the Arkansas River, and proceeded to Santa Fe (fig. 3.10). There, traders exchanged hardware, notions, textiles (including printed cotton calicos), and liquor from the United States for furs and skins, woolen blankets, silver pesos, saddles, and horses and mules.

Horses and mules in particular were in great demand but short supply in Santa Fe. As a consequence, in the winter of 1829–30, about 60 enterprising New Mexicans led by Antonio Armijo pioneered a pack trail to California, where animals were available. Known as the Spanish Trail because it followed an old Spanish slave-hunting route that led northwest from Santa Fe deep into Ute Indian country, this pack trail was extended southwest across the Great Basin and through Cajon Pass to Los Angeles (fig. 3.10). Travel occurred between about October and April, when temperatures were coolest and grazing grass was most plentiful. The New Mexicans traded their woolen goods for live-

stock in Los Angeles and at points along the California coast. Because there was some thievery, on their departure from California the New Mexicans would be escorted to Cajon Pass where Californios (native Spanish-speaking Californians) compared brands and bills of sale. Use of the Spanish Trail marked the first sustained contact between any of the four Spanish frontier outpost clusters.

The Spanish Trail and the Santa Fe Trail were used basically for trade. However, a small number of New Mexicans did migrate permanently to California by way of the Spanish Trail, settling along the upper Santa Ana River near Cajon Pass. In 1850 Antonio Armijo himself lived in Solano County north of San Francisco Bay. Some Anglos and French Canadians took the Santa Fe Trail and remained in New Mexico, marrying local women. Trade over the Spanish Trail ended in 1846–47; its volume and value had been minor compared with that on the Santa Fe Trail, which continued in use until the Atchison, Topeka and Santa Fe Railroad reached New Mexico in 1879. Indeed, New Mexico took on great importance for Mexico as the portal through which Americans imported their goods. This circumstance explains why, in a truce called in 1847 midway through the

Figure 3.12 Los Angeles, Looking East, as Sketched by Charles Koppel about 1853. Plaza in front of tower. (Courtesy Prints and Photographs Division, Library of Congress)

Mexican War, Mexico agreed to cede Alta California and to recognize the Nueces River as the boundary with Texas but refused to cede New Mexico. The war continued until February 2, 1848.

Alta California

As was the case in New Mexico, a relatively small number of traders and interlopers intruded upon Alta California during the Mexican era. Non-Spanish trading vessels appear to have been plying the coast of California as early as 1800. After 1821 such trade became legal. In July 1822 the first of many ships from Boston put in at Monterey harbor to register and pay taxes before trading for longhorn-cattle hides (to be used for shoes and leather goods) and tallow (to be melted for candles and soap). From Monterey these ships proceeded to a number of collection points, including San Francisco Bay (the port for San Jose), San Luis Obispo, Santa Barbara, San Pedro (the port for

inland Los Angeles, fig. 3.12), and San Diego (fig. 3.10). On the beach at San Diego hides would be cleaned, stretched, dried, and stored in buildings. The trading process would be repeated from north to south until sailors had enough hides to fill the ship's hold at San Diego. All this activity is beautifully chronicled by Richard Henry Dana Jr. in *Two Years before the Mast*, published in 1840. As a common seaman, Dana made the voyage from Boston around Cape Horn to California and back between 1834 and 1836.

By the time of Dana's visit, Alta California's Franciscans, whose Native American charges raised longhorn cattle on extensive mission lands, had become wealthy in this hide and tallow trade. But this soon ended. In 1834 civil authorities in Alta California began to replace the Franciscans with secular (nonmonastic) clergy and divested the missionary order of its lands, even those occupied by the missions themselves. Politicians restored these lands, containing the mission structures, to the Roman Catholic

Church in the 1860s. Known as secularization, this transition implemented policy that had been set in motion elsewhere in the Borderlands late in the Spanish era. In California governors re-granted the well-chosen mission lands as ranchos, some 500 of them by the end of the Mexican period. Thus, stockmen—usually Californios, but also a few recent Anglo intruders—became California's new wealthy elite.

Texas

Texas in the era of the Mexican republic (1821–46) developed quite differently from New Mexico and Alta California. Colonists, not traders, arrived in large numbers almost immediately after 1821. They had been encouraged to immigrate by a policy initiated by Spain at the close of her colonial administration whereby empresarios would be awarded land provided they introduce a minimum number of colonists. In 1820 Moses Austin, an American, applied for such a grant. When he died, his son, Stephen F. Austin, reapplied to the Mexican government and received a huge tract that straddled the lower Brazos and Colorado Rivers (fig. 3.10). In 1823 Austin established his headquarters at San Felipe on the lower Brazos, and cotton planters from the American South soon arrived with their slaves. Mexican authorities awarded additional empresario grants to a variety of peoples: to Anglos at Gonzales on the upper Guadalupe River, to Germans at Industry in the regranted northern reaches of the Austin grant, to Irish at San Patricio at the mouth of the Nueces River, and even to Mexicans at Victoria on the lower Guadalupe. None was as successful, however, as the first grant to Austin.

By the mid-1830s an estimated 30,000 Anglos outnumbered the old Tejano group six to one in Texas, and conflicts soon pitted one group against the other. Tejanos, found largely in San Antonio and along the lower Rio Grande, officially opposed slavery, and they questioned the political loyalty of the newcomers. Anglos, located mainly in the coastal plain east of San Antonio, found the political administration in San Antonio to be inept. The upshot was a revolt in which the Anglos (and some Tejanos) declared their independence, eventually defeated the Mexicans in battle, and in 1836 created the Republic of Texas. That Mexico did not recognize the republic never daunted the rebels, who in 1839 established Austin as their capital on the Colorado and who, by continuing to award empresario grants, encouraged further non-Mexican immigration. Many of the new arrivals were Germans who entered Texas at Indianola and made their way to Fredericksburg and other destinations in the Hill Country (fig. 3.10). In 1845, the United States annexed Texas as a state, a move that helped to trigger the Mexican War in 1846.

POLITICAL REALIGNMENT

The war between the United States and Mexico was clearly prompted by an American mentality—Manifest Destiny—that, by providential design, the United States should extend to the Pacific. It was by and large an unpopular war in the United States, but for Mexico it was disastrous (fig. 3.13). In taking Texas, the United States forced Mexico to recognize the Rio Grande (Mexico's Rio del Norte), and not the former line along the Nueces, as the border. The United States also forced Mexico to cede New Mexico Territory north of the Gila River and Alta California north of a line drawn west from the Gila near Yuma to the Pacific. In 1853 the American government instructed James Gadsden to purchase the area south of the Gila, which he did for $10 million, thereby furnishing the United States with a superior transportation corridor to southern California. The Gadsden Purchase finalized the present-day international boundary. The result was that the United States realized its Manifest Destiny by extending to the Pacific, and in the process Mexico lost half its national territory.

Living in this former northern half of Mexico were some 100,000 Mexicans, or about 1 percent of Mexico's total population. In the Treaty of Guadalupe Hidalgo (1848), these Mexicans were given one year to repatriate or they would become American citizens. Several thousand did move to the Mexican side of the Rio Grande—for example, from Laredo to Nuevo Laredo and from Doña Ana to Mesilla (fig. 3.13). Those who remained became Mexican Americans, some 75,000 of them in New Mexico and perhaps 12,000 each in Texas and Alta California. Because New Mexico had been only lightly intruded upon by Anglos, Mexican American proportions there remained uniformly

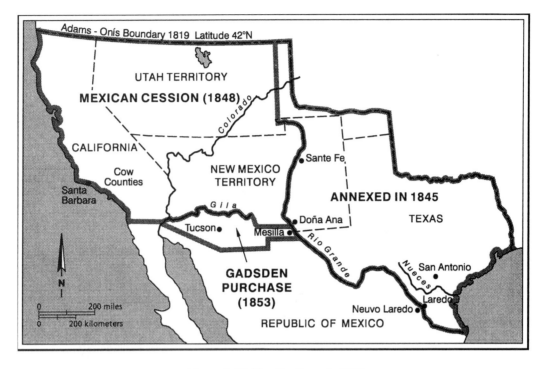

Figure 3.13 The Southwest, 1853

high. Heavy intrusion into Texas reduced Mexican American proportions everywhere except between the Nueces and the Rio Grande in south Texas; to this day this group makes up 70 to 80 percent of the population. In Alta California, immediately following the war, a heavy influx of gold seekers decisively reduced Mexican American proportions in the north. In the "cow counties" of southern California, so called because they remained overwhelmingly pastoral, percentages remained high until a real estate land boom in the 1880s brought in thousands of Anglos.

THE BORDERLANDS LEGACY

A Demographic Legacy

As a result of three geopolitical events—the United States's annexation of Texas in 1845, the Mexican Cession in 1848, and the Gadsden Purchase in 1853—some 100,000 Mexicans became Mexican Americans, at least nominally. Anglos for the most part engulfed the relatively small Tejano and Californio populations, al-

though pockets persist today in places like San Antonio and Santa Barbara (fig. 3.13). New Mexico's Hispanos, by contrast, were not immediately submerged, and what happened to them is one of the little-known stories in the annals of the Borderlands.

Drawing on a relatively large population reservoir, these Hispanos after 1848 aggressively expanded their frontiers—north to Colorado beginning in the early 1850s, and in the 1860s east across New Mexico to the panhandles of Texas and Oklahoma, west to Arizona, and south down the Rio Grande almost to the Mesilla valley. By 1900, about 140,000 Hispanos lived in these five states. Largely because of Anglo discrimination, they began to identify with their Spanishness as opposed to their Mexicanness. "Spanish" or "Spanish American" became their preferred self-referents when speaking in English. Roots that went deep into the Spanish colonial era, when now archaic Iberian speech patterns and folklore examples were introduced, seemed to justify this Spanish ethnic consciousness. In 1980, in the first census in which Americans could self-identify their ancestry, some 450,000 "Spanish," "Spanish American," or

Figure 3.14 Mission Santa Inés in the Late 19th Century (William Henry Jackson; courtesy Western History Department, Denver Public Library)

"Hispanic/Hispano(a)" people were living in New Mexico and its adjacent states.

Mexican Americans, a group that includes the self-consciously Mexican-Chicano element, have outstripped Hispanos numerically. ("Chicanos," a contraction of *Mexicanos*, identifies generally younger and often politically activist Mexican Americans.) In the latter 19th century only a few Mexican immigrants entered the southwestern states each year, but in the 20th century this trickle grew to a flood. Migrants poured in, especially to California, Texas, and Arizona, but also to Colorado and New Mexico and, after World War I, even to nonsouthwestern destinations like Chicago. By 1980 more than 8.7 million people, largely residents of the Southwest, listed themselves as "Mexican Americans" in the census, a number that did not include a million or more "undocumenteds." Unlike Hispanos, who are an indigenous people, these Mexican Americans are an immigrant people who constitute a separate subculture. Except for the most recent migrants, both groups are bilingual and bicultural, and neither has been fully integrated into American society. Both constitute a critically important Borderlands legacy.

A Landscape Legacy

The southwestern landscape displays the impress of the forebears of its present-day peoples. Geographer Wilbur Zelinsky's concept of the Doctrine of First Effective Settlement states that the first group to colonize an area effectively will be of singular importance in shaping the cultural landscape of that area, even though that first group may be small in numbers and later submerged by others. This doctrine certainly applies to Spaniards in their buildings and the way they organized their space. Even their place names persist to give a Hispanic character to Florida and especially to the American Southwest.

Many presidios and missions abandoned after Spanish and Mexican times gradually crumbled to ruins. Some that endured, however, became the nuclei around which larger settlements grew. For example, the communities that developed around the Tucson presidio and around Mission San Buenaventura became, through inertia, the Anglo–Mexican American cities of Tucson, Arizona, and Ventura, California. Missions that endured also inspired a distinctive "Spanish colonial" architectural style employed in domestic, civic, and ecclesiastic buildings. Many have been restored and attract thousands of visitors annually (fig. 3.14).

Civil communities had the power to attract; Los Angeles, Albuquerque, and San Antonio verify this principle, and a variety of colonial features persist in them. In the center of each is an open plaza, a church, and sometimes a palace of the governors, as at Santa Fe (fig. 3.6) and San Antonio. In Los Angeles, even the original pueblo boundaries are preserved as part of the street pattern as, for example, along Hoover Street. Rancho boundaries, as later surveyed by Americans, also persist as roads, private landownership boundaries, political (especially county) boundaries, railroad rights-of-way, power-line easements, and drainage ditches. They have also left their mark in street disruptions and irregularities.

Features built or laid out by a relatively few Spaniards have outlasted the builders to give character to a region now inhabited by millions of people of Spanish origin. The Borderlands area, particularly its southwestern segment, is one of America's genuinely distinctive cultural regions. It displays tangible evidence of America's enduring diversity.

ADDITIONAL READING

Bannon, J. F. 1970. *The Spanish Borderlands Frontier, 1513–1821.* New York: Holt, Rinehart & Winston.

———. 1978. *Herbert Eugene Bolton: The Historian and the Man, 1870–1953.* Tucson: University of Arizona Press.

Bolton, H. E. 1921. *The Spanish Borderlands: A Chronicle of Old Florida and the Southwest.* New Haven: Yale University Press.

Carlson, A. W. 1975. "Long-Lots in the Rio Arriba." *Annals of the Association of American Geographers* 65: 48–57.

Dana, R. H., Jr. 1946. *Two Years before the Mast.* 1840. Reprint, New York: World Publishing.

Gentilcore, R. L. 1961. "Missions and Mission Lands of Alta California." *Annals of the Association of American Geographers* 51: 46–72.

Jones, O. L., Jr. 1979. *Los Paisanos: Spanish Settlers on the Northern Frontier of New Spain.* Norman: University of Oklahoma Press.

Meinig, D. W. 1969. *Imperial Texas: An Interpretive Essay in Cultural Geography.* Austin: University of Texas Press.

———. 1971. *Southwest: Three Peoples in Geographical Change, 1600–1970.* New York: Oxford University Press.

Nelson, H. J., et al. 1964. "Remnants of the Ranchos in the Urban Pattern of the Los Angeles Area." *California Geographer* 5: 1–9.

Nostrand, R. L. 1970. "The Hispanic-American Borderland: Delimitation of an American Culture Region." *Annals of the Association of American Geographers* 60: 638–61.

———. 1975. "Mexican Americans circa 1850." *Annals of the Association of American Geographers* 65: 378–90.

———. 1992. *The Hispano Homeland.* Norman: University of Oklahoma Press.

Sauer, C. O. 1966. *The Early Spanish Main.* Berkeley and Los Angeles: University of California Press.

Spicer, E. H. 1962. *Cycles of Conquest: The Impact of Spain, Mexico, and the United States on the Indians of the Southwest, 1533–1960.* Tucson: University of Arizona Press.

Stoddard, E. R., R. L. Nostrand, and J. P. West, eds. 1983. *Borderlands Sourcebook: A Guide to the Literature on Northern Mexico and the American Southwest.* Norman: University of Oklahoma Press.

Weber, D. J. 1982. *The Mexican Frontier, 1821–1846: The American Southwest under Mexico.* Albuquerque: University of New Mexico Press.

———. 1992. *The Spanish Frontier in North America.* New Haven: Yale University Press.

4

France in North America

COLE HARRIS

The French engagement with North America began about 1500 and eventually influenced more than half the continent before France lost all her mainland North American territory following the Seven Years' War (1757–63). During this long period France made no spectacular North American conquests, developed a low regard for the potential of newly discovered midlatitude lands, and sent few colonists. Overall, North America was a marginal interest, never a preoccupation, and as a result France's long-term impact on the continent was far less than Spain's or England's. Yet France left her broad mark on North America politically in a country, Canada, which eventually and ironically would grow out of French beginnings, and culturally in the continuing presence of French as a North American language. More than this, the French effort in North America established a northern pattern of European outreach to the New World that would endure long after New France fell. In the first instance, this pattern revolved around staple trades, which, during the French period, were in fish and furs. Although one of these activities was confined to the Atlantic coast while the other drew traders into the interior, both detached capital and labor from France, placed them in North America, and tied them back to France by tight lines of trade. Eventually towns developed at crucial break-of-bulk points, and, because France and Britain warred in North America as well as in Europe, these towns became important garrisons, foci not only of trade but also of the military struggle for the continent. Apart from staple trades and towns, and somewhat detached from them, some immigrants turned to farming, usually introducing crops and agricultural techniques from northern France to settings where land was available and markets were poor. Staple trades, towns, and patchy agricultural settlements were the ingredients of which the pattern of the French penetration of North America, and of the northern economy, was composed.

THE 16TH CENTURY

During the latter half of the 15th century, an international fishery, pursued by English, French, Basque, and Portuguese fishermen, operated in the open Atlantic south of Ireland. When John Cabot made known New World fishing grounds, part of this fishery quickly reached out to exploit them, transferring a well-established European economy across the North Atlantic. Breton, Norman, and Portuguese fishermen were in waters around Newfoundland by 1502, perhaps earlier, and French and Spanish Basques were there a few years later. Before the end of the century dozens of ports from southern England to southern Portugal regularly sent fishing ships, each carrying an average of 25 men, to transatlantic fisheries. Of these ports some 60 were French. Usually the voyages were financed in the ports of embarkation, and labor was recruited locally. In 1577 an English captain, Anthony Parkhurst, estimated that there were 150 French ships in inshore waters around Newfoundland, and perhaps 3,000 to 4,000 men. These figures are probably low. It has recently been established that 47 fishing ships sailed for Newfoundland from Bordeaux in 1585, 49 from La Rochelle in 1559, and 94 from Rouen in 1555. In most years of the 16th century many more ships and men were sent annually from Europe to Newfoundland than to the Caribbean and Central America.

The attraction was one of the world's greatest fishing grounds in shallow waters along the Atlantic coast of North America from southern Labrador to northern New England (fig. 4.1). Cod could be caught in great numbers in relatively shallow water close to shore and on offshore banks at depths of 50 to 100 fathoms. Inshore waters were fished first, and the techniques that would dominate the inshore fishery for at least 200 years soon were well established. The ships that crossed the Atlantic were beached or anchored in New World harbors, where covered wharves were built (or repaired from the previous season) and boats assembled

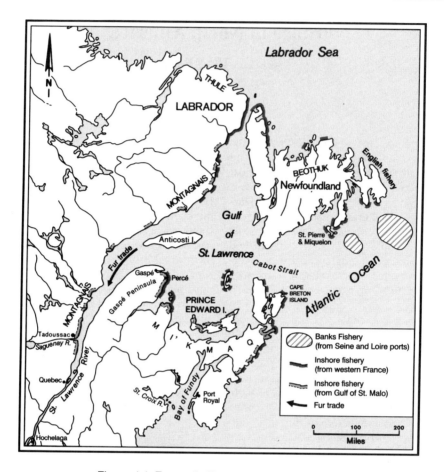

Figure 4.1 France in North America, 1600–1610

from prefabricated parts. Fishing took place from these boats operated close to shore by crews of three who fished with hempen lines and baited hooks. At the end of the day the fish were unloaded at the wharf, where they were headed, split, salted, piled for a few days, washed, and finally dried on beach cobbles, on branches cut and spread out for the purpose (*rances*), or on low drying platforms (*vignaux* or, in English, flakes). Drying required about ten good days, in each of which the cod had to be spread out, turned, turned again if rain threatened, and repiled at dusk. It was labor-intensive work. Shallop master, header, splitter, and salter required specialized skills, and the shore master had to balance the size of the catch, weather, shore crew, and departure date to produce as much well-cured dried cod as possible for quality-sensitive markets. But much of the labor was unskilled; peasants from overpopulated countrysides—even boys of eight or ten years—entered the fishery. At the end of the fishing season, shore installations were secured as much as possible against weather, Natives, and other fishermen, and the dried cod loaded aboard ship. Ship and crew returned to France.

The offshore fishery on the banks developed in the second half of the 16th century and was conducted by ships equipped to fish without landing in the New World. On the banks, perhaps 200 miles from Newfoundland, men stood in barrels on the deck and fished with long baited and weighted lines. The cod they laboriously hauled aboard were headed, split, and stored in the hold between layers of salt. This wet, or green, cod, much more perishable than the dry-cured variety, was marketed in northern France, principally along such rivers as the Seine and the Loire.

Until about 1575 the French inshore fishery focused on southeastern Newfoundland, the strait between Newfoundland and Labrador, and eastern Cape Breton Island. In all these locations it competed with Portuguese and Spanish Basque fishermen. On the Labrador shore, Basque whalers came in large ships (up to 600 tons) with large crews (up to 120 men) and built shore installations for rendering blubber that were even more labor intensive than the work camps of the cod fishery. Only after 1570, as the Danes reasserted control of the Icelandic fishery, did English fishermen cross the Atlantic in numbers; soon English raiding and piracy displaced other fishermen from southeastern Newfoundland. As this happened, the French fishery became more dispersed, considerably penetrating the Gulf of St. Lawrence.

The banks fishery made no regular use of the New World coast, and the inshore fishery, which did, relied on European labor. Yet the inshore fishery drew Europeans and Natives into contact, and trade in furs began early in the 16th century. At first Natives traded with fishermen, but as early as the 1550s small fur-trading companies detached themselves from the fishery and penetrated the Gulf of St. Lawrence. From 1580 French fur traders ventured each summer to Tadoussac at the mouth of the Saguenay River. Like the fishermen, they returned home each fall.

During the first century of French activity along the northeastern edge of North America, there was one major attempt to colonize, inspired by Spanish discoveries far to the south. In 1534, Francis I, king of France, authorized Jacques Cartier, a captain from St.-Malo, to explore west from the strait between Labrador and Newfoundland, hoping he would "discover certain islands and lands where it is said a great quantity of gold, and other precious things, are to be found." The French court dreamed of another Aztec or Inca empire for the plucking. Instead Cartier found a shore (the north shore of the Gulf of St. Lawrence) "composed of stone and horrible rugged rocks"; he thought the south shore of the Gulf of St. Lawrence was incomparably better, "the finest land one can see, and full of beautiful trees and meadows." He touched on Anticosti Island but missed the entrance to the St. Lawrence River. The next year, he was back with more ships and men and, directed by two Natives he had captured the previous year, sailed up the St. Lawrence River as far as the

agricultural villages of St. Lawrence Iroquoians near Quebec. Cartier and a few of his men went on to Hochelaga, a palisaded village on Montreal Island composed, Cartier said, of some 50 houses. He returned to spend the winter near Quebec, where 25 of his crew died of scurvy before Cartier learned of a cure from the Natives. As he left, Cartier captured several of them and got away to France.

Like the Natives who enticed Coronado and de Soto into the American West and South with tales of gold, Cartier's captives told the French what they wanted to hear. In the kingdom of Saguenay, not far beyond Canada, there were gold and silver, and people (at times with wings and without anuses) who wore woolens like people in France. Although such stories did not get the Natives home—all Cartier's captives, save one girl, were dead by 1539—Cartier set out again in 1541, this time with five ships, several hundred men and women, and livestock. He was to found a colony. The details of Cartier's second winter in North America, spent just above Quebec, are less clear than those of the first, but there was scurvy and there were repeated Native attacks. (Cartier's Native policy was reaping its reward.) In 1542 he packed up and left.

In their own terms the Cartier voyages were failures. The kingdom of Saguenay had not been found; the gold and diamonds Cartier brought back to France were iron pyrites and mica. Plantation crops could not be grown. There was no obvious route to Asia. The winter was daunting. For more than 60 years the negative results of these voyages discouraged the French from another attempt to colonize northeastern North America, but Cartier had expanded enormously European knowledge of the gulf and valley of the St. Lawrence and had established a powerful French claim to a major North American entrance. Basically, Cartier demonstrated the irrelevance in northern middle latitudes of a Spanish model of New World colonization and left the French where they had been in North America, that is, with an established cod fishery and an incipient fur trade.

FRANCE IN NORTH AMERICA IN 1600

In 1600 the numerous French settlements along the northeast coast of the continent were all seasonal work camps for a migratory, male labor force drawn from the Atlantic coast of France (fig. 4.1). There were no women. No society surrounded the fishery—the few Beothuk of Newfoundland did not frequent the fishing camps, at least not when the French were there. Life ashore was an extension of life aboard ship. The ships brought workers to a strange shore, perched them there for a time to accomplish a job, then withdrew them—vehicles of a transatlantic spatial economy that connected European capital, labor, and techniqe to New World resources. Because there was no alternative New World employment to bid up the value of their labor, fishermen bound for the New World received little more than other French fishermen. Because France was still an intensely regional country and shipowners recruited men from local hinterlands, there was much variety of local French ways within the common overall pattern of the fishery. Because no one intended to stay and because the leavings from one season could not be counted on to survive to the next, shore installations were quickly and minimally constructed. Behind the more frequented harbors the forest was cut a mile or two inland, while ramshackle wharves, drying platforms, and cabins lined the waterfront.

Perhaps a quarter of the French ships went to the banks and returned directly to France, usually to ports at the mouth of the Seine or the Loire. A large part of the wet (green) cod they carried was destined for the Paris market. The English, who by 1600 were well established in southeastern Newfoundland, deflected the French inshore fishery to the north and southwest. Most ships from western Normandy and northern Brittany (the Gulf of St.-Malo) headed for the northern peninsula of Newfoundland and the south coast of Labrador. French Basque shore installations were scattered along the south coast of Newfoundland, on northeastern Cape Breton Island, and on the Gaspé Peninsula in the western Gulf of St. Lawrence. By 1600 Spanish Basque and Portuguese competition was weakening as men and ships were commandeered for Spanish military ventures (including the Spanish Armada of 1588) and as inflation (initiated by New World bullion) increased costs for Iberian fishermen.

At the same time, the fur trade was well established in the western Gulf of St. Lawrence. It relied on Native labor, drew Native and European traders into direct annual contact, and quickly channeled European goods into Native economies in payment for furs. The points of annual contact between the westward outreach of European trade goods and the reciprocal flow of Native furs were familiar to European and Native traders. In 1600 a Huguenot, Chauvin de Tonnetuit, armed with a charter from the king, tried to establish a permanent trading post and year-round settlement at Tadoussac. The attempt failed, but a similar effort would be successful slightly farther west a few years later. Whereas the fishery spread a thin, discontinuous rim of French influence along the rocky shores of northeastern North America, the fur trade drew French people and influence inland, up the St. Lawrence.

A century of European contact probably spread European diseases among the Native peoples of what is now Atlantic Canada. Early in the 17th century a Jesuit missionary reported that the Mi'kmaq of today's Nova Scotia and New Brunswick

> are astonished and often complain that since the French mingle with and carry on trade with them, they are dying fast, and the population is thinning out. They assert that before this association and intercourse all their countries were very populous, and they tell how one by one the different coasts according as they have begun to traffic with us have been more reduced by disease.

Along the St. Lawrence River the agricultural Iroquoians whom Cartier encountered in the 1530s were gone in 1600. Perhaps European diseases killed them, but it is more generally assumed that the St. Lawrence Iroquoians were defeated and dispersed about 1580 either by Huron from north of Lake Ontario or by Iroquois from south of Lake Ontario (fig. 4.2). The St. Lawrence Iroquoians may have blocked the westward flow of European goods, thereby upsetting the balance of Native power and precipitating the attacks that proved fatal. As the French fur trade spread up the St. Lawrence after 1600, an unoccupied valley—an extraordinary change since Cartier's day—lay before it.

THE 17TH CENTURY

Chauvin de Tonnetuit's colony at Tadoussac had failed, but in 1604 another Huguenot trader, Pierre de Gua, sieur de Monts, also obtained a monopoly charter for fur trading and embarked

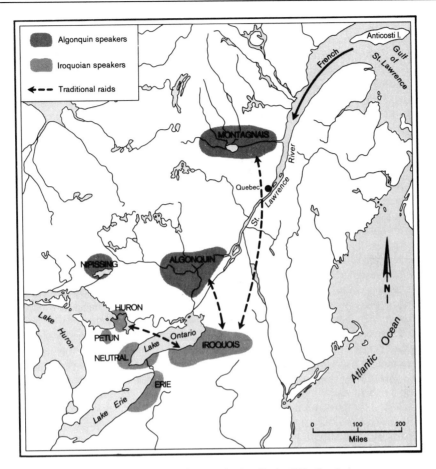

Figure 4.2 Native Groups in the Early 17th Century

with colonists. He went to the Bay of Fundy, established a first settlement on the St. Croix River (the present border between Maine and New Brunswick), and moved the next year to a more favorable location across the Bay of Fundy at Port Royal (fig. 4.1). By 1607 when de Monts's monopoly was terminated and he and most of his colonists returned to France, the feasibility of French settlement in the New World had been demonstrated. The next year de Monts's lieutenant, Samuel de Champlain, armed with a one-year trading monopoly, intent upon exploration, and aware that the Bay of Fundy was a cul-de-sac, went to the St. Lawrence River, where he selected a strong defensive site at Quebec, the head of navigation for large sailing ships, and built a post almost 1,000 miles from the open North Atlantic. The French were now on the St. Lawrence to stay.

Although Champlain had established a tiny outpost in a depopulated valley, Native peoples were not far away (fig. 4.2). Almost immediately Champlain was involved with them. To the immediate north and west were Algonquian speakers who lived primarily by fishing and hunting: the Montagnais in the Saguenay River valley, the Algonquin in the Ottawa River valley (called the Grand River by the French), and the Nipissing northeast of Georgian Bay. Around the eastern Great Lakes were Iroquoian speakers, agricultural people who raised corn, beans, squash, and tobacco, and who lived in large villages. Of the Iroquoians there were several groups: Huron south of Georgian Bay, Petun just west of the Huron, Neutral around the western end of Lake Ontario, Erie at the southeastern corner of Lake Erie, and Iroquois south of Lake Ontario in what is now upstate

New York. The Algonquian speakers lived in small, well-dispersed bands, but the agricultural Iroquoians were numerous and concentrated, with as many as 3,000 people in a single village. When Champlain arrived at Quebec, there may have been 20,000 Huron, as many Neutral, and almost as many Iroquois south of Lake Ontario. The St. Lawrence valley was a no-man's-land between the Iroquois to the south and southwest and the Montagnais, Algonquin, and Huron, in alliance, to the north and northwest.

Interested as he was in exploration and trade, Champlain had no choice but to plunge into this Native world and to take sides in its conflicts. In 1609 he sent a young man—Etienne Brulé—to live with the Huron, thereby establishing an alliance. That year and again in 1615 Champlain and his new Native allies launched campaigns into Iroquois territory, the second an ignominious failure to capture a well-fortified village south of Lake Ontario. Champlain was wounded and spent the winter of 1615–16 in Huronia. The French were becoming familiar with Native ways, had learned to use and repair birchbark canoes, and were acquiring a geographical knowledge of much of the Great Lakes basin. Champlain's last and most remarkable map, drawn in 1632, shows Lake Ontario, Lake Huron, and parts of Lake Superior with considerable accuracy, the largest addition to the European cartography of North America since Cartier. More telling in the long run, Champlain had committed the French to the Algonquin and the Huron—to trade with them, to warfare with their enemies, and, for the purpose of trade and movement, to the study of their languages and the adoption of many of their ways.

Yet in the first half of the 17th century, the French fur trade was confined to the St. Lawrence valley. Natives brought furs there. Initially the Algonquin controlled the trade, preventing French traders from ascending the Ottawa River and exacting tolls from the Huron and Nipissing who traveled to the St. Lawrence. Later, when Iroquois raids had weakened the Algonquin, the Huron and Nipissing came toll-free to Montreal. Jealous of their position as middlemen in the trade, they would not let French traders into the interior; Recollet and Jesuit missionaries were admitted to Huronia on condition that they did not trade. During these years Quebec, Trois-Rivières, and Montreal were outposts of French trade on the edge of a Native world.

Although French traders were excluded from the interior, the Native peoples of the Great Lakes basin faced immense new pressures. The Huron, Algonquin, and Montagnais were allied with the French along the St. Lawrence, the Iroquois were allied with the Dutch at the mouth of the Hudson River (fig. 4.2), and the two alliances competed with increasing violence. The demand for European goods and the diffusion of firearms (which the Dutch traded freely with their Native allies and the French withheld from theirs) intensified traditional animosities while disrupting balances of power. In 1634 European diseases, probably carried by Jesuit missionaries, reached the Great Lakes basin and killed approximately half its peoples. By 1639 there were only 12,000 Huron and Petun. Children and old people had been particularly vulnerable; most of the old men, the respected leaders of Native society, were dead. At the same time, villages with missionaries were divided between Christian and pagan factions. Economically, demographically, culturally, and militarily the precontact Native world of the Great Lakes basin was under intense assault, the region in ferment.

Eventually, the French-Huron trading system collapsed. Iroquois looting raids against populations weakened by disease and dissension turned to all-out warfare. At first the Iroquois blocked the Ottawa River. Then they turned to the population centers. In a series of well-organized campaigns, Iroquois warriors destroyed the Huron villages between 1647 and 1649, the Petun in 1649 and 1650, the Nipissing between 1649 and 1651, and the Neutral in 1651 and 1652. Refugees from these groups and others fled west and north, many of them to settle west of Lake Michigan. Except for the Iroquois south of Lake Ontario and the Shawnee at the forks of the Ohio and Mississippi Rivers (dispersed by the Iroquois in 1669 and 1670), the entire eastern Great Lakes basin south to the Ohio River valley was depopulated. The scholarly Jesuits burned their missions, thanked God that so many of the dead had been baptized, and were not again in the territory northwest of Lake Ontario until 1660.

After this horrendous depopulation of the Great Lakes basin, French traders began to venture beyond Montreal to reach Native groups west of Lake Michigan. Such trade was illegal—the Crown hoped to encourage Natives to return to Montreal—but almost impossible to

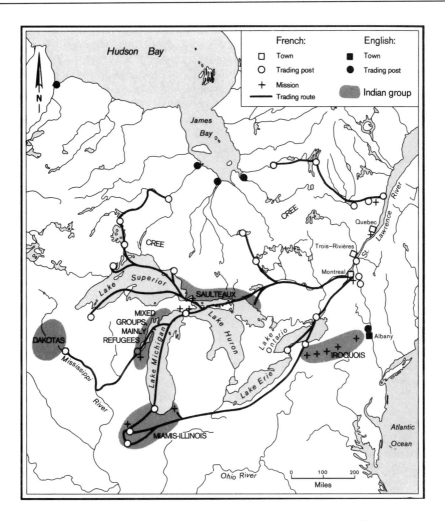

Figure 4.3 The Expanding French Fur Trade, 1679–1685

control. By the 1660s there were some 200 French traders and canoemen *(coureurs de bois)* in the west each year. When the Crown finally legalized the western trade in 1681, the number of coureurs de bois increased and Native trading journeys to Montreal stopped.

The French fur trade moved inland along the rivers (fig. 4.3). It depended on the birchbark canoe, Native guides, and traders who spoke Native languages and observed their ceremonials. A handful of French traders penetrated a huge territory, reaching out briefly to gather furs at what were soon prearranged trading places and to send them as quickly as possible to Montreal. Soon the lines of trade were hundreds of miles long, and the seasonal round-trip from Montreal became impossible. Posts had to be established in the interior and men left to overwinter in them. Fort de la Baie-des-Puants was established on Green Bay in 1670. By 1685 there were French posts on the Mississippi River (reached in 1673 and explored by La Salle to its mouth in 1682) and others north of Lake Superior, all on land that the Native peoples considered theirs and that they allowed the French to use in return for annual presents. In this fashion several hundred coureurs de bois operated a network of posts extending halfway across the continent and dominated the trade of the Great Lakes basin. Situated between Lake Huron and Lake Michigan, Michilimakinac became a major entrepôt, receiving furs from the interior and supplies and trade goods from Montreal.

The fur trade established the French on the Bay of Fundy (the heart of the territory called Acadia) and along the lower St. Lawrence (the entrance to the territory called Canada). In both locations the mixed, crop-livestock farming of northwestern Europe was feasible. Fur merchants were little interested in agriculture, which involved the expense of colonization. But the Crown judged that settlers would strengthen the French position in North America and provide a market for French manufactures, and hence stipulated in trading charters that merchant companies bring settlers. Halfheartedly, a few companies did. In this way agricultural settlement began, a by-product of the fur trade.

By 1654 there were perhaps 30 families near Port Royal. The Acadian population would grow from this tiny base, to which over the years a few men but virtually no women would be added from outside. In Canada the Crown created a large trading company, the Company of New France, in 1627, gave it land title and a monopoly of trade, and required it to establish 4,000 colonists in the next 15 years. This the company could not do, but over the years it sent some settlers and granted many seigneuries along the St. Lawrence River in the hope that seigneurs would become colonizers. In 1663 when the Crown revoked the charter of the Company of New France and took over the administration of Canada, there were perhaps 2,500 people of French descent along the lower St. Lawrence. Over the next decade the Crown sent about 1,000 women, many of them from poorhouses in Paris, and offered inducements to demobilized soldiers and indentured servants to stay in the colony. When royal interest in Canada waned after 1672, only 2 or 3 women and not many more men would emigrate from France each year, until the 1750s when some prisoners (salt smugglers) were sent out and soldiers were again induced to stay. In sum, this was a paltry migration of permanent settlers to Canada: over a century and a half only some 9,000 people who stayed, almost all young on arrival, most of them male, and only about 250 couples married in France. The fur trade, of course, depended on Native labor and required only a small resident white population, while agriculture as it developed along the lower St. Lawrence offered little to attract investment or labor. The ordinary emigrant who took himself to Canada faced the challenge of pioneering in a forested, northern setting, isolated from markets. In these circumstances very few French people chose to emigrate, and the Company of New France, seigneurs, and the Crown were all indifferent colonizers.

Agriculture in Acadia depended on tidal marshland around the Bay of Fundy (fig. 4.4). The Acadians diked these marshes, using sods reinforced by branches and logs to build broad dikes some six feet high. At intervals along the dikes there were sluice gates (*aboiteaux*) with clapper valves that closed to the tide. Land so diked would freshen in a few years and make excellent pasture or plowland. Soil fertility could be maintained by occasional flooding. The marshes along the Dauphin River at Port Royal were the first to be diked. By 1670 about 70 farm families lived there; by the 1680s the limited marshland at Port Royal was occupied, and settlement spread to the larger marshes at the head of the Bay of Fundy. Behind their dikes the Acadians planted wheat and legumes (beans and peas), their principal field crops, and raised cattle, sheep, and swine. On higher ground at the edge of the marshes they built small wooden houses, tended kitchen gardens and a few apple trees, and perhaps cleared a little upland. Supplemented by gatherings from forest and sea, such farms provided most of the needs of the families who worked them and a little surplus wheat and beef that entered a coasting trade southward to Boston.

After its small founding migration the Acadian population grew almost entirely from natural increase and was soon demographically balanced. Compared with peasant France, the rate of population growth was high, a result of a lower average marriage age for women and of lower infant and child mortality rates—reflections, presumably, of improved nutrition. By 1686 there were about 800 Acadians, almost all of them progeny of the founding families. The nuclear family was the primary unit of settlement, but adjacent farm families frequently had the same surname, and ties of consanguinity linked all the settlements around the Bay of Fundy. Acadian material culture, about which we know too little, must have reflected a selection of peasant ways from western France, supplemented by a few borrowings from the Mi'kmaq and adapted to the particular environment of the marshlands. Compared with French peasants,

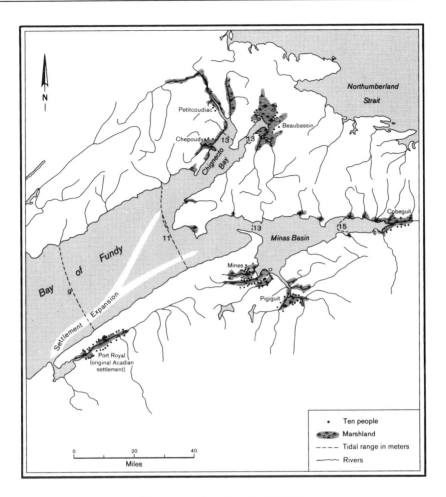

Figure 4.4 Acadian Marshlands

the Acadians were relatively detached from economic power. The seigneurial system (the French counterpart of the manorial system in England) was introduced in a few early land grants, but there is no evidence that Acadian farmers ever paid seigneurial rents for land. There were no royal taxes, although when the French held Port Royal, a governor and a few troops were usually there and a militia was raised locally. Commercial opportunity was limited because Acadia was a small catchment area for furs, there was no commercial fishing in the Bay of Fundy, and marshland farms produced crops and livestock that were available widely around the North Atlantic. In these circumstances Acadian society was not very stratified; people had enough to eat, but there was no

wealth. In 1686 the governor's small thatched house in Port Royal was only a little larger than the tiny Acadian houses nearby. Essentially, the marshlands provided a limited opportunity for the French peasant family but not for many other elements of French society. They became home to a people whose way of life, while French in most details, soon had no precise French counterpart.

The first farms in Canada emerged near Quebec in the 1630s. By 1692, date of an early Canadian census, some 10,000 people lived on farms along the lower St. Lawrence (fig. 4.5). All these farms were in seigneuries, tracts of land granted by the Crown, usually to persons or institutions of some eminence, in return for an oath of fealty and, in Canada, the expectation that they would

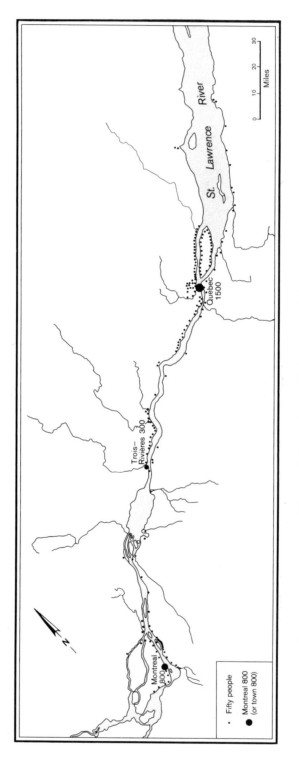

Figure 4.5 Population in St. Lawrence Valley, 1692

act as colonizers. The seigneurs, in turn, sub-granted land to tenants in return for an annual rent and charges for service (such as milling)—an essentially feudal hierarchy of rights and obligations. In Canada most seigneurs divided their seigneuries into farm lots, first along the river and then inland as demand warranted (fig. 4.6). From the beginning, farm lots were long and narrow, in any given area their long axes parallel to each other and roughly perpendicular to the river, their ratios of width to length approximately 1:10, and their area in the vicinity of 75 to 90 acres. This survey, introduced from Normandy, would have a long life in Canada. Long lots were easily surveyed; provided direct access to the river, the colony's highway; usually included a variety of vegetation and soil types; and enabled people to live on their own farms yet be fairly close to neighbors.

From the beginning, rural settlement was dispersed rather than nucleated. Farm families lived on their own land in houses 600 to 1,200 feet apart along the river and made their own agricultural decisions. The open-field village, in decline but still common in many areas from which emigrants had come to Canada, was not introduced. Lots were available for the asking somewhere along the lower St. Lawrence riverfront at any time during the 17th century. To be sure, the forest was a daunting barrier that made a farm virtually inaccessible to a destitute immigrant, and most men lived in Canada for some years as soldiers, indentured servants, or wage laborers before trying to farm. Many gave up or soon died. Still, the relative availability of land for farming raised the price of labor well above its French value. Slowly the forest yielded.

The Canadian farm, like the Acadian, was a mixed operation of a northwest European type. Fields were sown in a two-course rotation of wheat and fallow, occasionally in a three-course rotation with legumes and other grains (usually oats and barley) as well as fallow. The land was rarely manured, seed was poor, and after the initial high returns on newly cleared land, yields were low—as they were on pioneer farms throughout early North America. Yet with 30 acres cleared, such a farm produced about 100 bushels of wheat and probably carried two or three cows, as many swine, a few sheep, and perhaps a pair of oxen. A kitchen garden contained common French vegetables, herbs, tobacco, and usually a few fruit trees. The farm provided for

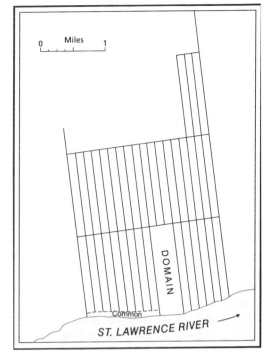

Figure 4.6 Farm Lots in a Hypothetical Seigneurie

most of the subsistence of a family, paid the seigneurial rent and milling charges and the tithe to the church (1/26 of the grain harvest) and had a modest surplus—some bushels of wheat, perhaps a pig or calf, perhaps some butter—for sale. Overall, it is estimated that 2/3 of the grain production of the countryside was required for domestic consumption and seed.

The market, however, was weak. A long decline in the price of wheat and other agricultural products in the 17th century was interrupted only when harvests were bad and farmers had little to sell. There were no agricultural exports—France or the French West Indies were too far away—and local markets in Quebec and Montreal were small. Canadian agriculture developed within this severe constraint. Farms raising many of the crops and livestock of northwestern France could be created. Families could live on them, engage in a lively local barter, and occasionally take some produce to market in one of the towns. Essentially, the countryside of the lower St. Lawrence admitted people to a limited economic opportunity that encouraged demographic rather than commercial expansion. In the early years young women married soon after puberty. Later, when the population was more balanced, they married, on average, at 19 or 20, still younger than women in France or in the English colonies. Families were large and life expectancy was relatively long. The population would double in less than 30 years, and most of the young would support themselves by creating farms much like those on which they had grown up.

Canadian rural society, like the Acadian, was never homogeneous, but neither was it sharply stratified. Save for millers and blacksmiths here and there, almost all heads of household were farmers. Farms of similar age were likely to be similarly developed. Before the end of the 17th century, in the areas of oldest settlement, a few peasants worked as much as 50 cleared acres, a substantial farm in Canada but nothing like the holdings of the wealthiest peasants in France. To a considerable extent the countryside developed within its own momentum, detached from the external economic influences that bore so heavily on the peasantry in France. The farm family and local rural community produced a high percentage of the goods and services they required. The local line of farmhouses along the river (the *côte*) became a loose rural neighborhood reinforced by consanguinity. The parish became a social unit of some importance, although without the responsibility, so onerous in France, to apportion royal taxes. A few merchants were in the countryside in the fall to buy grain and sell cloth, salt, and some ceramic and metal ware. Many peasants were in debt to them. In the early years seigneurs did not collect their rents because their sparsely settled seigneuries were unprofitable, but their legal rights were clear. As the population rose, seigneurs excercised more of their rights and demanded back debts. A few bushels of wheat a year could be a heavy charge for a largely subsistent farmer to pay. Edicts and ordinances from the governor and intendant—representatives of royal power—were read and posted in front of parish churches, and, in a colony frequently at war with the English or Iroquois, men drilled in local militias. In sum, the apparatus of commercial, landed, and state power was at hand in a countryside in which, compared to France, land costs were low, labor was expensive, and markets were poor. In such a

countryside, the most vigorous French transplant was the nuclear farm family.

Quebec and Montreal, the towns of early Canada, were centers of commerce, administration, and defense. At the head of deep-sea navigation on the St. Lawrence, Quebec was the colony's port. It received various imports from France (mostly manufactured goods and foodstuffs) and sent furs. Montreal, the point of transshipment from small ships and riverboats to canoes, was founded as a mission in 1642 and quickly became the focus of the interior fur trade. Until 1681 some Natives came to trade almost every year, while the expeditions of coureurs de bois that began in the 1650s and continued for the rest of the century were outfitted in, and eventually returned to, Montreal. The Canadian merchants who soon operated in these towns bought French goods, hired labor, operated interior posts, and sent furs to La Rochelle. Their warehouses lined the riverfront, and their commerce provided much of the vitality of these first French towns in North America. There were forts and troops in both towns; in 1688 Montreal was walled for protection against the Iroquois. As the colonial capital, Quebec was the residence of governor and intendant and of a considerable bureaucracy. The religious orders erected their finest buildings and maintained most of their staffs in the towns.

In the late 1660s the intendant Jean Talon established a shipyard and brewery in Quebec, a tannery nearby, and ironworks near Trois-Rivières and encouraged the preparation of masts and naval stores along the river below Quebec. But it was difficult to break the Canadian economy from its export dependence on furs and local dependence on farming. Most of Talon's initiatives collapsed when royal subsidies were removed, victims of the high cost and, often, inexperience of Canadian labor, the smallness of the local market, and isolation from external markets.

All the while, the French migratory fishery maintained a relatively static presence along the Atlantic coast. Techniques for catching and curing cod had changed little since the previous century, but the organization of the fishery became more concentrated, and, here and there, people began to overwinter. In France the fishery came to depend on a few ports: principally Havre-de-Grace (mouth of the Seine) and Sable d'Olonne (south of the Loire) in the green fishery; and St.-

Malo, Granville, La Rochelle, and the Basque port of St.-Jean-de-Luz in the dry. Firms that specialized in the transatlantic fishery operated out of these ports, sending out ships that were considerably larger (on average perhaps 90 tons) than those of the 16th century. Their destination in the northwestern Atlantic was limited in the north by Thule Eskimos, who drove French fishermen off most of the Labrador coast, and in the south by fishermen from New England, who increasingly controlled the Atlantic coast of Acadia. The English migratory fishery remained entrenched in southeastern Newfoundland. The French held the rest of Newfoundland and the Gulf of St. Lawrence. Along these French shores the fishery focused on proven, reliable harbors: Percé and Gaspé in the western gulf, Plaisance in southern Newfoundland, and a number of harbors along the bleak, icebound coast of northeastern Newfoundland (fig. 4.1).

Some fishing ships began to leave behind caretakers to look after shore installations over the winter. Eventually, a few merchants began to stay as well. Such men (called *habitants-pêcheurs* by the French and planters by the English) controlled at least one fishing property and a few boats, hired migrant labor, and purchased supplies from, and sold dry fish to, the ships that came each year from France. They were small links, close to the resource, in an elaborate transatlantic commerce. The advantages and disadvantages of the resident system were fiercely argued throughout the 17th century, but the system endured and gradually strengthened. As it did, women and children appeared in the fishing harbors; populations became a little more stable. Yet there were not many such residents. Plaisance in southern Newfoundland, the largest French settlement along the Atlantic coast of North America in the 17th century, had about 20 resident families in 1689. The settlement was a fishing camp with a few families and a small garrison added, a residential toehold in a still largely migratory French fishery that sent some 400 ships and 10,000 men across the Atlantic each year.

FRANCE IN NORTH AMERICA
ABOUT 1700

In 1700 fewer than 20,000 people of French background were scattered across North America from Newfoundland to the Mississippi (fig. 4.7). The overall pattern of their distribution had been set by the cod fishery and fur trade, and at the beginning of the 18th century many people still lived in, and many more worked seasonally in, the work camps of these staple trades. Directed toward rocky, inhospitable shores, the fishery had almost no New World multipliers, whereas the fur trade drew Europeans inland, generating towns and agricultural settlements. By 1700 Quebec and Montreal were well established, and most French speakers in North America lived on farms.

The fur trade continued to be riverine, expansive, and interracial; the cod fishery remained maritime, static, and European. The fishery, as it always had, relied on European labor, discouraged contact between Natives and Europeans, and drew fishermen to familiar shores year after year. The fur trade, dependent on an easily depleted continental resource and on Native labor, drew French traders far into the continental interior and linked Natives and Europeans. By 1696 there were some 20 French posts west of Montreal, 8 of them in the Mississippi watershed; all were tied in one direction to networks of Native trade and in the other by canoe routes to Montreal and by ship across the Atlantic to La Rochelle, the French port of entry for almost all Canadian fur. Yet both the cod fishery and the fur trade were staple trades dependent on overseas markets. Both created wilderness settlements dominated by the specialized techniques, work routines, and transportation connections of a staple trade and inhabited by migratory, male workforces. Put another way, both separated place of work from place of residence, detaching French capital and labor from their larger social contexts and placing them where neither tradition nor community, but rather the terms of work in a staple trade, would shape social relationships. In settlements near the resource a few trade-related tasks were accomplished by largely migratory workforces with as little expenditure as possible. In the fishery, wharves, dry platforms, washing cages, oil vats, and cabins were put up along a shore; in the fur trade, a few squared-log buildings could be constructed in days behind palisades erected with equal haste.

Although both the cod fishery and the fur trade depended on towns, the urban base of the cod fishery remained almost entirely transatlantic. Most ships, crews, and profits of the

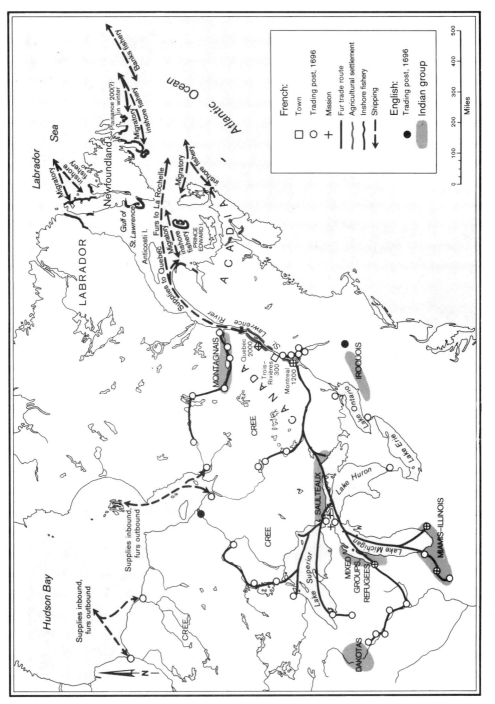

Figure 4.7 France in North America in 1700

fishery returned to France, strengthening French firms; imposing merchant houses were built in some French ports. As the fur trade pushed inland, however, it required New World towns. In Acadia, where the fur trade was small and scattered, Port Royal was barely a village in 1700. But in Canada in that year there were some 2,000 people in Quebec and perhaps 1,200 in Montreal. Although visitors from France described them as "miserable bourgs," they were by far the most comprehensive settings of French life in North America. Their waterfronts—the lower towns—were given to commerce: warehouses, stores, cabarets, and the artisanal activities of a port. Farther from the waterfronts, in the upper towns, land use was more open and institutional: forts and barracks; residences of officials; hospitals, churches, seminaries, and other buildings of religious orders. These towns were occupationally diverse and socially stratified, reproducing within the limits of such small places much of the fine meaning of French social hierarchy. They relied on the surrounding countryside for much of their food and on France or the North American interior for almost everything else. The availability of land in the countryside had driven up urban wages and probably had increased the mobility of labor, conditions that favored the importation of labor-intensive manufactures and discouraged skilled, local craftsmanship.

In 1700 about 1,200 people lived around the marshes of the Bay of Fundy and 13,000 in rural seigneuries along the lower St. Lawrence— the bulk of the resident French-speaking population of North America. In these rural settings the family farm was the primary unit of settlement and economy. People lived in small farmhouses, perhaps 18 x 28 feet, built of round or squared logs and usually thatched. The more durable houses had stone sills and either timber frame walls (variously infilled, but usually with squared logs laid horizontally) or solid walls of horizontal logs (usually cross-notched or dovetailed at the corners). Such building techniques had been common in medieval France when the forest was at hand, had largely lapsed when it was not, and reappeared where wood was again abundant. Houses built with them clustered around the Fundy marshes and lined the St. Lawrence River, one house much like its neighbor, one farm much like the next. Most crops,

livestock, tools, and agricultural practices came from France. Beyond the farm were the myriad relationships (some of blood) of the local community, usually a gristmill and a parish church, and perhaps a seigneurial manor only a little more pretentious than the peasant house. Farther away there was a town—a place that was known and sometimes visited—that sent out merchants who supplied goods beyond the capacity of local fabrication and took farm surpluses. In some areas there was still danger of Native attack, and for some young men there was contract labor in the fishery or the fur trade. But in large part the peasant horizon was local, and compared with France, there was more room for families. As the staple trades tended to detach specialized labor and capital from France, so these mixed agricultural economies tended to detach a peasantry. As Montreal and Quebec tended to reestablish French social and occupational variety, so the countryside tended to diminish both.

In 1700, as from the beginning, the French position in North America was contested. Thirty years before, in 1670, the Stuart court in England had granted the Hudson's Bay Company all the territory that drained into Hudson Bay. English forts, established on the bay at the mouths of the major rivers, began competing with the French for the interior trade. The English had replaced the Dutch at the mouth of the Hudson River and, allied with the Iroquois, were trading into the southern Great Lakes. There was a large English fishery in Newfoundland and English colonies, many times more populous than New France, along the eastern seaboard.

Nevertheless, at the end of the 17th century in North America, military momentum was with the French. French forces captured the English forts on Hudson Bay and James Bay in the 1680s, although the English recaptured one of them, Fort Albany, in 1693 and held it. French troops destroyed several Iroquois villages south of Lake Ontario in 1693 and 1697, forcing the Iroquois to treat for peace, although the Hudson-Mohawk route to the Great Lakes remained in Iroquois-English control. In 1690 a marine attack by New Englanders on Quebec failed miserably. In 1697 the French Crown, faced with a glut of beaver pelts, was confident enough to close most interior posts, assuming the Natives would return to Montreal. Far to the south it established three forts on the Gulf of Mexico—at Biloxi, at Mobile, and on the Mississippi River about 45 miles from its mouth—hoping to contain the English south of the Appalachians and to control access to the interior.

In fact the continental interior was vast and porous, and there was not nearly enough manpower to seal it off, least of all from illegal traders operating out of Montreal. In Newfoundland the predicament was similar. In 1696–97 a combined force of French troops and Canadians under Pierre Le Moyne d'Iberville sacked almost every English settlement in Newfoundland, but the English fishery returned when the attackers withdrew. In these years the one French loss in North America came a little later, in Acadia. The small fort at Port Royal withstood two assaults in 1707 but fell in 1710 to a force of some 3,500 New Englanders. By the terms of the Treaty of Utrecht (1713), which ended the long French-English war known as the War of the Austrian Succession, France confirmed English title to peninsular Acadia, ceded Newfoundland (while retaining fishing rights in the north), and returned the forts on Hudson Bay. France had bargained for European advantage with North American territory and had seriously weakened her North American position.

CHANGES IN THE EARLY 18TH CENTURY

The Treaty of Utrecht forced a number of adjustments. The French migratory fishery to northern Newfoundland continued much as before, whereas the French fishery in southern Newfoundland moved across Cabot Strait to Cape Breton Island (fig. 4.1), which was still in French hands, and quickly reestablished itself there. On Cape Breton Island, called Isle Royale by the French, the residential component of the fishery grew; some merchants adopted the New Englanders' practice of sending small schooners to the offshore banks. The best harbor on the island was at Louisbourg, where, in 1717, the French Crown decided to build a major fortification to protect the entrance to the Gulf of St. Lawrence. A geometrical town plan was superimposed on a straggling fishing village, and massive low walls, designed to withstand artillery bombardment, were slowly built. When completed in the 1730s, Louisbourg was the largest fortification in North America, an early-18th-century fortress town built in the precise military geometry of the Vauban style on a low, frequently foggy peninsula protecting an excellent harbor that had become one of the busiest in North America (fig. 4.8).

After the Treaty of Utrecht the French also moved quickly to restore their earlier position in the west. The ban on interior trade was lifted. Michilimakinac was reopened in 1712–13, and trade was soon restored to the Illinois and Michigan posts (fig 4.9). Agricultural settlement began in the Illinois country: at Vincennes on the lower Wabash River and at Kaskaskia on the Mississippi above the Ohio. Colonists came from Canada, which supplied and administered these settlements until the Illinois country was made part of the colony of Louisiana in 1717. By the early 1720s there were several posts along the lower Great Lakes from Fort Frontenac at the eastern end of Lake Ontario to Detroit, their purpose to exclude English traders, while French posts north of Lake Superior cut into Hudson's Bay Company trade. Detroit and Michilimakinac became major entrepôts, receiving supplies from Montreal and furs from the west. In the 1730s traders from Montreal reached the northern Plains, establishing posts on the Red and Assiniboine Rivers. By the 1740s they were on the Saskatchewan River, some 2,500 miles by canoe from Montreal. As the lines of the French carrying trade lengthened, more French labor was required in the west; by the early 1740s there are records of about 500 men leaving Montreal each year, most of them voyageurs hired to paddle canoes loaded with supplies and trade goods to specified destinations and to return with packs of fur.

To the south, France moved to strengthen her hold on the lower Mississippi River and, thereby, on the whole Mississippi valley. In 1717, after almost two decades during which French settlement along the lower Mississippi had been little more than a garrison, the Crown granted a merchant company title to, and a trading monopoly in, Louisiana for 25 years. The company was to establish 6,000 settlers and 3,000 slaves. The next year it founded New Orleans and began granting large properties that the company assumed would be worked primarily by indentured servants brought from Europe. Immigrants were recruited in France, the Low Countries, and Germany, and several thousand French convicts were sentenced to deportation to Louisiana. Few convicts left France, however,

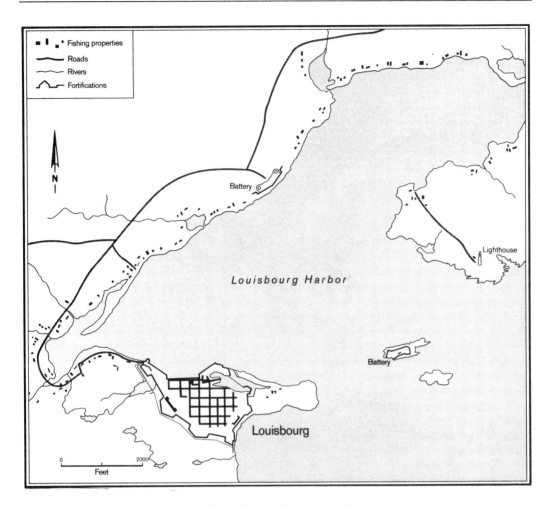

Figure 4.8 Louisbourg, 1742

fewer reached Louisiana, and only a handful survived there. Some Canadians arrived overland from Montreal, but white labor was scarce and expensive. In these circumstances the company turned increasingly to black slaves, the characteristic plantation labor force on the French sugar islands (Guadaloupe, Martinique, and St. Domingue, the western third of Hispaniola). By 1731 the company's monopoly had been terminated, and the Crown assumed control of Louisiana. Plantations worked by slaves were the principal units of production in a colony of about 4,000 non-Native people.

Yet an export staple was not established. Sugar was a marginal crop, not competitive with island production. Midlatitude grains grew poorly in a subtropical climate. Citrus fruits,

figs, and pineapples, which did well, had no export market. Cotton could not yet be ginned. Rice, indigo, and tobacco were more promising and became the principal plantation products, together with lumber and naval stores on some of the larger plantations. Furs and hides (deer and buffalo) from the interior were also exported, but, essentially, the struggling Louisianan economy depended on agricultural land, much of which was occupied by Natives. Initially amicable French-Native relations soured as Native lands were appropriated. Skirmishes and small wars broke out in which the Natives had the short-term advantage of surprise and the French the long-term advantage of firepower. Captured Natives were dispersed, many of them to St. Domingue as slaves.

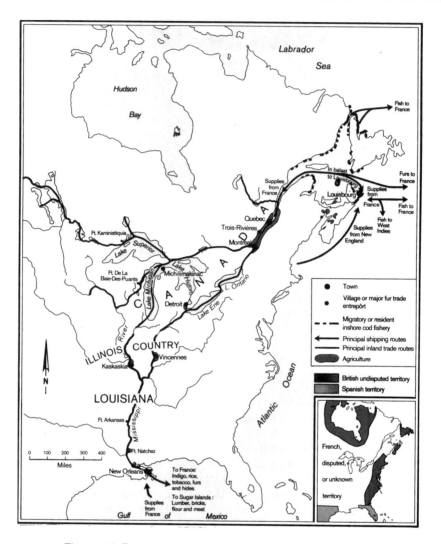

Figure 4.9 France in North America during the 18th Century

While these developments were taking place along the lower Mississippi, the very different settlements along the lower St. Lawrence and in Acadia expanded within well-established patterns. There was virtually no 18th-century immigration to Acadia and, until the last decade of the French regime, little enough to Canada. Birthrates remained high; in each area the average annual population increase was more than 2 percent, most of it absorbed in the countryside, where farmland was available. By 1740 there were about 40,000 French-speaking people in the St. Lawrence valley and some 8,000 around the Bay of Fundy. Settlement had spread along the St. Lawrence River, reducing the gaps between Quebec and Montreal, following minor tributaries, and extending well below Quebec on the south shore (fig. 4.10). All the habitable marshes around the Bay of Fundy were occupied by 1740, and Acadian settlement had begun on Prince Edward Island, called Isle St-Jean by the French (fig. 4.1). Agricultural practices did not change, but for a time there was a little more commercial opportunity because Louisbourg created a relatively accessible market. A little Acadian wheat and some cattle found their way there in most years, usually in small, Acadian-built ships. Merchants from Quebec also began

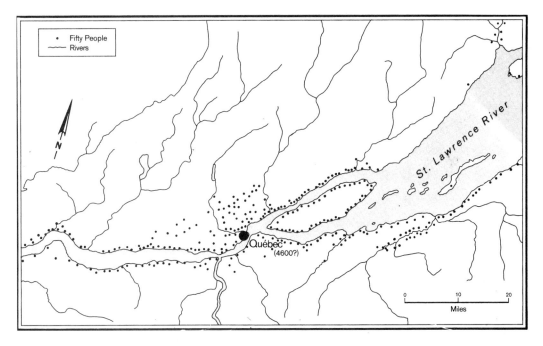

Figure 4.10 Population Distribution near Quebec, 1739

to supply Louisbourg and to expand their cabotage in the gulf (to supply fishing stations). From 1727 to 1742 an average of ten Canadian ships a year carried flour, meat, butter, and lumber to Louisbourg, and a few went on to the sugar islands. Then, in 1742, these trades were disrupted by the first of a succession of poor harvests along the lower St. Lawrence. Wheat prices rose, but there was no surplus for export, a condition that continued to the end of the French regime, putting a heavy lid on the agricultural economy, breaking a promising commercial connection between Canada and Louisbourg and a more tenuous one with the West Indies, slowing urban growth, and weakening the St. Lawrence colony.

With the impetus of expanding trade, Quebec grew quickly from 1727 to the early 1740s, but even in 1744 only some 4,700 people were in the town. Montreal was little more than half as large. The fur trade required the towns but generated little urban growth because most of the goods that traders exchanged for furs came from France. By 1744 agricultural exports had stopped; furs, a valuable export, required only two or three ships a year. Imports involved more ships, but the small colonial market for French

manufactures and foodstuffs and for West Indian molasses and rum was soon satisfied. The size of civil and clerical administrations, and even of garrisons, changed slowly. Quebec and Montreal were small, stable, preindustrial towns, their economies established and circumscribed, their populations growing slowly.

FRANCE IN NORTH AMERICA ABOUT 1750

In the middle of the 18th century France claimed a vast crescent of North America from the Gulf of St. Lawrence to the mouth of the Mississippi (fig. 4.9). Such a claim was intended to deflect European rivals; within much of New France the French deferred to Natives, who regarded the land as theirs and still controlled it. Yet the French dominated the two main continental entries and far outdistanced English traders in the interior, building posts and trading through thousands of miles of Native territory. French settlement was hardly in proportion: some 60,000 people of French descent along the lower St. Lawrence River, perhaps 2,000 along the lower Mississippi more than 3,000 miles

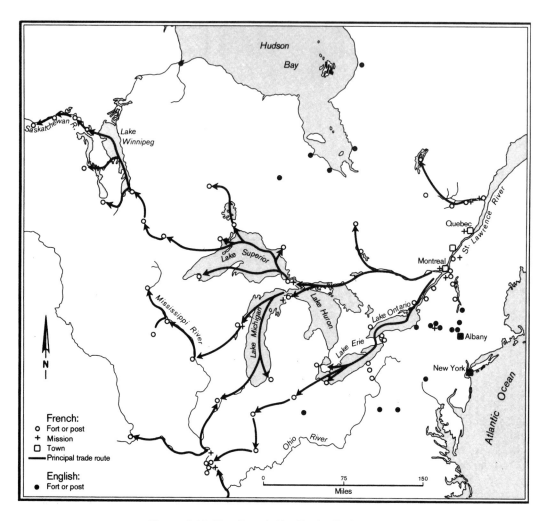

Figure 4.11 The French Fur Trade, Early 1750s

away, more than 1,000 in the Illinois country, a few hundred around the lower Great Lakes, more than 10,000 Acadians around the Bay of Fundy (most living in British territory), and just over 5,000 people on Cape Breton Island, including those at Louisbourg. After 150 years of French activity there were fewer than 80,000 French-speaking settlers in North America. The French migratory fishery, still large and inflexible, continued to northern Newfoundland and into the Gulf of St. Lawrence. Overall, the French-speaking settlements were a collection of patches strung somewhat diagonally across a continent, some linked to each other by trade, but the collection as a whole was dispersed, underconnected, and vulnerable.

In the early 1750s the French fur trade reached its zenith (fig. 4.11). Perhaps 700 men from Montreal Island and seigneuries nearby traveled west each year, many of them to overwinter at interior posts. English traders were checked along the Great Lakes, and Montreal traders competed around the large perimeter of Hudson's Bay Company trade. The whole Great Lakes basin and upper Mississippi valley were, briefly, in French control; in 1754–55, 80 percent of the North American fur trade was French, almost all of it passing through Montreal and Quebec and thence, in a few ships a year, to La Rochelle. In the same year almost a million quintals (one quintal equals 112 pounds, or about 50 kilograms) of dried and green cod from the French fisheries in the northwestern Atlantic returned to France in several hundred ships; a relatively tiny quantity of cod went to the sugar islands. A variety of agricultural products, naval stores, and lumber was shipped from New Orleans to the sugar islands or to France. These trades were not interconnected, and they largely bypassed the mixed farms along the lower St. Lawrence and in Acadia, on which most French-speaking people in North America lived. It is true, however, that Kaskaskia, Vincennes, and other French settlements in the Illinois country sent salt beef, pork, and flour to Louisiana. The farms at Detroit and near Montreal provided foodstuffs and manpower for the fur trade, and some farms near Quebec supplied the gulf fisheries. The ships that brought imports from France to Quebec usually sailed in ballast to Louisbourg, hoping for a cargo there. In the early 1750s the building materials and most foodstuffs imported at Louisbourg came from New England. Despite many official projects to the contrary, it had not proved possible to create an integrated commercial system out of the different, widely separated spatial economies of New France.

Therefore, there was no one urban hierarchy. New Orleans controlled the Mississippi trade north to the Illinois country, Quebec and Montreal controlled the St. Lawrence trade, and Louisbourg participated in North Atlantic trade. All were well connected to France and, excepting Quebec and Montreal, little connected to each other. Yet all were colonial French towns with important commercial, military, and administrative functions. Commerce dominated their waterfronts, and institutional buildings their upper towns. Merchants, colonial officials, and officers dominated their social structures. Urban society was sharply hierarchical, status conscious, and deferential, although, as in other towns of the day, people of very different standing lived side by side. In many ways the towns of New France resembled their French equivalents. Of course they were new, without centuries of architectural accretion, and they were composed of people of many regional backgrounds. In New Orleans there were many black and some Native slaves in a population of perhaps 1,200. In all the towns the cost of labor was high. There were no guilds, apprenticeship was much less defined than in France, and small labor-intensive manufactured goods were usual-

ly imported. In Quebec rough footwear was made locally, whereas most fine shoes came from France, although there were skilled craftsmen—wigmakers, cabinetmakers, sculptors, and silversmiths—as well as the rougher trades associated with the port and with construction. The oldest and largest of the towns of New France, Quebec was the most like a French provincial capital.

A good deal of Louisbourg was rebuilt as a Parks Canada project in the 1960s, after painstaking research; as a result its mid-18th-century appearance is remarkably accurately known. The architecture of all the principal buildings reflected current French taste, just as the layout of fortifications reflected current French military engineering. The appearance of lesser buildings, most of them of timber-frame construction variously infilled, was less bound to current style and more dependent on techniques of construction. Gardens, always small in Louisbourg, were laid out geometrically, as was the town itself, which, like New Orleans, was a rectangular grid of streets, walled. In Quebec and Montreal officials discouraged wooden buildings because of the fire hazard. By 1750 most houses were of stone, their shingle or plank roofs punctuated by plain dormers and massive chimneys. Usually they were built continuously on narrow lots. Size was gained by height; the largest houses of successful merchants had four stories above the basement. In New Orleans, where local stone was not available, most buildings were of timber-frame construction with brick infill. Otherwise the architectural styles and the techniques of construction of the northern towns also prevailed in New Orleans.

In 1750, as earlier, rural Acadia and Canada remained somewhat detached from this urban world. Some 13,000 Acadians had diked all the available marshes, and many of them, fearful of English intentions and short of land, were moving to Prince Edward Island, still in French hands. Acadian agriculture remained what it had been in 1700: mixed, largely subsistent, family centered, and primarily dependent on the marshlands. Acadian society may have become a little more stratified, although there is very little evidence one way or the other and no suggestion of wealth in any settlement around the Bay of Fundy. Now several generations removed from France, closely interrelated, and exposed to a common marshland environment, the Acadians had created a distinctive regional peasant culture.

By the early 1750s some 50,000 rural people of French descent lived along the lower St. Lawrence, almost all of them members of farm families. As the population grew, the countryside became somewhat more differentiated. There were now several agricultural villages housing a priest *(curé)* and perhaps the seigneurial family, a few artisans and perhaps a merchant agent or two besides farm families. More seigneurs were able to profit from their land rent and domainal farms; manor houses became more common and a little larger. A few merchants in Montreal and Quebec prospered from their dealings in the countryside, while a few farmers in long-settled areas near the towns worked as much as 75 acres of cleared land and relied on hired labor. Yet the continuing availability of land somewhere in the colony (if not near the parental farm) and the weakness of the export economy slowed the pace of social and economic differentiation. The countryside could still yield a rough living for most and was only slowly yielding much more for a few.

In the Illinois country, opportunities were quite different. The largest concentration of French settlement was in five villages, inhabited by some 1,000 whites and 500 black and Native slaves, along the Mississippi River between the Missouri and the Kaskaskia. Father Vivier, the Jesuit who served these settlements, estimated that two-thirds of their agricultural production was exported. Wheat, beef, pork, and some livestock on the hoof were sent to New Orleans, destined for the sugar islands. Corn, which was not exported, yielded abundantly and was the food of cattle, slaves, and Natives. The largest landholder in the village of Kaskaskia worked some 500 acres of arable land and owned 60 slaves (including some women and children) and many hundred cattle, swine, and horses. Almost 70 percent of white families were slaveowners. In the Illinois country, French settlement from Canada had reached a bounteous land suitable for arable and pastoral farming and within range of a market. A small, ethnically mixed population was growing rapidly, its economy vigorous, its society sharply stratified. Vivier considered the Illinois country the pivot of the French effort to hold the vast continental crescent between the Gulf of St. Lawrence and the Gulf of Mexico. In many ways he was right, but a few villagers far in the interior were a fragile pivot for continental ambition.

Almost 500 miles along the river south of Kaskaskia, a garrison (Fort Arkansas) at the mouth of the Arkansas River was the most northerly outpost of French settlement on the lower Mississippi and a way point for convoys to and from the Illinois country (fig 4.9). A few settlers had farmed there until driven off by the Chickasaw in 1748. At Natchez, some 190 miles farther south, there was another garrison, again penned in by the Chickasaw, and good but underused tobacco land. At Pointe-Coupée, halfway between Natchez and New Orleans, agriculture was more secure, tobacco being the principal crop. There was a German settlement 20 miles above New Orleans; below the town both banks of the river were occupied almost halfway to the sea. Throughout these plantations blacks considerably outnumbered whites (a census of 1763 enumerated 4,539 blacks and 2,966 whites along the lower Mississippi). Slaves were used to produce subsistent crops such as potatoes, corn, and vegetables and to work in rice, indigo, and tobacco fields. They also served as laborers in sawmills and brickyards and in the preparation of naval stores. Some 40 ships were reported to have called at New Orleans in 1750, most coming from Martinique and St. Domingue for lumber and bricks. The colony also exported a variety of goods to France—principally indigo, tobacco, rice, furs, and hides—but in 1750, as previously, Louisiana was a considerable financial liability to the French Crown. The settlements along the lower Mississippi were set around by hostile Natives and still had not established an export staple. After the initial burst of immigration in the first years of the merchant company, the population had grown very slowly.

CONCLUSION

The French position in North America, vast, scattered, and underpopulated, was lost during the Seven Years' War. In 1755, before the war officially began, British officials in Acadia, distrusting the French-speaking population they loosely governed and encouraged by Boston merchants who stood to earn lucrative contracts, decided to deport the Acadians. Many Acadians fled to Canada or to the Gulf of St. Lawrence, but many others were caught and sent to the English colonies to the south. When Louisbourg fell in 1758 after a massive siege, the French could no longer protect the gulf. Acadian refugees there were rounded up and sent to England or France. In 1759 another large British force laid siege to Quebec and, after a summer's bombardment, took the town. Surrounded, the French army in Montreal capitulated the next year. New France was lost. The British effort to take it had cost some £80 million, the French defense about 1/20 as much. At the end, as throughout, France's involvement in North America had been halfhearted. Furs from Canada were only 5 to 10 percent of the value of French colonial imports, 1 to 2 percent of the value of all imports. Louisiana had been an expense rather than a revenue. The fisheries seemed more important than either Canada or Louisiana. France bargained for them and, in the Treaty of Paris ending the Seven Years' War, retained fishing privileges in northern and western Newfoundland and two small islands, St. Pierre and Miquelon (fig. 4.1), south of Newfoundland. Canada and all of Acadia were ceded to Britain; Louisiana was ceded to Spain. From a French perspective the loss of New France was not devastating and might even encourage the English seaboard colonies, freed from French threat, to revolt.

In North America the fall of New France changed the control, but not the pattern, of the spatial economy. The Acadian lands were reoccupied by New Englanders who would soon practice much the same semisubsistent agriculture as their predecessors. Louisbourg was abandoned and demolished, but the fisheries continued, with the French migratory fishery now confined to northern Newfoundland and to St. Pierre and Miquelon. In the St. Lawrence valley Montreal and Quebec retained their older functions under new management. Their populations declined after the conquest, then grew very slowly. The countryside remained French-speaking, and rural life stayed much as it was. The connection with the west quickly resumed, employing the techniques and reoccupying and expanding the space of the Montreal fur trade at the end of the French regime. Increasingly the merchants were English-speaking. Plantation agriculture continued in the lower Mississippi valley, now in Spanish hands, to which, over the years, many Acadian refugees

made their way. The different economies of the former French possessions in North America were no more integrated than they had been under the French.

Early in the Revolutionary War American troops attacked Canada, assuming that the French-speaking inhabitants of the St. Lawrence lowlands, recently conquered by the British, would rally to the American cause. A few did; the invaders captured Montreal and laid midwinter siege to Quebec. But British troops held the town, local support for the Americans evaporated, and in the spring when British reinforcements arrived, the invaders fled. The old French colony along the St. Lawrence had held against its former enemies and at the end of the war was the core of the British position in North America. In the peace settlement of 1783 an international border was drawn from the St. Lawrence River through Lakes Ontario, Erie, Huron, and Superior, placing Grand Portage, the principal entrepôt on the north shore of Lake Superior, on the American side (fig. 4.9). A canoe route beyond Lake Superior to the northern Plains was barely retained, while the more southerly reach of the St. Lawrence fur trade into the Ohio valley and the Mississippi valley was lost. The small, vigorous, quite distinctive, but too belated settlements in the Illinois country would soon merge in the tide of American westward expansion. In the east, Newfoundland remained British, as did the territory the French called Acadia, renamed Nova Scotia.

Britain retained, in effect, the original French economies in North America: the cod fishery and the fur trade based on the St. Lawrence, the towns that the fur trade had created, and the semisubsistent agricultural economies that had emerged in its train—patches of settlement bounded by uncultivable land and separated by distance along the northern edge of North American agriculture. Over the years, the fur trade and cod fishery would continue, as detached as ever from each other. Other staple trades would reach into northern North American space, and towns would emerge to serve them. Agriculture would continue in patches, and none of the patches would be very well connected to each other. Economic, social, and political life would evolve within this fractured economic space, along the northern inhabitable edge of a continent, as it had done throughout the French regime.

ADDITIONAL READING

Clark, A. H. 1968. *Acadia: The Geography of Early Nova Scotia to 1760.* Madison: University of Wisconsin Press.

Courville, S. 1983. "Espace, territoire, et culture en Nouvelle-France: Une vision géographique." *Revue d'histoire de l'Amérique française* 37: 417–29. Translated as "Space, Territory, and Culture in New France: A Geographic Perspective," in G. Wynn, ed. *People, Places, Patterns, Processes* (Toronto: Copp Clark Pitman, 1990), 165–76.

Dechêne, L. *Habitants et marchands de Montréal au 17e siècle.* Montréal: Plon, 1974. Translated by Liana Vardi as *Habitants and Merchants in 17th-Century Montreal* (Montreal and Kingston: McGill-Queen's University Press, 1992).

———. 1994. *Le partage des subsistances au Canada sous le régime français.* Montreal: Editions du Boréal.

Eccles, W. J. 1969. *The Canadian Frontier, 1534–1760.* New York: Holt, Rinehart & Winston.

Greer, A. 1985. *Peasant, Lord, and Merchant: Rural Society in Three Quebec Parishes, 1740–1840.* Toronto: University of Toronto Press.

Harris, R. C. 1984. *The Seigneurial System in Early Canada: A Geographical Study.* Madison: University of Wisconsin Press, 1966. Reprint, Montreal and Kingston: McGill-Queen's University Press.

Harris, R. C., ed., and G. Matthews, cart. 1987. *Historical Atlas of Canada.* Vol. 1, *From the Beginning to 1800.* Toronto: University of Toronto Press.

Harris, R. C., and J. Warkentin. 1991. *Canada before Confederation: A Study in Historical Geography.* New York: Oxford University Press, 1974. Reprint, Ottawa: Carleton University Press.

Heidenreich, C. E. 1971. *Huronia.* Toronto: McClelland & Stewart.

Sauer, C. O. 1971. *16th-Century North America: The Land and the People as Seen by the Europeans.* Berkeley and Los Angeles: University of California Press.

Trudel, M. 1973. *The Beginnings of New France, 1524–1663.* Toronto: McClelland & Stewart.

5

The Colonial Origins of Anglo-America

ROBERT D. MITCHELL

> This enterprise may staye the spanishe Kinge from flowinge over all the face of that waste firme of America, if we seate and plante there in time.
>
> Richard Hakluyt, *A Discourse Concerning Western Planting,* 1584

> If you Plant, where Savages are, doe not onely entertaine them with Trifles and Gingles; But use them justly, and gratiously, with sufficient Guard nevertheless: And doe not winne their favour by helping them to invade their Enemies, but for their Defence it is not amisse. And send oft of them over to the Country that Plants, that they may see a better Condition than their owne, and commend it when they returne.
>
> Francis Bacon, *Of Plantations,* 1625

The "planting" of a new society, devoutly wished by the geographer and writer Richard Hakluyt and the philosopher-statesman Francis Bacon, has been enshrined by Americans in a complex vision of a heroic past, a unique mythology of creation. This vision, replete with references to rugged, individualistic pioneers winning the continent for civilization and culminating in the fight for freedom and independence, remains vivid in the popular, if not the scholarly, imagination. The revisionist scholarship of the 1960s to 1980s, on the other hand, has plunged us into debate about the origins of the new societies created in North America.

England entered the world of European colonization of the Americas rather late. Its principal achievement by 1700, more than 250,000 settlers distributed sparsely and discontinuously from southern Maine to South Carolina with few settlements more than 50 miles from the coast, appears modest in light of the demographic growth and territorial expansion of the 18th and 19th centuries. But viewed in comparison with Spanish colonization, with its marginal interests in North America, or French colonization, with its marginal locations in the north, English settlement proved quite successful. More important, this pioneer population was principally responsible for creating both the foundation for, and the delineation of, a new American culture and society that later generations gradually transformed into the more familiar world of the turn of the 21st century.

The study of Anglo-American origins is one of the more controversial issues in American historiography. Some observers have argued that the creation of the new society was based primarily on elements of English life that were transferred selectively across the Atlantic and, metaphorically speaking, transplanted in the new land, took root, and flourished. Continuity of life between the Old World and the New was, therefore, paramount. This view contrasted with the earlier interpretation of Frederick Jackson Turner, who emphasized the formative influences on a new society of a moving American settlement frontier increasingly distant from Europe. Others have argued forcefully that the characteristics of the new land itself were critical in defining the principal features of 17th-century life. Pioneer settlers had to adapt to a variety of environmental circumstances, seemingly familiar and unfamiliar. In so doing, they modified both their environments and their European heritages.

Debate has also ensued over the precise geographical configuration of these new colonial settlements. Are they best described in terms of a rapid convergence and simplification of English

Professor Mitchell was not available to review this chapter, and it appears here as in the first edition, with minor editing. The editors have composed an addendum, appearing at the end of the chapter, and have augmented the bibliography.

traits into three regions of cultural integration, the so-called hearths of southern New England, the lower Delaware Valley and southeastern Pennsylvania, and the tidewater Chesapeake? Or were early colonial settlements more diversified and more complex? If diversity is a more appropriate theme, what were the characteristics of its regionalism, and for how long did this diversity endure? And to what extent are the differences found in these early settlements to be explained basically in terms of distinctions made between communitarian, subsistence societies and those of more liberal, individualistic, and commercial orientation?

These issues and questions allow us to identify three major themes in our quest for Anglo-American origins. The first theme is the configuration and transfer of the values, institutions, and practices of English life to the Atlantic coast of North America during the 17th century. Second, we need to examine the spatial reorganization and landscape expression of these elements in new North American environments. Third, it is also important for us to identify the spatial and temporal changes that occurred in the colonies during the century and that provided the framework for continuity, expansion, and convergence during the 18th century.

ENGLAND ON THE EVE OF COLONIZATION

English administration of territories overseas was not a novel experience. As the largest, most populous, and most southerly area of the British Isles, England had administered territories in France until the middle of the 15th century. Later generations of Tudor monarchs devoted considerable attention to reorganizing the British Isles into an English-dominated national territorial system. Wales and Cornwall had been integrated into an English state structure by the middle of the 16th century. Scotland remained relatively untouched until the Union of the Crowns under James I in 1603. English monarchs devoted most attention to Ireland during the later 16th and early 17th centuries; and it was in Ireland that several early colonial founders—Humphrey Gilbert in Newfoundland, Walter Raleigh at Roanoke Island, and several members of the Virginia Company of London—received part of their training in colonization

and in the military subjugation of non-English populations. When the English turned their attention to transatlantic enterprises by the 1560s, therefore, they did so within the context of prior administrative, legal, and military experience.

The 4 million people who made up the English nation in 1600 were organized into some 40 shires or county communities, more than 700 boroughs, and about 9,000 rural parishes. English life was overwhelmingly rural, agrarian, and provincial. Only London, with 250,000 inhabitants, had more than 20,000 people. Even by the end of the century 85 percent of England's 6 million people still resided in the countryside (fig. 5.1). English life was thus characterized by considerable regional diversity, a diversity that tended to foster much insularity and provincialism. This provincial world, nevertheless, was focused on a widely shared set of values, symbols, and institutions. Belief in social order and stability, hierarchy and inequality, aristocracy and patriarchy, and individual responsibility within a recently transformed Protestant society was associated with symbols of nature and the pastoral, of communal and agrarian living, of emerging national identification and strong upper-class preoccupation with the past. The institutions that molded these characteristics into patterns of everyday living were those associated with family and kin, rural neighborhood and community, the manor and local government, church and parish, land and property, and civil and common law.

The conventional view of English regionalism holds that a basic division existed between a lowland zone of open-field arable farming associated with nucleated villages and hamlets in the south and east and an upland zone to the west and north of enclosed fields, hamlets, and dispersed farms, with more pastoral activities. It is now clear that rural England was more complex than this. We can identify several principal farming types, field systems, settlement patterns, and vernacular (folk) housing forms, all of which overlapped to create a myriad of regional subtypes.

In southern and eastern England, from which three-quarters of 17th-century colonists came, there were four principal regional societies and economies with several subtypes. In southeastern England, a wood pasture economy prevailed based on barley, wheat, and rye; peas and beans; and sheep, cattle, and localized pig production. This system was associated with irregular and

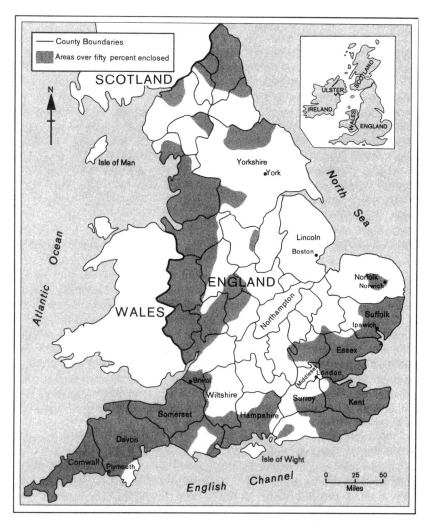

Figure 5.1 Early 17th-Century England

sometimes open-field systems and hamlets and dispersed farms in which timber-framed rectilinear houses predominated. In the Home Counties around London, large manors and individual farms produced wheat, oats, vegetables, cattle, and pigs in the valleys, shifting to sheep farming on the surrounding chalk hills. Midland England supported a more varied, mixed farming economy based on open- and common-field farming, with large villages under a strong manorial system in the east; this pattern gave way farther west to a more complex arrangement of villages and open fields interrupted by areas of enclosure and more dispersed settlement. To the east, barley, wheat, rye, oats, peas, and beans were commonly cultivated in association with cattle, pigs, and poultry; to the west, greater emphasis on rye, oats, cattle, and sheep was evident. Timber-framed rectilinear houses and hall-and-parlor houses were common throughout the region. In the southwest, a more open pasture economy prevailed based on barley and oats, plus cattle and sheep rearing. This system was associated with small enclosed fields, dispersed farmsteads, and long farmhouses with connected service buildings and merged into open-field systems, hamlets, and hall-and-parlor houses to the east.

Provincial England was also a relatively spatially restricted society. Country folk showed little interest in national affairs or even in regional issues. Strong association with place of birth, family loyalty, participation in community and church affairs, and limited contacts with the rest of the country fostered an often intense local attachment. Most people seldom strayed beyond the local parish and the local market town. Geographical mobility was discouraged officially among the lower classes of husbandmen, tenants, laborers, and paupers. Travel on roads and waterways was slow and limited, especially during periods of inclement weather. Within local communities the landowning classes, especially the aristocracy and the gentry who filled most provincial political and administrative offices, provided a continuity with the past. Their interest in family-inherited estates, political offices, trading connections, and genealogy and heraldry perpetuated the continuity of the local provincial scene.

Yet significant changes occurred in English society during the 17th century that affected both the pattern of emigration to the Americas and the relations between the mother country and her colonies. Foremost among these was the drive toward national-political integration alluded to earlier. This was exemplified by the concomitant establishment of the Ulster Plantation in northern Ireland (a colony of subjugation) and the Jamestown Plantation in Virginia (a trading venture) during the first decade of the century. It was expressed further in the bitter civil war of the 1640s, the subsequent Puritan republic of the 1650s, the restoration of a Catholic monarch in 1660, and the so-called Bloodless Revolution of 1689 that finally assured Anglican Protestantism as the faith in perpetuity of the British Crown.

A second measure of change was the increasing concentration of economic and political power in London and the challenges to the traditional order in the city and adjacent Home Counties. London became a magnet for the disaffected, the unemployed, and the ambitious provincials who were responding to long-run social and economic changes in the countryside. Agricultural reorganization in the form of increased farm enclosure (fig. 5.1), greater emphasis on commercial agricultural specialization, and a weakening of manorial institutions began to affect extensive areas of southern and eastern England by midcentury. The fragility of a 35- to 40-year life span generally made the

yeoman, husbandman, and lesser tenant and laboring classes, who constituted the bulk of rural populations, willing to accept authority, patriarchy, and inequality as part of the natural order of things. But vulnerability to famines, plagues, wars, and the economic decisions of larger landholders could lead also to social unrest, institutional modification, and religious revivalism. The spread of Puritanism (originally devised as a derogatory term) in the late 16th and early 17th centuries was one such response to perceived change.

Third, the emergence of new commercial and mercantile classes, partly supported by agrarian reform and by profits in New World ventures, began to produce a gradual redistribution of wealth, power, and status away from the traditional landowning classes to more urban-oriented merchants and artisans and to those farmers who sought to take advantage of the increasing pace of agricultural and trading enterprise. Many transatlantic migrants were derived from such populations, people ultimately unwilling to accept the limitations imposed at home on property ownership, wealth accumulation, social mobility, or religious practice.

The migrants to North America nevertheless brought with them a set of cultural assumptions about the world that was deeply embedded in the familiar provincial society of rural England. They expected to reproduce much of this world in their new surroundings in North America, within the limitations of their slim geographical knowledge. What distinguished their behavior above all was their sense of cultural mission that equated right with Christian faith, might with military power, social order with private property and individual worth, and civilization with the subdued pastoral and small-town landscapes of lowland England.

THE NEW WORLD ENVIRONMENT

The 60,000-odd English settlers who migrated to the American colonies before 1660 encountered a world both new and seemingly familiar. Glowing, propagandistic reports of early explorers and pioneer settlers gradually gave way to more measured, often critical views of the environments encountered. An almost universally expressed opinion was that the immense forested wildernesses found almost everywhere inland from the Atlantic coast were a challenge to civilized English settlers. The intellectual historian Perry Miller's evaluation of the Puritans' "errand into the wilderness" identified the particularly acute sense of mission transmitted to New England. Wild landscapes reflected wild people unable or unwilling to subdue nature for purposes of civilized settlement.

The environments encountered by the pioneer settlers, however, varied significantly in space and in time. Seventeenth-century climatic patterns appear to have been slightly cooler and drier than 20th-century patterns throughout the Atlantic region. Conditions were relatively temperate during the first two decades of colonization, with coastal climates perhaps a few degrees cooler and precipitation in general a few inches less than at present. In 17th-century terms, however, relatively harsh conditions prevailed during the 1630s and 1640s; a more temperate situation was the rule from the early 1650s until the extremely harsh winters of the 1680s and 1690s. A general amelioration of climate set in again until the deterioration of the 1730s and 1740s. These fluctuations, while locally variable, probably produced slightly shorter frost-free seasons than at present. This would mean about a 160- to-165-day season in eastern Massachusetts (some 50 days less than in southern England), 200 to 205 days in the Virginia tidewater, and 275 to 280 days in the South Carolina low country. What this meant in real terms for settlers north of the Carolinas, however, was that climatic patterns were more extreme than in the mother country: summers were hotter (by 10° to 20° F), drier, and more humid, and winters longer, colder (by 10° to 20° F), and snowier. While early settlers in Massachusetts could bemoan their settlement experience in a cold, barren, mountainous, rocky "desert," a visitor to South Carolina could write later that the climate in general was very pleasant and delightful. If the summer months were bothersome to some people, fresh air, shade, summerhouses, and cool baths provided relief.

What these experiences meant in ecological terms was that there were no major barriers, except the mixed deciduous forests (variously dense to open), to the direct transfer of English crops and farming practices to the colonies, although local adjustments had to be made. In New England, the rather stony, leached, and only moderately productive soils and frequently dry early summers tended to favor the growth of maize rather than wheat; the harsh winters created a need for more elaborate feed and shelter practices for livestock. In the Virginia tidewater, the hot, humid summers, brackish and saline water, and extensive marshlands made settlement more difficult, and the widespread occurrence of malaria initially caused higher death rates than farther north.

It was, however, the presence of the Native ("Indian") populations that provided the most significant encounters for the early settlers (fig. 5.2). It is clear from recent research that the Native societies that came into contact with the colonists were mere remnants of the populations that had occupied the Atlantic coastal zones during the early 16th century. Earlier calculations of a paltry 500,000 to 600,000 Natives east of the Mississippi have now been expanded at least fourfold to between 2 million and 2.5 million. Such numbers were not encountered during the 17th century because European contacts with Natives, through transmission of disease (smallpox, measles, influenza, bubonic plague) and warfare, had reduced those populations east of the Appalachians to probably less than 200,000 by the early 17th century.

It has been customary to suggest a broad homogeneity and unity of outlook among Native populations through such designations as the "Eastern Woodland Indians." But the unity can be recognized only at a macrolevel ("Native American" and "European") and the homogeneity scarcely at all. Beyond a general outlook or shared worldview, the diversity of Native life was even greater than that of English life. The Natives shared, nevertheless, not only a set of forested environments but also a philosophy of life that differed in significant respects from the assumptions entertained by the colonists. Fundamental to the Native American world was the indivisibility of the natural and human spheres of existence. The distinction between "man" and "nature" held so profoundly by the Europeans was incomprehensible to the Natives. This had important implications for their perceptions of, and access to, resources. Private ownership of land as an alienating right in perpetuity was unknown. Rights of access to land and water were more varied. Whether in the creation of long-term family hunting territories, privately used garden plots, or communal gathering and hunting practices, the general

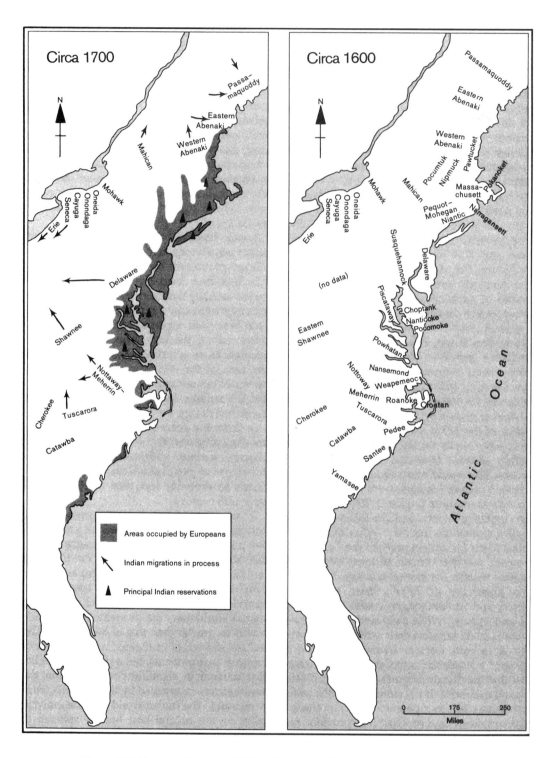

Figure 5.2 Eastern Seaboard Native American Groupings, 1600 and 1700

principle was usufructory. Rights of access were equated with rights of regular use; where persistent use had been terminated, rights of access were once again theoretically open. Thus the Dutch, who began occupying Manhattan in 1626, had "bought" the island for a mere 60 guilders from local Natives who were in the process of migrating farther north. These people no doubt were pleasantly surprised by the generous "gift" from the strange visitors for territory to which these Natives no longer had claim.

These basic differences in outlook were critical to contact, because the settlers who came under the aegis of English commercial companies eventually came to stay. The struggle for land that ensued has dominated relations between Natives and newcomers ever since. The settlers did not come to share the land but to alienate it from the Natives by purchase (from an English perspective), by manipulation, and by outright conquest. Even such a seemingly enlightened proprietor as William Penn could legitimize his acquisition of territory only through written treaty, contract, and purchase, means of land negotiation unfamiliar to the Natives. What justified the taking of these territories in English eyes was the belief above all that the Natives had not made sufficient or efficient use of the land. The English could do better.

There was some general relationship, although hardly a neat correlation, between Native economic, linguistic, housing, social, and political patterns in eastern America. In general, the hunting and gathering bands of Algonquian language stock that occupied much of northern and central New England were the smallest groups in numbers, the most nomadic (using portable tipis), and the least socially complex societies encountered by the early Europeans. From southern New England and central New York southward, however, an enormous variety of organizational patterns existed based upon a widely shared horticultural base of corn (at least four varieties), beans, squash, and several dozen other cultivated and wild plants used in the absence of domesticated animals except for small dogs and the feral turkey. Forest clearance was achieved through cutting and burning underbrush and girdling larger trees so that they rotted gradually. The ground was prepared with a rough hoe, and planting of corn, bean, and squash seeds was done with a

digging stick in mounds almost a foot high and four to six feet apart. New land was cleared on a regular basis as yields declined, in a system we describe today as a slash-and-burn field rotation cycle. Early colonists frequently described as "Indian old fields" areas cleared in this manner for cultivation or areas burned over for hunting purposes. The domesticated plant diet was supplemented by the gathering of wild roots, berries, nuts, and fruits, by both saltwater and freshwater fishing, and by the hunting of game (particularly deer).

It was this hunting component that most confused early English observers. Native preplow cultivation practices were comprehensible to the settlers, and indeed surplus Native crops helped the pioneers at Jamestown and Plymouth to survive the early years of agricultural experimentation and to make corn (maize) rather than European small grains a suitable foodstuff and feedstuff during the 17th century. Hunting, however, was a different matter. It was acceptable to the English as a sport indulged in mainly by the landed classes in England, but as a permanent occupation it offended the English sense of civilized humanity. Hunting of this kind was the mark of "savage" rather than civil behavior.

Europeans found a similar absence of a civilizing influence in Native social organization. Despite a gradual appreciation of the complexities of group arrangements from supraband organizations lacking clear leadership patterns to complex hierarchies and multiple chiefdoms, such as the Powhatan "confederacy" in tidewater Virginia and the "nations" of the Iroquois in central New York, and the generally larger populations and more stable settlements associated with such complexity, Europeans consistently refused to accept such characteristics as the mark of civilized people. What especially condemned the Natives from a European perspective was their "heathenism," their ignorance of the Christian god and of Christian salvation. English desire to acculturate and ultimately assimilate Natives into colonial society and culture was predicated on the elimination of the savage and the heathen elements of their lives, a proselytizing task that was adopted most intensely by the Puritan churchmen of Massachusetts. The transformation of the American wilderness into an English garden meant not only the introduction of English resource practices but also a cultural transformation of the Natives into a darker-skinned

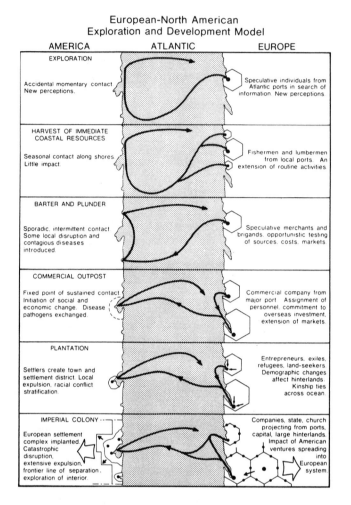

Figure 5.3 Transatlantic Interactions (after Meinig)

semblance of civilized English men and women. The subsequent history of relations between Native Americans and Euro-Americans has demonstrated the painful futility of such aspirations. The creation of colonial society was to be accomplished without serious Native participation. Intercultural contacts continued through trading connections, military alliances, and the survival of "mixed-blood" populations on reservations, but always within the larger context of a dynamically moving, contested, interior settlement frontier that was to leave the area west of European settlements as a temporary "reserve" for declining Native populations (fig. 5.2).

SETTLEMENT, POPULATION, AND TERRITORY

The early failures of private colonization schemes during the 1570s and 1580s, such as Gilbert's in Newfoundland and Raleigh's in North Carolina, partly convinced English administrators that the state should provide political, if not financial, aid in encouraging commercial trading companies to create permanent bases in North America. The establishment of such commercial outposts was an elaboration of informal and often haphazard contacts made previously by fishermen, lumbermen, speculative merchants, and illegal traders (fig. 5.3).

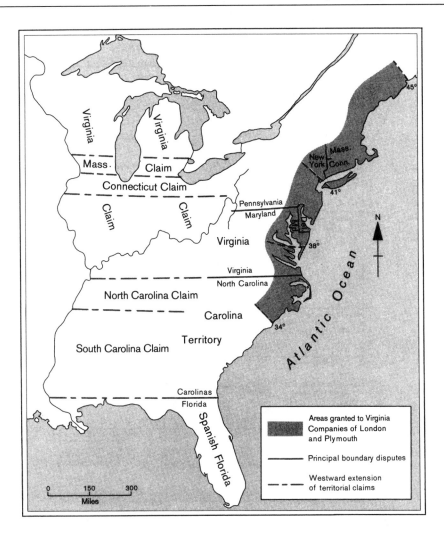

Figure 5.4 17th-Century America: Principal Territorial Disputes

More formal steps were taken in April 1606 with the founding of the twin companies, the Virginia Companies of London and Plymouth. Each company, reflecting the vague geographical knowledge of the time, was granted a wide swath of coastal territory within which to found profitable resource contacts (fig. 5.4). The St. George settlement in southern Maine was abandoned after the winter of 1607, but the Jamestown settlement, despite a shaky beginning, survived to provide the nucleus of the Virginia colony.

The Jamestown settlement arose in magnificent isolation until 1614, when the Dutch, who were emerging as the preeminent trading nation

in Europe, and who were already harassing Spanish convoys in the Caribbean, demonstrated an interest in the fur trade of the Hudson valley. They founded a trading post, Fort Nassau, just south of the future site of Albany, ten years before plans were made for a permanent settlement on Manhattan. Almost concomitant with these activities was the establishment of the Plymouth Colony north of Cape Cod by Puritan Separatists in 1620, which survived as a distinct colony until 1691. This was followed by the massive immigration (some 16,000 settlers) of more moderate Puritans to Massachusetts Bay and adjacent areas between 1629 and 1640. Farther south, Lord Baltimore founded his Maryland colony at

Table 5.1 American Colonies: Estimated 17th-Century Populations (in thousands)

Colony	1630	1640	1650	1660	1670	1680	1690	1700
New Hampshire	0.5	1.1	1.3	1.6	1.8	2.0	4.2	5.0
Plymouth	0.4	1.0	1.6	2.0	5.3	6.4	7.4	—
Massachusetts[a]	0.9	9.8	15	20	30	40	50	56
Rhode Island	—	0.3	0.8	1.5	2.1	3.0	4.2	5.9
Connecticut	—	1.5	4.1	8.0	13	17	22	26
New York	0.4	1.9	4.1	4.9	5.8	9.8	13	19
New Jersey	—	—	—	—	1.0	3.4	8.0	14
Pennsylvania	—	—	—	—	—	0.7	11	18
Delaware	—	—	0.2	0.5	0.7	1.0	1.5	2.5
Maryland	—	0.6	4.5	8.4	13	18	24	30
Virginia	2.5	10	19	27	35	46	53	59
North Carolina	—	—	—	1.0	3.9	5.4	7.6	11
South Carolina	—	—	—	—	0.2	1.2	3.9	5.7
Total	4.7	26	51	75	112	154	210	252

[a]Massachusetts includes Maine, and also Plymouth after 1691, although official totals do not reflect this.

St. Marys in 1634, and four years later a few score of Swedes and Finns established the short-lived colony of New Sweden (1638–55) on the lower Delaware River. From these tentative and discrete foundations, Anglo-America began to take shape. By midcentury, about 46,000 settlers had distributed themselves along the Atlantic coast and up the major river valleys from the rocky shores of southern Maine to the marshy lowlands of Norfolk, Virginia (fig. 5.5). Increasing settlement densities and geographical expansion were most evident in the Virginia tidewater and eastern shore, around Massachusetts Bay, and up the Hudson and lower Connecticut valleys.

Population grew to over 250,000 during the second half of the century. The latitudinal distribution did not change significantly, except for the first isolated settlements in the Carolinas around Pamlico Sound and Cape Fear in North Carolina and in the vicinity of Charles Town in South Carolina (fig. 5.5). But considerable settlement consolidation had occurred in eastern Virginia and the Chesapeake Bay in general, along the lower Delaware River, and along the northern coast from northern New Jersey to New Hampshire. Inland penetration had reached the general vicinity of the fall zone in Virginia and up the central Connecticut valley, but further expansion and consolidation failed to occur in the Hudson valley. The settlement of northern

and western New England, as well as most of New York and Pennsylvania and almost all of the Carolinas, therefore, was delayed until the 18th century.

Population growth patterns also reflected this general distribution (table 5.1). Rates of immigration varied considerably during the 17th century. Most colonies experienced very rapid rates of growth as a result of initial immigration, a pattern that generally slowed in the latter part of the century. Immigration rates tended to be highest during the 1630s and 1640s (especially in Virginia and Massachusetts), during the 1660s (especially in the Chesapeake), and during the 1680s and 1690s (especially in Pennsylvania and because of the Chesapeake slave trade). The results of these differential patterns by 1700 were two colonies with 55,000 to 60,000 settlers (Virginia and Massachusetts) and two others with 25,000 to 30,000 settlers (Maryland and Connecticut). New York's growth had proven to be erratic rather than steady until the 1690s, while Pennsylvania was in the process of attracting the most massive immigration levels of the entire colonial period.

Population growth and settlement expansion hardly occurred in a territorial vacuum. English colonial schemes contrasted starkly with the homogeneity and standardization that were more characteristic of official Spanish and French colonial policies. What is most remarkable

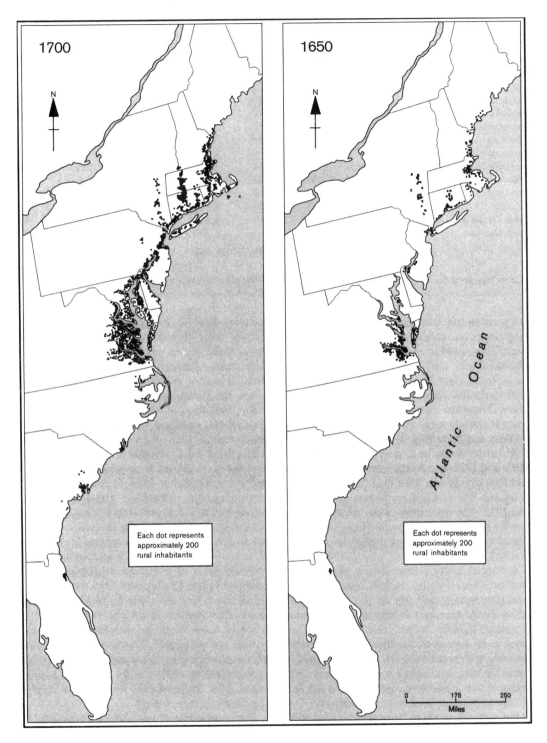

Figure 5.5 17th-Century America: Population Distribution (after Friis)

about the English experience was not only the volume and rate of population growth but also its institutional variety. Instead of one centralized and consolidated imperial system, there were 13 separate colonies (with Connecticut a consolidation of several colonies in the 1660s, Plymouth absorbed by Massachusetts in 1692, and Georgia founded in 1732). They were administered from London, to be sure, but each had its own distinctive political structure and operations. English colonies had been founded under a variety of schemes. Some, like Virginia and Massachusetts, began as company ventures only to become royal colonies under direct Crown administration; others, such as Maryland and Pennsylvania, originated as proprietary colonies in which the proprietors operated initially with little external interference; still others, notably Connecticut and Rhode Island, were chartered corporate colonies that had broken away from Massachusetts. This variegated arrangement reflected a practical, rather than an ideological, orientation in English colonialism. No other contemporary imperial system could have produced a Puritan Massachusetts, a Quaker Pennsylvania, and a Catholic Maryland.

Territorial variation and rivalry were not only the spice of colonial life, they were also the source of heatedly disputed boundary problems (fig. 5.4). Many boundary issues remained unsettled until after the American Revolution, while some lingered on into the 20th century. Such problems originated because of the diverse ways in which colonial grants were drawn up and because of the vagueness with which neat lines drawn on maps were translated on the ground. The most glaring omission was any sense of geographical understanding of the interior beyond the coastal zone. Many colonial grants and subsequent colony boundaries were simply latitudinal lines with overlapping claims and indeterminate western limits. Thus, eastern-bounded colonies such as Massachusetts and Connecticut, as well as those from New York southward, extended their territorial claims as far as the Mississippi River. Disputes between adjacent colonies were frequent, such as those engaging Connecticut and New York between the 1660s and 1728, Pennsylvania and Maryland between the 1680s and 1732 (a boundary finally surveyed by Mason and Dixon between 1763 and 1768), and Virginia and North Carolina between the 1660s and 1715. The resolution

of the status of interior lands beyond the Appalachians was to be one of the major problems facing the new nation in 1783.

Territorial organization below the colony level was based upon English conceptions of local government and private property. Population in the company colony of Virginia was organized initially on an irregular pattern of small units known as English hundreds, with monthly courts meeting at particular plantations. By 1634, an English county form of government was introduced that provided the initial foundation for local territorial organization in the colonies south of Pennsylvania (fig. 5.6A) and ultimately for all of the United States. Counties generally ranged in size from 200 to 450 square miles before devolving into new counties late in the century. County courthouses were located so that local residents could make the round-trip in no more than a day's ride. Although counties were often subdivided into, or synonymous with, church parishes, the parish system proved to be a less viable unit than in England, and counties remained the principal receptacles of civil government.

North of the Chesapeake, however, county systems were slower to emerge and were preceded, especially in New England, by townships (fig. 5.6B). The New England town or minor civil division reflected the more socially cohesive group settlement that characterized the region. Towns generally ranged in size from 50 to 100 square miles, much smaller and more intimate units of territorial organization than counties in the Chesapeake. The principal internal focus was the centrally located meetinghouse that functioned initially not only as the place for town meetings but also as the local church and social hall. This arrangement probably encouraged a greater sense of community and individual participation in decision making in New England than did the more loosely organized county system.

The acquisition of land was a prime goal of most 17th-century immigrants. Land grants were assigned on an individual basis generally on a fee simple (ownership) principle or on leasehold. The dispersed individual family farm and household formed the basic unit of social and spatial structure throughout the colonies. The result has been the most dramatic imprint of European culture on the American landscape: the creation of individual property (cadastral)

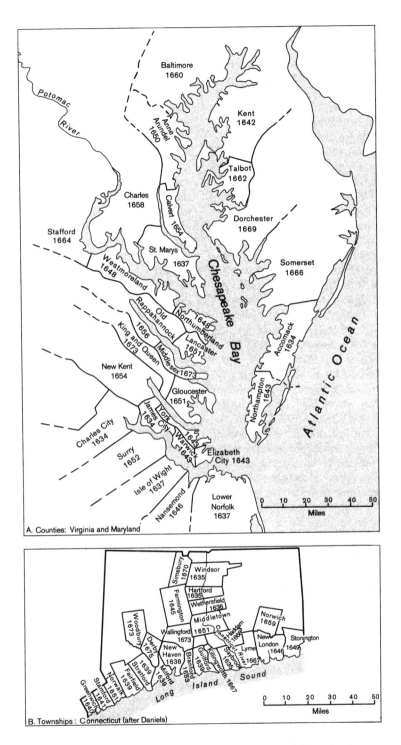

Figure 5.6 17th-Century America: Local Territorial Organization

boundaries outlined by fields, fences, walls, and town lots and delineating one private territory from another. Despite their common heritage, colonial land grant patterns varied considerably between colonies (fig. 5.7). In New England towns, for example, individual landholdings tended to be laid out in a more careful fashion than elsewhere, often accompanied by areas of common land for livestock (fig. 5.7A). In the Chesapeake, a more irregular metes and bounds survey system was employed, grants tended to be distributed more haphazardly along stream valleys, and overlapping boundaries led frequently to prolonged court litigation (fig. 5.7B). Grants were often assigned names, such as Ashley's Hope or Franklin's Folly, that highlighted the aspirations and the experiences of early landowners. A third cadastral form occurred in Dutch New York, where land was assigned under a modified manorial *(patroon)* system (fig. 5.7C). Large grants in the Hudson valley, sometimes exceeding 100,000 acres, were allotted by the Dutch West India Company to prominent colonial investors whose responsibility it was to redistribute some of the land in small parcels to long-term tenants. These three land assignment systems reflect, in a sense, the principal regional variations of 17th-century life that had emerged by the 1680s, the Chesapeake, New England, and the Anglo-Dutch world of New York–New Jersey.

THE CHESAPEAKE WORLD

The creation of a new society in tidewater Virginia ran counter to the creation of a normal English colony, because it proved to be a riskier venture than anticipated. The establishment of a trading station at Jamestown Island proved tenuous because of site limitations and the uncomfortable dependence on local Natives for sustenance. The direct transfer of English resource practices, moreover, was hampered by high death rates from malaria and poor nutrition, the initial failure of English grains, and the low nutritive value of native grasses for livestock. One of the first acts of adaptation was the adoption of Native staple foods and cultivation practices. Corn, beans, and squash were grown by means of hoe-hill cultivation methods without the use of the plow. (Plows remained rare objects in Chesapeake farming until the end of the centu-

ry.) A second adaptation was the "seasoning process" whereby new immigrants arrived in spring or early fall to avoid the summer heat, humidity, and disease. A third adaptation was the discovery in 1614, through trial and error, of the commercial viability of tobacco *(Nicotiana tabacum)*. This crop was to provide a profitable basis for the young settlement despite the belief of the colony's treasurer, Sir Edwin Sandys, that one could not build a colony on smoke.

The commitment to tobacco cultivation for export, however, required considerable amounts of land for its success. This had two important implications. First, land could be acquired only from the Native population. This produced a struggle for land with the Powhatan that by 1650 had resulted in two Native uprisings, the removal of their populations from the tidewater, and the creation of small spatial enclaves, or reservations, for the few surviving Natives. Second, tobacco cultivation in the absence of systematic crop rotation resulted in significant reductions in yields and soil fertility after 3 or 4 years. This encouraged the development of a field rotation system whereby additional acreages were cleared for cultivation, leaving former tobacco lands in prolonged fallow for up to 20 years. Land also became a device used by officials in Virginia and Maryland to attract immigrants through a headright system that granted anyone who brought in immigrants 50 acres per potential settler. This tactic highlighted the critical need for labor.

Tobacco production was a highly labor-intensive activity by English standards. Its 15-month cycle required heavy labor inputs for brush clearance, field preparation, transplanting, weeding, suckering, harvesting, drying, and packing in barrels (hogsheads) for delivery to ships for export to London. The Virginia Company's solution was to import large numbers of young male indentured servants from England. Thus, early Virginia society was characterized by distinct differences in social status between tobacco planters and their hired servants, a hierarchical structure that was to be magnified after midcentury by the immigration of sons of the English gentry sent to manage the family estates in the Chesapeake and to form the elite of colonial society. A second striking characteristic was the fact that few entire families came directly from England. This created initially a sexually unbalanced population and left many colonists with the responsibility of creating

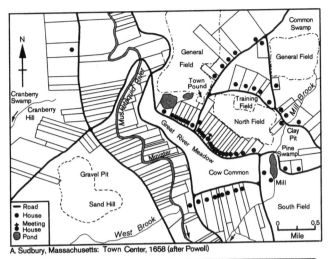

A. Sudbury, Massachusetts: Town Center, 1658 (after Powell)

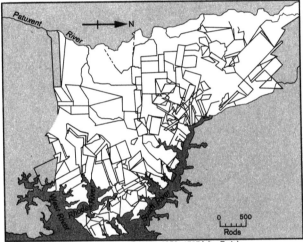

B. All Hallows Parish, Maryland: Initial Surveys, 1650–1707 (after Earle)

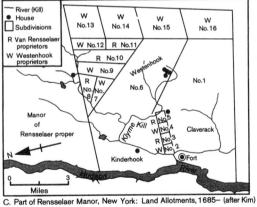

C. Part of Rensselaer Manor, New York: Land Allotments, 1685– (after Kim)

Figure 5.7 17th-Century America: Patterns of Land Subdivision

family structures without recourse to parental approval or extended family support.

The settlement consequences of a tobacco world were equally significant. Individual plantations were dispersed irregularly along the shores of the Chesapeake and up the major rivers, often spaced a mile or two apart (fig. 5.8). Early plantation structures were not designed to last. English cottages of simple rectilinear or hall-and-parlor design were built of wood, with the spaces between the planks wattled and daubed with clay and a wood-framed clay or stone chimney attached at one end. A tobacco barn—a simple log or plank structure for drying and curing the leaves during the winter—was the first outbuilding to be constructed. Only toward the end of the century were more elaborate frame housing structures built with board-and-batten exteriors to ensure insulation.

The establishment of Maryland in 1634, much to the consternation of Virginians, added a new element of diversity to the Chesapeake. Lord Baltimore had no intention of creating a tobacco colony on the Virginia model. Rather, his ideal was a semifeudal society based on manorial land tenure, a traditional landed gentry and aristocracy, a strong family nexus, nucleated village settlement, religious toleration, and a diversified economy of fur trading, mixed farming, and craft manufactures. Such a model of stability and hierarchy did not materialize, because the need to keep the colony solvent meant a commitment to rapid economic development, a commitment already worked out in Virginia. Thus, within a decade Maryland's pioneer generation was involved in a tobacco production system and an overseas trading link forged previously by its southern neighbor. The two colonies shared a tobacco-dominated world that was exporting between 4 million and 5 million pounds of tobacco annually to England by the 1650s.

Regional distinctions remained, however. At the colony level, Maryland's proprietary structure created an unusually divisive political tendency, the proprietary prerogative, whereby political decisions made by both elected and appointed officials could be ignored by the proprietor. This political tension was exacerbated by religious division. Many of the early landowners were Catholic, including several Jesuits eager to create a Catholic haven in the

Figure 5.8 A Maryland Tobacco Plantation (Historic St. Marys City)

colonies; most of the early indentured servants were English Protestants. This circumstance intensified the distinction between landowners and servants. Within both colonies there were also subregional differences. Virginia's three tidewater peninsulas, with their emphasis on water transportation, offered a rather different settlement experience from southern Maryland, where rivers offered fewer barriers to movement, and both areas differed from the more isolated Eastern Shore across the bay (fig. 5.6A).

Further touches to this Chesapeake world were made during the second half of the century. Between 1660 and 1700, the population of Virginia and Maryland increased from 35,000 to 88,000. Although immigration remained an important source of population, natural increase had become the principal contributor to growth. The first truly creole generation had been created in the Chesapeake by this time, a generation with no direct association with England. This undoubtedly further contributed to an "Americanization" of the region's inhabitants. Young women tended to marry at about 21 or 22 years of age and young men at about 24 or 25, at least two or three years earlier than their peers in England. Families were relatively small, with two or three surviving children per family, compared with five or six in New England, because women seem to have stopped having children earlier. Infant deaths remained common, and death rates were higher than in New England. Most people who survived could expect to live at least into their early 40s in the Chesapeake (and some lived into their 70s), during which time at least one-third of all adults were widowed and remarried, few grandparents existed, and orphans abounded.

The composition of the region's population also changed during the latter part of the century. The principal change was the shift from English indentured servant labor to African slave labor, beginning in Virginia during the late 1670s and in Maryland by the early 1680s. This shift, made initially for economic reasons, had profound effects on Chesapeake society because it raised important moral issues and it placed an already hierarchical class structure on a caste foundation. Slaves were permanently unfree, and their offspring were born automatically into slavery. Racial distinctions became an ingrained part of social differentiation; to be "negro" was to be unfree and ultimately to be inferior. Em-

ployed on plantations as field hands and domestic servants, Africans were to be excluded, like Native Americans, from the "normal workings" of an English colony.

Fewer than 1,000 Africans existed in the Chesapeake in 1660. Indentured servants continued to be imported from England at the rate of 1,000 per year. But during the 1660s, economic conditions in England improved, and the supply of servants dropped significantly by the early 1670s. At the same time, the increasing volume of slaves available from western Africa, principally for Portuguese Brazil and the Caribbean islands, had reduced the cost of a male slave. Between 1670 and 1700, more than 12,000 slaves were imported into the Chesapeake. The change was dramatic. Until the late 1670s in Maryland, for example, servants outnumbered slaves by more than 4 to 1; by 1700, slaves outnumbered servants by almost 4 to 1. Almost 15,000 slaves existed in the Chesapeake by this time, concentrated in the lower and middle peninsulas in Virginia and in southern Maryland, making up 15 percent of the Chesapeake's population. Slaveholding, however, remained an exception in the tobacco world. Fewer than 20 percent of all planters could afford slaves, and 90 percent of slave-owning planters owned only 1 or 2. The social basis of Chesapeake life, nevertheless, had been re-created on a vastly different basis from that of England, a fact that was to have dramatic repercussions for future American society.

Economically, the Chesapeake became increasingly immersed in a commercial tobacco world. Tobacco exports increased from about 9 million pounds in 1670 to 35 million pounds by 1700. These exports represented more than 80 percent of the total value of all mainland colonial goods sent to England by the end of the 17th century. Trade continued to be conducted on a straight consignment system whereby sloops and small ships would collect tobacco hogsheads from wooden landings along the rivers and deliver them to larger, ocean-going vessels anchored in the bay. The entire system was based on good fortune, trust, and credit. Planters lost all control over their product after it had left their landings, trusting that it would arrive safely in England, be sold for a good price by their merchant connections in London, the profits less commission be credited to their London accounts, and the goods that they requested arrive intact on the return voyage. No money changed hands, the credits from tobacco sales being balanced (and usually outweighed) by the debits of the planters' purchases in England. To add to the planters' concerns, tobacco prices fluctuated considerably during the century. They were high initially but stabilized at lower levels by the 1630s and declined further during the 1660s and 1670s, before plunging into prolonged depression for the rest of the century while fluctuating wildly from year to year.

Most planters rarely sent more than four or five hogsheads (variously weighing from 600 to 900 pounds each) to London in a season. This would have been the product of from 3 to 5 acres of land within plantations that ranged in size from 200 to 400 acres. A typical planter by the end of the century had between 15 and 20 acres cleared for crops, with more acreage (6 to 8) in corn than in tobacco or in English grains (4 to 5), as well as a kitchen garden of vegetables and herbs, a small apple or peach orchard, a few cattle, pigs, and perhaps sheep, a horse or two, and a collection of fowl. Labor would be supplied by some combination of servants and slaves such that each adult male could harvest 1 to 1.5 acres of tobacco.

The relative self-sufficiency of the plantation unit in terms of basic foodstuffs, feedstuffs, fuel, and clothing was enhanced by the pool of plantation craftsmen (especially carpenters, coopers, and blacksmiths) generally available within a five- to six-mile radius. This level of local support had important implications for the Chesapeake's settlement structure, particularly a distinct absence of towns.

The provision of local services and the conduct of the tobacco trade were highly decentralized throughout the 17th century. The dispersed arrangement of tobacco plantations, their relatively high level of self-sufficiency, the simple organization of the consignment system, the absence of further tobacco processing within the region, and the relatively limited demand for manufactured goods precluded the creation of an urban network. A service hierarchy did exist, but the highest-order place was London, 3,000 miles away. No settlement within the Chesapeake had attained more than 500 people. The new capitals of Virginia and Maryland, Williamsburg and Annapolis, respectively, were less than ten years old in 1700, and neither contained even a hundred houses. Local services were supplied by country storekeepers and merchant-planters. Activities at

county courts, ferry sites, and churches were periodic and intermittent and seldom sustained sufficient nodality to encourage further settlement concentration.

By the end of the century there was distinct evidence of regional homogeneity within the Chesapeake. The commitment to a tobacco plantation and slave system, with its consequent class structure, was widespread. Life was overwhelmingly rural, agrarian, dispersed, and decentralized. This was true whether one lived in peninsular Virginia, southern Maryland, or on the Eastern Shore. In the last region the first faint signs of dissatisfaction with the uncertain boom-and-bust life of tobacco production became evident. A few planters began to diversify their farm production by increasing their acreage of corn and wheat and improving their livestock production, a process of diversification that was to become more pronounced during the 18th century.

THE NEW ENGLAND WORLD

Despite a common English heritage, the settlers of early New England initially created a different settlement experience from their Chesapeake counterparts. The Plymouth and Massachusetts Bay Colonies brought a different kind of settler to America, who was to create a contrasting form of colonial society. The early Puritan colonists, of diverse persuasions, came with a distinct sense of purpose, even of destiny. Governor John Winthrop wrote in 1630: "For wee must consider that wee shall be as a citty upon a hill. The eies of all people are uppon us." Their desire to worship in their Protestant faith freely and without official interference created a distinctive pattern of population migration. People came more often in family groups, even occasionally as entire congregations, from specific locations in England. They encountered environments in southern New England that bore broad similarity to conditions they had left in western Europe. And they encouraged other Puritans to follow them in a kind of linked-chain migration that reinforced the regional characteristics of their home territories. The initial result was a more faithful attempt to reproduce the diversity of English provincial life than anywhere else in the New World.

The Separatist settlement at Plymouth remained isolated from the rest of New England until 1692, when the Confederation of New England was created under Massachusetts dominion. The 120 original Plymouth pioneers occupied a Native-held territory that had been devastated by disease in 1616, an event the new settlers viewed as providential, a conscious act of God that paved the way for their divinely inspired occupance. Despite a life of urban exile in London or the Netherlands, the settlers recreated much of the life they had remembered in provincial England. Indian corn, beans, and squash were integrated with the more familiar English small grains, peas, cattle, pigs, and fowl and the use of the plow into a closer reflection of English rural life than in Virginia. Settlements were organized into loosely arranged villages and then gradually into dispersed farmsteads. Houses, of rectilinear or hall-and-parlor design, were one- to one-and-a-half-story clapboard structures with central or end chimneys and thatched roofs. A small barn, cowshed, pigpen, garden, and apple and pear orchard generally completed the components of the "homelot." Farms, ranging from 30 to 100 acres in size, were relatively small by Chesapeake standards, but this excluded the common acreages used to pasture livestock. Spring wheat, corn, peas, beans, and squash were sown in May; English grasses were sown later to provide hay for wintering the animals; the wheat and vegetables were harvested in early August, while the corn was allowed to stand until September. Life in Plymouth Colony remained quiet and provincial until its 10,000 inhabitants were incorporated into Massachusetts in 1692.

The Massachusetts Bay Colony to the north proved to be a more dynamic settlement. Between 1629 and the early 1640s almost 16,000 immigrants came to Massachusetts and established Boston, named after its Lincolnshire counterpart (fig. 5.1), as a town focus and commercial port. Settlers came from a variety of English regions. Some had come from the communal, open-field, village worlds of parts of East Anglia and eastern Yorkshire. Others came from more individual enclosed-farm areas of Wiltshire and the "West Country." And still others had left such bustling East Anglian towns as Ipswich and Norwich. In their spread outward from Massachusetts Bay, they created townships within which they attempted to reproduce their familiar worlds of provincial England.

Within the semiplanned towns, land was assigned on an agreed-upon basis. In some towns this meant an initial attempt to create agricultural villages with elongated farmsteads of 20 to 30 acres radiating out from the village; in others, land assignment was made in individual lots of 100 to 200 acres on which each family established its own family farm; in still others, settlers founded small service centers in which merchants and craftsmen could conduct their activities most conveniently.

The end result of all this pioneering was a complex regional mosaic of colonial life, a series of "little Englands," subject to differential patterns of change during the rest of the century. Some towns remained relatively stable, with small families, low rates of population growth and turnover, and primarily subsistent and limited surplus agriculture. Such was the case in central Massachusetts (that is, the Connecticut River valley) and eastern Connecticut. Other townships, often immediately adjacent, appear to have experienced a contrasting situation of large families, rapid population growth, sharply declining human-land ratios, high rates of migration, and rapid transition to commercial agriculture. Such was the case around Massachusetts Bay, in the Narrangansett Bay area of Rhode Island, and in the lower and middle Connecticut valley.

There were, on the other hand, forces of centralization that mitigated these provincial variations. Foremost among them was the centralizing tendency displayed by the Massachusetts General Court in Boston in providing the legal and political basis for an acceptable Puritan commonwealth and by influential churchmen, such as John Cotton and Increase Mather, who provided the intellectual and spiritual basis for an acceptable Puritan life. Resistance to such conforming trends was a persistent feature of the early New England world. This caused a veritable diaspora from the Massachusetts Bay Colony itself of disaffected and disinherited settlers, most notably Roger Williams, who helped to found new settlements at Providence, Rhode Island (1636), at New Haven (1638), at Newport (1639), and in the lower Connecticut valley (late 1630s).

If religious beliefs and practices both united and divided early New Englanders, concern over the "Indian menace" created an English singularity of purpose. Two complementary attitudes developed toward the Native American.

First, the Puritans believed themselves to be superior to the Natives as users of land; this conviction was strengthened by the belief that it was God's will that they should subdue and conquer both the American wilderness and its inhabitants. The result was a series of skirmishes in Massachusetts during the 1630s that led to Native defeat and the first legal instigation of the reservation concept in North America. Further Native uprisings occurred during the 1640s (the Pequot Wars), as they did also in the Chesapeake, leading to further reduction in Native numbers and space, especially along the Rhode Island–Connecticut coast and in the lower Connecticut valley. By 1660, the few thousand remaining Natives in southern New England were largely confined to reservations (fig. 5.2). Only then did the second attitude, paternalism leading to proselytization, come to the fore. At least 14 "praying towns" comprising several hundred missionized Natives had been founded in Massachusetts, and several others existed in Plymouth Colony. Surviving Natives in these settlements were encouraged to convert to Christianity and to adopt an English farming way of life. Other, less assimilable Natives rallied around a new leader, Metacom ("King Philip" to the English), in 1675 in a last-ditch effort to retain their lands and their way of life. The failure of the uprising left all of southern New England in the hands of the colonists.

The early pattern of localism and regional diversity that characterized English settlement was modified during the 1670s, after two generations of settlement. By 1680, the 68,500 settlers of Plymouth, Massachusetts, Rhode Island, Connecticut, and New Hampshire (founded as a royal colony in 1679) were distributed from the coast of southern Maine south to New York and inland up the Connecticut valley to the New Hampshire border. Certain distinctive regional patterns had emerged by this time. The township, with its agricultural population, centrally located church and meetinghouse, and its small urban centers, remained dominant and spread wherever New England settlers migrated—to Long Island, the central Hudson valley, and to East Jersey. Almost everywhere, the rural settlement pattern was one of individual, dispersed farmsteads (fig. 5.9); outside of Plymouth only about 20 farm villages had been founded successfully, and few of these survived intact into the 18th century.

Distinct patterns of regional economy had also emerged by 1680. It is possible to identify at least three zones of economic activity. The broadest zone comprised the agricultural townships of eastern and central Massachusetts, northern Rhode Island, and central and northern Connecticut. Subsistence farming prevailed in these areas based on corn, wheat, barley, rye, flax, vegetables, fruits, cattle, pigs, and sometimes sheep. Farms ranged from 50 to 150 acres and were declining in size as they were subdivided for the next farming generation. Surplus products were few and were sold locally; labor was supplied by family members and an occasional hired hand. Communities tended to be close-knit and relatively egalitarian, to experience low levels of population turnover, and to have low levels of wealth differentiation. Much of the research on New England towns during the 1960s and early 1970s focused on such communities, thus creating an impression of all New England life during the 17th century as being stable, egalitarian, even harmonious. Such an interpretation has, in turn, been challenged by more recent research that suggests this image is less applicable to other New England areas.

This revisionist depiction is certainly more applicable to settlement evolution along Massachusetts Bay, where such foundings as Salem (1626) and Boston (1630) were predicated on port sites, fishing activities, craft concentrations, and mercantile trade. Boston came to dominate this relatively densely occupied region of small fishing villages, inland market centers, and compact commercial farms. The town became the regional entrepôt for most of southern New England, primarily because of its function as the center of Massachusetts government, the focus of craft and artisan activities, and its preeminence as the principal port for overseas trade, which was enhanced by its connections with prominent London merchants (fig. 5.10). The settlement, founded on a narrow peninsula, expanded inland on several areas of reclaimed land that almost doubled its area by 1700. Boston grew from 3,000 inhabitants in 1650, or some 20 percent of the colony's population, to almost 7,000 people in 1700, which made it the largest town in North America. With about 20,000 residents of the bay area living in urban centers by the end of the century, there was a growing demand for foodstuffs and processing

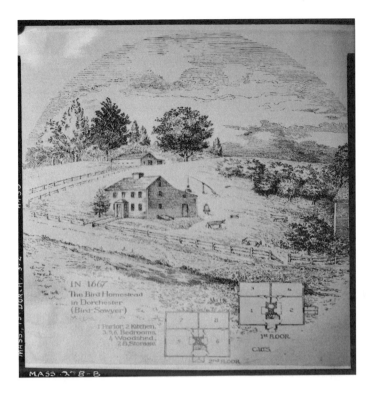

Figure 5.9 Farm Evolution in Massachusetts (Historic American Buildings Survey)

of raw materials. Farming in the region therefore became more commercialized, producing grains, meat, pork, and vegetables for Boston and its neighbors. Boston merchants, in turn, exported grain, cattle, naval stores, and dried codfish to western Europe and the Caribbean. They had extended their enterprise by the end of the century into shipbuilding and carrying goods for areas that possessed few vessels of their own. The evolution of trade around the Narragansett Bay followed a somewhat similar pattern. Newport, with a population about one-third that of Boston by 1700, dominated other urban centers, such as Providence, principally because it functioned as the outlet for corn, cattle, and sheep products from the large farms (200 to 300 acres) around the bay, and as a principal importer of molasses, sugar, and rum that were initially shipped to Boston to purchase imported English manufactured goods.

A third regional zonation emerged along the Connecticut coast and up the Connecticut valley as far as western Massachusetts. This region was characterized by small coastal towns, such as New Haven and New London, that were involved in local and coastal trade, and by rapidly growing centers in the Connecticut valley, such as Hartford and Springfield. The fertile soils of the valley helped to make the area the breadbasket of late-17th-century New England. Wheat, corn, barley, meat, and pork were the principal commercial products sent through local market centers to Boston or to the Caribbean. Farms were generally larger (200 to 300 acres) than in the subsistence farming areas outside the valley. Social stratification through land aggrandizement was more pronounced, tenancy was more common, and population turnover was more rapid than in adjacent subsistence areas. Merchant entrepreneurs, unlike the merchant-planters in the Chesapeake, were not content to make profits and accumulate debts but reinvested their earnings in land acquisition, lumbering, craft industries, and shipping. These investments, in turn, created further growth in the New England economy that was to distinguish the entire region's achievements from those of the tobacco-committed Chesapeake.

Figure 5.10 Boston's First Town House, 1657–1711 (Courtesy Harvard University Press)

THE ANGLO-DUTCH WORLD

The area that was to fall eventually between the Chesapeake and the New England settlements was quick to receive its own distinct European imprint. Five years after Henry Hudson, on behalf of the Dutch government, explored north of Manhattan in 1609 and brought back skins and beaver pelts, the Dutch established their fur-trading post at Fort Nassau. Thus began Dutch colonialism in the New World, which was to involve not only the New Netherlands but also ventures in Brazil, the Guyanas, and the Caribbean.

The New Netherlands, which stretched eventually from the lower Delaware River to Long Island and north to Albany, was an unusual and even paradoxical settlement. Founded as a centrally controlled company colony of the Dutch West India Company (1621), interested in the fur trade and in disrupting Spanish activities in the Caribbean, it was forced to establish a settlement policy that turned out to be more feudalistic in tone than anything created in the mother country. New Amsterdam, begun at the southern tip of Manhattan in 1624–25, created a focus for the colony. Within five years company settlers had built a fort and battery, about 30 tree-bark houses, and, symbolically, a stone countinghouse. All goods traded with the Natives or with the outside world had to pass through this new settlement. The company, advancing beyond Virginia Company practice, established three statuses. Highest in status were the wealthy, urban, merchant investors who formed the directorship of the company in the Netherlands; next were company employees, such as soldiers, clerks, and hired farmers, who received a subsistence and a salary in the New Netherlands; and third were autonomous individuals who received company benefits for deciding to emigrate to the New World at their own expense.

Yet the colony was plagued by a chronic labor problem that was exacerbated by the company's restrictive land policy. Control of the fur trade at Albany was to be a company monopoly. But even a successful trading colony required support services. The company's solution was to grant large tracts of land to prominent Dutch investors, described as patroons (patrons), who would be responsible for encouraging immigrants to settle on their lands. Land tenure was to be established on a feudalistic basis rather than on the freehold basis that was to become widespread in the English colonies. The result was that settlers would receive enough land to create working farms, called *bouweries,* but would remain as tenants, rather than owner-occupiers, subject to annual quitrent. Only four large patroonship grants were made during the Dutch colonial period, each with at least an eight-mile river frontage. But only the largest of these, the patroonship of Rensselaerswyck, which encompassed more than 800,000 acres on both sides of the Hudson River including Albany, successfully attracted settlers (fig. 5.7C). This patroonship had more than 200 tenants by 1650, but tenancy proved unattractive, population turnover was high, and few farming families were created.

The company's intent, therefore, to create a socially stratified society dominated by merchants and officials in New Amsterdam and Albany and by manorial landowners in the Hudson valley did not materialize. While the fur trade and coastal trade with the English colonies grew, agricultural settlement and development lagged. Despite a successful subsistence agriculture and even a trading surplus in wheat and rye, the chronic shortage of settlers encouraged the company to maintain a liberal immigration policy to attract colonists from any conceivable source. This policy had three long-term results. First, it encouraged an extremely culturally diverse population. As the leader of the Dutch Reformed Church described it in 1655, "[W]e have here Papists, Mennonites and Lutherans among the Dutch; also many Puritans or Independents, and many Atheists and various other servants of Baal under this Government, who conceal themselves under the name of Christians; it would create a still greater confusion, if the obstinate and immovable Jews came to settle here," which they did a few years later. More than a dozen languages were to be heard in the streets of New Amsterdam, spoken by people from English, Dutch, French Huguenot, Walloon, Spanish, and Scandinavian roots. Numerous German and African dialects added to the cacophony.

Second, many of the new immigrants who wished to take up land avoided the Hudson valley and dispersed into Long Island and New Jersey, where company policies were less stringently enforced. New England Puritans, who moved into eastern and central Long Island during the

1640s and 1650s, formed an integral part of the New Netherlands, and many swore allegiance to the Dutch colony. Other Puritans and Dutch settlers moved to New Jersey, opposite Manhattan, and along the lower Delaware River, where they encountered Swedish and Finnish settlers who had established fur-trading posts and small farms focused on Fort Christina (Wilmington, Delaware). New Sweden, however, was not to last, and its 500 settlers were incorporated into the New Netherlands in 1655, adding to the colony's already heterogeneous population. Third, the company's strong centralized control and the absence of local government institutions did not strike a responsive chord in many immigrants. The combination of cultural pluralism and weak public institutions was to produce increasing political factionalism and growing tension between the company and its settlers.

By the early 1650s, during the governorship of Peter Stuyvesant, the colony's population had barely reached 2,000 inhabitants. Despite reforms instigated by Stuyvesant that decentralized government and trade and granted land on a more liberal basis, the New Netherlands remained a weak and vulnerable colony. The fur trade was proving to be a disappointing investment, a Native invasion of Manhattan and adjacent New Jersey had disrupted settlement, and the English had enacted the first of their navigation acts, which were designed in part to reduce Dutch trade with English colonies.

Much of the growth of the New Netherlands occurred during the last decade of its existence, between 1654 and 1664. When the English captured New Amsterdam in 1664 they acquired a loosely defined colony of 8,000 settlers, about 5,000 of whom were of Dutch origin and another 600 of African origin. Population was unevenly distributed. More than a fifth of the population was located on Manhattan, 1,400 in New Amsterdam, and the rest in dispersed farms and the village of Haerlem. Half the remaining colonists occupied adjacent river valleys (kills) and flats of East Jersey and Staten Island to the west, Jonas Bronck's (Bronx) place to the northeast, and Long Island from the village of Breuckelen to the Puritan settlements of Southampton. The Hudson valley was thinly populated, with few concentrations of settlement between Manhattan and Beverwyck (Albany) except for the 100 settlers around Esopus (Kingston).

The Dutch legacy was more than a few place names and a great assortment of settlers. It included an operational fur trade, relatively good relations with the Iroquois, an extensive landholding system, and the entrepôt of New Amsterdam. The bustling, fortified town stretched as far north as Wall Street. On its narrow curving streets (except for Broad Way), stood some 200 three- and four-story, step-gabled, red-and-black-tiled row houses backed by kitchen gardens. There were more than 35 taverns, an imposing statehouse, the East River wharf, main canal, and windmill—all together presenting the most unusual urban appearance in 17th-century North America.

Few immediate changes occurred in the area as a result of the change in territorial control. Dutch cultural and property rights were upheld, and most settlers chose to remain. The land granted to the duke of York, however, was unwieldy. No serious attempt was made to pursue his claims in Maine and Connecticut, but the New Netherlands was divided by the granting of New Jersey to Lords Berkeley and Carteret. This broke the territorial unity of the Hudson valley and reemphasized the regional contrasts between East and West Jersey. By 1700, East Jersey's 8,000 settlers had had their Dutch heritage diluted by an influx of New England Puritans and Scots Presbyterians. West Jersey's 6,000 settlers represented a stronghold of English Quakerism, closely associated with Pennsylvania.

New York was to continue as an unusual colonial experience. It was to be a colony that had not originated with English settlers; its hastily assembled charter was to leave the duke of York with virtually absolute powers, to the detriment of representative government at the provincial level; and its persistent pluralism worked against unity and promoted local and regional rivalries. The result was a highly factional, dual colonial society in which Anglo-American influences were slow to replace the Dutch heritage.

The extensive land-grant system continued under the duke of York. The patroonship tradition was extended with the creation of 16 large manorial grants in the Hudson valley and on Long Island, ranging from a few thousand acres to almost 200,000 acres in size. No immigration requirements were stipulated, a leasehold system prevailed, and many manors became speculative enterprises. Yet survey boundaries were often vague and tenants difficult to attract. The result was a relatively slow growth in population until the 1690s (table 5.1).

The colony contained more than 19,000 inhabitants in 1700. They continued to be concentrated mainly on Manhattan (4,500 settlers) and on Long Island (7,000 settlers). Fewer than 5,000 settlers occupied the Hudson valley; most of them lived in isolated Dutch rural communities or in the settlements of Kingston, Albany, and Schenectady. Included in the provincial total were about 1,300 Africans, constituting 7 percent of the population; some were free, but the majority worked as laborers or domestic servants in Manhattan or as field hands on Hudson valley estates. Economic development and an increase in agricultural acreage occurred with the growth of population during the 1680s and 1690s. The fur trade continued to be an important, but declining, element in the colony's diversifying economy; it remained in the hands of Dutch traders in Albany. English officials, however, continued to seek Iroquois support for the struggle against the French. This strategy in effect allowed the Iroquois to play the English and French off against each other until the 1750s. Agricultural expansion on Long Island and intermittently in the Hudson valley took place along familiar colonial lines: general farming based on corn, European grains, and flax, with some specialization in wheat, beef, pork, apples, and, in some areas, small-scale lumbering. These characteristics were reflected in the occupational structure and export trade of the port of New York. Flour milling, brewing, and shipbuilding were prominent activities; bread and flour, furs, beef, pork, and lumber were major exports in the coastal and overseas trades. New York suffered, however, from the control exerted by Boston merchants in both of these trading arenas.

Anglicization of the colony was a process pursued only gradually by English officials. Although an English system of counties was introduced in 1683, Dutch cultural and social patterns remained intact. Indeed, the number of Dutch Reformed congregations expanded from 11 in 1664 to 29 in 1700. What emerged was an increasing factionalism between the older Dutch elite and the emerging Anglo-Dutch establishment. This tension came to a head in 1689 when a group of Dutch burghers rebelled unsuccessfully against the newer, more individualistic

tone set by an English administration. The result was a wholesale introduction of English institutions, from English common law and a new judicial system to the establishment of the Anglican Church in Manhattan and surrounding counties. Older Dutch settlers could only view these events with a sense of wry frustration. They were initiated by the new occupiers of the English throne, William and Mary, associated with the Dutch House of Orange.

TRANSPOSITION

The 1680s proved to be a watershed in the shaping of colonial America. Not only was coastal Native resistance eliminated by this time and the sustained commitment to slave labor initiated in the Chesapeake, but also two other events epitomized the ambiguous heritage of the 17th century. The first was the founding of Pennsylvania in 1681 by William Penn, a prominent member of the Society of Friends (Quakers); the second was the successful experimentation with rice cultivation in the vicinity of Charles Town, South Carolina, toward the end of the decade.

Pennsylvania, based on the utopian vision of Penn, was to emerge as the population phenomenon of the late 17th century. The colony increased from a handful of settlers in 1681 to almost 18,000 by 1700. Penn's policy of avowed religious freedom, easy land acquisition, and active overseas recruitment encouraged the first sustained immigration of continental Europeans to an English colony. German-speaking settlers, of both church (Lutheran, Reformed) and sectarian (Moravian, Mennonite) persuasions, mingled with English and Welsh Quakers in the rich farmlands of southeastern Pennsylvania. They created a diversified economy and society based on farms of 100 to 200 acres producing corn, small grains, and livestock products with the use of family and hired labor, together with a variety of small crafts, and the founding of the planned town of Philadelphia between the Delaware and Schuylkill Rivers. Pennsylvania thus came to symbolize the heterogeneous, yeoman-farming, free-labor world of the colonies north of the Chesapeake.

The creation of Charles Town, on the other hand, symbolized in exaggerated form the commitment to a more provincial, plantation-slave-staple world characteristic of the colonies south of Pennsylvania. The Carolinas, granted by Charles II to eight noblemen in 1664, had languished in uncertainty and neglect. The Spanish in Florida destroyed most settlement attempts made during the 1660s; a few isolated communities had survived in the Albemarle Sound section of North Carolina, where farmers had been trickling in from Virginia since the 1650s. English immigrants made a successful settlement at Charles Town, between the Ashley and Cooper Rivers, in 1670. The 1,000 settlers in the area by 1680 were exporting provisions to the English sugar islands and deerskins to England. The influx of planters from the heavily exploited island of Barbados during the 1680s quickened the search for a regional resource staple. The successful cultivation and husking of rice was achieved in the coastal uplands bordering the tidewater swamps by 1690, and exports to Portugal and the Caribbean had reached 400,000 pounds by 1700.

The commitment to rice production transformed a struggling farm population into a plantation society. Rice placed heavier demands on labor than did tobacco. The Fundamental Constitutions of Carolina, designed to create a colony neither "a numerous democracy" nor "an unrestrained aristocracy," became skewed in favor of the latter as the need for African slaves became paramount. The impact of slave labor was evident by 1700. Although North Carolina, with 10,700 settlers, had almost twice as many as South Carolina (5,700), only 4 percent of its population was slave, compared with almost 43 percent farther south. Slavery in early South Carolina showed another twist; more than 700 slaves were of Native origin, the result of wars and trade with inland Native groups.

CONCLUSION

"Thus in the beginning," wrote the philosopher John Locke, "all the World was America. The English colonist [has] thereby removed her from the state of Nature, wherein she was common, and hath begun Property." The imposition of a European world on a Native world, largely through the operations of English institutions, had created a new Atlantic America literally from scratch. What had been created was not simply a geographical extension of England. The process of migration and diffusion was itself a complex and selective one. Those who came and stayed founded a colonial system that was English in outline but American in content. Continuity existed between colonial and English societies, but often through more simplified and more hybridized agencies than were to be found in the mother country.

English visitors at the end of the century would have found much that was familiar. The virtual ubiquity of the English language would have permitted them to converse freely. They would have appreciated the dedication to the familiar values of liberty, property, and profit functioning through equally familiar, if less elaborate, legal, political, religious, and business institutions. The creation of boundaries, on the landscape and in the imagination, that had not existed previously would have met also with general approval: provinces, counties, and towns; property boundaries; fields with familiar crops and livestock; a skeletal road system; and the beginnings of urban life.

But in the transposition of the New World environment from a wilderness inhabited by savage heathens to the "middle landscape" of English pastoral civility, the experience had also transformed the colonists. The English visitors, if they had remained long enough and traveled far enough, would have found much to intrigue and even to disturb them. The sparseness of population, the often considerable distances between settlements, and the remaining vast stretches of forest might have proven unnerving. The summers would have been uncomfortably hot and humid, and the winters almost frighteningly cold and bitter north of the Carolinas. New crops, such as corn, squash, and tobacco, would have generated interest, but the generally casual and extensive nature of cultivation likely would have drawn expressions of disapproval. Countering such impressions would have been admiration for the relatively high material living standards, the ease with which land could be acquired, the ubiquity of dispersed farm units with recognizable architectural styles, and the generally egalitarian societies to be found, at least north of the Chesapeake.

Yet the creation of 17th-century Anglo-America was based not only on the successful exploitation of wild environments but also on the manipulation of non-European peoples. What might have given the visitors pause was the presence of two much modified European institutions, the reservation and the plantation. The shaping of early America had been accomplished at the expense of the Native population. Although English fascination with Native exoticism would remain, their world was upheld as an experience to which civilized Europeans could not revert. Violence, removal, and confinement were to be the consequences of Anglo-American advance. Although similar specialized staple-producing agricultural units could be found in southern Europe, the institution of slavery that accompanied such units in America had no English precedent. The perpetual enslavement of imported Africans, while rationally acceptable in economic terms, created moral, cultural, and racial fissures in colonial society that differentiated not only colony from metropolis but also colony from colony and social class from social class as Anglo-America began the 18th century.

ADDENDUM

Mitchell's essay, written in the mid-1980s, has stood up well to the passage of time. Were he composing it at the start of the 21st century, no doubt Mitchell would be giving fuller attention to labor issues, to matters of gender roles and the family, to the Atlantic Ocean and its coasts as a region, and to the opportunities for comparative study among communities. These subjects embrace gradual shifts in emphasis, not sharp changes of opinion.

Mitchell arranged his essay as regional studies of the Chesapeake, New England, and the Dutch enclaves and has even included a sketch of English life at the time of first overseas emigration. An alternative approach is to suggest underlying themes that might connect scattered parts of the text in fresh ways. Republication of this essay gives us the opportunity to rethink a body of material from a different angle. We ask, for example, how unified was America in 1700? There were few obvious intercolonial linkages up to that date, and Mitchell is clearly aware of the settlers' diversity. But did English migrants to mainland North America imagine their adopted home places to be small, freestanding entities, or components of some greater nation-in-waiting? Would such a greater nation-in-waiting have included Newfoundland and the West Indies? Mitchell, we believe, would argue the case

for a growing national sense, for his approach has been to find norms, similarities, and convergences. In paying little attention to Newfoundland and the West Indies perhaps he is saying that they were simply too peripheral. But we must ask whether such a coherent national vision had actually become evident before the 18th century. As we note contrasts and divergences among the early colonies, and the widely varying life experiences of disconnected little places, we are inclined to say "not yet."

Differences in territorial arrangement, shown in figures 5.6 and 5.7, suggest to us that comparing changes in these from one colony to another might shed light on the English struggle to establish the optimal manner of land distribution and control overseas. It would be the same sort of story in the early national period as the United States, after 1783, struggled with the allocation and management of America's inland regions. Some issues never go away. And what are the signals sent by the loose organization of the Newfoundland fishery and the high degree of regimentation in the West Indian cane fields, where corporations and partnerships prevailed and the sense of colonial government was much diminished? And what were the consequences of administrative dithering for the northern colonies—and especially for the timber-rich coast of Maine—during the years of conflict with France and its Native American allies between 1689 and 1713? These thoughts carry us into the substance of the following chapter on 18th-century America, by James Lemon; these two essays succinctly cover the historical geography of the prerevolutionary Atlantic seaboard.

The decline in English emigration toward the end of the century exacerbated an already tight labor situation in America—but in ways that may be compared from one situation to the next. English entrepreneurs found Native Americans suitable for the northerly trade in furs but inadequate in meeting many other colonial labor needs. One alternative source—Africans, captured and exiled—extended the American labor story to include the West Indies. Many small cultural enclaves there, suitable for comparison and contrast in their economic and labor structure, could add richly to the already varied list of mainland American situations. Perhaps 17th-century colonies were inclined to relate more to England than to their neighbors, but not always; an unheralded connection from Barbados to

Carolina, for instance, was a conduit for introducing slavery to mainland America. Identifying such a link raises questions of how family and household structure, gender roles, life expectancy, and even house types and spiritual expression were carried over from people in one colonial region to those in another. These differences, and their consequences, are identified in many of the works cited in the revised list of readings below.

Labor was a particularly desperate issue for the Dutch, in the Netherlands themselves as well as in Manhattan and the Dutch West Indies. Again, Native Americans and introduced Africans played contrasting roles, and these groups demonstrate a further point regarding marginalization. William Penn, some of the Dutch landlords, and even Lord Baltimore in the Chesapeake are, in our view, characterized by tolerance and egalitarianism, yet class structure and forms of isolation invariably became established with the earliest settlements. The many distinct tribal groups of Native Americans were repeatedly driven to, and beyond, the edges of the lands in which incoming Europeans took an interest; their marginalization was spatial. A different form of marginalization greeted African Americans, who found themselves living side-by-side with enterprising European masters while at the same time remaining worlds apart socially. Now, more than three centuries later, people of Native and African descent throughout North America continue to grapple with their place in the American fabric. Some of the themes raised in Mitchell's chapter have histories that seem to be without end.

ADDITIONAL READING

Allen, D. G., and D. D. Hall, eds. 1985. *17th-Century New England*. Charlottesville: University Press of Virginia.

Anderson, V. D. 1991. *New England's Generation: The Great Migration and the Formation of Society and Culture*. New York: Cambridge University Press.

Axtell, J. 1981. *The European and the Indian: Essays in the Ethnohistory of Colonial North America*. New York: Oxford University Press.

———. 1985. *The Invasion Within: The Contest of Cultures in Colonial North America*. New York: Oxford University Press.

Berlin, I. 1998. *Many Thousands Gone: The First Two Centuries of Slavery in North America*. Cambridge: Harvard University Press, Belknap Press.

Burke, T. E., Jr. 1991. *Mohawk Frontier: The Dutch Community of Schenectady, New York, 1661–1710*. Ithaca: Cornell University Press.

Cressy, D. 1987. *Coming Over: Migration and Communication between England and New England in the 17th Century*. New York: Cambridge University Press.

Cronon, W. 1983. *Changes in the Land: Indians, Colonists, and the Ecology of New England*. New York: Hill & Wang.

Daniels, B. 1979. *The Connecticut Town*. Middletown, Conn.: Wesleyan University Press.

Darby, H. C., ed. 1973. *A New Historical Geography of England*. Cambridge: Cambridge University Press.

Dodgshon, R. A., and R. A. Butlin, eds. 1978. *An Historical Geography of England and Wales*. New York: Oxford University Press.

Earle, C. V. 1975. *The Evolution of a Tidewater Settlement System: All Hallows' Parish, Maryland, 1650–1783*. Chicago: University of Chicago Department of Geography.

———. 1977. "The First English Towns of North America." *Geographical Review* 67: 34–50.

Everitt, A. 1972. *Changes in the Provinces: The 17th Century*. Leicester: Leicester University Press.

Fischer, D. H. 1989. *Albion's Seed: Four British Folkways in America*. New York: Oxford University Press.

Goodfriend, J. D. 1992. *Before the Melting Pot: Society and Culture in Colonial New York City, 1664–1730*. Princeton: Princeton University Press.

Greene, J. P., and J. R. Cole, eds. 1984. *Colonial British America: Essays in the New History of the Early Modern Era*. Baltimore: Johns Hopkins University Press.

Harris, R. C. 1977. "The Simplification of Europe Overseas." *Annals of the Association of American Geographers* 67: 469–83.

Henretta, J. A. 1978. "Families and Farms: *Mentalité* in Pre-Industrial America." *William and Mary Quarterly* 35: 3–32.

Horn, J. P. P. 1994. *Adapting to a New World: English Society in the 17th-Century Chesapeake*. Chapel Hill: University of North Carolina Press.

Innes, S. 1983. *Labor in a New Land: Economy and Society in 17th-Century Springfield*. Princeton: Princeton University Press.

———. 1995. *Creating the Commonwealth: The*

Economic Culture of Puritan New England. New York: Norton.

Jennings, F. 1975. *The Invasion of America: Indians, Colonialism, and the Cant of Conquest*. Chapel Hill: University of North Carolina Press.

Kim, S. B. 1978. *Landlord and Tenant in Colonial New York: Manorial Society, 1664–1775*. Chapel Hill: University of North Carolina Press.

Kupperman, K. O. 1984. "Fear of Hot Climates in the Anglo-American Colonial Experience." *William and Mary Quarterly* 41: 213–40.

Lemon, J. T. 1980. "Early Americans and Their Social Environment." *Journal of Historical Geography* 6: 115–31.

Martin, J. F. 1991. *Profits in the Wilderness: Entrepreneurship and the Founding of New England Towns in the 17th Century*. Chapel Hill: University of North Carolina Press.

McCusker, J. J., and R. R. Menard. 1985. *The Economy of British America, 1607–1789*. Chapel Hill: University of North Carolina Press.

McManis, D. 1975. *Colonial New England: A Historical Geography*. New York: Oxford University Press.

Meinig, D. W. 1986. *The Shaping of America: Atlantic America, 1492–1800*. New Haven: Yale University Press.

Merwick, D. 1990. *Possessing Albany: The Dutch and English Experiences, 1630–1710*. New York: Cambridge University Press.

Mitchell, R. D. 1983. "American Origins and Regional Institutions: The 17th-Century Chesapeake." *Annals of the Association of American Geographers* 73: 404–20.

Nash, G. B. 1982. *Red, White, and Black: The Peoples of Early America*. 2d ed. Englewood Cliffs, N.J.: Prentice Hall.

O'Mara, J. 1982. "Town Founding in 17th-Century North America: Jamestown in Virginia." *Journal of Historical Geography* 8: 1–11.

Perry, J. R. 1990. *The Formation of a Society on Virginia's Eastern Shore, 1615–1655*. Chapel Hill: University of North Carolina Press.

Powell, S. C. 1963. *Puritan Village: The Formation of a New England Town*. Middletown, Conn.: Wesleyan University Press.

Rutman, D. B. 1967. *Husbandmen of Plymouth: Farms and Villages in the Old Colony, 1620–1692*. Boston: Beacon Press.

Sauer, C. O. 1971. *16th-Century North America: The Land and the People as Seen by the Europeans*. Berkeley and Los Angeles: University of California Press.

Tate, I. W., and D. L. Ammerman, eds. 1979. *The Chesapeake in the 17th Century: Essays in Anglo-American Society and Politics*. New York: Norton.

Thompson, R. 1986. *Sex in Middlesex: Popular Mores in a Massachusetts County, 1649–1699*. Amherst: University of Massachusetts Press.

Webb, S. S. 1995. *1676, the End of American Independence*. Syracuse: Syracuse University Press.

Wood, J. S. 1997. *The New England Village*. Baltimore: Johns Hopkins University Press.

6

Colonial America in the 18th Century

JAMES T. LEMON

The founding of Pennsylvania in 1681 and of Georgia in 1732 confirmed what already had become clear: Europeans, mostly British, were permanent occupants of the most productive eastern margin of the New World. Between 1700 and 1775 the population of the eastern seaboard colonies (often called provinces) grew nearly ten times, as did the area occupied. The massive overtaking of the continent and of aboriginal lands, so conspicuous in the next century, was well under way, as colonizers filled the spaces between the discrete coastal settlements of the 17th century. Expansion reflected economic growth and in turn was a major factor in that growth. Economic specialization and diversification were becoming more evident, and for most whites living standards improved.

The result was an increased sharing of colonial experiences, leading toward greater homogenization among whites and broader regional behaviors. As the 18th century progressed, neither the Natives nor their allies in New France could hold back this inland movement. Yet, even as the French lost Quebec in 1759 and the British became undisputed masters of the land, British rules and regulations began to unravel in the colonies from New England southward. By 1775 many people, most removed by one or several generations from Britain, had come to see themselves as Americans first, even though the colonies seemed to be converging demographically and socially with the mother country. The first, and largest, colonial revolt in the New World was to produce a robust new nation that would put its own profound stamp on the world over subsequent centuries.

POPULATION: GROWTH, EXPANSION, AND COMPOSITION

Factors in Growth

By 1775 the population of the colonies had reached almost 2.5 million, compared with only 250,000 in 1700 (table 6.1). The tenfold increase was the result of a rate of growth averaging about 3 percent per year. This rate was rapid for the time, and thus the population jumped from 1/20 to 1/3 of Britain's. The gap continued to narrow after 1776, and by 1820 the population of the United States had overtaken Britain's. In contrast to Third World nations today with similar rates of growth, the colonies possessed the space, resources, and organization to maintain the highest average and probably most equitable standard of living in the world— at least for whites. Relatively few experienced starvation or even malnutrition. The gloomy late-18th-century prediction of the English reverend doctor Thomas Malthus—that the high population growth would eventually outstrip resources—was irrelevant in white, and even black, America.

Benjamin Franklin, newspaper publisher and social philosopher living in rapidly growing Philadelphia, described population change quite accurately in his *Observations Concerning the Increase of Mankind,* published at midcentury. He reported that marriages were occurring at a younger age and with greater frequency in the marriageable age group as the century progressed. As America's population closed in on Britain's, Franklin predicted that economic power would eventually shift across the Atlantic to America.

Birthrates persisted at a higher level in America than in England during the 18th century, especially in new settlements. American couples continued to marry earlier, leading to earlier births and adding more quickly to growth. They stopped sooner, however, so that the completed family size in America—5.5—was not much larger than the British figure of 5.0. Black reproduction rates gradually approached the white level, as the black sex ratio came into balance late in the century. Somewhat lower death rates, owing to healthier diets and a larger rural share, also contributed to growth. London was a death trap for many, in contrast to the far smaller colonial

Table 6.1 Estimated Populations of the American Provinces, 1700–1780 (in thousands)

Province or Colony	1700	1720	1740	1760	1780	Increase 1700–1780	% Total Pop. 1700	% Total Pop. 1775
(Maine)[a]	—	—	—	20	49			
(Vermont)[a]	—	—	—	—	48			
New Hampshire	5.0	9.4	23	39	88			
Massachusetts	56	91	152	203	269			
Rhode Island	5.9	12	25	45	53			
Connecticut	26	59	90	142	207			
NEW ENGLAND	93	171	290	449	714	7.5 times	37	26
% black	2				3[b]			
New York	19	37	64	117	211			
New Jersey	14	30	51	94	140			
Pennsylvania	18	31	86	184	327			
MID-ATLANTIC	51	98	201	395	678	13 times	21	24
% black	8				6[b]			
Delaware	2.5	5.4	20	33	45			
Maryland	30	66	116	162	245			
Virginia	59	88	180	340	538			
UPPER SOUTH	92	159	316	535	828	9 times	35	31
% black	23				37[b]			
North Carolina	11	21	52	110	270			
South Carolina	5.7	17	45	94	180			
Georgia	—	—	2.0	9.6	56			
LOWER SOUTH	17	38	99	214	506	30 times	6	17
% black	19				41[b]			
(Kentucky)[a]	—	—	—	—	45			
(Tennessee)[a]	—	—	—	—	10			
WEST	—	—	—	—	55		0	1
% black					17[b]			
TOTAL POPULATION[c]	251	466	906	1,594	2,780	11 times	100	100
% black	11				21[b]			

[a]Not organized as provinces or states by 1780. Maine part of Massachusetts; Vermont part of New York (disputed); Kentucky originally an extension of Virginia, and Tennessee of North Carolina.
[b]1775
[c]Imperfect sums because of rounding

cities. By later standards infant mortality remained high, yet probably three-quarters of colonial children survived to age 15, compared with two-thirds in England. Most could look forward to living the biblical three score and ten. American blacks were healthier and lived longer than those in the morbid working environments of the Caribbean sugar islands, though that could not compensate for their chattel status.

Immigration rose substantially after 1700 and was a prime contributor to America's rate of population growth being higher than England's. Between 1700 and 1775 about 370,000 Europeans and 250,000 Africans arrived. By one estimate, white immigrants added 25 percent to the population over this time, and of course they multiplied. But as the total grew larger, the immigrant share declined. By the 1770s perhaps only one white person in ten was born outside the colonies, the other nine thus having no direct memory of Britain. The impact of black immigration persisted longer because of the increasing importance of slavery, and blacks' share of the population nearly doubled to about one in five. An unknown but probably small number of settlers returned to their homeland, an option that blacks did not enjoy.

Distribution and Expansion

While all colonies grew, significant shifts in regional shares occurred (table 6.1; fig. 6.1). The upper South—the Chesapeake Bay area—and southern New England were the areas of oldest settlement, and together they dropped from nearly three-quarters of the total population to less than three-fifths. The Mason-Dixon line (the Pennsylvania-Maryland border) divided the population almost equally between South and North by 1775, and slavery confined almost 90 percent of the rapidly increasing black population south of the line. New England experienced the slowest growth, the lower South the fastest. Among individual colonies, Virginia maintained its lead, while Massachusetts, partly owing to a lower birthrate and also a shortage of good lands, yielded second place to Pennsylvania, the leading success story of the century.

By 1700 settlements were virtually contiguous from Norfolk, Virginia, to north of Portsmouth, New Hampshire (fig. 6.1). South of Norfolk only small, discrete settlements developed, the largest around Charleston. Penetration inland was still limited, being no more than 30 miles beyond tidewater except up the valleys of the Connecticut and the Hudson. Between 1700 and 1740 the strongest thrust inland was in Pennsylvania and into the backcountry of the upper South. Philadelphia was the major port of entry for immigrants. After 1740 the population of the lower South expanded greatly, and by 1775 colonists occupied almost all land east of the Appalachians, including many a fertile mountain valley. They were spilling out beyond the Appalachians in step with the rate of population growth.

Rural and Urban

Population was overwhelmingly rural. Densities varied with the timing of settlement, with access to seacoast markets, and with land quality. In Chester County, Pennsylvania (near Philadelphia), for example, by 1760 densities reached 30 to 40 persons per square mile. Densities remained lower than in much of rural England because offspring could choose to move west. Densities would once again start increasing after about 1790 with further agricultural and industrial intensification, and with them an expansion of wage labor. Before then, people had spread out over a larger space than actually required for their sustenance, driven by the lust for property. Landownership was the goal of most migrants from Europe, seeking to escape the constraints of courts, clergy, and crop failures. In 1775 only about 5 percent of the colonists lived in urban places, their farming being no more than garden plots. In fact, the proportion of urban dwellers fell during the 75-year period, even though most of the seaports and new inland towns grew. Regional variations were marked. The Chesapeake tobacco region, for example, was weakly urbanized, whereas urbanization in North and South Carolina was much greater.

CULTURAL COMPOSITION: ETHNICITY, RACE, AND RELIGION

America's white population became more heterogeneous during the 18th century, even in what had been hitherto the very English colonies of New England and Virginia. By 1775 those of English ancestry may have fallen to barely two-thirds of the white population. Estimates vary— a consequence of intractable data—but it is clear that other parts of the British Isles and German-speaking areas of western Europe sent many settlers. The so-called Scots-Irish from Ulster (northern Ireland) settled most thickly in parts of southeastern Pennsylvania, then also in the backcountry of that colony and of the South, and in New Hampshire. Welsh were most conspicuous in eastern Pennsylvania, lowland Scots in East Jersey and the Carolinas. German-speaking settlers arrived from the Rhine valley and Switzerland in increasing numbers until the onset of the Seven Years' War in 1755; few would come again until the mid-19th century. They too sought Pennsylvania primarily, and by 1775 about one American in ten was German. The Dutch had clustered in New York, adjacent East Jersey, and along the Delaware River since the 1620s, but their descendants made up only a small share. Except for some Germans, most settlers spoke, or came to speak, English. Ezra

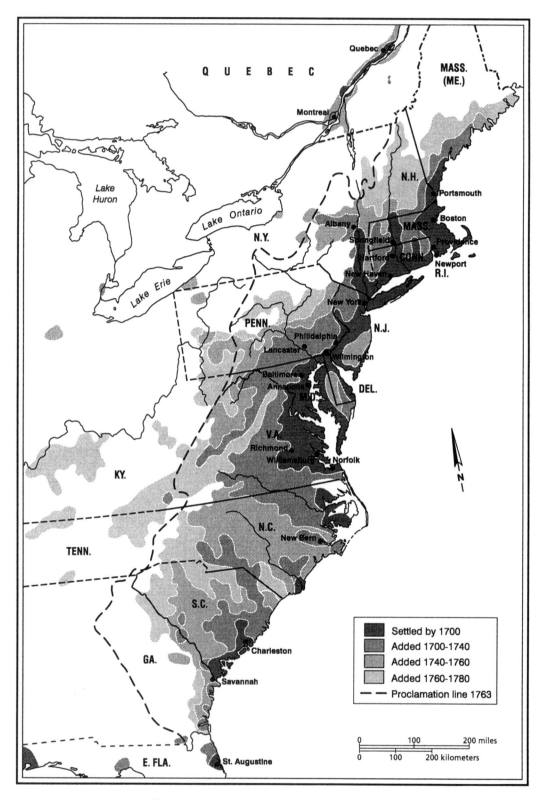

Figure 6.1 Population Distribution, 1700–1780

Styles of Connecticut predicted that English would "become the vernacular tongue of more people than any one tongue on Earth except the Chinese." Colonists of English ancestry were the dominant majority and chief bearers of institutions, and they could not be an ethnic group like the others.

The racial gulf between black and white and between Native and white was in each case enormous, and ethnic differences among whites pale in comparison. By 1775 blacks constituted one person in five, nearly double their share in 1700 (table 6.1). They were concentrated in the South, running up to almost 55 percent in South Carolina. In the North, only in New York City did blacks reach 10 percent. Over 90 percent were slaves, and even the few free blacks remained in the bottom rank of the social hierarchy. Few had hope of advancement; few held landed property. Black children learned early to defer to white masters and accept being sold as commodities. Rebellion could lead to severe punishment, and even death.

White mistreatment of Native Americans was of a totally different order. The decimation of eastern populations by European diseases had largely run its course by 1750. The Iroquois Confederacy in the colony of New York and the Cherokees and Creeks in the Southeast remained formidable adversaries for decades to come. But settlers pushed westward nonetheless, transgressing the settlement limit for the colonies defined by the British Proclamation Line of 1763 (fig. 6.1). This line followed the watershed between the rivers flowing directly into the Atlantic and those headed for the Mississippi or St. Lawrence. The great tension between whites and Natives concerned their perception of land; the liberal democratic power of whites, favoring freehold, ran roughshod over the collective order of the aboriginals.

Most whites were Protestant, but of many persuasions, and Roman Catholics were a small minority. The Church of England was the largest denomination, especially strong in the Chesapeake region. Bishops did appear eventually overseas, but traditional ecclesiastical arrangements were weakened considerably at first. Colonial Anglicans increasingly found themselves minorities, albeit of high status, as new groups moved in. The Episcopal Church (as the Church of England was called after 1776) retains its high status to the present, a sign that cultural continuity has been stronger than political orientation.

Eighteenth-century Americans replicated European regional and national denominations that arose out of the Reformation of the 16th century. Among Calvinists were Congregationalists of the Puritan tradition in New England, Presbyterians from Ulster and Scotland, and Reformed from some German states and the Netherlands in many colonies, particularly Pennsylvania. German-speaking Lutherans from other German states also favored Pennsylvania. Friends, known as Quakers, and as "plain folk" for their rejection of ostentation, dominated the earlier decades of Pennsylvania but located elsewhere as well. Mennonites, Amish, and various Baptist groups were plain folk also. Almost every conceivable Christian doctrinal strand was found in America. And later strands emerged, including Methodism of English origin in many areas and Unitarianism in New England. Some of the waves of evangelical fervor that periodically gripped many colonials originated there. The Great Awakening of the 1740s combined English and American nuances, spawning new groupings under charismatic leaders. Blacks gradually became Christian but not without weaving in traditional African customs.

Religious congregations were basic building blocks of local communities. At the same time, members of all denominations had to learn to live with one another. What had been national or regional churches overseas had become denominations in America. Historical interpretations, especially in the late 19th century, drew sharp distinctions in attitudes and practices among ethnic groups; recent scholarship is more reluctant to do so. European behavior was similar in most respects, notably regarding private property and diet. Further, none could escape the "Protestant ethic," emphasizing individual pursuit of success, enhanced greatly by the relatively open environment. Through Poor Richard's almanacs, Benjamin Franklin admonished his fellow countrymen to follow the rules of behavior that would lead to wealth and happiness.

SETTLEMENT PATTERNS AND SPATIAL ORGANIZATION

As European settlers spread themselves over the 18th-century landscape, they organized their households on freehold properties and these into formal communities. The terms rural and urban provide one spatial categorization. Another set concerns local, county, regional, and national levels of government and religious organization. Yet another way of thinking calls attention to the entrepreneurs and investors enmeshed in commerce locally and regionally, and in the British Empire and Atlantic trading networks globally.

The distinction between rural and urban settlement, though time-honored in the literature and censuses, cannot be rigidly applied to 18th-century America, just as it cannot be today. Cities were tiny by today's standards, and their residents were engaged with rural dwellers in government, voluntary bodies, and commerce. It is indeed true that the hustle and bustle of trading, of the courts, and of the ale- and coffeehouses were concentrated in densely built-up urban places. But country crossroad hamlets—with their clusters of a few houses, an inn with a tavern, and possibly a church—were everywhere and were hardly distinguishable from the countryside. In fact, reversing the picture, many functions associated with urban life were also found in the country—most obviously on large southern plantations.

A majority of rural households lived on their own land in farmsteads spatially separated at varying distances from one another. Agricultural villages, so common in many parts of Europe, were few, and of those that were established, only a handful survived for long. Such was the case in New England, despite several generations of historians who believed that Puritans had lived in tight spatial communities; new evidence indicates far more dispersal long before 1700. Likewise, in Pennsylvania, where founder William Penn sought to create tight community relations by settling people on home lots with fields at a distance, more or less like medieval villages, few agricultural villages survived. Even members of religious communities that demanded a strict code of behavior—Quakers, Mennonites, and Amish—lived on their own holdings, and Moravians, who had lived communally for a short time, gave up on the practice. The organizers of Savannah, Georgia, laid out a utopian landscape to settle marginal people off the streets of London, but that too failed. (Only Hutterites on the western plains have succeeded in maintaining villages on vast commu-

nally owned lands.) Separate and discrete holdings in America were replicating a process occurring in Britain. There, in stages over several centuries, the enclosure movement had resulted in the dispersal of farmsteads from villages and the fencing of medieval fields and common lands. Dispersed settlement was a sign of independence, of a liberalizing of society, and suited America.

As in Britain, irregularly shaped farm lots and fields were common during prerevolutionary generations (fig. 6.2). A few examples of long lots, mostly identified with the French, appeared adjacent to rivers. Roads were rarely straight over long distances, a fact still evident to today's motorists. An exception was in Pennsylvania, where settlers in the first two decades after 1681 occupied rectangular lots adjacent to straight roads (fig 6.3). Regularity indicated that survey occurred before settlement, whereas irregularity signaled that settlers had taken up land before officials had surveyed it. Sometimes the taking became a kind of free-for-all, as newcomers scrambled to be first on the best land, fertile and well watered. Oftentimes this process resulted in resurveying and court cases on overlapping claims. By 1775, however, regularity was becoming the norm, at least in northern New England. After 1783, the new federal government imposed the lot survey prior to settle-

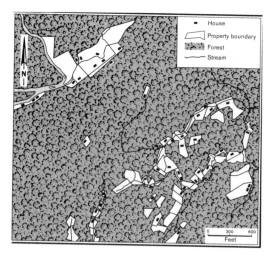

Figure 6.2 Dispersed Settlement in Northern New Jersey, Middle of the 18th Century.Density of forest overstated (after Wacker)

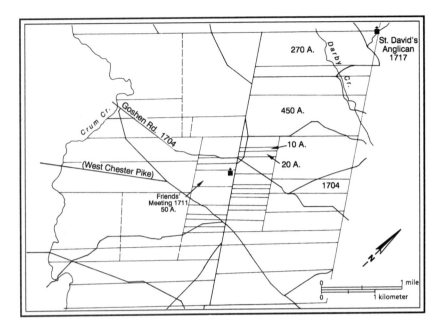

Figure 6.3 Newtown, Pennsylvania: A Failed Agricultural Village (after Lemon)

ment on land destined to be alienated to private citizens. This achievement is strikingly evident from the air. The officials took this initiative to speed up settlement and to earn revenue for government operations.

Colonial residents viewed land as freehold property and a sign of status. To the peasants and small farmers who came from Europe, where the much more spatially closed environments favored those few with power, the relatively open landscape in America was a resource to exploit both for use and for exchange. As in Europe, the more land one held and the better quality it was, the higher one's position in society. In the relatively egalitarian colonies white males owned thousands of parcels of land independently, yet through the decades better-off farmers amassed large properties and pulled ahead of their neighbors. Landownership was widespread in the North, but somewhat less so (among whites) in the South. Ownership was not quite absolute, for in some colonies settlers and their descendants had to pay quitrents (ground rents) to proprietors. The War of Independence wiped out these medieval hangovers in most cases, yet such laws prohibited encroachments on neighboring properties. Attempts by landlords ("patroons" in New York)

and others to settle peasant tenants tied to them by feudal dues largely failed. Married women could not own land; widows could, however, though often the male head would will property to his sons. As in many parts of Europe, in older settled areas where further division of a holding would jeopardize economic viability, the property went to one son, usually the oldest, a practice known as primogeniture.

Despite widespread landownership as the 18th century progressed, an increasing number of rural dwellers became tenants. Some tenant farmers in Pennsylvania were quite affluent because they occupied good, productive land; they seem to have reasoned that it was better to rent good land than own poor or more remote lands. Then too there were "inmates," the hired hands. Usually married, inmates lived with their families in a house on a plot of land that the owner granted them for use. In Maryland poor renters occupied the colony's own lands. Unmarried and married indentured servants resided in the households of sponsors of their overseas passage, but at the end of their term of service, probably few had been able to save enough money to buy land except in remote areas farther west. Sons of poorer owners, in New England and elsewhere, often worked as day laborers, and they too could move west and succeed on the land if they had the energy and enough capital to buy equipment and supplies. Another way to gain ownership was to trespass ("squat") on lands held by a very large landowner who held back tracts in the expectation of appreciated value. Seven years of occupation might confer title on the squatter. Needless to say, slaves, even when freed, had difficulty acquiring title to land. Although the image of a freehold paradise is marred by the great many tenants, laborers, and slaves, the belief (and in large measure the reality) generally was that, compared to Europe, owning land was widespread.

In the 18th century, as today, land was a commodity that could be bought and sold. Although many men willed their holdings to children, many others chose to sell when they saw opportunity elsewhere. Prices rose through the century on land adjacent to cities and where the soil quality was good. Leases were defined in money terms and often identified other obligations to the owner. When prices of goods dropped to low levels, farmers fell into debt, and not a few holdings passed to the hands of the sheriff and were sold at auction. At times groups of farmers protested collectively, but usually to little avail. The power of the state in maintaining property relations prevailed.

A family farmstead was composed of a house, barn, and other outbuildings, such as a chicken coop, piggery, smokehouse, bake oven, and springhouse for cooling. Some households added a separate apartment or rooms to the house for retired parents. On southern plantations owners built slave quarters and workshops for blacksmithing and other craft work. In the North, too, some built distilleries, cider presses, and weaving shops. Farmers divided the land into gardens and orchards, upland for crops, and moister meadows for hay and rough pasture; they usually retained some uncleared woodland. Even though land was increasingly viewed as a commodity, it continued as the chief means of sustenance.

Farmsteads connected to the local communities. Their lanes gave access to local public roads that in turn joined main regional routes. Farmers hauled their goods in wagons or carts, and for personal transport the more affluent drove carriages. A church or meetinghouse, a mill, a store, and an inn with a tavern were seldom far away, and sometimes these services were clustered in small urban places.

LOCAL GOVERNMENT: TOWNSHIPS AND COUNTIES

Farm families were citizens of minor civil divisions variously called townships, towns, hundreds, or parishes. Several townships together constituted counties (or, in South Carolina, parishes). Names were assigned by provincial officials, land developers, or the collective decisions of the first settlers. These names—whether harking back to the homeland, a saint, or the Bible or inherited from the aboriginal peoples—have persisted down to the present. Even though property was held freehold, no one could escape the institutional reality of living within a landscape organized by government. Every freeholder and many tenants had to pay taxes for local purposes, though these were very light by European standards. Male property holders, listed on tax rolls, elected their officials.

The size and shape of minor civil units and counties varied considerably, as did the terminology defining officials. When population densities rose, townships and counties were split into what residents and officials deemed to be more manageable units. Even so, northern counties remained larger than those in the South: 15,000 to 25,000 people in the 1770s compared to 5,000 (whites). In the Chesapeake tidewater region, for example, counties were only a quarter to a third the size of those farther north. Boundaries, like those of farm holdings, sometimes were arbitrary straight lines, but in more cases surveyors followed topographic features such as streams or lines of hills.

By 1700 provincial legislatures and councils had generally defined local and county powers, though the new colony of Pennsylvania still was experimenting, as some older ones had done earlier. The customary view of the division of powers between the lower level and the counties holds that in New England the town predominated, in the South the county, and in the Middle Colonies it was balanced. But such distinctions were not quite so sharp. The lower levels operated everywhere. In Pennsylvania an increasingly larger role emerged for township officials such as constables, overseers of the poor, road supervisors, fence viewers, and poundkeepers. But their power was circumscribed by limited taxing power. That local positions rotated among men suggests not only local, relatively egalitarian democracy, as in New England, but also that these positions were seen more as obligations and less as paths to higher status, as in the case of more sought-after county and provincial offices. As in New England, Pennsylvania township meetings elected officials and also nominated candidates for constables, who were then appointed by county justices. In New England, counties gradually became more important, as interactions intensified. County courts would quicken their activities in civil suits as well as criminal cases.

In the North male property holders elected some county officials, while provincial authorities appointed others—notably justices, who were the most powerful men in counties. Keeping public order was paramount: for instance, trying persons for criminal acts or resolving disputes over lot boundaries through civil suits. Male citizens sat on juries. Other officials kept records in courthouses regarding deeds and wills and other relevant matters of the public interest. In all colonies, as today, representatives to the legislatures assumed considerable influence over local and county affairs. Indeed, provincial governments had near sovereign constitutional power over the lower levels.

In the South the much smaller tidewater counties took on more local power than in the North. In Maryland, parishes, only created in 1692, were apparently not very important, because in 1776 revolutionary fervor abolished them. In Virginia, although counties were even smaller than in Maryland, parishes retained only a few functions, notably to raise money for clergy of the established Church of England. One of the more intersting secular obligations of the vestry of the parish was "land processing." Because inaccurate surveys had led to so many lawsuits, the provincial assembly ordered vestries to view property lines and renew markers every four years.

Local Community Bodies and Networks

Church congregations also provided social cement at the local level. But as in England, denominational preferences divided people, and theological disputes within congregations sometimes split neighbors. By 1700 more than one congregation operated in many local communities. Such was the case even in New England, where the Congregational churches arising from Puritanism had been established officially by provincial authorities, or again in Virginia and Maryland where the Church of England was the established denomination. Local congregations selected stalwart members to represent them at regional conclaves, mostly organized in hierarchical structures. Pennsylvania Quakers, for example, held monthly meetings for representatives from several local congregations and yearly meetings at Philadelphia.

The importance of other local rural institutions is hard to measure. Kinship ties were perhaps the strongest social glue, though mobility loosened bonds. Schools were still not mandated, though some provinces encouraged them. Often clergymen would attempt to teach children in a schoolhouse on land donated by a local farmer and erected by a group of interested parents. Urban schools catered to the children of the elite, though a few served poor immigrant children as well. Most learning of skills occurred at home.

Local trading and work patterns were not only for economic benefit but also brought people together socially, often across town and county lines. Barn raisings, quilting bees, and husking bees did not, however, bring out everyone in a neighborhood. Taverns were gathering places for some men; others created clubs; women created networks. Celebrations certainly were crucial for social cohesion. Funerals were as important as weddings and baptisms in bringing kin and neighbors together. These were occasions to discuss the problems presented by the weather, politicians, and merchants and, of course, to gossip.

Whatever the variations, the workings of local government and other ventures in each colony were basically the same, with the exception of relations to slaves. In fact, 18th-century Americans behaved in many respects like the British, and some scholars have argued that institutions became more Anglicized over the century. That case should not be surprising. Most new social situations involve experimentation, but once society is established, the usual ways of doing things will impose themselves. As in every community, some people were outsiders, some fell into poverty, and others climbed the social ladder.

Inheriting property was the surest way to affluence, and in this respect the American colonies were less like Britain. Given wider property ownership, deference to authorities in rural areas was weaker. In the North at least, at the local level, democracy prevailed more vigorously than in Britain. That would be America's greatest strength but also its greatest weakness. Social leveling did not stop some colonists from becoming richer than others, and, in the end, a class structure intensified in rural American communities. Without lords of the manor, against which people could clearly measure status, the distinctions were more subtle but in a sense more dangerous, as Alexis de Tocqueville warned Americans in the 1830s. In this most liberal of democracies, eventually the United States would show itself as the most inegalitarian country in the rich western world. It would have the greatest gap between rich and poor and would record the lowest voter turnouts because of a widespread sense that efforts to reduce such inequalities would be futile.

Higher Authorities

Everyone from Massachusetts to Georgia belonged to a province and also to Britain. Elective legislative assemblies represented their constituents. In many colonies, newer settled areas were underrepresented compared to older ones. This situation led to sectional tensions, based on a clash of interests. Nonetheless, enough unity of purpose within and among the colonies fueled opposition to Britain. Not long before 1700 the New England colonies, New York, and Maryland came under the direct rule of royally appointed governors, and New Jersey and the Carolinas would soon follow. Pennsylvania remained a proprietary province up to 1776. Georgia was a Crown colony, though in its early years James Oglethorpe, the driving force behind its establishment, chaired the board of trustees that administered the colony. While the governors (even those appointed by proprietors) and their executive councils were responsible to the Crown and Parliament overseas, the elective assemblies were run by colonial leaders, usually of elite economic status. Tensions between governors and legislatures were frequent, partly because information, often having to do with power, took weeks to cross the Atlantic and partly because of different aims. Not surprisingly, misunderstandings occurred, culminating finally in independence. The defeat of the French in Quebec, Acadia, and the West Indies in 1759 removed a major factor

in colonists' commitment to the Union Jack.

Colonial representation in the House of Commons in London might have headed off separation. As Britain, like America, moved haltingly toward wider representative government, it was not clear to enough people of authority in Britain how to reach a more democratic way of governing their overseas kinfolk. We need only to look to Canada, where it took from 1791 to 1931 (even 1982) to work out an acceptable system of self-government under the Crown. But most people in America could not wait, and in 1783, 13 colonies became states in a new union. The seemingly arbitrary boundaries of independence remained where they had been laid down, mostly early in the 17th century. No one would try to change state boundaries today, or for that matter many lower level ones either. Such is the power of inertia and the hold of place definitions.

Urban Development and Regional Organization

Boston, New York, and Philadelphia dated from the first days of their respective colonies, and each apparently had more than enough inertia and organizational capacity to serve as the focus for its region, even as rural growth outpaced urban. But rural population and economic growth induced the founding of more urban places, as perceptive promoters recognized the opportunities to service the increasing population. A hierarchy of towns—"central places" in geographers' terminology—was more obvious in all colonies in 1775 than it had been a century earlier. Larger places served larger regions and thus were fewer in number. The smaller the place, the narrower the range of services and the more limited its surrounding hinterland. Although some promoters had pretensions of greatness for their urban developments, few places could actually grow large. In general, population size reflected the importance of functions.

Colonial promoters established capitals as the seat of government for maintaining public order, facilitating commerce and trade, and focusing colonial social life. By 1700 Boston, New York, Philadelphia, Newport, and Charleston were well established as the main centers (fig. 6.1). All were seaports tied to London, the dominant political, economic, and social provider of power. They can be called network cities, connecting to the Atlantic world of trade and communication. Still, only Boston exceeded 5,000 persons. On Chesapeake Bay no large center appeared, the capitals of Maryland and Virginia being tiny. By 1775 Philadelphia and New York both had grown to about 25,000, equivalent to several provincial cities in the British Isles. They were followed by Boston, which, at 16,000, had stagnated since 1740; then came Charleston (12,000), Newport (11,000), and two new cities—Norfolk and Baltimore—each at 6,000. And there were now many more smaller places.

Philadelphia and its region provides the most comprehensive pattern of urbanization, the one closest to what central place theory proposes (fig. 6.4). In 1681 William Penn and his officials established the town site coincidentally with the founding of the province. Government operations, such as the provincial courts, the land office, and regulatory bodies, provided jobs there and, in turn, multiplied other occupations to supply them with goods and services. More lawyers clustered there than anywhere else. Merchants settled in town from the beginning and dealt with fur traders, inland shopkeepers, millers, and farmers. Those with sufficient capital built wharves and, in time, operated ships on the Atlantic. These ships, supplied with food from the Philadelphia region, exported produce to the West Indies and southern Europe and, in competition with British vessels, brought imports from Britain and the West Indies. Success led to shipbuilding that exceeded production in Boston. Skilled and unskilled employment rose with expansion; small-scale manufacturing grew.

Philadelphia became the premier printing and publishing center in the colonies. Benjamin Franklin was one of the earliest and most famous of these publishers, one of a handful of leading men who had power to shape society. For many years the leaders met primarily in the London Coffee House at the central waterfront, where ships landed from Britain. Reports of the latest military and political exploits and the dispensing of prices and fashions from the center of empire were of utmost importance to these regional leaders. By midcentury, Philadelphia had risen to the top among the larger cities on the continent; New York was nearly as large, because of the

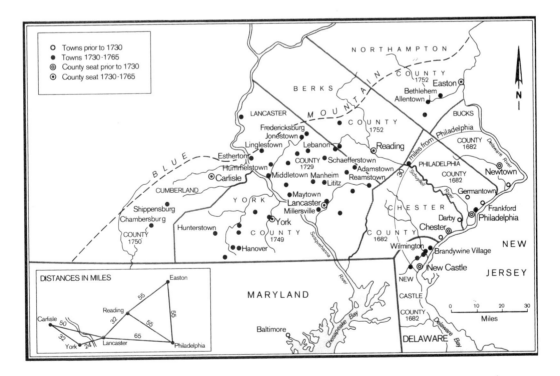

Figure 6.4 Urbanization in Southeastern Pennsylvania, 1652–1765 (after Lemon)

wealth of the region and the ingenuity of its merchants. Church life was prominent in colonial Philadelphia, and regional assemblies of Quakers and other denominations brought together leaders in local economic affairs, keen also to transact business. Symbolically, the most prominent church in the whole region was Christ Church, still standing today, its tall spire pointing to heaven. The city was also the locale of the first college in the province, and it led in public health measures and other social innovations. The quality of life gradually improved.

Philadelphia was always the richest place in the Pennsylvania colony, and eventually in America; it was a smaller replica of London. Many merchants garnered high incomes and great wealth because they acted as financiers in those days before banks had been established. They paraded their wealth by building fine houses, dressing in European finery, and riding in elegant coaches. Even successful Quakers could not resist the call of conspicuous consumption, to the disgust of their austere rural coreligionists. In midcentury some merchants organized an exchange, a predecessor of the later stock exchanges. At the same time, like London and other cities, Philadelphia attracted many of the poor from the countryside looking for opportunities. By midcentury the city had earned the title of "metropolis" from European visitors who were amazed at how rapidly it had grown in a few short decades.

Wealth could not have accumulated in Philadelphia without a prosperous hinterland that expanded into southeastern Pennsylvania and Delaware, southward into the backcountry of the upper South, and across the Delaware River into New Jersey. New central places emerged. The larger ones—Reading, York, and Carlisle—were county seats (fig. 6.4). For several decades, Philadelphia's commercial power so overshadowed county seats located along both sides of the Delaware River that they failed to grow strongly. But as settlement expanded and prosperity increased, the need for inland central places became apparent.

In 1729 an associate of the Penn family laid out Lancaster, and between 1741 and 1752 Thomas Penn, William's son, created four other county seats, coincident with the establishment of new counties; just before 1776 he established two more. Penn made money selling lots in these towns, which prospered because the planners had made the counties large enough that county seats did not crowd one another's territory and were sufficiently far from Phildelphia to encourage subregional commercial activity. European visitors noted that Lancaster, especially, resembled an English market town and was a miniature Philadelphia. Its central courthouse square surrounded by shops and warehouses was a busy place when farmers and residents of smaller urban places came to town. Lancaster had a post office too. As in Philadelphia, the local government paved the streets with stone, built bridges, ran the marketplace, and even piped water. Government and commerce worked together to make for prosperity.

Speculative land developers created more than 50 other urban places, in waves, between 1740 and 1775. Some were to be successful, most others not. The most prominent in the hierarchy was Harrisburg, named by the founder; after 1776 it became a county seat and subsequently the state capital. Others became mere villages. Smallest of all were the crossroad hamlets, spread out along main roads as frequently as every two miles; their taverns provided lodging and sustenance to wagoners and other travelers. Some places failed their founders altogether.

In some service-oriented towns small-scale manufacturing developed. Germantown, near Philadelphia, had a strong contingent of weavers and eventually specialized in stockings. Brandywine Creek above Wilmington, Delaware, fostered a string of waterpowered mills, grinding wheat to flour for export. Both could be considered cutting-edge cities of the day. Bethlehem, in Northampton County (fig. 6.4), combined mining, ironworks, and manufacturing with a strong religious orientation, and entrepreneurs built clusters of housing for their workers and families.

URBANIZATION ELSEWHERE

In New England the founding of a string of seaports and fishing villages had created a point pattern along the coast long before 1700. Boston, the capital of Massachusetts, had become the largest center in America, but increasingly Salem, Massachusetts, and Newport and Providence, Rhode Island, competed with it in the Atlantic carrying trade and in shipbuilding.

After 1740 Boston lost primacy in shipbuilding to Philadelphia and New York and also suffered from having to pay heavily for fighting several wars against the French farther north. Inland along the Connecticut River, Springfield continued as the dominant center, though Hartford emerged to compete with New Haven as the major focus of Connecticut. Our understanding of the degree of New England urbanization is clouded because towns, as local government units for which records were kept, could be totally rural or might be a mixture of rural and urban. It would appear that urbanization became much stronger after 1780 with the intensification of economic activity; even before 1775 Norwich began specializing in clothmaking and Lynn in shoemaking. While rural mills producing flour for export had induced urbanization in Pennsylvania, after 1775 textile mills would be a more powerful force for concentrating people in New England. The western part of New England increasingly fell under New York City's commercial dominance, as did East Jersey, Long Island, and the Hudson River valley. By 1775 New York was poised to surpass Philadelphia as the chief center in the American colonies. By 1810 it had in fact become the dominant financial city on the continent. Smaller urban places developed in New York's hinterland; the most notable was Albany, which, like Springfield, had started as a fur-trading post. Mill sites in northeastern New Jersey helped to lay the industrial foundations for that region.

The upper South—the Chesapeake region—experienced the most complex pattern of urban growth. Before 1700 urbanization had been slight and continued so throughout the 18th century. The tobacco trade was organized from London, and later Glasgow, to a far greater degree than was the grain and livestock production from the North, so merchant centers were absent. Northern merchants had much greater leverage in their dealings with British merchants than those in the Chesapeake. Also, many plantation owners shipped tobacco from their own wharves rather than having it collected in central warehouses. The richest planters controlled society, their large plantations doubling as urban places with many services. Development of strong secondary towns was further inhibited by the presence of too many small counties; courthouses often stood in the open countryside. De-

spite the promotion of English shire towns, none had appeared by 1700, nor did the creation of inspection warehouses in the 1730s and 1740s induce much urbanization. Agents (called factors) of Scottish merchants set up stores in the countryside, to the further detriment of commercial development. Williamsburg, created in 1699 as Virginia's capital, operated in a discontinuous seasonal fashion, quite unlike northern cities. The courts met quarterly, and only then did planters and merchants converge on the town. Annapolis, after 1694 Maryland's capital, languished for similar reasons.

Virginia and Maryland experienced profound settlement changes after 1740. As the Piedmont and Great Valley regions filled with settlers, these areas took on more of a northern colony quality of mixed grain and livestock farming. Even though it was not a capital, after 1760 Baltimore grew rapidly as a flour-milling center and port, competing with Philadelphia for regional control. Richmond emerged after 1730 as an important, if smaller, milling and shipping site and became capital of Virginia after the Revolution. Williamsburg, lacking commercial purpose, withered. Norfolk also rose to prominence early in the century, trading corn and livestock for West Indian rum and sugar. But Norfolk failed to pick up the wheat trade, so growth slowed. As in Pennsylvania, an inland pattern of secondary and tertiary towns, such as Frederick, Hagerstown, and Winchester, emerged.

In the lower South, Charleston, established in 1670, stood out as a capital and commercial center (fig. 6.1). Its inhabitants numbered 2,000 by 1700 but it experienced relatively slow growth until 1730. By 1775 its population had climbed to 12,000, about half that of Philadelphia and New York. Charleston merchants engaged in reexports and ship provisioning in the West Indies trade and financed the rice and indigo trades. In the 1760s they tapped the export wheat production of the backcountry, expanding southward from Pennsylvania and Virginia. Also, while northern merchants built country villas and Virginia's planters visited Williamsburg, South Carolina planters sought the summer sea breezes in their city mansions to escape the oppressive heat. Other coastal ports such as Savannah replicated Charleston. In North Carolina, urbanization was slight by 1775. Its coastal ports, such as Wilmington, remained small. Only inland, where the economy was similar to that of the North, did towns like Salem and, in South Carolina, Camden emerge.

Although American urbanization was tiny by later standards, the cities of the 18th century played a crucial role in organizing political, economic, and social power in their regions. They became more interconnected too. After 1790 the major cities grew more rapidly. Even though populist agitation forced New York, Philadelphia, and Charleston to give up their roles as state capitals to interior towns, they had the commercial and, increasingly, the manufacturing impetus to outstrip the aspirations of other places. London, too, lost its political role in America in 1776, but it would remain the commercial touchstone for America as the postrevolutionary new nation took shape.

MATERIAL LIFE:
AGRICULTURE AND RURAL INDUSTRY

In 18th-century America, monetary value had become firmly attached to property, labor, and commodities, even for barter in reciprocal trading. Although many deals were informally handled, written contracts were increasingly common. Merchants, shopkeepers, millers, and the more prominent farmers kept account books to track their dealings with others. Farmers frequently incurred debts, and only with high prices relative to other goods could they pay them off. Farmers and merchants alike encountered swings in prices—some short-term, some longer-term—but it was prices set in London that disciplined those in the colonies.

Anxious that the reputation of the region not suffer, governments hired regulators to maintain orderly trading and the quality of goods. Ensuring accurate weights and measures was also important, and taxes paid for all such services. The colonies operated in a relatively free-enterprise fashion, though there were limits. Nature imposed some of these constraints: rice, to take an extreme example, would grow only in South Carolina and Georgia. Comparative advantages favored some colonies over others. No one kept what are called today national accounts as measured by the gross domestic product, yet official correspondence did sometimes attempt to measure the relative importance of economic sectors, and in recent times scholars have estimated productivity.

Farming

In contrast to the present, farming engaged far more people and contributed a far larger share to the colonial economy. The production, processing, and distribution of food and fiber were highly decentralized and on a much smaller scale. Today the family farm struggles to survive, whereas in the 18th century there were few large operations apart from the big plantations in the South. Colonial farmers produced a wide range of crops and livestock needed for domestic use. This did not mean complete self-sufficiency, as has often been stated in earlier histories, because locally traded goods and services and European goods made their way into the rural economy. The number of improved acres was the prime determinant of how much produce was used at home and how much was traded. If colonial farmers specialized too much, they could be vulnerable to catastophic losses. Farm households had to be versatile in dealing with the many products from the land, and a gender and age division of tasks was evident. Despite experimentation, the few new techniques in caring for land and livestock and in processing during the prerevolutionary era gave rise to only a modest increase in productivity per person. Except for market gardens adjacent to cities, most land was not intensively worked.

Among grains, Indian corn (maize) and wheat (a "corn" in England) stood out. Wheat was more prominent in the Middle Colonies, and especially on the best land, and gradually diffused into the southern backcountry; corn was more extensive in New England and the tidewater South (fig. 6.5). Millers ground most of the wheat into flour, which was then baked into bread. Much of the wheat of the Middle Colonies entered trade, some to New England, where stem rust hindered wheat production, and increasingly overseas as markets opened up in the Caribbean during the 1740s. By the 1770s wheat was going to Britain, presaging North American supplies to come over the next two centuries. People ate most of the corn, primarily as cornmeal, but increasingly farmers fattened livestock with this great gift of the Natives, and in the South distilled it to make whiskey.

The other major crop was tobacco, principally from the Chesapeake tidewater region. As in the 17th century, it was the most valuable export. Over the 18th century, farmers had abandoned

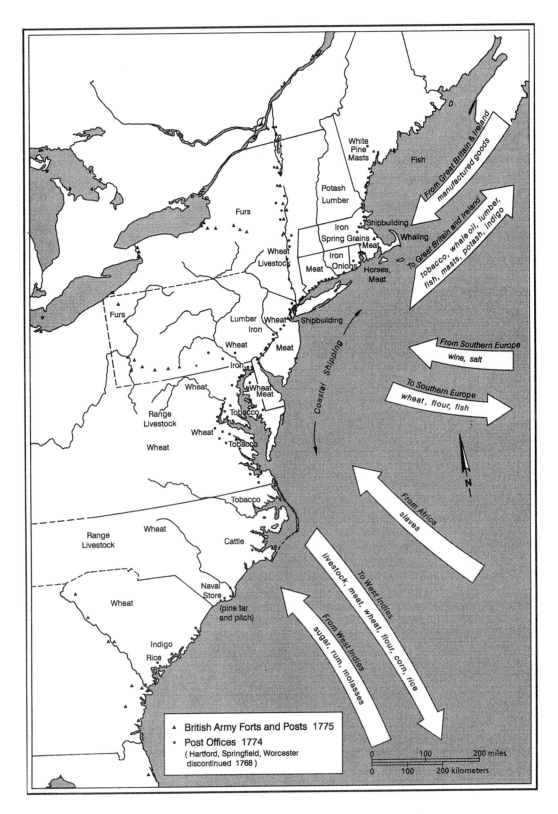

Figure 6.5 Colonial Trade and Economic Activity, 1775

tobacco in some areas but had expanded onto the Virginia Piedmont and into North Carolina. Large planters, favored by quality inspection beginning in the 1730s, increased their production at the expense of smaller farmers, whose production was often deemed "trash." The largest planters, working with slave labor, planted up to 60 acres; the small ones grew only an acre or 2. Over the century, planters diversified into more crops, especially wheat and corn.

Other grains and crops were less prominent. Distillers turned rye into whiskey, and brewers barley into malt for beermaking, though both were used in some breads. Oats fed horses primarily, but also people. In the lower South near the coast rice became increasingly important after 1730, principally for sale elsewhere. Farms and holders of small plots grew vegetables in kitchen gardens and produced fruit from orchards. Potatoes, added early in the century to the many vegetables initially brought from Europe, provided even more variety. Natives taught settlers that not only corn but also pumpkins, squash, and their styles of beans could be abundant and nutritious. Presses turned apples into cider, some of which was further converted into alcoholic beverages; American men did not shy away from alcohol. In the fall, surplus apples often ended up in pigs' stomachs. Maple syrup was a useful sweetener in New England and New York, though sugar imported from the West Indies was everywhere becoming increasingly important. Flax provided fiber for textiles and seeds for oil. South Carolina produced indigo, a source of blue dye that supplemented natural and imported dyes in coloring cloth. Hemp was another industrial crop, used to make rope and bags. Hay, from improved English grasses, clover, and alfalfa, was a major crop to sustain animals through the winter, though native grasses in watered meadows remained important too.

Livestock was as important as crops. In all regions pork in its various prepared forms was preferred over beef, while mutton and lamb were of less importance. Cows provided milk, some of which was converted into cheese and butter. For much of the year animals ranged on pasture and, in remote areas, into woods and in some places open prairie grassland. Horses or oxen plowed, harrowed, and pulled wagons and carts. As commercial production of wheat expanded—in eastern Pennsylvania, particularly—four-horse "Conestoga" wagons hauled wheat to merchant

mills on the Brandywine River and elsewhere. Most middle- and upper-income households had riding and buggy horses, while a few bred racing horses for speed. Sheep yielded wool for textiles, though imports of textiles and clothing from Britain exceeded local production. By midcentury, breeders had produced improved strains of livestock tuned to regional variations of climate, thus raising productivity. Chickens, geese, and ducks contributed their flesh, eggs, and feathers. The passenger pigeon (now extinct) and wild deer added protein; bees provided honey for sweetening.

Between 1760 and 1775 an average holding of 125 acres in Lancaster and Chester Counties in Pennsylvania devoted perhaps 25 acres to grain, including 8 to 10 in wheat and a further 8 in corn. Such a farm produced hay from another 20 acres, plus a few in flax and hemp and in vegetables and fruit. This average farm had 6 or 7 older cattle, 3 or 4 horses, 6 to 10 pigs, and 6 to 12 sheep, plus younger animals; these amounts varied depending on land quality. In New England, farms tended to be smaller, and in the plantation South on average larger, but there was great variation. The extent of woodland on farms decreased over the century in older settled areas, but large reserve acreages remained except near the bigger cities where they were depleted for firewood and shipbuilding.

Output per unit of land was much lower than today, largely as a result of superficial cultivation and low fertilizer inputs. Most 18th-century commentators pointed to an average of ten bushels of wheat per acre, about a quarter of today's figure. Yields from other grains were somewhat higher. Cattle and pigs were generally smaller than today. Critics of agriculture after 1750 complained of these low yields, but when one considers the relatively low density of population compared to Europe, production was more than adequate for home use, and even for local trade and export. Gardens, however, yielded abundantly and probably contributed more to food intake and balanced diets than scholars have realized. Commentators noted that farmers spread animal manure on orchards and other small acreages of intensively grown crops but rarely on grain fields or pastures. By 1760, however, lime had come into wider use as a rejuvenator of land. Higher yields in eastern Massachusetts in the early 1770s suggest more fertilizing had begun there. Crop rotation was also a growing practice, a common way to renew worn-out land by resting it with fallows of up to 20 years. Generally, however, improved care of the land had to await intensification of practices after 1776.

Contemporary observers noted with displeasure the limited use of labor-saving devices. Few new inventions were put into play. Farmers frequently hired day laborers, often the sons of poorer families, to mow hay. Other farm jobs, such as slaughtering livestock in the late fall and clearing land in the winter, also required outside help. Reaping grain demanded the most intensive use of labor, and farmers mobilized not only household members but also townspeople. Grain had to be harvested when exactly ripe. If it was cut too late, the seeds fell off the stalk and had to be gleaned off the ground one by one, a painstaking task. Following ages-old fashion, reapers bent down with short-handled sharp sickles, grasped a sheaf, and cut off a bundle of the stems near the ground. The introduction of long-handled scythes after 1760, fixed with cradles to catch the stalks as they fell, allowed harvesters to stand up straight, as in mowing hay, and thus be more productive.

Seasonally, farmworkers scythed the first crop of hay between May and July. They cut fall-sown wheat in the South in June, in New England in July, and spring-sown grains in August or later. After cutting, they set the grain sheaves upright in stooks in the fields to dry and in due course hauled them to the barn, where hands threshed with flails to remove the grain from the straw. Threshing could be done over a long period of time, though high prices in the summer might hasten the activity.

In the South the longer growing season permitted growing tobacco, rice, and indigo, each of which demanded substantial labor input. Planters were convinced of the need for slaves, who learned skills to deal with the great diversity of activity on plantations. Although by 1775 much of the South had turned to a more northern type of agriculture, thus reducing greatly the need for slave labor, the rise of cotton production following the Revolution saved the slave system for much of another century.

In slack seasons, especially in winter but also between sowing and harvesting, households engaged in crafts. Buildings and fences demanded care. Some farmers were skilled cabinetmakers, others carpenters and bricklayers. Still others

made clocks or cut hair; some peddled imported goods. In Pennsylvania men wove cloth, though in New England that job became a female occupation. Not all rural men classified themselves as farmers. Yet even justices of the peace, clergymen, blacksmiths, wheelwrights, coopers (barrel makers), and surveyors, for example, also usually put in crops and raised livestock, just as most farmers took on nonfarm tasks. Larger flour mills often operated for most of the year, but many smaller flour mills, sawmills, fulling mills (for cleaning cloth), and oil mills (for extracting oil from flaxseed) functioned only sporadically.

While men prepared the fields, tended the stock, cut wood, or sold produce, women churned cream into butter for sale. Women and older daughters everywhere spun yarn, much of which they sold through their own trade networks. Women were responsible not only for the household but also for the vegetable garden, flower beds, and fowl. Some women acted as midwives and tended the ill. Although married women did not have the right to hold property, without doubt they participated with their spouses in making decisions, and some probably kept the household accounts. As children grew older, their labor eased burdens. To lead comfortable and relatively independent lives, members of families had to be competent in a wide range of activities. Specialized labor, diversified but defined, was the character of rural life everywhere. Modest success meant that families could buy goods and services from others locally and goods from elsewhere in America and from overseas.

By 1775 the colonial iron industry turned out an estimated 15 percent of world production: 30,000 tons. Other than shipbuilding, it was the largest industry and the most labor intensive. All colonies produced iron from bog ore that was reduced in furnaces heated to high temperatures by charcoal. Since ore was located in hill country, owners were able to control large tracts of woods from which hardwood was cut to make charcoal. (Bituminous coal did not replace wood until after 1850.) In Pennsylvania, New Jersey, and Maryland more than 100 furnaces operated at midcentury. Some of these were large operations needing substantial capital inputs, and only the most affluent merchants had the money to invest. In the 1770s Hope Furnace in Rhode Island often employed 75 laborers at various seasons, half of them cutting wood. Owners organized company towns, providing housing and shops for workers.

Furnaces turned out pig iron that was further forged into bar and other kinds of iron, and modest amounts were made into much harder steel. Craftsmen and their helpers fashioned stoves, pots, kettles, and other finished products. Blacksmiths made horseshoes and bands for barrels, and wheelwrights were everywhere. The British Parliament tried unsuccessfully to retain such production at home, but colonial America was on the verge of the industrial revolution and would not be stopped. Although there were some experimental factories before 1776, only in the 1790s did textile mills appear, adding further momentum to the industrialization of postrevolutionary America.

TRADE: REGIONAL AND EXTERNAL

The pace of trade quickened over the 18th century, with widespread local trade intensifying. Until recently most scholars have underestimated the degree of interdependency among farmers. Around 1770, 90 percent of the corn and more than 80 percent of the wheat produced in Virginia were consumed there. Some goods were sold at formal markets, but more and more produce was handled by farmers through shopkeepers or merchants. In most towns, despite discouraging local laws, peddlers hawking produce competed successfully with marketplace stallholders. Drovers led range cattle from deep in the backcountry to fattening areas near cities, where slaughterhouses converted them to meat for urban dwellers and ship stores. Boats hauled cordwood down rivers to the cities for heating.

Regional deficiencies were apparent, and New England particularly was sometimes short of food. In 1771, 24 percent of Massachusetts households held acreages too small to feed themselves. When measured by grain alone, two households in five could not reach the minimum requirements for self-sufficiency—a calculation based on a conservative estimate of need, so the shortfall may have been even higher. Wheat and flour imports from the Middle Colonies compensated for the lack, and the inhabitants probably had to buy meat and hay too. Even so, the region did not suffer the agricultural crisis some scholars have claimed, as undernourishment

Table 6.2 Value of Exports to and Imports from England, 1700–1776 (in thousands of pounds sterling)

	Exports	Imports
1700	395	344
1720	468	320
1740	718	813
1760	761	2,612
1775	1,921[a]	4,202[b]
1776	104	55

[a]Prewar peak.
[b]Prewar peak year of 1771.

was not, it seems, widespread. New Englanders earned income through handling the largest share of the interregional trade and from reshipping imports. Boston's stagnation after 1740 was partly the result of other ports in the region appropriating a share of this traffic.

Most of the intercolonial trade was carried by coastal ships, but as roads improved, highest-value goods joined travelers on the increasing number of stagecoaches. Mail volumes among businessmen especially increased, the fastest moving by pony express, the less urgent by coach. The main highway (later U.S. 1) connecting Portsmouth, Boston, Providence, New Haven, New York, Philadelphia, Baltimore, and the Potomac River was the most intense information corridor; it remains so after more than two centuries, whether the mail is carried by road, rail, or air.

Much more is known about external trade than internal because customs and ship records exist. It is clear that colonial exports expanded enormously in the 18th century (table 6.2). To England alone the value of exports tripled between 1720 and 1770, then rose sharply in the 1770s. Even so, exports in these latter years amounted to only 9 to 12 percent of colonial output. Throughout the century the value of commodity imports outweighed exports, largely balanced by revenue from other sources. The terms of trade improved through the century; colonial commodity prices rose relative to import prices. The Navigation Acts restricted some colonial trade into channels set by Parliament, but they were not a major impediment to growth. Indeed, under the umbrella of the British Atlantic system protected by the British navy, the colonies prospered. Periodic downturns did, however, bring hardship to some.

Exports from the South generally exceeded those from the North by almost two to one by value. Between 1768 and 1772 (years for which complete customs accounts exist), the South sent out about three-fifths of the exports, the rest being divided about equally between the Middle Colonies and New England. By far the largest share (one-third) was tobacco from the Chesapeake. Rice, indigo, wheat, flour, bread, Indian corn, boards, and barrel staves were also important southern exports. Flour and bread were the major Middle Colonies contributions, followed by meat, iron, and potash. New England's list was even more diverse: fish, livestock, whale oil, potash, lumber, and masts stood out (fig. 6.5).

Great Britain, the West Indies, and southern Europe were the chief destinations of these exports. As the major enumerated commodity under the Navigation Acts, tobacco went to England. Shipments rose from an average of 17,000 to 25,000 tons in the 1720s to around 50,000 during the early 1770s. British dealers who organized the trade reexported much of it to France, despite periodic wars, and to other European countries. They thus earned the largest share of the profits, a principal cause of suppressed urbanization in Maryland and Virginia. As for other goods, most of the Carolina indigo traveled to England, and most of the grain, flour, and bread to the West Indies and, after 1750, increasingly to southern Europe. About two-thirds of the lower South's rice production found its way to the latter area. Northern Ireland favored flaxseed produced in the North. In all, between 1768 and 1772, ships hauled nearly three-fifths of colonial exports by value to Britain and Ireland, a quarter to the West Indies, and most of the remainder to southern Europe.

Imports grew more rapidly than exports. The West Indies sent sugar, molasses, and rum, though rum was distilled from molasses in all colonies, especially in New England, for export elsewhere in the colonies. Southern Europe provided wine and salt. But in 1760 the largest share, about four-fifths by value, came from Britain. Although colonial production rose in many goods, Americans simply could not get enough of a wide array of consumer goods manufactured in Britain or transshipped from India and the East Indies. An economic takeoff in the 1690s had triggered this activity. The famous

Boston Tea Party in 1773, a protest against taxation, demonstrated that tea had long since ceased to be a luxury. A traveler noted that "homespun was not for the exigencies of the masses," nor slaves either. Most English goods were cheaper than American manufactures and would continue to be so until 1820. The above commodity figures do not include the freight of human beings—slaves and indentured servants—that was needed if major economic expansion were to occur and profits to be made. Such trade was handled mainly by British ships.

Balancing the revenue shortfall from imports' exceeding exports took various forms. Colonists earned revenues in shipping and associated services like insurance and commissions for managing part of the trade. Merchants in the ports of New England and the Middle Colonies earned the largest part, thus partially explaining why the largest cities developed in the North. British investment in ironworks and shipbuilding provided capital. British military spending, especially during the Seven Years' War of the 1750s, also helped to balance the books. Metal money (specie) helped too, though only in small amounts. Recycling debt through bills of exchange, more or less like checks in later times, was a common procedure. As the colonies grew, the supply of this kind of money grew. In contrast to the findings of earlier scholars, modern research has shown that colonial indebtedness was not a burden. After 1776 British capitalists would be only too happy to supply investment capital to an indebted but growing America.

Economic Growth, Incomes, and the Distribution of Wealth

The colonial economy expanded in the aggregate between 1700 and 1775 to about £35 million sterling (over $4 billion in 2001) or about 40 percent of Britain's gross domestic product, compared to a tiny 4 percent in 1700. On a per person basis, however, productivity growth was only about one-half of 1 percent a year, far below what it would be in the next century. The evidence on imports suggests modest increases in income; the North and Middle Colonies experienced a large per capita jump at midcentury before receding to a level about 50 percent higher in 1775 than in 1730.

Increasing population was the main contributor to overall economic growth. New settlements clearly contributed the most to development; farmsteads, land clearing, and fencing in the first years amounted to an infinite rise, relatively, from zero. Subsequently the path in any particular place was haltingly upward as people added goods made at home or locally, or imported. The impact of improved business practices, faster ships, harvesting by scythes with cradles, and increasing services such as the post offices provided must not be undersetimated. Incomes in the white population rose to the point that they were on average probably the highest in the world, estimated at £13 per capita in 1774 (over $1,500 in 2001).

Wealth became more concentrated in fewer hands during the 18th century, leading to greater class differentiation. Most people were in what can be called the middle class, especially in rural areas of the North. A majority were landowners. These "middling sorts," as they were referred to then, were affluent enough to add goods for their comfort. But an elite and near elite class, composed of merchants, leading officials, lawyers, and some manufacturers, making up no more than 20 percent of householders, held over two-thirds of the total assets in 1775. This share had increased substantially over the century. The poor, perhaps 20 percent or more, fell further behind in relative terms, though some were able to rise up the ladder. Building poorhouses and hospitals to serve indigents were minimal steps to help what were considered the "deserving poor" such as the disabled and elderly. Marginal farmers agitated for the government to print more money and offer easier credit terms on land and business, as in the North Carolina Regulator Movement of the late 1760s and in Pennsylvania and Massachusetts. The presence of slaves in the South—two-fifths of the population—diverted attention from the wide gap between poor planters and the great wealthy planters, who emulated the leading rural gentry in Britain.

CAPITALIST SOCIETIES?

In 1744 a British traveler described Albany merchants as men whose "whole thoughts . . . turned upon profit and gain which necessarily makes them live retired and frugall." Writing in his annual *Poor Richard's Almanac,* Benjamin Franklin, arguably the quintessential American,

told readers the same thing: A penny saved is a penny earned. This manner has been called the Protestant ethic, though some Roman Catholics also exhibited the impulse. While it is clear that many first-generation merchants followed such admonitions, some scholars are not convinced that rural dwellers, the farmers, were committed to making money as the prime goal of living. No doubt many were frugal, but most were not seeking to maximize profits. Maximizing was hard to achieve in farming, but a minority in rural areas worked hard to become richer than others or were lucky to have produced the right goods at the right time. Real estate dealing was a major path to wealth, though, like trading, risky and vulnerable to cyclical downturns. It is futile in the end to ask whether colonial American society was capitalist or not. Powerful individuals dominated, but most people reached a level of competence and comfort beyond which they could not, or would not, push. Even today few people pursue making large amounts of money as an end in itself. The major difference between the 18th century and the present is that today most people work for others, whereas then a majority (excluding slaves) worked in and for their own households.

INDEPENDENCE

Intensified interprovincial communication and trade made independence for the colonies possible. The end of the French threat in 1763 took away a major reason for colonial adherence to the British Empire. Enemies thus were sought within the empire, rather than beyond it, and were not hard to find. The parliamentary imposition of special taxes, the Proclamation of 1763 to prevent colonial intrusion onto aboriginal land, and the Quebec Act of 1774 defining the interior of America as part of that province: all these actions angered the colonists from New England southward. But unifying opposition to George III and Parliament was not easy. A case can be made that separation was as much a matter of luck as good management, or was at least induced by bumbling in England. Whatever the reasons, separation did happen. In 1776 Americans formally embarked on redoing their institutions, though the legacy of British law, private property, and a willingness to truck and trade remained strong.

ADDITIONAL READING

Berlin, I., and P. D. Morgan, eds. 1993. *Cultivation and Culture: Labor and the Shaping of Slave Life in America.* Charlottesville: University Press of Virginia.

Cappon, L. J., B. B. Petchenik, and J. H. Long, eds. 1976. *Atlas of Early American History; The Revolutionary Era, 1760–1790.* Princeton: Princeton University Press.

Carson, D., R. Hoffman, and P. J. Albert, eds. 1994. *Of Consuming Interests: The Style of Life in the 18th Century.* Charlottesville: University Press of Virginia.

Daniels, B. C., ed. 1978. *Town and Country: Essays on the Structure of Local Government in the American Colonies.* Middletown, Conn.: Wesleyan University Press.

Earle, C. V. 1992. *Geographic Inquiry and American Historical Problems.* Stanford: Stanford University Press.

Earle, C. V., and R. Hoffman. 1977. "Staple Crops and Urban Development in the 18th-Century South." *Perspectives in American History* 10: 5–78.

Greene, J. P., and J. R. Pole, eds. 1984. *Colonial British America: Essays in the New History of the Early Modern Era.* Baltimore: Johns Hopkins University Press.

Gross, R. A. 1976. *Minutemen and Their World.* New York: Hill & Wang.

Henretta, J. A. 1991. *The Origins of American Capitalism: Collected Essays.* Boston: Northeastern University Press.

Hoffman, R., and P. J. Albert, eds. 1989. *Women in the Age of the American Revolution.* Charlottesville: University Press of Virginia for the United States Capital Historical Society.

Hood, A. D. 1994. "The Gender Division of Labor in the Production of Textiles in 18th-Century Rural Pennsylvania (Rethinking the New England Model)." *Journal of Social History* 27: 537–61.

Innes, S., ed. 1988. *Work and Labor in Early America.* Chapel Hill: University of North Carolina Press.

Jones, A. H. 1980. *The Wealth of a Nation to Be.* New York: Columbia University Press.

Kulikoff, A. 1992. *The Agrarian Origins of American Capitalism.* Charlottesville: University Press of Virginia.

Lemon, J. T. 1972. *The Best Poor Man's Country: A Geographical Study of Early Southeastern Pennsylvania.* Baltimore: Johns Hopkins University Press.

———. 1987. "Agriculture and Society in Early America." *Agricultural History Review* 35, pt.1: 76–94.

———. 1996. *Liberal Dreams and Nature's Limits: Great Cities of North America since 1600.* Toronto: Oxford University Press. See esp. chap. 3.

McCusker, J. J., and R. R. Menard. 1985. *The Economy of British America, 1607–1789.* Chapel Hill: University of North Carolina Press.

Meinig, D. W. 1986. *Atlantic America, 1492–1800.* New Haven: Yale University Press.

Merrens, H. R. 1964. *Colonial North Carolina in the 18th Century: A Study in Historical Geography.* Chapel Hill: University of North Carolina Press.

———, ed. 1977. *The Colonial South Carolina Scene: Contemporary Views, 1697–1774.* Columbia: University Press of South Carolina.

Mitchell, R. D. 1977. *Commercialism and the Frontier: Perspectives on the Early Shenandoah Valley.* Charlottesville: University Press of Virginia.

Nash, G. B. 1979. *The Urban Crucible: Social Change, Political Consciousness, and the Origins of the American Revolution.* Cambridge: Harvard University Press.

Rothenberg, W. B. 1992. *From Market-Places to a Market Economy: The Transformation of Rural Massachusetts, 1750–1850.* Chicago: University of Chicago Press.

Russell, H. S. 1976. *A Long Deep Furrow: Three Centuries of Farming in New England.* Hanover, N.H.: University Press of New England.

Rutman, D. B., and A. H. Rutman. 1994. *Small Worlds, Large Questions: Explorations in Early American Social History, 1600–1850.* Charlottesville: University Press of Virginia.

Shammas, C. 1990. *The Pre-Industrial Consumer in England and America.* Oxford: Clarendon Press.

Ulrich, L. T. 1991. *Good Wives: Image and Reality in the Lives of Women in Northern New England, 1650–1750.* New York: Vintage.

Vickers, D. 1994. *Farmers and Fishermen: Two Centuries of Work in Essex County, Massachusetts, 1630–1850.* Chapel Hill: University of North Carolina Press.

Wacker, P. O., and Clemens, P. G. E. 1995. *Land Use in Early New Jersey: A Historical Geography.* Newark: New Jersey Historical Society.

Wolf, S. G. 1993. *As Various as Their Land: The Everyday Lives of 18th-Century Americans.* New York: HarperCollins.

Wood, J. S. 1997. *The New England Village.* Baltimore: Johns Hopkins University Press.

Zuckerman, M., ed. 1982. *Friends and Neighbors: Group Life in America's First Plural Society.* Philadelphia: Temple University Press.

PART III

EXPANSION

1780s–1860s

What good man would prefer a country covered with forests and ranged by a few thousand savages to our extensive Republic, studded with cities, towns, and prosperous farms, embellished with all the improvements which art can devise or industry execute, occupied by more than 12,000,000 happy people, and filled with all the blessings of liberty, civilization, and religion.

President Andrew Jackson, 1830

The possession of land is the aim of all action, generally speaking, and the cure for all social evils, among men in the United States. If a man is disappointed in politics or love—he goes and buys land. If he disgraces himself he betakes himself to a lot in the West. If the demand for any article of manufacture slackens, the operatives drop into the unsettled lands. If a citizen's neighbours rise above him in the towns, he takes himself where he can be monarch of all he surveys.

Harriet Martineau, *Society in America,* 1837

And is this French Canadian nationality one which, for the good merely of the people, we ought to strive to perpetuate, even if it were possible? I know of no national distinctions marking and continuing a more hopeless inferiority. The language, the laws, the character of the North American continent are English. . . . It is to elevate them from that inferiority that I desire to give to the Canadians our English character.

Lord Durham, *Report,* 1849

7

The Geographical Dimensions
of a New Nation, 1780s–1820s

KENNETH C. MARTIS

In New York City on March 4, 1789, the new Constitution of the United States of America called for the first day of the first session of the First Congress. On April 6 both the Senate and the House of Representatives reached a quorum, organized, and, in a joint convention, counted the electoral votes and selected George Washington the first president of the United States. Washington took the oath of office on April 30. The United States of America officially began.

The Constitution of the United States and the early subsequent laws passed by Congress not only set the political organization of space of the new nation but also defined and enumerated the political, economic, and social freedoms that would dictate and guide the filling of this space. The United States in 1789 was the end product of a long historical and geographical process from the first British settlements at Jamestown and Plymouth, through the colonial period, the Declaration of Independence of July 4, 1776, the Continental Congresses, the Revolutionary War, and the Articles of Confederation government. Indeed, a unique culture of Europeans, Africans, and Native Americans had developed on the East Coast of North America.

The Treaty of Paris of 1783 officially ended the American Revolutionary War. This was the first significant setback in the overseas European colonial system that began in the late 1400s, would last nearly 500 years, and has remnants and legacies remaining today. Britain surrendered an area of nearly one million square miles, twice the area of the original 13 colonies. The new nation stretched from the Atlantic to the Mississippi River, south nearly to the Gulf of Mexico, and north to the Great Lakes (fig. 7.1). The new nation was larger than any country in western and central Europe, a thought unsettling to that continent.

For the British to cede—that is, give up—a territory of such extent was made possible by the terms of an earlier Treaty of Paris (1763) that ended the Seven Years' (or French and Indian) War. The British victory in the 1760s had virtually eliminated French claims from North America, and the Spanish had been relegated to lands in Florida and west of the Mississippi. British hegemony in eastern North American was virtually complete, at least with respect to its European rivals.

North Americans were relentlessly expanding westward, however, and to protect its newly acquired territory, Britain established the Proclamation Line of 1763. The line ran from Maine along the Appalachian Divide through central Georgia to the St. Marys River in Florida. The British deemed the trans-Appalachian region a Native reserve and banned American settlement beyond the Proclamation Line. Whether to protect the Native Americans, control them, or control the restive newcomers from the east, the proclamation did not work. Daniel Boone had blazed a trail through the Cumberland Gap and established Boonesborough in 1775. Throughout the late 1770s and 1780s many others pushed westward, and tens of thousands were in this region by 1783. The Americans were firmly ensconced beyond the crest of the Appalachians, and the American treaty negotiators in Paris in 1783 demanded—and got—this gigantic territory.

In the period from the 1780s to the 1820s—the Early American Period—the founders of the new American nation produced one the most significant advances in constitutional democracy, human rights, and individual freedoms in world history. However, in contradiction, Americans confronted, continued, and condoned the nonexistence of these rights and freedoms for the Native Americans and African slaves within their territory. In 1783 the geographical dimensions of the new nation were set. The question was now how this territory and nation would be organized and governed.

Figure 7.1 National Boundaries, State Land Claims, and the Public Domain

THE POLITICAL ORGANIZATION
OF SPACE

Federalism and the Size of States

The Constitution is the seminal document outlining many principles for the political organization of space in the United States of America, and decisions reached at the constitutional convention of 1787 are critical to understanding the political philosophy that underlies the basic governance of the United States. After the Treaty of Paris many Americans quickly realized that the Articles of Confederation government (proposed in 1777 and fully ratified in 1781) did not provide the political and economic structure for a unified and strong nation. The people with these feelings began to be called Federalists, and they called for a new structure with a stronger central government. Those with the opposite feelings, the Anti-Federalists, warned against a central power that could rule like the colonial power just overthrown. The drafting of a document that could unify 13 politically, socially, and economically diverse and far-flung geopolitical entities was a daunting challenge.

The 1783 treaty deeded a large territory, arousing one of the philosophical debates that pervaded the mid-1780s: the optimal size of a republic. Montesquieu and other political writers considered small units optimal, and the Anti-Federalists were drawn to these ideas. The Federalists rejected the idea that democracy and governance had geographical size limitations, however, as long as representation was just and equitable. The crafting of a government for an extensive republic was the challenge of the learned group of revolutionaries when the constitutional convention met in Philadelphia in the summer of 1787.

The political organization of modern nation-states can be categorized into two types, unitary and federal. Unitary countries have a strong central government in which power is concentrated and laws are somewhat uniform throughout the nation. Federal countries are made up of subunits (states, provinces, or departments) that are given some autonomy and have the power of making local laws. In the nascent political theory of the day, the framers of the Constitution were treading upon new ground. In a sense, both the Federalists and the Anti-Federalists envi-

sioned a federal state, one in which each former colony would retain some power. This basic political philosophy was evident not only in the drafting of the new Constitution but also in its interpretation in the first 50 years of government, during the Civil War, and over the 150 years since. The original constitutional debates were not really on the concept of federalism but on the kind of federalism: how much power the central government should have and how it would be distributed.

One of the central conflicts in the constitutional convention was between the large states and small states. Large ones (for example, Virginia) wanted representation in the federal government to be based on population. Not only would this arrangement give them enhanced power in the new government, but also many had already adopted this philosophy internally for their large areas and expanding populations. The small states (for example, New Jersey) preferred that representation in the new government be by state, each having an equal vote irrespective of population, as was the case under the Articles of Confederation. Many small states had adopted this philosophy internally, as it was well suited to their limited territory and static population. This concept of territorial representation was widespread in colonial America and staunchly from the British tradition. In the constitutional debates and votes, small states consistently lined up against large states on the issue of representation.

The conflict was resolved by the Great Compromise, which created the two-chamber legislative branch of the U.S. government. It remains today: a House of Representatives whose membership is based on state population size as counted and apportioned by a census every ten years, and a Senate with two members from each state irrespective of population size. The compromise was one of the chief factors enabling the Constitution to be ratified. Of course, this system is inherently federal and not completely democratic. In the 21st century the state of Wyoming has fewer people than the lower half of Manhattan or a typical Los Angeles suburb, yet Wyoming, New York, and California each have two senators. In the Senate at least, the citizens of Wyoming have more power than citizens of other states. Indeed, the states of the interior West have significantly more senatorial power than other regions of the United States.

Historically the West has always had a disproportionate share of power in Congress, beginning with the admittance of the trans-Appalachian states in the early 1800s.

A similar debate took place within individual states where, once again, thinkers argued that the colonial concept of legislative representation by town and county, regardless of population numbers, was undemocratic. During the Early American Period state legislatures adjusted, but only slowly and cautiously, and seemingly with reluctance, from the old system to the new. The decision to have two Senate seats per state, whatever the population, is the most obvious carryover from the colonial system of representation by territory.

Locating the Capitals

A major geopolitical event concerned the location of state capitals and the new national capital. A seaboard site for the legislature may have made sense in the Atlantic world of colonial days, but did it for a new nation that was increasingly expanding inland? All but two of the legislatures of the original 13 colonies voted between 1776 and 1812 to relocate their capitals (table 7.1). Part of the motivation was convenience, both for citizens to make their way to the seat of government and for authority to flow efficiently to all corners of the state. But leaders argued also that the more central the capital was to the population, the more democratic the government would be; the perception of being near the seat of power was important.

Those speaking for the small states with established and immutable boundaries—states such as Rhode Island and Delaware—had the luxury of placing their capitals near the geographic center with the assurance that the site was, and would remain, central also to the population. Those representing large states, with extensive unpopulated tracts, agreed that the capital should be near the demographic center but acknowledged that this position was certain to shift westward. It is noteworthy that Pennsylvania and New York were far slower in establishing their capitals—and Pennsylvania had to try twice—than were the smaller, well-settled states (table 7.1). The debate was almost constant in the large states until the 1810s, by which time they were sufficiently well settled that the distance between the political center and the demographic center had diminished into insignificance. An examination of the subsequent siting of new state capitals in the 19th century—and, indeed, of county seats, township schools, and government offices—shows a persistent American appreciation for the geographically central location. Distance mattered.

The location of the national capital was one of the first orders of business in the First Congress,

Table 7.1 Relocation of State Capitals, 1776–1812

State	Date of Removal Law	Old and New Capital Sites
Delaware	May 12, 1777	Newcastle to Dover
Virginia	June 12, 1779	Williamsburg to Richmond
Georgia	January 26, 1786	Savannah to Augusta (interim) to Louisville
	December 12, 1804	Louisville to Milledgeville
South Carolina	March 22, 1786	Charles Town to Columbia
North Carolina	August 4, 1788	New Bern (and others) to Raleigh
New Jersey	November 25, 1790	Burlington, Perth Amboy (and others) to Trenton
New York	March 10, 1797	New York City (and others) to Albany
Pennsylvania	March 30, 1799	Philadelphia to Lancaster
	February 21, 1810	Lancaster to Harrisburg
New Hampshire	1808	Portsmouth (and others) to Concord
Rhode Island	Rotating[a]	among Newport, Providence, East Greenwich, South Kingston, and Bristol
Connecticut	Rotating[a]	Hartford and New Haven

[a]The state legislature meeting place was shifted among selected towns.

Source: Zagarri, 151.

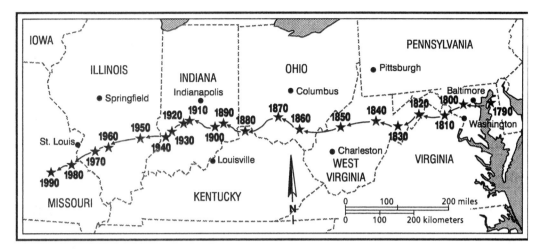

Figure 7.2 U.S. Center of Population, 1790–1990

which had assembled in New York City, the temporary seat of government; the inauguration of George Washington in 1789 had occurred there too. In 1790 the capital was moved to Philadelphia, a more central location, but still temporary. Conditions were far from satisfactory. Article 1, section 8, of the Constitution gives Congress the power "to exercise exclusive legislation in all cases whatsoever, over such district (not exceeding ten miles square) as may, by cession of particular states, and acceptance of Congress, become the seat of the government of the United States." James Madison and others agreed that ease of attendance demanded a central situation. Madison added that "the feelings of the component parts of the community" (that is, all sections, including the South) must be considered.

Dozens of locations were reviewed, from New York south to Virginia. Political intrigue and vote trading were rampant in the determination, and in the end, centrality again played a key role. The permanent new national capital would be on the Potomac River. The Potomac was between the North and the South, but historians consider this decision not to have been a question of a slave section versus a free section since the capital would be located partly in Maryland and partly in Virginia, both slave states. The Potomac was also central in the geography of population (fig. 7.2), and it would provide river access to the interior and the westwardly expanding population. Congress gave President Washington the power to choose the exact site of the District, and in 1800 the capital

was finally moved from Philadelphia to the District of Columbia. Again, as in the location of state capitals, the newly emerging ideas of democracy, republicanism, and representation influenced geographic location and the political organization of space.

LAND CESSIONS AND THE PUBLIC DOMAIN

The States

Although by the Treaty of Paris in 1783 the British officially ceded trans-Appalachian land to the Confederation government, the former colonies had coveted and claimed this territory far back into the colonial period. Eight of the 13—Massachusetts, New Hampshire, Connecticut, New York, Virginia, North Carolina, South Carolina, and Georgia—had claims to western lands (fig. 7.1). Some early colonial charters were vague with respect to boundaries, especially the western end. Not only did the colonies claim these lands and eye them for revenue, but also many wealthy and influential individuals and land speculators were involved. Determining which level of government would have jurisdiction over state claims to trans-Appalachian land is one of the first critical issues faced by Americans after the Declaration of Independence.

Virginia had the largest western land claim. After long and arduous debate, Virginia agreed in 1781 to give up all lands north of the Ohio

River, and the Articles of Confederation, drafted in 1777, were finally ratified. Interestingly, Thomas Jefferson's argument within the Virginia legislature to give up these claims was that he feared that democracy at the state level could not be assured over such a large area. New York, with the second-largest claim, turned over its lands in 1782, followed by Virginia in 1784. While most ceding took place in the 1780s the last formal surrender, by Georgia, did not occur until 1802. All ceded lands were now part of the public domain. The only other piece of disputed territory was Vermont, claimed by both New York and New Hampshire. These claims were settled in 1791, and the United States admitted the first new state, Vermont, in that year.

The western lands most settled by Americans were eastern Kentucky (further ceded by Virginia in 1789) and central and eastern Tennessee (ceded by North Carolina in 1790). In fact, in the First Congress Kentucky was a separate Virginia congressional district and sent a Virginian to the House of Representatives. Likewise, the Tennessee region of North Carolina was a separate district and sent a North Carolina member to Congress. After these areas were ceded, Kentucky was admitted as the 15th state in 1792 and Tennessee the 16th in 1796. Because of their early settlement history, both Kentucky and Tennessee were given title to the lands within their boundaries. All future states, except West Virginia and Texas, would go through a territorial process of federal government supervision before admittance. At the beginning of the territorial process the federal government held ownership of all land as part of a public domain. However, before the public domain could be disposed of, the rights of the Natives had to be addressed.

Native Americans

The confrontation between Native Americans and European Americans is one of the saddest aspects of American history. Active hostilities began with the first British settlements and lasted to the end of the Plains Indian wars in the 1870s and the termination of organized resistance in the late 1880s. Sporadic confrontations, legal battles, and legacies continue into the 21st century.

The general English colonial policy was to claim sovereignty rights over large areas, while at the same time recognizing the soil rights (or tillage rights) of each tribe. The English believed that European occupance of the land could only be achieved by treaty. Treaties in theory were legal documents in which autonomous Native nations ceded land to the Crown or one of its colonies. In many cases, however, the sequence started with settlers moving in and confrontation resulting, followed by wars and only then by a treaty.

The British cession of the trans-Appalachian lands to the United States in 1783 had grave consequences for the Native Americans. By the Proclamation Line of 1763 British authorities had set aside this area as a Native reserve and had prohibited American settlement beyond the mountains. This area was legally now in the hands of the Americans, however, Proclamation Line or not, and pent-up demand after the Revolutionary War, as well as a rapidly increasing population in the East, caused thousands of American settlers to go west seeking land. A new era of conflict and wars between Natives and migrants began in the 1780s and was destined to last for decades. The U.S. government generally continued the British precedent of proclaiming sovereignty but was prepared to recognize soil rights and negotiate treaties. The Northwest Ordinance of 1787 demonstrates good intentions. Article 3 reads: "The utmost good faith shall always be observed towards the Indians; their lands and property shall never be taken from them without their consent; and, in their property, rights, and liberty, they shall never be invaded or disturbed, unless in just and lawful wars authorized by Congress; but laws founded in justice and humanity, shall from time to time be made for preventing wrongs being done to them, and for preserving peace and friendship with them."

Hundreds of treaties were contracted with tribes between the Appalachians and the Mississippi River from the 1780s through the 1820s. Most were preceded by intrusive white settlement, confrontation and resistance by the Natives, war, peace, intrigue, and fraud—and only at the end the treaty itself. This process continued relentlessly westward until the late 1820s (fig. 7.3). The major eastern tribes all signed treaties with the federal government as new settlement slowly pushed west, first along river routes and then on better farmland inland. Some tribes still legally held land in the 1820s: the Cherokee in Georgia, North Carolina, and

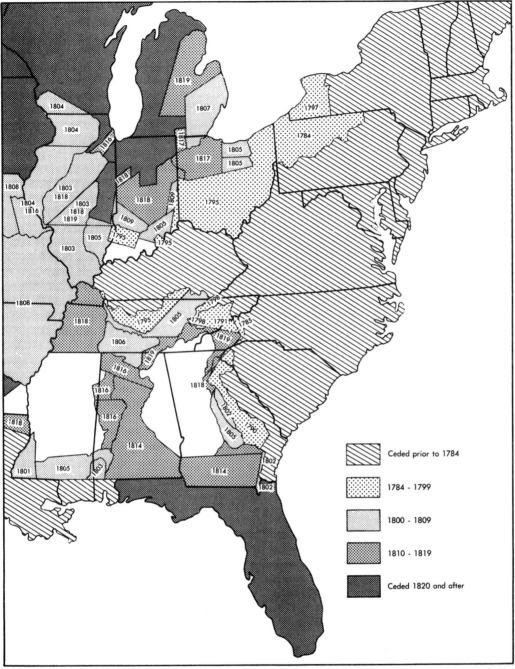

Figure 7.3 Native American Land Cessions, 1784–1819

Tennessee; the Creek in eastern Alabama; the Chickasaw in northern Mississippi; and the Choctaw in central Mississippi.

American Native policy in the East changed under the presidency of Andrew Jackson, elected in 1828. In his first message to Congress, he declared that Natives could no longer be treated as independent sovereign people with soil rights and in total control of their land. The upshot was the Indian Removal Act of 1830, one of the most despicable laws in U.S. history ever to be passed. All remaining Native Americans east of the Mississippi River would be removed—forcibly if necessary—from their ancestral lands to an area west of the Arkansas Territory, now the state of Oklahoma. Congress chose to disregard the fact that by this time many of the remaining eastern Natives—particularly the Cherokee—were assimilated into American society. The Cherokee had developed a written language, practiced democratic ways in tribal governance, and had converted to Christianity, and some had intermarried with whites. Many of them were sedentary commercial farmers or owned businesses, and some even owned black slaves and participated in plantation cotton cultivation. The Cherokee fought the Removal Act in court, but, in spite of the sympathy of Chief Justice John Marshall and others, lost all substantive rulings. The final treaty, in 1833, included a cash settlement. The U.S. Army carried out the removal to Oklahoma, and the subsequent Trail of Tears route west turned out to be a long march in which a quarter of the Cherokee died from hardship and starvation.

As a radical interpretation, the Euro-American and Native American relationship in the East from the 1780s to the early 1830s may be seen—to use a very modern term—as slow, methodical ethnic cleansing. Another interpretation is that outright warfare was much less common than popularly supposed, that there were conflicting tribal claims in many areas, and that the American government tried to continue treaty arrangements with a people who were slow to adapt, especially with respect to such areas of low Native settlement as the vast hunting grounds. In fact thousands of Natives, and many settlers, were killed by war. Yet tens of thousands of Native Americans became integrated into settled American society, and millions of citizens today trace their heritage in part to Native ancestry. The final fact, however, is that owing to treaty, war, geno-

cide, intimidation, removal, or integration, Natives are found today in the eastern United States in only a few small areas.

LAND DIVISION

The Europeans viewed North American land, its soil and accompanying natural resources, as an incredibly valuable storehouse of riches for the taking. From the earliest Dutch purchase of Manhattan Island from the Native Americans to the British and then the American treaties, land was slowly ceded by the original occupants to the migrants. From the earliest colonial settlements, through the westward march of the American frontier, to today's speculative urban and suburban housing and property markets, many Americans have viewed land as primarily a commodity to be examined, bought, improved, sold, and resold, hopefully all for a profit. This view of the earth differs radically from the Natives', who by tradition held land in common, considered some as sacred, and, in general, viewed land as "Mother Earth." Native American tribes had few formal boundaries, but they did organize space in informal and functional ways. Each tribe occupied certain spaces that they considered exclusively theirs. Many intertribal conflicts were over land and resources, exacerbated by differing mental maps each group held of their respective spaces.

The concept of formal, private landownership and its transfer may be traced back to postfeudal Europe and beyond and has important legal and geographical consequences; it needed the support of a formal legal system. Ownership and occupancy must be defined in written words in a document such as a land deed. To ensure accuracy and the orderly transfer for all buyers, sellers, and adjacent landowners, the message in these words was, in America, more and more frequently delimited on maps. Surveyors would demarcate the tangible expression of those deeds by physically staking or marking boundary points on the ground itself. Furthermore, all documents would require secure and locally accessible housing in, say, a county courthouse.

Metes and Bounds

In North America, administrators used three basic methods of property land division: metes and bounds, rectangular, and French long lots. In the original 13 colonies, plus Vermont, Kentucky, and Tennessee, the metes and bounds system prevails. Named land features (both physical and human) describe and enclose property parcels. It is a British tradition and was refined in North America with the use of compass directions and measured distances as surveying techniques grew more complex in the 1700s. Properties defined by metes and bounds were usually oddly shaped, and many times had no straight lines (fig. 7.4). A hypothetical survey deed might read as follows: "Starting at the large willow tree on the Boston Post Road at the corner of the Kent property, follow the high ridge line west to York Creek, follow York Creek some distance upstream until the pointed rock outcrop, then go 200 poles distance N 50° E compass direction along the Franklin property line, then at the deer salt lick follow the animal trail down toward the Boston Post Road, then back to the origin point." In North America, chains, poles, perches, and rods were standard measures of distance, arcane units long since converted into miles, feet, and inches. In places where there were no outstanding ground features, surveyors drove stakes or pins or constructed stone monuments. Identification became problematical with the passage of time, for trees died, streams changed course, and property owners came and went.

Rectangular System

The majority of the American states have been laid out in rectangular land surveys, and no other large area of the earth has such a system of geometric land division lines. Several factors contributed to its popularity in the Early American Period: improved understanding of geometry and surveying techniques, the emerging American heritage of land as a commodity to be bought and sold, the need for government revenue on a systematic basis, the capabilities of individual farming families, and the sense of democracy inherent in offering small equal-looking squares of land.

The origin of the American rectangular land

Figure 7.4 Metes and Bounds Land Division in Western Pennsylvania (author)

survey system is generally credited to Thomas Jefferson—another major decision of his that has had a lasting effect upon the American landscape. After the Treaty of Paris in 1783, the Confederation Congress put Jefferson in charge of drafting a policy on use of and disposal of the public domain. Out of his expertise as a surveyor and his revolutionary zeal came a land division system in keeping with his enlightened, democratic, western scientific mind, and Congress incorporated it (with minor alterations) into the Land Ordinances of 1784 and 1785. The rectangular survey placed on the public domain a uniform geometric grid based on latitude and longitude lines; it had no regard for features of the natural landscape (fig. 7.5a). Starting from east-west baselines and north-south ranges, surveyors divided the land into square townships six miles on each side (fig. 7.5b). Townships were further divided into 36 "sections" each one square mile (or 640 acres); sections could be further divided into halves, quarters, and even quarter-quarters, these latter being 40 acres each. The pattern and the standard farm size for the settling of the American frontier were set.

Jefferson's plan was steeped in political geography. He visualized a democracy of "independent yeoman farmers," each on a family farm of a quarter section or quarter-quarter section. His believed that the township would make the ideal size for a democratic rural community and anticipated that townships governments would be run by local people who shared a common space and lived in proximity. Land, including title, was to be given free to this yeomanry.

But Congress had other plans and in the Northwest Ordinance Act of 1787 ruled that land would be sold, thus providing revenue for the federal government. Under this act, the rectangular survey came into use first in the Northwest Territories, a part of the public domain north of Kentucky and west of Pennsylvania and Virginia. Geographer and surveyor Thomas Hutchins ran what came to be called the Geographer's Line west from a spot on the north (west) shore of the Ohio River where it crossed Pennsylvania's western boundary (fig. 7.6), demarcating the north boundary of the original Seven Ranges of Ohio. The first public domain land was sold there, and the first U.S. federal

Figure 7.5a Aerial Photograph of the Rectangular Land Survey System in Nebraska (author)

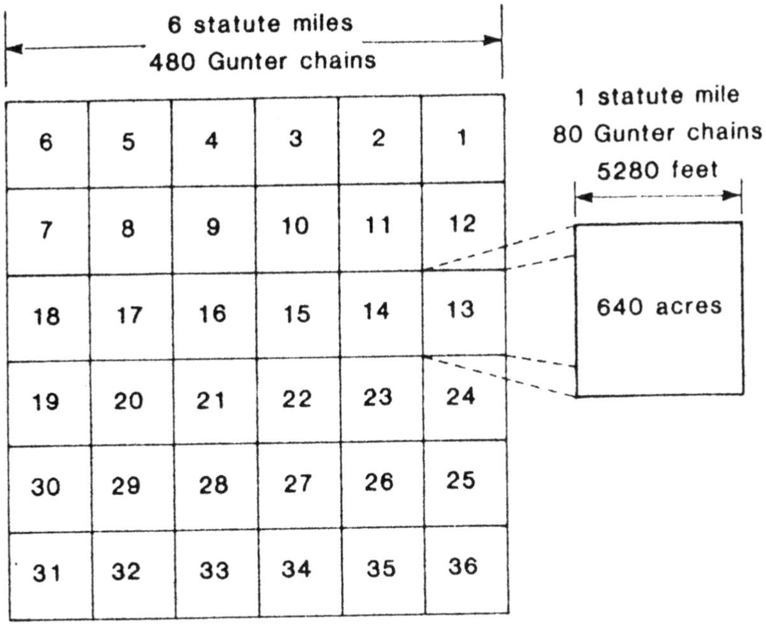

Figure 7.5b American Rectangular Land Survey System

land office opened in Steubenville. Eventually Ohio was divided into 19 survey districts, and in all but 1, townships and the grid pattern dominated. The exception was the Virginia Military Reserve, where both rectangular and metes and bounds surveys can be found. Farther west, where no European settlement occurred prior to land division, entire states would be surveyed in rectangular fashion. Some, such as Colorado, Utah and Wyoming, even have all their state boundaries as survey lines. Texas did not participate in the federal rectangular survey but had a similar system, as do many parts of Canada.

French Long Lots

The first permanent French settlement in North America was at Port Royal (now Annapolis Royal, Nova Scotia) in 1605. From this date until 1763 the French claimed and settled a vast area of North America, including Acadia (now the Maritime Provinces), the St. Lawrence River valley, the Great Lakes region, and the Mississippi River valley. French place names in these areas provide evidence of exploration, settlement, claim, or influence. In all areas where permanent French settlement occurred, a land division into long lots is found (fig. 7.7). In this system, parcels of land may be ten times as long as they are wide and are laid out in successive parallel ranges back from a river or road. It is most pervasive and most visible today in Quebec and Louisiana, easily discernible from the air or on topographic maps.

The objective of the long-lot system was to give all settlers direct access to cheap water transportation and river resources. In some cases in Louisiana, long lots also provided for an equitable division of the best nonswampy levee land; in Quebec people shared equally in the narrow band of alluvial soils in the river valleys. Where population numbers outgrew waterfront sites, a second row of long lots was surveyed along a road parallel to the river, and further rows—*rangs* in French—were added as needed. The narrow lots meant that houses were built close together, giving a sense of community quite in contrast to the farmhouses in the rectangular system, standing isolated on their square properties. Although long lots served their purpose in the early settlement period, the French system of inheritance caused lengthwise subdivision, frequently making parcels too narrow to be worked efficiently. Beginning with the opening of the Erie Canal in the 1820s and throughout the 19th century, agricultural competition

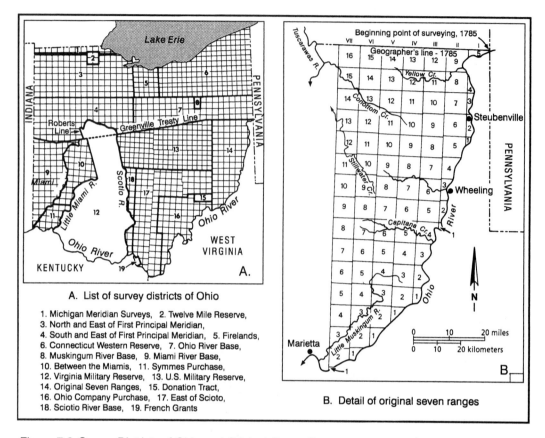

A. List of survey districts of Ohio

1. Michigan Meridian Surveys, 2. Twelve Mile Reserve,
3. North and East of First Principal Meridian,
4. South and East of First Principal Meridian, 5. Firelands,
6. Connecticut Western Reserve, 7. Ohio River Base,
8. Muskingum River Base, 9. Miami River Base,
10. Between the Miamis, 11. Symmes Purchase,
12. Virginia Military Reserve, 13. U.S. Military Reserve,
14. Original Seven Ranges, 15. Donation Tract,
16. Ohio Company Purchase, 17. East of Scioto,
18. Sciotio River Base, 19. French Grants

B. Detail of original seven ranges

Figure 7.6 Survey Districts of Ohio and Original Seven Ranges. Virginia Military Reserve (12) and Original Seven Ranges (14)

from large farms in other areas of the United States and Canada grew. In recent years long-lot properties have been reconsolidated along the St. Lawrence and Mississippi Rivers not only for larger agricultural units but also for industrial and residential uses.

When President Jefferson negotiated the purchase of the Louisiana territory from France in 1803, areas of French (and Spanish) settlement became subject to the rectangular survey system. This was also the case upon the purchase or annexation of other large areas such as Florida (in 1819), the Mexican southwest (in 1845), and Oregon (in 1846). In almost all cases acceptance of U.S. citizenship by the long-term European occupants entitled them to keep their land. The rectangular survey was drawn only in areas where no previous land division existed, as in California where the so-called Spanish Land

Grant areas, usually a version of metes and bounds, remain visible.

POPULATING THE TRANS-APPALACHIAN REGION

The Frontier in American Geography

The first U.S. census in 1790 enumerated a population of nearly 4 million people (table 7.2). By 1820 population had more than doubled, to over 9.5 million and by 1830 had more than tripled to nearly 13 million. Numbers were increasing by over a third each decade, an incredible rate of growth. More than 97 percent of Americans lived east of the Appalachians in 1790 (table 7.3 and fig. 7.8); just a few had made it west, mostly to Kentucky and Tennessee. However, by

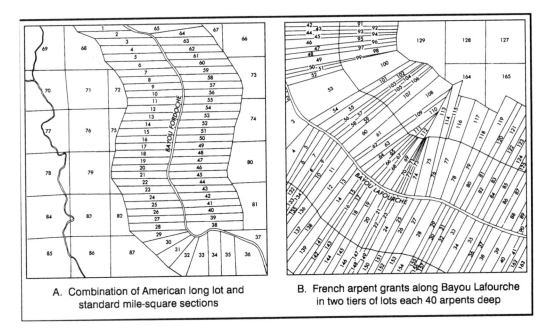

A. Combination of American long lot and
standard mile-square sections

B. French arpent grants along Bayou Lafourche
in two tiers of lots each 40 arpents deep

Figure 7.7 Long Lots in Southern Louisiana

1820 over 2 million lived across the mountains, nearly 25 percent of the population. Westward expansion was well under way (fig. 7.2). In 1790, 95 percent of the population was rural and mostly agrarian, and even the ten largest urban places were tiny (table 7.4). Forty years later, urban places were indeed larger, for trade was growing and industrialization was under way, but Americans were still over 90 percent rural. Population growth in this era meant taking land for farms in the West.

The frontier defines American population expansion beginning in the 1780s and continuing for fully a century. The frontier was the meeting place of white settlement, wilderness, and Native Americans—a steadily shifting locale for self-sufficient living that Americans considered wild, primitive, and dangerous. Despite the risks, the push factors in the East—crowding and worn-out and expensive land—and the pull factors of opportunity and inexpensive fertile farmland in the West lured millions of people.

One of the most famous articles in American historiography linking geography and history is the 1893 classic by Frederick Jackson Turner, "The Significance of the Frontier in American History." Turner contends that Americans were not simply transplanted Europeans but products of the American experience, of which a

Table 7.2 U.S. Population, 1790–1830

Census Year	Population	Decade % Increase	Places 2,500+	% Rural	% Urban	% White	% Black (slave/free)
1830	12,860,702	33.4	90	91.2	8.8	81.9	18.1 (86.2/13.8)
1820	9,638,453	33.1	61	92.8	7.2	81.6	18.4 (86.8/13.2)
1810	7,239,881	36.4	46	92.7	7.3	81.0	19.0 (86.5/13.5)
1800	5,308,483	35.1	33	93.9	6.1	81.1	18.9 (89.1/10.9)
1790	3,929,214	—	24	94.9	5.1	80.7	19.3 (92.1/7.9)

Source: U.S. Bureau of the Census

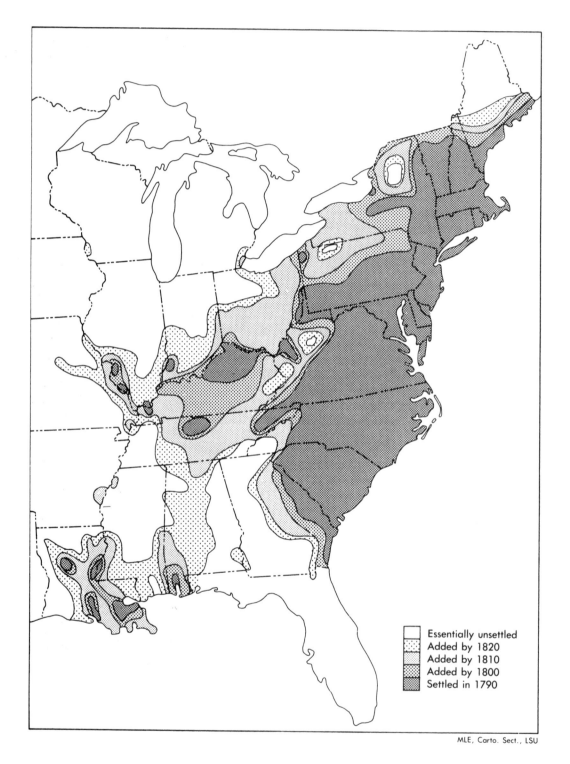

Figure 7.8 Expansion of Settlement, 1790–1820

Legend:

- Essentially unsettled
- Added by 1820
- Added by 1810
- Added by 1800
- Settled in 1790

Table 7.3 Population of the States 1790–1830

State	1790	1800	1810	1820	1830
Old States—Atlantic Coast States					
Maine[a]	96,540	151,719	228,705	298,335	399,455
New Hampshire	141,885	183,858	214,460	244,161	269,328
Vermont	85,425	154,465	217,895	235,981	280,653
Massachusetts	387,787	422,845	472,040	523,287	610,408
Rhode Island	68,825	69,122	76,931	83,059	97,199
Connecticut	237,946	251,002	261,942	275,248	297,675
New York	340,120	589,051	959,049	1,372,812	1,918,600
New Jersey	184,139	211,149	245,562	277,575	320,823
Pennsylvania	434,373	602,365	810,091	1,049,458	1,348,233
Delaware	59,096	64,273	72,674	72,749	76,748
Maryland	319,728	341,548	380,546	407,350	447,040
Virginia[b]	747,610	886,146	983,152	1,075,069	1,220,978
North Carolina	393,751	478,103	555,500	638,829	737,987
South Carolina	249,073	345,591	415,115	502,741	581,185
Georgia	82,548	162,686	252,433	340,989	516,823
New States—Trans-Appalachian States					
Kentucky (1792)	73,677	220,955	406,511	564,317	687,917
Tennessee (1796)	35,691	105,602	261,727	422,823	681,904
Ohio (1803)		45,365	230,760	581,434	937,903
Louisiana (1812)			76,556	153,407	215,739
Indiana (1816)		5,641	24,520	147,178	343,031
Mississippi (1817)		7,600	31,306	75,448	136,621
Illinois (1821)			12,282	55,211	157,445
Alabama (1821)		1,250	9,046	127,901	309,527
Missouri (1821)			19,783	66,586	140,455
United States	3,938,214	5,300,336	7,208,586	9,592,008	12,733,677

[a]Maine is part of Massachusetts until becoming a separate state in 1820.
[b]Western Virginia is part of Virginia until becoming the separate state of West Virginia in 1863.

constantly moving frontier was the most significant part. Here class distinctions lessened, political equality grew, unlimited economic opportunity existed, and individualism flourished. The frontier experience began with the Atlantic coast colonial settlements and moved westward until what the U.S. census, Turner, and others recognized as the closing of the frontier in the 1880s. Many have described the frontier as a line moving steadily westward, as in Georgia (fig. 7.8). However, there are many instances of its leapfrogging ahead while other areas have been bypassed; there is no easy generalization. Turner's thesis evokes many possible questions. Can the American fascination with firearms today be traced back to the frontier experience? Is the American disregard for the environment until the 1960s a legacy of the promise of endless natural resources on the frontier?

Heading for the Best Land

The surge of Americans across the Appalachians beginning in the 1780s and 1790s was guided by geographical features both on the grand and local scales. In a region with virtually no roads, rivers were the highways into the wilderness, first and foremost. They not only afforded access to settlement and promise of future commerce but also were potential paths for exporting products. The Great Lakes served a similar function, making land near Lake Erie in Ohio and southern Ontario, for example, quite desirable. Rivers, the Great Lakes, and their connecting

Table 7.4 Top Ten U.S. Urban Places, 1790 and 1830

1790 Rank	Place	Population	1830 Rank	Place	Population
1	New York, N.Y.	33,131	I	New York, N.Y.	202,589
2	Philadelphia, Pa.	28,522	2	Baltimore, Md.	80,620
3	Boston, Mass.	18,320	3	Philadelphia, Pa.	80,462
4	Charleston, S.C.	16,359	4	Boston, Mass.	61,392
5	Baltimore, Md.	13,503	5	New Orleans, La.	46,082
6	Northern Liberties, Pa.*	9,913	6	Charleston, S.C.	30,289
7	Salem, Mass.	7,921	7	Northern Liberties, Pa.*	28,872
8	Newport, R.I.	6,716	8	Cincinnati, Ohio	24,831
9	Providence, R.I.	6,380	9	Albany, N.Y.	24,209
10	Marblehead, Mass.	5,661	10	Southwark, Pa.*	20,581

*District
Source: U.S. Bureau of the Census

canals were the focus of the western transportation system until the advent of the railroads in the 1840s.

Beyond the Appalachians the river systems flow westward in the Mississippi River watershed. Access to the West was through natural gaps in the mountains, and here adventurers had beaten tracks—perhaps too grandly called roads—to the headwaters of navigable rivers. The Wilderness Road passed through the Cumberland Gap in Tennessee; the National Road reached the Ohio River at Wheeling, Virginia (after 1863 West Virginia), in 1818. The Mohawk Gap west of Albany was navigable above the rapids at Schenectady, routing people onward to Buffalo. Land on or near the Ohio River and major tributaries such as the Kanawha, Tennessee, and Wabash became particularly valuable; land sales in the original Seven Ranges in southeastern Ohio were strongest near the river. Population grew sufficiently that Ohio became eligible for statehood and was admitted as the 17th state in 1803 (fig. 7.9). In Louisiana, long settled by French, Spanish, and French Acadians, American penetration boomed after the Louisiana Purchase in 1803 (fig. 7.8). Settlement spread up the river from New Orleans, and Louisiana became the 18th state (and the first noncontiguous one) in 1812 (fig. 7.9).

Topography and soil significantly influenced settlement geography. Areas of sand, rock, swamp, and otherwise poor soil occurred widely, and prospective farmers shunned them in favor of fertile soils, well-drained and of good texture. Flatness is always a priority in agriculture, and high relief and steep slopes make farming, especially commercial farming, difficult. Two trans-Appalachian areas that had all the good features were the Bluegrass Region of north central Kentucky and the Nashville Basin of north central Tennessee. The geologic formation and underlying bedrock made the soil in these places exceptional, and the beauty and richness of the rural landscape are still evident today. These areas leapfrogged the frontier line and were settled early in the national period (fig. 7.8).

Appalachia, especially the plateau area, had many of the features settlers tried to avoid. Many parts had high relief, no flat land, and thin acidic soils produced by steep slopes and the native deciduous forest. Much of Appalachia was thinly settled or vacant, and this is the case even today. Settlers subsisted by augmenting their small farm production by hunting, fishing, and gathering. Some settlement did occur in the early American period, but as better land and commercial farming developed farther west and transportation routes opened up across the mountains, Appalachia became more and more bypassed and isolated. The Erie Canal, opened in 1825, is the prime example of this process, providing inexpensive water transportation to and from New York City and the Northeast. By linking the Hudson River at Albany across the Mohawk Valley with Buffalo on the Great Lakes, the canal allowed commercial farming to boom in southern Ontario and Ohio. Increased migration occurred in these areas and farther

Figure 7.9 Creation of New States, 1791–1848

west, increasing economic links and trade between the Northeast and the Old Northwest decade by decade in the period leading up to the Civil War.

The rectangular land survey system was devised in part to sell the public domain in an orderly sequence, and so to provide a steady stream of revenue to the federal government. Administrators in Washington envisioned that, following the signing of a particular treaty with the Natives, Congress would authorize a survey of the area involved, establish a land office, and send in survey teams. Land auctions and sales would be held, title established, and settlement would begin. However, reality was not orderly, and grabbing the best land was far more sensible to prospective settlers than awaiting bureaucratic instructions. Speculators, land companies, and individuals eyed obvious town sites—a river fording point, a junction of two rivers, a harbor, a mountain pass, a defensive position—and these lay well ahead of the frontier and surveyed land.

In fact, then, settlement was likely to start with white squatters—called "actual settlers" in the Land Ordinance of 1785—jumping ahead of survey lines into Native territory and claiming the best lands. Natives naturally enough confronted these apparent impostors, battles ensued, and the U.S. Army was called in to restore order and in some cases expel the squatters. Only at this point was the sequence approved by Congress likely to be followed: treaty signed, survey authorized, land office established, surveyors sent, and land sold. Predictably, disputes arose everywhere between squatters and those who had purchased, or sought to purchase, the same parcels in the intended way. Congress recognized the preemption rights of squatters (protection against land speculators and eligibility for gaining title to claimed land without competition) expressed in many state admittance laws and land laws but at the same time passed "intrusion acts" intended to prohibit squatting. A half-century of uncertainty over squatting and preemption was largely resolved between 1830 and 1841, and all that time trans-Appalachian America had been filling up.

FREE SPACE AND SLAVE SPACE

The American Revolution and the accompanying call for political and economic freedom brought to the fore the most cruel contradiction in American society: "life, liberty, and the pursuit of happiness" for some, and death, slavery and entrenched misery for others. So aware of the contradiction were the framers of the U.S. Constitution that it does not contain the words "slave" or "slavery." In their discussion of the census population figure that would be used for the apportionment of seats in the House of Representatives, the framers deemed slaves to be "other persons" and counted each as three-fifths of a human being. When discussing the end of the slave trade in 1808, the Constitution speaks of the "importation of such persons," thus recognizing the existence of slavery de facto, and therefore condoning it. The status of slavery was left up to each individual state, in conformity with the philosophy of federalism. Eventually the states decided on the fate of their fellow human beings along sectional and regional lines.

Like the general population, slavery in British colonial America had been concentrated east of the Appalachian mountains. While slavery was legal and found in every colony, over 95 percent of the slaves were located in the South, concentrated in the tobacco areas of eastern Virginia and Maryland and the Delmarva Peninsula and in the rice and cotton areas of the coastal Carolinas and Georgia. Beginning in the revolutionary period every northern state passed emancipation laws, effective immediately or gradually; they had little to lose, and the moral argument was compelling. Vermont was the first area to ban slavery, in 1777, and Massachusetts the first state, in 1780; New Jersey was the last state in the North to abolish slavery, gradually, beginning in 1804. Some northern states with gradual laws did not rid themselves of slavery completely until the 1840s. By this time the boundary between Pennsylvania and Maryland had taken its place as a clear divide in American geography. Called the Mason-Dixon Line (after its surveyors), it separated the northern "free" states from those to the south, which continued to allow slavery. The Mason-Dixon Line became the symbolic boundary dividing one nation into two different societies moving in two different directions.

The first federal census in 1790 did the earliest count of the racial composition of the United States and reports a population that was one-fifth of African descent (table 7.2). Because of the extremely large European immigration in the 19th century, the percentage of African Americans in the United States was never again so high. Absolute numbers nevertheless grew at a very fast rate until the beginning of the Civil War in 1861, and slavery spread geographically despite the end of the slave trade. The 1790 census also revealed that a slowly increasing percentage of the black population was free, concentrated in the North and especially in the New York City area and in other towns wherever state emancipation laws were coming into effect. In the political fervor of the 1780s even the Virginia legislature liberalized the laws with respect to manumission, and thousands of blacks gained their freedom in this period. Blacks with money could also buy their own freedom, and many skilled laborers did so. Concentrations of free blacks in eastern Virginia and Maryland, and even in some scattered parts of the coastal South, are signs of this process, which was well in evidence by 1830 (table 7.2).

In the 1780s and 1790s not only was the morality of slavery being debated but also in many places its economics. Would "the peculiar institution" survive in competition with free labor and subtropical products grown in other parts of the world? Industrialization in Europe, and eventually in New England, increased the demand for cotton for the textile industry. Eli Whitney's 1793 invention of the cotton gin, which separated the cotton fiber from the pesky cottonseeds, assured the inland spread of cotton in a continuous band across the subtropical American South. This circumstance, along with the need for a long growing season, in turn allowed the profitable growing of cotton with slave labor. Other subtropical products—rice and sugar cane—followed, and the labor-intensive nature of all three gave continuing force to the slave system. One of the first western areas of plantation slave agriculture was southern Louisiana, along the Mississippi River. The area is flat, with rich alluvial soil regenerated by the river, and is well suited for sugar cane. Cotton plantations pushed settlement up the river into the Mississippi and Arkansas Territories and even as far north as western Tennessee and the boot of Missouri. And cotton helped push the frontier westward across the South from Georgia into Alabama and Mississippi and, later, as far as eastern Texas.

The other major component of the plantation slave labor system was tobacco, for which climate is much less restrictive. Tobacco was also a labor-intensive crop and also in great demand, for both export and internal markets. As population grew and new lands opened up, tobacco cultivation spread west from the colonial hearth in eastern Virginia, the Eastern Shore of Maryland, and North Carolina. The spread was discontinuous, jumping over the Appalachians to the Bluegrass of Kentucky, the Nashville Basin of Tennessee, and eventually as far west as Missouri. Thus the slave South was actually two Souths: a tobacco region bordering the northern free states, and a cotton region far from them.

Statehood Two by Two

The geopolitics of states' permitting slavery or not became more and more evident in the Early American Period, and the subject increasingly confrontational. Economic and social differences between North and South dated back to the colonial period, were subdued during the Revolution, but arose again in the constitutional debate and in discussions regarding location of the national capital. The first contested presidential election, in 1796, highlighted the emerging sectional differences in political parties, and the delicate balance of power between free states and slave states became more and more sensitive in Congress. In 1803, the year Ohio became eligible for statehood, there were eight free states and eight slave, making an equal balance of power in the Senate (table 7.5). The Northwest Ordinance of 1787 banned slavery in all new states formed out of this territory, so Ohio entered as a free state, tipping the balance to the North. Equality was restored with the admission of Louisiana as a slave state in 1812. For several decades thereafter, states were admitted in pairs, one slave and one free, to retain sectional balance. Indiana was paired with Mississippi in 1816–17, likewise Illinois with Alabama in 1818–19 (fig. 7.9).

The next territory eligible for statehood under the territorial population provisions was Missouri, a border region with both northern and southern elements in its geography and the origins of its migrants. Missouri applied for admission as a slave state, and when northerners vigorously resisted, the issue was resolved by admitting as a free state Maine (a breakaway from Massachusetts), which became the 23rd state in 1820; Missouri was then admitted as a slave state in 1821, once again restoring balance. However, to placate the North, the Missouri Compromise of 1820 and 1821 banned slavery in any future states to be established north of latitude 36°30' N, the southern boundary of Missouri. This decision temporarily soothed sectional stress, and this line became another of the sacred symbolic divides in American historical geography. Later, when the Missouri Compromise line was seemingly violated, sectional stress would bring the nation to civil war.

The admittance of Missouri in 1821 brought to 9 the number of new states created out of the trans-Appalachian West in less than 30 years. Missouri took the organized states far beyond the Mississippi River into the fringes of the Great Plains. After Missouri there was a noticeable pause in the admittance of new states. The next pair—Arkansas and Michigan—entered in 1836 and 1837, bringing western representation in the Senate up to nearly 40 percent (11 states) among the 26 states at that time (table 7.5).

Migration to the West was continuing at a fast pace in the new nation's first half-century, filling in the good land in the newly created states. The number of members of the House of Representatives from the West continued to grow with each decennial apportionment. Virginia, which was by far the largest state in 1790 (table 7.3), had slipped to third place by 1830, and Ohio had risen from nowhere to fourth. Indeed, in 1830 Ohio was larger than 10 of the original 13 states. Eastern Virginia was stagnating while Ohio was vibrant. Since the size of the congressional delegation is used to determine the size of the electoral college, the West had increasing influence in both congressional and presidential politics. Clearly the West was growing in both population and political power; a new section was emerging.

OLD STATES VERSUS NEW STATES

The needs and desires of the trans-Appalachian population, and the conditions in which they lived, were significantly different from, and even in contradiction to, those of the long-settled areas along the Atlantic Coast. As western power increased, tension between West and East intensified. It was manifested most clearly in three major issues before Congress: land sales, internal improvements, and tariff policy. These

Table 7.5 Slave States and Free States, 1790–1860

Southern Slave States	Northern Free States
Deep South	New England
Virginia	Maine
North Carolina	New Hampshire
South Carolina	Massachusetts
Georgia	Connecticut
Tennessee (1796)	Rhode Island
Louisiana (1812)	Vermont (1791)
Mississippi (1817)	
Alabama (1819)	Middle Atlantic
Arkansas (1836)	New York
Florida (1845)	New Jersey
Texas (1845)	Pennsylvania
Border	Old Northwest
Delaware	Ohio (1803)
Maryland	Indiana (1816)
Kentucky (1792)	Illinois (1818)
Missouri (1821)	Michigan (1837)
	Wisconsin (1848)
	Great Plains
	Iowa (1846)
	Minnesota (1858)
	Kansas (1861)*
	Pacific Coast
	California (1850)
	Oregon (1859)

*Kansas is included in the report called for by the law enabling the 1860 census; hence it is included in this table.

three concerns are intricately linked, and how they were addressed gives a clear picture of the emerging economic geography of the period.

Congress envisioned obtaining vast revenues by selling the public domain in parcels as large as 5,760 acres (nine sections). This approach would make sales so expensive that, in effect, only speculators and large land companies, often with New England money, could purchase them. Westerners and those in sympathy with Jefferson's "independent yeoman farmer" argued instead for a liberal policy: inexpensive (or even free) land, to be sold in small parcels, and only to actual settlers. They sought a generous credit system and squatters' preemption rights. This disagreement came to the fore in the Land Sale Act of 1796, and it clearly favored the eastern view. Each plot was to be no smaller than 640 acres and sell at a price not lower than $2.00 per acre, payable within one year. An outlay of $1,280 and a parcel of that size were absurdly beyond the needs and resources of most family farmers, capable of tending perhaps 40 acres and lucky if they saw $200 gross in a year. As the West gained population and power, the more liberal land policy indeed gradually arose, encouraging migration westward and favoring the common smallholder. Successive Congresses reduced the land price and minimum size and gave preemption rights; private companies, such as newly emerging insurance companies in New England, entered the credit business. The Homestead Act of 1862 was the culmination of 80 years of debate and shifting regional attitudes; thereafter settlers could claim up to 160 acres for free.

The second great East-West issue to emerge out of the Early American Period concerned internal improvements: the building and maintenance of roads, bridges, canals, harbors, river channels, locks, and dams. An early debate, before 1800, questioned the role of each level of government—national, state, and local—in such activity. Many commentators felt it was unconstitutional for the federal government to be involved in internal improvements and held that the states, or indeed private money and private companies, should do this work. The old seaboard states had always thought that Atlantic coast harbor improvements deserved federal support, yet they balked when the new western states began to ask for federal help for their internal improvements. The Atlantic states felt western improvements were being made at their expense, not only by cutting into their revenue but also by making western areas more accessible and thus luring away their young people and reducing land prices in the East. As a result, most early transportation improvements were done under private, state, and local auspices.

The admittance of Ohio, the first public domain state, in 1803 renewed the debate over internal improvements. In 1807 President Jefferson's secretary of the treasury, Albert Gallatin, proposed the building of a national road linking the Potomac River at Cumberland, Maryland, with Ohio. A year later he went further, proposing to Congress a vast spending bill for general internal improvements. While this initiative was shelved, Congress did pass the National Road legislation after great debate, and federally funded construction began in 1811. The precedent of federal involvement in western internal

improvements was set. The National Road—U.S. Route 40 today—reached Wheeling on the Ohio River in 1818 and eventually central Illinois in the late 1830s.

Tariffs were the subject of the third confrontation between East and West. The debate on the amount of taxation on imported goods has been incessant. In the 21st century it is about the North American Free Trade Agreement, the World Trade Organization, or granting most-favored-nation trading status to China. In the early 1790s it concerned Alexander Hamilton's *Report on Manufactures* and his support of high import tariffs to help create American industry. Industry and manufacturing, even of the smallest variety, had been prohibited in the colonies, and even after the Revolution the British continued to regard their former colonies strictly as suppliers of agricultural products and natural resources and consumers of British manufactured goods. American homegrown industry, such as textiles and iron, increased, but this growth required protective tariffs. In 1818 and again in 1824 Congress passed massive new tariffs.

Import tariff policy was linked directly to land sales and internal improvements. Tariffs and land sales were the source of revenue for the federal government. Low land prices called for high tariffs, which meant that imported goods were expensive for the common person. High tariffs were good for the emerging manufacturing areas of the Northeast but would mean retaliatory tariffs by other nations for imported cotton, which was not good for the economy of the South. High tariffs meant more money for western internal improvements that would encourage land sales but also high-priced goods for the yeoman farmer. Tension between the regions and sections was seemingly unavoidable.

THREE SECTIONS

The Early American Period witnessed the development of the West as a new region of the nation. By the 1820s, the United States had three clearly recognizable sections, as spoken of in the literature: Northeast, South, and West. Each section had its own political agenda. All were developing unique and specialized regional economies, linked to one another and to a larger growing world economy, especially in areas bordering the North Atlantic Ocean. In no more than four or five decades, Americans had set up a political, economic, social, and transportation infrastructure new to the world. They were ready to compete vigorously in the coming decades.

ADDITIONAL READING

Berkhofer, R. F., Jr. 1972. "Jefferson, the Ordinance of 1784, and the Origins of the American Territorial System." *William and Mary Quarterly* 29: 231–62.

Block, R. H. 1980. "Frederick Jackson Turner and American Geography." *Annals of the Association of American Geographers* 70: 31–42.

Cappon, L. J., B. B. Petchenik, and J. H. Long, eds. 1976. *Atlas of Early American History: The Revolutionary Era, 1760–1790.* Princeton: Princeton University Press.

Clayton, A. R. L. 1992. "'Separate Interests' and the Nation-State: The Origins of Regionalism in the Trans-Appalachian West." *Journal of American History* 79: 39–67.

Hamilton, Alexander. 1791. *Report on Manufactures.* House Report 31, 2d Cong., 1st sess., December 5.

Hilliard, S. B. 1984. *Atlas of Antebellum Southern Agriculture.* Baton Rouge: Louisiana State University Press.

———. 1972. "Indian Land Cessions." *Annals of the Association of American Geographers* 62, Map Supp. 16.

Jacobs, W. R. 1969. *America's Great Frontiers and Sections.* Lincoln: University of Nebraska Press.

Martis, K. C. 1993. *The Historical Atlas of State Power in Congress, 1790–1990.* Washington: Congressional Quarterly.

Meinig, D. W. 1986. *The Shaping of America: Atlantic America, 1492–1800.* New Haven: Yale University Press.

———. 1993. *The Shaping of America: Continental America, 1800–1867.* New Haven: Yale University Press.

Mitchell, R. D. 1991. *Appalachian Frontiers.* Lexington: University of Kentucky Press.

Paullin, C. O., and J. K. Wright. 1932. *Atlas of the Historical Geography of the United States.* Washington: Carnegie Institution.

Prucha, F. P. 1990. *Atlas of Indian Affairs.* Lincoln: University of Nebraska Press.

Silbey, J. H., ed. 1991. *The United States Congress in a Transitional Era, 1800–1841: The Interplay of Party, Faction, and Section.* New York: Carlson.

Turner, F. J. 1893. "The Significance of the Frontier in American History." *Annual Report of the American Historical Association for the Year 1893.* Washington: American Historical Association.

U.S. Department of Commerce, Bureau of the Census. 1975. *Historical Statistics of the United States from Colonial Times to 1970.* Washington: U.S. Government Printing Office.

U.S. Department of the Interior, Geological Survey. 1976. *Boundaries of the United States and the Several States.* Washington: U.S. Government Printing Office.

———. *National Atlas of the United States.* Public Land Survey System, www.atlas.usgs.gov/plssm.html.

Zagarri, R. 1987. *The Politics of Size: Representation in the United States, 1776–1850.* Ithaca: Cornell University Press.

8

Beyond the Appalachians, 1815–1860

CARVILLE EARLE

Few countries have grown so fast on so many fronts in so short a time as the United States between the American Revolution and the Civil War. In just eight decades, Americans expanded their territory 3-fold, their population 15-fold, their economy 20-fold, and their urban population 30-fold. They also prospered. Americans in 1860 had twice as much income per capita as they did in 1780, and their economy ranked third in riches after Britain and France. These achievements are all the more remarkable in comparative perspective. In a world mostly accustomed to stagnating economies at best and decaying ones at worst, the United States seemed a beacon of growth, prosperity, and progress.

The remarkable success of the American economy in the first half of the 19th century has focused attention on two issues: the pace of American economic growth—that is, the increase in income per capita—and the breadth of economic development—that is, the investments in transportation, communications, urbanization, and manufacturing that help transform agricultural economies to higher levels of productivity. Given the size and geographical diversity of the United States, the growth and development of the American economy necessarily resulted in varying regional patterns. During the years between the fall of Napoleon and the American Civil War, a predominantly commercial, agrarian nation was transformed into a mosaic of three distinctive and specialized economic regions. The northeastern states increasingly specialized in manufacturing located in large urban centers; the South persisted on an agrarian course with emphases on cotton, slavery, and plantations; and the West, including the Ohio River and Great Lakes basins, shifted toward diversified grains and livestock, usually produced on family farms with free labor and marketed through an elaborate urban transport system.

This chapter accents the contributions of trans-Appalachian agriculture to American economic growth and development. My principal propositions are, first, that expansion into this vast region, stretching from the Great Lakes to the Gulf of Mexico and from the Appalachians to the 100th meridian, greatly increased the aggregate and per capita outputs of the American economy; second, that these productivity changes are attributable to the evolution of three specialized agricultural regions, the Cotton, Corn, and Wheat Belts; and third, that these staple crops, with their distinctive requirements for production and marketing, shaped the geographies of labor, rural settlement, urbanization, and commodity marketing in their respective regions.

ECONOMIC GROWTH AND DEVELOPMENT

The spectacular achievements of the American economy between 1815 and 1860 have occasioned a rich literature and three separate, if overlapping, interpretations. The first and the best-known of these interpretations stresses investments in social overhead capital and a leading sector of growth—railroads—as preconditions for economic "takeoff" and sustained growth. The second thesis, associated with Douglass North's regional export-base model, attributes national economic growth to regional specialization and interregional trade. The third thesis sees growth as the consequence of intraregional changes in agricultural productivity and the developmental ramifications of staple crops. What follows is a brief review of these three theories and the criticisms of them.

The United States in 1800 was, according to Walt Rostow, a preindustrial economy poised for rapid economic growth. This transition hinged, however, on substantial investments in social overhead capital that Americans channeled into transportation infrastructure: first for roads, river navigation, and canals, and later for the extension of railroads. These innovations dramatically lowered transport costs, facilitated commerce and exchange within the nation, and effected a "transportation revolution." Although some of Rostow's critics have discounted the significance of railroads in American economic development, even they would concede that transportation improvements played a crucial role in the expansion of the American market.

Rostow's emphasis on the nation's aggregate economic performance tends to obscure the enormous regional variations and interdependencies in the American space economy. As Douglass North has reminded us, American economic growth was simultaneously a spatial process of regional specialization and interregional trade. In North's view, the United States divided after 1815 into three specialized macroregions—the industrial Northeast, the cotton South, and the grain-and-livestock complexes of the Middle West—all linked by interregional trade flows. In this interdependent economy, cotton was king. The cotton South generated sizable export earnings, provided the Midwest and the Northeast with a large market for their provisions and manufactured goods, and thereby stimulated interregional trade, economic growth, and development in the nation at large.

North's regional model of economic growth touched off a volley of empirical criticism. It soon became evident that the antebellum trade flows theorized by North, however plausible in theory, simply did not exist. Several studies documented the modest volume of trade in western provisions to southern markets; others demonstrated that most southern planters produced sufficient corn and pork for their own needs, thus obviating the need for western provisions. Nor was there much evidence for southern consumption of northeastern manufactures. In the end, only one of North's interregional trade links—the commodity flows between the Northeast and the Middle West—has survived scholarly scrutiny.

The breakdown of North's model poses some vexing questions. Why did Americans defy the economic principle of rationality and the economic theory of comparative advantage, regional specialization, and trade? More specifically, why did southern cotton planters raise their own corn and hogs at a time when cotton specialization would have ensured them greater profits, fostered regional complementarity, and encour-

aged the provisions trade with the Middle West? And further, if southern planters spent so little on midwestern provisions and northeastern manufactures, then where did they spend their sizable earnings from the cotton trade?

The collapse of North's thesis of interregional trade has encouraged alternative interpretations that emphasize the intraregional nature of economic growth. Diane Lindstrom's study of greater Philadelphia chronicles the process of growth within one relatively autonomous region. In her view, population growth and internal markets provided the engine for Philadelphia's economic development. In response to the expansion of aggregate consumer demand in the region, entrepreneurs in Philadelphia enlarged the scale of their operations and invested in manufactures that displaced the importation of foreign goods. In Lindstrom's model, as in Adam Smith's, growth is a function of the size of the market, the division of labor, and the sectoral shift to manufacturing. The problem with this neoclassical interpretation is that all of the United States was not Philadelphia. One is left to ponder why New York City and Boston developed in quite different ways, or why the cotton South preferred an agrarian commercialism over industrialization, or why the West tended to reenact Philadelphia's experience after 1840.

One of the difficulties with these theories of American economic growth is their tendency to neglect agriculture. In a nation where the majority of the population practiced farming or planting and where, as late as 1860, agriculture contributed perhaps 60 percent of commodity output, it can hardly be ignored. Robert Gallman has called attention to agriculture's very substantial contribution to productivity gains beginning in the 1820s—a decade when the Erie Canal commenced operation and settlers began pouring into the trans-Appalachian country. Four decades later, on the eve of the Civil War, these western states and territories produced three-fourths of the nation's cotton crop, three-fifths of its corn, and nearly half its wheat. One of the principal sources of agricultural productivity was the emergence of specialized regions—the Cotton, Corn, and Wheat Belts west of the Appalachians. In the Wheat Belt of the upper Midwest, for example, introduction of the reaper in the 1850s increased both acreage per worker and output per worker. Meanwhile, in the Corn Belt of the lower Midwest, riding cultivators sped up the process of corn tillage and permitted farmers to plant more acres per worker. And in the Cotton Belt, the westward migration of production into the relatively drier regions of the Mississippi Valley reduced the extent of weed invasion and, in turn, increased the acres a single worker could cultivate. In each of these regions, environmental and technological changes boosted agricultural output per worker by 25 percent or more.

In addition to these contributions to productivity, the staples of wheat, corn, and cotton shaped the trajectories of regional economic development west of the Appalachians. Each crop imposed distinctive production and marketing requirements on its respective region, each with ramifications for rural labor, settlement patterns, and regional urban wage rates in the first instance; and transport development and urbanization in the second. Perhaps the most important requirement of staple production is the seasonal nature of the demand for labor; the key distinction is between the broadcast grains, such as wheat, that require few days of labor, mainly at harvest time, and the planted crops, such as cotton and corn, that require multiple days of effort, particularly in tillage. Wheat farmers consequently preferred to hire day laborers for the short harvest of early summer, while cotton planters preferred slaves for the many days of planting, tillage, and picking. Rural settlement reflected these divergent demands for labor, with northern farmers residing on family farms and drawing on rural laborers, and cotton planters residing on plantations and relying, when possible, on slave labor.

The seasonality of rural staples also influenced the development of cities owing to seasonal effects on urban wage rates. In farming regions, rural laborers experienced long periods of unemployment, and hence they accumulated small annual earnings; consequently, a relatively low urban wage was usually sufficient to induce them to migrate to city jobs. Conversely, rural whites in the cotton South labored much of the year either as small planters or as overseers; hence rural earnings were higher, as were the urban wages required to lure white workers to the city. Contemporary estimates from the 1850s suggest that unskilled urban wages in the Cotton Belt were double those in the upper Middle West; in other words, a midwestern urban entrepreneur could hire two workers for every one

hired by his southern counterpart. The seasonality of broadcast cereal farming thus created a pool of cheap rural labor that was especially favorable for urban growth and the expansion of manufactures.

The urban wages prevailing under staple regimes go a long way in explaining the remarkable differences in city sizes in the Middle West and the South, but these differences also reflected variations in the marketing requirements of regional staples. Commodities such as wheat, corn, and livestock products were perishable, heavy, and bulky, and this meant that marketing costs were considerably higher than for cotton or tobacco. For example, corn shipped from the Illinois farm gate to New York City in the 1850s carried a 50 percent price margin, which was distributed among the various middlemen in the region's urban transport system. Cotton, by contrast, customarily carried marketing margins of just 7 to 10 percent. Total earnings for staple marketing rarely accounted for more than a fifth of the economic base of northern or southern cities; still, these expenditures provided the financial foundations for regional urban systems and the scaffolding for urban and industrial growth.

These three theoretical perspectives on the takeoff of the American economy—the transportation revolution, regional interdependence, and the exacting requirements of staple agriculture—come to a point in the trans-Appalachian region before 1860. The several geographical processes unfolding there would transform the region and underwrite the exceptional achievements of the early American economy.

THE POLITICAL-ECONOMIC CONTEXT FOR AMERICAN TAKEOFF

In 1815 the Atlantic world was at peace and would remain so, more or less, for several generations. In the afterglow of Napoleon's defeat, European statesmen boasted of having created a balance of international power and a durable peace. Americans meanwhile were relieved that the war-weary British had decided to conclude the War of 1812 in a draw. With peace in sight, Americans envisioned "halcyon days" and "flush times," the resumption of international trade, the expansion of domestic investment, and a general prosperity.

Americans adapted swiftly to the new political-economic environment. Their relative prosperity as neutral traders during the Napoleonic Wars notwithstanding, Americans welcomed the outbreak of peace and the prospects of unfettered trade. With peace at hand, Americans joined with Europeans in the belief that international markets would operate at maximum efficiency and sustain limitless economic growth and development. In this instant of renewed economic confidence, Americans laid the foundations for a transportation revolution.

THE TRANSPORTATION REVOLUTION AND TRANS-APPALACHIAN AGRICULTURAL EXPANSION

The American takeoff into economic growth took place amidst this buoyant atmosphere of peace and anticipated prosperity. Transport improvements led the way. Two years after the Napoleonic Wars, the state of New York authorized funds for the construction of a canal—the Erie—that would link midwestern grain farmers with New York City and European markets. In that same year, Mississippi River entrepreneurs touted a new era shortly after the shallow-draft steamboat the *Washington* made the trip upstream from New Orleans to Louisville in just 25 days. Both events signaled confidence in the international economy and the trans-Appalachian region, provided that Americans could overcome the high costs of inland transportation. This was a large proviso given the prohibitive costs of wagon transport. With overland freight rates running in excess of 15 cents per ton-mile on even the best roads, farmers rarely shipped agricultural goods more than 100 miles overland.

Navigable rivers and flatboats offered a far cheaper mode of transport for midwestern farmers. Downriver rates for flatboats were less than 2 cents per ton-mile as early as 1800. At these rates farmers near Pittsburgh found it cheaper to ship their goods over 1,700 miles down the Ohio and Mississippi Rivers to New Orleans and then several thousand miles by ship to Philadelphia than to ship them 300 miles overland. The drawback of flatboats was, of course, that they could not operate upstream. To solve this problem, entrepreneurs along the Mississippi turned to steamboats, which sharply lowered upstream freight rates after 1817 (fig. 8.1).

But neither the steamboat nor the flatboat served the entire trans-Appalachian region. Canals promised greater accessibility. New York's Erie Canal, opened in 1825, carried interregional trade between the upper Midwest and eastern markets, and the various Ohio canals constructed during the late 1820s and early 1830s served as intraregional feeder routes into the Great Lakes and then on to the Erie system. By 1830 Ohio ranked second in canal mileage after New York and had surpassed the Empire State a decade later. As canal construction proceeded, freight rates tumbled to less than a cent per ton-mile by the early 1840s (fig. 8.1).

The trans-Appalachian country had secured two transport outlets for its products by the early 1840s (fig. 8.2). Exports from the northern third of the region moved via intraregional canals to the lakes and then to the Erie Canal or St. Lawrence River; those of the southern two-thirds, via flatboat and steamboat down the Mississippi trunk line to New Orleans. Rail lines added a third outlet during the 1840s and 1850s. Although the Baltimore and Ohio Railroad had introduced the steam locomotive in 1828, and despite the wide recognition of the potential of railroads, rail systems diffused slowly, perhaps because of the heavy investments required. As late as the mid-1840s, investments in rail and canals were nearly the same—in 1840, for example, nearly $15 million in canals and $14 million in railroads. Most of the early rail investments went into the northeastern states, but as freight rates fell and after the British opened their grain markets to foreign producers in 1846, investment shifted westward. In 1851 the Middle West accounted for a third of U.S. rail investment; in 1853, more than half. As annual investments in midwestern railroads rose to nearly $50 million, investments in canal construction plummeted to just $4 million. The result by the late 1850s was an elaborate intraregional rail net in the Middle West and a handful of trunk-line routes to eastern markets. The former served as a feeder system for the main interregional routes: the Great Lakes and Erie Canal system, the southern river route, and, in the 1850s, direct rail lines to New York City, Philadelphia, and Baltimore. The Grand Trunk Railway, opened through British North America in that same decade, provided a direct route eastward from Michigan to tidewater on the St. Lawrence River and at Portland, Maine. In the Midwest, rail-

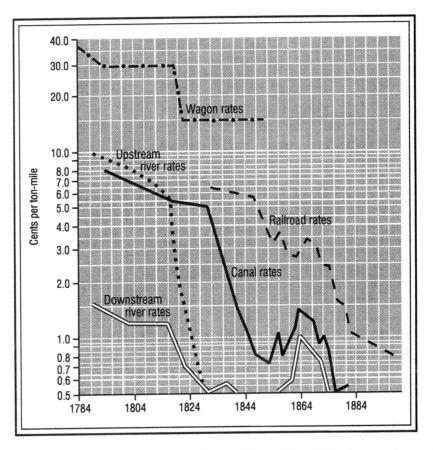

Figure 8.1 Freight Rates in the United States, 1784–1900 (after North)

roads radiated from the principal entrepôt cities. On the northern perimeter, the rail hubs in Cleveland, Toledo, Detroit, Chicago, and Milwaukee expedited the flow of agricultural goods to the Great Lakes or interregional rail routes. On the southern and western perimeter, the regional hubs of Cincinnati and St. Louis gathered the shipments of interior produce for dispatch by river to New Orleans. To these entrepôts must be added the interior rail hubs of Indianapolis and Dayton, serving farmers in the eastern Corn Belt (fig. 8.2).

The trans-Appalachian country north of the Ohio River was well served by river, canal, lake, and rail carriers. By 1860 the region contained a third of the nation's rail mileage, and the vast majority of its farmers had ready access to distant markets. Few of them lived more than 20 miles from low-cost transportation routes (fig. 8.3).

Accessibility was not as widespread south of the Ohio River, yet river navigation in tandem with short rail connectors proved to be highly effective in the southern states. Rail mileage in this region increased from 400 to 4,000 miles between 1850 and 1860. Although a few railroads such as the Mobile and Ohio, the New Orleans, Great Northern, and Jackson, and the Mississippi Central competed directly with the main river routes, the vast majority of southern lines connected interior planters to river ports. The South's principal cities lay along the trunk-line rivers: New Orleans and Memphis on the Mississippi River, Louisville on the Ohio River, and Mobile and Montgomery on the Alabama River; or on tributary rivers: Nashville on the Cumberland, and Chattanooga on the Tennessee. But despite the plenitude of rivers and the supplemental rail network in place by 1860, inaccessibility presented problems in large sections of the

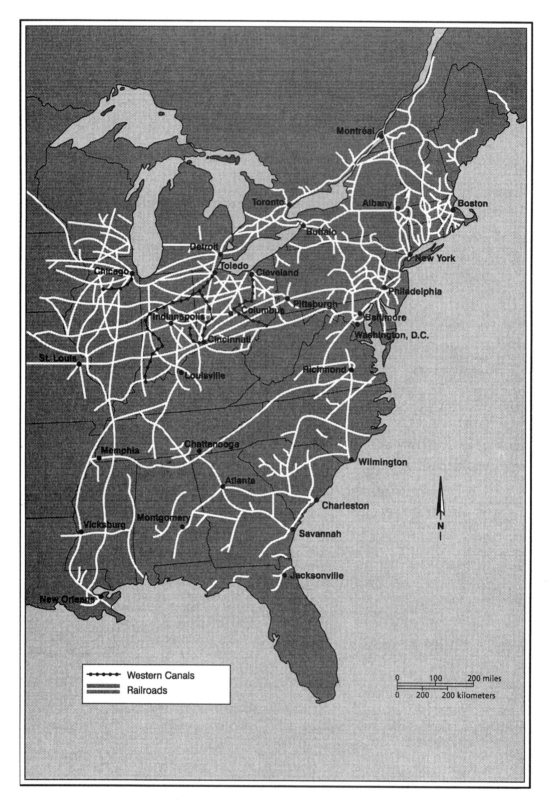

Figure 8.2 Railroads and Western Canals, 1860

trans-Appalachian South. A journey of 20 miles or more separated planters and farmers from rail lines or navigable rivers in large areas of the South, in eastern Kentucky, east-central Tennessee, north-central and southeastern Alabama, southern Mississippi, southwestern Louisiana, and northwestern Arkansas (fig. 8.3). Conversely, midwestern rails offered far greater accessibility by 1860; isolated areas had been reduced to tiny islands located on the margins of the Corn and Wheat Belts.

As accessibility to low-cost transportation spurred economic development and population growth in the trans-Appalachian West, the region's share of the nation's population rose from just one-seventh in 1810 to over two-fifths in 1860. During the early years, settlements were concentrated along rivers in the Mississippi Valley states. As of 1820, nearly half the people in the region lived in Kentucky and Tennessee. Two decades later, thanks in large measure to the success of the Erie Canal and Ohio's feeder-canal system, population growth had shifted northward. Ohio's population soon rivaled that of Kentucky and Tennessee; by 1860, following the spread of the intraregional rail net over the Middle West, that region contained the three most populous states in the trans-Appalachian country and more than 60 percent of its total population Even more impressive was the expansion of improved agricultural land. While the Midwest's population grew 13-fold (from 1 million to 13 million) between 1810 and 1860, improved acreage increased 18-fold (from 4.4 million to 80.6 million acres); improved acreage per capita doubled, with the most sizable gains occurring between 1810 and 1820.

As the transport revolution cascaded over the Appalachians, American agriculture experienced a dramatic reorganization. With just two-fifths of the American population in 1860, this new agricultural heartland produced three-fourths of the nation's cotton, three-fifths of its corn, half of its wheat, and a large share of whiskey, hemp, tobacco, sugar, livestock, and livestock products. Of all these western products, cotton was king. New Orleans was the destination for almost two-fifths of all American cotton as early as 1825. A decade later the Crescent City and Mobile accounted for half of all cotton receipts, and by 1860 these two cities together with the youthful Texas ports received

three-fourths of the South's entire crop. No other American commodity export could rival cotton. The fiber contributed 39 percent of the value of American exports from 1816 to 1820, 63 percent from 1836 to 1840, and about half thereafter.

The trans-Appalachian country also aggrandized the production of cereal grains and livestock, albeit more slowly than was the case with cotton. Midwestern farmers produced just 15 percent of national wheat output in 1820, but 31 percent in 1840 and 46 percent by 1860. More significantly, the Middle West dispatched ever larger shares of its wheat to domestic and foreign markets. In 1820, the region exported no more than 12 percent of its wheat crop, almost exclusively downriver to New Orleans. Two decades later, on output of 26 million bushels, that proportion had doubled to about 27 percent, with 300,000 barrels of flour going to New Orleans and 5 million bushels of wheat going eastward along the Erie Canal. And the proportion jumped again with the rise of prices following the British repeal of their protectionist Corn Laws (referring to wheat) in 1846. By 1860, regional exports of 56 million bushels of wheat represented 70 percent of the Midwest's total output. Like cotton planters to their south, wheat farmers in the Midwest were inextricably bound to extraregional markets on the eve of the Civil War.

The trans-Appalachian West also increased the production of corn and corn derivatives such as livestock, pork, beef, and whiskey. Less than a quarter-century after the Napoleonic Wars, the middle section of the area—states in the Ohio Valley, together with Tennessee, Iowa, and Missouri—produced nearly 60 percent of the nation's corn crop. Unlike the overwhelmingly commercial orientation of cotton and wheat, however, corn (or its equivalents in livestock, meat, and whiskey) contributed relatively modest amounts to regional exports. In 1839, less than 3 percent of the region's corn output of 188 million bushels left the region. That proportion had risen to almost 9 percent of the 492-million-bushel crop in 1857. At this time wheat farmers and cotton planters were exporting 70 and 90 percent of their crops, respectively. In sum, the overwhelming bulk of Midwestern corn and livestock remained in the region for household consumption or for intraregional markets.

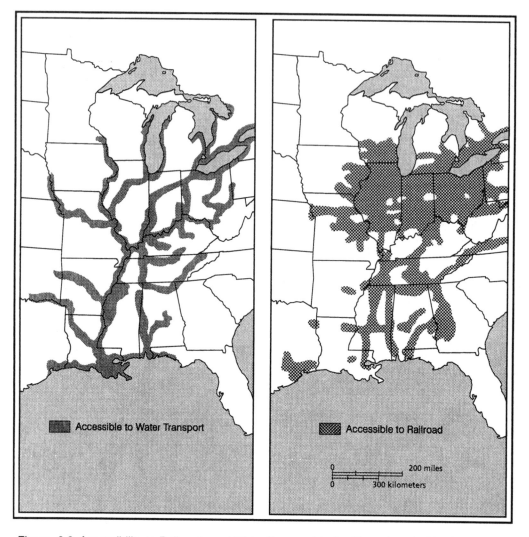

Figure 8.3 Accessibility to Railroads and Water Transport in the Trans-Appalachian West, 1860

FARMING PATTERNS IN THE TRANS-APPALACHIAN COUNTRY

The extension of commercial agriculture progressed rapidly after 1815. Cotton planters relied on distant markets as early as 1820; the same may be said for midwestern wheat farmers by the 1850s. Corn and livestock farmers, however, had just begun the transformation when the Civil War erupted; their thoroughgoing commitment to distant markets awaited postwar improvements in refrigerated transport and institutional changes in the regulation of the meatpacking industry. Nonetheless, an elabo-

rate, multimodal transportation system provided most farmers and planters with access to interregional and international markets.

Three gateways connected the Middle West with external markets. These were, in chronological order, the southern river routes, the northern Erie Canal system (later complemented by rail), and the eastern rail lines of the Pennsylvania and the Baltimore and Ohio Railroads. Of the three routes, the southern dominated western trade until the mid-1830s, when the Erie Canal–Great Lakes–Ohio feeder-canal system began making inroads. By 1850 the northern route had captured half the shipments from

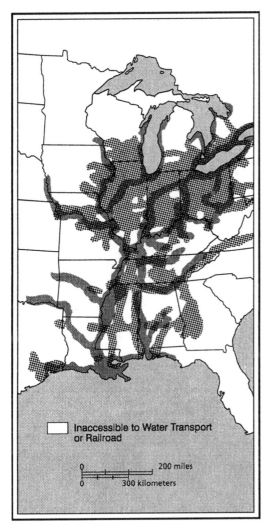

Inaccessible to Water Transport or Railroad

0   200 miles

0   300 kilometers

Figure 8.3 (continued)

reversed direction and shipped over 90 percent of its products upriver to the termini of the eastern railroads—Wheeling and Pittsburgh—by 1860.

The centerpiece of the southern route was the Mississippi River and its navigable tributaries. In the earliest years of settlement, flatboats offered cheap downriver freight rates. Lacking alternative low-cost transportation, western settlement congregated along navigable waterways. The successful adaptation of shallow-draft steamboats to southern waters in the 1810s reinforced the pattern of riverine settlement. Steamboats lowered upstream freight rates and permitted New Orleans to dispatch imported goods as far north as the Ohio valley. By the mid-1820s, nearly half of the Crescent City's trade originated in the Ohio valley, the other half coming from the Mississippi valley south of St. Louis. Well over half of the interior receipts at New Orleans consisted of diverse provisions— corn, flour, pork, beef, and whiskey—mostly from the Ohio valley. Bulk grain shipments were rare, however, because wheat spoiled in the heat and humidity, and in any event, New Orleans had modest storage facilities. For similar reasons, merchants there favored cornmeal and barreled corn (in the ear) over sacked corn (shelled) until the mid-1830s.

During its period of western hegemony, New Orleans and its tributary towns upriver flourished. As the principal entrepôt for a drainage basin of over 1 million square miles, New Orleans enjoyed a rapid rise in river receipts, from less than 100,000 tons of goods in the 1810s to 1.2 million tons by 1840. During its heyday in the 1830s, the busy port received 2,000 to 3,000 flatboats and steamboats annually and transshipped the bulk of these goods on to ocean-going vessels. From a small city of some 17,000 persons in the 1810s, the Crescent City had risen by 1840 to 102,000 and fifth rank among all American cities; it was almost precisely the size of Baltimore. Upriver from New Orleans, hundreds of landings, wood stations, towns, and cities connected the river traffic with interior producers. Of the various settlements along this trunk line in 1840, the three largest lay in the Ohio valley: Cincinnati, with 46,000 people and 1,600 miles from New Orleans, was the sixth largest city in the nation; Pittsburgh had 31,000 people and was 2,063 miles distant; and Louisville had 21,000 persons and was

the West, while the southern river route retained just 45 percent. The rapid expansion of commerce via the Erie Canal reflected its capture of the grain trade of the upper Midwest, on the periphery of the Great Lakes. The southern route, which had taken virtually all midwestern trade prior to 1830, accounted for 62 percent in 1835, 44 percent in 1844, and just 29 percent in 1853. The Erie route, meanwhile, had captured nearly 40 percent of the trade by 1840 and more than 60 percent by 1853. Even the lower Midwest along the Ohio River diverted its trade from the southern water route. Cincinnati, which shipped more than 90 percent of its goods south in 1853,

1,442 miles distant. St. Louis was 1,242 miles up the Mississippi and ranked fourth in this group with a population of 16,500 (fig. 8.1).

The growth of cities tributary to New Orleans was closely tied to their trade in diversified, bulky, and perishable provisions. These cities assembled the produce of their hinterlands and then improved its value by reducing bulk and perishability. Corn, for example, was shelled and sacked, barreled, milled into meal, or made into whiskey. Wheat was ground into flour. Livestock was slaughtered and barreled in brine or cured into bacon and hams. Cincinnati's booming meatpacking industry earned it the title of "Hogopolis" by 1840. In these cities, the pace of commercial life was brisk; in the summer they received wheat, in the fall and winter hogs, and in the spring corn.

Closer to the river mouth, ports were smaller and quieter than the bustling cities upriver. A town of several thousand was a rarity, and trade was generally dull except in the cotton shipping season between August and November. Located at intervals of roughly 75 to 100 miles along the river, a good day's journey by steamboat, these towns served principally as collection points and markets for local cotton planters. Baled cotton was carted to these towns by slaves and small white planters and, requiring neither processing nor elaborate storage facilities, just sat awaiting the arrival of the steamboats headed downstream. New Orleans, which dominated the interior trade, increasingly shared the cotton trade with the neighboring port of Mobile, Alabama, at the mouth of the Alabama River. Mobile serviced the successful cotton planters of central Alabama and northeastern Mississippi. Cultivating the rich prairie soils and bottomlands along the Alabama, Tombigbee, and Black Warrior Rivers, these planters produced fine yields of cotton and shipped the "lint" via steamboat to Mobile. By the late 1830s, cotton receipts in Mobile amounted to almost half those of New Orleans, and the young port housed more than 20,000 persons—about the population of Louisville.

The hegemony of New Orleans over the western trade endured until the late 1830s, when the northern gateway—the multimodal system of western canals, lake boats, and Erie Canal boats—offered unusually stiff competition that stretched south into central Ohio and northwest along the edges of Lakes Erie and Huron. As this northern trunk-line route expanded, the populations of the principal lake ports assumed a rank-size distribution: in 1840 Buffalo (population 18,000) was about twice the size of the second-ranked Detroit, triple third-ranked Cleveland, and quadruple fourth-ranked Chicago. During the next decade, however, the western ports grew faster, and Chicago, with nearly 30,000 people, moved into second place, and Milwaukee challenged Detroit for third.

Although the northern gateway stimulated urban growth, the lake ports were smaller than the river ports on the southern route. The northern ports specialized in handling bulk grains, particularly wheat and corn, and they lacked many of the processing industries associated with the Ohio River ports. Consequently, the largest lake port in 1850—Buffalo, with 42,000 people—was slightly smaller than Louisville, about half the size of Pittsburgh, and a third the size of Cincinnati.

The pace of urban growth on the northern route accelerated, however, with the spread of railroads into the Middle West after 1846. Before that date, shipments via the lake system had to be suspended each November because of wind and ice, and they were not resumed until spring. The interregional rail routes overcame this obstacle by permitting year-round shipments of higher-value goods. These new routes also encouraged investment in facilities for processing wheat and livestock. In Chicago, for example, processors shipped increasing quantities of flour and dressed hogs—the latter in winter, to take advantage of natural refrigeration. Live hogs and cattle, destined for the tables of urban easterners, also moved through Chicago's enormous stockyards. By 1860, 15 rail lines funneled staples into Chicago; in that year the city's storage capacity for grain exceeded the total tonnage of the southern cotton crop. The rail lines brought people, too, as the city's population swelled to 112,000. Meanwhile, Buffalo, at 81,000, had lost ground, as much of the trade that only recently had gone via the Erie Canal now traveled east by rail. The other lake ports of Detroit, Cleveland, Milwaukee, and Toronto held their own with populations of 40,000 to 45,000 (fig. 8.4).

Chicago's exceptional growth—travelers regarded it as an American wonder—was predicated on two connections: the city's transport links to the East (via rail and the Erie system),

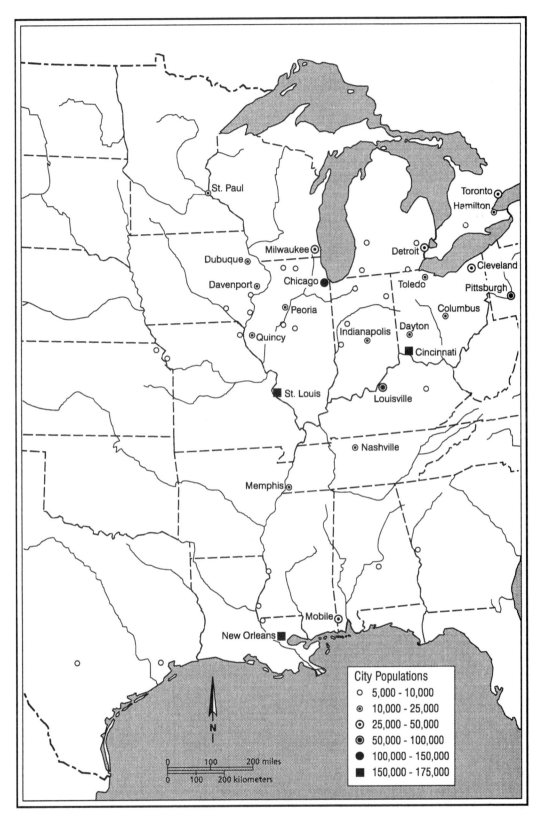

Figure 8.4 Trans-Appalachian Cities, 1860

and its proximity to two emergent agricultural regions: the Wheat Belt of northern Illinois and southern Wisconsin, and the Corn Belt (with its associated hogs and cattle) of central Indiana and Illinois. The focus of these regions to the north and west would prove especially favorable for Chicago.

By the eve of the Civil War, the commerce of the trans-Appalachian West had been thoroughly restructured. Although the largest cities were still located on the old southern route—New Orleans, St. Louis, and Cincinnati ranged between 160,000 and 175,000 people—the bulk of the trade of the Old Northwest now flowed through the eastern and northern gateways. The lake ports, especially Chicago, advanced more rapidly than the river ports to the south. New Orleans, once the master of the Mississippi valley, suffered sizable losses of its hinterland. Although the Crescent City in 1860 retained the lucrative cotton trade of the lower Mississippi and some of the provisions trade from the Tennessee and Cumberland valleys, the city's share of the trans-Appalachian trade had diminished to about 25 percent, scarcely any of which came from north of the Ohio River.

REGIONAL ECONOMIC SPECIALIZATION AND PRODUCTIVITY

The radical realignment of western commerce and the shifting loci of urban growth were part and parcel of a broader restructuring of agricultural regions west of the Appalachians. As this extensive territory assumed the role of the nation's agricultural heartland, it also divided into specialized chambers. Three distinctive regions were put into place in the two decades before the Civil War: the Wheat Belt of the upper Middle West, the Corn-Hog Belt of the lower Middle West and the upper South, and the Cotton Belt in the lower South (fig. 8.5). Supplementing these was a series of more localized regions: the coniferous forests of Wisconsin and Michigan where lumbering occurred, scattered areas of burley tobacco and hemp production in the upper South, and the sugar country of subtropical Louisiana.

These emergent agrarian regions exhibited a tendency to drift westward. "Westering" is usually regarded as a natural and inevitable product of frontier expansion, but in actuality it involved a host of interrelated climatic, agronomic, and technological factors. Consider the case of cotton. Three-fourths of the nation's cotton in 1860 was raised west of the Appalachians, and 55 percent came from just three states: Alabama, Mississippi, and Louisiana. Within these states, cotton production was concentrated in three areas: the rich alluvial bottomlands of the Mississippi valley from Baton Rouge to Natchez and its tributaries in the state of Mississippi, the black prairies of central Alabama and northwestern Mississippi along the Tombigbee River, and the "Delta" region south of Memphis on the Mississippi River.

More than that of any other western crop except sugar, the geography of cotton was influenced by climate. The optimal conditions for cotton include a long growing season of 200 or more frost-free days. Today the 200-day isoline runs from the Georgia–South Carolina border northwest to the tip of southeastern Missouri and then west to Oklahoma, but in the mid-19th century a cooler temperature regime shoved this line farther to the south. The antebellum Cotton Belt thus evolved in a region that was one to two degrees cooler than at present and that was drier as well. The area of drier conditions formed a triangle with its apex in the Mississippi valley and its base extending from Alabama to Texas, a triangle that enclosed the core of the Cotton Belt in the 1850s.

The gravitation of cotton into this triangle represented a rational response to more optimal agronomic conditions. This cooler and drier zone minimized two of the severest problems for cotton producers: weed growth and fungus diseases. In the first instance, drier conditions retarded the invasion of crabgrass into the cotton fields during the critical tillage period, the first two months of the plant's growth. Unlike planters in the rainier Old South, who regularly complained that cotton required tilling four times or more in spring, western planters usually escaped with just three cultivations. And because tillage was the principal bottleneck in cotton planting, this reduction in the frequency of cultivation permitted commensurate increases in cotton acreage per worker (of three to four acres) and in output per worker. In the second instance, drier conditions also meant that cotton disease was a less severe problem for western planters than for their eastern counterparts, who

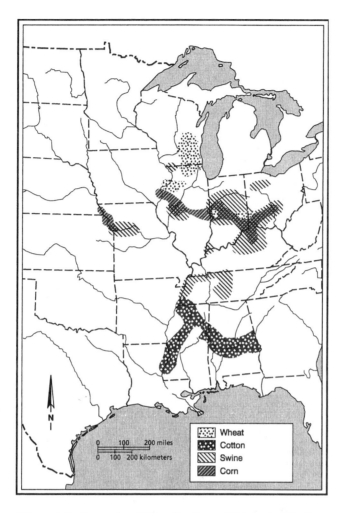

Figure 8.5 Generalized Core Regions of Staple Production
in the Trans-Appalachian West, 1860

searched in vain for solutions to cotton-plant rust.

Although wheat stood at the opposite latitudinal extreme from cotton, it too shifted westward before the Civil War. In the early 1840s Ohio led the nation in wheat production, but by 1860 the center of the Wheat Belt had shifted several hundred miles northwest to northern Illinois and southern Wisconsin. To be sure, this migration was facilitated by the easy access afforded by rail and lake carriers, yet many areas of the Midwest enjoyed similar locational advantages. More critical, perhaps, was the drier and cooler climate in the new home of the Wheat Belt. The plant diseases of wheat rust and "wheat blast" that plagued farmers in Indiana and Ohio in the 1850s were far less serious in the upper Midwest. And the latter region had two other advantages. First was its location on the prairie margin. Unlike the open prairie lands to the south, the uneven surface of ridges and trees here moderated winter soil temperatures and reduced the risk of winter killing from heaving and thawing. Secondly, the relatively drier springs in the prairie margin permitted a shift from sowing wheat in the fall to doing so in the early spring. The chance of winter kill was avoided altogether, and there was still sufficient time for maturation. Although other areas of the country persisted in raising wheat in the 1850s, none of them rivaled the spatial concentration of production in the Wheat Belt, and few rivaled it in yields.

Corn, the third great crop of the trans-Appalachian region, flourished in a wide variety of environments from the Gulf of Mexico to the Great Lakes, but its core region lay in a belt between 39° and 41° N latitude and a longitudinal range from Columbus, Ohio, to Davenport, Iowa. Corn Belt farmers specialized in feed corn and, on the belt's eastern margins, hogs and cattle (fig. 8.5). In the creation of this region, climatic conditions once again played a key role. To the south a rainier environment presented considerable problems for row-crop tillage. Weeds such as Johnson grass, Bermuda grass, and yellow nutsedge were chronic pests, invading cornfields and demanding more tillage and labor than in the Corn Belt. Moreover, southern grasses often demanded tedious hand-hoed tillage while Corn-Belt farmers escaped with lighter cultivations. This may explain why riding cultivators were so much more popular in the Corn Belt than in the South, where these new machines were relatively ineffectual on vigorous weeds. In any event, tillage rates tended to be faster in the Corn Belt, and farmers responded by increasing their acreage in corn, in some cases doubling the per worker acreage of southern corn farmers. North of the Corn Belt, cooler temperatures constrained corn production. Although the Corn Belt today extends as far as 44° N latitude, conditions were generally cooler in the mid-19th century, and corn's optimal thermal limits (a heat supply of 50°F or more for a period of four to five months) were exceeded beyond 42° to 43° N, or roughly Wisconsin's southern border (fig. 8.6).

Favorable climate alone would not have made the Corn Belt into a preeminent agricultural zone. Equally important was the intensive railroad construction that lashed the region together during the 1850s. Few areas of the nation rivaled the rail mileage constructed in southeastern Ohio, central Indiana, and central Illinois at that time. Between 1849 and 1853, Indiana added more than 1,000 miles of rail lines (half of the state's total mileage as of 1860), and southwestern Ohio acquired most of its antebellum trackage. Indianapolis, served by seven lines, and Dayton, served by five, emerged as rail hubs. The feverish pace of railroad building was prompted in part by specialization and trade

within the Corn Belt. The new rail lines facilitated shipments of cash grain from Illinois and Iowa to the hog growers on the eastern margins of the Corn Belt. Although the new railroad companies soon suffered from overbuilding, intense competition, and declining profits, corn farmers and hog raisers reaped the advantage of lower freight rates. Cheap transport fostered subregional differentiation: the western Corn Belt specialized in feed grain destined for the livestock markets of Chicago, St. Louis, and other Mississippi River ports or the eastern corn-hog complex; the eastern Corn Belt specialized in hogs destined for Ohio River packers and pork markets in the South or for eastern cities such as Baltimore, Washington, and Philadelphia.

The westward migration of antebellum agriculture involved far more than the spread of commercial farming and planting into new lands. These specialized belts of cotton, wheat, and corn also accelerated the pace of American economic growth. Between 1839 and 1859 the American population rose by 60 percent. In the same period, agricultural output doubled, a surge made possible by environmental-agronomic conditions more favorable west of the Appalachians than to the east. Cooler and drier weather in the Mississippi and Ohio valleys conferred an ecological advantage on the producers of row crops. Drier conditions during the growing season retarded weed growth among the rows of cotton and corn, thereby reducing labor input at tillage and increasing acreage per worker. In these areas, three cultivations in May and June usually sufficed, while four or more cultivations were customary to the east. Given the roughly 60 days available for tillage and at the usual tillage rate of an acre per worker per day, a western laborer could cultivate somewhere between 19 and 20 acres, while a laborer in the humid East could tend just 15 acres or less. By easing the tillage constraint, drier conditions permitted a 25 percent increase in labor output. Productivity gains were even higher in the Corn Belt of the 1850s as the introduction of riding cultivators lifted capacity above 20 acres. Operating at twice the manual speed, these new machines proved particularly successful in the Illinois prairies, where light plowings sufficed. They were far less successful to the east and south of the Corn Belt where humidity was greater and weeds grew more vigorously; here

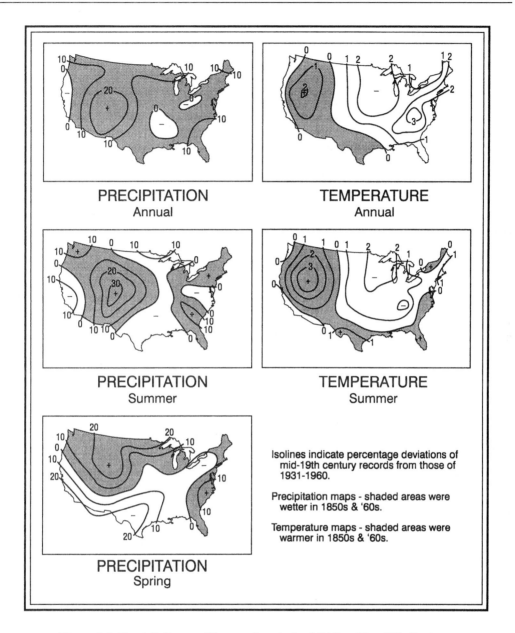

PRECIPITATION
Annual

TEMPERATURE
Annual

PRECIPITATION
Summer

TEMPERATURE
Summer

Isolines indicate percentage deviations of
mid-19th century records from those of
1931-1960.

Precipitation maps - shaded areas were
wetter in 1850s & '60s.

Temperature maps - shaded areas were
warmer in 1850s & '60s.

PRECIPITATION
Spring

Figure 8.6 Precipitation and Temperature in the Middle of the 19th Century,
Compared with 1931–1960

the tedious method of hand-hoeing persisted.

Wheat farmers also enjoyed gains in output in the course of the grain's westward migration. Yields rose from the 20 bushels per acre typical of Ohio to around 30 in the Wisconsin-Illinois border area. The region's gently rolling topography allowed mechanical reapers to operate with little difficulty, easily superseding broadcast sowing. While the reaper surely sped up the harvest rate, the precise gain remains controversial; an improvement of 20 to 50 percent over the hand rate of an acre a day appears most plausible. What this meant was that during the intense ten-day span of the wheat harvest, a worker using a reaper might harvest 12 to 15 acres as compared to perhaps 10 acres using a scythe or cradle. The superior productivity of the Wheat Belt over eastern producers boils down to this: a yield advantage of 10 bushels per acre, an acreage-per-worker advantage of 2 to 5 acres, and an overall advantage of 20 to 50 bushels per worker over and above typical eastern outputs of 200 bushels per worker. The Wheat Belt conferred a productivity gain of somewhere between 10 and 25 percent.

The American economy thus achieved substantial productivity gains from the western extension of agriculture, the emergence of specialized crop regions, and the presence of more favorable environmental conditions. Of the various gains, perhaps the most significant occurred in row crops and more specifically in labor output. Cotton and corn experienced a 25 percent gain in acreage per worker while broadcast grains (most notably wheat) enjoyed a gain of 10 to 25 percent. Enhanced western productivity was evident also in yields per acre. In the 1850s, yields in the Wheat Belt were half again those of eastern farmers. The advantage was somewhat smaller in the Cotton and Corn Belts. Fresh, fertile soils accounted for some of these differences, but just as important were the more subtle environmental advantages of the West— drier growing seasons, fewer weeds, and reduced risks from plant disease. These agroecological advantages provided sound economic reasons for the western drift of agricultural production and specialization amidst the expanding national and international markets of the first half of the 19th century.

STAPLE REGIONS AND SETTLEMENT SYSTEMS

Although productivity gains accrued in all of these new agricultural regions, their systems of rural and urban settlements were distinctive indeed. At one extreme was the southern Cotton Belt with its dispersed rural plantations, many though not all with slaves, and small towns; at the other extreme was the Wheat Belt replete with family farms, seasonal wage laborers, and a hierarchy of towns and cities. Somewhat more ambiguous were the settlements in the Corn Belt, drawing as they did upon slave labor south of the Ohio River and upon free labor north of it.

These variations in settlement systems represented regional adaptations to staple crops and their unique labor requirements. In the Wheat Belt, the demand for labor was highly seasonal, skewed as it was to the frantic summer harvest of ten days to two weeks. Wheat was a "few-day" crop, and hence farmers hired seasonal wage labor mainly at that time. Even at the high daily wages prevailing in the Wheat Belt in the 1850s, a hired hand at harvest cost only about $20 per year as compared to about $60 for a year-round slave. In the Cotton Belt, by contrast, planters preferred slaves when they could afford them because cotton demanded labor from spring planting and tillage to late-summer and autumn picking. This demanding "multiple-day" crop required no fewer than 120 days of labor stretched out over an eight-month period; hence cotton planters rarely, if ever, hired wage-workers since their costs were double those of a slave.

Corn is the most interesting American staple because it was an "intermediate-day" crop and because corn farmers were often ambivalent about the most efficient supply of labor. As a row crop, corn required considerable attention during the three to four months from spring planting through early summer tillage, but thereafter the crop placed fewer demands on labor. Harvesting did not have the urgency that was associated with wheat or cotton because farmers had several options. Sometimes they left corn in the field well into winter, when, fully dried, it was harvested casually by family members; other times they let the corn be mowed down by grazing livestock; in still other instances they had the corn cut, shocked, barned, and shelled as soon as it was ripe. Corn farmers spent more time worrying about the labor bottleneck during spring tillage, in what they called the "crop season"—the four months from April through July. By the 1850s, corn farmers in the Midwest had discovered that the annualized costs of hiring a wageworker for the crop season were nearly the same as purchasing and sustaining a slave laborer. Consequently, corn growers south of the Ohio River, where slavery was legally permissible, often used slaves, while midwesterners continued to use hired hands. But many midwesterners also recognized the economic superiority of slave labor, and during the 1850s not a few of them advocated the advantages of slavery for corn farmers north of the Ohio River.

The unique labor requirements of wheat, corn, and cotton were reflected in the settlement systems of their respective regions. In the Wheat Belt, family farms drew upon three sources of farm labor: sons, local agricultural laborers and townsmen, and seasonal workers arriving by train from Chicago, Milwaukee, and other points. Of the three, sons were the most reliable. A wheat farmer assisted by a teenaged son could expect to harvest 20 acres; on that certainty, farm families confidently planted 20 acres of wheat in the fall or early spring. The reliability of family labor was an inducement for high fertility; in Illinois, for example, women in 1860 averaged over four children during their childbearing years. Local men made up a second and somewhat less reliable source of harvest labor—a reservoir that typically constituted a fifth to a third of the adult male labor force in the Wheat Belt. The third and least reliable source was itinerants who came from more distant cities and regions in search of harvest work. The convergence of these labor flows at the time of wheat harvest made for a bustle of activity, but the numbers of workers were soon spread thin. And since most farmers rarely had access to more than a few harvest workers, most farms were of modest size. The average wheat farm in 1860 consisted of perhaps 50 to 70 acres in improved land and double or triple that amount in total acreage. Of the improved land, less than half was in wheat (somewhat more if farmers used mechanical reapers), and the rest was planted with corn, oats, rye, barley, and grass. Every farm had livestock too, but the numbers of swine and cattle in the Wheat Belt were modest when compared to farms in the Corn Belt.

This landscape of moderate-size family farms and seasonal laborers sustained a quite formidable series of urban systems. Chicago and Milwaukee, the principal entrepôts for the Wheat Belt, had broken into the middle and upper ranks of American cities by 1860, and hinterland towns such as Peoria and Rockford also flourished. Urban growth and wheat farming were clearly intertwined, but just how? The most obvious link between country and city was the marketing and forwarding of staple commodities via urban centers. But according to calculations by Earle and Hoffman, the contribution of marketing to the urban economic base cannot alone explain the large sizes of Wheat Belt towns and cities. More decisive was the tie between wheat farming and labor supply. Rural underemployment was a fact of life for farm labor in the Wheat Belt owing to wheat's acutely seasonal production regime. The short harvest made it extremely difficult for rural workers to accumulate capital and climb the agricultural ladder toward farm ownership. For most rural workers the Wheat Belt represented a waystation for migration, either westward to cheaper lands on the frontier or eastward to the region's burgeoning towns and cities. The plight of the underemployed wheat laborer thus was a bonanza of cheap labor for the Wheat Belt's urban entrepreneurs. In the 1850s, for example, the transfer wage—that is, the annual amount required to lure a rural farmhand from the countryside to an unskilled city job—stood at about $180 to $200 per year in Chicago. It may have been the lowest in the nation and was about half the level of unskilled wages paid in cities in the cotton South. Urban entrepreneurs in the Wheat Belt could hire more workers per unit of labor cost than could their counterparts in the rest of the nation. Consequently, even though the urban systems of Chicago and Mobile were sustained by nearly identical regional economic bases, Chicago and its hinterland towns employed nearly twice as many workers in their labor forces.

The rural and urban landscapes of the Corn Belt had much in common with the Wheat Belt to the north. Corn farmers also resided on family farms of modest size and hired rural wage labor, except for those living south of the Ohio River, where slaves were often used. Similarly, cities and towns were integral features of the Corn Belt. Indeed corn farmers were served by the second- and third-largest cities in the Midwest: Cincinnati in the eastern half of the region, and St. Louis in the western. Chicago made inroads among corn farmers in central Illinois and central Indiana.

These morphological similarities in the landscapes of the Corn and Wheat Belts are somewhat misleading, however, because they tend to obscure certain fundamental differences in the seasonality of corn production and labor supply. As noted earlier, corn is a row crop that imposes its heaviest labor demands during the crop season from April through June. In these crucial months, the tasks of tillage largely determined how much corn a farmer could plant. In the 60-day tillage period, a good worker who tilled an acre a day and who cleared each field thrice might cultivate a maximum of 20 acres of corn. Some farmers managed to increase corn acreage by introducing riding cultivators, but the diffusion of this machine in the Corn Belt before 1860 was modest. Farm expansion hinged on the availability of rural laborers. Although these workers accounted for between an eighth and a third of the Corn Belt's total rural labor force, their numbers were insufficient to satisfy every farmer. Thus, the typical Corn Belt farm in central Illinois in 1859 had 163 acres, yet only 105 were improved. Still, Corn Belt farms were somewhat larger than those in the Wheat Belt, perhaps because corn farmers also used their hired hands for harvesting wheat and other small grains, and for haying during the crop season.

The Corn Belt further differed from the Wheat Belt in its emphasis on livestock, and most especially swine. By 1860 the eastern half of the Corn Belt had effectively integrated corn and swine production; hogs were occasionally turned loose in the corn fields, but more typically the standing crop was cut, taken to the barn, and fed on demand. In the western half of the Corn Belt, swine were less numerous; here corn was cut, shocked, shelled, and shipped to external markets as feed grain for livestock.

The corn-hog complex typical of southwestern Ohio and east-central Indiana also appeared south of the Ohio River, but producers in the Kentucky Bluegrass and Nashville Basin suffered sharp setbacks during the 1850s. At the beginning of that decade, Tennessee and Kentucky led the nation in swine production per capita, and middle Tennessee tripled the national average. By 1860, however, these states had experienced a 20 percent decline in numbers of hogs and had surrendered national leadership to Indiana and Illinois. Although improved animal weights offset some of the decline, these gains could not compensate for the collapse of the market for corn and pork in the Cotton Belt. Beginning in the 1840s, Cotton Belt planters in Alabama, Mississippi, and Louisiana had begun diversifying their operations, raising corn, cowpeas, and swine along with cotton and concurrently providing most if not all of the food required on their plantations. In these cotton states, corn production rose by 18 percent during the 1850s as compared with a gain of just 5 percent in the upper South; simultaneously, the numbers of swine in the cotton states fell by less

than 5 percent as compared with a 20 percent drop in the upper South. Such diversification of production in the cotton South thus deprived the upper South of its principal market for corn and pork.

The family farms and the sizable cities and towns in the Wheat and Corn Belts gave way to a landscape of plantations and small county towns in the Cotton Belt. The settlement fabric in the lower South was woven out of three strands: the heavy labor demands of cotton, the rationality of slave labor, and the possibility of expanding slavery (fig. 8.7). Cotton required many days of labor, from the late winter seeding through spring planting and tillage to fall picking. Because of these lengthy demands, cotton planters who sought to expand operations found it cheaper to acquire slaves than to hire wage-workers. Expansion was obstructed, however, during the prosperous 1850s, when the price of prime male slaves rose from $1,500 to $2,000, a level far exceeding the resources of family plantations that grossed perhaps $300 a year from cotton. As a result, many small planters turned to their wives and children for help, and plantations without slaves increased from 39 percent of all plantations in the cotton South in 1850 to 48 percent in 1860. Even in the highly productive Mississippi alluvial region, already legendary for its grand slave plantations, the proportion of those without slaves rose from 20 to 36 percent in that same decade, and in the Cotton Belt of central Alabama, from 21 to 29 percent. The ownership of slaves became concentrated numerically among the largest planters (those having 15 or more slaves) and spatially in the fertile areas of the Mississippi valley and the black prairie lands of central Alabama and northeastern Mississippi (fig. 8.7).

Adding slaves to the plantation labor force does not, however, seem to have resulted in increasing returns on cotton production. Scale economies were at best modest because cotton output was so closely regulated by a worker's tillage capacity. No matter how many slaves were added to the plantation, each slave's limit remained at 15 to 20 acres of row crops. To be sure, large planters tried to circumvent the bottleneck by compelling slaves to cultivate from sunup to sunset, rain, shine, and holidays, and in gang systems, but these strategies produced only marginal gains. From an economic standpoint, therefore, a large plantation was little more than

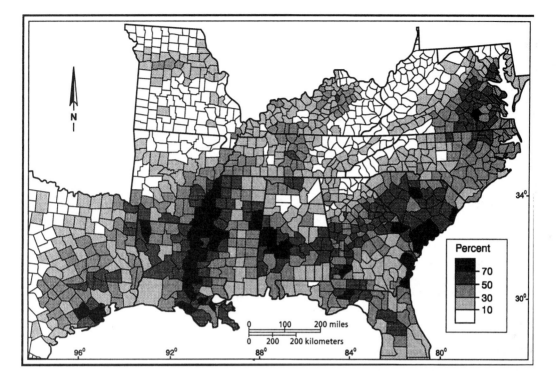

Figure 8.7 Slaves as a Proportion of Total Population, 1860

an enlarged version of the many smaller plantations cultivated with family labor. That is not to say that the social organization of large plantations did not differ; indeed, scholars of the slave experience have pointed out the ironic virtues of large slave plantations in offering slaves a richer cultural life, preserving African American folkways, and providing a greater measure of economic mobility within the slave system.

Plantations large and small also shared in the economic diversification that began in the depression of the 1840s and accelerated in the boom times of the 1850s. In switching some of their cotton land into corn and hog production, southern cotton planters behaved in a seemingly irrational fashion. Perhaps, as some scholars have suggested, planters allocated cotton and corn acreage in a two-to-one ratio, customarily planting 12 acres of cotton for every 6 of corn as a hedge against the uncertainty of cotton prices. When prices fell, planters were at least able to feed themselves and their families. But in the late 1840s, and especially in the 1850s, cotton prices were not falling. Quite the contrary:

prices rose rapidly in response to international prosperity and Britain's heavy investment in textile mills. During a period of rising cotton prices, diversification for the purpose of self-sufficiency seems unlikely.

A more plausible explanation is to view diversification as a planter strategy for maintaining soil fertility. Soil exhaustion had long been a serious problem for cotton planters, and they had few ways to combat it. Wearing out the land and migrating west to fresh lands had been one option, customary until the early 1840s. Another possibility, applying guano or commercial fertilizers, was exorbitantly expensive. Then a third option arose with the discovery by soil scientists of the nitrogen-fixing properties of leguminous plants. With this knowledge, planters devised an ingenious crop rotation—corn and leguminous cowpeas with cotton—and restored soil fertility far more cheaply than by other means. They began by planting exhausted cotton land in corn in the spring, and in July, after corn tillage was done, they intercropped cowpeas in the corn rows. By fall, as the cowpeas climbed the corn stalks, their roots were restoring nitrogen to the worn-out soil. Planters then turned their hogs into the fields to mow down the corn and the cowpeas. The following spring, the restored land was available for two more years of cotton, and when fertility declined again, the land was turned back into corn and cowpeas. This rotation assured the planter steady cotton yields as well as adequate supplies of corn and pork—much to the dismay of producers in the upper South.

The southern cotton plantation was by 1860 a diversified agricultural production unit that relied on either family or slave labor. Plantations produced cotton for the market, corn and cowpeas for swine, and corn and pork for human consumption. In their effort to prevent soil exhaustion, cotton planters had devised a remarkably self-sufficient domestic economy. Although the adoption of crop rotation and diversification was widespread in the cotton South, these processes seem to have progressed furthest among the largest slave plantations such as those in the Natchez District on the Mississippi. Despite their numerous slaves (50 or more were usual), their wealth, and their material opulence, these large plantations produced cotton, corn, hogs, and cowpeas in almost precisely the same manner as did their smaller neighbors. Small cotton planters also were relatively prosperous during the 1850s, even though the rapid rise in slave prices prevented them from pursuing the expansion path of slave acquisition taken by their wealthier neighbors.

AGRICULTURAL REGIONS AND THE COMING OF THE CIVIL WAR

The economic superiority of slaves in the cotton South and free labor in the Wheat Belt was unambiguous, but matters were not so clear in the Corn Belt. In the production of cotton, slaves were far more efficient than hired labor, and their acquisition provided opportunities for increasing the scale of operations. Consequently, plantations with more than 1,000 acres and 100 slaves were juxtaposed with small farms solely reliant on family labor. Conversely, in the production of wheat, seasonal wage labor was far more efficient, but the practice of hiring daily or monthly wageworkers seriously crimped expansion possibilities. The seasonal labor pool mobilized at harvest was always insufficient for the

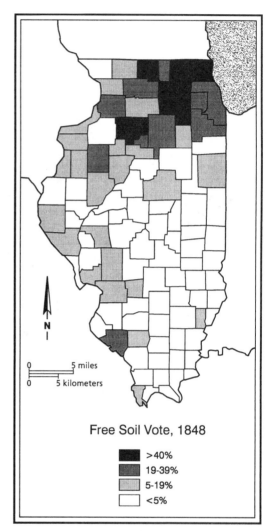

Free Soil Vote, 1848

■ >40%
▨ 19-39%
▦ 5-19%
□ <5%

Figure 8.8 (see caption to the right)

needs of all wheat farmers. Although some farmers expanded wheat acreage by adding mechanical reapers, mechanization of the farm was still in its infancy. Consequently, very large wheat farms were uncommon, and such a scale of operation awaited the postbellum period, when massive seasonal labor pools were transported by passenger trains to the vast wheat farms in the Great Plains. In sum, large agricultural holdings were possible in the cotton South, although these coexisted with family plantations, while farm size was constrained by labor scarcity in the Wheat Belt of the Middle West. The landscape there generally consisted of fam-

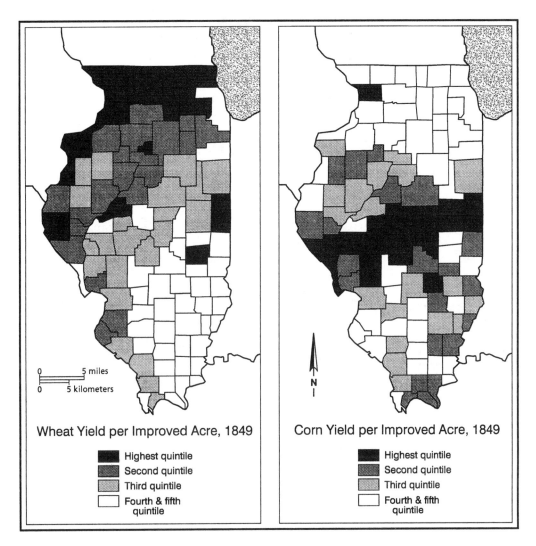

Wheat Yield per Improved Acre, 1849

- ■ Highest quintile
- ▨ Second quintile
- ▫ Third quintile
- □ Fourth & fifth quintile

Corn Yield per Improved Acre, 1849

- ■ Highest quintile
- ▨ Second quintile
- ▫ Third quintile
- □ Fourth & fifth quintile

Figure 8.8 Antislavery Politics and Agricultural Production in Illinois during the Late 1840s

ily farms of 100 to 200 acres supported by substantial numbers of landless rural laborers.

For corn farmers faced with intermediate demands for seasonal workers, the choice of labor systems was invariably problematic on both moral and economic grounds. They tended on the whole to be ambivalent about the preference for slaves or wage labor. As noted by Alexis de Tocqueville in the 1830s and Frederick Law Olmsted in the 1850s, some corn farmers preferred slaves while others hired labor for the crop season. This choice was merely an economic one where slavery already existed. But north of the Ohio River, where slavery had been prohibited by various state constitutions, local advocacy of slavery's superiority in corn farming inflamed political and moral passions. During the 1840s, not a few Corn Belt farmers in the Midwest proclaimed the economic advantages of slavery and openly advocated its legalization through state constitutional conventions. On a purely economic basis, the pro-slavery position of these corn farmers made some sense in 1850, when the costs of hiring a free worker for four months were virtually identical with the annualized costs of a prime male slave. It made even more sense over the next ten years, when free wages rose more rapidly than slave prices.

Slavery gained a decisive advantage, the annual costs for free labor standing at $72 and for slave labor only $60.

Although the nation was preoccupied with the debate over the extension of slavery into the western territories of Kansas and Nebraska, a far more critical struggle over slavery threatened to erupt in the Middle West. When Corn Belt farmers, many of them from northeastern states, proposed the extension of slavery into Illinois, Indiana, and Ohio, wheat farmers in the upper Middle West—for whom slavery was uneconomic as well as immoral—responded by giving vigorous support to antislavery political parties. The 1848 presidential election returns in Illinois exposed the unstable fault line that divided antislavery wheat farmers and ambivalent or pro-slavery corn farmers (fig. 8.8). In this election, the candidate for the antislavery Free Soil Party, Martin Van Buren, drew the vast majority of his support from northern wheat-farming areas. This geographical division deepened during the 1850s. Following the controversial Kansas-Nebraska Act in 1854, which decisively repealed the Missouri Compromise of 1820 that had prohibited slavery north of 36°30' N latitude, the Wheat Belt threw its support solidly behind the newly risen antislavery Republican Party. In the campaigns of 1858 and 1860, the Wheat Belt provided crucial support for Abraham Lincoln's unsuccessful bid for the Senate and his victorious campaign for the presidency.

But if the pivotal role of the Middle West on the eve of the Civil War has been eclipsed by the debate over slavery in the western territories, it is worth recalling that both of the leading presidential candidates in 1860, Lincoln and Stephen Douglas, were from Illinois and that Lincoln's narrow margin of victory was won largely in his home state and in Indiana. To be sure, Lincoln won the election by a comfortable margin in the electoral college, but these results are deceptive. Had just 18,000 voters in Illinois and Indiana and 500 in California switched their votes to the leading opposition party, Lincoln would have been denied a majority in the electoral college. The election would have been thrown into the House of Representatives, where undoubtedly he would have lost. The Middle West, and most especially the wheat farmers on its northern margins, preserved Lincoln's narrow victory and virtually

guaranteed the secession of the southern states.

Southerners understood correctly Lincoln's goal of preserving the union and eradicating slavery, but they did not fully appreciate the basis of his fear. The greatest danger in slavery was not its existence in the South, nor even its extension into the western territories; the real danger, in Lincoln's mind, lay in the expansion of slavery into the middle-western Corn Belt. Lincoln had witnessed the constitutional and electoral offensives of Corn Belt farmers on behalf of slavery. He had witnessed the antislavery reaction that barely defeated the advocates of slavery in the state constitutional conventions and that lost to them in the 1858 Senate race. But Lincoln's presidential victory did nothing in the end to change the economic advantage of slaves over free labor in the Corn Belt. He understood that efforts to legalize slavery in the Middle West would persist until labor costs in the Corn Belt shifted in favor of free labor—unlikely anytime soon—or until the institution of slavery was eliminated altogether as an economic choice. As long as slavery existed in the United States, corn farmers would be tempted to adopt it. Lincoln thus would have appreciated the observations of a perceptive southerner who noted that "where a real interest, and a question of abstract morality conflict in a Yankee's mind, abstract morality will suffer a grievous overthrow." Under these circumstances, the abolition of slavery may have been Lincoln's only viable alternative to the nationalization of "the peculiar institution."

CONCLUSION

The story of trans-Appalachian settlement between 1815 and 1860 is bittersweet. On the one hand, the occupation of the region resulted in marvelous economic achievements. Agricultural productivity gains were substantial as the region responded to external markets and transport improvements through regional specialization. It is fair to say that the trans-Appalachian region had assumed the role of the nation's agricultural heartland by 1860. Its endowments were considerable. Aside from excellent and extensive navigable rivers and gentle topography, much of the area enjoyed a relatively cooler and drier climate than at present. These subtle climatic differences made farming and planting easier and more productive.

In the mosaic of specialized staple regions that emerged, each region developed distinctive patterns of rural and urban settlement. In the Cotton Belt, plantations ranged from small family operations to very large-scale slave production units. The economic advantages of slavery in cotton production provided an expansion path that was unavailable for farmers in either the Wheat Belt or the Corn Belt, who perforce relied on less reliable pools of seasonal wageworkers. In the Wheat Belt, farm sizes were constrained by the labor bottleneck in the ten days to two weeks during harvest, while in the Corn Belt they were fixed by tillage capacity during the two months of May and June. Not until after the Civil War would the mechaniza-tion of corn tillage and the wheat harvest reduce the stringency of these constraints on the small family farm.

The bitter side of trans-Appalachian development is, of course, the economic viability of slavery in the plantation South and, by the 1850s, in the lower Midwest. The superior efficiency and profitability of slavery for corn farmers jeopardized the delicate geopolitical balance that had been constructed out of assorted compromises in the first half of the century. In this case, however, it was midwestern corn farmers rather than the southern slavocracy who represented the vanguard of slave expansion. As of 1860, the economic geography of labor and staple crops, and most notably corn, had pushed the nation toward its greatest impasse.

ADDITIONAL READING

Andreae, C. A. 1997. *Lines of Country: An Atlas of Railway and Waterway History in Canada.* Toronto: Stoddart.

Bidwell, P. W., and J. I. Falconer. 1941. *History of Agriculture in the Northern United States, 1620–1860.* Washington: Carnegie Institution, 1925. Reprint, New York: Peter Smith.

Bogue, A. G. 1963. *From Prairie to Cornbelt: Farming in the Illinois and Iowa Prairies in the 19th Century.* Chicago: University of Chicago Press.

Curti, M. 1959. *The Making of an American Community.* Stanford: Stanford University Press.

David, P. A. 1975. *Technical Choice: Innovation and Economic Growth.* Cambridge: Cambridge University Press.

Davis, C. S. 1974. *The Cotton Kingdom in Alabama.* Philadelphia: Porcupine Press.

Earle, C. 1992a. *Geographical Inquiry and American Historical Problems.* Stanford: Stanford University Press.

———. 1992b. "The Price of Precocity: Technical Choice and Ecological Constraint in the Cotton South, 1840–1890." *Agricultural History* 66: 25–60.

Earle, C., and R. Hoffman. 1980. "The Foundations of the Modern Economy: Agriculture and the Costs of Labor in the United States and England, 1800–60." *American Historical Review* 85: 1055–94.

Fishlow, A. 1965. *American Railroads and the Transformation of the Ante-Bellum Economy.* Cambridge: Harvard University Press.

Fogel, R. W., and S. L. Engerman. 1974. *Time on the Cross: The Economics of American Negro Slavery.* 2 vols. Boston: Little, Brown.

Gallman, R. E. 1972. "Changes in Total U.S. Agricultural Factor Productivity in the 19th Century." *Agricultural History* 46: 191–210.

Gates, P. W. 1960. *The Farmer's Age: Agriculture, 1815–1860.* New York: Holt, Rinehart & Winston.

Genovese, E. 1965. *The Political Economy of Slavery.* New York: Pantheon.

Gray, L. C. 1958. *History of Agriculture in the Southern U.S. to 1860.* 2 vols. Washington: Carnegie Institution, 1932. Reprint, New York: Peter Smith.

Haites, E. F., J. Mak, and G. Walton. 1975. *Western River Transportation: The Era of Early Internal Growth, 1810–1860.* Baltimore: Johns Hopkins University Press.

Hilliard, S. B. 1972. *Hog Meat and Hoecake: Food Supply in the Old South, 1840–1860.* Carbondale: Southern Illinois University Press.

Hudson, John. 1994. *Making the Corn Belt: A Geographical History of Middle-Western Agriculture.* Bloomington: Indiana University Press.

Jakle, J. 1977. *Images of the Ohio Valley.* New York: Oxford University Press.

Kelsey, D. P. 1972. *Farming in the New Nation: Interpreting American Agriculture, 1790–1840.* Washington: Agricultural History Society.

Klingaman, D. C., and R. K. Vedder, eds. 1975. *Essays in 19th-Century Economic History.* Athens: Ohio University Press.

Lindstrom, Diane. 1978. *Economic Development in the Philadelphia Region, 1810–1850.* New York: Columbia University Press.

McManis, D. 1964. *The Initial Evaluation and Utilization of the Illinois Prairies, 1815–1840.* Chicago: University of Chicago, Department of Geography.

Meinig, D. W. 1993. *The Shaping of America: Continental America, 1800–1867.* New Haven: Yale University Press.

Muller, E. K. 1976. "Selective Urban Growth in the Middle Ohio Valley, 1800–1860." *Geographical Review* 66: 178–99.

North, D. C. 1966. *The Economic Growth of the United States, 1790–1860.* New York: W. W. Norton.

Parker, W. N., ed. 1970. *The Structure of the Cotton Economy of the Antebellum South.* Washington: Agricultural History Society.

Paullin, C. O., and J. K. Wright. 1932. *Atlas of the Historical Geography of the United States.* Washington: Carnegie Institution.

Phillips, U. B. 1929. *Life and Labor in the Old South.* New York: Grosset & Dunlap.

Potter, D. 1976. *The Impending Crisis, 1848–1861.* New York: Harper & Row.

Pred, A. 1980. *Urban Growth and City Systems in the United States, 1840–1860.* Cambridge: Harvard University Press.

Rostow, W. 1960. *The Stages of Economic Growth.* Cambridge: Cambridge University Press.

Scheiber, H. N. 1969. *Ohio Canal Era.* Athens: Ohio University Press.

Shob, D. E. 1975. *Hired Hands and Plowboys: Farm Labor in the Midwest, 1815–1860.* Urbana: University of Illinois Press.

Taylor, G. R. 1951. *The Transportation Revolution, 1815–1860.* New York: Holt, Rinehart & Winston.

Ward, D. 1971. *Cities and Immigrants: A Geography of Change in 19th-Century America.* New York: Oxford University Press.

Whitaker, J. W., ed. 1974. *Farming in the Midwest, 1840–1860.* Washington: Agricultural History Society.

Wright, G. 1978. *The Political Economy of the Cotton South.* New York: W. W. Norton.

———. 1986. *Old South, New South.* New York: Basic Books.

9

The Northeast and Regional Integration, 1800–1860

PAUL A. GROVES

At the dawn of the 19th century the United States had fewer than 5.5 million inhabitants, of whom about 900,000 were slaves. Life expectancy at birth remained low (40 years), the country was largely rural (94 percent of the population was nonurban), transportation and communications were poor, and the population was concentrated along the eastern seaboard from Georgia to New Hampshire. Almost three-fifths of the U.S. population lived north of the Potomac River; most of the remaining two-fifths resided to the south, with a small fraction west of the Appalachians.

Increasing levels of urbanization and industrialization in the North and the increasing dependence of the South on a rurally based, staple-crop economy reinforced the distinction between the Northeast and the South throughout the first half of the 19th century. In 1800 the four largest cities in the United States— New York, Philadelphia, Baltimore, and Boston—were all in the Northeast. Of the 33 settlements defined as urban in 1800, 28 were in the Northeast. Yet, the Northeast was not highly urbanized in 1800, for only 1 in 10 of its residents lived in urban places; in the South the proportion was about 1 in 50. The slave population was strongly concentrated in the South, with only Maryland of the northeastern states having a large slave population.

This pattern was transformed as the new nation emerged in the decades prior to 1860 (fig. 9.1). Westward expansion pushed the settlement

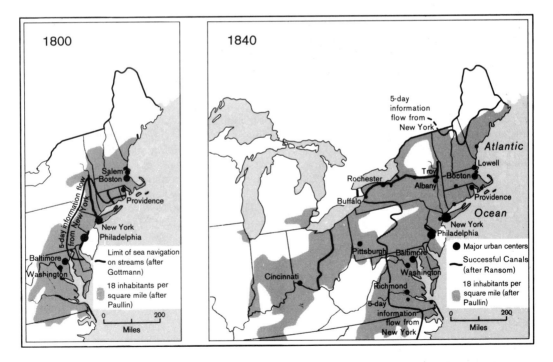

Figure 9.1 Northeast: Urban Centers and Population Density, 1800 and 1840

Table 9.1 U.S. Population by Region, 1800–1860 (population in thousands)

	1800	1820	1840	1860
Northeast	3,040	4,862	7,343	11,468
	(57)	(51)	(43)	(36)
South	2,208	3,917	6,369	10,260
	(42)	(41)	(37)	(33)
West	49	839	3,408	9,785
	(1)	(8)	(20)	(31)
Total U.S.	5,297	9,618	17,120	31,513

Note: Figures in parentheses indicate proportion of total U.S. population.

In this and all other tables the Northeast is defined as New England (Maine, New Hampshire, Vermont, Massachusetts, Rhode Island, and Connecticut) plus the Mid-Atlantic states (New York, New Jersey, Pennsylvania, Delaware, Maryland, and the District of Columbia).

frontier beyond the Mississippi River (table 9.1), while new forms of transportation (steamboats, canals, turnpike roads, and railroads) bound the existing ecumene more tightly together. Foreign trade and the capital accumulated by merchants in the seaport cities provided an economic base for the rapid growth of the major mercantile centers. The transformation of the national economy through the dual processes of industrialization and commercialization of agriculture placed new demands on both urban and rural America. The cities received not only migrants from rural areas but also, and increasingly, immigrants from western Europe. During the period from 1820 to 1860, between 5 million and 6 million immigrants, the majority of Irish and German origin, landed in the United States. Their numbers swelled the city populations of New England and the Mid-Atlantic states; few settled in the southern states.

At the beginning of the 19th century, therefore, the Northeast was the most economically developed region in an infant national economy. It was an area ready to take advantage of the shifting fortunes of international trade and of early transportation developments. It was the first region in North America to experience the impact of industrialization. Industrial growth transformed the landscape of eastern Massachusetts, southern New Hampshire, and Rhode Island and created additional impetus to growth of the other mercantile cities. The Northeast was a

core area with a periphery that would extend generally westward as transportation and trade pulled it into a closer economic relationship with the core. For the Northeast this meant bridging the Allegheny section of the Appalachians. Once this was done, an emergent Middle West would be linked more fully with the Northeast and would itself experience the impact of urbanization and industrialization. The Northeast, in this view, can be seen as a staging ground for extending economic development to, for example, Ohio, Illinois, Indiana, and Michigan.

As the American economy grew, each of the four major northeastern seaports developed a network of economic relationships with its hinterland and, more important initially, with the Atlantic trade. Standing at the contact of these two realms, one inward-looking and the other outward-looking, the seaports assumed the role of "hinges" linking the development of these two foundations of the national economy. The period from 1790 to 1807 was one of massive maritime expansion, and the mercantile cities of the Northeast were the prime beneficiaries. New York, during this period, took a commanding lead among American seaports.

During the period from 1800 to 1860, the Northeast lost its role as the major populated region of the United States. It accounted for 57 percent of total population in 1800, but this proportion declined to 36 percent by 1860. By the latter date, the population of the United States was about equally divided among the Northeast, the South, and the Middle West (table 9.1). Yet, the Northeast accounted for almost two-thirds of manufacturing employment and 17 of the 30 cities in the nation with populations of 25,000 or more (table 9.2). Of course, its population was not static; an increase of 8.5 million included a disproportionate number of the foreign-born population.

The Northeast was an innovative area throughout this period. Here, the dual and inextricably linked processes of urbanization and industrialization initially played out. Transportation improvements produced more efficient links to other regions; yet by 1860, the emerging national economy occupied only the area east of the Mississippi River. The problems of urban-industrial growth—shortage of housing, poor urban amenities, child labor, immigrant populations—were all found initially in the Northeast. The area grew from a sparsely populated region

Table 9.2 U.S. Cities of 25,000 Population or More by Region, 1800–1860

	1800	1820	1840	1860
Northeast	4	4	6	17
South	—	2	2	5
West	—	—	1	8
Total U.S.	4[a]	6[b]	9	30

[a]Includes Boston (24,937).
[b]Includes Charleston (24,780).

Note: The suburbs of New York (Brooklyn), Philadelphia (Spring Garden, Northern Liberties, Kensington, Southwark), Boston (Charleston, Roxbury, Dorchester, and Cambridge), and Pittsburgh (Allegheny) are included in the population totals for those cities in this and all subsequent tables.

with major urban development limited to main ports, to a core area that acted as innovator and director of a growing nation. Such developments created a number of tensions. First was the tension between the larger dominant cities and their hinterlands, particularly if the latter were congruent with the political unit of the state. New York, for example, early in the century experienced the distinction and perceived prejudice toward New York City at the expense of "upstate." The dominance of Baltimore within Maryland provides another example. Second, within each of the regions, growing tensions emerged between rural areas and rapidly growing urban centers. The rural areas were afflicted with changing market conditions related to western competition and with the growing demands of the northeastern cities for labor as well as for food and raw materials. Agriculture was in flux over much of the early 19th century, and reorganization and readjustment took their toll. Third, within the major urban areas a cleavage developed between the older native-born populations and the newer immigrant populations over competition for work and housing. Finally, increased political tension between the North and the South had particular impact on border states like Maryland.

TRADE AND TRANSPORTATION

The period from 1790 to 1810 marked a high point in America's dependence on foreign trade

as a means of development. The leading sectors in the period of substantial economic development from 1793 to 1807 were the shipping and export industries, the latter including exports of American products as well as the reexport of foreign goods. War between Britain and France (the Napoleonic Wars) lasted, with one major interruption, from 1792 to 1815. This tied up the shipping trade of France, Britain, and major European countries and gave the neutral United States a massive advantage in world trade. The United States transported sugar, coffee, cocoa, pepper, and spices from the West Indies to Europe and carried manufactured goods from Europe to the rest of the world. In addition, domestic exports grew as cotton production spread through the South and demand increased from the cotton textile plants of Britain.

Foreign trade was generally more important to the economy than domestic trade until the second decade of the century. In 1790, exports totaled $20.2 million, reexports $0.3 million, and imports for domestic use $23.5 million; the figures for 1807 were $108.3 million for exports, $59.6 million for reexports, and $85.1 million for imports. The passage of the Embargo Act in 1807, followed in 1809 by the Nonintercourse Act, slowed U.S. trade expansion, and the outbreak of war between the United States and Britain in 1812 brought an end to the era. For example, exports in 1808, as a result of the 1807 Embargo Act, were only 20 percent of the total for 1807.

The decade from 1810 to 1820 has been called the great turnabout in American economic development. During (and after) the decade, foreign trade declined relative to domestic trade as the hinge seaports looked increasingly to the national, rather than the international, economy. The early period of foreign-trade prosperity had permitted capital accumulation and laid a foundation for future economic expansion. The capital market was made more efficient through the extension of banking and insurance. An influential merchant and banking clan evolved, the growth of urban centers increased the domestic market, and turnpike roads were built to permit foodstuffs to be moved to the expanding seaports. Most of these gains from trade accrued to the Northeast, particularly to the ports of New York, Boston, Philadelphia, and Baltimore. Between 1790 and 1820, New York's population grew fourfold, Boston's threefold, Philadelphia's more than twofold, and Baltimore's nearly fivefold. In addition, New York established a dominance that it would never relinquish.

Short intraregional movements dominated domestic trade prior to the War of 1812. Henry Adams commented in 1800: "In becoming politically independent of England, the old thirteen provinces developed little more commercial intercourse with each other . . . than they had maintained in colonial days. . . . Each group of States lived a life apart." Such internal trade as occurred at the beginning of the 19th century was mostly confined to the immediate hinterlands of the seaports. Boston engaged in commerce with eastern Massachusetts and northern New England, Philadelphia with the Delaware valley and southeastern Pennsylvania, Baltimore with the Chesapeake Bay and western Maryland, and New York with the Hudson valley, Connecticut, and northern New Jersey. Accessibility by natural waterway, whether river or bay, was the major determinant of hinterland size.

After the War of 1812, the settled areas west of the Alleghenies remained commercially isolated, but the Northeast and South began an increasing level of trade. The Northeast, particularly via New York, redistributed European and domestic finished goods, while the South's increasing commitment to cotton and other staples, such as tobacco, sugar, and rice, produced a reciprocal trade. Trade was based on available, inexpensive transportation that highlighted waterway movement (sea, river, canal) over land travel (turnpike, road). Until the advent of interregional railroad networks in the 1850s, the availability of water transportation set the lines of trade. Cost limited the role of overland transportation in long-distance trade. An 1816 Senate committee report indicated that importing a ton of goods from Europe cost about $9, or roughly the cost of moving the same ton of goods 30 miles overland. Such high costs did not totally prevent overland movement. In the early 1820s, prior to the opening of the Erie Canal, the turnpike from Philadelphia to Pittsburgh carried about 30,000 tons of goods annually, and the National Road from Baltimore to Ohio about 10,000 tons. However, most roads were the initial, albeit short, link for producers (whether farmers or manufacturers) to move their merchandise to the steamboat, canal barge, or sailing vessel, unless the goods were sent by wagon directly to nearby ports.

While the coastal trade was an important economic component in the growth of the four major northeastern seaports, each attempted to enlarge its hinterland area in other ways. New turnpikes, particularly in New England, provided an improved road system and expanded the area of commercial agriculture. A few major turnpikes—for example, the Lancaster Turnpike—were financially successful, and by 1815 fairly good roads linked eastern Pennsylvania, New York, New Jersey, and southern New England to the seaports. Nevertheless, building costs for turnpikes were high, and travel remained slow and expensive. The humble country road still provided the initial link for most farmers to the major carriers of merchandise—the river, and later the canal and the railroad.

The building of the Erie Canal (1817–25), financed by the state of New York, demonstrated the advantages of significant hinterland expansion. New York City, via the Erie Canal and its feeders, tapped into the Great Lakes and the upper midwestern market in a strikingly short period of time. The Erie Canal was the major element in a series of canals connecting it to other important water transportation routes. For example, the canal to Lake Champlain and the Oswego Canal, linking the Erie Canal to Lake Ontario, succeeded financially. More importantly, they extended the role and regional dominance of New York City. Other major cities attempted to follow suit. Construction of the Chesapeake and Ohio began in 1828 and extended canal transportation some 184 miles from Washington, D.C., to Cumberland, Maryland. Philadelphia, attempting to address the potential loss of trade to New York, completed the Main Line Canal, which included a portage railroad, to Pittsburgh and the Ohio valley in 1834. Other canals, including the Delaware Division, linked the anthracite fields of eastern Pennsylvania to the Delaware River and Philadelphia. These in turn were connected by canals across New Jersey or New York State and became important as carriers of anthracite coal to New York City and New England markets. By 1840, the nation had 3,326 miles of canals, but few were long-term financial successes. The Erie, Champlain, Oswego, and anthracite canals were the notable exceptions.

After 1846, the railroad, the steamship, and the telegraph became the standard means of transportation and communication. In 1840, 3,328 miles of railroad line had been built in the nation, almost two-thirds of which was in the Northeast. Most of these early railroads served essentially as feeder lines to the existing canal system or were radial passenger lines from the ports to their inner hinterlands. By the outbreak of the Civil War, railroad mileage nationally had reached 30,636, with railroads extending across the eastern third of the country. Between 1851 and 1854, the Erie, the Baltimore and Ohio, the Pennsylvania, and the New York Central Railroads provided all-weather overland transportation from the Northeast to the Middle West. While an intensification of the system in the Northeast occurred and many independent lines were combined, most traffic still remained within its own system. For example, even as late as 1860, more than 80 percent of the traffic on the Pennsylvania and the Baltimore and Ohio Railroads did not move beyond those respective systems.

As the railroad spread west, so too did the telegraph. Now communication was not bound to overland transportation time. This benefited the bankers, investors, and entrepreneurs of the Northeast by supplying information necessary for economic decisions. The advent of the ocean-going steamship after 1848 confirmed the role of New York and other Atlantic ports as the American termini of transatlantic runs.

Large volumes of trade linked each pair of major northeastern cities. The only weak link was between Philadelphia and Baltimore, which were separated by a roundabout sea route to the south of Cape Charles at the mouth of Chesapeake Bay. The coastal commodity flows between these cities between 1820 and 1860 were of three types: agricultural or raw material production from the port of origin, manufactures produced in the port of origin or its hinterland dependents, and redistributive shipments. Boston receipts included flour, corn, oats, and other grains from Baltimore, Philadelphia, and New York, both for the city's own use and for the mill towns of its hinterland. Also to Boston came hides and leather from Baltimore, Philadelphia, and New York for the boot and shoe industries of the area around Lynn; anthracite coal, steam engines, and manufactured goods from Philadelphia; and foreign imports from New York. Philadelphia receipts included shoes and textiles from Boston both for local consumption and for redistribution, and English dry goods and other foreign imports from New York. New York coastal receipts included shoes and textiles from Boston, many of which local merchants forwarded to the West and South; industrial commodities from Philadelphia, many of which were reshipped to southern ports; coal from Philadelphia; and flour, coffee, and tobacco from Baltimore. Baltimore's acquisitions included leather products from Boston, foreign imports from New York, and manufactured goods from Philadelphia.

This massive coastal water traffic was not, however, the totality of interurban trade. Each of the four major cities had an important set of connections to those smaller urban places in its own hinterland. Boston had trade with the coastal ports of Maine and the closer ports of Salem and Portsmouth; Baltimore had the Chesapeake Bay commerce and the downstream Susquehanna River trade. Philadelphia traded with places along the Delaware River as well as with areas to the west of the city, especially after completion of the Main Line Canal to Pittsburgh in 1834. New York had a flourishing coastal trade with Providence, Bridgeport, New Haven, New London, and Norwich and, most significantly, an important river trade with Albany and such smaller Hudson valley towns as Poughkeepsie, Newburgh, and Kingston. Before the opening of the Erie Canal in 1825, there were large flows of flour and grain from Albany to New York and of imports and manufactured goods in the opposite direction. After the opening of the Erie Canal, this traffic increased dramatically, sufficient to propel Albany to the 6th-largest urban center in the Northeast by 1840. By 1860, Buffalo, Albany, Troy, Rochester, and Syracuse, a line of cities paralleling the Erie Canal, were among the 20 largest places in the Northeast (table 9.3).

While interaction within the developing northeastern system was high, important connections also existed to the South (particularly New Orleans and Mobile), as a function of the cotton trade, and to Europe. New York's cotton triangle was the most important component of this trade. At the three corners of the cotton trade were the cotton ports of New Orleans, Mobile, or Charleston; the European ports of Liverpool or Le Havre; and New York. While a normal direct run of cotton from, say, New Orleans to Liverpool would seem logical, New

Table 9.3 Northeast U.S.: Population of Major Urban Places, 1800–1860 (by 1860 population rank; population in thousands)

	1800	1820	1840	1860
New York	61	131	360	1,093
Philadelphia	62	109	220	566
Boston	25	54	119	298
Baltimore	27	63	102	212
Buffalo	—	—	18	81
Pittsburgh	—	7	31	77
District of Columbia	14	33	44	75
Newark	—	—	17	72
Albany	5	13	34	62
Providence	8	12	23	51
Rochester	—	—	20	48
New Haven	4	7	13	39
Troy	—	5	19	39
Jersey City	—	—	3	37
Lowell	—	—	21	37
Syracuse	—	—	—	28
Hartford	4	5	10	27
Portland, Maine	4	9	15	26

Note: Populations of less than 2,500 are not included.

York acquired a strong grip on the cotton trade by channeling cotton from the South through New York to Europe. The return run from Europe to New York carried imported merchandise as well as immigrants. New York then shipped these goods to the southern ports, for consumption there or redistribution up the Mississippi-Ohio River system. New York merchants consolidated the city's position after 1822 by establishing regularly scheduled packet lines to the major cotton ports of Europe, although by the late 1830s and early 1840s Boston was capturing an increasing share of the trade.

Through its trade and manufacturing growth in the first half of the 19th century, the Northeast became the most diversified and developed region in the emerging national economy. By 1860, the Northeast, South, and Middle West were recognizable regional entities, displaying distinctive features. However, the nature of the linkage between these three regions has been subject to varying interpretations. Fishlow concluded that "interregional exchange was a prominent feature of American antebellum development but not as a result of interdependence among all regions." In particular, what developed in trade between the Northeast, the South, and the Middle West was not trilateral, but bilateral, trade. Trade between the South and the Middle West was always of limited importance to both regions in the antebellum period. The South was not a major market for midwestern produce nor in dire need of imported foodstuffs. In its rate of growth this trade stands in sharp contrast to exchange between the Middle West and Northeast. While consumption of midwestern produce by the North and South was at approximate parity in 1839, the former absorbed three times as much by 1860. Flow patterns diverged most distinctly in the 1850s as the extension of east-west transport routes drew the commerce that had once been transshipped via New Orleans. From the beginning, high-valued merchandise was able to bear the cost of transportation and entered the Middle West from the Northeast; by 1839 the Middle West already depended more heavily upon the Northeast than the South for its imports. By 1860, the advantage had grown enormously; almost ten times more western purchases came from the Northeast than up the Mississippi River. This occurred in the context of a rapid increase in the domestic market. The North, unlike the South, always fared better in exports to other regions than abroad. The Northeast found itself during the early 19th century in a dynamic role, with urbanization and industrialization proceeding on a broader scale than elsewhere, but also with the need to respond to competition from the Middle West, particularly in agricultural produce. For example, whereas New England's consumption of wheat and corn exceeded its production of these crops between 1839 and 1859, the states from New York to Maryland, which had always been deficit states in corn, moved from a surplus in wheat production in 1839 to a deficit in 1859. This was a direct effect of western competition. Thus, traditional crops like wheat became less important as agriculture reorganized to take advantage of the expanding urban markets.

READJUSTMENT AND REORGANIZATION

As the American ecumene increased in size and the Northeast established itself as the economic

Table 9.4 Northeast U.S.: Production of Selected Crops, 1840–1860 (thousands of bushels, except where noted)

	1840	1850	1860
Wheat	31,960	36,175	30,514
	(37.7)	(36.0)	(17.6)
Corn	46,939	70,590	84,564
	(12.4)	(11.9)	(10.1)
Oats	56,418	62,425	83,032
	(45.8)	(42.3)	(48.1)
Rye	13,987	12,020	13,680
	(75.0)	(84.7)	(64.8)
Barley	3,548	4,172	5,962
	(85.2)	(80.7)	(37.7)
Hay[a]	7,989	9,662	10,420
	(78.0)	(69.8)	(54.6)
Potatoes	78,160	45,237	65,324
	(72.0)	(68.8)	(57.3)

Note: Figures in parentheses equal proportion of total U.S. production.

[a]Thousands of tons

core of the new nation, a series of readjustments in the Northeast's economy occurred. Nowhere was this clearer than in agriculture. The U.S. census agricultural reports, beginning in 1840, identified two dimensions of change in northeastern agriculture. First, production in corn, oats, barley, and hay increased from 1840 to 1860, while production of wheat, rye, and pota-

toes showed an absolute decline (table 9.4). All crops (with the exception of oats) showed a relative decrease, however, so that the proportion of U.S. crop production accounted for by the Northeast declined. Second, the Mid-Atlantic states were more productive than New England (table 9.5). By 1860, New England was producing a larger proportion of U.S. hay and potatoes in comparison with its population size but a lower proportion of most other crops. In the Mid-Atlantic states production of rye, barley, oats, hay, and potatoes was disproportionately large.

Until the second decade of the 19th century, agriculture in the Northeast had incorporated few of the changes identified with the agricultural revolution in England. While pockets of commercial farming existed, many farms were still self-sufficient units, growing food for home use and trading small surpluses at the local store for salt, sugar, or iron products. Cultivation was expensive and exploitive, systematic crop rotation and fertilizers generally absent, and livestock neglected. Oxen were the main draft animals, and cattle were relatively poor producers of either meat or milk. Where commercial agriculture existed, it was tied, locationally, to adequate transportation. Thus, for example, early in the century the Hudson and lower Mohawk valleys were specializing in wheat production and the Connecticut valley in corn.

Table 9.5 Northeast U.S.: Concentration of Selected Crops and Animals, 1840–1860

	1840		1850		1860	
	N.E.	M.S.	N.E.	M.S.	N.E.	M.S.
Wheat	0.2	1 2	0.1	1.2	01	0.7
Corn	0.2	0.4	0.2	0.4	0.1	0.3
Rye	0.8	2.2	1.0	2.6	0.7	2.2
Barley	1.5	2.2	0.7	2.6	0.8	1.1
Oats	0.5	1.3	0.5	1.3	0.6	1.6
Hay	2.3	1.6	2.1	1.6	2.1	1.3
Potatoes	2.5	1.3	2.6	1.4	1.9	1.5
Dairy cows	—	—	0.8	0.9	0.8	0.9
Hogs	0.2	0.5	0.1	0.3	0.1	0.3
Sheep	1.5	1.3	0.9	0.9	0.8	0.8

N.E. = New England. M.S. = Mid-Atlantic states. Numbers equal crop production or animal numbers by region as % of U.S. total, divided by population by region as % of U.S. total. Thus in 1850, New England's proportion of total U.S. rye production was equal to its proportion of the U.S. population.

The advent of large-scale commercial agriculture depended strongly on the growth of regional, nonfarm demand and effective transportation to move farm goods to the urban markets. Thus, as the Northeast urbanized and developed a transportation infrastructure, farmers could specialize in what they could produce best and move their products to market at ever decreasing cost.

Initially, agriculture in the Northeast was adjusting to changing intraregional conditions—massive population growth, increasing levels of urbanization, and the development of manufacturing. Industrialization drew young men and women to the factories, but the resultant urban communities provided large and consistent markets for foodstuffs. The Northeast responded in two ways. First, the techniques of farming were improved sufficiently to provide partial competition with the Middle West. Second, and more important, a shift to crops and livestock responded directly to the new economic conditions of the Northeast. It was in this latter area that agricultural invention and innovation appeared as never before.

While agricultural societies, such as the Philadelphia Society for Agriculture, founded in 1785, flourished throughout the region, they were elitist and impractical. A more effective organization for the diffusion of new ideas, the agricultural fair, was started in 1810 in Pittsfield, Massachusetts. The Berkshire Agricultural Society was established to perpetuate this custom, and by 1858 a list of such boards and societies in the United States numbered over 900. These societies through their fairs demonstrated machinery and exhibited livestock; some operated experimental farms and imported improved cattle. In 1862 the federal government showed its direct interest in the agricultural sector by establishing the U.S. Department of Agriculture. Its duties were to "acquire and to diffuse . . . useful information on subjects related to agriculture." Through the diffusion of information by these channels, farmers became more scientific; they had, in effect, accepted their own agricultural revolution.

The growing cities and towns of the Northeast created a strong demand for perishable products that needed to be grown close to markets, such as dairy products, eggs, and vegetables, as well as for beef, pork, mutton, dray horses, carriage horses, and the hay and grain to feed such animals. Around each major city market gardening and dairy industries developed. The production of fluid milk was of particular importance and continued to expand as other facets of the dairy industry, notably cheese and butter production, moved westward. Feeding cattle for beef concentrated in the Connecticut valley, which supplied the Brighton Market near Boston, and in southeastern Pennsylvania to the west of Philadelphia. Many of these cattle were locally raised, but cattle increasingly came from the Middle West. Specialization in butter- and cheese-making developed north of New York City and in upstate New York after the completion of the Erie Canal. Around other cities the sale of fluid milk had largely supplanted cheese and butter production by 1840.

Eastern wool production enjoyed its greatest prosperity in the 1830s. The domestic manufacture of woolen goods was firmly established, and by 1840 the farmers of the Northeast accounted for 60 percent of the country's sheep. Wool production was limited to the hilly regions of the Northeast on marginal land largely unfit for crops. With their fine wool, merino sheep had been imported from Spain to Vermont as early as 1810. Their wool commanded premium prices, and by the 1830s merino sheep were widely distributed over the Northeast, with an attendant improvement in flocks.

A second transforming influence, western competition, caused eastern farmers to adjust still more. The opening of the Erie Canal in 1825 and the extension of the railroad system beyond the Alleghenies in the 1840s brought steadily increasing quantities of western products to eastern markets. From the Middle West came wool, wheat, and pork in large quantities and at prices low enough to discourage northeastern production. Sheep raising in New England declined nearly 50 percent between 1840 and 1850, with a further 35 percent decrease in the following decade. Eastern wheat growers, suffering from soil deterioration and crop blights, could not compete with midwestern wheat. In 1840, the three major wheat-producing states (in rank order) were Ohio, Pennsylvania, and New York; by 1860 they were supplanted by Illinois, Indiana, and Wisconsin. Buffalo, for example, received 1 million bushels of wheat from the Middle West in 1840, but by 1855 more than 8 million bushels came to the Great Lakes port. The driving of cattle from Ohio to the eastern markets had practically ceased by 1860; cattle were now sent east by railroad. Hog production in the Northeast also declined; the number of hogs in New England, for example, dropped from 749,000 in 1840 to only 326,000 in 1860. Hogs could be brought in by railroad, as with cattle, to be slaughtered at the market.

If northeastern farmers lost their ability to compete with western wheat, wool, and pork, they focused even more on their advantage of proximity to the large urban centers of the region. More attention was given to vegetable farming and supplying fluid milk. Cheese- and butter-making also increased. By 1860 the Northeast accounted for more than 70 percent of the nation's cheese production and more than 50 percent of its butter. More hay and forage were grown in 1860 than in earlier years, potato production (particularly in Maine) increased dramatically, and orchards were planted to supply the cities' needs. The fruit and vegetable industry was dependent upon a middle-class urban market, improved transportation, and nursery production of young trees. All of these were in place by 1860.

Thus, urban demand and western competition changed agriculture in the Northeast. Local farmers were forced to specialize in milk, butter, cheese, vegetables, fruit, and hay, which because of their bulk or perishability escaped western competition and found markets in the expanding urban centers close by.

INTEGRATION AND DIFFERENTIATION

The wholesale-trading mechanism was the basis for the development of the largest places in the Northeast's urban hierarchy. Geographer James Vance's basic thesis holds that "the earliest support for enlarged cities, beyond the encouragement offered by the population in the close vicinity, comes from wholesaling—only a single entrepôt in each major region will rise to large city size on the basis of wholesale trading." Thus, the early mercantile cities acted as points of collection and distribution in an enlarging and westward-expanding urban system. They competed for regional and national domination as new forms of transportation (canals, railroads, steamships) provided the potential for more efficient linkages in external trade as well as in internal expansion. The mercantile

cities of Boston, New York, Philadelphia, and Baltimore dominated the Northeast and the nation for much of the 19th century. A coastal settlement pattern existed in 1800, with a regional economy severely curtailed by limited transportation facilities. As the trading complex developed, the interior entrepôt serving as a "primary collecting point for resources shipped back to the original entrepôt" was formed. In the case of New York City (the major mercantile center), Albany, Rochester, and Buffalo can be identified as interior entrepôts by 1840. Consequently, the Northeast as a region became more spatially integrated and more urbanized than either the Middle West or the South.

After 1820, the early mercantile cities, building on their trade and wholesaling functions, invested progressively in manufacturing. In Philadelphia manufacturing came earlier and in greater volume than in its neighbors of New York City and Baltimore. To the north, merchant capital, especially from Boston and Providence, industrialized the basically rural landscape of eastern Massachusetts, New Hampshire, and Rhode Island through the development of the cotton textile and shoe industries. Thus, a second set of midsized places developed as industrial towns. By 1830, a number of these towns such as Lynn, Springfield, Lowell, and Warwick had emerged in New England. To the south the new federal capital of Washington, D.C., also emerged.

The Mercantile City

The mercantile city was focused on the waterfront (fig. 9.2). There the functions of the city were performed: vessels were loaded and unloaded, goods and materials awaiting distribution into the city or farther inland were warehoused, items were repackaged for transshipment to other domestic and overseas ports, and various financial transactions occurred in the financial houses and merchant exchanges. Beyond the waterfront lay the courthouse, the final arbiter of mercantile conflict. All these functions were organized with reference to the "point of attachment" (the docks) to the outside world (fig. 9.2). Still further beyond lay the residences of the wealthy. Charles Dickens described Baltimore in 1842 as "a bustling busy town with a great deal of traffic of various kinds and in particular of water

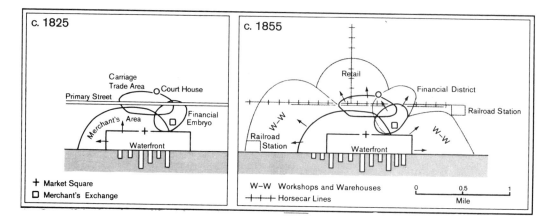

Figure 9.2 The Mercantile City and the Emergence of Downtown (after Muller)

commerce. That portion of the town that it most favors is none of the cleanest it is true; but the upper part is of a very different character and has many agreeable streets and public monuments." Thus the middle and upper classes separated themselves from the commercial waterfront area. Noxious industries such as tanning and slaughtering and large land-using industries like brickmaking and shipbuilding occupied the city's periphery.

The mercantile city was also compact. The fact that most people moved on foot and most goods by horse and cart produced a highly condensed city structure. Residential and land use densities were high. Baltimore in 1830 packed its 81,000 residents into an area measuring 2 1/4 miles by 1 mile, and no part of the built-up area was more than 1 mile from the developed waterfront. Not until 1827 in New York and the 1850s in most other large cities was the horse-drawn omnibus introduced. This provided for the privileged few—25,000 riders per day in New York in 1837—an escape from the high density.

Many people worked at their place of residence. Except for commerce-serving (shipbuilding, ship repairing) and entrepôt industries (processing of tobacco, sugar, and other raw materials), the dominant form of manufacturing organization was the artisan shop. Here, production, sales, and residences occurred in the same location. The vast majority of tailors, bakers, cobblers, tobacconists, and blacksmiths were organized in this manner. There were few large manufacturers. In the early 1830s probably no

more than 10 factories with 100 or more employees existed in all of the major mercantile cities of the Northeast combined. In New York, the largest plant employed 200 workers; in Baltimore, the Stockton and Stokes coach-making operation employed 80; in Boston no establishment employed more than 100. While small-scale, predominantly artisan manufacturing characterized mercantile cities, steam power was beginning to be used in foundries, machine shops, and cotton textile plants. Baltimore in 1833 had 32 steam-powered plants, using small horsepower engines. By 1838, 45 plants in Baltimore and 59 in Philadelphia used this newer form of power.

Industrialization

As the sequential transportation improvements of canal, steamship, and railroad more fully integrated the area east of the Mississippi, the Northeast experienced the parallel growth of industrialization and urbanization (table 9.6). The mercantile cities acted as source areas for capital for merchant capitalists who were seeking new areas for investment. Three distinct industrial locational patterns emerged: the New England form of small- to medium-sized town dominated by manufacturing (Lowell, New Bedford, Lynn, Lawrence, Manchester); the large city (New York, Philadelphia, Baltimore, Boston) building on its mercantile heritage; and the processing centers (Albany, Rochester, Troy) concentrated along the Erie Canal transportation corridor (fig. 9.3).

Early industry in the Northeast was predominantly household manufacture (the "family factory"), in which farm homes were the units of production. The process was self-provision, "a fertile ground in which invention might germinate," and thus from the basically rural areas of southern and eastern New England came a flood of inventions. Samuel Slater set up the first cotton-spinning mill at Providence in 1790. It used waterpower, the energy for the American industrial revolution. The first true industrial city in America, as opposed to the existing large mercantile centers, was Lowell, established by "The Proprietors of the Locks and Canals of the Pawtucket Falls of the Merrimac River in Massachusetts." The growth of the national market (to nearly 10 million people by 1820) and demands by New England shippers for goods to trade increased the pressure on domestic manufacturers to produce more staple products, for example, cheap and durable textiles, metal products, and woodenware. The first industry to which the new American system of manufacture was applied was, as in Britain, cotton textiles.

Earlier developments in the cotton-textile industry in such places as Pawtucket and Slatersville had been relatively small, producing yarn and thread for use in hand weaving, and had used whole families as their labor forces. In 1814 Francis Cabot Lowell and Patrick Jackson organized the Boston Manufacturing Company, utilizing capital earned in the shipping trades. They built their first mill in that same year at Waltham. It was an integrated mill, using baled cotton purchased from southern merchants to produce a plain, coarse, inexpensive white sheeting. The enormous success of the Waltham mill encouraged other Boston capitalists to imitate the undertaking. The next great venture was at Lowell, followed by mills at Chicopee and Holyoke in Massachusetts, Nashua and Manchester in New Hampshire, and Biddeford and Lewiston in Maine. In 1850, the Merrimack Manufacturing Company in Lowell employed 2,145 operatives, and five other mills had employment exceeding 1,000 each. Five years later, 52 integrated mills in Lowell employed 13,187 people, of whom nearly 9,000 were women. Boardinghouses were constructed initially to house the female workers attracted from the surrounding areas by employment opportunities in Lowell. By the 1850s, however, many immigrant women worked in the mills, particularly in the lower-paid cording and spinning departments. The Irish in Lowell were "a dominant factor of Lowell life" by 1860, and this was repeated in other mill towns like Manchester and New Haven. Large mills in a rural setting with their attendant boardinghouses, interlaced with industrial canals to harness the waterpower, characterized this archetypal industrial town. The mill towns that developed in northern New England as a consequence of the Waltham enterprise had their antithesis in the Providence region. While the Boston-financed cotton-textile plants of eastern Massachusetts were large integrated plants and highly dependent on female labor, the Providence-financed Rhode Island–Connecticut cotton factories were smaller and relied more on male labor.

This phase of industrial-urban growth produced a new set of cities with industrial, rather than mercantile, origins (fig. 9.4). While the wholesaling functions for the Waltham-system cities remained in Boston and Portland (Maine), the mill towns attracted retail trade. Providence

Table 9.6 Northeast U.S.: Manufacturing Data, 1860

	Establishments		Employment		Average Employment per Establishment	Value Added ($000's)	
New England	20,871	(14.8)	391,836	(29.9)	13.9	223,076	(26.1)
Middle States	53,286	(37.9)	551,243	(42.0)	10.3	358,211	(41.9)
Northeast	74,158	(52.7)	943,079	(71.9)	12.7	581,287	(68.0)
Rest of U.S.	66,475	(47.3)	368,167	(28.1)	5.5	272,970	(32.1))
Total U.S.	140,633	(100.0)	1,311,246	(100.0)	9.3	854,257	(100.0)

Note: Numbers in parentheses equal proportion of U.S. total.

grew upon demands generated by the small industrial towns of Rhode Island and Connecticut, as well as upon its function as the port from which southern cotton was redistributed to local mills. By 1860 both Lowell and Providence were among the 25 largest cities in the United States.

An important effect of a rapidly growing dominant industry, cotton textiles being no exception, is the linkages created by that industry—forward linkages in the form of consumer goods such as men's clothing and cotton goods, and backward linkages expressed in an important demand for textile machinery. Many textile mills produced their own machinery, but as the industry grew larger in scale, specialized textile machinery producers emerged. These firms often, in turn, broadened their production line to include machine tools, stationary engines, and locomotives. For example, the Lowell Machine Shop began as a textile machinery manufacturer, but by 1845, with a labor force of 900 men, it was producing other kinds of machinery, locomotives, and stationary engines. The backward linkage into textile machinery had further important linkages into the iron casting, metalworking, and machine tool industries. This

process of demand created through both forward and backward linkages was of increasing importance to the emergence of the United States as an industrial nation by the 1860s.

The woolen industry and the production of boots and shoes matched the cotton-textile industry in its concentration in New England. Each of these industries was strongly geared to a national, rather than local, market and operated at scales substantially above the average for the United States. Massachusetts was the dominant location for both industries. In the 1850s, the value of the output from the New England woolen mills increased dramatically, and by 1860 the region accounted for two-thirds (by value) of U.S. production. By midcentury the boot and shoe industry of New England adopted the factory system, and the sewing machine was transforming the industry in a parallel manner to that experienced in the clothing industry. In terms of employment, the boot and shoe industry became by 1860 the largest manufacturing industry in the nation and was highly concentrated in eastern Massachusetts, particularly in Lynn and Worcester. For boots and shoes, as with the cotton and woolen industries, Boston was the dominant wholesaler, with probably 50

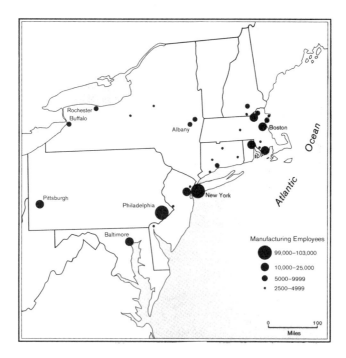

Figure 9.3 Northeast: Manufacturing Cities, 1860

percent of the footwear output remaining in the Northeast. In similar fashion, close to 75 percent of the coastal shipment of cotton goods from Boston remained in the Northeast.

The introduction of steam power brought yet another element to the New England manufacturing complex. The Waltham system, expanding in the mid-1840s, reproduced the Lowell industrial model by both utilizing waterpower and engaging female labor lodged in boarding-houses at Lawrence. At the same time, the Wamsutta Company in New Bedford created a cotton mill based on steam power and male labor drawn from the existing port town. Lawrence and New Bedford demonstrate two distinct forms of industrial development using different power sources and labor segments, albeit at a large factory-scale level. Fall River, originally dependent on limited waterpower to expand, had by 1860 converted to steam power and was on the threshold of preeminence as a cotton-textile town.

Outside of New England, the major cities dominated manufacturing employment. While Boston accounted for only 11 percent of Massachusetts's manufacturing employment, New York, Philadelphia, and Baltimore employed 45 percent or more of their respective states' industrial workers (table 9.7). New York and Philadelphia had especially large numbers of industrial workers, four times larger than their nearest rival. Like all large cities, they benefited from high levels of local demand, but they slowly sought to expand their markets in certain products from local to regional and national levels. Thus, a broad range of manufacturing output with a handful of dominant industries characterized their industrial profiles. In Philadelphia in 1850 textiles and the clothing trades hired about one-third of all industrial workers. The building trades, boot and shoe manufacture, heavy industry, and metalworking all absorbed between 5 and 10 percent of the labor force, and five more industries, including hat-making, food production, and printing, employed between 2 and 4 percent. New York showed a similarly broad mix: textile mills, garment factories, ironworks, breweries, distilleries, flour mills, meatpacking plants, and the largest shipyard in the nation producing ocean clippers, sailing vessels, and steamships. In all the major port cities, agricultural processing was also important; consequently sugar refining, flour milling, brewing,

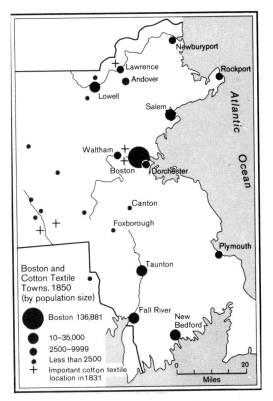

Figure 9.4 Cotton Textile Towns in Eastern Massachusetts, 1831 and 1850

and slaughtering were part of the urban landscape.

Three other factors encouraged the industrial development of these large seaport cities. First, as the dominant port cities, they were the recipients of vast numbers of immigrants. The availability of labor, a problem in New England industrialization, was not a concern for the large-city manufacturer. The immigrant populations swelled city labor forces while adding to the burgeoning consumer market. By 1860, foreign-born residents exceeded one-quarter of the population in all but one (Washington, D.C.) of the ten largest cities of the Northeast (table 9.8). African American populations were insignificant except in the "border cities" of Baltimore and Washington, D.C.

Second, these cities, as a function of their mercantile dominance, were points of capital accumulation where entrepreneurs saw opportunity through investment in manufacturing. They also possessed the physical structures—

Table 9.7 Northeast U.S.: Manufacturing Data for Selected States, 1860

	% of U.S. Population	% of U.S. Manuf. Employment	Female % of State Manuf. Employment
Massachusetts	3.9	16.6	32.7
Boston (11.2)			
Lowell (6.1)			
New Bedford (5.2)			
New York	12.3	17.6	23.1
New York (44.8)			
Pennsylvania	9.2	16.9	17.8
Philadelphia (44.6)			
Pittsburgh (5.0)			
Maryland	2.2	2.2	23.6
Baltimore (59.4)			
New Jersey	2.1	4.3	23.0
Newark (33.7)			
Rhode Island	0.6	2.5	36.0
Providence (34.3)			

Note: Figures in parentheses after the important manufacturing centers show proportion of state manufacturing employment.

port facilities, warehousing, and transportation connections into their enlarging hinterland areas—and the banking and insurance institutions necessary for integrated output.

Third, the availability of steam power allowed a higher concentration of particular manufacturing types than would otherwise have been the case. Waterpower sites limit industrial concentration; steam power has no such built-in constraint. Yet steam power was not used in all industries and in all sizes of industrial establishments. It was more expensive at this time than waterpower at virtually all locations in the Northeast; thus its utilization required evidence of strong necessity. In Philadelphia in 1850 only 10 percent of all employers used steam engines or waterwheels. In Baltimore in 1860 only 7 percent of 1,147 manufacturing establishments used steam power. The application of steam power related more to product than to size of enterprise. This relationship was clear in Baltimore in 1860. Fewer than 5 percent of all industrial plants in the city employed more than 50 workers, and these establishments accounted for more than one-half of all employment. Yet, such large-sized establishments accounted for fewer than 30 percent of steam-powered plants. The

concentration of steam power was associated with particular industries: iron foundries, metalworking, machine production, food processing, and planing and woodworking.

Albany and Troy formed an industrial district at the eastern terminus of the Erie Canal. It was an important center for lumber, brewing, and flour milling, as well as one of the nation's major iron producers. In addition, Troy had important cotton mills. Rochester and Buffalo, at the western end of the Erie Canal corridor, were points of connection to the increasingly important midwestern wheat states. Flour milling dominated their manufacturing. Rochester, for example, had only 2 cotton mills to go with its 23 flour mills.

By 1860 mercantile cities were industrializing, and factory towns were fast becoming urban. The Northeast contained 72 percent of the nation's manufacturing employment and 68 percent of its "value added" by manufacturing. Size of establishment in the Northeast was twice the national average. Of 23 cities in the nation where manufacturing employment exceeded 5,000, only 6 were outside the Northeast (table 9.9). New York and Philadelphia dominated, with 15 percent of the nation's manufacturing

Table 9.8 Northeast U.S.: Foreign-Born and African American Proportions of Population in the Ten Largest Cities, 1860

	% of Foreign-Born in Total Population	Most Numerous Foreign-Born Group	Next most Numerous Foreign-Born Group	% of Af. Am. in Total Population
New York	48	Irish	German	2
Philadelphia	29	Irish	German	4
Boston	36	Irish	British-American	1
Baltimore	25	German	Irish	13
Buffalo	46	German	Irish	1
Pittsburgh	37	Irish	German	2
District of Columbia	18	Irish	German	18
Newark	37	Irish	German	2
Albany	34	Irish	German	1
Providence	25	Irish	English	3

employment. Although challenged by the newer midwestern centers of Cincinnati, St. Louis, and Chicago, these two, plus Baltimore and Boston, were edging toward metropolitan status. They dominated large hinterland areas; were industrial, wholesaling, and financial centers; and were important beyond their statistical status as the points of organization within the emerging national economy. Between 1840 and 1860 the Northeast was the primary area of urban manufacturing innovation, a model (albeit imperfect) that would be restructured and modified as the nation grew and that itself would be subject to readjustment in process.

The Nation's Capital

While economic power became vested in the large cities of the Northeast during the antebellum period, the nation's political center was a new, planned city straddling the Potomac River. Section 8 of Article 1 of the Constitution gave Congress power to set up "a district not exceeding ten miles square" to be "the seat of the government of the United States." The Residence Act of 1790 gave the president the power to choose a location on the Potomac River. President Washington chose a site that included the existing settlements of Georgetown and Alexandria. Once the site had been selected, Washing-

ton acted with dispatch to hire Pierre Charles L'Enfant to plan the city. The plan, drawing heavily for inspiration on European designs, was essentially a grid overlaid with a radial pattern. The President's House (today's White House) and the Capitol were to be joined by a grand avenue (the Mall). The federal government moved from Philadelphia to Washington in 1800. Thus, a new city was born with an initial population of some 14,000 people, including extant populations of 3,000 people in Georgetown and 5,000 in Alexandria.

The District of Columbia grew dramatically during the first half of the 19th century. As the nation grew, the federal capital assumed greater responsibilities and attracted population, both white and African American. African Americans, in particular, sought to locate in the capital, and by 1860, they made up 18 percent of its residents, a far higher percentage than that found in any city to its north. As a political and administrative town that had incorporated into its boundaries the bustling ports of Georgetown and Alexandria, Washington's commercial aspirations were tied strongly after 1828 to the construction of the Chesapeake and Ohio Canal to Cumberland, Maryland. The canal experienced limited success, particularly after the construction of the Baltimore and Ohio Railroad westward from Baltimore. Washington would not become a trade center, nor would it develop a manufacturing base. This potential was undermined when, in 1846, the federal district lost one-third of its total area with the retrocession back to Virginia of the area south and west of the Potomac, including Alexandria. By 1860, however, Washington, D.C., had 75,000 residents, a population not attained through mercantile strength or an industrial base but largely through its attractions as the nation's capital.

THE NORTHEAST IN 1860

Although between 1800 and 1860 its proportion of the U.S. population fell by 20 percent, the Northeast, in the words of David Ward, "supported a sizable industrial production and was the center of the expanding American economy." In 1860, with 37 percent of the total U.S. population, the Northeast contained 72 percent of all American manufacturing employment. Only 12 percent of the U.S. population lived in

Table 9.9 Northeast U.S.: Manufacturing Cities with 5,000 or More Manufacturing Employees, 1860

	Population	Manufacturing Employment	Manuf. Employ. as % of Pop.	Female % of Manuf. Employ.
New York	1,092,791	102,969	9.4	25.2
Philadelphia	565,529	99,003	17.5	30.9
Boston	297,673	24,445	8.2	22.8
Newark	71,941	18,851	26.2	27.4
Baltimore	212,416	17,054	8.0	27.4
Lowell, Mass.	36,827	13,236	35.9	65.3
New Bedford	22,300	11,297	50.6	5.9
Pittsburgh	77,233	11,151	11.9	19.1
Providence	50,666	11,142	22.0	26.8
Lynn, Mass.	19,083	9,588	50.2	39.0
Troy, N.Y.	39,235	8,826	22.5	54.6
New Haven	39,267	7,474	19.0	42.0
Lawrence, Mass.	17,639	7,150	40.5	55.4
Manchester, N.H..	20,107	7,000	34.8	64.9
Rochester	48,204	6,706	13.9	21.4
Albany	62,367	5,821	9.3	22.9
Buffalo	81,129	5,578	6.9	6.2

Note: Outside the Northeast, only Cincinnati (29,501 manufacturing employees), St. Louis (9,352), Richmond (7,474), Louisville (6,679), Chicago (5,360), and New Orleans (5,062) had 5,000+ manufacturing employees in 1860.

cities of 25,000 or more, but 21 percent of the Northeast's population resided in cities of that size (table 9.10). Thus, the Northeast was in the forefront of the linked processes of industrialization and urbanization. It was, in short, the central area of economic organization for the entire American economy. As Thomas Cochran has observed, "while the United States of 1850 . . . was still agricultural as measured either by employment or production, its Northeast had gone through the first and critical phases of industrialization." It was the economic core from which manufactured goods, in particular, were sent to less urbanized areas and to which farm products flowed. Large markets permitted higher levels of specialization. Thus, the first firms producing for a national rather than a regional or local market were in the Northeast, manufacturing textiles, clothing, boots and shoes, and stoves. The industries of the towns and cities of the Northeast became the basis for the emerging Manufacturing Belt. David Meyer has argued that "by 1860 . . . the key regional industrial systems of the manufacturing belt were established." This belt stretched from St. Louis to Baltimore and Chicago to Detroit, but it was the

Table 9.10 Northeast U.S.: Population, Urbanization, and Industrialization, 1860

	Total Manufacturing Employment		Female % of Manufacturing Employment	% of Total U.S. Population	% Population in Cities of 25,000+
New England	391,836	(29.9)	32.9	10.0	15.2
Mid-Atlantic	546,243	(41.7)	20.8	26.5	28.3
Northeast	938,079	(71.6)	25.9	36.5	20.9
U.S. total	1,311,246	(100.0)	20.6	100.0	11.9

Note: Percent of U.S. total in parentheses.

eastern region that was dominant.

The "new" Northeast was a prototype for many of the processes—economic, political, social, and cultural—that were played out on a larger scale as the American ecumene enlarged. Perhaps the most important was the development and linking of mass production and mass consumption. As real family incomes improved in the Northeast, city retail structures were increasingly democratized. In 1862 A. T. Stewart opened his modern department store in New York City. This symbolized the realization that the consuming public was able to purchase more than basic necessities. Such consumer palaces were, as Daniel Boorstin has indicated, "symbols of faith in the future of growing communities." They identified the central business district of the American city into the 20th century.

While the Northeast by 1860 was the most economically diversified and advanced region within the nation, not all parts of the region shared equally in these impressive gains. Areas of northern New England, the Appalachians, and the Alleghenies remained relative backwaters. If urbanization and industrialization produced positive economic results, they also produced many negative social effects. In 1850, almost 60 percent of the total number of foreign-born inhabitants lived in the Northeast. The region's towns and cities at that time were often overcrowded, with poor housing, inadequate urban services, and limited transportation. Yet they were productive, innovative, and bustling. The marked social and economic differences (as well as incipient racial cleavages) that increasingly characterized the American city as the 19th century unfolded were evident in the Northeast by the onset of Civil War.

ADDITIONAL READING

Adams, H. 1964. *The United States in 1800.* Ithaca: Cornell University Press.

Bidwell, P. W., and J. I. Falconer. 1941. *History of Agriculture in the Northern United States, 1620–1860.* Washington: Carnegie Institution, 1925. Reprint, New York: Peter Smith.

Boorstin, D. J. 1973. *The Americans: The Democratic Experience.* New York: Random House.

Cochran, T. C. 1981. *Frontiers of Change: Early Industrialism in America.* New York: Oxford University Press.

Cochrane, W. W. 1979. *The Development of American Agriculture: A Historical Analysis.* Minneapolis: University of Minnesota Press.

Crowther, S. J. 1976. "Urban Growth in the Mid-Atlantic States, 1785–1850." *Journal of Economic History* 36: 624–44.

Danhof, C. H. 1969. *Change in Agriculture: The Northern United States, 1820–1870.* Cambridge: Harvard University Press.

Dickens, C. 1843. *American Notes and Reprinted Pieces.* London: Chapman & Hall.

Doucet, M. J. 1982. "Urban Land Redevelopment in 19th-Century North America: Themes in Literature." *Journal of Urban History* 8: 299–342.

Dublin, T. 1979. *Women at Work: The Transformation of Work and Community in Lowell, Massachusetts, 1826–1860.* New York: Columbia University Press.

Fishlow, A. 1964. "Antebellum and Interregional Trade Reconsidered." *American Economic Review* 54: 352–64.

Gates, P. W. 1960. *The Farmer's Age: Agriculture, 1815–1860.* New York: Holt, Rinehart & Winston.

Gilchrist, D. T. 1967. *The Growth of Seaport Cities, 1790–1825.* Charlottesville: University Press of Virginia.

Glasco, L. 1975. "The Life Cycles and Household Structures of American Ethnic Groups." *Journal of Urban History* 1.

Gottmann, J. 1961. *Megalopolis: The Urbanized Northeastern Seaboard of the United States.* New York: Twentieth Century Fund.

Groves, P. A., and E. K. Muller. 1979. "The Emergence of Industrial Districts in Mid-19th Century Baltimore." *Geographical Review* 60: 159–78.

Hershberg, T., ed. 1981. *Philadelphia: Work Space, Family, and Group Experience in the 19th Century.* New York: Oxford University Press.

Kirkland, E. C. 1961. *Industry Comes of Age: Business, Labor, and Public Policy, 1860–1897.* New York: Holt, Rinehart & Winston.

Licht, W. 1995. *Industrializing America: The 19th Century.* Baltimore: Johns Hopkins University Press.

McIlwraith, T. F. 1976. "Freight Capacity and Utilization of the Erie and Great Lakes Canals before 1850." *Journal of Economic History* 36: 852–77.

McClelland, P. D. 1997. *Sowing Modernity: America's First Agricultural Revolution.* Ithaca: Cornell University Press.

Meyer, D. R. 1983. "Emergence of the American

Manufacturing Belt: An Interpretation." *Journal of Historical Geography* 9: 145–74.

Muller, E. K. 1977. "Regional Urbanization and the Selective Growth of Towns in North American Regions." *Journal of Historical Geography* 3: 21–39.

———. 1980. "Distinctive Downtown, Fashioning the American Landscape." *Geographical Magazine* 52: 747–56.

Pred, A. 1966. "Manufacturing in the American Mercantile City: 1800–1840." *Annals of the Association of American Geographers* 56: 307–38.

———. 1973. *Urban Growth and the Circulation of Information: The United States System of Cities, 1790–1840.* Cambridge: Harvard University Press.

———. 1980. *Urban Growth and City-Systems in the United States, 1840–1860.* Cambridge: Harvard University Press.

Rothenberg, W. B. 1992. *From Market-Place to a Market Economy: The Transformation of Rural Massachusetts, 1750–1850.* Chicago: University of Chicago Press.

Taylor, G. R. 1951. *The Transportation Revolution, 1815–1860.* New York: Holt, Rinehart & Winston.

———. 1967. "American Urban Growth Preceding the Railway Age." *Journal of Economic History* 27: 309–39.

Trollope, A. 1862. *North America.* London: Chapman: & Hall.

Vance, J. E., Jr. 1970. *The Merchant's World: The Geography of Wholesaling.* Englewood Cliffs, N.J.: Prentice Hall.

———. 1977. *This Scene of Man: The Role and Structure of the City in the Geography of Western Civilization.* New York: Harper & Row.

Ward, D. 1971. *Cities and Immigrants: A Geography of Change in 19th-Century America.* New York: Oxford University Press.

Ware, C. F. 1931. *The Early New England Cotton Manufacture.* Boston: Houghton Mifflin.

Warner, S. B. 1972. *The Urban Wilderness: A History of the American City.* New York: Harper & Row.

Wood, J. S. 1984. "Elaboration of a Settlement System: The New England Village in the Federal Period." *Journal of Historical Geography* 10: 331–56.

Wyckoff, W. 1988. *The Developer's Frontier: The Making of the Western New York Landscape.* New Haven: Yale University Press.

10

British North America, 1763–1867

THOMAS F. MCILWRAITH

In 1755 John Mitchell published "a map of the British and French Dominions in North America" (frontispiece). The patchwork of territorial units bears scant resemblance to today's provinces and states, yet this map was used until the early 20th century to fix boundaries as English-speaking people took over the continent largely explored by the French. Mitchell used modern English names throughout, anticipating the end to "the French Dominions," still eight years away. When the end came, two British islands—St.-Pierre and Miquelon, off Newfoundland—were ceded to France and continue to this day as token remnants of the once great French claims in North America. Elsewhere, from Florida to Hudson Bay, from Newfoundland to the Mississippi valley, along the Atlantic seaboard, across the Appalachians, and around the Great Lakes, the land in 1763 was British.

Britain was supreme at sea, and 18th-century North America was ocean oriented. That grip diminished over the next 100 years as America developed a landward focus. Mitchell's map was barely into its second edition when the American Revolution occurred, outdating it once more; the Monroe Doctrine (1823) and the Reciprocity Treaty (providing for free trade) between the United States and British provinces (1854–66) reinforced the trend away from Europe. Old coastal ports linked overseas came to share attention with Ohio and Ontario, where self-standing transport and town systems were evolving. Land took on value and domestic economies grew up; social structure went far beyond simple kin and family organization. Settlement frontiers generally advanced, but some sputtered and stalled and occasionally even retreated. Despite its unimaginable vastness, in some places America was actually becoming crowded by the 1860s.

AN OVERVIEW

The subject of this chapter is those parts of North America never included within the United States. Figures 10.1 and 10.2 show population change and trends in selected economic indicators for this broad northerly territory and are the basic elements upon which to build an account of a century of achievement.

Fewer than 300,000 people lived and thrived in British North America in the 1760s, about two-thirds of them Native and one-third European. No more than 10,000 Natives remained in the Atlantic region, survivors of much larger populations 150 years earlier. Nearly 80,000 occupied the Great Lakes woodlands and the extensive regions from Hudson Bay westward to the Rockies and were active participants in the European fur trade. The remainder—100,000 on the Pacific slopes, in the Mackenzie valley, and throughout the Arctic—had yet to see white faces.

Of the Europeans, some 70,000 were French-speaking Roman Catholics, mostly family farmers subsisting in the St. Lawrence valley. Traditional husbandry, limited involvement in the fur trade, and a decaying feudal social structure (seigneurialism) in the shadow of the walled towns of Quebec and Montreal placed this group on the outer margins of world affairs in the middle of the 18th century. Another 20,000 or so were slightly nearer the center of the action, in the Atlantic cod fishery. Half of these traveled annually from Europe to the fishing banks and perhaps never saw land; the remainder fished out of countless villages sprinkled around the mainland shores and eastern parts of Newfoundland. Several thousand first-generation New Englanders occupied the Bay of Fundy shores, often taking up farmlands recently vacated by French Acadians, who had been expelled by the British between 1755 and 1757. A commercial, aggressive spirit characterized these people. Halifax, a military town of 8,000 persons founded in 1749, was the sole outpost of British urbanity beyond the 13 colonies.

Scientific and artistic evaluation added new depth to understanding America. Titus Smith Jr. (botanist), William Logan (geologist), Louis

Agassiz (geomorphologist), Paul Kane (artist and ethnologist), and military topographer-artists such as J. F. W. Desbarres, Thomas Davies, and James Cockburn established beyond question that a huge landmass with manageable vegetation and climate lay open for settlement and use. By the 1860s, British North America had more than 3 million inhabitants, ten times that of a century earlier (fig. 10.1).

In 1867, the provinces of Ontario, Quebec, New Brunswick, and Nova Scotia united to form a federation, Canada, with its own legislature. Newfoundland, Prince Edward Island, Manitoba, and British Columbia looked on with interest, and all but Newfoundland joined within six years. Had Huck Finn's balloon drifted northeastward on that mass of humid Gulf of Mexico air that regularly makes a friendly invasion of eastern Canada, he would have gazed down on a patchwork of regions virtually indistinguishable from those in his own country. British traditions persisted in Canada, enlivened by a reviving French element and a growing sense that the differences, whatever they might be, had to be defended. Identifying, celebrating, and maintaining "Canadianness" is a lasting legacy of the century when British North America turned inland from the sea.

THE CHANGING NATIVE WORLD

Between the 1760s and 1860s many Native groups were overtaken by alien cultures, both European and displaced Native, with predictable loss of patrimony. By and large the surrender was without violence, but military alliances, commerce, stewardship of land, mission work, and attitudes toward benevolence all changed, irreversibly accelerating the erosion of Native independence. By 1867 episodes of assimilation, deportation, isolation, neglect, and extinction had occurred, and it is clear that Native people were becoming misfits in their own lands.

The Eastern Woodlands Groups

In the Atlantic region, Native and European were well acquainted by the 1760s (fig. 10.3). Some 10,000 hunters and gatherers took game in the interior of Newfoundland, the northern Appalachians, and the north shore of the Gulf of St. Lawrence during the winter and migrated to the coasts for summer fishing. Their rhythm matched the seasonal migrations of European fishermen, large numbers of whom appeared offshore each spring and then retreated overseas in the late fall. Here was a potential complementarity, but the Natives could teach Europeans little about the Grand Banks cod fishery offshore.

As the New Brunswick shorelines filled with white settlements after 1783 and timber camps began appearing in the interior about 1800, the 3,000 to 4,000 surviving Mi'kmaq and Malecite there quietly gave up their old migratory ways. A few tried, unsuccessfully, the western Newfoundland fur trade in the 1830s. These Roman Catholic peoples had been allies of the Acadian French expelled in the 1750s and were among the first victims of British neglect of Natives in British America. The Beothuk of Newfoundland fared far worse, cornered on their island and hunted to apparent extinction in the 1820s; the Innu of Labrador may be survivors of this carnage. The least affected in this period were the Naskapi of the north shore of the Gulf of St. Lawrence. Poor harbors and land hopeless for forestry or farming assured that this coast would remain largely undisturbed well into the 20th century.

Woodland peoples living north of the Great Lakes pursued similar seasonal patterns, migrating to the interior in the winter and to the larger lakes in the summer. Here the remote wintering grounds, rich in fur, interested the Europeans, and a partnership developed between Algonquin in the woods and Europeans at the shores. But it was not a symbiosis, and as European self-confidence and knowledge of the land grew, the Europeans took over the middleman role. By the 1820s the Algonquin in a wide arc south of Hudson Bay were ravaged by disease brought on by starvation and cultural destitution. The Roman Catholic and Anglican Churches by 1850 were offering spiritual support and welfare, but to less than half the number of Natives of a century earlier.

Throughout the Great Lakes the end of French rule left a power vacuum. Those Natives allied with Britain in the American Revolution were given sanctuary on dedicated reserve lands north of Lakes Erie and Ontario after 1783, and many fought for Britain one last time in the War of 1812. Britain's subsequent attempt to make

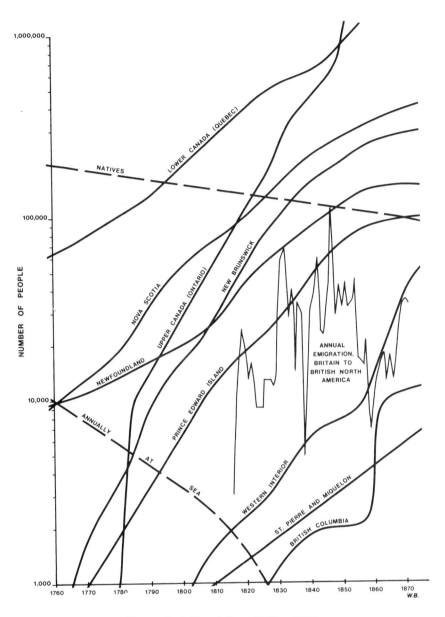

Figure 10.1 Population, 1760s–1875

the agricultural Mohawk into family farmers appeared reasonable, but failed; to try it on the Algonquin, nomadic hunters, was a naïve affront. The suspension of annual gift-giving and withdrawal of good farmland from the reserves further eroded good relations. Some Natives were relocated to remote areas of poor land, such as Manitoulin Island in Lake Huron. Old partnerships dissolved, and the Natives were shunted aside.

The Western Interior, Pacific, and Arctic

Ojibwa and Cree living northwest of Lake Superior had been drawn into the parklands and plains before 1800 by the energetic rivalry between fur

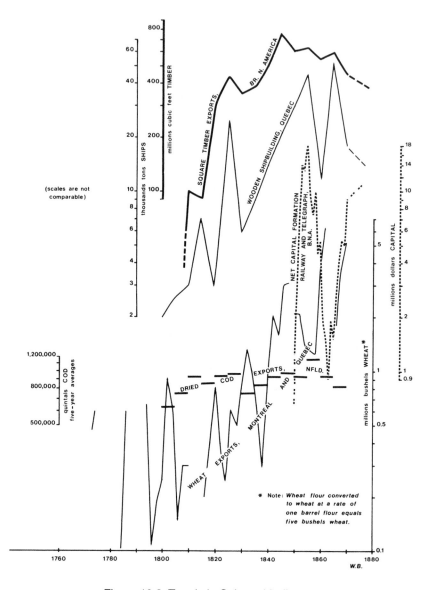

Figure 10.2 Trends in Selected Indicators

traders from Montreal and Hudson Bay (fig. 10.3). Here they joined the Assiniboine, and once they had accepted the horse and buffalo hunt central to grassland life, they could not readjust to the forest. Even a few Iroquois went west from Lake Erie, but for most Woodland peoples the grasslands were incomprehensible. The Black Hawk wars of the 1830s were the desperate strikes of frightened peoples pressed to the wall—in this case unfamiliar grasslands.

Following the company's incorporation in 1670, the Hudson's Bay Company fur trade had gradually spread to the plains. For a century trapping and transporting were done by the Natives, but after 1770 the Montreal rivalry drew Europeans inland (fig. 10.3). The Natives' role as intermediaries had so diminished by 1790 that many turned to hunting bison and marketing their meat and hides. Food production was taken over by a few thousand Scottish settlers in the 1820s, however, and when the supply of buffalo robes ended with extermination of the great bison herds by 1865, Native independence came to an end.

Enlightened conservation measures initiated by the Hudson's Bay Company after 1821 could not reverse the ecological damage of the rivalry, and outbreaks of diseases such as measles added to the misery. A long, peaceful coexistence had quietly fallen apart. From the transition sprang the Métis, mixed-blood peoples (mostly French-Native) who numbered more than 8,000 in 1857. Their rebellious reaction to alleged British disdain for civil rights brought troops, a police force, and settlers into the Manitoba region after 1870, assuring the final demise of traditional grassland societies.

First Nations peoples of the Pacific Coast had yet to encounter Europeans in the 1760s. British, Spanish, and Russian explorers' ships first appeared late in the 18th century, and Alexander Mackenzie, employed by Montreal traders, arrived overland in 1793. Each was at the extreme outer limits of their respective overseas trading systems and posed little threat. Northwest coast tribes were among the most advanced culturally of any in America, and in the benign climate they had evolved rich economies and societies in the rivers and estuaries and at sea. An estimated 100,000 Natives easily held their own initially against foreign approaches.

European exploitation of the Pacific and intermontane regions rarely involved Natives. Nootka and Haida only briefly joined the new sea otter fur trade with China at the turn of the 19th century. Tlingit of Alaska provided some foodstuffs for the Russians, but smallpox in the 1830s ended the relationship. There was no market for salmon they caught, and First Nations people did not engage in the whale hunts developing after 1820. The Hudson's Bay Company acquired Pacific coast rights after 1821 and started selling farm lots on Vancouver Island in the 1840s to augment its own farm production at Fort Langley, but Natives were not involved. When gold drew 20,000 fortune seekers inland to New Caledonia in 1858, the Native population was halved to 30,000 within 15 years, largely again because of disease.

The far north remained the undisturbed home to several thousand tundra people—Dene and others—and Inuit throughout the 100 years. A Moravian mission established in Labrador in 1771 was exceptional, and the Hearne, Mackenzie, Parry, and Franklin expeditions and Hudson's Bay Company forays as far as the Yukon and eastern Alaska were purely exploratory. The tundra lacked furs, and lands east of Hudson Bay did not start producing them until the mid-19th century. American whalers appeared at Southampton Island and in the Beaufort Sea after 1860, signaling new enterprise, but until that time missionaries, not traders, were the principal influence.

Europeans regarded Native Canadians as useful guides and hunters, but little more. When the hunt was over—the furs depleted or the foe vanquished—these people were not further drawn into the new European world. It is remarkable that beaver pelts found a ready market at the very moment in history when explorers started reaching inland in America, for neither wheat nor wood pulp nor iron ore, had they been sought, would have produced the same working arrangement. Hunting was a Native habit, and we may speculate that the fur trade, for all its recorded destructiveness to traditional societies, nevertheless softened the impact of the meeting of the two cultures. The relatively peaceful relationship that had existed between the two groups may be seen as a legacy of the fur trade.

TIDAL BRITISH NORTH AMERICA

Territorial and Political Geography

The Treaty of Paris, closing the Seven Years' War in 1763, divided authority northward from Massachusetts (which then included Maine) into four parts (fig. 10.4). The British province of Nova Scotia was the old Acadian area, and Quebec the entrance to the fur trade; both had vague or arbitrary inland limits. Newfoundland (a British claim but not a colony) and St.-Pierre and Miquelon (French territory) provided each mother nation with landing places for the Atlantic fishery.

The American Revolution made it necessary to fix the northeastern boundary of the United States, and it was resolved at the Atlantic coast in 1817 and inland in 1842. No other international decisions were called for in the region,

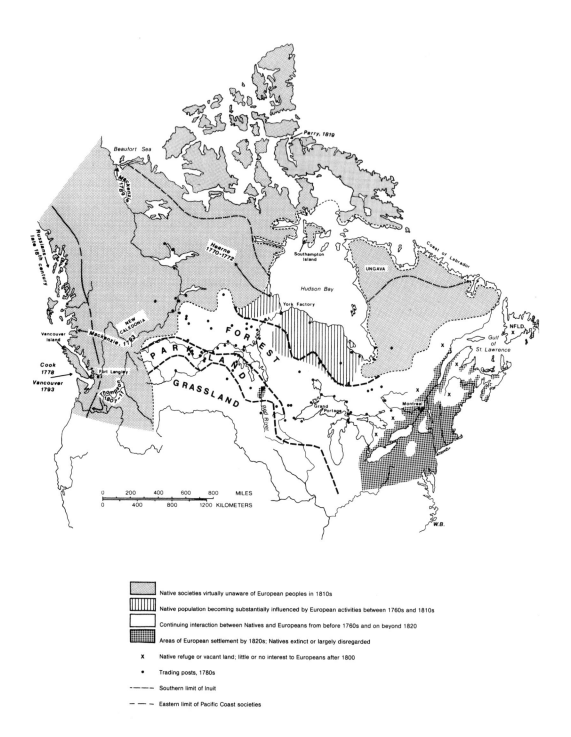

Beaufort Sea

Mackenzie 1789

Russians late 18th century

Hearne 1770-1772

Perry, 1819

Southampton Island

Coast of Labrador

UNGAVA

Hudson Bay

York Factory

NEW CALEDONIA

Vancouver Island

Mackenzie 1793

Cook 1778

Vancouver 1793

Fort Langley

Thompson 1807

FOREST

PARKLAND

GRASSLAND

Red River

Grand Portage

Montreal

NFLD.

Gulf of St. Lawrence

0   200   400   600   800   MILES
0   400   800   1200   KILOMETERS

W.B.

Native societies virtually unaware of European peoples in 1810s

Native population becoming substantially influenced by European activities between 1760s and 1810s

Continuing interaction between Natives and Europeans from before 1760s and on beyond 1820

Areas of European settlement by 1820s; Natives extinct or largely disregarded

X   Native refuge or vacant land; little or no interest to Europeans after 1800

•   Trading posts, 1780s

‒ ‒ ‒   Southern limit of Inuit

‒ ‒ ‒   Eastern limit of Pacific Coast societies

Figure 10.3 Native Northern America, 1760s–1820s

but substantial refinements occurred within the British jurisdiction. By 1784 Nova Scotia had been fragmented into four pieces; this resulted in a scatter of parochial settlements, and all attempts at reunification, starting as early as the 1830s, have failed. The shores of Newfoundland were passed back and forth with Quebec and were opened to French and Americans for landing and curing fish but supposedly not for settlement. Any hope of achieving political unity was thwarted by the international character of the fishery.

Britain's claims on the Pacific, dating from Cook's discovery in 1778, were challenged at various times by Spaniards, Russians, and Americans. Had the boundary line eastward from the coast been drawn before 1815, precedent suggests that the Columbia River would have formed part of it. By the time the stakes became high enough to force a solution in the 1840s, however, Britain was satisfied with simple geometry. Extending the line along the 49th parallel westward across the Cordillera in 1846 suggests that Britain was only moderately committed to the Pacific region. The dominance at sea persisted, however, and in 1866 the colonies of Vancouver Island and New Westminster merged as the province of British Columbia.

The Seaward Focus

Settlement of Newfoundland, Labrador, and the lower north shore of the St. Lawrence is the unpremeditated result of changed perceptions of the local marine resources (fig. 10.5a). Between 1780 and 1830, 100,000 people (three-quarters of them Irish) established new homes in the coves from Bonavista around the southeast coast of Newfoundland and westward to Fortune Bay. More than 3,000 French (Acadians and St. Pierrais) and British occupied the west shore, though it was supposed to be for landing purposes only. Another 10,000, mostly from Jersey, settled the Gaspé region, and 900 more fished out from the Magdalen Islands.

As early as the 1740s, British seasonal fishing parties started passing the winter in Newfoundland as guardians of the drying tables and other modest assets that marked the beginnings of the dried-fish industry. This was conducted from shore in small boats and was more lucrative than the ship-based salted-fish industry it was destined to supplant by the early 19th century. This new cod economy set the scene for permanent family settlement after 1780 (fig. 10.6). Installation of a year-round governor in Newfoundland in 1807—his predecessors had been on hand only during the summer—and the establishment of private property ownership rights in the next decade confirmed that a real colony was in the making.

European wars between 1793 and 1815 contributed further to declining annual migration and brought about the demise of the great English West Country fishing merchant monopolies. Cheaper foodstuffs from New England transformed Newfoundland into an American outpost by 1840. A new marketing strategy, the truck system, evolved in the Gaspé to control local fish stocks against overharvesting by larger and larger numbers of solo operators. Resident managers kept fishermen perpetually indebted to them by supplying fishing gear in exchange for guarantees to buy the season's catch. And the catch could be substantial, for year-round residence permitted the development of other fisheries. The number of seals taken off Labrador and in the Gulf of St. Lawrence increased sevenfold between 1805 and 1830. A winter cod fishery, with light salting, developed along the south shore of Newfoundland, and salmon, lobster, mackerel, and herring all were attractions for a swelling American market after 1820.

This world turned on cod, however, and when the English market declined about 1840, severe underemployment resulted throughout Newfoundland. Farmers, fishermen, and nonfishing landholders reverted to the jack-of-all-trades conditions of isolation, even as life elsewhere in America was tending toward specialization. Newfoundland was slipping behind. The simpler, subsistent way of life persisted until the 1960s, when the provincial government undertook a massive—some would say draconian—program to close hundreds of tiny outports and resettle residents in larger centers. Now, at the beginning of the 21st century, the survival of many of these places is threatened because of the closure of the entire cod fishery in the early 1990s.

Between 1760 and 1810 the rest of the Atlantic coast was alive with new and revitalized settlement, much of it by refugees. Nearly 3,000 German and French Protestants were

Figure 10.4 British American Territorial Organization, 1763–1867

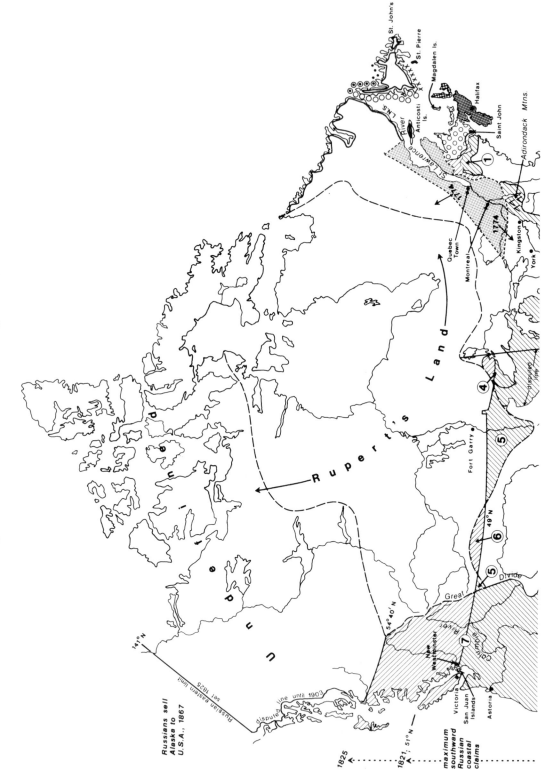

38° N

42° N

0   200   400   600   800   MILES
0   400   800   1200   KILOMETERS

80° W

W.B.

Mississippi River

Ohio River

Cairo

② ③ ②

Nova Scotia 1763

  subdivided into St. John's Island, 1769 (renamed Prince Edward Island, 1798)

    New Brunswick, 1784

    Cape Breton Island, 1784 - 1820 (formerly Ile Royale)

Newfoundland 1763

  including Coast of Labrador to 1774, and after 1809

    Lower north shore (L.N.S.) to 1774, and 1809 - 1825

    Anticosti Island and Magdalen Islands to 1774

Quebec 1763

  expanded to Ohio and Mississippi rivers, and Rupert's Land, 1774

  including Coast of Labrador, 1774 - 1809

    Lower North Shore, 1774 - 1809 and after 1825

    Anticosti Island and Magdalen Islands after 1774

France 1763: St. Pierre and Miquelon Islands

  fish-curing rights on Newfoundland Island, 1774 - 1783 ••••••••

  1774 - 1904 ⊙⊙⊙⊙ 1783 - 1904 OOOO

xxxxxx **United States 1818**

  fish-curing rights on Newfoundland Island

Territorial Claims and Disputes Resolved 1783 - 1867

  To British North America

  To United States

① Maine boundary, fixed 1842

② Trans-Appalachian area, unchallenged by British 1774

③ Quebec Act claim, conceded by British 1783

    and confirmed by treaty 1815

④ Quetico region, dispute 1826 - 1842

⑤ Rupert's Land, to U.S.A. 1818

⑥ Louisiana Purchase land, to Britain 1818

⑦ Oregon-Columbia region, dispute 1818 - 1846;

    San Juan Islands boundary, fixed 1871

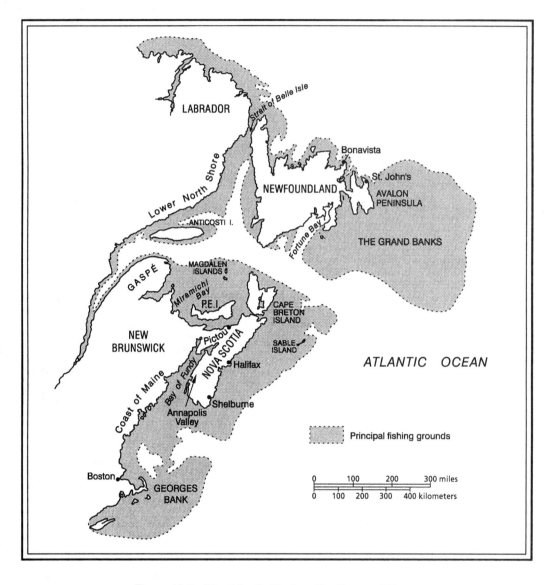

Figure 10.5a The Atlantic Region: The Seaward Focus

fleeing religious oppression; 35,000 United Empire Loyalists were displaced by the American Revolution; the free blacks of Halifax had escaped slavery. By 1800 as many as 8,000 of the Acadians deported in 1755 had returned, joining descendants of the 2,000 who never left. Thousands of Highland Scots—Roman Catholic, conservative, and committed to family—came voluntarily. New Englanders had been spreading northward along the Maine coast for years, and for 7,000 of them the Bay of Fundy was the next stopping place.

Newcomers fished for oysters and scallops; carried coal, timber, or gypsum; built and worked ships; or filled hundreds of positions in naval services centered in Halifax during the Napoleonic Wars. Others turned to farming in the limited pockets of suitable land in the Annapolis River valley, at the head of the Bay of Fundy, along the Miramichi, or on Prince Edward Island, "the garden of the gulf." The old Acadian marshlands were worn out, however,

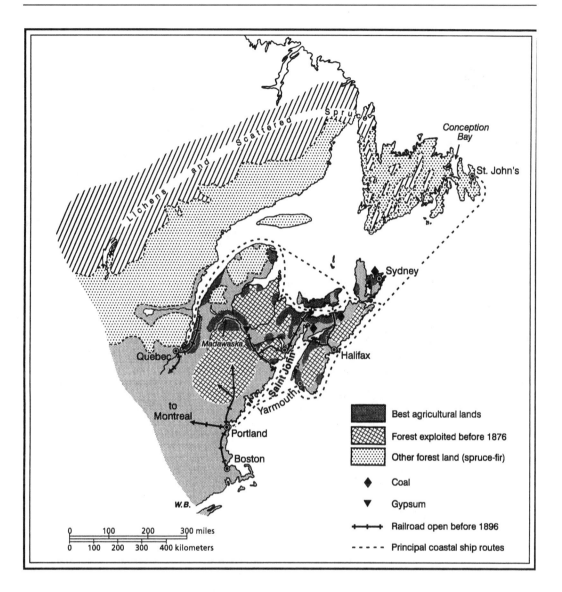

Figure 10.5b The Atlantic Region: The Landward Focus

and elsewhere yield was uncertain. People who had been starving in Cape Breton in 1833–34 were exporting surplus produce to Newfoundland in the late 1840s. Three thousand United Empire Loyalists migrated to the rocky shore at Shelburne, Nova Scotia, in 1784, only to find that farming was hopeless. By 1790 all but 300 had moved on, mostly to the Lake Ontario region. Shelburne symbolizes the inability of the Maritimes to be agriculturally self-sufficient, let alone be a food exporter.

Inland Atlantic Canada

Inland Atlantic Canada was for the most part heavily forested and of great value in an age of wooden shipping. When the Revolution placed Maine's mast and ship timber beyond reach in 1776, Britain looked to the interior of New Brunswick (fig. 10.5b). From 1806 until 1849 preferential tariffs further encouraged exploitation of these hardwood and pine forests, and ruthless, undisciplined cutting allegedly occurred.

Figure 10.6 A Newfoundland Outport: Brigus South, Newfoundland, 1963
(Courtesy C. Grant Head)

Land management and environmental concern were absent, and even the great Miramichi forest fire of 1825 seemed like a minor episode. A complex system of inward provisioning and outward log drives developed in the basins of the rivers Saint John, Restigouche, and Miramichi, and an imperfect symbiosis evolved between woodsmen and bush farmers. Timber created massive demands for export cargo space before the 1850s, and many a vessel sailed once only, eastward, and was dismantled overseas for reusable timbers and lumber. The crews and ships' fittings returned on immigrant vessels.

Timber preferences ended in 1849, but markets held up for a further period owing to the Reciprocity Treaty (duty-free trade in primary products) with the United States between 1854 and 1866 and to a shipbuilding industry that had chosen to stay with wood despite the rise of steam and iron. Decline of the New Brunswick forest industry was gradual, and until nearly

1900 Maritime yards were building small wooden vessels for the coastwise trade and fishing, becoming ever more anachronistic and less competitive as time wore on.

Land in interior New Brunswick was poor, and removing the forest was not generally a prelude to agriculture. The Saint John River valley was exceptional, Loyalist country where a mixed dairy and grain economy served the city of Saint John. Far upstream, and spilling over into what would become Maine and Quebec, lay the "republic" of Madawaska, another enclave of good farmland that was developing as a major potato region, rivaling Prince Edward Island's potatoes. Eastern Nova Scotia, central New Brunswick, Gaspé, Cape Breton, and Newfoundland provided no more than the most meager subsistence.

In 1828 the General Mining Association was organized in Halifax to develop the coal reserves at Sydney, Pictou, and the Chignecto isthmus. Coal exports offset declines in other sectors, and production of gypsum, grindstones, lime, and bricks provided further income. But Pennsylvania anthracite and bituminous coal held the edge over Nova Scotia in eastern American markets, especially after 1866. At one time favored colonies of Britain, the Maritimes were becoming colonial outposts of the United States, but without special status.

Tidal Towns and Transport

By the 1840s, transformation of Newfoundland's fishery to a New World operation was complete, and the final step was the emergence of Newfoundland's entrepôt. The choice of St. John's as the seat of government clinched its position as the successor to Waterford, Bristol, and Plymouth overseas. No other colonial town so dominated its hinterland as did St. John's; its population of 29,000 in 1870 was about one-fifth that of the entire island.

Halifax was founded in 1749 for defensive reasons, similar to the French forts at Plaisance, Newfoundland (1690–1713) and Louisbourg (1713–58). Merchant Loyalists and pre-Loyalists who settled there saw this town of 3,000 as inheritor of the trading mantle borne by Boston prior to the Revolution, and Halifax was indeed a vital landing in the British Empire throughout the Napoleonic Wars. After 1815, however, the dockyard was transferred to Bermuda, leaving only a diminished peacetime naval role and failing hopes of Halifax ever becoming a manufacturing town.

Despite its reduced importance, Halifax grew from 10,000 to 25,000 people in the half-century before Confederation. Political hostility toward Boston was followed by economic rivalry. Halifax became the focus for coastwise traffic from Yarmouth to Cape Breton and for reshipping. American grain, British manufactures, West Indian sugar products, local minerals, and dried fish were exchanged there, and reciprocity and the American Civil War kept the warehouses busy. But Halifax was poorly situated to become British North America's New York; that distinction was Montreal's. The rerouting of Cunard ocean liners away from Halifax to terminals in Quebec and New York in the 1840s symbolized the plight of Halifax and, as the polemicist T. C. Haliburton suggested, Nova Scotia's fading sense of confidence.

From its founding by Loyalists in 1784, Saint John, New Brunswick, grew rapidly to a shipbuilding center of 10,000 by the 1830s, drawing upon the timber and foodstuffs in its upriver hinterland. From then until nearly 1860 Saint John was the leading city of the Maritimes, outranking Halifax in manufacturing strength. Forty percent of the nonfishing tonnage built in Atlantic Canada at midcentury was from Saint John, only 13 percent from Halifax. A suspension bridge spanned the harbor mouth in 1853, a visible step not matched in Halifax until the next century. The promise of railroad links to Montreal or Boston added to the euphoria, but in the end, a conservative business community hanging on to a technologically obsolete, labor-intensive industry sealed Saint John's fate.

Staples production and frequent food shortages made the Maritimes dependent on others and vulnerable to political pressures. Manifest Destiny—the U.S. doctrine that viewed British North America as diminishingly British and ripe for American takeover—was a persistent threat. Boston's proximity to the Maritimes, plus New York's improved access to the St. Lawrence and Lake Ontario in the 1820s, threw British America into a defensive posture and prompted discussions of overland transport between the two colonial regions. A celebrated military trek across the Appalachians north of the Madawaska region in the winter of 1813 had demonstrated the isolation of the Atlantic and inland areas. Britain was invincible at sea, but security within British North America was another matter.

A proposal to build an all-British railroad between New Brunswick and Montreal in the 1840s won the support of Loyalists in the Saint John valley (fig. 10.5b). But the cost of crossing the empty country around the hump of Maine was excessive, and British entrepreneurs in the St. Lawrence–Great Lakes region chose instead to build a railroad on the shortest route to the sea, southeastward from Montreal and terminating, in 1853, at Portland, Maine. Economic motives prevailed over political, and a ferry between Portland and Saint John or Halifax would have to do. This was not a solution to satisfy nationalists, and winter passage was problematical, yet it stood until an all-Canadian route was completed in 1876.

Improved internal communication was making the Maritimes more integrated. Railroads offered shortcuts between Halifax and the Bay of

Fundy (1857) and between Saint John and the Gulf of St. Lawrence at the Prince Edward Island ferry terminal in 1869 (fig. 10.5b). Other lines reached Pictou and Fredericton, the New Brunswick capital. But the sea was a continuing influence, and a mixed system of land and water facilities persisted in the Maritimes long after railroads had achieved sole supremacy further west.

The Maritimes were not swallowed up by the United States, but neither did they fall in comfortably with the British colonial territory around the Great Lakes. By 1850, central Canada was emerging as the focus of colonial power, and a well-defined farming belt, being supplemented with industry, was established between the Detroit River and the lower reaches of the St. Lawrence River. The Maritime colonies were tied to this region only slightly by kin and tradition and even less by economy, and gradually they drifted further towards the periphery of North American affairs. Only two—Nova Scotia and New Brunswick—joined with Quebec and Ontario in the Canadian confederation of 1867, and they did so only reluctantly. Prince Edward Island joined in 1873, on promise of an internal railway; the Newfoundland referendum to unite with Canada was held in 1948 and was carried by only a slight majority.

The Atlantic region demonstrates cultural persistence through isolation. Land valued as a base for fishing was cursed for its weak farming potential. The idea of owning land for its own sake—the engine that drove so much of inland settlement—remained weak, especially in Newfoundland. Isolation reinforced the homogeneity of individual settlements, preserved today as a patchwork of dialects, fraternalism, and vernacular buildings. Much of North America looked like a construction camp in the 19th century, but in Atlantic Canada that phase had long since passed. By 1867, it was a postpioneer region with a lingering commitment to staple commodities, ill suited to the processes of industrialization and urbanization that were moving to center stage elsewhere in the continent. Atlantic Canada was one of the first regions of decline in North America.

The Pacific

Fort Victoria, founded on Vancouver Island in 1843, was to British interests on the Pacific what Halifax had been a century earlier: a fixed presence against aggressive Americans. The colony of Vancouver Island was formed in 1849, three years after the Oregon Treaty had set the mainland boundary along the 49th parallel and left the fort uncomfortably close to the United States (fig. 10.4). In 1862 Victoria, with a population of 6,000, became headquarters for the British navy on the Pacific, replacing Valparaiso, Chile. It largely shed its American tone and developed the cultured English image that has been its hallmark ever since.

The Fraser River gold rush in 1858 gave the Pacific region a second focus. Twenty thousand adventurers scrambled inland 600 miles by boat and pack trail, only to leave within a few years after the workings ran out. More enduring were wool, tallow, and hides, marketed since the 1840s, and canned salmon (replacing the salted variety) and coal. The trees were so large that only those that could be felled directly into coastal waters were readily merchantable until new logging machines came into use in the 1880s. San Francisco was a major market. Unlike the Maritimes, British Columbia had a future. In 1871 it became a Canadian province, the western anchor of the Dominion, on condition that an overland railroad be built.

QUEBEC AND ONTARIO

Territorial and Political Geography

In 1763 British officials declared outline boundaries circumscribing the new province, Quebec (fig. 10.4), and proposed free landownership. Assimilation of the French was presumed to be both proper and inevitable, and a handful of new administrators were expected to oversee the process. Seigneurial life changed imperceptibly, however, while chaos on the Native lands throughout the Great Lakes threatened several hundred traders. The need for further new rules was evident, continuing the succession of attempts to fit French traditions into the broader Anglo-American continent. At the start of the 21st century there is still no satisfactory resolution.

With the Quebec Act (1774), Britain expanded Quebec territory to the confluence of the Ohio and Mississippi Rivers and guaranteed French institutions—religion, language, law, land system—throughout. But just ten years later the north shores of Lakes Ontario and Erie began filling with British Loyalists who resented French customs, especially seigneurial duties. They were modern North Americans, bent on owning land, not renting it. In 1791 the Constitution Act accommodated them by severing a portion of old Quebec and setting up a new, inland colony—Upper Canada—with British institutions.

Quebec shrank to a remnant—Lower Canada—with much the same limits as in 1763. Its Frenchness intensified, buoyed by natural population increases of between 3 and 4 percent annually. A mild uprising against entrenched British authority in 1837 renewed British calls for assimilation; French resolve for *la survivance* deepened. Many perceived the union of Upper and Lower Canada in 1841 (named the Province of Canada) as a sinister move to outnumber them, and many believed that two outbreaks of cholera in this era were extermination plots. In fact, by midcentury the French presence was unassailable, and the legal end to seigneurialism in 1854 was a minor postscript to the transformation of French Canada into a solid North American entity. If territorial unity may be listed as a factor in survival and in the roots of Quebec nationalism, then the decision to establish Lower Canada in 1791 surely stands as a turning point.

In 1867 the Province of Canada split again, becoming the provinces of Quebec and Ontario in the new Canadian federation. For the British, creating a national government structure to which more provinces might be added was an act of unification and held promise of great progress. For the French, confederation was a partnership of provinces with different histories. These are two very different impressions of one event. Quebec nationalism smoldered for a century while Canada grew from sea to sea but erupted in the 1960s and has set the tone of domestic politics ever since.

The Quebec Act of 1774 set the boundary through the middle of Lake Ontario and Lake Erie as far west as 80° W longitude (Erie, Pennsylvania, today), leaving a tract of undefined jurisdiction between the crest of the Appalachians and Lake Ontario (fig. 10.4). Soon after the Declaration of Independence American settlers began moving through the Mohawk River valley into this region, taking possession. Through this territory would pass the Erie Canal in 1825—the best inland route south of the St. Lawrence—and the Genesee valley region around Rochester would become one of America's great wheat-growing regions.

The Erie Canal region very nearly was part of postrevolutionary British America. It might have filled with United Empire Loyalists and remained the home of the loyal Iroquois nations, which were, instead, uprooted and placed on reserve lands in the Grand River valley north of Lake Erie. In place of naval engagements on the Great Lakes in the War of 1812, there would have been skirmishes along the crest of the Appalachians. Buffalo and Rochester would have been Canadian cities, Genesee wheat a British product, and New York City not the great mart that it became. But the middle-of-the-lakes boundary line of 1774 held, and by treaty in 1783 it was extended to the western end of Lake Superior. The value of having the Great Lakes drainage basin under a single jurisdiction was forfeited, and two generations later, railroads would make even the idea of unified watersheds altogether irrelevant to regional interaction.

Further territorial decisions affirmed the inevitability of what the American pamphleteer William Gilpin called "the hereditary line of progress." British negotiators continued to lack the resolve of their American counterparts, and Canadians have viewed these decisions at least partly as sellouts. These included the 49th parallel, which sliced across the plains in 1817, and its extension from the Rocky Mountain crest to the Pacific in 1846, the Maine–Quebec–New Brunswick boundary (1842), the Quetico area (1842), and the San Juan Islands (1871) (fig. 10.4). Canada was firm in at least one instance, however, rejecting an American attempt in the 1840s to buy a strip of land around the north flank of the Adirondack Mountains for a proposed all-American canal between the St. Lawrence River and Lake Champlain.

Settlement and Economy

Upper and Lower Canada were a single economic unit, and settlers speculated in Crown land near Toronto and in seigneuries near Montreal for a common reason. The entire area was exposed to continental expansion, pioneer agricultural spirit, the rise of a commercial economy, and budding industrialization. Localized environmental, cultural, and economic conditions produced varied responses, but the quest for wealth was universal.

A few dozen Scots took over the Montreal fur trade and, with experienced French voyageurs working for them and with the security of the Quebec Act, mounted an intense, debilitating rivalry with the Hudson's Bay Company. Until 1802, when war caused prices to slump, furs accounted for two-thirds of the value of Quebec exports, and grain, spirits, and wholesaling also prospered, especially in the 1790s. Montrealers made the first improvements to St. Lawrence River navigation, built a road between Lake Ontario and Georgian Bay in 1795, and consolidated Fort William, on Lake Superior, at the start of the canoe-and-road portage route westward to the Red River. Montreal traders stretched as far inland as preindustrial technology would allow. Overextension killed their enterprise in the 1820s, and 60 years would pass before the railroad once again placed Montreal interests firmly in the prairie economy.

Between 1784 and 1791, 10,000 United Empire Loyalists from the United States established rural communities along the British shores of Lakes Erie and Ontario, at the western end of the St. Lawrence River, and in the Eastern Townships directly north of New England (fig. 10.7). They made up only 2 percent of the estimated 500,000 Anglo-Americans opposed to the Revolution, but many more came later, adding to the 100,000 English-speaking residents who were established on the British side of the Great Lakes by 1810. The Americanness of Upper Canada by 1815—fully 75 percent—was a defining factor in the longer history of the province but did not alter the outcome of the War of 1812.

Loyalism looks like a noble gesture to one's sovereign but might equally be seen as a polite, thin veil over simple economic motives and geographic reality. Settlers chose Canada because it was the next place inland offering accessible, good farmland at the end of the 18th century. Loyalists and others were eligible for free land grants, either in recognition of wartime service or simply by being there. Americans who supported the Revolution could receive land in the United States, so it would appear that few land seekers in 1800 were unable to acquire a choice piece somewhere in America. It was a buyer's

market in a porous borderland, and each country was trying to consolidate its sovereignty by establishing a resident population.

Upper Canada was to be a planned community. Lieutenant-Governor John Graves Simcoe (1791–96) fancied a British class system of town lots, gentry estates, and land reserves for the Anglican Church and the Crown. Military regiments would be the focus of town life, and a rectangular grid of roads would bind town and countryside together with geometric elegance. This plan was as ill suited as the seigneurial system had been, however, and only the gridwork of farm lots and roads, somewhat adapted to physiography, materialized. Too few true settlers opened farms, and speculative holdings ran to 50,000 acres in some cases. By 1819, the year absenteeism was outlawed, three-quarters of Upper Canada land south of the Canadian Shield was in private hands, yet barely 10 percent was cleared for farming (fig. 10.8).

Upper Canada came to life in the half-century after 1820, becoming rather less "Yankee" but no less English-speaking as overseas migration resumed following decades of war. Settlers filled the gaps of the Loyalist era in an ethnic and denominational brocade quite unlike the frontier zone of the United States. Group settlements, such as the McNab and Talbot communities (fig. 10.7), were rare, and utopian communities were scarcer still. Some 150,000 new persons came into the St. Lawrence valley between 1825 and 1832, principally Scots, Ulster Scotch-Irish, and English. They included artisans, families escaping the gloom of industrial towns, and prosperous farmers seeking still greater fortune. Military pensioners added an element of gentility here and there, frequently introducing a type of mixed farming quite out of step with the export-based style. Several thousand immigrants put off taking up land, at least temporarily, to build the Welland and Rideau Canals, the two showpiece public works projects of the period. These heavily capitalized stone structures brought substantial quantities of British specie into an economy always strapped for cash.

Pioneering immigrants paid a small registration fee that allowed them a few years to start farming and gain land title. For most it was their first experience with landownership, and success lay in the unpaid labor of men, women, and children toiling together. There was no money for building roads, and it was rare indeed for professional builders to make a farm or mill for a client. It was typical woodland pioneering, at the rate of 1 or 2 acres cleared per year, until a manageable farm unit of about 35 acres of field was achieved. Even allowing for woods, two farms could easily be made on one survey lot of 100 acres. Each successful settler was thus a speculator, holding an attractive parcel for the children or for sale to later farm-makers.

Immigration numbers soared in the 1840s (fig. 10.1). Upper Canada's population doubled in 10 years and had surpassed Lower Canada's by 1851. The annual amount of new farm acreage in Upper Canada rose from 10,000 in 1825 to more that 200,000 within 20 years, and the total farmland exceeded that of Lower Canada about 1855. Many of the 80,000 fleeing the Irish famine of 1847 went into farming on the last substantial tract, the Grey-Bruce highlands, rapidly filling with Scots too. Others cut trees, built railroads, and took industrial jobs in the towns. Some heard of greater opportunities in the American Middle West and moved on. There even was talk of Manitoba, where private landownership became legal after 1840; a steamboat on the Red River and a wagon road to Edmonton in 1859 improved access. But such talk was premature when places like Illinois were such attractive alternatives.

The era of easy land in Ontario was drawing to a close by 1860. Farm prices rose, farmers built fences to define individual properties, and they started draining wetlands. The province sought to continue the settlement process by once again offering free lands along colonization roads running into the Canadian Shield (fig. 10.7), but word spread during the 1850s that little decent land existed in those parts. Among those moving on west after midcentury were children of immigrants for whom the original family farm could not be further subdivided. This was not 18th-century New France with its long lots riven into unmanageable slivers but a far more rootless society in which families, not lands, were split up.

As Upper Canada and the Eastern Townships filled, the landscape mellowed (fig. 10.9). But an undercurrent of instability persisted, part of the process of cultural mixing. Church buildings, often three or four in a single village, signaled the diversity. Anglicans, Catholics, Methodists, Presbyterians, Baptists, and various

sects all endeavored to reestablish spiritual consciousness in raw communities. The Methodists —the roots of today's United Church of Canada—became predominant, their circuit riders acting as wandering central places for a scattered flock, while the Church of England stayed put in misguided anticipation of parishioners' coming to it. The circuits faded with urbanization, leaving a populist church strongly in place.

Rural French society remained introverted, pioneering on vacant land within the familiar seigneuries. Even the Catholic Church seemed to have forsaken its people, the number of priests actually falling between 1760 and 1830 while the population grew seven times. It was a resolute, self-sufficient body of habitants that finally overflowed the seigneurial confines in the 1830s and moved on to the farmlands of the Eastern Townships and adjacent Upper Canada or the barrens of the Gaspé. They filled timber camps from the Ottawa River valley to Lake St. John and took up new industrial jobs in Montreal and southern New England. Wherever they went, they became interspersed with English-speaking people, and in the timber areas along the Laurentian fringes to the north, intermarriage of French and Irish Catholics was commonplace. Fears that French survival was still threatened made emigrants to the United States in the 1860s look unpatriotic, and an element of divine inspiration drove settlement schemes in northern Quebec sponsored by the revitalized Roman Catholic Church.

Canada was the agricultural heartland of British North America (table 10.1), and wheat was the principal product (figs. 10.3 and 10.13). Wheat and flour made up one-third to one-half of all Upper Canada tonnage shipped down the St. Lawrence in the second quarter of the 19th century. A well-established farm could produce enough wheat to make flour annually for 60 people. The best land lay west from the Grand River toward the American border, where the growing season was 40 days longer than at Quebec City. Severe winters determined that spring-planted wheat be grown east of Kingston, despite its lower market price.

Between 1815 and 1846, Canadian wheat received preferential status in Britain under the Corn (i.e., wheat) Laws. In addition, Canadian millers benefited from the special status given to flour of American wheat imported into Britain if ground in British North America. After 1832,

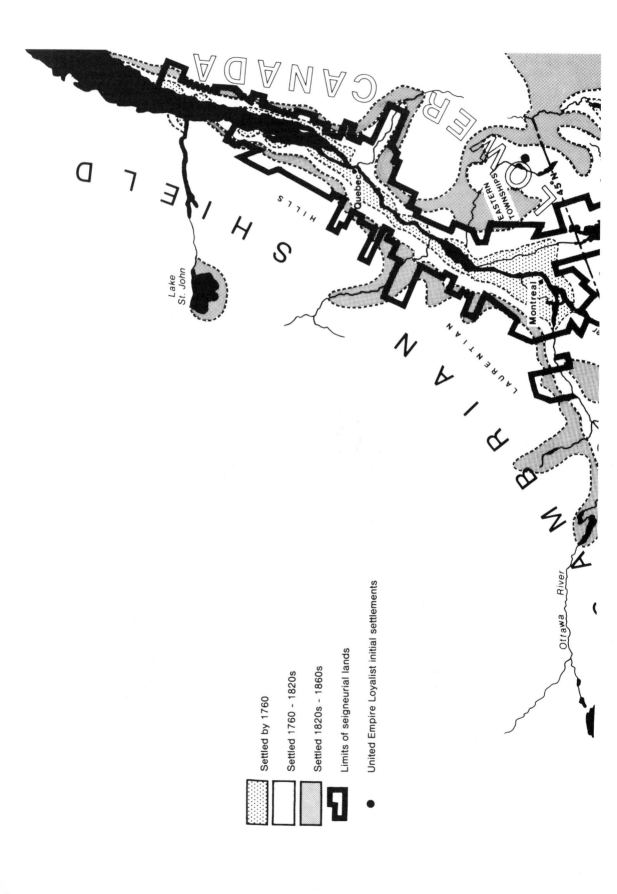

Settled by 1760

Settled 1760 – 1820s

Settled 1820s – 1860s

Limits of seigneurial lands

United Empire Loyalist initial settlements

Figure 10.7 Upper and Lower Canada

however, substantial quantities of Upper Canada wheat and flour were diverted to Lower Canada as that region switched from export grain to livestock and mixed farming for local markets. Foodstuffs from Upper Canada were routed through the Erie Canal to supply the booming American cities, and in 1835 and 1836 British wheat surpluses briefly flowed overseas to cover deficiencies in the United States. Upper Canada occupied a fallback position, a place to turn to when all other wheat sources failed, a land of barns bursting with surplus in those years when supply exceeded needs.

Ontario's prominence in wheat declined after 1860. The alternation of wheat and fallow, so hard on the soil, was gradually replaced by a crop rotation that included wheat perhaps only one year in seven. Better-educated farmers appreciated that restorative crops—clover, peas, or grasses—planted in the intervening years offered an opportunity for raising livestock, and the mixed-farming economy that emerged was well suited to serve the needs of more and more city dwellers. Seasonal roads were rebuilt for year-round use, school attendance increased, log houses disappeared, and a rural tenantry of farm laborers developed. These were all signs that the new province of Ontario had passed beyond the pioneer stage.

Beyond the good farmlands lay the Canadian Shield and Appalachian uplands, cloaked with forests and underlain with minerals. By 1820, the hardwoods and pineries of the Ottawa River valley and many smaller streams were providing millions of board feet of square timber cheaply rafted to the port of Quebec for overseas shipment (fig. 10.2). When preferential duties ended in 1849, merchants turned to the huge inland American market for construction lumber, and that trade built up substantially with reciprocity in 1854.

Mines were rare before Confederation. Several bog iron sites and two iron ore pits were developed, and a major silver strike was made on Lake Superior in 1868. Stone was quarried in limited quantities for construction, as well as a great deal more brick clay. Brick and brick-veneer houses were showing up on farms and in towns throughout Ontario by 1870, many decoratively colored in combinations of red and buff. Glacial sands and gravel were uncovered in the course of railroad construction after 1850 and became the source of the all-weather road essential to mixed farming. Petroleum was first pumped near Sarnia in 1859, the year it was also discovered in Pennsylvania.

Transport and Urban Places

Wheat and flour traders found the Great Lakes an imperfect transport system, and their inability to deliver the first big crop in 1802 highlighted the problem. Whichever nation built the better transport facilities would carry the exports of the vast, rich American Middle West fronting on Lakes Erie and Michigan. Montreal, gatekeeper

Table 10.1 Farmland and Population, 1851

	Land Cleared for Farming		Population		
	(000's) acres	%[a]	(000's)	%[b]	
Upper Canada	3,000	35	900	33	3.6 acres per
Lower Canada	3,500	40	900	33	capita in 3/4 of all cleared farmland
New Brunswick	800	9	300	11	2.4 acres per
Nova Scotia	1,000	11	400	14	capita in 1/4
Prince Edward Island	400	4	80	3	of all cleared
Newfoundland	little	1	150	6	farmland
Total	8,700+	100	2,730	100	

[a]Percent of total land cleared for farming.
[b]Percent of total population.

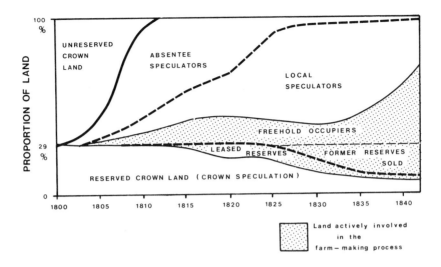

Figure 10.8 Land Disposal in Upper Canada, Hypothetical Example

for the trade of Upper Canada, was pitted against New York City. The Erie Canal was a bold technological step that gave Americans access to Lake Erie for barge-load traffic in 1825 and set the British to catching up (fig. 10.10). By 1832 the Welland and Rideau Canals had matched it, but already the Oswego branch of the Erie assured Americans that Lake Ontario traffic could still find its way to the Hudson. By the time steamboat canals had been completed on the St. Lawrence in 1847, tonnage through Albany was five times that passing Montreal, and the enlarged, rebuilt Welland Canal was being used at less than one-seventh of its capacity.

Outscored on the water, the British continued the challenge in the 1850s with the first of several bursts of railroad construction. The Grand Trunk Railway would provide year-round transportation for the intensively settled stretch of Canada between the Michigan border and Quebec City and divert American traffic from the Erie Canal to the St. Lawrence (fig. 10.11). Its completion in 1860 was politically significant, but it turned out to be debt ridden and underutilized, somewhat out of step with the swelling north-south trade. Other pre-Confederation railroads served mainly as shortcuts for established water routes. During the 1850s four lines opened between Lake Ontario and Lake Huron, and half a dozen more were chartered. Each reinforced Canadian-American interaction, as did

railroads between Montreal and New England. Gradually gaps were filled in—with bridges across the Niagara River in 1854 and 1873, ferries at Sarnia and Windsor in the 1860s—and international through routings were possible once track gauges became uniform in the 1870s. But by then American railways had already established direct links between Chicago and New York entirely bypassing the Great Lakes, the Grand Trunk, and Canada.

Canadian railroad entrepreneurs focused on long-distance, rather than local, business: a line to bring cordwood from the Canadian Shield to heat Toronto houses, another carrying ice from Lake Simcoe, several sending lumber from the Ottawa valley or Laurentian highlands to American markets. Only gradually were wayside stations and side tracks added. But as mixed farming developed, the milk train came to be part of the railroad's repertoire, enhancing its role as a regional carrier and creating the dominance of the terminal town.

Urban morphology varied with tradition. In French Canada linear street-villages—*rangs*—retarded the emergence of nucleated settlements. Mill sites and churches were the most usual nodes away from the river landings, and with the exception of Montreal and Quebec, virtually no communities numbered more than 5,000 inhabitants (table 10.2 and fig. 10.11). Lower Canada's population in towns of 1,000 or

Table 10.2 Urban Characteristics, 1851 and 1871

Towns (population)	Lower Canada		Upper Canada	
	1851	1871	1851	1871
25,000 plus	76[a]	73	22	25
5,000–25,000	0	9	29	29
1,000–4,999	24	18	49	46
Number of people in towns of more than 1,000	131,000	229,000	139,000	327,000
Percent of total population in towns of more than 1,000	14.7	19.2	14.6	20.2

[a]Numbers are percentages of total urban population.

more fell from 25 percent in 1760 to 10 percent in 1825 and still had not recovered 40 years later. In 1825, only 1 French person in 20 lived in a town, compared with 1 English person in 3.

Upper Canada and the Eastern Townships were, in contrast, born to trade, and a hierarchy of nucleated settlements was evident during the farm-making era (table 10.2). Snow-packed winter roads, lakefront granaries, and lake boats had served the grain trade adequately and also had introduced mills, warehouses, merchant forwarders, and bankers, scattered widely and poised to serve industrialization as it developed in the 1860s. Vigorous campaigns began in the 1840s to finance plank roads, and then railroads, to bind it all together. The number of manufacturing firms in Upper Canada rose from 60 in 1841 to 260 in 1867. Textiles and machinery in the Grand River valley, woolens west of Ottawa, farm machinery in Lake Ontario shore towns, and a wide variety of machine shops in Hamilton and Toronto were signs of a manufacturing sector that would blossom from this small-town base after 1867.

Toronto, a major new city of the 19th century, grew from 2,000 in 1825 to 67,000 in 1867, the third-ranking city in British North America. As relations between Britain and the United States warmed after 1820, the threat of Manifest Destiny diminished and was replaced by the new challenge of economic dominance, first commercial and later industrial. Toronto belonged to this new order, emerging as the main city along Lake Ontario by consolidating the importing function and becoming the provincial capital. In the 1830s a dozen towns strove for

Figure 10.9 The Rural Ontario Landscape (author)

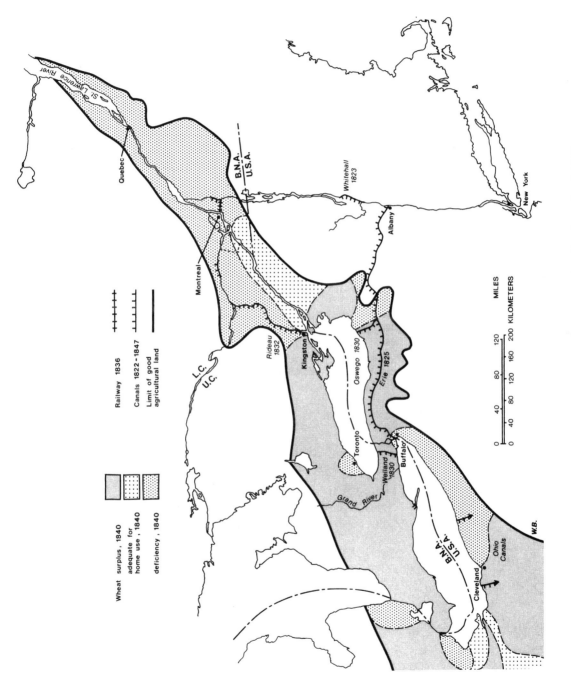

Figure 10.10 Wheat Production in the Great Lakes Region, about 1840

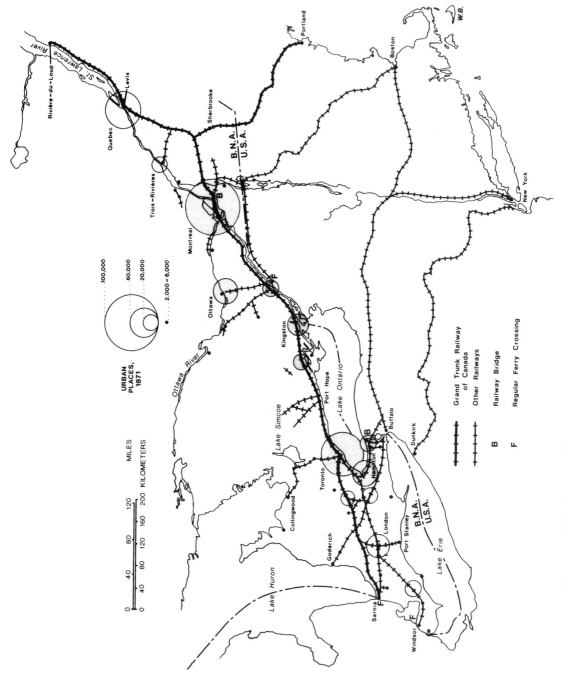

Figure 10.11 Railways of Canada and Selected Main Lines in the United States, 1853–1869

preeminence, all involved in exporting grain and many in due course holding railroad charters. But all fell back, with the wholesale center of Hamilton the last to go (in the 1870s), as more and more main roads and railroads converged on Toronto. Toronto had a fine harbor and a lakefront transport corridor built on reclaimed land and was about to embark upon a substantial program of municipal services that would assure undeterred growth and the spatial specialization of functions familiar to industrializing cities of the time. Its course was set.

Montreal became the metropolis of the St. Lawrence valley and eclipsed both Quebec City, the anchor of New France for two centuries, and Kingston, a onetime French fort at the outlet of Lake Ontario. Montreal's population passed Quebec's in the 1770s, and by 1815 a line of steam tugboats on the river was drawing overseas transshipment activity away from the port of Quebec. Montreal's wall was demolished in the 1820s, and despite loss of the fur trade, the economy accelerated after the harbor was rebuilt in 1832. Commerce dominated manufacturing through most of the century. A fine townscape emerged (fig. 10.12), crowned by Mount Royal Park, laid out by Frederick Olmsted, designer of New York's Central Park. Rejecting the 18th-century Atlantic world and adopting a continental role propelled Montreal to the forefront of Canadian cities, where it stayed for nearly a century.

Quebec, a staple-export depot and a military and administrative center, became marginalized. Overseas timber exports faded after 1860, and the last British garrison was withdrawn in 1871. The railway line with which Quebec entrepreneurs intended to reclaim control of the Great Lakes became instead a feeder to Montreal. Quebec salvaged the role of provincial capital in 1867 but was as poorly situated as Saint John or Halifax to participate in the emerging continentality of British North America. As for Kingston, it had experienced a brief glorious moment as provincial capital between 1841 and 1844, and some fine buildings were constructed. But stripped of that function and no longer a naval base (an 1817 treaty with the United States forbade warships on the Great Lakes), Kingston entered a long, gentle decline.

Both Montreal and Toronto were establishing relatively independent regional markets by midcentury, supplementing their traditional roles in international trade. Such an enduring rivalry developed that Canada today has no clearly primate city. The immiscibility of the French- and English-speaking groups is part of the explanation, but so too is economic geography. Aggressive entrepreneurs in each region carved out niches for themselves with considerable success, and neither could buy out the other. In 1822, English-speaking Montreal merchants tried without success to annex themselves to Upper Canada. Had this goal been achieved, quite possibly Toronto would be alone at the top today.

The administrative separation between 1791 and 1841 had been critical, and by the 1820s Upper Canada was well on its way to becoming the heartland of British America. People thought expansively—large farm lots, big canals, fine stone mills, steamboats—and never doubted that growth would catch up sooner or later. While T. C. Haliburton ridiculed Nova Scotia's dithering, the spirit of progress flourished a thousand miles inland. Unlike those of old Quebec, residents of Upper Canada spoke the common North American language, were growing wheat demanded in the United States, and dwelt astride the westward routes. It was in the thick of the continental action, and while that meant power, it also presaged the danger of becoming a pawn of the United States, a threat that would become more acute as industrialization developed.

INSIDE AND OUTSIDE

British military officers stationed in Canada commonly passed the time painting or sketching or writing novels, poetry, and plays. Captain John Richardson was one of this dabbling fraternity, and his 1834 play, *Wacousta*, dramatized a garrison mentality that was rooted far back in the country's history. To Richardson, early Canada was characterized by an inside—within fortress walls a sanctuary for the Europeans—and an outside, filled with savages. This is arguably an inversion of reality, for the Natives were actually the insiders and the Europeans the interlopers, but Richardson's image has been perpetuated in the literature, and by 1867 the roles had indeed become reversed in much of British North America. Throughout the Great Lakes, St. Lawrence, and Atlantic regions, Native reserves were the emaciated remains of the inside that Natives had always considered home, now occupied by intruders poised on the brink of industrialization and urbanization.

British North America of the 1860s was a vast landmass, scantily populated and far from unified. The one recognizable heartland, Quebec, had little of the procreative powers of continent-wide settlement displayed by New England or the Pennsylvania-Chesapeake area. The Maritimes received migrants into small homogeneous, conservative communities that were inconsistent with continental norms. Ontario was yet to attain clear definition, a crossroads where English, Scots, Irish, Maritimers, New Englanders, Pennsylvanians, and New Yorkers all were awkwardly thrown together in one of America's principal eclectic landscapes. Ontario in 1867 was to the future Canada what Pennsylvania had been to the United States a century earlier. But whereas the Quaker State had distanced itself socially and economically from Britain, Ontario (and Canada generally) was unable to put the same mileage between itself and the United States. There was no clean start, wrenching though that might be, that spells independence, and therein lies the root of Canada's continuing self-doubt.

The cultural landscape of the 1860s must have shown the effect. New York temple-style houses stood on the Ontario shore of Lake Erie, and Cape Cod houses in southwest Nova Scotia. The Pennsylvania barn was appearing in western Ontario, while handsome middle-class terraces of New York–Boston–Edinburgh brownstones ascended Montreal's mountain (fig. 10.12). Even the seigneurial lands were sprouting American classical or British Gothic styles in place of generations-old Norman structures, and Virginia rail fences ran everywhere. Particularly in Ontario, the cultural landscape was still raw, and new structures, rather than altered ones, were normal. Distinctively Canadian landscapes were rare.

British North America was immature, certainly beside Britain, but even in relation to the United States. It was a place for pragmatists, not

Figure 10.12 A Montreal Terrace in the 1860s. Mount Royal rises behind.
(Courtesy McGill University, Montreal)

philosophers or dreamers. There were no transcendentalist thinkers, no Hudson River school artists, no Tench Coxe to eulogize industrialization. Only in Quebec an author—F. X. Garneau—and a subject—"la survivance" (French survival)—stirred men's hearts. The skyline was still mainly trees, or dories at sea; steeples and chimneys were scarce in this horizontal landscape. The United States had a Middle West in which to develop agricultural populism, while Canada had only the impenetrable Canadian Shield with its tradition of hit-and-run staples exploitation. That all-important "middle ground" between city and wilderness, of which Leo Marx has written, was yet to be found. Instead of extolling a warm inside, Canadian literature has dwelt on the dark, gothic, wilderness, and survival themes that led Captain Richardson to see the vast land as outside his comprehension.

British North America did display one distinctive, abiding link to the old country: the use of the name Victoria. From coast to coast the monarch's name was applied to towns, bridges, railways, steamboats, municipal halls, townships, a Methodist mission, a coal mine, and countless streets, as well as later to an entire era. Victoria Day, the queen's birthday, is still a statutory holiday. It is ironic that many of these Victorias owed their well-being principally to the United States. Victoria, British Columbia, lay just beyond the reach of San Francisco, while residents and horses from Victoria County, New Brunswick, found seasonal employment in southern Maine. Victoria Foundry, Hamilton, and the Victoria Railway, northeast of Toronto,

had American investors and American customers.

Here, then, was British North America in the 1860s, subtly different from the United States but enough so that the border, for all its porosity, was a discernible influence. Within British America, the Atlantic region was more and more outside the oceanic world, yet it never became truly inside North America with Confederation; British Columbia was much the same. Many from the east coast found their metropolitan focus in Boston, where a club for Maritime expatriates was formed in 1853. Quebec, once on the fringes of the Atlantic world, created its own enclave on the fringes of the North American world and continues to struggle for its place in America. Ontario started beyond the fringe but found its inland location was consistent with the emergent continental orientation. Canals and railroads had made Ontario accessible, jut as deep keels and fore-and-aft rigging had opened the oceans three or four centuries earlier. Ontario's problem has been to reconcile overseas and North American ambitions, and the province has found itself both inside and outside at the same time. The western interior plains were central to a vanishing way of life for Natives and mixed bloods but, along with the Arctic and Cordillera, were external to the current focus of human activity in North America. The Confederation year, 1867, has been recognized as a political benchmark. Huck Finn would have wanted a new map, but for life in British North America it was neither an end nor a beginning.

ADDITIONAL READING

Bliss, J. M. 1987. *Northern Enterprise: Five Centuries of Canadian Business.* Toronto: McClelland & Stewart.

Dictionary of Canadian Biography. 1966–2000. Toronto: University of Toronto Press. See esp. vols. 4–10.

Duffy, D. 1986. *Sounding the Iceberg: An Essay on Canadian Historical Novels.* Toronto: ECW Press.

Gentilcore, R. L., ed. 1993. *Historical Atlas of Canada.* Vol. 2, *The Land Transformed, 1800–1890.* Toronto and Montreal: University of Toronto Press / Les presses de l'université de Montréal.

Greer, A. 1985. *Peasant, Lord, and Merchant: Rural Society in Three Quebec Parishes, 1740–1840.*

Toronto: University of Toronto Press

Harris, R. C. 1997. *The Resettlement of British Columbia: Essays on Colonialism and Geographical Change.* Vancouver: University of British Columbia Press.

Harris, R. C., ed. 1987. *Historical Atlas of Canada.* Vol. 1, *From the Beginning to 1800.* Toronto and Montreal: University of Toronto Press / Les presses de l'université de Montréal.

Harris, R. C., and J. Warkentin. 1991. *Canada before Confederation.* 1974. Reprint, New York: Oxford University Press.

Houston, C. J., and W. J. Smyth. 1990. *Irish Emigration and Canadian Settlement: Patterns, Links, and Letters.* Toronto: University of Toronto Press.

Lecker, R., ed. 1991. *Borderlands: Essays in Canadian-American Relations.* Toronto: ECW Press.

Mannion, J. J., ed. 1986. *The Peopling of Newfoundland: Essays in Historical Geography.* 2d ed. St. John's: Memorial University of Newfoundland.

McCallum, J. 1980. *Unequal Beginnings: Agriculture and Economic Development in Quebec and Ontario until 1870.* Toronto: University of Toronto Press.

McCann, L. D., and S. Gunn. 1998. *Heartland and Hinterland: A Geography of Canada.* 2d ed. Scarborough, Ont.: Prentice Hall Canada.

McIlwraith, T. F. 1997. *Looking for Old Ontario: Two Centuries of Landscape Change.* Toronto: University of Toronto Press.

Meinig, D. W. 1986. *The Shaping of America: Atlantic America, 1492–1800.* New Haven: Yale University Press.

———. 1993. *The Shaping of America: Continental America, 1800–1867.* New Haven: Yale University Press.

Norrie, K. H., and D. Owram. 1991. *A History of the Canadian Economy.* Toronto: Harcourt Brace Jovanovich.

Ouellet, F. 1980. *Economic and Social History of Quebec, 1760–1850.* Ottawa: Carleton University Press.

Ray, A. J. 1996. *I Have Lived Here since the World Began.* Toronto: General Publishing.

Vance, J. 1995. *The North American Railroad: Its Origin, Evolution, and Geography.* Baltimore: Johns Hopkins University Press.

Wynn, Graeme. 1981. *Timber Colony: A Historical Geography of Early 19th-Century New Brunswick.* Toronto: University of Toronto Press.

PART IV

CONSOLIDATION

1860s–1920s

The depravity of the business classes of our country is not less than has been sup-posed, but infinitely greater. The official services of America, national, state, and municipal, in all their branches and departments . . . are saturated in corruption, bribery, falsehood, mal-administration. . . . The great cities reek with respectable as much as non-respectable robbery and scoundrelism. . . . I say that our New World democracy . . . is, so far, an almost complete failure.

Walt Whitman, *Democratic Vistas,* 1871

I understand that you are going to stay some time in California. Do you mind my giving you a little advice? . . . Do you understand anything about revolvers? . . . Then you are safe. . . . You invite your own death if you lay your hand on a weapon you don't understand. No man flourishes a revolver in a bad place. It is produced for one specified purpose and produced before you can wink.

Rudyard Kipling, *From Sea to Sea,* 1889

The truth is, that the majority of non-Anglo-Saxon immigrants since the Revolution, like the majority of Anglo-Saxon immigrants before the Revolution, have been, not the superior men of their native lands, but the botched and unfit: Irishmen starving to death in Ireland, Germans unable to weather . . . the post Napoleonic reorganisa-tion, Italians weed-grown on exhausted soil, Scandinavians run to all bone and no brain, Jews too incompetent to swindle. . . . Here and there, among the immigrants, of course, there may be a bravo, or even a superman . . . but the average newcomer is, and always has been, simply a poor fish.

H. L. Mencken, *Prejudices,* 1923

11

Settling the Great Plains, 1850–1930:
Prospects and Problems

DAVID J. WISHART

The finest soil you ever dreamed of—a veritable land of Canaan.
O. E. Rolvaag, *Giants in the Earth,* 1927

A nameless, blue-green solitude, flat, endless, still, with nothing to hide behind.
O. E. Rolvaag, *Giants in the Earth,* 1927

Throughout O. E. Rolvaag's epic novel of Norwegian settlement in southeastern South Dakota in the 1870s, a central conflict divides the pioneers' reactions to the Great Plains. The soil is so rich that the head of the pioneer family becomes almost drunk with excitement as he plans the empire he will build in this "Promised Land." His wife, however, confined to their crude sod house surrounded by vast plains, sees only the isolation and grinding poverty of frontier life. This conflict between the fertile promise of the soil and the practical difficulties of living in a remote and climatologically marginal land is a primary defining characteristic of the settlement of the Great Plains.

The Great Plains is an extensive, sometimes flat, but generally rolling, area stretching from the coastal plain of Texas to the coniferous forests of Canada, and from the Rocky Mountains to a largely indistinct merger with the Middle West and the South to the east. The international boundary between the United States and Canada bisects the northern Plains along the 49th parallel, marking no major division on the land but offering a political basis for dividing the region for purposes of study into the American Great Plains and the Canadian Prairie Provinces. This chapter focuses on the American Great Plains.

The Great Plains was settled late and rapidly, but with considerable difficulty, by Euro-Americans. Pioneer settlement began with the Kansas-Nebraska Act of 1854, progressed westward in waves of advance and retreat, and ended with the dust bowl and depression of the 1930s. Although abandoned lands were quickly put back into cultivation as soon as the rains returned and prices recovered after 1940, the era of pioneer settlement was over. A region of net in-migration became a region of net out-migration.

The two main environmental problems that have faced settlers in the Great Plains are climatic variability and sheer distance. The climatic hazards are many—extreme summer and winter temperatures, tornadoes, blizzards, hail, and high winds—but the key factor is periodic drought. Periods of 35 days or more without rain can be expected each year, and extended droughts of years' duration have occurred on about a 20-year cycle since the area was opened to Euro-American settlement. Not all parts of the Great Plains are equally susceptible to drought. In general the frequency of 30-day droughts increases westward across the Plains. The major extended droughts of the 1890s and 1930s desiccated the entire region. The dry years of the early 1950s, however, affected mainly the southern Plains, while North Dakota and Montana received near normal precipitation. Rainfall also varies locally so that, quite literally, one farmer's good fortune may be another farmer's failure. Despite agricultural adjustment, efforts by optimists to increase the rainfall, and government aid, which provides some cushion against drought, the pulse of life on the Great Plains still reverberates to the rhythm of the fluctuating climate.

The problem of distance, on the other hand, has been progressively overcome through transportation improvements. The significant innovations were the railroad and the automobile. The railroads extended into the Great Plains after 1860, breaking settlers free from the Missouri River, which had previously been their main link to the markets and supplies of the eastern United States. The railroad became, in Isaiah Bowman's words, "the forerunner of development, the pre-pioneer, the baseline of agriculture." In the areas between the rail lines, distance remained a serious problem until the 1920s, when automobiles came into common use, revolutionizing mobility and giving a new flexibility to settlement decisions. Even at the beginning of the 21st century, however, isolation remains a reality of life on the Plains, particularly in the sparsely populated interstices between the main lines of transportation and settlement.

The settlers who advanced to the western borders of Iowa and Missouri in the early 1850s were not daunted by the environmental problems of the Plains. Enthusiasm for the organization of Nebraska Territory was at a fever pitch. Even before the Kansas-Nebraska Act had officially opened the central and northern Plains to Euro-American settlers, a provisional government for Nebraska had been formed in Missouri, and frontiersmen had crossed the Missouri River and were squatting on Native American lands. Far from being dismissed as a desert, a reputation given to the area by the early 19th-century explorers Zebulon Pike and Stephen Long, the Great Plains were now praised in the Missouri newspapers as a "beautiful country … soon to belong to the white man, and be made to blossom like a rose."

EASTERN NEBRASKA BEFORE 1870

To sponsoring politicians like Stephen A. Douglas of Illinois, the main purpose of the Kansas-Nebraska Act was to open up a corridor for a transcontinental railroad that would unite the country from coast to coast. To the local settlers, Nebraska and Kansas Territories offered new opportunities for cheap land, speculation, and the various activities associated with supplying other settlers. First, however, the area had to be bought from the Native Americans, and this involved a major shift in federal Indian policy.

Since 1803, when President Jefferson purchased Louisiana from France, the Great Plains had been seen as a depository for Native Americans who were blocking the progress of westward expansion in the eastern United States. In the 1820s and 1830s the relocation of the Cherokees, Choctaws, Chickasaws, Creeks, and Seminoles from the southeastern United States to Indian Territory (later Oklahoma) and of the Shawnees, Delawares, Wyandots, Ottawas, and many other groups into what is now Kansas put this removal policy into practice. By the late 1840s, however, with tens of thousands of emigrants crossing the central Great Plains to Oregon and California each year, the "Permanent Indian Frontier" was no longer feasible, and it was replaced by the reservation policy. The indigenous peoples would be restricted to small areas that were remnants of their former domains or in Indian Territory.

By 1858, Native Americans had ceded much of what would become the states of Kansas and Nebraska in the following decade (fig. 11.1). The Native Americans (or some of each people, at least) generally gave their consent to these sales, but as Secretary of the Interior Caleb Smith admitted in 1862, "It is well known that they have yielded to a necessity which they could not resist." Forced to sell by pressure from the federal government and by their own desperate circumstances, they relinquished their lands for a pittance. The Pawnees, for example, were given 22 cents an acre for almost 10 million acres in central Nebraska and were left with a 288,000-acre reservation on the Loup River.

Payments to the Native Americans generally were made in kind—agricultural equipment, seeds, livestock, clothes, and food—and the services of blacksmiths, laborers, and farmers. The objective was to break them of their communal and nomadic ways and to convert them into individual farmers so that they would become self-sufficient and ready for assimilation into the larger American society when the frontier again enveloped them. This spatial restriction and cultural assault only added to the turmoil of the Native Americans of the eastern Plains, whose populations had been decimated by epidemics of cholera and smallpox over the preceding century. Moreover, the reservation policy was never given a chance to work because settlers encircled the remaining Native American lands in the following two decades, and many tribes were pressured into migrating to Indian Territory.

With most of the indigenous peoples cleared from the eastern portions of Kansas and Nebras-

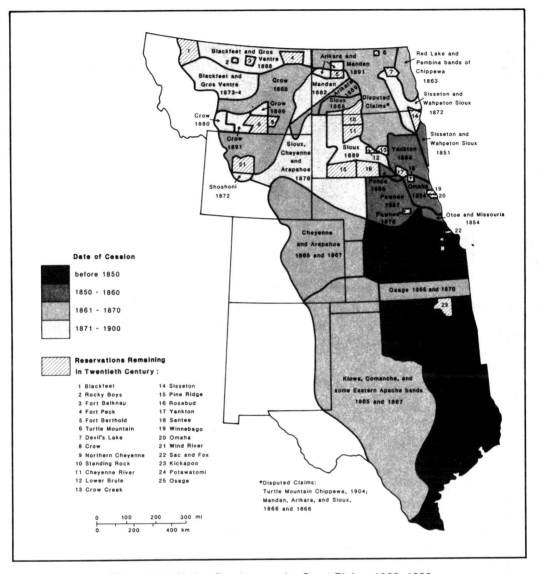

Date of Cession

- before 1850
- 1850 - 1860
- 1861 - 1870
- 1871 - 1900

Reservations Remaining in Twentieth Century:

1 Blackfeet	14 Sisseton
2 Rocky Boys	15 Pine Ridge
3 Fort Belknap	16 Rosebud
4 Fort Peck	17 Yankton
5 Fort Berthold	18 Santee
6 Turtle Mountain	19 Winnebago
7 Devil's Lake	20 Omaha
8 Crow	21 Wind River
9 Northern Cheyenne	22 Sac and Fox
10 Standing Rock	23 Kickapoo
11 Cheyenne River	24 Potawatomi
12 Lower Brule	25 Osage
13 Crow Creek	

*Disputed Claims:
Turtle Mountain Chippewa, 1904;
Mandan, Arikara, and Sioux,
1866 and 1868

Figure 11.1 Native Cessions on the Great Plains, 1860–1890

ka territories, the way was open for resettlement by European immigrants and by Americans. By 1860, the counties adjacent to the Missouri River in Nebraska, plus a wider belt of counties in Kansas, had population densities of more than two persons per square mile (fig. 11.2). Most settlers stayed near the Missouri valley, where abundant timber and water and access to imported supplies made pioneering relatively easy. The main westward extensions of population were along the Platte and Kansas River valleys, but virtually every stream and creek flowing into the Missouri had its own small fingers of settle-

ment. Open prairies were avoided because it was too difficult and costly to break the sod.

By 1860 there were 28,826 settlers in Nebraska, already well in excess of the local Native American population. The majority came from previous frontier areas in Ohio, Illinois, Iowa, and Missouri. Almost one-quarter were foreign-born, with British, Irish, and Germans the dominant groups. Settlers came by steamboat from St. Louis, disembarking at the various towns along the river, or they crossed by ferry from Iowa and Missouri, paying a $1 fare for their loaded wagon and team of horses. As is

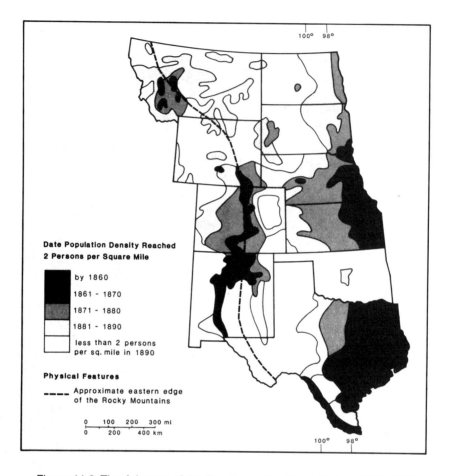

Date Population Density Reached
2 Persons per Square Mile

by 1860

1861 - 1870

1871 - 1880

1881 - 1890

less than 2 persons
per sq. mile in 1890

Physical Features

▬ ▬ ▬ ▬ Approximate eastern edge
of the Rocky Mountains

Figure 11.2 The Advance of the Frontier on the Great Plains, 1860–1890

typical of frontier areas, the settlers were most-ly young adults and children, and men outnumbered women.

Before 1862 most of the land was purchased under the Preemption Act of 1841, which allowed settlers to buy 160 acres at $1.25 an acre. Former soldiers could obtain 160 acres free through government-issued land warrants. After 1862 the Homestead Act introduced the era of virtually free land: any adult citizen or person who intended to take out citizenship could file for 160 acres of public land, pay a nominal registration fee, and after residing on the land for five years and showing proof of cultivation, receive title from the government. Homesteaders could also receive immediate title after six months by paying $1.25 an acre. Land values in Iowa already averaged $2.50 an acre in 1860, so

the attraction of the new frontier areas, with cheap or free land, was strong.

Yet Nebraska was not really a farming frontier in these early years of settlement. In 1860, no county had more than 7 percent of its land area in improved pasture or crops. Agricultural technology was limited, and although land was cheap, the costs of cultivation and fencing were high. Corn was the main frontier crop, followed by oats and potatoes. Most of the harvest was locally consumed, although after 1858 a small surplus was marketed in St. Louis and Colorado.

Almost three-quarters of the population in territorial Nebraska lived in nucleated settlements, from small hamlets of fewer than 20 people to embryonic towns like Omaha and Nebraska City. By 1856, Omaha had 200 buildings and 1,200 inhabitants and was a bustling commercial center with warehouses, hotels, stores, a bank, and blacksmith shops. Like Sioux City to the north and Kansas City to the south, Omaha grew as an outfitting center linking the frontier areas to a national trade network. The main economic activities of Omaha's population were construction, wholesaling, and speculation. City lots already cost $1,000 to $2,000 in 1860 and were increasing in value at a rate of 50 percent a year. More immediate profits were to be made in the rapidly developing cities than on the land.

As in most frontier areas, geographic and occupational mobility was high. Many settlers moved on to Colorado, Utah, and California after only a short stay in Nebraska. The small town of Omadi in northeastern Nebraska, for example, was virtually depopulated by an exodus to the Colorado mines in 1859. Across the Missouri River from Omadi, in Sioux City, 66 percent of the 142 workingmen who were there in 1860 were gone a decade later. Mobility was particularly high among young, low-income laborers, many of whom stayed in Sioux City only long enough to earn a down payment on land. People with large investments in the community tended to stay, forming a socioeconomic elite who dominated Sioux City at least until the 1890s.

Nebraska's population had increased to 122,993 by 1870, and Kansas had almost three times that number. The Civil War and a nationwide financial crisis beginning in 1857 had slowed settlement, but even with these constraints, densities of more than 50 persons per square mile were common along the Missouri River in both states. Railroads had enhanced the positions of Sioux City, Omaha, and Kansas City as gateways to the Plains, and the economic structures of these towns were far more complex than they had been in 1860. Railroads penetrated west of the Missouri, and the Kansas Pacific and Union Pacific spanned the Plains. The railroads permitted the expansion of commercial farming, and by 1870, 52 percent of Nebraska's population were farmers.

Settlers advanced westward along the Platte and Kansas valleys to about the 98th meridian (fig. 11.2). This is the line that historian Walter Prescott Webb designated an "institutional fault" between the humid East and the semiarid Great Plains. Webb believed that settlers halted at this boundary, stalled until adjustments could be made in institutions and ways of life. It is true that significant adaptations were made in the process of settling the High Plains to the west of the 98th meridian but, contrary to Webb's thesis, there was no hesitation at this line, at least not in the central Great Plains, where the advance of the frontier was spearheaded.

EASTERN DAKOTA TERRITORY IN THE 1870s AND 1880s

Before the Railroads

Dakota Territory, like the eastern portions of Kansas and Nebraska, was a prerailroad frontier in its early years. In 1870 settlers were concentrated in the southeastern corner of the territory, in the river valleys of the Missouri and its north bank tributaries, the James, Vermillion, and Big Sioux (fig. 11.3). The Yankton cession of 1858 had prepared this area for resettlement. The Yanktons were given a reservation of 430,000 acres on the north side of the Missouri, just west of the town that adopted their name. The reservation was well suited for agriculture, and by the mid-1870s many of the Yanktons were cultivating individual plots, raising sheep, and wearing "citizens' dress." Still, living conditions were poor and death rates high. Vaccination prevented major losses from smallpox and cholera, but pulmonary and respiratory diseases continued to take a heavy toll. The Yankton agent attributed the high death rate to "extreme poverty," poor housing, and the harsh climate, but the rapid change in diet from traditional foods to government provisions (white flour, sugar, and lard, primarily) must also have weakened resistance.

There was no rush of settlers to Dakota Territory until 1868. The disruption and inflation of the Civil War years slowed migration to the frontier in general, and cheap land was still available in the more accessible and temperate regions of eastern Nebraska and Kansas. Locally, drought and grasshopper infestations in 1864 and 1865, and violent clashes with the Santee Sioux in Minnesota and bands of the Lakota to the west of the Missouri River after 1863, gave the new territory a bad reputation. By 1868, with economic recovery, a growing military presence on the northern Great Plains that eventually subdued the Native Americans and the arrival of the Illinois Central Railroad at Sioux

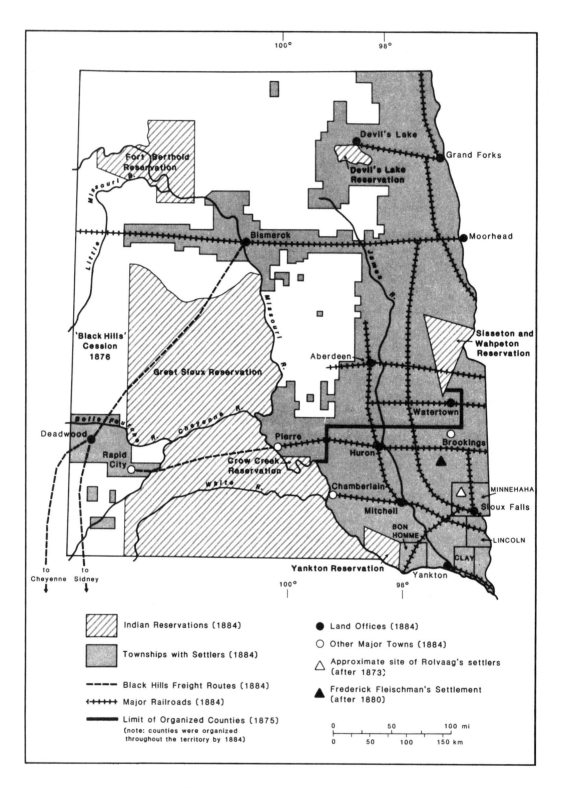

Figure 11.3 Dakota Territory in 1884

City, the stage was set for the first Dakota boom.

Sioux City was the main entry point into Dakota Territory until 1873. After reaching the railhead at Sioux City, settlers boarded steamboats for Yankton or Vermillion, then headed up the James and Vermillion River valleys to the nearest available cheap land. The completion of the Dakota Southern Railroad from Sioux City to Yankton in 1873 facilitated this process, and the Dakota Southern carried thousands of Americans (mostly from Minnesota and Iowa), Norwegians, Swedes, Czechs, German Russians, and Hutterites to their new homes. In 1871 the Immigration Bureau was established, and representatives were dispatched to the New York docks and the Chicago rail terminal to lure immigrants with glowing reports of Dakota Territory. Germans from the steppes of Russia were particularly sought because they were already skilled grassland farmers.

Most immigrants, however, found their way to the frontier by following well-defined migration routes that connected previous neighborhoods and social networks in Europe, often through intermediate settlements in the Middle West, to new emerging communities in Dakota Territory. It was not so much a process of planned group migration (although this did occur, as in the case of the Hutterites) as a reassembling over a period of years of families and acquaintances who were linked through letters and native-language newspapers.

In Dakota Territory, migrants settled "in neighborhoods of their own." Swedes, for example, concentrated in Clay County, to the east of the Vermillion River; Czechs, German Russians, and Hutterites settled in Bon Homme County, to the west of the James; and Norwegians pushed up the Big Sioux River into Lincoln and Minnehaha Counties (fig. 11.3). Even within national groups, immigrants tended to cluster in communities that reflected their regional origins in the old country.

The first Dakota settlement boom ended in 1873 when the nation entered a five-year period of economic depression. Settlers also had their first protracted exposure to the environmental hazards of the Plains. Extremely cold winters and irregular rainfall brought hardship to many settlers, and the grasshopper plagues of 1873, 1874, and 1876 finally left the region destitute. Crop failures and high interest rates combined to produce large numbers of farm foreclosures.

This period of settlement is captured vividly in Rolvaag's *Giants in the Earth,* a work of fiction, but one with a true sense of time and place. Rolvaag's settlers had been fishermen in central Norway who migrated by steamship to Quebec. They set out for the frontier, pausing in southeastern Minnesota, where there were well-established Norwegian communities. After filing a homestead claim at the Sioux Falls land office in the spring of 1873, Per Hansa and his family and friends pushed out into the prairies. Fifty miles northwest of Sioux Falls the settlers stopped at Spring Creek, a site that had been selected by one of the men in the previous fall (fig. 11.3). They stayed close together, settling adjacent quarter sections, knowing that they would need the group support.

Per Hansa came to the frontier with only $30, which meant improvisation and deprivation. The improvised home was a sod house, which was regarded as a temporary structure until such time as timber, an expensive item in the early years of settlement, could be imported for frame buildings. Timber for fuel and for the willow thatch on the sod buildings was hauled 35 miles from the valley of the Big Sioux. Potatoes were the initial sod crop, but the Norwegian settlers were convinced that this was "soil for wheat, the king of all grains." The wheat crop flourished until the grasshoppers descended, leaving the fields stripped to the soil.

The settlers stayed only because poverty had deprived them of the ability to leave. They persisted through the hard times, and by 1881 Per Hansa owned 480 acres. In addition to the initial homestead, he probably had purchased 160 acres through the Preemption Act and another quarter section through the Timber Culture Act (1873), which had been passed in an effort to increase the number of trees on the Great Plains.

The community survived through combined effort. One of their number served as a schoolteacher, another as a justice of the peace, and soon a frontier minister brought organized religion to Spring Creek. Other Norwegians settled nearby. But the Plains environment continued to threaten the settlers. Per Hansa finally died in a blizzard while attempting to reach a doctor in the James River valley.

Many migrants to Dakota Territory, particularly the Americans, came to the frontier alone. Frederick A. Fleischman, for example, homesteaded in Kingsbury County in 1880 (fig. 11.3).

He started with $425, with which he built a small frame house and invested in a wagon, a team of horses, and some farm machinery. Fleischman paid to have 20 acres of prairie broken, and in the fall of the first year he harvested 181 bushels of wheat. Encouraged by his initial success, he returned to Wisconsin, married, and brought his wife back to the Dakota homestead in time for spring planting. Eventually, the Fleischmans raised ten children, a valuable asset on a family farm.

In 1882 a good harvest produced an income of $1,242, enough to cover expenses and provide a comfortable living by the standards of the time and place. But the price of wheat went in a downward spiral after 1882 and did not recover until after the drought and depression of the 1890s. While many others failed, the Fleischman family endured because of luck, intelligence, and austerity. They were lucky in starting farming during two years of good rainfall and high wheat prices, which allowed them to gain a foothold. When wheat prices fell, they diversified, so that even during the hard times there was some income from the sale of eggs, milk, lard, and meat. But the family survived mostly because they tightened their belts. In 1894 when the income from the farm was only $95, they became virtually self-sufficient and spent only $30 on groceries and provisions. Conditions improved after 1895, and the Fleischmans enjoyed a period of relative prosperity in the first two decades of the 20th century.

The Impact of the Railroad

By the late 1870s, Dakota Territory was a railroad frontier experiencing a surge of population growth. In the year following June 30, 1879, more than 2 million acres of government land were disposed of under the Homestead, Preemption, and Timber Culture Acts. This was more than one-quarter of all the land alienated in the nation that year. From 1880 to 1883, 200,000 settlers moved into east-central Dakota Territory. This was a zone of overlap between the Corn Belt of southeastern Dakota, which had been largely settled before 1873 via the Missouri River, and the emerging Spring Wheat Belt, which was settled after 1878 in an east-west movement of people following the railroad tracks (fig. 11.3).

The arrival of the railroads at the eastern border of Dakota Territory and their extension westward after 1878 eclipsed Sioux City's role as gateway city to the northern Great Plains. A series of formerly insignificant towns, such as Sioux Falls and Grand Forks, became the main portals for settlers heading west and the primary exit points for agricultural products destined for eastern markets. The railroads also truncated the Missouri River route. Steamboat traffic declined after a peak in 1867, and Chicago and Minneapolis supplanted St. Louis as the main wholesaling centers for the northern Plains.

The railroad changed the pace and nature of pioneering. Settlers were recruited by railroad companies that wanted their government land grants filled with people and their boxcars filled with grain. The railroad companies joined the Immigration Bureau in sending agents to Europe and New York, and throughout the United States they set up booths at county fairs to demonstrate the rich agricultural rewards of settling on the northern Plains. Most immigrants now boarded trains for the frontier, unless the trip was of a short distance or the price of a ticket too high. They came by the thousands in the spring, often to be met at the station by railroad representatives who would direct them to their quarter sections. This recruitment process displayed a strong ethnic bias. Non-English-speaking immigrants from northern Europe and Russian German Mennonites were sought because it was believed that they would "work harder, complain less, and produce more than anyone else."

Settlers were tied to the railroad by their reliance on wheat, which accounted for 60 percent of all the improved land in the new state of North Dakota in 1889. Wheat farmers were obliged to live within 20 miles of the railroad because haulage over a longer distance would consume all their profits. The Census Bureau estimated that it "costs the ordinary farmer more to carry each bushel of wheat a mile than it now does the railroad to carry a ton."

The North Dakota settlers included native-born Americans from the Middle West, first-generation Canadians from Ontario, German Russians in their tightly organized communities, Germans directly from Europe and German Americans from Wisconsin, and tens of thousands of immigrants from the overpopulated rural districts of Norway and Sweden. On the frontier the non-English-speaking settlers tended to marry within their groups, preserving the ethnic mosaic that was established with the initial settlement. These groups, however, mingled in the course of making a living. Occupational and geographic mobility was a way of life; 40 percent of North Dakota homesteaders worked off their farms for periods during the early years.

After 1880 the frontier was much more closely tied to national economic networks than it had been in previous years. The nationwide system of railroads, a national bank system, and vertically integrated corporations that controlled the supply and distribution of products all brought the frontier into closer contact with the more settled parts of the country. Mail-order houses and canned goods introduced diversity to the consumer on the frontier. The Fleischman family, for example, expanded its diet after 1895 to include imported fruits and vegetables and a wide variety of canned goods.

This was an era of increasing economic specialization, and the range of goods and services that the new Plains towns offered reflected this trend. In addition to the general store, there were now butcher shops, hardware stores, grain elevators, and lumberyards. Whereas the small establishments were generally locally owned, most frequently by native-born Americans, the elevators and lumberyards were controlled by large companies based outside the region. By 1889 Minnesota was producing one-third of the nation's lumber, much of it destined for the treeless northern Plains, and corporate giants such as Pillsbury of Minneapolis dominated the grain trade.

The morphology, spacing, and prospects of the towns were largely dictated by the railroad. The central courthouse square plan, common in the eastern United States, was replaced on the northern Plains by the "T-town," where the main street was laid out perpendicular to the railroad tracks, which were flanked by grain elevators, lumberyards, and standardized depots. The railroad companies spaced the towns along the tracks to serve as grain-collection points for the surrounding farms. This relatively dense settlement fabric was an anachronism within a few decades of its creation. Established in a horse-and-buggy era when the extent of a town's hinterland was limited by slow and costly movement, the towns were too many when the automobile expanded the range of circulation in

the 20th century. Those distant from the lifeline of the railroad, in particular, could not compete, and many stagnated and died. The growing mechanization of agriculture, resulting in increased farm sizes and declining rural population, also removed customers from the services upon which the economy of the small towns depended. The towns that survived, either because of favored location or enterprising citizens, benefited from the extra business that had previously been conducted at smaller, more local centers.

While the eastern Great Plains was filling up with settlers, Native Americans, miners, and cattlemen occupied the drier and more remote country to the west of the 100th meridian. After the Civil War, hundreds of thousands of cattle were driven north from Texas each year to the boomtowns at the railheads in Kansas and Nebraska, where they were bought and shipped to eastern markets. The cattle were moved in even greater numbers to the western ranges in Colorado, Montana, and Dakota Territory, where gold and silver discoveries had created bustling exclaves of settlement in 1859, 1862–64, and 1874, respectively. The final destinations for the drives were the reservations of Indian Territory and the northern Plains. Meat and stock were furnished to Native Americans as one form of payment for their lands and as an alternative to the bison, which by the 1870s was facing extinction. Nothing symbolizes the deteriorating circumstances of the indigenous peoples of the Great Plains as accurately as this shift from bison hunting, which had allowed mobility, independence, and effective resistance, to the "feeding" policy on the reservations, which emphasized dependency and defeat.

THE WESTERN GREAT PLAINS, 1865–1900

Restricting the Native Americans

By 1865, while the Native Americans of the eastern Great Plains were making difficult adjustments to reservation life, the nomadic hunters of the western Plains remained relatively unchallenged in the possession of their lands. In fact, the 1851 Treaty of Fort Laramie had defined and confirmed the territories of the Lakotas, Cheyennes, Arapahoes, Crows, Assiniboines, Gros Ventres, Mandans, and Arikaras in an attempt to reduce intertribal conflict over contested hunting grounds. The Treaty of Fort Laramie also recognized the right of the United States to establish roads and military posts in these territories. This clause became a contentious issue after 1862, when gold was discovered in Montana and miners converged on the northern Rockies. Army posts were built along the Missouri River and along the Bozeman Trail through Wyoming to protect the two main routes to the goldfields. Relations between the United States and the western tribes deteriorated to a state of intermittent warfare that continued until the last resistance was stamped out on the snow-swept Plains of Wounded Knee, South Dakota, on December 29, 1890.

The federal government's response to the escalating conflict on the western Plains after the Civil War was the Peace Policy, a combination of brutal military suppression and well-intended paternalism. The emphasis of the Peace Policy varied from time to time, depending on who was commissioner of Indian affairs, and from place to place, according to degrees of Native American resistance. At the heart of the Peace Policy was the idea of the reservation. Native Americans would be collected into two large districts, one in Indian Territory, the other to the west of the Missouri River in Dakota Territory. This would not only remove Native Americans from the central Plains, where the advance of settlers was most rapid, but would also restrict the movements of the bison hunters, tying them down to specific places where government agents could teach them "self-sustaining habits."

In 1867 and 1868, at the Councils of Medicine Lodge Creek (Kansas) and Fort Laramie (Wyoming), vast areas of the western Plains were sold to the United States. At Medicine Lodge Creek, the Kiowas, Comanches, Southern Cheyennes and Arapahoes, and some bands of the Apaches ceded their lands on the High Plains of Texas, New Mexico. Colorado, and Kansas and were placed on reservations in Indian Territory. At Fort Laramie, the Crows, Northern Cheyennes and Arapahoes, and the seven bands of the Lakotas agreed to major cessions of their hunting grounds in return for subsistence rations and guaranteed reservations. The Crows, for example, received a cash-equivalent of 3.6 cents an acre for 30 million acres of land in Wyoming and Montana and a 6-million-acre reservation to the south of the present town of Billings (fig. 11.1).

In subsequent years, the reservations created by the Treaty of Fort Laramie were reduced through additional cessions of lands, often in direct violation of earlier treaties. The 1876 surrender of the Black Hills by the Lakotas and the Northern Cheyennes and Arapahoes, for example, was made under duress and without the necessary signatures of three-quarters of the tribal population. The Black Hills cession is still unfinished business, a matter of dispute between the federal government and the Lakotas and between the Lakotas and the Northern Cheyennes.

The Peace Policy distinguished between those Native Americans who capitulated and settled on the reservations and those who resisted and continued their independence. As Commissioner of Indian Affairs Francis Walker explained in 1872, "The Indian should be made as comfortable on, and as uncomfortable off, their reservations as it was in the power of the Government to make them." On the reservations, missionaries were appointed as agents in the hope that they would reduce administrative corruption and put the Native Americans on the Christian path. Massive amounts of rations were delivered to the agencies to sustain and pacify the Natives. The rations were given to the heads of individual families so that the power of the chiefs and the communal basis of their societies would be weakened. Frequently agents withheld rations as a punishment or means of coercion.

The feeding policy did not work well. Rations were dispensed irregularly from agencies located predominantly along the Missouri River. This was convenient for the government, which could transport the bulky annuities by steamboat, but difficult for the Native Americans, many of whom still camped in bands in remote parts of the reservations. Not until 1890 were substations established to dispense rations more locally. Even then, many of the nonfood rations that the government handed out were quickly sold to traders for a few cents. The shelves of the secondhand store in Gordon, Nebraska, just to the south of the Pine Ridge Reservation, were well stocked with government clothes in the 1890s, sold by Lakotas at a going rate of 25 cents for a pair of shoes and 75 cents for a suit of clothes.

Off the reservations Native Americans found it increasingly difficult to resist the growing force of the American military. By the 1870s there were 25,000 troops on the northern Great Plains. The number of military posts was increased from 3 in 1860 to 38 in 1878. Most of the forts were located at the agencies along the Missouri River and served the dual function of regulating the Native Americans and keeping the river route open. Forts were also built on the western Plains to protect railroad and telegraph construction crews, as well as on the routes to the goldfields. The extension of the railroads into the Plains, improving communication lines for the army, and the virtual elimination of the bison herds, depriving the Native Americans of their economic base, foreshadowed the end of their resistance. After the massacre at Wounded Knee the military presence on the northern Plains was greatly reduced.

Despite statements to the contrary in various treaties, the Indian Office saw reservations as only temporary expedients on the way to assim-

ilation. This was made clear in 1887 when the Dawes Act imposed allotments, an action that had been under consideration for decades. Each Native American would be given an individual plot, generally 160 acres, and encouraged to farm. The remainder of the reservations, after allotments had been made, would be sold as "surplus lands" to settlers. The result was another massive erosion of the Native American land base. The 1.7-million-acre Fort Peck reservation in eastern Montana, for example, was created in 1888 as a redefined homeland for 1,178 Yanktons and 713 Assiniboines (fig. 11.1). During the following 20 years the Yanktons and Assiniboines lived on rations, produce from small gardens, and income from grazing leases. Allotments were introduced on the reservation in 1908. By 1912, 700,000 acres had been allotted, mainly along the southern border of the reservation, and the remainder of the reservation was opened to settlers. The proceeds from the sales

Figure 11.4 Guthrie, Oklahoma, May 2, 1889 (Courtesy Oklahoma Historical Society)

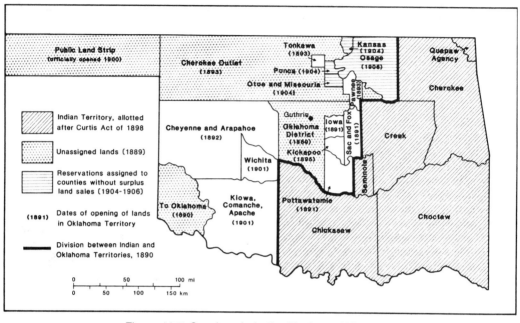

Figure 11.5 Cessions in Indian Territory, 1889–1906

were put into irrigation projects and cattle purchases, but even in 1925 fewer than 5,000 acres
were in crops, and many Native Americans were
still dependent on rations.

Allotments were also the means of extin-
guishing Indian title to much of Indian Territory. The first area to be opened for settlement was
the unassigned Oklahoma District, which was
filled by a stampede of homesteaders on April
22, 1889. Towns sprang up on the prairie
overnight, tent and clapboard cities of men (very
few women at first) where the military maintained a semblance of order (fig. 11.4). Settlers
came from all parts of the United States, attracted by country that offered better prospects than
the drought-prone lands that remained as frontier in Kansas and Nebraska.

In 1890, Indian Territory west of the lands of
the Five Civilized Tribes was redefined as Oklahoma Territory. With the exception of the
Kansas, Osage, Ponca, and Otoe and Missouria
reservations, which were converted into counties and allotments without surplus land sales,
the reservations in Oklahoma Territory were allotted and the surplus lands sold to settlers in
the decade following 1891 (fig. 11.5). The eastern part of Indian Territory, home to the Five
Civilized Tribes since the removals of the 1820s
and 1830s, was largely allotted during the first

decade of the 20th century. The Cherokees,
Creeks, Choctaws, Chickasaws, and Seminoles
gave up their special status as self-governing
nations following the Curtis Act of 1898 and
took out citizenship along with their allotments.
In 1907 Indian Territory and Oklahoma Territory were combined into the new state of Oklahoma.

The transition to farming on individually
owned plots was made more successfully on
the eastern than on the western Great Plains.
Many of the Omahas in eastern Nebraska, for
example, and the Pawnees in eastern Oklahoma
Territory, were farming on allotments and living in frame houses by 1900. But on the drier
western Plains, which had never been farming
country, attempts to cultivate the land generally failed. On the Pine Ridge Reservation in the
1890s, corn, turnips, and other vegetables did
germinate but were "scorched away" in the
heat of the August sun. Consequently, very few
Lakotas were settled on allotments by 1900.
Unless irrigation was provided, as on the Crow
Reservation in Montana, grazing proved a more
successful adaptation to changed circumstances for the Native Americans of the western
Plains, but rations continued to be a main
means of subsistence well into the 20th century (fig. 11.6).

The Black Hills Mining Frontier

In 1874, long-standing rumors of gold in the Black Hills were confirmed as fact. By the end of 1876 (before the Black Hills had been officially ceded from the Native Americans), there were 5,000 people in Deadwood and another 15,000 in mining camps within a ten-mile radius. In 1879 a correspondent for the New York Tribune visited Deadwood. He found a lively town. Frame buildings, adorned with sham fronts to give a "metropolitan appearance" lined the main street (fig. 11.7). The residential areas consisted of small "but tastefully built cottages," with a Chinese quarter at the bottom of Main Street. Deadwood had gambling halls, opium dens, an "abundance of saloons," a variety theater, schools, churches, and three banks, each with more than $500,000 in deposits. Wage rates were high, but so was the cost of living, because of the need to import food and other supplies. Profits were to be made as readily in supplying the area as in mining. One enterprising man brought $3,000 worth of goods up from Cheyenne in 1877 and sold them within a day for $10,000. Deadwood was also full of lawyers because mining gave rise to "almost endless" litigation.

Deadwood, like Denver and Helena but unlike most Plains towns, was founded without the aid of the railroad. The first tracks did not reach the Black Hills until 1886, when a branch line was laid north from the Chicago and Northwestern at Chadron, Nebraska, and Rapid City was not connected east by rail to Pierre until 1905. The lure of gold and silver was strong enough to pull settlers hundreds of miles ahead of the railroad. Moreover, unlike wheat, gold would bear the high costs of overland transportation. So for more than a decade Deadwood and other mining areas in the Black Hills were connected to the outside world only by difficult, and often dangerous, stagecoach routes. Before 1880, the most important connections were to Sidney, Nebraska, and Cheyenne, Wyoming. After 1880, when the Chicago and Northwestern reached Pierre and the Northern Pacific pushed west through Bismarck, the Black Hills were increasingly supplied overland from the east (fig 11.3).

As in Colorado and Montana, the presence of a large mining population in the Black Hills was a strong incentive for local food production. By 1879 the valleys of the Black Hills were supplying wheat, oats, and potatoes to the mining camps. The development of stock raising on the Plains around the Black Hills was even more significant. The first drives from Texas into southwestern Dakota Territory (other than to the reservations) took place in 1877, as soon as the land was acquired from the Native Americans. For a brief period cattlemen dominated the western Great Plains from the Rio Grande to the Canadian prairies.

Figure 11.6 Ration Day Issue at the Commissary, between 1889 and 1891
(Courtesy Nebraska State Historical Society)

Figure 11.7 Main Street, Deadwood, Dakota Territory, circa 1860
(Courtesy Nebraska Sate Historical Society)

The Open-Range Cattle Kingdom

The "day of the cattleman" actually lasted about two decades, from 1866 until the late 1880s. It was one of the few occasions when the region was integrated lengthwise, instead of being fragmented by lateral connections to the east and west (fig. 11.8). The predominant east-west orientation was reestablished in the 1880s when much of the open range was settled and fenced by homesteaders.

The transfer of almost 6 million steers from Texas to the railheads and ranges of the central and northern Great Plains from 1866 to 1885 made patent economic and ecological sense. During the Civil War, when the conventional outlets to eastern markets were blocked, a reservoir of more than 3 million cattle built up in the Coastal Bend and Cross Timbers regions of Texas and spilled over onto the southern High Plains. The economic logic of the cattle drives, as the entrepreneur Joseph G. McCoy realized in 1866, was that a three-year-old steer worth less than $10 in Texas would bring as much as $70 at the New York market. McCoy was instrumental in creating the first Kansas cattle town at Abilene in 1867, where cattlemen could meet buyers and where the Kansas Pacific Railroad provided the link to eastern markets.

The ecological reason for the trail drives involved the complementary nature of the southern and northern ranges. The southern Plains of Texas, with their mild winters, were excellent breeding grounds where a herd could increase its numbers by 80 to 90 percent each year. But the cattle did not add flesh well on the mesquite grass of Texas. On the northern Great Plains, on the other hand, severe winters kept the annual calf "crop" at less than 45 percent, but cattle fattened well on the nutritious short-and mixed-grass prairie. A two-year-old Texas steer could add 200 pounds in two years on the Montana range at a cost of no more than $1.25 a year. The four-year-old steer would be worth $25 to $45 at the railhead. The trail drives, therefore, consisted of one- to two-year-old steers that were moved to the northern ranges for fattening and mature steers that were driven to the cattle towns and shipped directly to the packinghouses in Kansas City and Chicago.

As the period progressed, the cattle trails and transshipment points were dislodged westward as the railroads penetrated the Plains, drawing the farming frontier in their wake. Quarantine laws enacted to prevent the spread of Texas (splenic) fever from the longhorns to the local cattle also caused the trails to veer to the west. Abilene flourished from 1867 to 1872, then surrendered the trade to Ellsworth and Wichita. By 1877 fences and quarantine legislation blocked

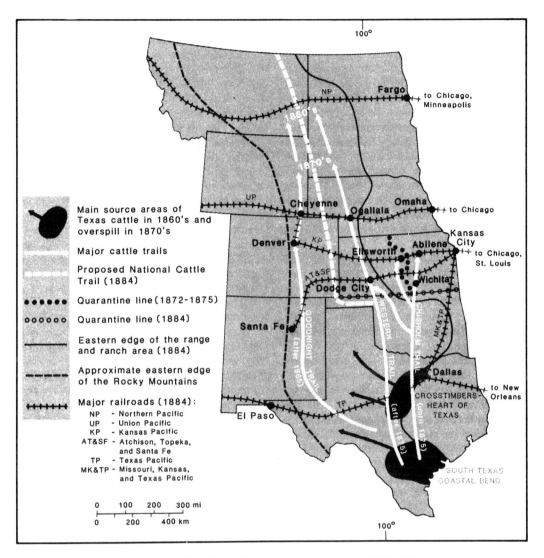

Figure 11.8 The Open-Range Cattle Kingdom, 1866–1887

the Chisholm Trail to Wichita, and Dodge City took over as the major cattle town. Dodge City and Ogallala, Nebraska, were the main trans-shipment points in the 1880s during the last years of the open-range cattle era on the central Great Plains (fig. 11.8).

The cattle towns were both more and less than their reputations: less, because they were never as violent as legend has made them; more, because they were important commercial centers, with banks, saloons, hotels, grocery and clothing stores, bootmakers, lawyers, and prostitutes, all connected in one way or another to the cattle trade. They were temporary boomtowns that cashed in on the cattle trade and then made the necessary adjustment to the more mundane world of serving the surrounding ranching and farming population.

By 1885 there were an estimated 7.5 million cattle on the western Plains from Indian Territory to the Canadian border. Settlement patterns on the open range were oriented to the streams because cattle needed to graze within six miles of water. The herdsmen secured the rights to the land along the rivers, often by manipulation of the land laws. In the Nebraska Sand Hills, for example, stock owners employed their herders at "liberal wages" to take out Timber Culture claims in the lush hay meadows that lie between the dunes. These were used "rent free, tax free, and interest free" for many years with no pretense at fulfilling the conditions of the law. By 1885, many herdsmen on the northern Plains were fencing the range in order to gain firmer control over the water supplies and in anticipation of the wave of homesteaders that was about to engulf them.

Many of the early cattlemen who grazed their herds on the open range were typical frontier entrepreneurs who had moved to the West at an early age and accumulated capital in such activities as trading or land speculation. They were owner-operators who made the most of the "golden age of ranching," when their control of the open range was unchallenged, prices were high, and the only overhead was the cost of stock cattle. After 1880 these individual owners and small partnerships were bought out by major corporations and foreign investors. In Cheyenne County, in the Panhandle of Nebraska, the 13 operators who controlled the range in 1880 had sold their interests to two corporations—the Ogallala Land and Cattle Company and the Bay State Live Stock Company—by 1885. This same process of consolidation of holdings on the open range occurred throughout the western Great Plains in the early 1880s. Standard Oil controlled large acreages in the Cimarron Strip in Indian Territory (using Oil as a brand), and European aristocrats invested heavily in the industry in Colorado, Wyoming, and Montana.

This second wave of investment was only just beginning when the bottom dropped out of the industry. The Texas cattlemen suffered greatly after 1884, when Kansas extended its quarantine laws against splenic fever across the entire state, blocking the northern drives (fig. 11.8). On the northern Plains, overstocking of the range led to a deterioration in the quality of the cattle. The poor quality, combined with the accumulation of years of high production that resulted in oversupply at the markets, caused the price of beef to fall from $5.60 per 100 pounds at Chicago in 1884 to $4.75 in 1885. Collusion between the major meat companies, Armour and Swift of Chicago and Kansas City, also kept the market prices low. The final blow was dealt by the severe winters of 1886–87 and 1888–89,

which reduced the herds by 40 to 60 percent throughout the northern Plains. The owners tried to recoup their losses by dumping their remaining stock on the market, and the price of beef at the Chicago stockyards plummeted to $3.75 per 100 pounds by 1889.

Even if the cattlemen had survived these economic and climatic reversals, their period of control of the western ranges was over. The whole weight of the federal government, as expressed in the land laws, favored the homesteader over the cattleman. In ideology, at least, it was considered un-American for a few owners to dominate the range where thousands of homesteaders could settle. The Texas cattle interests made a last attempt to salvage their industry by introducing a bill in Congress in February 1885 to establish a national cattle trail, a six-mile-wide "free highway" stretching from western Indian Territory to Canada that would be reserved from private ownership (fig. 11.8). But the grid of barbed wire fences was rapidly being laid across Kansas and Nebraska, choking off the trails and restricting the open range to smaller and smaller areas and to remote refuges, such as the Montana Plains.

Homesteading on the Western Great Plains, 1878–1900

In 1890 the U.S. Census Bureau declared that the unsettled area was "so broken into by isolated bodies of settlement" that it was no longer possible to identify a distinctive frontier line. A surge of settlement in 1878 and 1879, then again from 1883 to 1887, carried the farming frontier across the mythical barriers of the 98th and 100th meridians into the short-grass Plains of Kansas, Nebraska, and Colorado. By 1890, this westward-moving frontier had merged with the irrigated oases that were scattered along the Colorado piedmont. To the north, the new state of South Dakota was settled to the Missouri River (with an outlier of 32,559 people in the Black Hills), and the railroads were rapidly pulling the spring-wheat frontier across North Dakota. To the south, the resettlement of Oklahoma and Indian Territories was imminent, and Oklahoma District already appeared on the population map (fig. 11.2).

In Texas the southern frontier had been blocked at the eastern edge of the Great Plains from 1860 to 1875 by the Kiowas and Comanches, which may explain why Walter Prescott Webb, a Texan, believed that the entire Great Plains frontier stalled at the 98th meridian for several decades. Even when the Native American threat was removed, farmers were slow to migrate west of the Cross Timbers because of remoteness from markets and the prevailing belief (fostered by the cattle ranchers) that West Texas would never be farming country. The extension of the railroads beyond the Cross Timbers and through the Panhandle after 1880 changed both the image and the economic potential of West Texas, prompting, and to a great extent promoting, the boom of 1887–90. The cotton frontier advanced 100 miles along its entire length, and in the Panhandle wheat fringed the railroad tracks that cut through the heart of sparsely populated cattle country.

On the central Great Plains, settlers were seduced into the marginal farming lands beyond the 100th meridian by years of good rainfall (particularly 1883–87) and an intense propaganda campaign launched by federal and state agencies, town site promoters, and the railroads. To a large degree this was a speculator's frontier, with genuine farmers following on the second wave of settlement. Speculation varied in scale from local entrepreneurs who filed claims for the purpose of relinquishing them when the area became more settled and land values climbed, to absentee landlords like William Scully, who amassed 225,000 acres of farmland in Illinois, Missouri, Kansas, and Nebraska. Nowhere was the discrepancy between the ideal of the yeoman farmer and the reality of the speculator's frontier more blatant than in Nance County, in central Nebraska, which was created out of the abandoned Pawnee reservation in 1879. Virtually all the land was sold by 1883, with 14 individuals or partnerships each acquiring more than 2,500 acres. Most of the land was resold to settlers within a few years of purchase, indicating the intent of speculation. This was particularly ironic, because the Pawnees had been preached to for decades that the way to become an American was to work diligently on a 160-acre plot.

The promoters of Plains settlement had at their disposal a "perfect recruiting device" in the theory that rainfall was "following the plow." The illusion was inculcated into the receptive minds of the settlers that rainfall would increase as they broke the prairie sod and planted trees. Scientific backing for the idea came from Samuel Aughey and Charles D. Wilber in Nebraska and Franklin B. Hough of the Department of Agriculture, who theorized that loosening the soil and planting trees would make more water available for evaporation, leading to saturation of the atmosphere and increased rainfall. Constructing facile arguments from dubious experiments, Aughey, Wilber, and Hough predicted that the Great American Desert would soon be transformed into a "rain belt" through the farmers' own efforts. School textbooks, state atlases, railroad promotional pamphlets, local horticultural societies, and the Federal Division of Forestry all conveyed this hopeful, but fallacious, message. Many scientists disclaimed the theory, but the settlers were left alone to realize its folly in the desperate years of the 1890s.

There was nothing illusory, however, about the value of the railroads in easing the burdens of settling the western Great Plains. Branch lines sprouted from the main tracks after 1878, making it easier for settlers to get into the country and bringing supplies and markets closer to formerly isolated communities. By 1885 virtually all of Nebraska east of the 98th meridian was within 12 miles of a railroad, and even in the western part of the state the Burlington, Union Pacific, and Sioux City and Pacific railroads brought the frontier into close contact with the more settled parts of the country.

The editors of the widely read journals *Rural Nebraska* and the *Nebraska Farmer* advised the settler to bring $200 to $300 to the frontier to cover the costs of housing, fencing, and sod breaking. But many settlers moved with little except hope for the future. They could not afford railroad land or other accessible land that had already been improved. So they moved out ahead of the main wave of settlers and stuck it out in isolated areas, waiting years, often in vain, for the tracks to be laid into their counties.

One such settlement occurred in Osborne County in north-central Kansas. The first farmers reached the area in the 1870s, driving ranchers into the hills, then out of the district altogether. Most came with very little, one settler reportedly bringing "nine children and eleven cents." This was a self-contained community; there was no other choice, because the nearest railroad station was 60 miles away. A settler with a few cows was considered rich. Food was plain and entirely locally raised; sorghum molasses was the settlers' sugar, rye their coffee, and cornmeal their staple. The main crop was corn, planted in small fields with the aid of an ax, worked with a hoe, and cut with a knife. Wild plants, such as dandelion leaves, sheep sorrel, and plums, added some variety to the diet and kept scurvy at bay. The settlers lived in sod houses, often shoveled out of banksides, sometimes with flowers planted on the roofs (fig. 11.9). At their best, the sod houses were efficiently insulated dwellings, staying warm in winter and cool in summer; at their worst, they were dark and dank, infested by mosquitoes and bedbugs, and offering attractive shelter for rattlesnakes. Life was tedious and lonely, especially for the women, who worked in the fields, made the clothes, kept the house, and walked great distances to sell butter, lard, and eggs at the nearest town. Despite these hardships, the old-timers who told these stories to Kansas historian John Ise remembered their pioneer days with fondness, recalling a simpler life when friendships were binding and the connection with the land brought a satisfaction that had since been lost.

Lying at the heart of Webb's thesis is the argument that settlers could not advance onto the western Great Plains until major adjustments were made in their "ways of life and living." There is no doubt that various inventions— Glidden's barbed wire, for example, and the self-governing windmill, both of which came into general use in the 1880s—facilitated settlement. But adaptations to the semiarid grasslands took place slowly and in face of opposition from settlers who did not want, or did not have the means, to change their methods of farming. It was easier to believe that the environment was adapting to them by becoming more humid.

Corn remained the dominant crop throughout western Kansas, western Nebraska, and even eastern Colorado in the 1880s. In years of good rainfall, corn thrived on the newly turned sod and was useful both as a feed and as a food crop. But corn could not endure the drought that returned in 1887 and lasted, with only brief respites, until 1896. The drought desiccated the western Great Plains from the Texas Panhandle to the Canadian prairies. In eastern Colorado, rainfall fell from its average of 16 inches a year to 8 inches in 1895. Grasshoppers and low market prices compounded the farmers' distress. Large parts of the western Plains were depopulated. Abandoned farmhouses, boarded-up towns, and the stream of broken settlers, their futures foreclosing with their farms, stood as stark evidence of what Harlan Barrows called "the first great crushing defeat" of the American farmer.

The population map for 1900 shows this dramatic retraction of the frontier in the central Plains, despite the renewed immigration that occurred after 1896. Many of the failed settlers

Figure 11.9 "Our Home": Dugout near McCook, Nebraska, 1890s
(Courtesy Nebraska State Historical Society)

headed for the newly opened lands in Oklahoma Territory, which filled up so quickly that by 1900 there was no evidence on the population map to suggest that the area had been held out of American settlement for 50 years. The bands of population density ran across Oklahoma from Kansas to Texas without refraction (fig. 11.10).

The drought forced adjustments on the farmers of the western Plains. The illusion of increasing rainfall was finally laid to rest, and irrigation and dry farming were advocated as more realistic solutions to the problem of moisture deficiency. New drought-resistant crops, such as Turkey Red wheat, gradually replaced corn, and in eastern Colorado many farmers turned to livestock raising. A more accurate view of the area was forged from the failures of the 1880s and 1890s, but as with every drought on the Great Plains, many of the lessons were quickly forgotten when the rains and prices revived.

20TH-CENTURY FRONTIERS

A comparison of the 1900 and 1930 population density maps for the Great Plains states clearly reveals that much of the area was settled on 20th-century frontiers (fig. 11.10). In fact, more land was disposed of under the Homestead Act (and its enlarged versions of 1909 and 1916, giving 320 and 640 acres, respectively) from 1898 to 1917 than in the previous three decades. From 1900 to 1910, millions of acres were plowed up in central North Dakota, western Kansas and Nebraska, and parts of western Texas and Oklahoma. From 1910 to 1919 the main thrust of settlement was through western North Dakota into eastern and central Montana. When another devastating drought and a rapid decline in wheat prices halted the settlement boom on the northern Plains after 1919, the focus shifted to the southern Plains. This was the last great farming frontier in the United States. It was also the prelude to the dust bowl.

By the 1920s at least five major agricultural regions could be distinguished on the Great Plains. In the south, the Cotton Belt extended west across the red soil prairies of central Oklahoma and out onto the fertile sandy loams of the Texas High Plains as far west as Lubbock. To the north, stretching from the Texas Panhandle to western Nebraska, lay the Winter Wheat Belt. Separating the Winter Wheat Belt from the Spring Wheat Belt of the Dakotas and Montana was the western extension of the Corn Belt, an area of mixed crop and livestock production characteristic of northern Kansas and southern and eastern Nebraska. On the western fringes of the Great Plains in south-central Montana, Wyoming, western South Dakota, and with an eastern outlier in the Nebraska Sand Hills, cattle and sheep raising were the primary economic activities, unless irrigation allowed local crop production.

Each of these agricultural belts was oriented to, and largely controlled by, cities located mainly to the east of the Great Plains. The railroad provided the essential connections, and only the most isolated parts of the Plains remained more than 25 miles from the tracks. Fort Worth, for example, was the "gateway and focus of West Texas," channeling cotton and livestock products to the East. The Texas Panhandle, however, was connected by the Atchison, Topeka, and Santa Fe to Kansas City, the capital of the Winter Wheat Belt. Omaha, and ultimately Chicago, were the main hubs of the Corn Belt, while Denver's Plains hinterland extended from eastern Colorado and western Kansas to Wyoming. On the northern Plains, Minneapolis millers and bankers, in alliance with the railroad companies, controlled the storage, pricing, transportation, and marketing of spring wheat.

The diversity of farming types tends to obscure common characteristics of early-20th-century Plains settlement. These were mechanized frontiers where settlers came, and left, by railroad and automobile. They were frontiers where the small farmer had a poor chance of success; the marginal nature of the environment necessitated large acreages, which were difficult to work without the new gasoline-powered tractors and combines and prohibitively expensive to fence. Few people had the resources for such heavy capital investments, unless they went into debt and faced the consequences of foreclosure when grain prices went on a downward spiral, as they did in the 1920s. Increasingly, this was a speculator's frontier where a few people with money and ambition could acquire vast holdings by manipulating the land laws or buying out failed small farmers for a few dollars an acre. Many of the failed farmers, or settlers too poor to buy good farming land in the first place, became tenants. By 1930, more

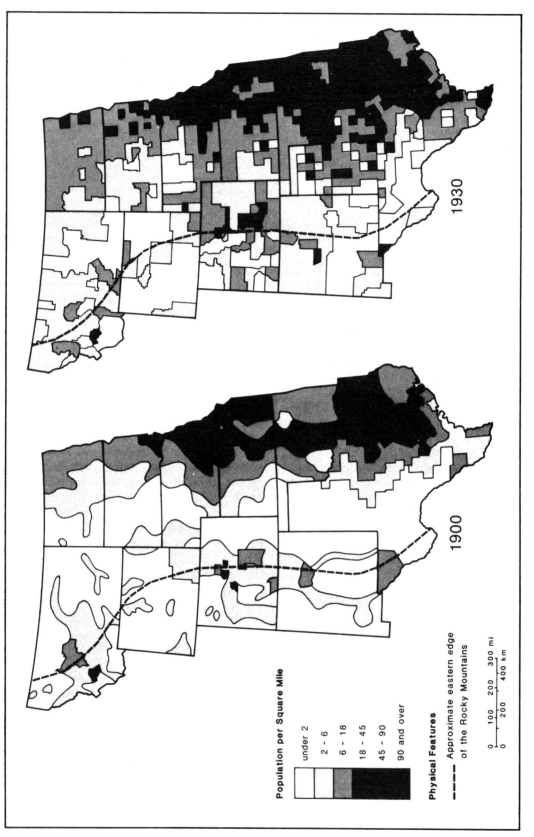

Population per Square Mile

under 2

2 – 6

6 – 18

18 – 45

45 – 90

90 and over

Physical Features

– – – Approximate eastern edge
of the Rocky Mountains

0   100   200   300 mi
0   200   400 km

1930

1900

Figure 11.10 Population Density on the Great Plains, 1900 and 1930

than 60 percent of the farmers in Texas and Oklahoma were tenants, and in general the Great Plains was second only to the South as a region of tenancy. Finally, agriculture on the Plains (particularly in the Wheat Belts) became monocultural, where a single crop dominated the landscape, producing ecosystems that were highly simplified and, therefore, highly unstable.

Pioneering in Montana, 1900–1930

Even as late as 1910 only 4 percent of Montana was improved for agriculture. Most of the improved land was in the Rocky Mountain valleys, where oats and wheat had been grown since the 1860s to feed the mining population. By 1905 some irrigated agriculture was practiced on the Montana Plains, in the valleys of the lower Yellowstone and Milk Rivers, but eastern and central Montana was primarily open-range country thinly populated by cattlemen, sheepherders, and Native Americans.

The cattlemen came into Montana in the 1880s, some driving their stock across the mountains from the Pacific Northwest. The cattle thrived on the blue grama and needle-and-thread grasses, and by 1894, the year the Montana open-range business peaked, the eastern two-thirds of the state was organized into 17 large roundup districts. The Native Americans, including the Blackfeet, Gros Ventres, and Assiniboines, posed no threat to the newcomers. They had ceded their homelands in the last three decades of the 19th century and were confined to reservations located mainly in the dry grassland country to the north of the Missouri and Milk Rivers (fig. 11.1).

The Montana homestead boom began in 1909, following the passage of the Enlarged Homestead Act. The railroads were already in place to bring the settlers in. In the peak year of 1910, 21,982 homestead applications were filed at the Montana land offices, almost as many as in all the years from 1869 to 1905 combined. Homestead entries continued to be made at an average rate of 14,911 a year until 1919. Most of the settlers came from North Dakota, Minnesota, and other midwestern states, with western Canada and Washington also important source areas.

Montana received above-average rainfall from 1906 to 1915, and farmers enjoyed bumper crops. Then drought struck in 1916, intensified in 1918 and 1919, and lasted through the early 1920s. Homestead filings decreased sharply. With the reestablishment of grain production in western Europe and Russia after the war, wheat prices were halved from 1918 to 1921. Farmers who had considered it their patriotic duty (as well as the route to success) to borrow more money, buy more land, and grow more wheat during the war years found themselves faced with declining land values and debts that they could not pay. By 1925 one out of every two Montana farmers had lost his or her land through foreclosure. Even the drought and depression of the 1930s took a lighter toll on Montana than the collapse of the 1920s.

The drought aggravated the already terrible living conditions on the Montana reservations. When Hugh L. Scott, a member of the Board of Indian Commissioners, inspected the Blackfoot and Fort Belknap Reservations in 1920, he found the range desiccated and the tribal cattle starving. Many of the Native Americans were also starving. Conditions were particularly severe among the traditional full-bloods, who lived separately from the other residents. Most were old, many were blind, and all were dependent on government relief. The Native Americans were inadequately clothed and poorly sheltered, and the sanitary conditions at the agency boarding schools were described as "dangerous." Scott observed that many of the homesteaders in the vicinity of the reservations were also destitute, but, unlike the settlers, the Native Americans had nowhere else to go.

In 1930 Isaiah Bowman, president of the American Geographical Society, visited Garfield County, located on the dry, short-grass plains of eastern Montana. He found a sparsely populated frontier, predominantly ranching country, without a single mile of railroad or telegraph line. Garfield County's infant mortality rate was one of the highest in the United States, and the landscape of sod houses and tarpaper shacks stood as witness to the recency and impermanency of settlement. Bowman saw signs of "amelioration" in living conditions: the increased ownership of automobiles, the appearance of frame dwellings, and the prospect, always a year or two ahead, that the railroads would extend into the county, putting the rancher and dry farmer on an equal competitive footing with producers in more accessible areas. But the railroads never came to Garfield County, and the trend of declining population that was already under way in 1930 has continued to the present.

The End of Pioneering:
The Southern Great Plains
in the 1920s and 1930s

The last extensive area of the Great Plains to be plowed up and settled was the short-grass country of western Texas and Oklahoma, eastern Colorado and New Mexico, and southwestern Kansas (fig. 11.10). The boom began in 1900, as soon as rainfall and confidence recovered from the setbacks of the 1890s, accelerated under the stimulus of wartime grain demands, continued despite dry years in 1910 and 1915 and falling wheat prices in the 1920s, and ended in 1931 with the return of the Great American Desert to the Plains.

From 1920 to 1930, the High Plains counties of Texas, Oklahoma, and Kansas added 197,045 people, an increase of 260 percent. This land was perfect for mechanization—extensive, flat, and without the impediments of stumps and stones. Soon the farmers were investing in gasoline-powered tractors, disc plows that pulverized the surface soil, and combines that could harvest 500 acres in two weeks. By 1930, more than three-quarters of the farmers in the Winter Wheat Belt owned combines.

The refined transportation and production technology gave rise to a new type of entrepreneur, the absentee, or suitcase, farmer. Farming from a distance was already under way by World War I (and in fact had been common at a local level since the beginnings of Euro-American settlement), but the big expansion occurred in the Spring and Winter Wheat Belts in the 1920s. Suitcase farmers typically owned widely dispersed lands that they visited for only a few weeks each year to harvest one crop and plant the next. They concentrated on wheat as offering the best chance for short-run profits. By 1933, in nine counties in western Kansas, more than one-quarter of the farmers lived more than one county away from their lands; most were from the established wheat country of central Kansas. Some of the absentee owners were farmers back home; others were bankers, lawyers, doctors, real estate agents, even preachers. In one sense, the suitcase farmers were making an intelligent adjustment to farming on the semiarid margins by spreading their risks from place to place and from occupation to occupation. In another sense, they epitomized the attitude that land was no more than a context for making money. The landscape of suitcase farming, with its absence of dwellings, or at the most a tent or portable bunkhouse, was a surface expression of the fact that farming was becoming divorced from attachment to place.

As farmers moved out into the southern Plains, agricultural experts urged them to diversify and to practice dry-farming techniques. But farmers were reluctant to diversify because, despite the risks, wheat had a better chance of producing a salable product than any other crop and was well suited to mechanized production. Moreover, there is an inertia to farming, an investment in experience and specialized equipment, and few farmers had the savings to see them through the transition to a more diversified base. Farmers did adopt drought-resistant varieties of wheat. They also learned from their own or their neighbors' successes and failures to plant early so that the crops were well established before the intense heat of the summer and to cultivate frequently to establish a moisture-preserving mulch. But other recommended techniques, such as well irrigation and summer fallowing, were largely avoided by farmers intent on maximizing short-run profits or, quite simply, surviving.

Dry farming was not enough to secure settlement on the southern Great Plains when drought and depression struck in the early 1930s. By 1937, 20 counties in the southern High Plains, centered on the Panhandles of Texas and Oklahoma, were severely damaged by wind erosion, and the forage value of the range had been depleted by more than 75 percent. In Cimarron County, Oklahoma, in the very heart of the dust bowl, virtually no wheat was harvested from several hundred thousand acres. Mortgages on land and debts on equipment could not be met. By 1934, the total rural debt in the county was $4.75 million, or $5,500 per farm. Over the decade the farm population fell by 40 percent. The agricultural collapse brought down entire communities, as banks closed, implement dealers lost their markets, and real estate dealers lost their clients. The pioneer settlement of the Great Plains came to an end in the worst ecological disaster in American history.

POSTSCRIPT

In 1936 a committee of experts presented its recommendations to President Roosevelt concerning the future of the Great Plains. The committee blamed the dust bowl on the settlers' lack of understanding of the differences between the humid environments of the eastern United States and the subhumid lands of the Great Plains. The problem lay not only in unadapted methods of farming but also, and more fundamentally, in "attitudes of mind" that had been ingrained through generations of pioneering in the country east of the Plains. These included beliefs that nature must be conquered, that resources are limitless, and that landownership carries privileges but not obligations. These assumptions had powered frontier expansion, but on the Plains they came up against environmental limits and resulted in ecological catastrophe.

Among its recommendations, the committee urged that most of the land in dry farming, particularly the wheat and cotton regions, should be put into pasture for livestock. This recommendation echoed the earlier advice of John Wesley Powell and Willard Johnson, both of whom had recognized that the Great Plains was not merely an extension of the Middle West but a distinctive region of inconstant climate and variable agricultural potential. It is significant that all three critical appraisals came in, or at the end of, a serious drought, when adversity brought a temporary realism and willingness to look at the region as a whole. It is also significant that their recommendations were largely forgotten as soon as the hard times passed.

By 1950, fully 90 percent of the land plowed up in the 1920s was back in crops. In addition, several million acres that had never been plowed were put into wheat in the central and northern Great Plains by 1950. Despite stabilizing influences, such as government subsidies, built-in crop insurance, and improved varieties of crops and methods of farming (including expansion of irrigation and widespread use of summer fallow), crop failure is still common on the Plains, particularly in the recurring drought years, as in the early 1950s and mid-1970s.

Meanwhile, as agriculture has become more capital intensive, the trend of rural depopulation has continued. The number of farms in Nebraska declined from 134,000 in 1935 to 70,000 in 1973 and has continued to decrease since that time. The rural landscape is emptying. Abandoned farmhouses, their porches sagging and windows gaping, stand as evidence of a time when the Great Plains was the last great agricultural frontier for homesteaders. No doubt future booms will restore prosperity, if not population, to the Plains. But if the past offers any lesson, it is equally certain that drought and depression will never be far behind.

ADDITIONAL READING

Alwin, J. A. 1981. "Jordan Country: A Golden Anniversary Look." *Annals of the Association of American Geographers* 71: 479–98.

Barrows. H. G. 1962. *Lectures on the Historical Geography of the United States as Given in 1933.* Chicago: University of Chicago Department of Geography.

Bowman, I. 1931. *The Pioneer Fringe.* New York: American Geographical Society.

Fite, G. C. 1981. "Agricultural Pioneering in Dakota: A Case Study." *Great Plains Quarterly* 1: 169–80.

Frazier, I. 1989. *Great Plains.* New York: Farrar Straus Giroux.

Great Plains Committee. 1937. *The Future of the Great Plains.* 75th Cong., 1st sess. House of Representatives, Doc. 144, February 10.

Hewes, L. 1973. *The Suitcase Fanning Frontier.* Lincoln: University of Nebraska Press.

Holt, O. M. 1885. *Dakota.* Chicago: Rand McNally.

Hudson, J. C. 1985. *Plains Country Towns.* Minneapolis: University of Minnesota Press.

Ise, J. 1935. "Pioneer Life in Western Kansas." Pp. 141–54 in *Economics, Sociology, and the Modern World,* ed. N. E. Himes. Cambridge: Harvard University Press.

McIntosh, C. B. 1975. "Use and Abuse of the Timber Culture Act." *Annals of the Association of American Geographers* 65: 347–62.

Pelzer, L. 1936. *The Cattlemen's Frontier.* Glendale, Calif.: A. H. Clark.

Raban, J. 1996. *Bad Land: An American Romance.* New York: Pantheon Books.

Richardson, C. H. 1968. "Early Settlement of Eastern Nebraska Territory: A Geographical Study Based on the Original Land Survey." Ph.D diss. University of Nebraska.

Rolvaag, O. E. 1927. *Giants in the Earth.* New York: Harper & Row.

Silag, William. 1982. "Citizens and Strangers: Geographic Mobility in the Sioux City Region, 1860–1900." *Great Plains Quarterly* 2: 168–83.

Webb, W. P. 1931. *The Great Plains.* Boston: Ginn.

Wishart, D. 1994. *An Unspeakable Sadness: The Dispossession of the Nebraska Indians.* Lincoln: University of Nebraska Press.

Worster, D. 1979. *Dust Bowl: The Southern Plains in the 1930s.* New York: Oxford University Press.

12

The Far West, 1840–1920

JEANNE KAY GUELKE AND DAVID HORNBECK

Geographers know that environments do not cause or determine human settlement patterns and uses of nature, but environments do establish certain opportunities and constraints for societies. Environmental risks and benefits may be assessed and managed differently by different groups, depending on their economies, political systems, level of technology, and beliefs. Once the cultural and environmental attributes of people and places are studied, students of "history on the ground" can begin to understand the logic behind societies' decisions about settlements, natural resources, transportation, and other important themes.

The environmental setting thus seems to be a useful way to introduce the historical geography of the western United States, where extremes of climate and land forms offered a wide range of opportunities and constraints. The map of physical features of the Far West (fig. 12.1) shows a series of north-south-oriented mountain ranges, both large and minor. As moist air from prevailing westerlies blows toward the west coast from the Pacific Ocean, it is forced up over the coastal ranges of mountains, and subsequently over the Cascade and Sierra Nevada ranges. The rising air cools and drops its moisture on the windward side of the peaks, more at the cooler high elevations. The eastbound air is then relatively dry in the "rain shadow," unable to acquire much moisture from either the arctic or the subtropical air masses that it encounters as they seasonally advance from Canada and Mexico. The western valleys and low peaks of the interior are also blocked from moist air surging north from the Gulf of Mexico by the massive Front Range of the Rockies, so only a few of the larger interior ranges, like the Wasatch Mountains flanking Salt Lake City, Utah, can trap enough moisture themselves to generate year-round flowing streams and dense forests. Aridity is also pronounced during summers in coastal southern California, with its Mediterranean-type climate.

The interior south-central plateau country consists of a series of geological "stair steps," terminating in the great bend of the Colorado River in the Grand Canyon. The plateau's climate and natural vegetation resemble either the mountains or the drylands, depending on the elevation at any particular location.

Moving around the Far West, one sees a land of contrasts: abundant precipitation and forests in coastal or high, relatively inaccessible places, with deserts or sparse grasslands on the level land in between. Only the high elevations and Pacific Northwest coast receive as much precipitation as the eastern states. Salt Lake City receives about 14 inches per year, and most of the desert lands under 10 inches. There are few navigable rivers across this vast area; only the Columbia River of Washington and Oregon carries anywhere near the volume of water of the significant eastern U.S. rivers.

Under such dry conditions, natural vegetation and soils develop very slowly, and once disrupted, they are slow to reclaim their former ground. Yet desert soils can be surprisingly fertile and productive once the mountain waters are diverted to crop irrigation.

Each group that settled the Far West had a slightly different solution to the challenges and advantages these landscapes presented, and these varied with the group's culture or ethnicity, their values, time of settlement, and the particular environmental configuration. Thus, it may not be wise to speak of the West as a single region. There were and remain many Wests: the diverse Native American Wests, the Wests of Anglo settlers in such different environments as the rain forest of western Washington State and arid Utah, the diverse Hispanic Wests of California missions and private ranches. Overlaid on these were the expansionist territorial goals of Spain, Britain, Russia, Mexico, and the United States, as well as the personal individual goals of Native people and subsequent settlers: Chinese laborers, gold and silver miners, and

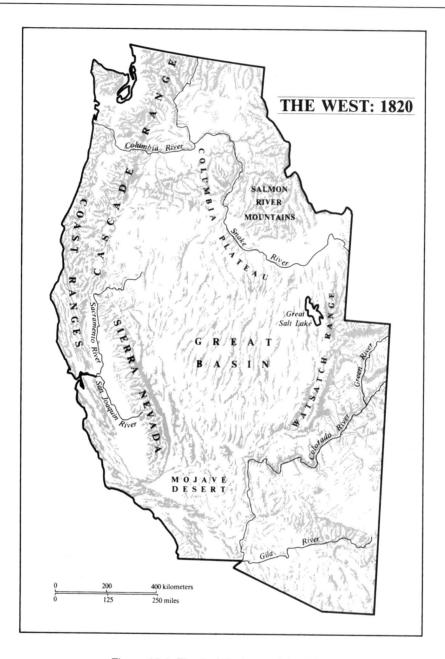

Figure 12.1 Physical Features of the West

religious refugees like the Mormons. Indeed, to many of these interested parties, the West was not West at all. It was *El Norte* to Mexicans, a voyage east to Russian fur traders and Chinese immigrants, and a journey south to British Canadian fur trappers.

PRE-EUROPEAN ABORIGINAL OCCUPANCE

"Diverse" is probably the most apt description of the first inhabitants of the Far West. Approximately 250 tribes, or ethnic units, spread over the area in varying patterns and distributions (fig. 12.2). The area was extraordinarily complex linguistically, with about 22 major language families split over 116 mutually unintelligible languages. The most fragmented area was California, with 14 language families and about 80 mutually unintelligible tongues.

Although differences among Native inhabitants were great, there were places where subsistence patterns were similar enough to group tribes regionally on the basis of greater subsistence similarities within regions than between them. These economic features can be grouped into five broad regions: the Northwest Coast, the Columbia Plateau, California, the Great Basin, and the Southwest. This regional division rests on specific ecological adjustments, because the overriding feature of all Native American tribes in the Far West was their mixed diet of wild plants, seeds, land mammals, and fish. Gathering, hunting, and fishing were in some combination the main bases of Native economies, with gathering usually dominant.

Fishing was the paramount activity for the Northwest coastal tribes. Fishing was also extensive in the northwest plateau region, where salmon was the dietary mainstay, with wild roots and berries providing the balance of the Native subsistence base. In California, marine resources dominated among the coastal and riverine environments, while outside these narrow ecological bands, acorns and pine nuts were important foods. Great Basin inhabitants tended to gather many types of xerophytic plants, although seed-bearing plants prevailed. In the Southwest, domesticated crops like corn (maize) were an important part of the diet, with wild plants of lesser importance. Throughout the Far West, Native Americans also acquired food resources from their neighbors (who usually lived in different ecological zones) through ceremonial feasts, trade, raids, or common consent to joint access to an area. Hunting was both common and an important activity, but it nevertheless tended to be secondary to an alternative secure plant-resource base.

There was a strong relationship between environmental quality and aboriginal population density. In general, the marine and riverine environments, with their wealth of food sources, supported higher population densities than the interior regions and the areas away from rivers. Permanency and compactness of communities

followed a similar pattern, ranging from seminomadic family camps of 10 people in the arid Great Basin to permanent villages of 1,000 or more along the rich Santa Barbara coast. California, by far the most densely populated region, was the home of some 300,000 Native Americans. With about 5 percent of the land area of the United States, California contained at least 12 percent of its total Native population.

While the Europeans were ever conscious of Native people after contact, few whites appreciated the extent of the Natives' dependence on the local environment for their livelihoods. For example, early American ranchers appropriated desert peoples' springs and overgrazed their edible seed-bearing grasses with little regard for their subsistence patterns and needs. As white settlers' cropping and trading expanded into extensive colonization and farms, substantial disruption in the gathering and hunting environments of Native Americans in turn caused a decline in their numbers. For example, California's indigenous population declined from 300,000 in 1770 to less than 30,000 by 1870. European diseases cannot be overlooked as an important factor in the decline of Native populations, but the alteration of their land base was equally significant.

EXPLORATION

The first European efforts to appropriate the region, beginning in the American Southwest, were by Spanish explorers in the 16th century, searching for the fabled Seven Cities of Cibola. Spain sought to acquire more of the riches that Cortés enjoyed in central Mexico. Treasure, however, was not to be found. It took two centuries for Spain to receive any reward, and when it came, it was in the guise of spiritual rather than material wealth. The Christianization of the Native Americans along the California coast, in central Arizona, and in the upper Rio Grande valley of New Mexico was the only reward Spain received for 200 years of effort. The British and Russians also entered the Far West in the latter part of the 18th century. They focused their energies on the Pacific Northwest and sought riches from the exploitation of beaver, sea otter, and trade with local Natives. The United States quickly followed Britain into the Pacific Northwest, competing for similar rewards.

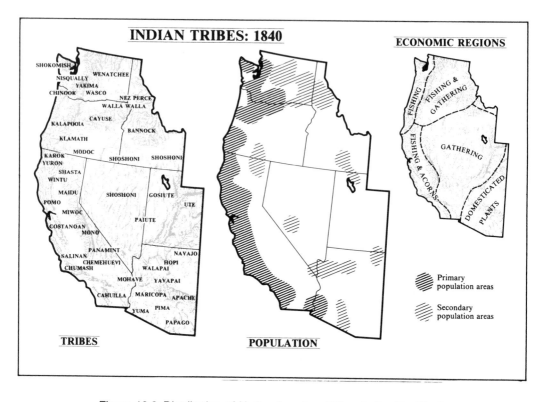

Figure 12.2 Distribution of Native American Tribes in the Far West

These early excursions by Spain, Britain, Russia, and the United State not only revealed the broad extent of the area and its diverse environments but also brought about conflicting territorial claims.

Although American seamen had traded along the northern Pacific Coast in the latter part of the 18th century and an American ship had navigated a short distance up the Columbia River in 1792, the United States's involvement in the Far West did not begin in earnest until the Louisiana Purchase in 1803. The Lewis and Clark expedition not only surveyed the geography of the upper Missouri River, Rocky Mountain, and lower Columbia River regions between 1804 and 1806 but also brought public attention to the Far West by illustrating its varied and abundant resources (fig. 12.3).

The Lewis and Clark expedition was followed by a far-reaching plan of John Jacob Astor, whose Pacific Fur Company attempted to occupy the Columbia River basin in 1811. He planned to send an overland party via the Missouri, Snake, and Columbia Rivers to rendezvous at the mouth of the Columbia with a ship sent around Cape Horn. From there the parties would trade for furs in the Pacific Northwest in order to ship them to China. The War of 1812, the tremendous distances involved, and local difficulties with Native Americans spoiled Astor's bid to establish a fur-trading center, but the venture was not a total failure. The expedition established Fort Astoria at the mouth of the Columbia River, signifying yet another U.S. claim to the Far West. The expedition also blazed a new trail across the Rocky Mountains to the Pacific Ocean, which with its famous South Pass would eventually become the Oregon Trail. However, the Far West was so far removed from the pioneer fringe of the eastern United States, as Astor's venture well illustrated, that distance remained a formidable problem.

Between 1820 and 1840 one of the most colorful and unique "frontier types" in American history, the mountain man, hunted and trapped in the region for one of the many fur-trading companies or for himself. The mountain men explored the Far West in search of beaver pelts and adventure, defying Mexican law and causing considerable alarm among British trappers entering the Oregon Country from Canada.

During the 1830s, American trappers and traders made their way across the Rockies into the Far West in greater numbers, exploring its resources and extolling its beauty. Joseph Walker, Jim Bridger, Kit Carson, and many others so successfully defined the Far West that, by the 1840s, would-be farmers, miners, and merchants made their way west along easily identified trails. The mountain men accomplished a great deal. They established important overland routes like the Santa Fe and Old Spanish Trails to California, discovered mountain passes through formidable mountain barriers, sent thousands of furs down the Missouri River into the American economy, brought about confrontation between the Americans and the British in the Oregon Country and the Spanish in California, and identified fertile valleys for future farmers.

Yet, for all that was known by the 1840s, the Far West remained to be mapped. Beaver were overtrapped, and mountain men, so familiar with every corner of the country, became the guides for a new kind of explorer—those who would begin to map the Far West. The government needed more information about the vast expanse of territory at its western boundary, accurate locations of topographic features, and, especially, detailed maps of possible routes westward. Charles Wilkes, John C. Fremont, and William H. Emory were among those early government explorers who began to provide this needed detail on maps. The California gold rush of 1848 stimulated a whole new need for maps, those that located and identified mineral resources. These, in turn, brought new government-sponsored surveys into the Far West. As permanent settlement advanced into the area in the 1850s, government surveys turned toward mapping another potential resource of the Far West, its agricultural land.

U.S. ACQUISITION OF THE FAR WEST

The mountain men and traders who explored and exploited large areas of the Far West did not establish permanent territorial rights for the United States. In the first quarter of the 19th century,

Spain, Britain, Russia, and the United States each laid claims to parts of the area. Just as Europeans showed little sensitivity toward Native American natural resource needs and rights, they also viewed Native land claims as immaterial or extinguishable through treaties designed to promote imperial interests. Although most Americans would date the founding of their nation to 1620 with English Pilgrims in Massachusetts, Spain sent permanent settlers to New Mexico as early as 1598. But Spanish territorial claims were reduced in 1819 by the Adams-Onís treaty, in which Spain surrendered to the United States all of its claims north of 42° N. The agreement further provided for a western boundary to the Louisiana Territory. The treaty between the United States and Spain left Russia, Britain, and the United States all jockeying for the Oregon Country. At first, Russia attempted to seize a share of the Oregon Country by asserting territorial rights as far south as 51° N latitude, but the Monroe Doctrine and the size and presence of the British navy forced Russia to reconsider. In 1824 and 1825, Russia signed treaties limiting its claim as far south as 54°40' N latitude.

With Spanish and Russian claims thus limited, only the United States and Britain were left to vie for the Oregon Country, the last unclaimed part of the Far West. Rather than press for immediate and permanent division, the parties signed a treaty of joint occupancy. Britain based its claims to Oregon on the coastal explorations of James Cook in 1778 and George Vancouver in 1792 and the overland explorations of Alexander Mackenzie. The strongest claim in Britain's favor was that the London-based Hudson's Bay Company owned permanent fur-trading posts in the area. Neither Britain nor the United States wanted to quarrel over so distant a land, however. Thus in 1827, they renewed their joint occupancy of the Oregon Country indefinitely, with the proviso that either nation could end the agreement with one year's notification. In the 1820s Oregon could have gone to either nation, the territory being awarded to the nation that was able to attract the greater number of permanent settlers. Britain was clearly winning the race during the 1820s and 1830s.

Religion helped to settle the Oregon Country for the United States. Beginning in 1834, a number of churches began to establish missions in the area to convert Native people to Christianity.

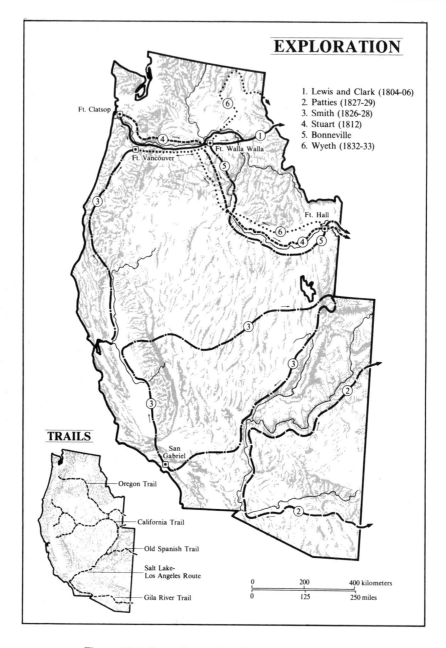

EXPLORATION

1. Lewis and Clark (1804-06)
2. Patties (1827-29)
3. Smith (1826-28)
4. Stuart (1812)
5. Bonneville
6. Wyeth (1832-33)

Ft. Clatsop
Ft. Vancouver
Ft. Walla Walla
Ft. Hall

TRAILS

San Gabriel

Oregon Trail

California Trail

Old Spanish Trail

Salt Lake-
Los Angeles Route

Gila River Trail

0   200   400 kilometers
0   125   250 miles

Figure 12.3 Early Exploration Routes in the Far West

Glowing letters describing agricultural possibilities began to circulate throughout the United States, causing widespread interest in the Oregon Country. The United States also experienced an economic downturn in 1837, and Oregon became the prime focus for westward migrants. By 1846, approximately 8,000 American settlers permanently occupied the lower Willamette Valley. Facing increasing American settlement, Britain ceded the Oregon Country to the United States and agreed to the present-day boundaries between Washington State and British Columbia.

Religion also helped to establish an Anglo-

American toehold in the Great Basin in 1847, when 1,500 members of the Church of Jesus Christ of Latter-day Saints, or Mormons, immigrated to the strip of land between the Wasatch Mountains and the Great Salt Lake in what was then Mexican territory. Under their charismatic leader, Brigham Young, Mormons hoped to avoid the religious persecution they had experienced in the Middle West and to establish their own communitarian, utopian territory. They developed irrigation networks to channel mountain snowmelt onto dry valley floors and grazed livestock on the undeveloped or nonarable lands around their villages. By 1850 their numbers approached 12,000, owing to continued immigration supported by an active program of religious conversion east of the Mississippi and abroad.

While initial settlement of Oregon and the Great Salt Lake area can be characterized as pioneering efforts by transplanted settlers from the eastern states and the Middle West, the settlement of California was entirely different. Spain had occupied California since 1769. When the Anglo-Americans finally arrived, they found a preexisting society. California's early Hispanic population derived from colonization by administrators, soldiers, agriculturists, and missionaries. Spain, however, did not people its new land vigorously, and California's non-Native population reached only 3,000 by 1821, when independent Mexico began to govern California. Under Mexico, California's non-Native population grew to approximately 12,000 by 1845, mostly concentrated at settlements along the coast. Los Angeles was the largest town, but new arrivals began to populate the Sacramento valley on the eve of the war between Mexico and the United States. Hispanic California in the 1840s was hardly in a position to resist the westward push of Anglo-American settlers. Isolated from the major settlements of Mexico, rural, and few in number, California's population was unable to stem the aggressive tide of Anglo-American immigrants claiming the land as their rightful and manifest destiny.

Manifest Destiny was the ideology that the United States had an obvious and God-given natural right to extend its western boundary to the Pacific Ocean (fig. 12.4). To some Americans it was an aggressive philosophy calling for military expansion into the Far West, while others viewed it as an idealistic, nonviolent program for settlement. The many faces of Manifest Destiny were complicated and often contradictory, but at its simplest it provided a nationalistic philosophy and a justification for geographical expansion. A push westward would assure the possibility of the rich trade with eastern Asia and prevent European designs on the West. The United States would gain control of strategically important San Francisco Bay and be in a better position to control and educate the "backward" Native Americans and Mexicans. The target for Manifest Destiny was the Pacific Coast, for here was the terminus, the culmination of the westward march of American settlement.

Throughout the 1830s and 1840s, a few Americans and other foreigners came to California because Mexican cattle ranching produced a profitable cowhide and tallow trade by sea between California and Boston. Others came to take up the land. For the most part, these newcomers settled in the interior Central Valley, because the coastal areas between San Diego and San Francisco continued to be occupied by Mexicans. With increasing numbers of Americans on Mexican soil, the annexation of Texas by the United States against the wishes of Mexico in 1845, and growing jingoistic attitudes throughout the United States, war broke out between Mexico and the United States in 1846. When the war ended in 1848, the United States added virtually the entire Far West to its land area. The Gadsden Purchase in southern Arizona and New Mexico in 1853 completed the contiguous territory of the United States (fig. 12.4). By the end of the war, California's population was about 16,000, but the discovery of gold in 1848 caused such a tremendous influx of people that by 1850 the U.S. census enumerated more than 93,000 people in the state.

AGRICULTURAL SETTLEMENT OF THE FAR WEST

By 1848 the U.S. government's sweep across the continent was nearly complete. The Far West offered new and exciting vistas that would delight Anglo-Americans and engage their imaginations. Yet only three areas had permanent Anglo-American settlement at the time of acquisition by the United States: the Willamette valley, the Wasatch front, and coastal California. For Anglo-Americans, these three centers

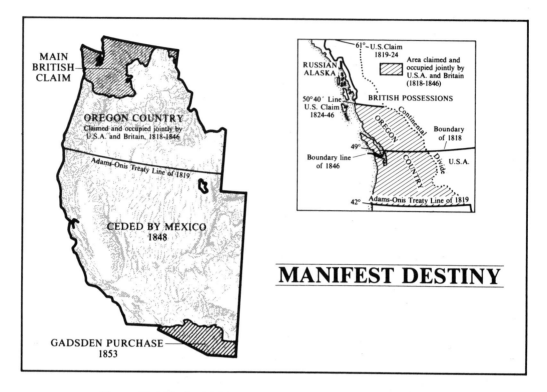

Figure 12.4 Territorial Acquisition as a Result of Manifest Destiny

would serve as staging areas from which more extensive colonization would be undertaken. They also served as population clusters capable, under the U.S. Constitution, of meeting the requirements to become territories and, later, states. Thus Anglo-American colonization of the interior of the Far West initially depended on three "centers" located on the western and eastern rims of the region as a whole (fig. 12.5).

Agriculture in the Far West was difficult, beset with the problems and hardships of unfamiliar climates and varying physical conditions. Unlike the humid East, where familiar and traditional agricultural methods and crops could be transferred from one area to the next, the Far West, like the Great Plains, required modifications and adaptations in farming methods and types of crops grown. The three settled areas each exhibited a distinct set of environmental and locational problems. Farmers in Oregon, where agriculture was most advanced, coped with clearing heavily forested land and considerable rainfall. Mormon settlers struggled with digging ditches for their first efforts at irrigation

farming. Much of the agricultural land in California along the accessible coast was already occupied by the Mexican *rancheros* for extensive cattle grazing. New California farmers had to cope not only with raising crops far from the urban markets but also with bewildering, long summer drought.

Yet, the rapid population growth caused by the gold rush quickly made farming a successful commercial enterprise in California. The northern coastal section attracted the most immigrants, although increasing numbers of newcomers were drawn to the rich and fertile Central Valley. After 1880 southern California began to attract large numbers of immigrants, and by 1890 California had two major population centers, San Francisco and Los Angeles.

Of these three settled areas, the Willamette valley environment was most like the eastern frontier, and many of the newcomers came from Missouri, Indiana, Illinois, and Kentucky. The actual settlement of the valley began in 1841; within a year, more than 100 hopeful settlers arrived in the region. They formed a provi-

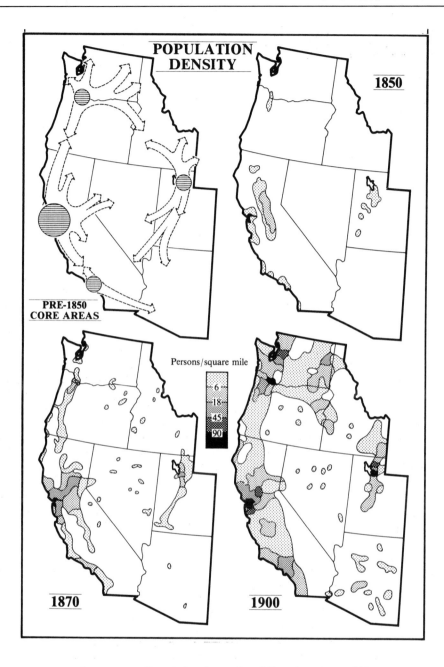

Figure 12.5 Population Spread and Density, 1850–1900

sional government in 1843, and 1,000 new settlers arrived in that year alone (fig. 12.6). With
the organization of the Oregon Territory in
1848, the population continued to increase
steadily to more than 13,000 inhabitants by
1850, 90 percent of whom lived in the

Willamette valley. In the 1850s migrants moved
north into the Cowlitz valley and south into the
Rogue River and Umpqua valleys. Although the
California gold rush provided many settlers
with the initial impetus to move west, gold miners willing to pay high prices for farm goods

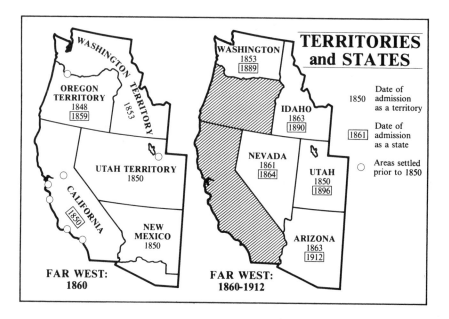

Figure 12.6 Development of Political Boundaries in the Far West

and forest products led many other newcomers to turn north to the fertile lands and the forests of southern Oregon. The discovery within Oregon of gold on the Rogue River in 1851 caused a rush that brought even more people to southern Oregon, many of whom found farming ultimately more profitable than mining.

The region north of the Columbia River was separated from Oregon in 1853 and named Washington Territory (fig. 12.6). The new territory, particularly the areas around Puget Sound, also benefited from California's rapid surge in population. Here were excellent harbors, vast forests, abundant waterpower for mills, and the prospect of a ready and seemingly insatiable market for timber and lumber in San Francisco.

On the eastern side of the Cascades and west of the Rockies is an area of more than 200,000 square miles drained by the Columbia River and its tributaries. Bypassed by early pioneers who thought the country too dry for exploitation, the area around Walla Walla, Washington, began to gain a few settlers by the late 1850s. As miners flooded the region after the discovery of gold along the branches of the Snake River, these early farmers found a ready market in the new mining areas. As word spread, more and more settlers began to take up land throughout what

would become known as the Inland Empire of eastern Washington.

From their headquarters in Salt Lake City on the eastern rim of the Far West region, the Mormons sent missionaries throughout the United States and other countries to preach their faith and urge converts to resettle in Utah. The response was immediate. Salt Lake City became a staging area for thousands of converts beginning new lives in Mormon settlements in the Great Basin and the Colorado Plateau. From 1847 through the 1870s, the number of Mormon settlements increased by 100 and extended from Idaho south into Arizona.

Mormon settlement of the arid valleys followed a well-defined set of procedures, much like those used by Spain to settle its northern frontier in North America. First, exploring parties found locations with good water and pasturage where settlements could be established viably. Church leaders then issued a call for settlers, and, as the new settlers arrived, communal efforts under the direction of village leaders established an irrigation system for agriculture and surveyed streets and lots within a town. Central to Mormon settlement was the village surrounded by large fields to which villagers commuted. The villages were planned with wide streets, irrigation ditches, and large blocks divided into homes and gardens.

After 1862 Americans in the Far West used the Homestead Act to settle still-vacant rural land, but the best farmlands and ranch lands were taken by the 1870s. Overly optimistic homesteaders continued to file claims on marginal lands, but few could remain economically competitive.

The Far West did not appear at first to have a great future in farming, as there was no economical way to reach eastern markets and labor was in short supply. However, experimentation in crops and methods demonstrated that agriculture could be profitable (fig. 12.7). As new areas opened to settlement and railroads began to solve the problems of isolation, dryland farming and irrigation offset rainfall deficiencies, and the introduction of new kinds of machinery compensated for labor shortages. By 1880, when the Far West was essentially integrated into the national economy, the region had over 14 million cultivated acres with a considerable proportion devoted to specialized commercial crops. Bonanza wheat farms spread throughout the Central Valley of California, fruit and vegetable farms extended all along the coast, and cattle ranches dominated southern California. In the Pacific Northwest, mixed grain, vegetables, and fruit had emerged as the primary crops. The Mormons emphasized a mixed agriculture and cattle-grazing economy. Although they specialized in a few crops like sugar beets, they paid more attention to self-sufficiency and local markets from mining towns and immigrants passing through Salt Lake City en route to the Pacific.

Between 1900 and 1910 western agriculturists stabilized their crop patterns, more carefully assessed their environments, established markets, solved transportation problems, and significantly increased the amount of irrigated acreage. In California, wheat declined in importance as a commercial crop, to be replaced by irrigated, higher-value fruits and vegetables. In the Willamette valley and west of the Cascades, mixed farming continued, while dairy farms and fruit orchards emerged as commercially viable enterprises. The Great Basin briefly boomed as a major sheep-ranching area after 1890, because sheep proved more tolerant than cattle of dryland grazing conditions. After 1880 the rolling hills of the Columbia plateau transformed into one of the premier wheat-growing regions in the United States, known as the Palouse. Characterized by huge farms, large amounts of machinery, and a single crop, this boom resembled the earlier patterns of the wheat bonanza in California.

The Columbia plateau was the last viable agricultural frontier in the Far West. Farmers who followed thereafter were forced into the marginal lands of deserts or dense mountain forests. Farming much of the remainder of the Far West required costly capital inputs, primarily for irrigation, costs that were too much for private individuals to bear. If new areas were to be farmed, it would have to be with the federal government as a partner. The government, in turn, moved to assist agriculture by building dams in sections of Idaho and central Washington to stimulate irrigation and fruit production. The Roosevelt Dam on the Salt River provided central Arizona with water—the prime ingredient for its agricultural base. In California, damming of the lower Colorado River in the 1900s turned the Imperial Valley into a veritable winter garden. By 1920 these and many other government-sponsored projects illustrated that profitable commercial agriculture in the Far West had to depend on the twin inputs of irrigation and government capital.

The population of the Far West increased fivefold between 1860 and 1890; yet the three early settlement areas continued to dominate the overall settlement pattern (table 12.1). The population of the Far West tripled between 1890 and 1920 to almost 7 million. Each state increased in population, but California continued to outpace its western rivals. Washington overtook Oregon as the second-largest state, primarily on the basis of the large number of newcomers taking up agricultural land in eastern Washington. The major change in the settlement pattern during this 30-year period was the rapidly increasing population of southern California and the retreat of overly optimistic homesteaders from the Great Basin's drier lands. By 1920 the earliest settled areas remained important population centers, and the basic settlement patterns of today had been established. Americans had successfully and progressively occupied the periphery of the Far West but left most of the Great Basin and mountain slopes to the federal government in the form of national forests and the unclaimed public domain, used for extensive sheep and cattle ranches.

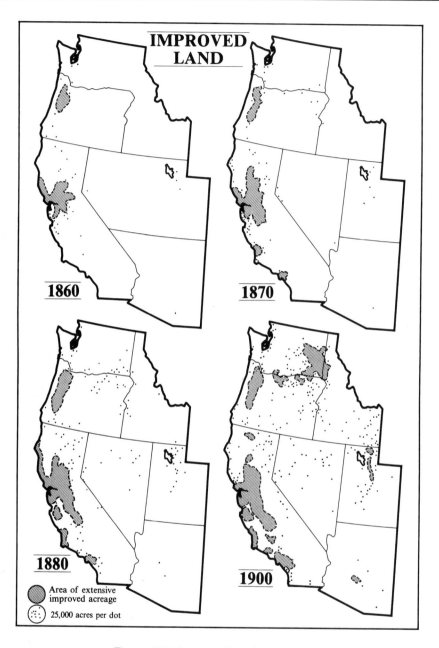

Figure 12.7 Improved Land, 1860–1900

URBAN DEVELOPMENT
AND MINERALS EXPLOITATION

Across the Far West, but especially for California, the discovery of gold or silver in the mountains and foothills brought a tide of miners who sought instant wealth. For many, their stays in the mining districts were only temporary. If they "struck it rich," they might return home; if unsuccessful, they might move to the next new mining area to open. With each new mining boom the local economy changed suddenly from a pastoral, subsistence-oriented economy to one of commerce, services, and industry. Yet

Table 12.1 Populations of the Far Western States, 1850–1920 (in thousands)

	1850	1860	1870	1880	1890	1900	1910	1920
Arizona	—	—	10	40	88	123	204	334
California	93	380	560	865	1,213	1,485	2,378	3,427
Idaho	—	—	15	33	89	162	326	432
New Mexico	62	94	92	120	160	195	327	360
Nevada	—	7	42	62	47	42	81	77
Oregon	13	53	91	175	318	414	673	783
Utah	11	40	87	144	211	277	373	449
Washington	—	12	24	75	357	518	1,142	1,357
Total	179	585	921	1,513	2,484	3,216	5,465	7,220
% of U.S.	0.7	1.8	2.4	3.0	3.9	4.1	5.8	6.7
Total U.S.	23,067	31,184	38,116	50,189	63,070	77,257	93,402	107,436

mining brought about rapid change in the agricultural sector as well because a rural farm population was needed to provide food and draft animals for it (fig. 12.8). Eastern or British capital further boosted economic development, even when it was apparent that the goldfields or silver mines were producing diminishing returns for the labor and capital invested in them. But many mining communities were short-lived, once high-grade ores played out or became too expensive to extract. But new mining districts held out the promise of new riches, such as southern Oregon in 1852, the Colorado Rockies and the eastern Sierras in the late 1850s, western Washington and Idaho in the 1860s, and scattered regions throughout the Great Basin until 1890. Copper mining in Arizona supported five major districts by 1900. In another example of eastward expansion, many miners moved from California to the new districts.

Early mining was basically a set of individual treasure hunts on a grand scale. Mining transformed by around 1865 into a capital-intensive industry controlled by large companies that employed miners as wage laborers. Both types of mining generated the capital that catapulted mining districts into highly urbanized economies.

The vast amounts of wealth pouring out of the mines combined with the limited areas of good farmland close to the mines made the region's population remarkably urban in nature. Western cities and towns were an integral part of the frontier that preceded, rather than followed,

most agricultural settlement. The urban frontier of the Far West was an uncoordinated and detached set of mining camps, speculative towns, market centers, military posts, religious communities, railroad towns, and port cities, often competing for recognition and for control of a hinterland. Literally thousands of western settlements were founded between 1850 and 1880, although failure rates were high. Towns located in the earliest settled areas had an initial advantage as financial and administrative centers, however, and often became focal points of early city growth. Large regional cities developed in the Willamette valley, the Great Salt Lake region, and in coastal California, where an urban network was already in place from the days of Hispanic settlement (table 12.2).

San Francisco, the primary port city and gateway to the mining regions of California, grew rapidly in the 1850s. New mining strikes in landlocked Nevada, along with an expanding local agricultural base, assured San Francisco of a strong economy. By 1860, with a population of 234,000, it dwarfed its nearest rivals and was beginning to establish hegemony over the entire Far West. San Francisco became a great commercial emporium, almost a city-state, commanding lumber and agricultural products from the Pacific Northwest, gold and silver from the interior, and cattle from southern California. The region immediately surrounding San Francisco Bay reflected its dominance: Sacramento, San Jose, and Oakland, ranging in size from 9,000 to 16,000 inhabitants in 1870,

Table 12.2 Major Cities in the Far West, 1860–1920 (population in thousands)

	1860	1870	1880	1890	1900	1910	1920
San Francisco	57	150	234	299	343	417	507
Sacramento	14	16	21	26	29	45	66
San Jose	—	9	13	18	22	29	40
Oakland	2	11	88	49	67	150	216
Los Angeles	4	6	11	50	103	319	577
Long Beach	—	—	—	1	2	18	56
San Diego	1	2	3	16	18	40	74
Portland	3	8	18	46	70	207	258
Salt Lake City	8	13	21	45	54	93	118
Seattle	—	1	4	43	81	237	315
Spokane	—	—	—	20	37	104	104
Phoenix	—	—	—	3	6	11	29
Tucson	—	3	8	5	8	13	20
Albuquerque	—	—	—	4	6	11	15

were essentially satellites of San Francisco. By 1880, San Francisco (fig. 12.9) and its surrounding region was the most urbanized area in the West and contained a population of almost 360,000, greater than all other cities in the Far West combined or any single western state outside of California.

Other emerging large cities in the Pacific Northwest between 1850 and 1880 responded to local settlers' needs for goods and services, but their early growth also greatly depended on San Francisco's voracious appetite for raw materials and agricultural products (fig. 12.10). Portland was founded in 1845 as a market center for the Willamette valley and later became a commercial leader for exporting products from the Columbia River basin to San Francisco. Although Portland reached eventually into the interior and commanded the trade for Oregon, in reality the town was little more than a second-order center dominated by San Francisco. Seattle, founded in 1851, remained hardly more than a mill town supplying lumber to San Francisco until the last decade of the 19th century.

The urban center least dominated by San Francisco was Salt Lake City. As the headquarters of the Church of Jesus Christ of Latter-day Saints since its establishment in 1847 and with thousands of converts arriving in the city yearly, Salt Lake City was assured of constant growth. Local businesses also took advantage of its isolated position astride one of the major overland trails to the West, outfitting westbound travelers. When the transcontinental railroad reached Utah in 1869, landlocked Salt Lake City and nearby Ogden thrived. When silver mines opened in Utah in 1869, attracting "gentiles" to the territory, Mormon agriculture benefited from these new markets for its produce and livestock. As the Mormons already occupied the best agricultural land, and mines tended to locate in nonfarmable mountains, a kind of mutual, if mistrustful, economic relationship developed. By 1880, 400 towns had been founded in the Great Basin, mostly along the western edge of the Rocky Mountains from Idaho to Arizona. While not rivaling San Francisco in commerce or mining, Salt Lake City firmly controlled its own hinterland. It maintained its distinction and separateness from both San Francisco and Denver, Colorado, 500 miles to the east.

After 1880, many cities took advantage of continued immigration, consolidated early economic gains, and moved out from under the hegemony of San Francisco. Although San Francisco, Portland, and Salt Lake City continued to attract urban dwellers, the transcontinental railroads helped other cities establish their respective urban identities. For example, Ogden was a quiet Mormon agricultural town before it became a major railroad depot after completion of the transcontinental railroad at Promontory, Utah, in 1869.

The last two decades of the 19th century and the early years of the 20th century can be characterized as a period of emergence for those newly maturing cities that challenged and eventually surpassed the original centers of American settlement. With the aid of the railroads, Los Angeles grew from 11,000 in 1880 to 577,000 in 1920, surpassing San Francisco as the largest city in the Far West. Seattle's population increased during the same period from 3,500 to 315,000, making it the largest city in the Pacific Northwest. Long Beach, Tucson, and Phoenix would eventually become large cities, but their major growth would come later in the 20th century.

Cities in the Far West lacked the strong industrial base of their eastern counterparts. Instead, they had large service and distribution sectors, well out of proportion to their modest manufacturing and agricultural bases. San Francisco was the 9th-largest U.S. city in 1880, yet it ranked only 25th in manufacturing. Although the cities' need to import agricultural products during the early years of urban growth stimulated specialized agricultural development in the immediate areas, western city growth quickly exceeded the capability of local farmers to satisfy urban demands. To satisfy their needs for food, cities like San Francisco reached well beyond their immediate hinterlands, stimulating agricultural development throughout the Far West.

TRANSPORTATION

Notwithstanding strong markets within the region for agricultural crops, the ability of far western farmers to market their crops outside of the region came with the railroads and associated improvements in shipping methods. In general, the entire economic spectrum of the Far West closely followed the development of transportation, although good roads would wait until the 1920s. During the last quarter of the 19th century, the railroads opened up vast stretches of the region to profitable settlement, encouraged immigration, stimulated urban growth, and set in motion new economic patterns.

The first railroad to span the Far West was completed in 1869. By 1883, four transcontinental railroads were in operation: the Union Pacific–Central Pacific, the Southern Pacific, the Santa Fe (Atlantic & Pacific), and the Northern

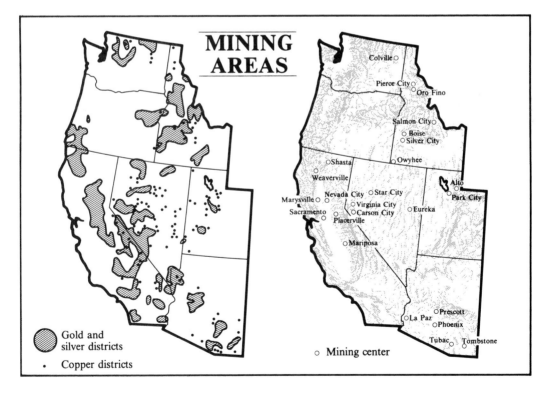

Figure 12.8 Mining Towns and Districts of the Far West

Figure 12.9 San Francisco, 1874 (Courtesy California State Library)

Pacific (fig. 12.11). A fifth, the Great Northern, was extended from the Great Lakes to Puget Sound in 1893. Other short lines added to the system, crisscrossed the Far West, and connected cities or mining areas with nearby urban centers.

The addition of railroads to the Far West had an immediate impact on the economy. Before the first rail lines spanned the continent, Portland and especially San Francisco used their coastal locations to great advantage. As port cities, they could control the flow of goods into and out of the interior. The railroad broke up this regional monopoly by allowing other cities to reach eastern manufacturing and trading firms directly. Eastern firms flooded the Far West with cheap manufactured goods and undercut local western manufacturers. Quick to capitalize on the emerging western markets, the railroads encouraged, and often sponsored, an eastward flow of raw materials, thereby obtaining profits from freight in both directions. The railroads also brought in new capital. Before 1870 mining had been the major source of capital for the de-

velopment of agriculture, irrigation projects, lumbering, fishing, and manufacturing and for the railroads themselves. With the Far West more easily accessible after 1870, however, eastern capital became more prevalent in the development and exploitation of western resources. As this capital moved into the Far West on a large scale, the economy began to move toward a "colonial" economy, in which western raw materials were exchanged for eastern manufactured products.

The transportation transformation of the Far West brought about by the railroads significantly modified rural settlement as well as urban growth patterns. Railroads controlled vast amounts of land awarded to them by the government as inducements for railroad construction, and they enticed new settlers to come west and buy railroad land. In this manner, railroads opened the wheat country east of the Cascades, California's San Joaquin valley, southern California, and central Arizona. The railroads in these areas meant not only new settlements but

Figure 12.10 Astoria Harbor, Oregon, 1881 (Courtesy Oregon Historical Society)

also a shift from extensive livestock grazing to cereals raised on smaller landholdings, and eventually to irrigated specialty crops.

The most spectacular effect of the railroad was on urban growth. The Far West was a dynamic region, with constant movement and change, particularly in the development of new towns. Each new town competed to become a metropolitan center, but without a rail facility its chances of survival were slim. The railroads were instrumental in founding new towns and also in enhancing those already in existence. Seattle, Tacoma, and Spokane grew quickly after the arrival of a railroad. Probably no city owed its growth to the railroad more than Los Angeles, a city so often associated with the automobile. The city of Los Angeles was in the enviable position of having two rail connections with the East, the Southern Pacific and the Santa Fe. The competition between the two lines resulted in fares so low that thousands of settlers were encouraged to come to Los Angeles and buy land from the largest landowners in the area, the railroads.

EMPTY LANDS?

Compared with the eastern United States, and even with much of the Great Plains, one of the most striking features of the Far West today is its vast extent of uncultivated open land. Despite the land rushes, urbanization, and boom industries of past and present, there simply is a lot of open space in the Far West. "Open" space yes, but not empty space.

Native people, for example, did not simply vanish as a "first stage" of white frontier expansion. Although their numbers dwindled through European diseases, loss of habitat and food resources, and military struggles, Native people still claimed vast portions of the West. By 1850 the federal government realized that it could no longer simply solve its "Indian problem" by removing eastern Natives to Indian Country west of the Mississippi, because settlers were already moving into the Great Plains and streaming into California and Oregon. But, with a system of small reservations loosely patterned after the paternalistic California mission system, Native people could be isolated from settlers and forced to yield their most valuable lands. The legacy of this policy was the establishment of numerous reservations throughout the West, mostly between 1854 and 1884 and mostly concentrated on arid lands deemed worthless by the whites. Although most reservations were quite small, the Navajo and Hopi lands of the Four Corners area enclosed the entire northeastern section of Arizona. The integrity of Indian Country continued under threat, however, as the government pressured Native Americans to cede more of their land and as the Dawes Act (General Allotment Act) of 1887 required many Native families to claim their own "allotment" individually, generally a quarter section of 160 acres of reservation land. Any "surplus" land not claimed by registered members of a particular tribe or nation was then thrown open for settlement by whites. Since the tribe or nation collectively no longer owned the allotments, many Native Americans eventually sold or leased their land to whites, leaving behind a fragmented pattern of landownership within the larger reservation boundaries. These factors help explain why a small-scale map of reservations in the United States shows most of them in the western United States, but a large-scale map of reservations would show much of the actual acreage in non-Native hands.

The Dawes Act further provided for a system of government-run boarding schools. The act required Native children to attend them and forbade them to speak their ancestral languages or to practice their traditional religions. Such pressures strongly pushed Native people toward further accommodation to Anglo-American society.

Hispanic Americans also continued to occupy the Far West, particularly in their early homes in coastal California, Tucson, and the upper Rio Grande valley extending from Colorado through New Mexico and El Paso, Texas. Initially overwhelmed by the influx of Anglo-Americans, they subsequently expanded their numbers through continuing immigration from Mexico, particularly following the Mexican War and after 1900. Many of these individuals moved across the border and between various job opportunities within the United States. Despite an association today of Mexican migrants with farm labor, many 19th-century Mexican migrants moved to the larger border cities like

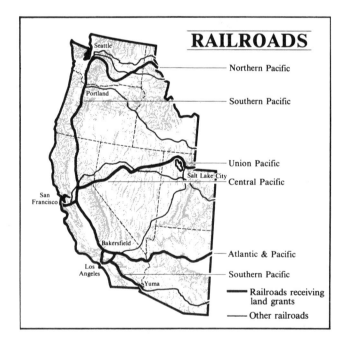

Figure 12.11 Major Railroad Routes in the Far West, 1883

Los Angeles or to mining- and railroad-based communities, where they formed ethnic neighborhoods within the urban West.

Smaller numbers of other newcomers spread throughout the West in ways that do not readily conform to the Anglo-American concept of westward expansion. If the Far West was simply "home" to Native people and El Norte to Spanish-speaking settlers, it was a voyage east to Asians, principally from China. Beginning in 1850 single men from the south of China immigrated via San Francisco, expecting to stay just long enough to earn money and to send it home to their families. However, many stayed on and moved throughout the Far West, mining gold, building railroads, and starting small businesses, such as fishing. Extreme ethnic prejudices forced many of them to accept jobs the Anglos did not want to (or could not) fill. For example, many Chinese became domestic workers or used their cooking and cleaning skills to open restaurants and laundries. Major cities like San Francisco developed large permanent Chinese districts (Chinatowns), but even smaller interior mining towns like Park City, Utah, developed Chinese neighborhoods during their mining boom days.

Bowing to ethnic prejudice, Congress passed several anti-Chinese exclusionary immigration laws starting in 1882. From peak numbers in 1880, the Chinese population began to decline; with so few female Chinese immigrants there was little natural increase. From over 102,000 Chinese reported for the western states in 1880 (when they accounted for nearly 97 percent of the total U.S. Chinese population), just under 39,000 remained in the West by 1920, principally in West Coast cities.

In terms of land area owned, the federal government would have to be considered the principal occupant of the Far West. Most of the acreage of U.S. land in public range lands, national forests, national parks, military lands, and federal water reclamation projects lies west of the Great Plains (fig. 12.12). When Native American trust lands are included, over half of the surface area of Utah, Nevada, Alaska, Wyoming, Idaho, Oregon, and Arizona is federal land. Even highly urban California is 45 percent under federal management. The comparable figure for the eastern states is generally under 9 percent. How did this imbalance happen? The explanation lies in federal policy for the disposal of the public domain. In the Far West, as in the central states, settlers could claim lands under the 1841 Pre-emption Act and 1862 Homestead Act through a visit to the nearest General Land Office. Even a quarter section of 160 acres, however, was insufficient to maintain a desert or mountain ranch, just as explorer John Wesley Powell predicted. The federal government offered further inducements for settlement; the Desert Land Act of 1891, for example, offered settlers up to 320 acres so long as individuals would irrigate their land to raise crops. The settlers who moved to the most marginal of the remaining unclaimed lands in the Great Basin, however, seldom completed the probationary period of their patents. Thus, vast expanses of seemingly empty western lands are lands once cultivated, then abandoned. And the driest, steepest, rockiest arable lands simply went unclaimed.

Not so in the mountains where precipitation, particularly in the Northwest, supported the growth of tall spruce, pine, and fir sawtimber. Miners, settlers, and railroad builders took what they needed. Lumbermen often commenced logging and sawmilling operations based upon the "free" lumber of the public domain.

From eastern travelers word got back to Washington, D.C., about unparalleled scenic attractions of the Far West: the geysers of Yellowstone, the impressive cliffs facing California's Yosemite Valley, the Grand Canyon of the Colorado River in Arizona. Logging or private development placed some of these special places under threat.

An 1891 act of Congress gave the president the right to withdraw public lands as forest reserves. Presidents Harrison, McKinley, and especially Theodore Roosevelt established most of the West's national forests in mountain environments in this fashion. Today about 10 percent of the United States lies within national forest boundaries. Because so much of the eastern United States was privately owned by 1890, most of these national forests are in the Far West and Alaska.

When President Ulysses S. Grant set aside Yellowstone as a special reserve in 1872, there was no thought of a system of American national parks. Other western parks followed piecemeal, variously managed by the U.S. Army, the Department of Agriculture, and the Department of the Interior, which also controlled the public

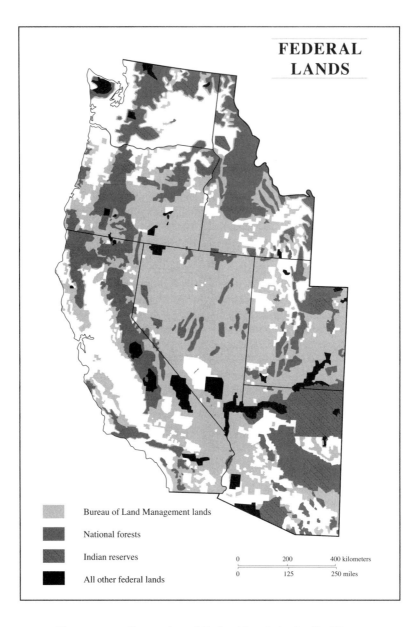

FEDERAL
LANDS

Bureau of Land Management lands

National forests

Indian reserves

All other federal lands

| 0 | 200 | 400 kilometers |
| 0 | 125 | 250 miles |

Figure 12.12 Categories of Federal Lands in the Far West

domain. Sometimes wealthy philanthropists simply donated money to the government to establish parks or to purchase private inholdings within them, as the government dedicated little funding for its growing set of parks. Congress established the National Park Service under the Department of the Interior in 1916. Although national park status required an act of Congress, the Antiquities Act of 1909 permitted the president to withdraw sensitive lands under his own signature. A number of present-day western national parks were initially established as national monuments under this system.

The closure of the remaining public domain to settlement would not come until the drought and depression of the 1930s devastated the remaining arid lands, which ranchers used extensively for sheep and cattle range. The Bureau of Land Management, established in 1934, put the sizable remnants of the public domain—used, but neither officially patented or purchased by individuals nor claimed by another federal land management agency—firmly and indefinitely under the control of the Department of the Interior.

NATURAL RESOURCES CASE STUDY: WESTERN WATER RIGHTS

One might argue, as westerners do, whether federal control of so much of the region's land and forest resources is a desirable or undesirable outcome. It may be useful to compare a critical natural resource for which no comparable federal government framework exists: water resources. Except for the coastal Pacific Northwest and the mountain surfaces too cold and steep to be cultivated, water is the limiting factor in western urban and agricultural development. Most of the level lands receive less than 20 inches of rainfall per year; extensive areas receive less than 10. So the challenge to agriculturalists has been to divert runoff from the mountains, where it is abundant, to the fertile, level soils, where it is not. Beginning with pre-Columbian cliff dwellers, the Far West's farmers have addressed this problem with irrigation canals and ditches.

A complicating issue of water scarcity has been a western approach to water rights. The western territories and states generally avoided the eastern systems of "riparian rights," where each occupant along a stream had the right to remove water for use. They adopted the Spanish doctrine of prior appropriation, or "first come, first served." Where water was insufficient for all comers, a principle of fairness implied that the first individuals or communities to claim or withdraw a specified spring or amount of stream flow had priority. Accordingly, water rights could be bought or sold independently of the land through which the water flowed. (In reality, the principal beneficiary was often the family at the head of the ditch who clandestinely took the most water, independent of the doctrine of prior appropriation.) As water networks and policy developed, private companies managed many irrigation systems whose shareholders held water shares.

Water rights issues were troubling enough to individuals, but municipalities and California fruit growers began to purchase water rights from ranchers, essentially foreclosing some arable valleys from further development. In areas that were irrigated with imperfect knowledge of soil drainage, such as the Owens valley of eastern California or the lower-elevation fields in western Utah, waterlogging and sometimes salinization occurred to such an extent that fields had to be abandoned. The Owens valley's fate as a farming area was sealed in the early 20th century, when the city of Los Angeles purchased most of its water rights and transported water from the Owens River to the city via an aqueduct. The Hetch Hetchy valley (near Yosemite and rivaling it in beauty) was dammed in 1913 to send water to San Francisco. Because ranchers and farmers were often the prior owners of water on the basis of their ancestors' earlier settlement history, both governments and other interests like municipalities have had to subordinate their goals and concerns to those of agricultural interests.

CONCLUSION

One overriding theme that appears throughout the historical geography of the Far West, from aboriginal occupance to the early 21st century, is diversity, reflected in its biophysical environments as well as in its human populations. Native American occupance displayed tremendous differences from place to place. The differences went unnoticed, for the most part, by early trapper-explorers, who were more concerned with environmental exploitation. The human ecology of Native people and the explorer yielded to a varied political geography once Spain, Britain, and the United States began to compete geopolitically for the Far West. Each approached the region from different perspectives and directions, and each in turn created regional frontiers that would remain throughout the 19th century and influence and anchor the West's growth and development. Once the United States had quieted all competing imperial claims to the land, it faced the prospect of developing an economic and population geography that was not, and would never become, a cultural mirror of its eastern "heartland." The discovery of gold in California, and the subsequent rush to claim it, heightened and extended the diversity of the entire area. Mining, instant urbanization, specialized agriculture, and spiraling economic growth intensified differences that, in turn, engraved its human geography.

The Far West should not be considered merely as an extension of a continually westward-moving frontier from the Atlantic but also as the home of Native Americans, as an eastward-moving frontier from the Pacific, or a northward-moving frontier from Mexico, each with its own historical geographies.

Western historians of the past tended to view western history as a triumphal expansion of Euro-American civilization. Today western historians are more apt to question its moral and environmental costs, such as dispossession of Native Americans and the despoliation of the natural environment to accommodate growing water demands. Although these tragedies are by no means restricted to the American West, they have tended to cause more serious repercussions owing to a more recent (and therefore ideally more enlightened) settlement history and more ecologically fragile mountain and desert habitats.

ADDITIONAL READING

Allen, B. 1987. *Homesteading the High Desert.* Salt Lake City: University of Utah Press.

Allen, J. L. 1975. *Passage through the Garden: Lewis and Clark and the Image of the Northwest.* Urbana: University of Illinois Press.

Arrington, L. J. 1958. *Great Basin Kingdom: An Economic History of the Latter-day Saints.* Cambridge: Harvard University Press.

Barth, G. 1975. *Instant Cities: Urbanization and the Rise of San Francisco and Denver.* New York: Oxford University Press.

Bowen, M. E. 1994. *Utah People in the Nevada Desert: Homestead and Community on a 20th-Century Farmers' Frontier.* Logan: Utah State University Press.

Bowen, W. A. 1978. *The Willamette Valley: Migration and Settlement on the Oregon Frontier.* Seattle: University of Washington Press.

Conzen, M., ed. 1990. *The Making of the American Landscape.* Boston: Unwin Hyman.

Dicken, S. N., and E. Dicken. 1979. *The Making of Oregon: A Study in Historical Geography.* Portland: Oregon Historical Society.

Fogelson, R. M. 1967. *The Fragmented Metropolis: Los Angeles, 1850–1930.* Cambridge: Harvard University Press.

Frantz, K. 1999. *Indian Reservations in the United States.* Chicago: University of Chicago Press.

Goetzman, W. H. 1966. *Exploration and Empire: The Explorer and Scientist in Winning the American West.* New York: Alfred A. Knopf.

Hornbeck, D. 1983. *California Patterns: A Geographical and Historical Atlas.* Palo Alto: Mayfield.

Jackson, R. H. 1981. *Land Use in America.* London: Edward Arnold.

Jolinek, L. S. 1979. *Harvest Empire: A History of California Agriculture.* San Francisco: Boyd & Fraser.

Jorgenson, J. G. 1980. *Western Indians: Comparative Environments, Languages, and Culture of 172 Western Indian Tribes.* San Francisco: W. H. Freeman.

Limerick, P. 1987. *The Legacy of Conquest: The Unbroken Past of the American West.* New York: W. W. Norton.

Lotchin, R. W. 1974. *San Francisco, 1846–1856: From Hamlet to City.* New York: Oxford University Press.

Luckingham, B. 1982. *The Urban Southwest: A Profile History of El Paso, Albuquerque, Tucson, and Phoenix.* El Paso: Texas Western Press.

McKee, J., ed. 1985. *Ethnicity in Contemporary America: A Geographical Appraisal.* Dubuque, Iowa: Kendall/Hunt.

Meinig, D. W. 1968. *The Great Columbia Plain: A Historical Geography, 1805–1910.* Seattle: University of Washington Press.

Merk, F. 1963. *Manifest Destiny and Mission in American History: A Reinterpretation.* New York: Alfred A. Knopf.

Peterson, R. H. 1977. *The Bonanza Kings: The Social Origins and Business Behavior of Western Mining Entrepreneurs, 1870–1900.* Lincoln: University of Nebraska Press.

Pomeroy, E. 1966. *The Pacific Slope: A History of California, Oregon, Washington, Utah, and Nevada.* New York: Alfred A. Knopf.

Reps, J. W. 1979. *Cities of the American West: A History of Frontier Urban Planning.* Princeton: Princeton University Press.

Rodman, P. 1963. *Mining Frontiers of the Far West, 1848–1880.* New York: Holt, Rinehart & Winston.

Rodman, P., and R. W. Etulain. 1977. *Frontier and the American West.* Arlington Heights, Ill.: AHM Publishing.

Wheat, C. I. 1957–63. *Mapping the Trans-Mississippi*

West, 1540–1861. 5 vols. San Francisco: Institute of Historical Cartography.

Winther, O. O. 1964. *The Transportation Frontier, 1865–1890.* New York: Holt, Rinehart & Winston.

Wishart, D. 1979. *The Fur Trade of the American West, 1807–1840: A Geographical Synthesis.* Lincoln: University of Nebraska Press.

Wyckoff, W., and M. Dilsaver, eds. 1995. *The Mountainous West: Explorations in Historical Geography.* Lincoln: University of Nebraska Press.

13

Population Growth, Migration, and Urbanization, 1860–1920

DAVID WARD

During the period of mass immigration that began in the mid-1840s and ended in the mid-1920s, the population of the United States increased from about 17 million to more than 105 million (table 13.1). This sixfold increase was unparalleled elsewhere in the Western industrializing world; the populations of the United Kingdom and Germany, for example, grew at about half that rate. Even before the onset of mass immigration, extremely high rates of natural growth had doubled the population of the new nation in less than 25 years, but toward the end of the 19th century natural growth rates declined as the excess of births over deaths diminished. During the 1870s, death rates were as high as 22 per 1,000 and birthrates exceeded 40 per 1,000. By the decade of World War I, death rates had declined to about 15 per 1,000, but birthrates had dropped more dramatically to just over 25 per 1,000.

Net migration rates fluctuated from decade to decade, reaching a maximum of 10 percent between 1880 and 1885 and, after declining to less than 3 percent during the depression of the mid-1890s, increased once again to a level of 7 percent between 1905 and 1910. The proportion of the white population born abroad increased from about 13 percent in 1850 to almost 20 percent in 1890 and then declined to 17 percent by 1920, but the proportion of people of foreign birth and parentage together reached its maximum level of 45 percent in 1920 (table 13.1). Overall, immigration probably doubled the rate of growth among those of European ancestry, but in the absence of a substantial immigrant contribution, the relative proportion of African Americans in the total population dropped from more than 15 percent in 1850 to less than 10 percent in 1920.

As in many parts of Europe, a rapid rate of urbanization accompanied this unparalleled rate of growth among the white population. Unlike Europe, the diverse resources of an un-developed frontier stimulated high levels of interregional migration to nonurban settings as well. Between 1790 and 1850, the urban proportion of the total population more than tripled to reach 15 percent and increased by a similar margin in the succeeding six decades, so that by 1910 more than 45 percent of the population lived in urban settlements (table 13.1). Toward the turn of the century, the city-ward movement of people far exceeded migration to a greatly diminished frontier. By 1920, the population of the United States surpassed 100 million, and for the first time a narrow majority was urban.

The impact of foreign immigration on both the size and the ethnic composition of the American population had long aroused anxieties among the native-born, and in 1924, entry restrictions, which had been applied to East Asians as early as the 1880s, were extended to include all foreigners. Thereafter, a precipitous drop in foreign arrivals compounded the longer-term effects of a declining rate of natural growth and brought to an end a period of unprecedented population growth.

Table 13.1 U.S. Population Composition and Growth, 1840–1920 (in percentages)

	Population (in millions)	Urban	African Am.	Foreign Parentage	Foreign Born
1840	17.1	10.8	16.8	n.d.	n.d.
1850	23.2	15.3	15.7	n.d.	12.9
1860	31.4	19.8	14.1	n.d.	17.9
1870	39.8	25.7	13.5	19.0	19.6
1880	50.2	28.2	13.1	22.5	17.8
1890	62.9	35.1	11.9	25.0	19.9
1900	76.0	39.7	11.6	27.6	18.1
1910	92.0	45.7	10.7	27.8	18.0
1920	105.7	51.2	9.9	28.0	16.9

n.d. = no data

THE ORIGINS AND DESTINATIONS
OF MIGRANTS

Restrictive legislation was in part provoked by changes in the volume, sources, and destinations of immigrants after about 1880. Approximately 33 million foreigners entered the United States in the century prior to comprehensive immigration restriction, but only one-third of this total had actually arrived by 1880. During the succeeding 40 years, an average of about 6 million people arrived in each decade, with more than 8 million newcomers entering the United States in the first decade of the 20th century (table 13.2). Prior to 1880 about 85 percent of all immigrants came from the British Isles, British America (Canada), the German states, Switzerland, Scandinavia, and the Low Countries. But, during the decade of World War I these areas accounted for barely 20 percent of the total arrivals because the source areas of immigrants after 1880 expanded from northwestern Europe to include southern and eastern sections of the continent. Immigrants from the Austro-Hungarian and Russian Empires as well as from Mediterranean Europe provided more than one-half of the new arrivals in the last decade of the 19th century and overwhelmingly dominated the immigrant stream from Europe in the two subsequent decades (fig. 13.1). Immigration from Latin America and East Asia also increased markedly after 1880. Although their contribution to the total flow remained less than 10 percent, both groups had a pro-found impact on the populations of western states.

Debates on the desirability of immigration increasingly focused on the tendency of the more recent arrivals to congregate in the slums of large cities of the Northeast and Middle West. On the basis of both Old World sources and American destinations, a distinction was made between "old immigrants" who had arrived before about 1880 and "new immigrants" who had landed after that date. The distinction became the source of prejudicial evaluations of the new immigrants and the basis of the ethnic quotas that were established by the immigration restriction legislation of the 1920s. In contrast, the contributions and experiences of the old immigrants were reevaluated in a more positive light. Northwest Europeans were viewed as part of the broader culture from which American values were derived. Their rapid assimilation into American society was further facilitated by their participation in the frontier movement and their more balanced distribution between urban and rural settings. With the striking exception of the Irish, most old immigrant groups contributed to the settlement of the midwestern frontier in larger proportions than most new immigrants. Parts of the rural Middle West were, however, a mosaic of ethnic communities, and for most groups assimilation was not necessarily rapid.

In contrast to the Middle West, immigrants from both southern and eastern Europe were more urbanized than the earlier arrivals from

Table 13.2 Decennial Immigration to the United States, 1820–1919

	1820–1829	1830–1839	1840–1849	1850–1859	1860–1869	1870–1879	1880–1889	1890–1899	1900–1909	1910–1919
Total in millions	0.1	0.5	1.4	2.7	2.1	2.7	5.2	3.7	8.2	6.3
% of total from:										
Ireland	40.2	31.7	46.0	36.9	24.4	15.4	12.8	11.0	4.2	2.6
Germany[a]	4.5	23.2	27.0	34.8	35.2	27.4	27.5	15.7	4.0	2.7
United Kingdom	19.5	13.8	15.3	13.5	14.9	21.1	15.5	8.9	5.7	5.8
Scandinavia	0.2	0.4	0.9	0.9	5.5	7.6	12.7	10.5	5.9	3.8
Canada[b]	1.8	2.2	2.4	2.2	4.9	11.8	9.4	0.1	1.5	11.2
Russia[a]	—	—	—	—	0.2	1.3	3.5	12.2	18.3	17.4
Austria-Hungary[a]	—	—	—	—	0.2	2.2	6.0	14.5	24.4	18.2
Italy	—	—	—	—	0.5	1.7	5.1	16.3	23.5	19.4

[a]Continental European boundaries prior to the 1919 settlement.
[b]British America to 1867; Canada includes Newfoundland; Canadian immigration was not recorded between 1886 and 1893.

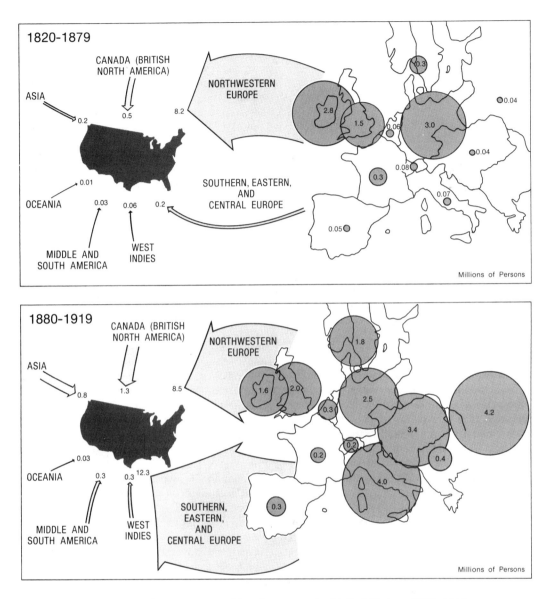

Figure 13.1 Source Areas of Immigrants to the United States, 1820–1919

northwestern Europe (table 13.3). Indeed, some ethnic and national groups of the new immigration settled almost exclusively in cities. More than 80 percent of all Poles, Hungarians, and Italians lived in cities. The exception among old immigrant groups was the long-established Irish, who remained the second most urbanized group in 1920. Almost 87 percent of the Irish-born lived in cities; only Russian immigrants exceeded this proportion. Fewer than 70 per-

cent of some other new immigrant groups were classed as urban. Among the recently arrived Yugoslavs and Czechs, for example, the degree of urbanization was little different from that of the longer established German-born.

Although some ethnic and national groups of the new immigration settled almost exclusively in cities, as late as 1920 old immigrants still accounted for almost half of the foreign-born urban population. For example, while only

Table 13.3 Urban Residence of Foreign-Born White Population, 1920

	Percent of Group Urban	Percent of Total Foreign-Born Urban Population	Total Foreign Populations (in millions)
Foreign-born white	75.5	100.0	10.36
Russia	88.6	12.0	1.24
Ireland	86.9	8.7	0.90
Italy	84.4	13.1	1.36
Poland	84.4	9.3	0.96
Hungary	80.0	3.1	0.32
United Kingdom	75.0	3.4	0.86
Austria	75.0	4.2	0.43
Canada	74.5	8.1	0.84
Yugoslavia	69.3	1.1	0.12
Germany	67.5	11.0	1.14
Czechoslovakia	66.3	2.3	0.24
Scandinavia	54.6	6.5	0.34

two-thirds of the Germans were urban residents, they accounted for 11 percent of the total foreign-born population of American cities. Only the newly arrived Russians and Italians contributed more to the total foreign population (table 13.3). This suggests that the distinction of the "old" and the "new" clearly neglected the effects of length of residence in the new country on both the distribution and the assimilation of immigrants, and it also obscured major differences in the experiences of individual groups within each category.

Changes in the proportion of immigrants with urban destinations were probably no greater than among native-born Americans who migrated before and after 1880. Some of these native-born urban migrants were, of course, the children of immigrants who had settled on the land earlier in the century. Others were southern-born African Americans who established patterns of migration that were to expand dramatically once foreign immigration was restricted.

These cumulative geographic consequences of rapid population growth, high rates of migration, and accelerated urbanization resulted from literally millions of individual decisions that were provoked by an almost endless combination of specific motives. Most migrants were in search of new employment, and at any

given time, information on the availability of opportunities in specific destinations was restricted. Moreover, centers of expanding employment were rarely fixed, and information was often incomplete, if not erroneous. Consequently, migration was rarely a single event, and frequent moves were often responses to expanding agricultural and mining frontiers and to the growth of manufacturing industries in the Northeast and Middle West. High rates of population turnover in both urban and rural settings took place throughout the second half of the 19th century. The large volume, high frequency, and sequential pattern of migration usually occurred in the form of a network or "chain" of destinations within which relatives and friends provided short-term security and reliable information.

Frequent migration and population turnover did not obliterate the cumulative locational effects of the selective migration of different ethnic, religious, and racial groups from their ancestral or adopted source regions. Although most immigrants shared their new destinations with other groups, and although in time many of their ancestral traits disappeared, their ethnic identities in the United States were often associated with their initial regional concentrations, rather than with their cultural hearths in the Old World. Long before mass immigration, English immigrants to the New England and Chesapeake colonies, when they spread westward, were identified as "Yankee" and "southern" rather than as English American. Similarly, French colonists to Quebec and Acadia retained their original, New World labels long after their subsequent moves to Louisiana and New England, respectively. The Mormons, defined by their religious beliefs, were originally organized in upstate New York but today are most closely identified with their adopted state of Utah. Other groups have retained their immigrant label, even though their ethnic identity is also closely associated with their original concentrations within the United States. People of Norwegian ancestry, for example, are strongly associated with sections of Wisconsin and those of Swedish descent with parts of Minnesota.

These uneven patterns of distribution in part record national and regional differences in the impact of industrial capitalism, which set well-defined limits to the routes and destinations of most migrants. The disruptive effects of industrialization on rural crafts, domestic manufacturing, and farming virtually forced emigration from many parts of Europe. During the 1840s, crop failures savagely compounded this agrarian distress, and these critical conditions in the Old World rather than any complete awareness of opportunities in the New World probably initiated mass emigration. Once established, however, the immigrant flow also responded to upswings and downswings in the American business cycle and to regional shifts in economic growth within the United States.

THE INITIAL IMPACT OF MASS IMMIGRATION, 1860

The regional destinations of those foreigners who had arrived in the first surge of mass immigration were clearly established by 1860. Of more than 4 million foreign-born people, 37 percent were concentrated in the Mid-Atlantic region and an identical proportion in the Middle West, while another 11 percent were to be found in New England (fig. 13.2). Fewer than 10 percent of the foreign-born had settled in the South,

and the majority of these people were concentrated in Baltimore, New Orleans, Louisville, and other ports and river towns that encircled that predominantly rural region. Most old and new immigrants avoided the South throughout the entire period of mass immigration. A commercial agricultural system largely based on the intensive use of black labor and a decidedly slow rate of industrialization offered few attractions to foreign immigrants.

Prior to the start of mass immigration, native-born Americans had moved westward in substantial numbers, and each coastal concentration of colonial Americans had expanded in a somewhat latitudinal fashion. Most migrants from the Southeast (Georgia and South Carolina) moved into the lower Mississippi valley, while those from the Mid-Atlantic region pushed west along the Ohio valley into the middle Mississippi valley. Those from the upper South (Virginia, Maryland, and North Carolina) migrated to both sections of the Mississippi valley, while the majority of New Englanders moved into the Great Lakes region by way of the Mohawk Gap, through which the Erie Canal was dug. The westward extension of this northern trajectory

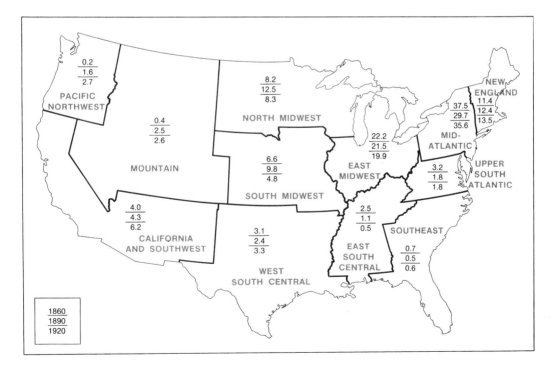

Figure 13.2 Regional Distribution of Foreign-Born Immigrants: 1860, 1890, and 1920

of frontier settlement lagged far behind those farther south, for New Englanders had initially found land available in upstate New York and Upper Canada (Ontario). By the time New Englanders began to settle the westerly sections of the Great Lakes region, they were joined by large numbers of immigrants primarily, but not exclusively, from the German states and Scandinavia. The pioneer populations of Wisconsin and Minnesota included extremely high proportions of foreigners. The Irish contribution to this proportion was, however, decidedly modest. Consequently, the regional distributions of the Irish and continental Europeans exhibited some striking contrasts as early as 1860.

These regional tendencies are revealed by a crude index of deviation that indicates the degree to which a given group is under- or overrepresented in relation to regional distribution of the population as a whole (table 13.4). The index has been computed for regional clusters of states on the basis of similarities in their ethnic compositions (fig. 13.2). The Irish were heavily overrepresented in the Northeast, and although immigrants from the German states were also well represented in the Mid-Atlantic region, there were relatively few of them in New England. The Germans were as highly overrepresented in the Middle West as the Irish were in New England. Of all immigrant groups, the English were the most evenly distributed among these regions, and only in Missouri, Iowa, and the Kansas Territory were they slightly underrepresented. The Scots closely paralleled the settlement patterns of the English, but the Welsh were strongly overrepresented only in the Mid-Atlantic region. Of the other smaller groups, those from British America (Canada), including many whose parents were born in the British

Isles, were strikingly prominent in New England and some sections of the Middle West, while immigrants from Scandinavia, Holland, and Switzerland were almost exclusively concentrated in Michigan, Wisconsin, and Minnesota.

Although substantial proportions of most immigrant groups had participated in the settlement of the Middle West, the Irish were a notable exception. To be sure, Irish laborers were involved in the construction of canals, railroads, and cities in the West, but very few settled on the land. Famine conditions yielded a high proportion of impoverished and sickly migrants who lacked the skills and resources to move beyond the ports of arrival. Indeed, in the absence of specialized cheap passenger services, Irish immigrants became the westbound ballast of Atlantic sailing ships, compensating in revenue for the difference in bulk between eastbound cargoes of raw materials and return loads of manufactured goods. The New Brunswick lumber trade, in particular, provided cheap passages to the Maritime Provinces (Canada), from where many Irish immigrants moved on to New England. Eventually, the greater frequency of ships between Liverpool and New York directed the Irish immigrant traffic to that latter port.

The majority of German immigrants also landed in New York, but initially the routes of commodity commerce had influenced their destinations too. Many German-speaking people from Alsace-Lorraine and adjacent sections of the Rhine valley traveled to the United States on cotton freighters returning from Le Havre to New Orleans. They moved on to the Middle West by way of the Mississippi valley. Immigrants from northwestern Germany utilized the

Table 13.4 Regional Representation of Selected Foreign-Born Groups, 1860 (index of deviation)

	Ireland	Germany	England	Scotland	Br. America
New England	1.9	0.2	1.0	1.2	2.8
Mid-Atlantic	2.0	1.4	1.7	1.6	1.0
E. Midwest	0.7	1.6	1.3	1.2	1.4
N. Midwest	1.3	3.6	2.6	1.9	2.7
S. Midwest	0.7	1.6	0.8	0.8	0.8
Total (000's)	1,611	1,301	432	109	250

Note: Index of deviation = percent group / percent total population in each region.
See figure 13.2 for regional boundaries.

Table 13.5 Regional Representation of Northwest Europeans, 1890 (index of deviation)

	Ire.	Ger.	Eng.	Scot.	Wales	Can.	Nor.	Swe.	Den.	Swit.	Hol.	Boh.[a]
New England	3.0	0.3	2.0	2.2	0.5	5.2	0.1	1.0	0.4	0.1	0.1	0.1
Mid-Atlantic	2.2	1.5	1.7	1.6	2.3	0.5	0.2	0.5	0.4	0.7	1.0	0.5
E. Midwest	0.7	1.5	1.1	1.0	1.0	1.3	0.6	1.3	0.8	1.3	2.6	1.8
N. Midwest	0.7	2.6	0.9	1.2	1.1	2.0	11.8	5.0	4.8	2.0	2.1	3.8
S. Midwest	0.5	1.2	0.8	0.8	0.8	0.5	0.9	1.5	2.3	1.5	1.2	2.5
Mountain	1.0	1.0	3.7	3.3	4.5	1.7	1.2	3.1	6.8	2.6	0.5	0.2
Pacific N.W.	0.7	1.0	1.7	2.4	2.0	2.4	3.4	2.9	3.1	3.3	0.6	0.3
Total (000's)	1,872	2,785	908	242	100	981	323	478	133	104	82	118

[a]Bohemia.

Note: Index of deviation = percent group / percent total population in each region.
See fig. 13.2 for regional boundaries.

tobacco ships that plied the route from Bremen to Baltimore, from where the majority moved inland by way of the Ohio valley. Others found their way to New York after short voyages across the North Sea to the ports of the east coast of England and then overland to Liverpool. Once the emigrant traffic became a specialized and scheduled service and the pressures for immediate emigration subsided, the vast majority of all foreigners arrived at New York. With the rapid development of steamship services after the Civil War, this dominance became even more pronounced. Deteriorating and at times catastrophic conditions in the Old World strongly directed the initial courses of emigration, but, increasingly, economic growth in the United States became decisive in the regional allocation of immigrants.

REGIONAL DESTINATIONS, 1860–1890

Following the resumption of mass immigration with the end of the Civil War, the majority of immigrants continued to come from northwestern Europe, and most arrived during two major surges that peaked in the early 1870s and again in the mid-1880s. The completion of a transcontinental railroad system and the rapid advance of trunk lines into the western states had facilitated the westward expansion of settlement and development. Railroad construction had been rewarded by huge government grants of land adjacent to their routes, and consequently, the railroads had a vested interest in the rapid alienation of their holdings. To speed up settlement,

they sent agents to Europe to publicize the potential of their holdings and provided special discounted fares from rural Europe to the American West. Several midwestern states created immigration agencies that also facilitated the diffusion of information on conditions and opportunities on the American frontier, but it was the personal networks of knowledge, compiled from emigrants' correspondence, that provided the most persuasive influences on the decision to migrate.

Under these circumstances, the proportion of immigrants who moved directly inland from the ports of arrival increased markedly. In 1860, approximately equal proportions of immigrants were housed in the Mid-Atlantic region and in the Middle West, but by 1890 about 45 percent of all foreign-born residents lived in the latter region and just under 30 percent in the former (fig. 13.2). While many immigrants continued to settle in Ohio, Michigan, and Illinois, the largest gains occurred in Wisconsin, Minnesota, and the Dakotas. Here, immigrants often formed a majority of the new settlers. Farther south in Iowa, Missouri, Kansas, and Nebraska the substantial native-born migration exceeded that of foreigners. Scandinavian, Dutch, Swiss, and German immigrants were all well represented in varying degrees throughout the Middle West. With the exception of the Germans in the Mid-Atlantic region and the Swedes in New England, these groups were not prominent in the Northeast (table 13.5). Although they were often identified as new immigrants, almost 120,000 Bohemians (Czechs) were recorded in the U.S. census of 1890, and their regional distribution was little different from that of other groups from continental northwestern Europe. In particular, there were marked concentrations of Czechs in and around Omaha, Nebraska. The Swiss and Scandinavians were also overrepresented in the Pacific Northwest and the northern sections of the Rockies. Throughout this vast expanse of new settlement, newly arrived immigrants often reestablished and even elaborated their ancestral patterns of life in the form of church-centered or congregational societies. Although they quickly adapted to the agricultural practices and market orientation of American life, many rural groups have retained a distinct ethnic identity to this day. Among many striking examples of these persisting ethnic groups are the Dutch in and around Kalamazoo, Michigan, and the Swiss of New Glaurus, Wisconsin.

California attracted some of the immigrant groups who had settled the Middle West and the Northwest, but the British, Irish, Italians, and Portuguese were also well represented. The prominence of the Chinese and Mexicans, however, set the distinctive ethnic tone of California and adjacent sections of the Southwest. Mining and railroad construction extensively used Chinese labor, but by the mid-1880s the increasing volume of immigration from East Asia had provoked not only hostility but also exclusionary legislation. In 1890, almost 107,000 Chinese immigrants lived in the United States, more than three-quarters of them concentrated in the cities and larger towns of northern California and the Pacific Northwest. Although there were only 2,200 newcomers from Japan, they also concentrated on the West Coast, where more than three-quarters of their total worked primarily in intensive horticulture (table 13.6). The Mexican presence in California was, of course, partly a consequence of annexation in 1848. By 1890 almost 30 percent of the 77,800 people of Mexican birth in the United States were recorded there. Almost all the remainder lived along the border in Arizona, New Mexico, and Texas.

This period also saw the final stages of the relocation of Native Americans on western reservations. In 1890, the census recorded fewer than 60,000 Native Americans. About one-quarter of them were concentrated in various parts of the northern Middle West, another third lived in California, and the majority of the remainder were dispersed throughout the Southwest and mountain regions (table 13.6). Throughout the 19th century, the continued decline in their numbers accompanied these enforced migrations of Native Americans, and this trend persisted until the 20th century. The majority of Native Americans were assigned to reservations, where they attempted to maintain their tribal institutions in unfamiliar, isolated, and often distinctly unpromising environments.

Between 1860 and 1890, the number of African Americans increased from 4.4 million to 7.5 million, but their proportional contribution to the national population declined from 14.1 to 11.9 percent. African Americans were as highly concentrated in the South in 1890 as they had been in 1860, despite the emancipation of slaves in 1863. While the proportion of whites living in the Old South, east of the Mississippi, declined from 22 to 18 percent, that of African Americans dropped from 78 to 72 percent (fig. 13.3). These losses were compensated for by

Table 13.6 Regional Distribution of Selected Minority Groups, 1890 and 1920 (as percentage of total U.S.)

	1890				1920			
	Native America	Mexico	Japan	China	Native America	Mexico	Japan	China
Southwest	36.7	29.8	56.4	68.9	28.6	34.6	65.5	48.9
Pacific N.W.	8.4	0.2	18.9	11.9	5.5	0.2	19.4	8.9
Mountain	9.1	1.1	1.5	9.3	10.0	2.9	9.0	4.9
W. South Central	2.7	66.8	1.0	1.1	24.8	56.6	2.5	56.6
Total (000's)	59[a]	78	2	107	244	486	82	44

[a]Excludes Native Americans in Indian Territory and on reservations.
See figure 13.2 for regional boundaries.

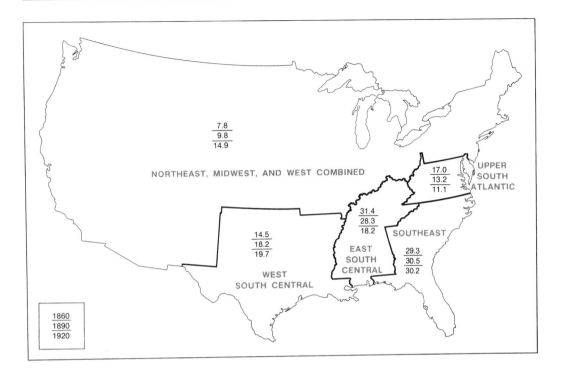

Figure 13.3 Regional Distribution of the African American Population: 1860, 1890, and 1920

gains in southern states west of the Mississippi, and, consequently, more than 90 percent of African Americans still resided in the South in 1890. Like the population of the South as a whole, African Americans were overwhelmingly rural, but those who lived outside the South were concentrated in Philadelphia, Baltimore, Washington, St. Louis, Kansas City, and other cities that bordered on the South.

Before 1890, the vast movement of people to the Middle West often deflected attention from the substantial impact of immigration on the industrialization and urbanization of the Northeast. Immigrants from England, Scotland, and Wales joined the native-born in the skilled sectors of the expanding mining, metalworking, and textile industries, and in 1890 they were much more strikingly overrepresented in the Northeast than in the Middle West (table 13.5). The regional distributions of the English and the Scots were quite similar, but the Welsh remained concentrated in the Mid-Atlantic region and were poorly represented in New England. The Irish remained relatively underrepresented in the Middle West and were more highly concentrated in the Northeast than in 1860 (table 13.5). The Irish had begun to obtain employment in the semiskilled sectors of several manufacturing industries, but the majority worked as day laborers or domestic servants or were employed in the workshops of so-called sweated trades. In New England, they shared their regional predominance with the Canadians, who had originally come from the English-speaking sections of the Maritime Provinces and Newfoundland; but after the Civil War the French-speaking Québécois also moved there in large numbers. The latter often competed with the Irish for jobs in the textile industry. English-speaking Canadians were able to enter the skilled trades, within which advancement to petty proprietorship was still possible. In the Mid-Atlantic region, where the Canadians were not prominent, German immigrants often dominated these small-scale skilled trades.

Overall patterns of migration and settlement established before the Civil War during the first surge of mass immigration were maintained during the influx of the early 1870s and mid-1880s. To a much greater degree than in subsequent decades, these immigrants moved directly to the farms and small towns of the agricultural interior. Farther south and especially in the Southwest, native-born migrants dominated. Substantial numbers of immigrants from the British Isles and to a lesser degree from Germany concentrated in the industrial centers of the Northeast. On the West Coast, where immigrants were also well represented, newcomers from non-European sources had already established a distinctive tone to that region's ethnic pluralism. Generalizations about the old immigrants exaggerated the assimilative effects of their settlement on the frontier, and in any event, many of them also responded to industrial developments in northeastern cities. Moreover, these same generalizations overlooked the impact of non-European immigration on the West and Southwest. During the mid-1880s, several new groups made their appearance in the immigrant stream, and their regional destinations were quite different from those of most of their predecessors.

REGIONAL DESTINATIONS, 1890–1920

Immigration from northwestern Europe continued at a relatively high level until the turn of the century, but by the time immigration was restricted in 1924, the proportion arriving from these areas was less than 20 percent (table 13.2). Nevertheless, considerable numbers of immigrants from these long-established sources continued to settle in the regional destinations of their predecessors. The increase in immigration from southern and eastern Europe began slowly in the 1880s, when more than 750,000 people came from these more remote sources and accounted for about 15 percent of the total. By the first decade of the 20th century this proportion had increased dramatically to well over two-thirds of total immigration. Foreign arrivals declined slightly in the subsequent decade because of the disruptive effects of World War I.

Changes within Europe strongly influenced these shifts in the source areas of immigrants. Diminishing rates of population growth, combined with economic development, greatly reduced the incentives for emigration from many parts of northwestern Europe. In contrast, the disruptive impact of industrialization on rural societies, which had afflicted northwestern Europe earlier in the century, finally diffused to many once remote areas of southern and eastern Europe. Quite apart from these economic considerations, political persecution in the form of pogroms greatly accelerated the emigration of Jews from the Russian Empire, while the removal of restraints on movement within the Austro-Hungarian Empire also facilitated emigration from Central Europe.

The changing labor needs of the American economy were also critical in this reorientation of immigrant source areas. The United States was one of the pioneers of the second phase of those technological and organizational innovations that marked the later stages of the industrial revolution and the transition from entrepreneurial to corporate capitalism. Many longer-established immigrants and especially their American-born children moved into the growing managerial and clerical strata of the labor force, but an even more voracious demand for semiskilled and unskilled labor could no longer be supplied from northwestern Europe. The bulk of this new employment was concentrated in the industrial cities of the Northeast; but just as the agricultural frontier had strongly influenced the destinations of immigrants before 1890, a second, more intensive frontier of manufacturing attracted immigrants as it spread from the Northeast into the eastern sections of the Middle West. Between 1890 and 1920 the earlier decline in the proportion of immigrants living in the Mid-Atlantic region was reversed, and by 1920 almost 36 percent of the foreign-born lived there (fig. 13.2). The proportions in the eastern Middle West and New England remained relatively stable, and by 1920 well over two-thirds of the total foreign-born lived in the three regions that formed the expanded industrial core of the American economy, often described as the American Manufacturing Belt.

These changes in the regional distributions of the foreign-born clearly indicate the predominant destinations of recently arrived immigrants from southern and eastern Europe. As early as 1890 the concentration of southern and eastern European immigrants in the Mid-Atlantic region was especially pronounced; in addition, there was a strong representation of Italians in New England and of Poles in the eastern

Table 13.7 Regional Representation of "New" Immigrants, 1890 and 1920 (index of deviation)

	1890						1920					
	Italy	Rus.	Aus.	Hun.	Greece	Pol.	Italy	Rus.	Aus.	Hun.	Greece	Pol.
New England	1.2	0.9	0.3	0.4	0.6	0.5	2.1	1.7	0.9	0.5	2.9	n.d.
Mid-Atlantic	2.8	2.2	2.4	3.5	1.4	1.4	2.8	2.3	2.1	2.4	1.1	n.d.
East Midwest	0.5	0.7	0.7	0.8	0.9	1.9	0.6	1.1	1.5	1.8	1.3	n.d.
Total (000's)	183	183	123	62	2	147	1,610	3,871	3,130	1,111	176	n.d.

Note: Index of deviation = percent group / percent total population by regions.
See figure 13.2 for regional boundaries.

Middle West (table 13.7). Thirty years later, these initial patterns had been maintained, but East Europeans and Greeks were now strongly overrepresented in the eastern Middle West. The Italians alone of the new immigrants were weakly represented in the eastern Middle West, while in New England they now shared their prominence with the Russian-born, who were primarily of Jewish background (table 13.7). Despite their greatly reduced proportional contribution to the total immigrant stream, northwestern Europeans also concentrated in the industrial core region and, with the exception of the Irish, continued to be well represented in the Middle West and the Far West. The regional distributions of these old immigrants showed few overall changes between 1890 and 1920 (tables 13.5 and 13.8).

The large cities of the industrial core region were also the primary destinations of African American migrants from the South. During the 1870s and 1880s, the net loss of African American migrants from the South amounted to about 130,000. During the 1890s, when emigration from Europe dropped from the extremely high levels of the previous decade, the South incurred an even greater loss of more than 250,000 African Americans. After a slight decline in net migration from the South between 1900 and 1910, the northward flow increased dramatically during World War I, when emigration from Europe was virtually impossible. During this decade the South experienced a net loss of more than 450,000 African American migrants, most of whom moved to the cities of the Northeast and the Middle West. With the restriction of foreign immigration in 1924, the migration of African Americans became the largest single source of new unskilled labor; in many respects

it defined the beginning of a third major era of migration. By 1920 these new patterns of migration were well established. The decline in the African American population of the Old South, which had begun before 1890, increased markedly thereafter. Although the Old South housed just over two-thirds of the total African American population by 1920, 10 percent now lived in the Northeast and eastern Middle West (fig. 13.3).

Immigration from both Canada and Mexico also increased substantially after 1890 and especially during World War I. Their long-established regional patterns remained unchanged. More than 70 percent of the French Canadians in the United States were concentrated in New England (table 13.8), and more than 90 percent of those of Mexican birth were spread along the border states of the Southwest (table 13.6). In California both the Mexican- and Japanese-born populations had increased, but the Chinese had declined after legislation excluded newcomers. Unlike the Japanese and Mexicans, who were closely associated with different aspects of intensive horticulture, the vast majority of the Chinese lived in distinctive ethnic quarters, or "Chinatowns," in many of the large metropolitan cities.

THE PREDOMINANCE OF URBAN DESTINATIONS

Throughout the period of mass immigration, cities were the original destinations of most immigrants, and many of the children of those who initially settled in small towns or rural areas also eventually moved to larger communities. Between 1890 and 1920, however, almost all the newcomers from southern and eastern Europe moved directly to the cities of the expanding industrial core region. Like the Irish and Germans before them, the proportional representations of each of the major ethnic groups of the new immigration varied considerably from city to city within the Northeast and Middle West. Even though the percentages of Irish and Germans in the foreign-born populations of American cities declined by 1910, they still tended to predominate in different groups of cities (fig. 13.4). The cities of New England continued to house large proportions of Irish-born and relatively few Germans, while these proportions were reversed in the port cities of the Great Lakes (Milwaukee, Buffalo, Detroit, Toledo, Chicago, and Cleveland) and in Cincinnati, St. Louis, and St. Paul. In the more than 50 cities with populations greater than 100,000 in 1910, only 3—New York City, Jersey City, and San Francisco—had higher than average proportions of both German- and Irish-born, but many cities of the Mid-Atlantic region housed close to the average proportions of both groups (for example, Rochester, Newark, Pittsburgh, Syracuse, Paterson, Albany, and Philadelphia). In contrast, most southern and western cities housed less than average proportions of both groups.

Slavic and Hungarian immigrants from the Russian and Austro-Hungarian Empires found their way to major centers of heavy industry in the valleys of Pennsylvania and eastern Ohio and the ports of the Great Lakes. Consequently, the port cities of the Great Lakes, which had long housed substantial German-born popula-

tions, became major centers of eastern European settlement. Other German-dominant cities that did not become centers of heavy industry, such as Cincinnati and St. Louis, housed relatively small proportions of the new immigrants. Few Slavs moved to the Irish-dominated cities of New England, but they did work alongside the Irish in the heavy industrial cities of the Mid-Atlantic region where the Irish and Germans were more evenly represented. Precise measurements of the proportional representation of different Slavic ethnic groups in various cities are not always possible from the census record. Although immigrants from the Austro-Hungarian Empire included some German-speaking people, the majority were Slavs and Hungarians, who were well represented in Pittsburgh and several of the cities of the Great Lakes. With the notable exception of Bridgeport, Connecticut, they were sparsely represented in the cities of New England (fig. 13.5).

In contrast, immigrants from Russia and Italy were only weakly represented in cities with high proportions of people from the Austro-Hungarian and German Empires. They were, however, particularly prominent in the larger cities of New England and the Mid-Atlantic coast and especially those with highly diversified and consumer-oriented industries (Boston, Providence, New Haven, New York City, Paterson, Newark, and Philadelphia). Most immigrants from the Russian Empire were of Jewish background; they found employment in the rapidly growing clothing industry that had long been associated with the use of sweated immigrant labor in small work-

Table 13.8 Regional Representation of Northwest Europeans, 1920 (index of deviation)

	Ire.	Ger.	Eng.	Scot.	Wales	Can.	Nor.	Swe.	Den.	Swit.	Hol.	Fr. Can.
New England	3.2	0.3	2.0	2.2	0.4	7.7	0.2	1.4	0.5	0.3	0.2	10.4
Mid-Atlantic	2.0	1.2	1.4	1.4	2.0	0.7	0.2	0.6	0.4	0.9	0.9	0.3
East Midwest	0.8	1.6	1.1	1.1	1.2	1.4	0.5	1.3	0.8	1.3	2.3	0.6
North Midwest	0.6	2.7	0.6	0.6	0.8	1.2	10.0	4.5	4.1	1.8	2.4	1.1
South Midwest	0.6	1.4	0.5	0.5	0.8	0.4	0.9	2.7	5.7	2.7	1.3	0.4
Pacific N.W	0.7	0.9	1.8	2.3	2.0	2.6	4.0	1.3	2.5	1.2	1.6	0.1
Mountain	0.8	0.6	2.0	1.9	2.8	1.4	1.8	3.1	3.0	2.9	1.4	0.6
Southwest	1.1	0.9	1.8	1.8	1.4	1.9	0.6	1.2	2.1	2.8	0.7	0.1
Total (000's)	1,037	1,686	814	255	67	1,138	364	626	189	119	132	308

Note: Index of deviation = percent group / percent total population in each region.
See Figure 13.2 for regional boundaries.

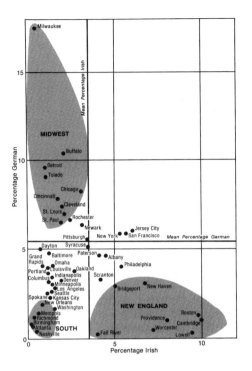

Figure 13.4 Proportion of "Old" Immigrants in American Cities, 1910

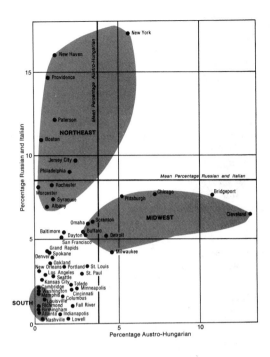

Figure 13.5 Proportion of "New" Immigrants in American Cities, 1910

shops or homes. They were also conspicuous in the rapidly expanding retail sector of not only the large cities of the Northeast but also most major metropolitan centers of the Middle West and the Far West. Southern Italians were especially prominent in cities once dominated by Irish immigrants. Although Italians replaced the Irish in the ubiquitous activities of day laboring, they were also well represented in retailing and other small proprietary activities.

THE IMMIGRANT WITHIN THE CITY

It has generally been assumed that most immigrants initially clustered in the slums of the inner city and then gradually dispersed into suburbs. The term "ghetto" is often applied to these inner-city concentrations of immigrants. This American usage of the term has its origins in the settlement of large numbers of East European Jews in American cities during the last two decades of the 19th century. The term rapidly lost its exclusive association with Jewish settlement and was widely used to refer to

the residential quarters of other newly arrived European immigrants and eventually to the inner-city concentrations of African Americans and Hispanics. Like the term "slum," the ghetto referred to those parts of the city where congested and unhealthy living quarters and isolation from the remainder of urban society combined to create pathological social conditions. In the ghetto, exotic migrants unfamiliar with American culture exacerbated the problems of the slum.

These negative impressions of the ghetto were part of the more general sense of apprehension at the change in the composition of foreign immigration discussed earlier. These distinctions between the old and the new immigration were, perhaps, somewhat exaggerated, for immigrants had been closely associated with the slums of large northeastern cities long before the ghetto became a focus of concern. The residential quarters of Irish and German immigrants who settled in American cities during the middle decades of the 19th century were not described as ghettos, but contemporary observers complained of unsanitary living arrangements, social problems, and the immigrant threat to American institutions. Nevertheless, to a greater degree than earlier immigrants from northwestern Europe, the more recent arrivals from southern and eastern Europe were assumed to be ill prepared for residence and employment in the American city and for participation in American society and politics. Deprived of contact with the host society, they would encounter a slower and more painful process of assimilation.

By 1900 the ghetto had become a symbol of the failure of the American dream not only in regard to material advancement but also because it was associated with pathological social conditions and the "corruption" of American democracy. The image provided justification for efforts to improve the environment of the immigrant and also for campaigns to exclude further immigration from southern and eastern Europe. Following the implementation of immigration restriction, this negative image of the ghetto and its residents was retained to describe the social and living conditions of Hispanic migrants from Mexico and Puerto Rico and African Americans from the South, who replaced Europeans in the inner sections of American cities. These new ghettos became more extensive and more enduring than any of the earlier concentrations of European immigrants. In the extent of their segregation, the persistence of their poverty, and the degree of their social disorganization, the African Americans' experience in the American city now symbolizes the most extreme manifestation of ghetto conditions. The term "ghetto," like the term "slum," projects a negative image of the migrant experience of the American city, but this image is in many respects both oversimplified and incomplete.

THE ENVIRONMENT OF THE GHETTO

The overcrowded and often unsanitary conditions within the ghetto are not a matter of debate. Overcrowded rooms, congested lots, and inadequate utilities contributed to high mortality, the neglect of domestic cleanliness, and the breakdown of family life. These apparent consequences of the adverse environment of the ghetto did, however, differ greatly both between and among immigrant groups. While age-standardized death rates were substantially higher in the

inner-city slums than in the growing suburbs, the rates within the congested immigrant quarters were extremely varied. For long, mortality and especially infant mortality among African Americans had greatly exceeded that of other minority groups, and during the 19th century Irish death rates were much higher than those of other immigrants from northwestern Europe. Of the diverse immigrants from southern and eastern Europe, the death rates of Russian Jews were generally much lower than those of Italians in adjacent dwellings and also somewhat lower than those of longer-established immigrant groups who lived in substantially less crowded conditions. The magnitude of environmental effects on African American and Irish mortality rates was compounded by the degree and longevity of the groups' impoverishment both before and after migration, while low rates among Jewish immigrants were influenced by their prior adaptations to congested living conditions in the Old World.

The moral life of those who survived in the harsh environment of the ghetto was also presumed to be in constant danger. Congested quarters with overcrowded rooms threatened the moral fabric of family life, and these environmental pressures were further aggravated by the tendency of migrants to be young, single, or married men without families. They were prepared to work in undesirable jobs and to endure appalling living conditions so that they might save funds sufficient to advance their prospects in their homeland. Moreover, the frequency with which immigrants took lodgers into their already crowded homes was viewed as a serious threat to domestic morality and family stability. Many lodgers, however, were relatives or friends, and standards of family privacy were not necessarily any different from those that had long prevailed in the Old World. Many temporary migrants became immigrants and made arrangements for their families to join them. While the prevalence of single-parent households or high proportions of young unmarried men among the early arrivals from southern and eastern Europe was often viewed as an indicator of family disintegration, relatives residing in several locations often provided support and resources whenever migration was frequent and gender selective. These households consisted of dispersed and itinerant individuals, and despite the social costs of separation, families did not necessarily disintegrate but rather adapted to the consequences of frequent migration.

Originally, these temporary migrants from southern and central Europe were distinguished from northwest Europeans who came to the United States as families with every intention of permanent settlement. In many respects, however, the Irish migration to the United States was initially an extension of seasonal movements within the British Isles, which could no longer accommodate the impact of famine. Throughout the 19th century, the uneven effects of industrialization on artisans, small farmers, and agricultural laborers had made temporary out-migration an increasingly essential part of rural life in many once remote sections of Europe. This process began as a spasmodic seasonal event over short distances and eventually developed into an intercontinental labor market involving lengthy sojourns in the New World. The rapid growth of labor migration toward the turn of the century was associated with the shift in the source areas of European emigration. Many Irish and many southern Europeans viewed migration to the United States as a temporary measure. Only after it became clear that return from a somewhat hostile environment was impossible did the Irish reluctantly interpret their departure from Ireland as an involuntary eviction.

The Irish quarters of the major northeastern seaports and some of the manufacturing towns of New England aroused great concern, even though the vast majority of urban residents lived in cramped and poorly serviced accommodations. Impoverished at the time of their arrival and confined to the most menial occupations in the United States, the Irish were described as intemperate, criminal, disorderly, and immoral. It has been assumed that the Irish were condemned to the slums of their adopted cities for a life term, but it is now clear that they were extremely mobile and moved frequently within the United States in search of employment. Although the movements of the Irish to northeastern cities were more gender balanced than those of southern Europeans, most females sought employment in resident domestic service and most males were itinerant laborers. These gender-divergent employment patterns often created single-parent households and a critical dependence upon networks of friends and relatives. The initial experience of the Irish in the New World was somewhat exceptional among northwest Europeans, but just as the new immigration included some families, the old included some labor migrants.

By the turn of the century these anxieties about the Irish had diminished, and consequently, the social problems of the ghetto were associated with southern and eastern Europeans. Similarly, in the more recent past, the prejudicial judgments about southern and eastern Europeans have been obscured as the social problems of African Americans and Hispanics have been magnified. Some authorities stress profound differences between the experiences of European immigrants and the more recent migrants to the inner city, but in the organization of their movements around the resources of relatives and friends, African Americans and Hispanics have established adaptations to deprivation that have many precedents. Certainly, current concerns about the damaging effects of the gender division of labor on the family patterns of African American migrants resemble early and often insensitive native-born reactions to Irish immigration. High levels of recorded criminal behavior have also supported negative or defamatory interpretations of the ghetto. And, too, the corrupt administration of public services, institutionalized crime, and the prevalence of adolescent gangs offended dominant legal and moral precepts, but they also revealed a highly organized and elaborately regulated pattern of life.

Even those quarters that began as colonies of labor migrants and where the environment of the ghetto exacted its mortal toll eventually established social networks based not only on family and friends but also on ethnic institutions. Some of these institutions were transplantations of long-established, ancestral organizations that were rapidly adapted to meet new demands in an unfamiliar setting. The organizational activities of both secular and religious institutions were not viewed as an appropriate antidote because they tended to delay or obstruct assimilation. These "separatist" developments simply compounded the fears of those who viewed assimilation as conformity to an American Protestant world, but for many immigrants the ghetto served as a "decompression chamber" within which familiar faces and associations mediated the newcomers' encounter with the American city.

The organization of parochial schools, fraternal lodges, and political associations revealed a level of institutional development that was inconsistent with many negative evaluations of the social life of immigrant quarters. The term "urban village" has been coined to describe quarters where economically deprived remnants of these distinctive ethnic subcommunities persisted over several generations. Initially, these positive reports about the social organization of ethnic groups were regarded as exceptions worthy of comment and as scarcely numerous enough to call into question the negative image of the ghetto. Social disorganization and pathological behavior are no longer regarded as unavoidable outcomes of migration to, and prolonged residence in, the inner city slums, and increasingly, ghettos have been described in a fashion that is more sensitive to the adaptations of their residents to their deprivation and discomfort.

THE SPATIAL SETTING
OF THE GHETTO

Just as negative interpretations of the ghetto assumed that the social isolation of segregated quarters compounded the damaging effects of the environment, some revisionist viewpoints have related the social networks and institutional fabric of the ghetto to high levels of residential concentration. In short, both interpretations share a similar view of the spatial setting of the ghetto. From the negative perspective, residential dispersal would substitute the elevating influences of American society for the contagious moral degradation of the ghetto. From the opposing viewpoint, this process would undermine ethnic communities. These assumptions about the degree to which immigrants were segregated in ethnically homogeneous inner-city quarters have also been qualified. During the period when the term "ghetto" was first applied to immigrant quarters, the majority of newcomers did live in congested quarters bordering on the central business district or specialized industrial areas. The threatened expansion of business activities into adjacent residential areas had resulted in their abandonment by upwardly mobile families, but the rate of abandonment was quite varied. Accordingly, most immigrant groups settled in several relatively small districts that they

shared with at least one other group, while quite different nationalities often dominated the intervening areas. Industrial areas were often located on the edge of large cities, or they formed the nucleus of new urban settlements; under these circumstances, more homogeneous ethnic quarters were often established in new, hastily built housing.

At times, the rate of immigration greatly exceeded the supply of available housing, and despite extremely high levels of overcrowding, some immigrants were forced to seek housing in many parts of the city. This problem was especially severe during the middle decades of the 19th century, when the first major wave of mass immigration greatly exceeded the available housing in both the northeastern seaports and the newly established cities of the Middle West. Some Irish and German immigrants did concentrate in congested housing near the waterfront and warehouses, but the rate at which established Americans vacated these neighborhoods was much too slow to provide accommodation for newcomers who quickly accounted for a third or more of urban populations. Although existing dwellings were hastily converted into multifamily tenements and their grounds were filled with cheap new structures, these developments could not meet the rapidly growing demand. Many immigrants were forced to settle in shantytowns on the edge of the city, like migrants to the cities of the less-developed world today. Others clustered on poorly drained, filled land vacated by those who were able to afford more desirable sites.

In mid-19th-century cities the small-scale and scattered locations of much urban employment also diminished the degree of immigrant concentration. Many immigrants were involved in the direct service of wealthy families or small proprietors and lived where they worked, in the homes or shops of their employers. German immigrants to mid-19th-century cities were on the whole better represented in the petty proprietary artisanal occupations. They moved to newly settled parts of the Middle West and were especially prominent in the ports of the Great Lakes and the river towns of the Ohio valley. Here, in the absence of a large preexisting housing stock, they formed somewhat more extensive ethnic settlements than in the Northeast. In Milwaukee, for example, the Germans were usually more strongly concentrated than were the Irish but were also scattered in several clusters rather than in one district. Substantial numbers of those in the service and food trades were to be found mixed in with their Irish and native-born clienteles. Only toward the end of the 19th century, when employment was more abundantly available in the adjacent sections of the central business district, did centrally located immigrant quarters house the majority of newcomers, who were increasingly drawn from southern and eastern Europe.

Although the expansion of the central business district blighted and diminished the supply of inner-city housing, it was also a major source of employment for new immigrants. Despite the substandard housing, residence close to the abundant and diverse employment opportunities of the central business district offered advantages unavailable in more desirable residential areas. Immigrant employment was often insecure and seasonal, and it usually entailed long and awkward working hours for which neither the schedules nor the routes of the emerging city streetcar systems were appropriate. Because the growth of the central business

district was often spasmodic and different land uses expanded at varying rates, long-lived immigrant settlements were maintained on stable margins. Indeed, some groups were able to settle near those sections of the business district that provided the bulk of their employment. In most northeastern and midwestern cities, the most striking examples of this relationship were the proximity of Russian Jews to the clothing workshops and Italians to the fresh food markets.

The effects of this selective expansion of the central business district and the cumulative consequences of two major waves of immigration were especially striking in Boston (fig. 13.6). During the middle decades of the 19th century, the Irish had settled in many sections of the city, including the northern and southern margins of the central business district. The expansion of commercial facilities rapidly displaced the Irish from the southern edge of the business district, but the northward expansion of business was extremely modest, and the Irish settlement there persisted to the end of the 19th century. By 1905, the Irish were abandoning

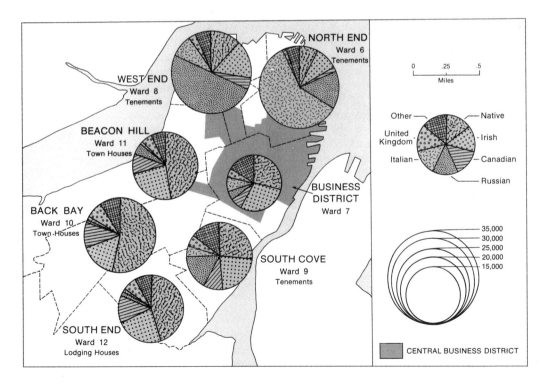

Figure 13.6 Immigrants in the Inner City: Boston, 1905

the North End and other sections of the inner city of Boston to newly arrived Russian Jews and southern Italians. Italians were rapidly becoming the predominant group in the North End and in East Boston, while Russian Jews concentrated in the West End and to a lesser degree in the South End (fig. 13.6). Nevertheless, both the North and West Ends continued to house not only residual Irish populations but also modest proportions of other immigrant groups, while in the South End no one ethnic group predominated.

Moreover, immigrant settlement in the inner city did not form a complete zone around the central business district, because in Beacon Hill and Back Bay an affluent population of native parentage still prevailed. In these districts, immigrants were highly dispersed since they provided resident domestic service and local services. This mosaic of ethnic residence was not confined to the inner city. Newcomers as well as longer-established immigrants also concentrated in Roxbury, at that time considered to be an inner suburb. The leading ethnic institutions and amenities were usually associated with the largest and often earliest concentrations of particular groups, and while these quarters were usually identified as the ghetto, they housed only a minority of each group. These fragmented and complex residential patterns resulted from the uneven availability of cheap housing near appropriate sources of employment at the time of initial settlement.

Although the movement of Puerto Ricans to New York and other northeastern cities did not reach large proportions until after World War II, the settlement of Mexicans in the cities of southern California and the Southwest increased substantially in the 1920s, as did that of southern-born African Americans in northeastern and midwestern cities. Mexicans encountered relatively small concentrations of European ethnic groups, but like East Asians, they tended to be segregated in small but extremely homogeneous districts. African Americans were initially unable to compete with European immigrants for quarters near the central business districts of northeastern and midwestern cities. Prior to World War I, they had settled in the back alleys and rear lots of substantial dwellings, as they had for generations in southern cities. This somewhat dispersed and decidedly limited supply of housing proved to be inadequate for the increased flow of migrants during World War I. Confronted with a densely occupied inner city and an increasingly racist housing market, African Americans were forced to settle in those sections of the inner suburbs where speculative overbuilding had created a supply of vacant middle-income housing suitable for subdivision. New York's Harlem, Boston's Roxbury, and Chicago's South Side all indicate the degree to which the initial foci of African American ghettos were established beyond the outer fringes of the inner-city settlements of European immigrants.

After World War I, further increases in the cityward movement of southern African Americans transformed these small nuclei into ghettos that became more extensive and more enduring than any of the earlier concentrations of European immigrants. Similarly, with the expansion of migration from Mexico, extensive and exclusive Hispanic settlements described as barrios developed in cities of the Southwest and southern California. These developments created an extent and level of residential segregation unprecedented among European immigrants, and distinctions among European ethnic groups appeared to be of minor consequence when compared with those between African American, Hispanic, and white. The suburban dispersal of the descendants of European immigrants and their presumed assimilation into a homogeneous, but white, American society further emphasized these new distinctions. The more recent minorities of the inner city have encountered many obstructions in their efforts to follow the suburban course of their predecessors. While it is clear that the ghettos formed after 1920 have proven to be more extensive and persistent than earlier concentrations, the presumed relationships between suburbanization, social mobility, and assimilation of the former residents of the inner city have been questioned.

SUBURBANIZATION AND ASSIMILATION

Although the social problems of the slum and the ghetto were often simplified or exaggerated, suburbanization facilitated efforts to alleviate the environmental disabilities of the inner city. Despite the modest impact of public intervention on living conditions in the inner city, suburbs by the late 19th century appeared to provide a partial solution to the housing problem for a progressively larger proportion of the urban population. From this perspective, the ghetto could be viewed as the temporary residential quarters of newly arrived immigrants, from which they or their immediate descendants would eventually disperse into the growing suburbs. Since suburban populations were presumed to be defined by social and economic status and stage in the life cycle rather than by ethnic heritage, social and residential mobility was associated with final assimilation into American society. Certainly, revised positive interpretations of the social world of the ghetto were more consistent with assumptions about the material advancement and suburbanization of immigrants and their descendants than the ones that stressed the pathological social consequences of the ghetto environment.

While levels of residential segregation among most of the descendants of European immigrants were lower than those of their migrant ancestors, these changes do not necessarily record a simple trajectory from inner-city ghetto to integrated suburb. Modest proportions of some groups retained some sections of their original ethnic quarters, and the dispersed larger community continued to patronize the long-established ethnic institutions and amenities there. Suburban movements did not always take the form of dispersal from an inner-city concentration but occurred in the form of a contiguous wedgelike expansion in one or two well-defined directions. Eventually the inner margins of this wedge were abandoned, and among highly mobile groups a completely suburban residential pattern was established. Under these circumstances, new suburban foci of ethnic institutions were developed, and today they are frequently as closely associated with the ethnic heritage of their clientele as were their original inner-city quarters. Although the original ethnic communities of the inner city were based upon an overlapping mosaic of neighborhoods, the ethnic associations and networks that serve the needs of suburban residents were not necessarily dependent upon high levels of residential concentration. Ethnicity may thus have had a diminishing influence upon suburban residential differentiation, but some ethnic identities and associations persisted despite suburbanization.

If diminished levels of residential segregation have been viewed as measures of suburban dispersal and, by inference, of assimilation, in many cities both the rates and the dimensions of these changes were quite modest. In contrast, suburbanization involved dramatic improvements in the quality of the living environment and in access to avenues of occupational mobility. From this perspective the experiences of immigrants and especially their descendants have been envisaged as a set of escalators on which the rate of advancement varied from group to group. In general, it was assumed that the course of upward advancement followed an almost natural or inevitable order, in which long-established groups were expected to hold the most remunerative and desirable occupations and newly arrived migrants the least secure and lowest-paid jobs. In short, with each successive wave of immigration, the ethnic division of labor was altered as newcomers entered the lowest strata of the labor force and the descendants of earlier immigrants moved on to more rewarding positions. While many, perhaps the majority, of newcomers initially worked in unpleasant and poorly rewarded jobs, they assumed they would return to their homeland with their accumulated savings or that they or their children would eventually gain access to more remunerative employment. In each phase of immigration some newcomers were able to avoid the lower floors, while others were condemned to prolonged residence on the ground floor long after the arrival of more recent immigrants.

In many respects, a preoccupation with the environmental deficiencies and social isolation of the ghetto and the slum has obscured the degree to which the fluidity or rigidity of the ethnic division of labor influenced the material predicament and residential patterns of the most-deprived minority groups. The damaging effects of inner-city life varied considerably among diverse residents, and both the environmental and spatial attributes of ghettos have been reinterpreted in a fashion that is more sensitive to the positive adaptations of their residents. Nevertheless, these adaptations were strained beyond their limits whenever deliberate exclusion or depressed economic conditions blocked access to avenues of economic advancement. Today, levels of residential segregation among African Americans and some

Hispanics are far higher and more persistent than they were among the migrant generation of European groups. The inner city today is more isolated not only from the remainder of urban society but also from the increasingly decentralized urban employment opportunities than it was during the era of European immigration. The boundary between the inner city and the suburb has for long been the graphic expression of apparently temporary blockages in the process of social mobility. During the 1890s these obstructions presented a more permanent look and aroused anxieties about the impact of the "new" immigration, and today similar concerns about impoverished minorities have provoked questions about the desirability of immigration.

REGIONS AND CITIES
IN A PLURAL SOCIETY

Despite the proverbial geographical mobility of Americans and the loss of many overt ethnic traits among the children of immigrants, the regional destinations of the immigrant generation have proved to be quite persistent. Certainly, many of the descendants of northwest European immigrants have joined those with a longer American ancestry in the movement to the Pacific Coast. By far the most conspicuous change in the distribution of ethnic groups has been the movement of African Americans to the cities of the Northeast and Middle West. Overall, however, the regional representations of different ethnic groups have resulted from an incremental process of migration of varying volume and composition. Regional destinations were often established on the basis of new opportunities; occasionally they were the unavoidable outcome of pressures to emigrate. Networks of information and family ties often reinforced these initial patterns of settlement.

The cities of each major region also displayed variable ethnic profiles, but for each major phase of immigration certain general observations about ethnic residential patterns may be made. The term "ghetto" was used to describe the common disabilities of immigrant quarters. This negative view, however, has been substantially modified, as have interpretations of the suburban movement as a process of rapid assimilation. Emigration certainly profoundly altered the ancestral cultures of most American immigrants, but these changes were already under way before their departure. Moreover, while these alterations were often in the direction of a single, well-defined national culture, some aspects of ethnic identity were voluntarily redefined or preserved through discrimination. This persistent, if changing, pluralism of American society is directly derived not only from the complex composition of several major phases of migration but also from the varied geographic consequences of each migration flow.

ADDITIONAL READING

Barton, J. J. 1975. *Peasants and Strangers: Italians, Roumanians, and Slovaks in an American City, 1890–1950.* Cambridge: Harvard University Press.

Borchert, J. 1980. *Alley Life in Washington: Community, Religion, and Folklore in the City, 1850–1970.* Urbana: University of Illinois Press.

Conzen, K. N. 1976. *Immigrant Milwaukee, 1836–1860: Accommodation and Community in a Frontier City.* Cambridge: Harvard University Press.

Glazer, N., and D. P. Moynihan. 1970. *Beyond the Melting Pot.* Cambridge: MIT Press.

Golab, C. 1977. *Immigrant Destinations.* Philadelphia: Temple University Press.

Gordon, M. M. 1964. *Assimilation in American Life.* New York: Oxford University Press.

Groves, P. A., and E. K. Muller. 1975. "The Evolution of Black Residential Areas in Late-19th-Century Cities." *Journal of Historical Geography* 1: 169–92.

Hershberg, T., et al. 1979. "A Tale of Three Cities: Blacks and Immigrants in Philadelphia, 1850–1880, and 1970." *Annals of the Academy of Political and Social Science* 441: 55–81.

Higham, J. 1955. *Strangers in the Land: Patterns of American Nativism, 1860–1925.* New Brunswick: Rutgers University Press.

Philpott, T. 1978. *The Slum and the Ghetto: Neighborhood Deterioration and Middle-Class Reform in Chicago, 1880–1930.* New York: Oxford University Press.

Piore, M. J. 1979. *Birds of Passage: Migrant Labor and Industrial Societies.* New York: Cambridge University Press.

Smith, T. L. 1978. "Religion and Ethnicity in America." *American Historical Review* 83: 1155–85.

Steinberg, S. 1981. *The Ethnic Myth: Race and Ethnicity and Class in America.* New York: Atheneum.

Taylor, P. 1971. *The Distant Magnet: European Emigration to the United States.* New York: Harper & Row.

Thernstrom, S. B. 1978. *The Other Bostonians: Poverty and Progress in the American Metropolis, 1860–1970.* Cambridge: Harvard University Press.

———, ed. 1982. *The Harvard Encyclopedia of American Ethnic Groups.* Cambridge: Harvard University Press, Belknap Press.

Ward, D. 1971. *Cities and Immigrants: A Geography of Change in 19th-Century America.* New York: Oxford University Press.

———. 1982. "The Ethnic Ghetto in the United States: Past and Present." *Transactions of the Institute of British Geographers* 7: 257–75.

———. 1989. *Poverty, Ethnicity, and the American City, 1840–1925: Changing Conceptions of the Slum and the Ghetto.* Cambridge: Cambridge University Press.

Yancey, W. L., et al. 1976. "Emergent Ethnicity: A Review and Reformulation." *American Sociological Review* 41: 391–403.

Zunz, O. 1982. *The Changing Face of Inequality: Urbanization, Industrial Development, and Immigrants in Detroit, 1880–1920.* Chicago: University of Chicago Press.

14

The National Integration of Regional Economies, 1860–1920

DAVID R. MEYER

The national economy transformed from a set of regional economies with low levels of interchange in 1860 to a continental set of integrated regions by 1920, but much of this shift had occurred by 1890. The South struggled as its cotton areas declined, even as settlement west of the Mississippi River added new regions of resource production, including cotton. These new supplies competed with output of older regions as wholesalers and commodity firms took advantage of improvements in transportation and communication to forge a national market in agricultural, lumber, and mineral commodities. Therefore, regional producers specialized in commodities in which they had competitive advantages; those could include market access or quality of natural resource endowment. Manufacturers who predominantly utilized raw materials in production gained access to low-cost inputs and could ship their outputs to other regions. Some manufacturers who produced high-value, low-bulk goods achieved economies of scale, such as through greater use of machinery. A select number of these firms created innovative management organizations that exploited the increased efficiency of transportation and communication media to dominate national markets. The twin trends of aggregate growth within each region and enhanced specialization of regions spurred demands for improvements in transportation and communication. Nevertheless, heightened regional integration and increased specialization did not operate in a simple circular and cumulative cycle. Transportation and communication costs fell erratically, and intraregional changes, including innovations in production, accumulation of capital, and learning by doing could boost supply and lower prices; that, in turn, caused shifts in the flows of natural resources and manufactures among regions.

The American economy had unique advantages compared to that of other nations at this time, because it offered a continental-scale, free-trade zone that economic actors could access to purchase inputs and market products. Their actions powered prodigious economic growth; the following indices (beginning with 1870, except for mining, which begins with 1880) indicate the scope of this change. Population grew by 2.7 times, but the economy as a whole (gross national product) surged by 7.4 times, measured in constant dollars. Per capita gross national product, consequently, rose by 2.5 times, giving Americans more resources to purchase a wider array of goods. Farm and lumber output increased 3.0 and 2.7 times, respectively, roughly equal to population growth. However, mineral output jumped 7.3 times, and manufactures surged 7.7 times. The enormous growth of these two sectors reflected structural change in the economy from agriculture to industry. An analysis of changes in the integrating mechanisms of transportation and communication provides a lens to view the evolution of regional specialization in agriculture, lumbering, mining, and manufacturing; the core-periphery organization of the national economy culminated from these specializations.

REGIONAL ECONOMIES IN 1860

Most regional economies lay east of the Mississippi River in 1860; they had a moderate level of integration with each other. Each region had a metropolis with financiers and wholesalers who dominated economic exchange with a surrounding hinterland. These intermediaries of capital controlled both intraregional trade and the limited amount of interregional trade. Eastern regions were becoming significant markets for midwestern agriculture, especially meat, wheat, and corn. The East supplied approximately equal volumes of manufactures to the Middle West and South, but the most rapidly growing part of this trade was to the Middle West. An unknown share of this trade was made up of foreign manufactures; southern trade probably had a higher share from foreign producers. Southern cotton moved to northern and foreign markets.

Orientation of midwestern trade to the East had solidified by 1860. Long-distance, efficient connections via one through mode did not exist yet, but combinations of railroad and water (lake, river, and canal) transport bound both regions. By the 1850s, massive quantities of midwestern agricultural produce moved eastward on the Erie Canal, but railroads emerged simultaneously to compete with eastern canals. They also redirected trade away from the Ohio-Mississippi River route and its New Orleans outlet. By the early 1850s, five major railroads reached from the East to the border of the Middle West: the Pennsylvania to Pittsburgh; the Baltimore and Ohio to the Ohio River; the New York Central and New York and Erie Railroads to Lake Erie; and the Northern Railroad and Vermont Central from Boston to Ogdensburg, New York, at the east end of Lake Ontario. Within the Middle West, extensive networks of railroads were constructed during the 1850s that focused on each of the regional metropolises of Cleveland, Detroit, Cincinnati, Milwaukee, Chicago, and St. Louis, but a few lines also linked these metropolises with each other by 1860 (fig. 14.1).

Therefore, by 1860, the United States stood at an early stage in the emergence of a continental space economy. Interregional trade within both the East and the Middle West rose, and trade between these two sections swelled. Eastern metropolises, especially New York, and the burgeoning western metropolis of San Francisco, which served the Pacific Coast mining communities, had a tenuous long-distance bond by ocean. The eastern links of Portland and its Oregon hinterland passed through San Francisco. Gold miners and fur traders in the Rockies had connections with the Middle West and the East through metropolises such as St. Louis, but these links remained small scale. In 1860, for example, Colorado housed only 34,000 people, and farm and ranch expansion into the Great Plains had just begun. On this base of growing interregional trade came major changes in transportation (railroad) and in communications (mail and telegraph), which helped forge a highly integrated national space economy by the end of the century.

TRANSPORTATION AND COMMUNICATION CHANGES

The railroad justly deserves its status as the pivotal integrator of the national space economy between 1860 and 1920 and as a key component of late-19th-century economic growth. Although commodities moved by rail throughout the East and Middle West in 1860, the 30,626 miles of track did not make up an integrated network (fig. 14.1). The standard gauge (4 feet 8 1/2 inches) existed on only about half of the track. Therefore, most freight carried by major eastern railroads, such as the New York Central, Pennsylvania, and Baltimore and Ohio, did not travel beyond their respective lines. Incompatible gauges and lack of bridge crossings at major rivers, such as the Ohio and the Mississippi, hindered long-distance, continuous connections between the East and the Middle West. Railroads within the South also used different gauges, and few north-south lines existed. Gauge differences and gaps in the network added high transshipment costs to railroad use.

This loosely coordinated railroad network altered substantially during the 30 years following 1860. Increases in through freight and improvements in the network reinforced each other over time. During the 1860s, difficulties of transporting Civil War troops and supplies focused attention on the lack of a coordinated network and led to federal pressure for change. Congress legislated the use of the standard gauge on transcontinental railroads, reinforcing its demands for rail network integration. The growth of the grain trade stimulated demands for integration that would lower costs to move midwestern grain to eastern markets and transshipment ports for export. By 1880 about 81 percent of the railroad mileage was standard gauge, a sharp rise over the 1861 proportion of 53 percent. That jump, coupled with the fact that railroad mileage in 1880 was triple that in 1861, represented a vast addition to standard-gauge mileage; by 1890, almost all track had that gauge.

The enormous growth in railroad track mileage effectively bound all parts of the nation by 1890. Little new track was added during the Civil War, but within the short span of nine years (1866–75) the rail net doubled from 36,801 to 74,096 miles. The map of railroad lines in 1880 (fig. 14.2) exhibits the blanketing of the eastern half of the nation by railroads, and the West Coast had two links, the Union Pacific–Central Pacific and the Southern Pacific, to the Middle West. By 1887 the rail net had doubled again to 149,214 miles, and by 1920 it had reached 259,941 miles, within 1,000 miles of the maximum mileage of the 20th century.

Construction concentrated in three boom pe-
riods during the 30 years after the Civil War (table 14.1). During the initial period, 1868–73, completion of the first transcontinental railroad provided a dramatic event when the Central Pacific and Union Pacific lines met at Ogden, Utah, in 1869. The West obtained almost half of the new railroad track as extensive construction served the growing number of farms in the

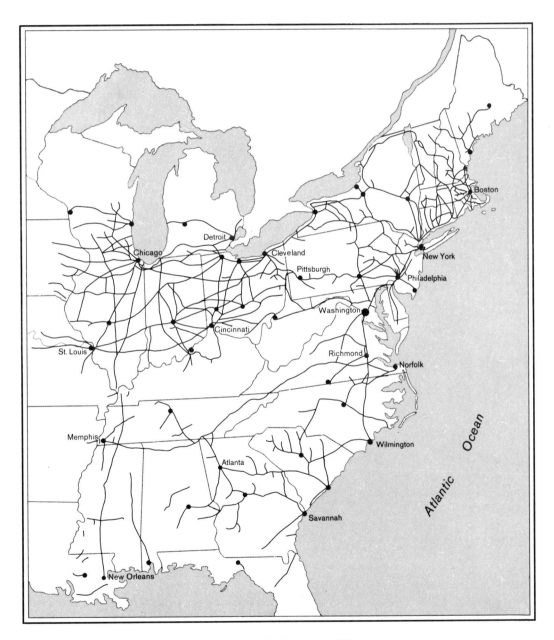

Figure 14.1 Railroads in 1860

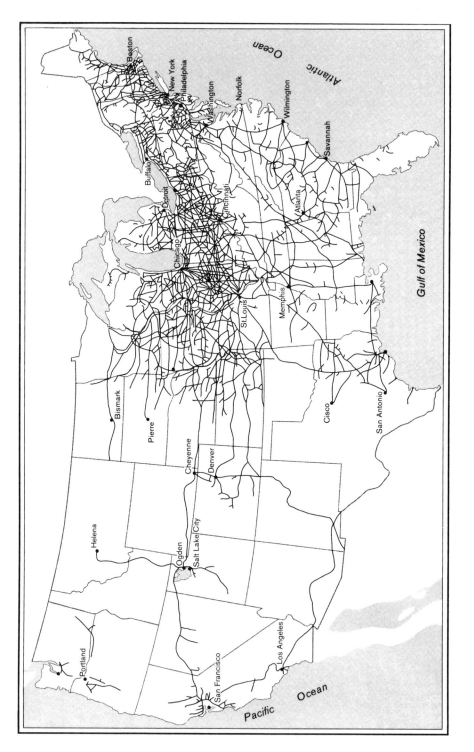

Figure 14.2 Railroads in 1880

Great Plains. Total numbers of farms in North and South Dakota, Nebraska, and Kansas quadrupled from 13,000 in 1860 to 52,000 in 1870 and then quadrupled again to 220,000 in 1880. The second period, 1879–83, witnessed even greater railroad expansion on the Great Plains. Numerous new routes connected the Plains and the Pacific Coast, and when European demand for grain and meat surged after 1879, railroads provided low-cost transportation from Plains farms to eastern ports, such as New York, Philadelphia, and Baltimore. During the third period, 1886–92, sizable mileage was added in the West, and the South gained the second-highest share. Western expansion of the railroad network dominated during all periods (table 14.1); therefore, by the 1890s the entire West, including the Pacific Coast, was integrated with the rest of the nation. Equally significant, during all periods the rail net intensified in areas of highest population density and earliest agricultural and industrial development—East, Middle West, and South. The South received about half of the new mileage, yet it made up just one-third of the national territory. By 1890 the railroad network linked most places in the nation; subsequent network intensification filled in the interstices.

Technological changes and organizational innovations also boosted railroad efficiency. Steel rails replaced iron rails because they offered greater durability and could withstand heavier loads. More-powerful locomotives and larger freight cars increased train capacity, and a host of inventions, such as the automatic coupler and air brake, improved operations. Organizational innovations, becoming standard during the 1870s and 1880s, effectively coordinated the

growing volume and complexity of traffic. Functional divisions established within railroads handled different responsibilities, and firms revolutionized accounting to organize data on enormous flows of goods. Railroads devised cooperative arrangements to move commodities long distances, such as fast freight and express companies, bills of lading, and car accountant offices. Bills of lading recorded goods, routes, and charges, and each railroad kept a copy. The car accountant office of a railroad monitored its own cars as well as those of competitors on its tracks. Aggressive financiers such as Jay Gould created larger railroad systems and encouraged defensive tactics by other railroads. Two of Gould's competitors, J. Edgar Thomson, president of the Pennsylvania Railroad, and the Vanderbilts, who controlled the New York Central, organized large railroad systems that covered the Middle West and the East. Cornelius Vanderbilt piously criticized railroad speculation by financiers such as Gould; however, Vanderbilt could not resist stock manipulation when the opportunity arose, as when he inflated the number of shares of the New York Central in 1868. By the 1880s, large railroad systems became characteristic of railroad organization throughout the nation.

Expansion of the rail network and technological and organizational innovations combined to make railroads one of the most productive economic sectors in the late 19th century. Between 1870 and 1910, railroad productivity, the change in railroad output (e.g., volume of freight moved) relative to railroad input (including locomotives, cars, and track), rose at an average annual rate of 2.0 percent, compared with 1.5 percent for the economy as a whole. This productivity supported a decline in freight rates from 2.6 cents per ton-mile in 1859 to 0.75 cents in 1910. The vastly expanded railroad network and falling rates stimulated an enormous increase in the amount of goods shipped. The number of ton-miles shipped grew 30-fold from 2.6 billion in 1859 to 80 billion in 1890 and more than tripled again to 255 billion in 1910. These flows contributed to, and were affected by, heightened specialization of regions.

Communication and transportation changes in the late 19th century were inseparable. Communication improvements provided critical control and coordination functions necessary to

Table 14.1 Railroad Mileage Constructed by Region for Selected Periods (percent of total U.S. mileage)

Region	1868–1873	1879–1883	1886–1892
East	21	8	7
Midwest	16	19	15
South	16	13	24
West	47	60	54
Total	100	100	100
No. of miles	24,589	39,553	46,818

move swelling volumes of commodities efficiently over the expanding national transport network. The mail and telegraph served as the long-distance communication media; a national telephone network did not exist until after 1910, two decades after effective integration of the national space economy. The enlarging railroad network became the major carrier of long-distance mail. Concurrent with the growing volume of mail from the 1850s to the 1870s, the post office implemented organizational and operational changes to handle large volumes of long-distance mail shipments with numerous origins and destinations. From its inception in the 1840s, the telegraph became a nationwide system along with the railroad, as telegraph lines were strung along railroad rights-of-way and the railroad used them to coordinate trains. By the mid-1860s, the telegraph provided instantaneous nationwide communication for business, and by 1866 Western Union had formed as the first national multiunit company in the United States. The first long-distance telephone lines, on the other hand, did not enter service until the late 1880s, and an extensive network east of the Mississippi River did not exist until at least 1907. The long-distance network finally reached Denver in 1910 and San Francisco in 1915. Therefore, the telephone did not play a significant part in the rise of a national space economy. Improvements in mail and the telegraph enabled firms to control and coordinate exchange with each other and within each firm. Reductions in time to transport commodities and to communicate information diminished the relative amount of goods held in transit and in inventory. Firms gained wider access to information to make business decisions and to respond rapidly to business problems. These improvements lowered costs for the entire economy and facilitated greater regional specialization of production.

REGIONAL SPECIALIZATION

Regional specialization in production is the domestic equivalent of the principle of comparative advantage, which helps explain specialization and trade among nations. A region specializes in production of those commodities in which it has the greatest relative efficiency. Some of this output is usually consumed within the region that produces it, but export of the commodity to other regions forms the basis of specialization. Regions change their specialization as new regions enter production of a commodity; thus, earlier-settled regions may have to change specialties. This dynamic process operated vigorously between 1860 and 1890 because new regions entered the production of commodities with access to national markets via transportation and communication improvements. Emerging specializations in agriculture, lumbering, mining, and manufacturing proceeded at different rates.

Agriculture

Agricultural products are bulky, heavy, and low in value relative to their weight; therefore, transport cost reductions after 1860 lengthened shipping distances markedly. Decline of railroad transport costs in the 50 years following 1860 meant that biophysical conditions, especially soil, slope, and climate, increased in significance. Regions with favorable environmental conditions for a given crop produced it at lower cost than less favorably endowed regions, even if the former faced longer distances to markets than the latter. A region near the market and favorably endowed environmentally had both advantages. Although transport costs declined, they remained salient; therefore, regional specialization of agriculture that emerged after 1860 reflected both the effect of distance and the enhanced significance of biophysical conditions.

In 1860, regional agricultural specialization remained limited. Environmental factors dominated in the location of cotton in the South; cotton requires a long growing season (200 frost-free days or more) and a moist spring and summer followed by a dry, cool autumn. Greater output of wheat, corn, cattle, and hogs in the Middle West during the 1840s for shipment to the East had some environmental bases. Flat, rich soils of midwestern farms produced crops at lower cost per acre than hilly eastern farms, whose soils in many places also suffered from degradation. This regional specialization had restricted scope; only one-third of the national territory had entered production. Corn farmers concentrated somewhat more in the Middle West, but numerous farmers grew corn in the East and South. Large numbers of farmers grew wheat in the East, although few grew it in the South. Cattle raising stayed ubiquitous, except for a concentration in eastern Texas. Distance from eastern markets chiefly determined midwestern specialties. Low land costs and large farms gave wheat growers in the Middle West a competitive advantage over those in the East. In 1860, the typical midwestern farm had 140 acres, 30 percent more than the 108-acre eastern farm, and could make greater use of machinery to produce low-cost wheat. Corn, cattle, and hog farming also responded to distance from market. Farmers fed corn to hogs and a variety of grains to cattle; they shipped meat to market in salted form or drove animals to market. Meat, as well as corn in the form of whiskey, had high value per unit weight; thus, they withstood long-distance transport. However, agricultural settlement was limited west of the Mississippi, and long-distance transport costs of low-value, bulky products still remained high as of 1860. These factors restrained regional specialization, but that changed over the next three decades.

By the 1920s, regional agricultural specialization had altered dramatically (fig. 14.3). The continental United States comprised broad regions of specialized agriculture, which had mostly emerged by the 1890s and stayed remarkably intact throughout the 20th century. There were two major exceptions: the demise of the traditional Cotton Belt in the Piedmont of the Carolinas, Georgia, and Alabama; and the introduction of soybeans, especially to midwestern agriculture. East of the Mississippi River, recently settled areas of the Middle West had large increases in improved acreage, while earlier-settled areas there also added farmland (table 14.2). Sparsely farmed areas in Minnesota, Iowa, Missouri, the Willamette valley in Oregon, and the Central Valley and selected coastal areas in California also experienced large expansions of improved farmland. In the 1870s, new areas of expansion in the previous decade added substantial amounts of farmland, while older-settled midwestern areas added less. The new lands of the 1870s were in the eastern Great Plains, and these areas, along with California's Central Valley, continued to add farmland during the 1880s. Large areas also came under cultivation for the first time: the Red River valley of North Dakota and Minnesota; the eastern third of the Dakotas; western Nebraska and Kansas; eastern Washington; and southern California near Los Angeles. Most increases in farmland during the 1890s occurred in the eastern Great Plains and in eastern Washington, whereas the western Plains added most of the new farmland following 1900. Except for arid portions of the western Great Plains, most agricultural lands that defined the emerging regional specialization were farmed by 1890.

As the Middle West and West added agricultural lands after 1860, other lands in the East and South were withdrawn from cultivation; however, these withdrawals stayed small before 1890 (table 14.2). During the 1860s, parts of southern New England experienced a decline in cultivated land, a continuation of antebellum trends. The southern Piedmont also declined significantly, but this probably resulted from Civil War dislocation. In the following decade, additions to cultivated lands in other areas roughly balanced the declining agricultural

Table 14.2 Change in Improved Farmland, 1860–1920

U.S. Census Region	Number of Acres (millions)			Percent Change	
	1860	1890	1920	1860–1890	1890–1920
New England	12.2	10.7	6.1	(12.3)	(43.0)
Middle Atlantic	26.8	31.6	26.6	17.9	(15.8)
East North Central	41.2	78.8	87.9	91.3	11.5
West North Central	11.1	105.5	171.4	850.5	62.5
South Atlantic	34.9	41.7	48.5	19.5	16.3
East South Central	25.9	35.7	44.4	37.8	24.4
West South Central	7.3	30.6	64.2	319.2	109.8
Mountain	0.2	5.5	30.1	2,650.0	447.3
Pacific	3.4	17.6	23.9	417.6	35.8
Total United States	163.1	357.6	503.1	119.3	40.7

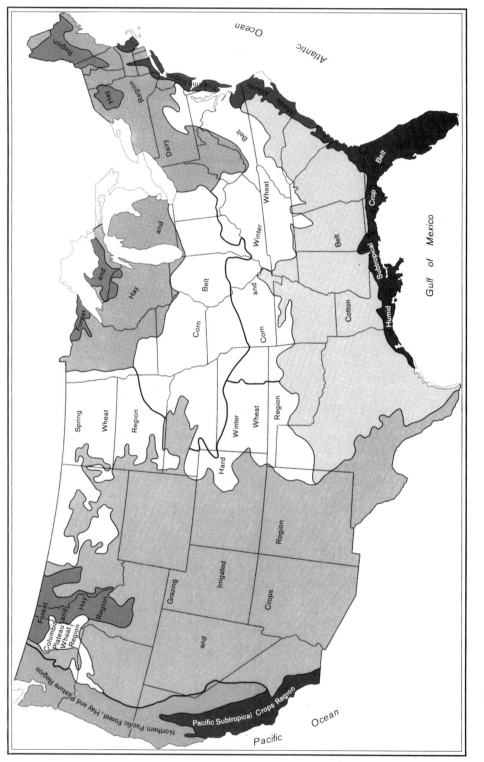

Figure 14.3 Agricultural Regions in 1920. Almost the entire eastern seaboard is included in the Fruit and Vegetable Belt.

lands of the southern Piedmont. A similar balance existed in New England: the northern half declined, while the southern half reversed course and added agricultural land. Beginning in the 1880s, declines in agricultural land became more widespread. In the South only southern Texas had a significant decline, but in the North a broad area from eastern Ohio to New England began to lose agricultural land. In the 1890s the decline in New England agriculture accelerated and New York continued its decline. Substantial quantities of farmland ended production in the arid areas of the Great Plains, especially in Texas. Subsequent decades witnessed a decline in agriculture in the hilly and poor-soil areas of the South, Middle West, and East. Nevertheless, this shrinkage in improved farmland remained modest compared to large increases during the period 1860–1920. Therefore, the emerging regional specialization of agriculture resulted from the addition of previously unexploited areas and a shift in types of agriculture in older farming areas, rather than from large-scale declines in older areas.

Technological change in agricultural machinery had minimal impact on the emergence of specialized agricultural regions, with the important exception of the wheat regions. Basic principles of most agricultural machinery manufactured in the late 19th century were known by 1860. Iron and steel plows and harrows for tilling the soil, reapers and other harvesters for cutting grain, and threshers for separating grain from the rest of the plant boosted labor productivity. Cotton picking remained hand labor. Improved farm machinery permitted the operation of larger farms by a given number of workers, but this had little direct impact on regional specialization in the areas of the Middle West and East settled by 1860. The Middle West already had specialized in corn and wheat, and new machinery mostly opened drylands to wheat farming. Low yields per acre meant that economical farms had to be large, but farming large acreage required machinery.

The most important specialized wheat regions entered production by 1890 (table 14.3 and fig. 14.3). They emerged through successive advancing waves, consolidations, and retreats, stimulated by rising domestic demand, fluctuating foreign demand, and drought. The Spring Wheat Belt emerged in the expansion of 1878–85 in the

Table 14.3 Leading Wheat and Corn States, 1860–1900

1860	1870	1880	1890	1900
Leading Wheat States				
Illinois	Illinois	Illinois	Minnesota	Minnesota
Indiana	Iowa	Indiana	California	North Dakota
Wisconsin	Ohio	Ohio	Illinois	Ohio
Ohio	Indiana	Michigan	Indiana	South Dakota
Virginia	Wisconsin	Minnesota	Ohio	Kansas
Pennsylvania	Pennsylvania	Iowa	Kansas	California
56%	56%	53%	50%	49%
Leading Corn States				
Illinois	Illinois	Illinois	Iowa	Illinois
Ohio	Iowa	Iowa	Illinois	Iowa
Missouri	Ohio	Missouri	Kansas	Kansas
Indiana	Missouri	Indiana	Nebraska	Nebraska
Kentucky	Indiana	Ohio	Missouri	Missouri
Tennessee	Kentucky	Kansas	Ohio	Indiana
Iowa	Tennessee	Kentucky	Indiana	Ohio
Virginia	Pennsylvania	Nebraska	Kentucky	Texas
Alabama	Texas	Tennessee	Texas	Kentucky
Georgia	Alabama	Pennsylvania	Tennessee	Oklahoma
71%	72%	79%	81%	76%

Note: Percentages indicate proportion of total production accounted for by the listed states.

Red River valley of the eastern Dakotas and western Minnesota, and a second wave, 1913–16, expanded the region into the western Dakotas and eastern Montana, displacing cattle ranching. The Kansas portion of the Winter Wheat Belt and the Columbia Plateau wheat region also formed by 1890. At that time, the Central Valley of California had become a major wheat producer; it expanded initially in the 1870s and had diversified by 1910. The emergence of these wheat regions remained integrally bound to the expanding railroad network. In addition to the transcontinental railroads, an elaborate network of westward-branching railroads reached into the eastern margins of the Great Plains by 1880 (fig. 14.2). They connected to the termini of Minneapolis, Kansas City, and Chicago, which, in turn, linked to East Coast metropolises.

In the Plains, only large-scale wheat farms were profitable; typical farms reached sizes of 150 to 200 acres by the 1880s. Some farms in the Red River valley and California's Central Valley, termed "bonanza farms," reached 1,000 acres or more, and a few in North Dakota were 25,000 to 100,000 acres. Financed by external investors, these farms had corporate organizations, precursors of 20th-century corporate farms. Large cattle ranches preceded these huge farms 10 to 20 years earlier, but the crop planting of the bonanza wheat farms reached impressive proportions with large plows, reapers, and threshers. Although the portable steam-powered thresher was invented before 1860, the rise of the specialized wheat regions gave a major impetus to its adoption. These threshers became common features in all wheat regions by 1880, and bonanza farms were their principal users.

The internal homogeneity of the specialized wheat regions that emerged between 1860 and 1890 made them unusual in American agriculture; other regions had more diverse agriculture because moister climates permitted a wider variety of crops. Before 1890 older wheat-growing areas in the Middle West and East did not decline in absolute terms, but they declined relatively as new specialized regions supplied net additions to domestic and foreign demand. As late as 1890, Illinois, Indiana, and Ohio stayed among the nation's six leading wheat states, but by 1900 only Ohio remained in that group (table 14.3).

Cattle and sheep raising also were established

throughout the West by 1890, but the expanding wheat frontier, continuing a process that began in the 1860s, encroached on the eastern margins of livestock production between 1890 and 1920 (fig. 14.3). Texas stayed the leading cattle state during the period 1860–1920; its cattle population rose from 2.9 million to 6.2 million over that time span. However, as a share of the national total, Texas cattle declined from 17 percent in 1860 to 9 percent in 1920. During the 1880s, cattle ranching spread throughout the western Plains and the Far West, and by 1890 a degree of specialization had arisen. Western ranches bred and raised young calves for shipment by rail to Corn Belt farms in eastern Nebraska, eastern Kansas, Iowa, and Illinois for fattening. Large-scale cattle ranches, a logical adaptation to the need for substantial acreage of arid land to support each animal, became common in the West by the 1870s. Irrigated pasturage, which permitted intensive grazing, developed between 1870 and 1890 along river valleys draining from the Rocky Mountains. By 1890, irrigated acreage totaled 2.7 million, but not all was pasture; major growth in irrigated land came in the following 20 years, and by 1910 the acreage totaled 11.6 million. Cattle are associated typically with the West, yet sheep in the Mountain and Pacific regions actually outnumbered cattle in every state in 1890 and 1920, except Arizona in 1890 (table 14.4). Both sheep and cattle were widely distributed across the Mountain and Pacific regions,

Table 14.4 Number of Cattle and Sheep in the West, 1890 and 1920 (in thousands)

Region	Cattle		Sheep	
	1890	1920	1890	1920
Mountain				
Montana	668	1,269	1,859	2,083
Idaho	192	715	358	2,356
Wyoming	674	875	713	1,860
Colorado	641	1,757	718	1,813
New Mexico	559	1,300	1,249	1,640
Arizona	263	822	102	882
Utah	154	506	1,014	1,692
Nevada	202	356	273	881
Pacific				
Washington	184	573	265	624
Oregon	406	851	1,780	2,002
California	1,050	2,008	2,475	2,400
West total	4,994	11,031	10,807	18,233

with the exception of arid areas of Arizona and Nevada and of heavily forested areas of Oregon and Washington. High prices made sheep profitable during the period 1860–1920, and they could tolerate short grasses, cold weather, and semiarid conditions in the Rocky Mountains and bordering areas.

The rise of the Corn Belt (fig. 14.3) between 1860 and 1890 had integral bonds with westward expansion of wheat and growth of western cattle ranching. Corn is a superior feed for cattle and hogs, and the emerging Corn Belt had ideal conditions for growing corn—fertile soil and warm, humid summers. As national demand for meat rose, demand for corn as feed increased. A combination of large output per acre and high price per bushel made corn more valuable per acre than wheat in the evolving Corn Belt; so it dominated there. Wheat shifted westward to low-cost, drier lands. Corn's westward expansion halted when it reached the approximately 20-inch-per-year rainfall line in the eastern Dakotas and western portions of Nebraska and Kansas. Changes in the top ten corn states from 1860 to 1900 document the emergence of this Corn Belt (table 14.3). In 1860, the four leading states—Illinois, Ohio, Missouri, and Indiana—represented the older core of the region, and southern states, where corn was a traditional human food and animal feed, also remained important corn producers. During subsequent years Iowa, the core of the Corn Belt, rose to its leading position; Kansas and Nebraska joined the ten largest producers during the 1870s and moved rapidly upward in later years. In addition to cattle and hogs bred and raised locally, the Corn Belt specialized in fattening western-bred cattle, a feasible practice only because the railroad provided low-cost transportation from western ranch country. Therefore, the Corn Belt emerged by 1890 as an intermediate link in providing meat for midwestern and eastern urban markets. South of the Corn Belt, an east-west band, loosely termed the "Corn and Winter Wheat Belt," had formed (fig. 14.3). This region had less-fertile soils and hilly topography; consequently, agricultural output per acre stayed lower. The Ozarks of southern Missouri typify this region, which also contained the specialty-tobacco-growing area of Kentucky that accounted for 25 percent of national output in 1860 and 45 percent by 1890.

In contrast to the Corn Belt, the Pacific Coast's specialization in fruits and vegetables for national markets remained in its infancy in 1890, but the base was in place for enormous expansion during the period 1890–1920 (fig. 14.3). Two thousand miles, two mountain ranges, and deserts separated it from the nearest midwestern markets, and East Coast cities were an additional thousand miles away. Not surprisingly, wheat became the first specialty crop grown in the Central Valley of California for nonlocal markets. It moved to those markets by slow ships or followed the one transcontinental railroad link from northern California. The Pacific Coast settlements, whose economies were based on mining, lumbering, cattle ranching, and wheat growing, were the chief markets for fresh fruits and vegetables from 1860 to 1890. During this crucial learning period, farmers grew a wide variety of fruits and vegetables and developed irrigated farms in the 1880s. Two transcontinental railroads were completed by 1880, and within ten years an additional two links became available, so that all sections between the Canadian and Mexican borders had eastern connections. During the 1870s, refrigerated rail cars reached sufficient capabilities to handle transcontinental shipments of perishable fruits and vegetables, thus meeting a crucial requirement for marketing produce outside the Pacific Coast. Coordination of the complex transcontinental production, transportation, and marketing of these perishables required more time, but this problem could not be resolved fully until large shipments were initiated.

Irrigated land in California grew fourfold between 1890 and 1920, and by the latter date 4.2 million acres were irrigated. Farmers grew fruits and vegetables in the Central Valley and in the coastal valleys from San Francisco to San Diego. The state became a leading supplier of winter fruits and vegetables to eastern markets and year-round supplier of a wide range of subtropical fruits grown only in southern California. By the 1920s, California provided one-third of the nation's winter vegetables; two-thirds of its oranges; three-fourths of its grapes, prunes, and figs; and almost all of its lemons, almonds, and apricots. Oregon and Washington contributed small amounts of fruit prior to the mid-1880s, but their production increased following the completion in 1883 of the Northern Pacific Railroad, which linked Puget Sound with Minnesota and the midwestern rail network. By the

1890s, the Pacific Northwest specialized in apples, pears, peaches, and cherries. Irrigated fruit and vegetable agriculture in the Southwest—Arizona and the bordering Imperial Valley of California, and New Mexico—arose after 1890 and had developed only modestly as of 1920.

Southern agriculture continued to rest on climatic advantages of a long growing season and ample rainfall. Florida's subtropical location conferred benefits analogous to those in southern California. After 1890, Florida emerged as a leading citrus area and secondarily as a supplier of winter vegetables to northern markets (fig. 14.3). By 1919 it ranked second to California in citrus fruit production and third by value of vegetables grown. The sugarcane area of Louisiana had been a specialized producer since the 1820s, and following a slow period of recovery after the Civil War, it regained large-volume production during the period 1890–1920. Sugarcane production was always a highly capitalized enterprise consisting of large farms (1,000–3,000 acres), small railroads for moving cane to sugar mills, and large steam-powered refineries on farms. As far back as the 18th century, the Carolina-Georgia tidewater had specialized in rice, but rice growing emerged later along the Gulf Coast. In the 1880s, settlers from the Middle West began irrigated rice farming in a 250-mile band along the southwestern Louisiana and southeastern Texas Gulf Coast. Extensive use of agricultural machinery, combined with ideal soil and climatic conditions, resulted in highly productive rice farms that competed in Asian markets, even though the latter had lower-cost labor. The Cotton Belt became well established by the 1840s, and by 1860 it extended from the Carolinas to eastern Texas and southeastern Arkansas. After 1860 it expanded westward in Texas and northward in Arkansas and, after 1890, into southern Oklahoma; these new lands had richer soils than older cotton-producing areas (fig. 14.3). After 1890, efforts to avoid the advance of the boll weevil encouraged the northward and westward movement of cotton. Export markets took about two-thirds of the steadily growing cotton output in the late 19th century. The lack of a suitable mechanical cotton-picker contributed to maintaining cotton as a labor-intensive crop during the years 1860–1920.

Crystallization of the corn and wheat regions, including their dominance of cattle and hog production, forced adjustments both in older eastern agriculture and in the area from Michigan to eastern Minnesota that had developed between 1840 and 1870. This latter area had a variable combination of cool, humid climate, poor soils, and hilly topography that often precluded efficient use of farm machinery. The East lost its competitiveness in corn, wheat, cattle, and hogs before 1860, and the upper midwestern band of farm counties lost their competitiveness during the next several decades. Adjustments took two forms that had started in the East before 1860: a Dairy Belt emerged across the northern tier of states, and an intensive truck gardening region emerged in the East from Carolina to Boston (fig. 14.3). Throughout both areas large urban demand for milk, vegetables, and dairy products influenced the form of these newer agricultural regions.

The Dairy Belt housed two sets of products with different locational patterns based on transport cost and value. Liquid milk for human consumption is valuable but expensive to transport, whereas butter and cheese have high value per unit weight and transport cost is less important. Following 1860, improvements in milk handling and refrigeration made consumption of fluid milk safer, and perfection of refrigerated railcars after 1870 permitted long-distance transport of dairy products. Fluid milksheds, the hinterlands from which cities acquire their fresh milk, had first emerged within short distances of eastern cities during the 1840s. Growing efficiency and density of the railroad network permitted these milksheds to expand significantly outward from metropolises and industrial cities in the East and Middle West during the 30 years following 1860. Dairy farms near cities produced fluid milk, whereas cheese and butter became a specialty of the dairy farms across the northern tier of states more distant from large cities. An area between central New York State and northeast Ohio specialized in cheese before 1860, and by the 1870s southern Wisconsin also produced cheese for export to eastern markets in refrigerated railcars. By 1890 the Dairy Belt had completed formation and acquired its typical crop pattern of about half of the arable land in hay and pasture for feeding dairy cattle. Pockets of specialized fruit production also arose in the region, especially along the east and south shores of the Great Lakes in locations that provided protection from frost and low winter temperatures. Smaller-scale dairy specialization also arose around all the nation's large cities; for example, even rapidly growing Pacific Coast cities acquired small adjacent dairy areas.

The term "truck gardening," which signifies vegetable production for nearby city markets, evolved as a shorthand phrase after motor-powered wagons were introduced early in the 20th century, but the East Coast vegetable region emerged much earlier in response to demand from burgeoning populations in the metropolises of Boston, New York, Philadelphia, and Baltimore and in numerous small industrial cities surrounding them. The post-1860 growth of the East Coast urban belt, coupled with gradually rising incomes, stimulated demand for vegetables. Improvements in canning during the Civil War spurred output of summer vegetables beyond the immediate needs of summer consumption. When large shipments of fresh vegetables from California and Florida began after 1890, a specialization in fresh vegetables between the East Coast and these other states occurred. California and Florida supplied fresh vegetables to East Coast markets in the winter and spring, while the East Coast supplied summer vegetables. California and Florida provided subtropical fruits and vegetables all year. On the East Coast, vegetable production specialized by area: potatoes in Maine and Long Island, onions in Massachusetts and Connecticut, and tomatoes from New Jersey to Maryland. Farms grew some fruits, such as cranberries in eastern Massachusetts and peaches in southern New Jersey. At a smaller scale all metropolises and large cities in the rest of the nation developed fresh-vegetable zones surrounding them, but none has ever equaled the East Coast region.

Most of the broad pattern of 20th-century regional specialization in agriculture existed by the 1890s; it rested on an 87 percent increase in farm output between 1870 and 1890. During the 30 years following 1890, farm output grew by 63 percent, but this somewhat smaller percentage rise consisted of an enormous absolute increase, because the 1890 base was much larger than the 1870 base. Transportation and communications improvements following 1860 facilitated an emerging regional specialization simultaneously with the entrance of new lands into production. Settlers moved to western agricultural frontiers either because significant local markets for agriculture existed, such as mining

or lumbering areas, or because opportunity existed to produce for the national market. The emergence of new agricultural regions required, in turn, that older regions adjust their agriculture to remain competitive in national markets.

Lumbering

Widespread distribution of forests in the United States, excluding the lightly populated, arid areas of the West, precluded the lumber industry from becoming as regionally specialized as agriculture throughout most of the 1860–1920 period. Specialized lumber districts emerged, but before 1880 firms sold lumber chiefly within the region or in nearby regions. In subsequent years, flows became more prevalent from the Pacific Northwest and the South to deficit areas in the East and Middle West. Because trees take 20 to 30 years, or more, to grow to commercial size, lumbering inevitably depleted this resource; therefore, a consistent theme of the period is the rise and decline of lumber areas (table 14.5).

Maine, New York, and Pennsylvania were major suppliers of eastern lumber prior to 1860, but between 1860 and 1890, with the exception of a few short periods of recovery, Maine and New York declined relatively. However, Pennsylvania, especially the northern Susquehanna River basin, remained nationally prominent (table 14.5). From the 1870s to the mid-1890s, the Great Lakes states of Michigan and Wisconsin became the largest lumber producers; in 1880, they accounted for 29.3 percent of national employment, and they had larger, more heavily capitalized lumber firms than the East had. They first supplied markets in their states, other Great Lakes states, and along the Mississippi River and then supplied an increasing volume of lumber to the East and the Great Plains. A decade or more before the decline following the mid-1890s, Michigan and Wisconsin lumberers purchased timberland on the Pacific Coast and in the South to assure future production.

The Pacific Coast achieved national prominence after 1890. Throughout the 1860–1920 period, its heavily capitalized lumber industry served markets on the West Coast and export markets around the Pacific basin. Rapidly growing markets in California spurred its lumber industry to the lead before 1890. In 1880, California, with 10.2 percent of national employment, stood second nationally to Michigan and far

Table 14.5 Leading Forestry Employment States, 1880–1920

Percent of Total Employment		
1880	1900	1920
20.5 Michigan	9.3 Pennsylvania	11.7 Washington
10.2 California	8.8 Michigan	7.6 Michigan
9.4 Pennsylvania	7.7 Washington	6.8 Minnesota
8.8 Wisconsin	6.1 California	6.5 Wisconsin
5.0 Minnesota	5.5 Wisconsin	5.8 Maine
4 0 New York	4.9 Minnesota	5.1 Oregon
3.0 Maine	4.1 Arkansas	4.0 California
2.6 Missouri	3.9 Louisiana	3.8 Louisiana
2.5 Georgia	3.6 Georgia	3.3 Pennsylvania
2.4 Alabama	3.3 North Carolina	3.1 New York
31.6 all other states	42.8 all other states	42.3 all other states
100.0 total	100.0 total	100.0 total
55,931 employed	140,599 employed	217,378 employed

ahead of the other Pacific Coast states of Oregon and Washington (table 14.5). The redwood lumber industry centered around Humboldt Bay and its city of Eureka in northern California. After 1880 Oregon and Washington grew rapidly as lumber states. Local markets contributed to their growth, as well as the increased demand from California and Pacific basin markets. Completion of the Northern Pacific Railroad in 1883 did not immediately stimulate exports to the East; those shipments were small until the late 1890s, when the Great Lakes lumber industry finally began to decline. By 1900, California had slipped to fourth rank nationally in forestry employment, whereas Washington had surged to third rank; Oregon still did not reach the top ten in employment. Within 20 years Washington had become the nation's leading lumber state and Oregon had moved up to sixth place.

The large expansion of the lumber industry in the South began in the 1880s; before that time, its markets remained local. In 1880, Georgia and Alabama ranked ninth and tenth nationally. Growing markets in the East, whose demands could not be fully met by eastern mills, and the decline of competition from the Great Lakes states after the mid-1890s supported steady growth of southern lumbering that served local, midwestern, and eastern markets. By 1900, Arkansas, Louisiana, Georgia, and North Carolina occupied the seventh through tenth places in forestry employment, and together they accounted for 14.9 percent of the nation's

lumber employment (table 14.5). By 1920, lumbering had emerged as regionally important in the Great Lakes, Pacific Coast, and the South; older lumber areas in the East also had revived (Maine and New York), and Pennsylvania, though slipping, remained in the top ten states. Even so, imports from Canada began to rise because U.S. lumbering could not keep up with demand. Although specialization in lumbering did not reach equivalence to that in agriculture, some locations relied heavily on the lumber industry for their livelihood—especially Washington, Oregon, Maine, and numerous scattered sites throughout the southeastern states.

Mining

In the latter part of the 19th century, mining output grew twice as fast as manufacturing output, as metals replaced most wood in manufacturing and the expanding national economy required larger quantities of energy resources for power. Coal was essential to the livelihood of the nation during the period 1860–1920. It powered factories, railroads, steamboats, steamships, ferries, elevated railways, and elevators; it heated homes, offices, stores, and factories; and it was used to make iron and steel. For the years 1885–1905, industries and households consumed about 40 to 45 percent of coal, railways consumed a similar share, and the iron and steel industry consumed about 12 to 17 percent. Annual coal production soared at a compound an-

Table 14.6 Iron Ore Production, 1879–1920

	Percent of Total Iron Ore Mined				
	1879	1890	1900	1910	1920
Minnesota	0.0	5.6	35.7	56.1	58.4
Michigan	23.0	44.5	36.0	23.3	25.9
Wisconsin	0.5	5.9	2.7	2.0	1.5
Alabama	2.4	11.8	10.0	8.4	8.7
Tennessee	1.3	2.9	2.2	1.3	0.6
New York	15.8	7.8	1.6	2.3	1.4
Pennsylvania	27.4	8.5	3.2	1.3	1.1
New Jersey	9.5	3.1	1.2	0.9	0.6
All other states	20.0	9.8	7.4	4.4	1.9
Total U.S. (%)	99.9	99.9	100.0	100.0	100.1
Total U.S. (000's of long tons)	7,120	16,036	27,553	57,015	67,604

nual growth rate of 6 percent from 1860 to 1920, about half again as fast as the 4 percent real growth rate of the economy (measured by gross national product), testimony to coal's critical contribution to the nation's well-being. Translated into quantity terms, annual coal output rose over 20-fold, from 26 million tons to 562 million tons. As of 1860, consumption of anthracite coal, a hard mineral that gave a clean, slow burn, exceeded consumption of bituminous coal by about 10 percent. The Scranton–Wilkes-Barre area of northeastern Pennsylvania produced virtually all of the nation's anthracite, but its high cost limited consumption outside of nearby iron and steel mills, factories, and cities in Pennsylvania, New York, New Jersey, and New England.

Bituminous coal—softer, dirtier, plentiful, and low cost—became the fuel of choice. By the 1880s its annual production exceeded that of anthracite by two times, and by 1920, its annual production was five times larger. Pennsylvania, West Virginia, Ohio, Kentucky, and Illinois accounted for about 80 percent of bituminous coal production during the years 1880–1920, providing most of the East and Middle West access to cheap coal. After 1860 bituminous coal from the western side of the Appalachians became the principal fuel for the rapidly growing iron and steel industry. Coal was transformed into coke, and by 1890 the Connellsville region of southwestern Pennsylvania (near Pittsburgh) and northern West Virginia produced half of the nation's coke. Pig iron smelted with bituminous

coal and coke comprised 13 percent of all pig iron smelted in 1860, and this share rose to 85 percent by 1900.

As late as 1879, more than half of the iron ore that industry needed was mined in the East, in New York, New Jersey, and Pennsylvania. The shift to richer deposits occurred rapidly after 1879 (table 14.6). Lake Superior mines in Michigan and Wisconsin expanded after the Sault Ste. Marie Canal, connecting Lake Superior and Lake Huron, opened in 1855; it provided a clear passage to the lower Great Lakes. By 1890 the eastern mines' share had fallen below 20 percent, and half of the iron ore now came from the Lake Superior district. During the 1880s two other important iron ore districts commenced production. The area around Birmingham, Alabama, reached 11.8 percent of national production by 1890; over the next 30 years its percentage declined slightly. The Mesabi Range of northern Minnesota, the nation's richest iron ore area, developed slowly; by 1890, it accounted for only 5.6 percent of ore mined. However, within a decade its output surged to more than one-third of the nation's and by 1910 had climbed to more than 50 percent; the Lake Superior district declined simultaneously to about one-quarter. These relative changes in iron ore mining coincided with absolute expansion in all districts to serve the burgeoning iron and steel industry in the East and Middle West. Expansion of the Lake Superior mines in the 1860s initiated the pattern of input linkages for the industry, which persisted well into the 20th century. Ore freighters tied Lake Superior–Mesabi mines to iron and steel mills along the lower Great Lakes or to rail connections at ports for transporting ore to inland mills in eastern Ohio and western Pennsylvania. Connellsville coke moved by river barge and rail to the mills.

The Keweenaw Peninsula of Michigan was a major supplier of copper before 1880. However, depletion of the best ore deposits required development of distant mines in the West, which could not enter production until completion of the transcontinental railroads and feeders to them. Butte, Montana, developed first, followed by several Arizona districts. By 1889, Butte and Arizona accounted for 43 percent and 14 percent, respectively, of national production, whereas Michigan accounted for 39 percent. Relative shifts continued during the subsequent 30 years. In 1919, Arizona had become the nation's chief producer with 47 percent, whereas the Butte and Michigan districts had declined to 16 percent and 19 percent, respectively. New districts had emerged in Utah, Nevada, and New Mexico; their combined production rose from less than 2 percent in 1889 to 17 percent in 1919. By 1920, western districts, located far from the Manufacturing Belt in the East and Middle West, accounted for 80 percent of the nation's copper.

Copper, coal, and iron ore mining were heavily capitalized businesses between 1860 and 1920. Although folklore immortalized gold and silver miners as rugged individuals who braved all odds to mine precious minerals, in fact, large, heavily capitalized firms took over mining after the easily reached veins had been exhausted within the first few years of a mine's existence. The 1860s witnessed the start of numerous gold and silver mining districts. Following the California gold rush of the preceding decade, Nevada became prominent with the discovery of the Comstock Lode near Reno. Butte, Montana, gold and silver mines also opened in the 1860s. Colorado experienced several successive mining booms, including the Central City district in the 1860s, the Leadville district in the late 1870s, and the Cripple Creek district in the 1890s. Because refined gold and silver had high value per unit weight, railroads were not essential; therefore, this mining began in the West earlier than other mineral mining. In 1870, mines in the Great Lakes states still accounted for 60 percent

of the nation's lead. During the 1870s, the famous tristate district in southwestern Missouri and border parts of Oklahoma and Kansas commenced production. This district, which also had zinc, by 1920 accounted for one-third of all lead mined. Few lead mines opened in the West until the 1880s, when railroad feeder lines brought connections to the transcontinental trunk lines. During that decade, lead districts in Colorado, including the famous Leadville district, and Nevada emerged; they followed earlier Utah lead mines near the transcontinental railroad. These western districts accounted for about two-thirds of production during the 1880s. Mining in the Coeur d'Alene district of Idaho, which was to become the nation's most productive, did not begin until the 1890s.

Oil, the last of the major minerals exploited during the late 19th century, played a greater, long-lasting role in regional development. Initial important oil production began in the 1860s near Titusville in northwestern Pennsylvania. Through most of the 19th century, oil served chiefly for lighting and as a lubricant for machinery. Fuel oil and gasoline did not become consequential until about 1910, after the appearance of the automobile. Transportation quickly became crucial to oil development because oil was bulky, difficult to handle, and of low value. Short branch railroads were quickly employed to link oil fields to the nearest trunk rail lines. In the 1870s, short pipelines linked to the main railroads, and within a decade networks of long-distance pipelines had emerged. John D. Rockefeller early recognized the value of forming large, integrated oil companies that combined acquisition, refining, and distribution. In reference to Standard Oil's takeover of much of Cleveland's oil-refining capacity in the early 1870s, he reputedly responded to a refusal to sell a refinery: "You can never make money, in my judgment. You can't compete with Standard. We have all the large refineries now. If you refuse to sell, it will end in your being crushed."

Pennsylvania and other portions of Appalachia remained the leading oil producers until 1900 (table 14.7). The Ohio-Indiana field became a major producer in the mid-1890s and continued for about a decade. During the first few years after 1900, new discoveries in the Gulf Coast (Texas) and in southern California saw these fields grow rapidly. The last major

Table 14.7 Crude Petroleum Output by Region, 1900–1919

Field	Percent of Total Crude Petroleum Output				
	1900	1905	1910	1915	1919
Appalachian	57	22	13	8	8
Ohio-Indiana	34	17	3	2	1
Illinois	—	—	16	7	3
Kansas-Oklahoma	1	9	28	44	51
Gulf Coast	—	27	5	7	6
California	7	25	35	31	27
Others	1	—	—	1	4
Total %	100	100	100	100	100
Total production (millions of barrels)	64	135	210	281	378

fields to develop were in Kansas-Oklahoma and Illinois after 1905. Two fields dominated by 1919: Kansas-Oklahoma and California. The large distances that separated newer oil fields from major consuming areas forced the oil industry to devise an elaborate system of production, transportation, refining, and distribution, which spanned the nation by the first two decades of the 20th century. Many of the nation's largest oil corporations existed by 1910, including Standard, Gulf, Texaco, Union, and Sun. Mining districts had tight integration with the national space economy by 1890, and as new resources such as oil emerged, they also quickly became part of a national market. Given the close tie between mining and manufacturing, it is not surprising that manufacturing also made major strides toward national market integration before 1890.

Manufacturing

A variety of factors—transport cost, labor cost, and agglomeration economies—influence the choice of manufacturing location. Raw-material processing manufactures such as sawmills, flour mills, and smelting involve large weight loss of waste material or convert material to a more suitable form for transportation; they locate near raw-material sites. Other manufactures for which transportation is important locate near the market; examples are bread and bricks. These manufactures have high transport costs for final products because they are perishable, delicate, or of low value relative to their weight. Some manufactures do not need such proximity and

are termed "regional market" manufactures. Firms in each region produce them, but they cannot be shipped outside the region because the cost is too high; during the mid-19th century, examples included furniture, paper, and iron foundry products (heavy metal components and machines). Transport costs are not factors in location for "multiregional" or "national market" manufactures, such as textiles, drugs, and gloves, because those costs are small proportions of final sale prices. Other industrial location factors such as special labor advantages (e.g., low wages) or agglomeration economies also may be important. Agglomerations of industries linked in production sequences may occur because of savings in transport cost between plants or because of the need for access to information about production requirements. Examples are carriage-parts manufacturers located near carriage factories, or auto-parts producers near auto factories.

Between 1860 and 1880 the relative importance of these location factors changed, producing a concentration of most industry in the American Manufacturing Belt (fig. 14.4). This great industrial region persisted as the nation's manufacturing core through much of the 20th century. Its emergence became inseparable from the westward-expanding natural resource sectors of agriculture, lumbering, and mining. By the 1860–80 period, a set of regional industrial systems emerged that fixed the belt's outline. In each region, the metropolis's firms in finance, wholesaling, warehousing, and transportation provided services to manufacturers who located locally or in an industrial city in the hinterland.

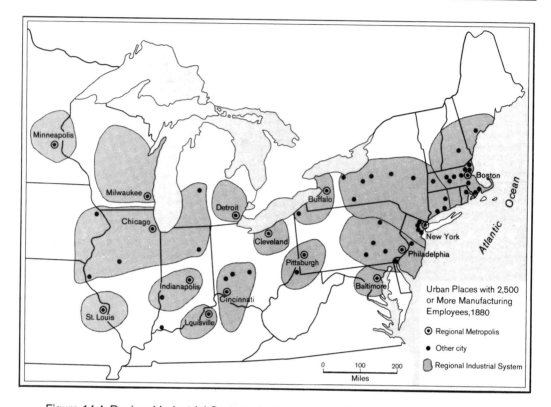

Figure 14.4 Regional Industrial Systems in the American Manufacturing Belt about 1880

Examples of the provision of metropolitan services are Boston for cotton-textile manufacturers in New England, Philadelphia for iron manufacturers in southeastern Pennsylvania, and Chicago for agricultural machinery firms in northern Illinois.

Prior to 1860, and especially before 1840, most industrialists served demands originating in their own region. Four sources of demand were significant: household consumers, urban infrastructure, the natural resource sector, and intra- and interregional trade. Households demanded a diverse set of manufactured products that included clothes, furniture, stoves, houses (lumber, doors, and windows), and food (flour, sugar, spices, and meat). City growth stimulated demand for construction materials such as bricks, lumber, pipes, glass, nails, and hinges. Two important components of the natural resource sector—agriculture and extraction and processing—demanded manufactures. Commercial agriculture required construction materials such as lumber, nails, and hinges to build fences and barns. Farmers also needed implements such as axes, hoes, and rakes, and machinery such as plows, harrows, mowers, reapers, and threshers. The extraction and processing sectors required extensive manufactures. Mining employed hand tools and machinery for crushing and smelting, and lumbering used saws and sawmill machinery. Food processing such as flour milling used water- and steam-powered machinery, and meatpacking used hand tools. Intra- and interregional trade stimulated diverse manufactures. Containers such as boxes and barrels were needed in large quantities. Steamboats ran with steam engines, and railroads used locomotives and cars (foreign producers supplied most of the rails).

These four diverse sources of demands for manufactures stimulated a crucial set of manufactures that are called the "pivotal producer durables." They included iron foundries, machine shops, and machinery firms. Because a wide variety of industrial processes used their products, they emerged simultaneously with other manufactures. They equipped factories for production and supplied ongoing needs for parts and machinery; many products, such as steam engines and locomotives, were themselves machines. Each regional industrial system developed a producer durables sector.

As settlers moved into each new region before 1860, a regional system of manufacturing emerged. The East Coast industrial systems, developed in the 1790–1820 period, centered on Boston, New York, Philadelphia, and Baltimore. These industrial systems also produced the first national market manufactures, such as textiles in Boston's hinterland, hardware in New York's hinterland, and drugs and chemicals in Philadelphia's hinterland. In a successive manner the industrial systems of Pittsburgh and Cincinnati emerged in the 1810–40 period and those of St. Louis, Detroit, Cleveland, Chicago, and Milwaukee in the 1840–60 period. Therefore, by 1860 the key regional industrial systems of the Manufacturing Belt were already established.

Comparable industrial systems did not emerge in the South before 1860, even though the region experienced westward settlement, like the Middle West. The reasons for limited manufacturing in the South are complex and disputed. The South and the North housed factories of similar size and profitability, and both areas had comparable types of manufactures. Nevertheless, the South had substantially lower aggregate demand for many manufactures produced for markets in a region. White population size and density in regions around metropolises such as Charleston, Mobile, and New Orleans was lower than around midwestern metropolises such as Cincinnati and Cleveland. Because slave owners invested their capital in slaves, not land, and moved as soil became exhausted, they had little commitment to investments in fixed infrastructure of urban places and transportation projects. Large plantations maintained self-sufficiency in many everyday items, and owners restricted slaves' consumption patterns. This limited transportation and consumer activity and kept urban populations small. Therefore, local and regional manufacturers faced relatively low demands for consumer market goods, urban infrastructure products, and transportation goods such as wagons and locomotives. These manufacturers also faced few demands for agricultural equipment because slaves did most of the work. The small volume of this wide variety of manufactures kept demands for the producer durables sector

equally small. Before 1860, the South's demand for these diverse regional manufactures remained less than those of both the Middle West, which grew simultaneously, and the East, which had emerged earlier.

The expanding volume of manufactures shipped between regions during the years 1840–60 foreshadowed sweeping changes in industry that took place after 1860. Manufactures produced for intraregional markets continued to expand from 1860 into the 1880s in the East, and, especially in the rapidly industrializing Middle West. Even as this growth occurred, some regional market firms increasingly produced for markets in other regions, and firms targeted multiregional and national markets in new manufactures. This inhibited later-settled and lagging regions from acquiring manufactures; therefore, regional-market manufactures ceased serving as the foundation of a region's industry. Technological knowledge, efficient factories, and marketing networks were solidly established in the industrial systems of the Manufacturing Belt; thus, the belt eventually stopped expanding westward around 1880. Industrial systems of the Manufacturing Belt grew enormously as each developed specialties for multiregional and national markets, and this regional industrial specialization increased markedly after 1890. Increased efficiency of transportation and communication supported this specialization.

Industrial systems of the Manufacturing Belt had achieved national dominance by 1860, and they maintained their position in 1900. The value-added share of interstate trade in manufacturing that each industrial section contributes measures the relative importance of that section in interregional commerce. The Manufacturing Belt accounted for the overwhelming majority of interregional trade in manufacturing in both 1860 and 1900. In 1860, southern New England was a leading national manufacturer of textiles, paper, leather products, fabricated metals, nonelectrical machinery, and instruments. The Mid-Atlantic section led in food, apparel, furniture, printing and publishing, rubber, leather, primary metals, nonelectrical machinery, transportation equipment, and instruments. In contrast, the Middle West had only modest importance in food, lumber and wood products, and furniture. By 1900, southern New England remained a leader in

Table 14.8 Manufacturing Specialization in Regional Metropolises, 1880

	Persons Employed in Manufacturing	Foundry and Machine-Shop Products		Selected Other Industries		
New York City (inc. Brooklyn)	274,939	5.0	(0.9)	17.8	(3.0)	Clothing, men's
				4.7	(5.2)	Clothing, women's
				3.9	(1.9)	Printing & publishing
Philadelphia (inc. Camden, N.J.)	189,897	5.7	(1.1)	25.6	(17.8)	Misc. textiles
Chicago	79,414	6.2	(1.2)	1.3	(0.9)	Agricultural implements
				10.7	(1.8)	Clothing, men's
				6.2	(2.8)	Furniture
				9.4	(9.4)	Slaughtering & meat-packing
Boston (inc. Cambridge, Chelsea, & Somerville)	68,403	6.4	(1.2)	13.6	(2.3)	Clothing, men's
				3.4	(8.5)	Musical instruments
				5.4	(2.6)	Printing & publishing
Cincinnati, Ohio (inc. Covington & Newport, Ky.)	59,190	6.6	(1.2)	6.0	(3.2)	Carriages & wagons
				15.7	(2.7)	Clothing, men's
				6.2	(2.8)	Furniture
				1.9	(1.9)	Slaughtering & meat-packing
Baltimore	56,338	4.7	(0.9)	19.8	(3.4)	Clothing, men's
				19.4	(17.6)	Fruits & vegetables, canned & preserved
Pittsburgh (inc. Allegheny)	43,401	8.1	(1.5)	13.4	(14.9)	Glass
				39.6	(7.6)	Iron & steel
St. Louis, Mo.	41,825	8.3	(1.6)	6.8	(1.2)	Clothing, men's
				3.2	(3.2)	Liquors, malt
				5.4	(2.6)	Printing & publishing
Cleveland	21,724	11.7	(2.2)	1.7	(5.4)	Brooms & brushes
				13.8	(2.7)	Iron & steel
Milwaukee	20,886	7.0	(1.3)	20.6	(3.5)	Clothing, men's
				5.0	(5.0)	Liquors, malt
Buffalo	18,021	12.0	(2.3)	4.4	(101.4)	Glucose
				1.4	(36.0)	Refrigerators
Louisville	17,448	9.0	(1.7)	4.7	(2.1)	Furniture
				7.9	(6.6)	Tobacco, chewing, smoking & snuff
Detroit	16,110	6.4	(1.2)	5.0	(2.4)	Printing & publishing
Minneapolis-St. Paul	10,574	5.6	(1.1)	7.2	(3.4)	Flour
Indianapolis	10,000	13.1	(2.5)	6.4	(3.0)	Printing & publishing
				8.9	(8.9)	Slaughtering & meat-packing

Header note: Percent of Total Manufacturing Employment and Location Quotient[a]

[a]Location quotient (in parentheses) is computed as $(CM_i/CM_t) / (NM_i/NM_t)$ where CM_i and CM_t are respectively a city's employment in industry i and total manufacturing employment, and NM_i and NM_t are respectively the national employment in industry i and total manufacturing employment.

textiles and leather products but had declined in numerous other manufactures. Its rise to dominance in rubber production was an exception. The Mid-Atlantic section remained a leader in apparel, printing and publishing, leather, primary metals, nonelectrical machinery, and instruments; it declined significantly in food and rubber. In contrast, the Middle West made substantial gains in food, lumber and wood products, furniture, fabricated metals, nonelectrical machinery, and transportation equipment.

A rich texture of specialization among both metropolises and small industrial cities existed as early as 1880 (tables 14.8 and 14.9). Some metropolises had 20 percent or more of their manufacturing employment in a single manufacture. Such high percentages occurred in men's clothing and fruit and vegetable canning in Baltimore, men's clothing in Milwaukee, miscellaneous textiles in Philadelphia, and iron and steel in Pittsburgh. The location quotient, which measures the percentage of a city's employment in a manufacture relative to the national percentage employed in that manufacture, is a better indicator of specialization. Large location quotients indicate a high degree of specialization. Metropolises that had high specialization in manufactures included Baltimore with fruit and vegetable canning, Boston with musical instruments, Chicago and Indianapolis with slaughtering and meatpacking, Milwaukee with malt liquor (beer), Philadelphia with miscellaneous textiles, Pittsburgh with glass and iron and steel, Cleveland with brooms and brushes, Buffalo with glucose and refrigerators, and Louisville with tobacco (table 14.8). Foundry and machine-shop products, indicative of the pivotal producer durables sector, were well represented in all metropolises.

Similarly, small industrial cities in the hinterlands of metropolises had high shares of their industrial labor force in some manufactures, and they were highly specialized relative to the nation (table 14.9). A high percentage of industrial workers were employed in furniture in Grand Rapids; miscellaneous textiles in Paterson; distilled liquors (whiskey) in Peoria; agricultural implements in Springfield, Ohio; and cotton goods in Taunton, Massachusetts. Compared with national employment (location quotients), the most specialized cities were Columbus with carriages and wagons, Grand Rapids with furniture, Peoria with distilled

liquors, and Springfield with agricultural implements. Some of the small industrial cities such as Fort Wayne and Taunton even specialized in foundry and machine-shop products. This degree of specialization in both metropolises and small industrial cities indicates that some of their manufactures sold in multiregional and national markets by 1880.

Iron and steel and cotton textiles, both old manufactures, and electrical machinery, a new one, exemplify diverse changes in manufacturing between 1860 and 1920. The iron and steel industry is sometimes considered the epitome of changes in late-19th-century manufacturing, but its firms were always atypically large, compared with firms in other industries. By 1860 the iron industry already had acquired some characteristics that anticipated changes over the next 60 years. East of the Appalachian Mountains many large iron firms had used anthracite coal from the fields of northeastern Pennsylvania long before 1860. Blast furnaces that produced pig iron and rolling mills that transformed pig iron into rails and bar iron clustered in river valleys and other areas near the large metropolises of Boston, New York, and Philadelphia. Most iron firms on the west side of the Appalachians still employed charcoal as fuel for blast furnaces, but use of coke had begun. Charcoal blast furnaces scattered throughout rural areas for easy access to timber supplies for making charcoal. In contrast, rolling mills, which used coal to power steam engines, located in Pittsburgh and at numerous sites along the Ohio River, as well as in other midwestern metropolises such as Buffalo, Cleveland, Detroit, and Chicago.

A trend of increasing integration and rising scale of firms began in the 1860s with the start of Bessemer steel manufacture. To manufacture steel efficiently required close integration between blast furnaces, which produced pig iron, and the Bessemer converter, which made steel from pig iron. At the same time, blast furnaces increasingly adopted Connellsville coke; this freed them from rural locations because coke was transported more easily than charcoal. Blast furnaces and Bessemer converters could be located near one another, and the large output of Bessemer converters encouraged firms to include rolling mills in Bessemer steelworks. Firms achieved efficiencies by close integration of the sequences of steel manufacturing. Large

Table 14.9 Manufacturing Specialization in Small Industrial Cities, 1880

	Persons Employed in Manufacturing	Percent of Total Manufacturing Employment and Location Quotient[a]		
		Foundry and Machine-Shop Products	Selected Other Industries	
Albany-Troy	34,219	13.5 (2.5)	12.7 (2.4)	Iron and steel
Columbus, Ohio	5,490	7.0 (1.3)	13.8 (7.3)	Carriages and wagons
			9.7 (1.9)	Iron and steel
Fort Wayne	2,735	34.6 (6 5)	11.4 (2.1)	Lumber, sawed
Grand Rapids	5,172	5.3 (1.0)	34.9 (15.9)	Furniture
Paterson	19,799	14.2 (2.7)	59.2 (6.2)	Misc. textiles
Peoria	4,067	5.2 (1.0)	26.5 (132.5)	Liquors, distilled
Springfield, Ohio	3,970	6.8 (1.3)	59.9 (42.8)	Agricultural implements
Taunton	5,154	23.9 (4.5)	28.9 (4.3)	Cotton goods
Worcester	16,559	14.4 (2.7)	14.6 (2.9)	Boots and shoes
			14.4 (2.8)	Iron and steel

[a]Location quotient (in parentheses) follows the percent of total manufacturing employment for the given industry. For computation see footnote in table 14.8.

integrated steelworks appeared in some locations such as Pittsburgh and Johnstown in Pennsylvania and Chicago, Illinois, but the parts remained separate at other places. The open-hearth iron and steel process became important after the 1880s. It operated at a smaller scale than the Bessemer process, but by 1890 the trend toward large, integrated iron and steel mills was firmly established. Average capital investment for rolling mills rose sixfold from $156,000 in 1869 to $967,000 in 1899, and by 1917 at least 16 integrated iron and steel companies had assets of $20 million or more each; 3 of them were among the nation's 10 largest industrial corporations. As demand for steel shifted from railroad rails to higher-quality steels, the open-hearth process increasingly became the preferred method of production.

After 1860, midwestern and western railroad expansion provided important sources of demand for steel, which was met by large Bessemer rail mills in Pittsburgh and Chicago. Midwestern demand for bridges, structural parts, and machinery also undergirded the iron and steel industry expansion. Therefore, the industry gradually shifted to the Middle West, although eastern mills still remained important suppliers for eastern demand. Growing use of Lake Superior iron ore and Connellsville coke, along with

demand of midwestern markets, encouraged the location of iron and steel mills at points that minimized transport costs to acquire inputs and distribute outputs to markets. Between 1890 and 1920, major concentrations of blast furnaces and integrated mills existed in Pittsburgh and along the river valleys surrounding it, including the Ohio, Mahoning (Youngstown, Ohio, vicinity), and Shenango (Sharon, Pennsylvania, vicinity), and in Buffalo, Cleveland, Detroit, and Chicago. In the East the iron and steel industry concentrated at fewer sites as the scale of firms increased. By the early 20th century, New England's iron and steel industry had declined, and larger mills located in eastern Pennsylvania and Baltimore. Birmingham, Alabama, which had local deposits of iron ore and coal, became the leading southern center for steel after 1888.

Firms implemented organizational changes as the size of iron and steel plants increased and the plants concentrated at fewer locations. Andrew Carnegie, the foremost innovator in implementing organizational changes in the industry, applied experience gained as one of the managers of the Pennsylvania Railroad, the pioneering business organization that introduced modern management techniques to large-scale firms. The crux of Carnegie's approach in his firm, Carnegie Steel, was a fanatical attention to cost control. He claimed that "one of the chief sources of success in manufacturing is the introduction and strict maintenance of a perfect system of accounting so that responsibility for money or materials can be brought home to every man." The organizational structure and cost-reporting system that Carnegie implemented gave him control of all facets of Carnegie Steel. By the 1880s, some large individual firms such as Carnegie Steel were multifunctional, multilocational enterprises that combined mills, iron ore, and coal mines in one organization. When U.S. Steel was organized in 1901 as a "combination of combinations," large integrated firms had been in existence for more than a decade. For most of the 1860–1920 period, iron and steel firms served regional and multiregional markets from individual plants. Transport costs remained sufficiently important that it was not feasible to serve a national market from one region.

The cotton-textile industry followed a somewhat different trajectory of development after 1860. Its input, cotton, had high value per unit weight and little weight loss in manufacture, and the product, thread and cloth, also had high value per unit weight. Therefore, transportation costs never constrained the location of the cotton-textile industry. Although the industry was widely scattered initially, once economies of scale in manufacture were achieved and marketing channels established, it had concentrated in New England as early as 1830, with smaller concentrations in eastern New York and in Philadelphia and its vicinity. New England's dominance in cotton textiles persisted as late as 1890, when it accounted for about three-fourths of the nation's spindles, a figure unchanged from 20 years earlier. The exploitation of most waterpower sites by 1870 forced the industry to expand with steam power. Firms chose coastal locations and other non-waterpower sites. By the early 1870s, Fall River, Massachusetts, had surpassed the old center of Lowell, Massachusetts, and New Bedford, near Fall River, became a major center by the 1880s. Other older textile centers along the Merrimac River from Lawrence, Massachusetts, to Manchester, New Hampshire, and along the Maine coast continued to expand up to 1890. However, rapid growth of cotton textiles in the southern Piedmont from North Carolina to Georgia between 1870 and 1890 signaled future changes; textile cities,

such as Augusta and Columbus in Georgia, emerged. In 1900, the South had about 25 percent of the nation's spindles and by 1914 about 40 percent. Northern industry did not decline absolutely during these years; rather, southern industry grew faster. Most southern expansion rested on locally owned firms, not relocation of northern mills. Southern Piedmont capital achieved more profitable employment in cotton textiles than in cotton growing, and low-wage labor in the Piedmont provided a competitive labor supply.

Although the telegraph used electricity starting in the 1840s, the electrical machinery industry and its closely allied components of lighting and traction first developed in the late 1870s. Electrical machinery quickly became a national-market industry dominated by General Electric and Westinghouse. In the late 1870s arc lighting was perfected for street lights, and during the 1880s numerous companies emerged to build dynamos for the lighting companies that appeared in many cities. Equipment firms often started lighting companies. Already in the late 1880s, consolidation commenced as capital requirements rose. Thomas-Houston, one of the leading firms, was headquartered in Boston with its main plant in nearby Lynn. The brightness and flickering tendency of arc lighting made it impractical in homes. Thomas Edison invented the incandescent lamp, and by 1882 the first power station to light the lamps was built in Manhattan. Edison Electric Light Company was formed in 1878 to build machinery, encourage development of power stations, and produce lamps. In 1886 the Schenectady works of Edison's company opened, and Edison General Electric Company was founded in 1889 as a combination of eight companies. Pittsburgh's Westinghouse Electric Company became a vigorous competitor of the Edison firm in the mid-1880s. Combination continued in 1892, when Edison's firm merged with Thomas-Houston to form General Electric. Thus, by the mid-1890s, Westinghouse and General Electric dominated the electrical machinery industry; they built locomotives, electric railcars, and power station machinery. The dominant centers in the 1890s consisted of three of their modern plants: General Electric's Lynn and Schenectady works, and Westinghouse's Pittsburgh works. The electrical machinery industry took only 10 to 15 years to move from inception to national-market stature. Because the industry required skills closely related to nonelectrical machinery, leading firms of this "new" industry located in the Manufacturing Belt.

Late-developing regions in the 19th century such as the Great Plains, Southwest, and Pacific Northwest had limited opportunities to acquire manufactures, except for residual local- and regional-market ones such as lumber-planing mills and diversified iron foundries. Some regional-market manufactures such as iron and steel shifted to multiregional-market scale, and new manufactures such as electrical machinery quickly became national market in orientation. Entrepreneurs outside the Manufacturing Belt did not have the skills to compete successfully in new national-market manufactures. Given the outline of the belt (fig. 14.4) and changes in transportation, communication, and manufacturing, the belt probably had formed no later than the 1860–80 period. By the 1890s, industrial systems within the belt became significantly more specialized, and interchange increased considerably both among them and between them and areas outside the belt. The South missed joining the belt by 1860; its acquisition of cotton textiles during the period 1860–1920 was an exception and rested on its low-labor-cost advantage. The Great Plains, Rocky Mountains, Pacific Coast, and Southwest were settled too late and at too low a population density to acquire most manufactures. The exceptional industries consisted of resource processing such as canning, lumber milling, and smelting that were raw material oriented and followed the exploitation of natural resources.

CONCLUSION

Transportation and communication improvements, along with organizational changes in business, undergirded the expansion of the United States to a continental set of integrated regional economies between 1860 and 1920. This nationalization of the economy progressed at varying paces in different economic sectors. Most agricultural regions had integrated by 1890, but some late specializations emerged in the Southwest (Arizona and New Mexico) and the western part of the northern Plains (Montana, western Dakotas). Lumbering lagged somewhat behind agriculture in reaching a con-

tinental scale of integrated regions. Specialization for multiregional lumber markets within the East, Middle West, and Pacific Coast prevailed before 1890, and some long-distance shipments between them occurred before 1890, such as from the Middle West to the East. Mining became highly specialized among regions by 1890. Some widely distributed minerals, such as coal, moved chiefly within regional and multiregional markets. Yet, industrial minerals and precious metals moved long distances before 1890. Even oil, moderately distributed at least among several regions, quickly evolved into a complex network of national production and distribution when output increased significantly between 1890 and 1910. Industrial specialization among regions emerged earliest. Some regions served multiregional and national markets before 1860, especially New England, and others produced for markets outside the region by 1880. Some manufactures were still evolving into national-market manufactures, and many new national-market manufactures arose after 1880. But only regional industrial systems that emerged by the 1860–80 period could specialize at a national scale. At a broader level of generalization, a large core, the Manufacturing Belt, emerged between 1860 and 1880, and a vast periphery of resource regions formed to provide specialties such as agricultural products, lumber, and minerals to this core in exchange for manufactures. This core-periphery organization of the national economy persisted from about 1880 until the mid-20th century.

These patterns of spatial expansion, regional economic growth and specialization, increasing interregional exchange, and reorganization of regional economic activity (cotton textiles, for example) in the U.S. economy between 1860 and 1920 had significance within a larger geographical context. By the 1900–1920 period, regional economic development in next-door neighbor Canada complemented U.S. development. Lumbering in New Brunswick and Maine as well as in Washington and British Columbia were part of the same resource development. On the Canadian prairies, the wheat farms of the southern portions of Manitoba, Saskatchewan, and Alberta abutted the wheat farms of Minnesota, North Dakota, and eastern Montana. And Canada's heaviest concentration of manufacturing, extending from Montreal, Quebec, to Windsor, Ontario, stretched alongside the U.S.

Manufacturing Belt from New York to Michigan. From an international perspective outside North America, the United States had gained new stature in the North Atlantic industrial world as a result of its enormous internal development. Even before 1860, U.S. agricultural output had surpassed that of western Europe. By 1871, the United States's population of more than 42 million and its coal production of over 50 million tons had passed the dimensions of the new, united state of Germany. By the late 1890s, it had surpassed the United Kingdom, the original "workshop of the world," in coal and steel production and in total manufacturing output. Thus, the United States entered the 20th century as the leading industrial nation in the world.

ADDITIONAL READING

Anderson, O. E. 1953. *Refrigeration in America: A History of a New Technology and Its Impact.* Princeton: Princeton University Press.

Armstrong, J. B. 1969. *Factory under the Elms: A History of Harrisville, New Hampshire, 1774–1969.* Cambridge: MIT Press.

Brown, J. K. 1995. *The Baldwin Locomotive Works, 1831–1915.* Baltimore: Johns Hopkins University Press.

Chandler, A. D. 1977. *The Visible Hand: The Managerial Revolution in American Business.* Cambridge: Harvard University Press, Belknap Press.

Cox, T. R. 1974. *Mills and Markets: A History of the Pacific Coast Lumber Industry to 1900.* Seattle: University of Washington Press.

Cronon, W. 1991. *Nature's Metropolis: Chicago and the Great West.* New York: W. W. Norton.

Gordon, R. B. 1996. *American Iron, 1607–1900.* Baltimore: Johns Hopkins University Press.

Gordon, R. B., and P. M. Malone. 1994. *The Texture of Industry: An Archaeological View of the Industrialization of North America.* New York: Oxford University Press.

Greever, W. S. 1963. *The Bonanza West: The Story of the Western Mining Rushes, 1848–1900.* Norman: University of Oklahoma Press.

Johnson, E. R., et al. 1915. *History of Domestic and Foreign Commerce of the United States.* 2 vols. Washington: Carnegie Institute of Washington.

Kirkland, E. C. 1962. *Industry Comes of Age: Business, Labor, and Public Policy, 1860–1897.* New York: Holt, Rinehart & Winston.

McMurry, S. 1995. *Transforming Rural Life: Dairying Families and Agricultural Change, 1820–1885.* Baltimore: Johns Hopkins University Press.

Modelski, A. M. 1984. *Railroad Maps of North America: The First Hundred Years.* Washington: U.S. Government Printing Office.

Perloff, H. S., et al. 1960. *Regions, Resources, and Economic Growth.* Baltimore: Johns Hopkins University Press.

Pred, A. 1966. *The Spatial Dynamics of U.S. Urban-Industrial Growth, 1800–1914.* Cambridge: MIT Press.

Pursell, C. 1995. *The Machine in America: A Social History of Technology.* Baltimore: Johns Hopkins University Press.

Schlebecker, J. T. 1975. *Whereby We Thrive: A History of American Farming, 1607–1972.* Ames: Iowa State University Press.

Schwartz, S. I., and R. E. Ehrenberg. 1980. *The Mapping of North America.* New York: H. N. Abrams.

Shannon, F. A. 1945. *The Farmer's Last Frontier: Agriculture, 1860–1897.* New York: Holt, Rinehart & Winston.

Sitterson, J. C. 1953. *Sugar Country: The Cane Sugar Industry in the South, 1753–1950.* Lexington: University of Kentucky Press.

Stradling, D. 1999. *Smokestacks and Progressives: Environmentalists, Engineers, and Air Quality in America, 1881–1951.* Baltimore: Johns Hopkins University Press.

Taylor, G. R., and I. D. Neu. 1956. *The American Railroad Network, 1861–1890.* Cambridge: Harvard University Press.

Temin, P. 1964. *Iron and Steel in 19th-Century America: An Economic Inquiry.* Cambridge: MIT Press.

Vance, J. E., Jr. 1995. *The North American Railroad: Its Origin, Evolution, and Geography.* Baltimore: Johns Hopkins University Press.

Ward, D. 1971. *Cities and Immigrants: A Geography of Change in 19th-Century America.* New York: Oxford University Press.

Warren, K. 1973. *The American Steel Industry, 1850–1970: A Geographical Interpretation.* Oxford: Clarendon Press.

Williamson, H. F., and A. R. Daum. 1959. *The American Petroleum Industry: The Age of Illumination, 1859–1899.* Evanston, Ill.: Northwestern University Press.

Williamson, H. F., et al. 1963. *The American Petroleum Industry: The Age of Energy, 1899–1959.* Evanston, Ill.: Northwestern University Press.

15

The Impact of Industrialism and Modernity
on American Cities, 1860–1930

MICHAEL P. CONZEN

Urban life in America in the decades following the Civil War spread widely across the continent, speeded up in daily pace, and took on undeniable new complexity. These changes paralleled the transcontinental colonization effort, but even more they reflected the impact of strident industrialization and the new modernity it engendered. The Civil War, although it affected cities variously in the short term north and south, was at most a regional accelerant or retardant in this broader pattern of shift. The engines of change were technological innovations in production and transport, reflected in the variable speed of adoption from place to place.

These changes encompassed the extension of the national network of cities to exploit the western portions of the continent and the onset of major industrialization, particularly in the developed Northeast. The resulting economic growth and social adjustment recalibrated the human use of time and space within the larger cities. This altered pace trickled down through the urban hierarchy, especially after the war, affecting even the smaller regional centers, so that "city" life became even more sharply distinct from the rural and small-town existence that the majority of Americans understood and took to be the norm. To the extent that the altered quality and timbre of urban life were the product of changing urban scale and economic functions, such trends are better understood in the context of the evolving national system of cities.

SHAPING A NATIONAL CITY SYSTEM

Cities have always been essential articulation points in the national flows of investments, commodities, labor, and services. What changed remarkably in this period (1860–1930) was the share of national production emanating from urban places and thus the proportion of the na-

tional population concentrated in cities to achieve it. As late as 1860, 4 out of 5 Americans still lived in completely rural surroundings—that is, in settlements with less than 2,500 inhabitants—whereas by 1920 the total number of urbanites finally outnumbered those in rural areas. While these particular benchmark dates exhibit clear and simple ratios, the thrust of deep change in the settlement fabric of America was longer lived and more variable than these figures suggest.

The American system of cities has always been part of a transatlantic and, indeed, a global network of trade and economic control. During the colonial period crucial links to metropolitan cities in Europe, principally London, were more important than links between American towns, keeping them in a state of dependency and primitivism as a regional urban "system." During the 19th century this relationship changed to one of high interdependence and somewhat increased closure with greater American autonomy in general economic relations. In such a context, the sweep of American urbanization during the 19th and early 20th centuries falls into three broad phases that can be bounded roughly by the years 1840, 1880, and 1930 (table 15.1). This phasing is composite, incorporating not only economic growth cycles, with their own complex periodicities, but also the deeper structure of overall urban production and consumption, reflecting long-run investments in infrastructure and habitual social relations. The 1840s and 1850s initiated a midcentury period of unprecedentedly rapid urban growth, a period in which the Civil War failed to slow or reverse any index of national urban growth. Between 1840 and 1930, the census year 1880 marks a major turning point after which the shift away from agricultural occupations doubled and the urban proportion climbed more vigorously. It was to take the Great Depression of the 1930s to puncture this long record of urban florescence.

Table 15.1 Measures of American Urban Growth, 1840–1930

	Pre-1840	1840–1880	1880–1930
No. of urban places (over 2,500)	131	939	3,165
Average number new towns per annum	2	20	45
Urban population as % of total population	10.8	28.2	56.2
Rate of increase in urban share	1.1	4.4	5.6
Average decadal % change in urban population	56.4	67.3	37.7
Nonagricultural labor force as % of total	36.9	48.7	78.4
Average decadal % change in nonagricultural labor force	2.6	2.9	5.9

Note: Figures apply to the end date in each period.

Considering the dramatic developments in the nation's economy during the later 19th and early 20th centuries—expansion of the agricultural, pastoral, and timber domains; major mineral discoveries; transport innovations on a continental scale; immigration; regional specialization; massive but regionally selective industrialization; and the burgeoning of commerce that wove these elements together—it is appropriate to explore how the national system of cities functioned to mold, and be molded by, the regional structure of this economic transformation. Geographical change in the city system can be separated into three major components that describe distinct but interrelated processes: spatial expansion, functional differentiation in city roles, and economic integration. These processes operated simultaneously, but with greater or lesser power in any given period or region.

Expansion:
Ocean to Ocean and Points in Between

The Period 1840–1880

The urbanization that occurred between 1840 and 1880 is evident in the sheer growth in "urban places" from 131 to 939. Many villages in the established regions along the northeastern

seaboard benefited from rural migration and foreign immigration and blossomed into small towns and cities, thickening the urban settlement cover. Much more dramatic was the geographical reach of the expansion with the rise of towns beyond the Appalachian Mountains.

Migrants across the mountains had by 1840 already created many towns in the Ohio valley, anchored by Pittsburgh and Cincinnati—testimony to the agricultural wealth of the region and the utility of the river as an avenue of commerce. To this was added the healthy growth of Louisville and the emergence of places like Covington and Evansville (for evidence of the expansion of the upper levels of the city system, see figure 15.1). The South in 1880 was deep in the throes of recovery from the economic dislocations of the Civil War, and the urban pattern there was changing. Earlier the region had been structured to depend upon peripheral entrepôt towns such as Savannah, Mobile, and New Orleans, but now some inland centers—Atlanta and Memphis, in particular—were emerging as nationally significant urban places.

Meanwhile, the upper Middle West had developed a yeoman economy of mixed grains and livestock, whose huge trade surpluses spawned a well-spaced network of large and medium-sized cities centered upon Chicago and reaching as far as St. Paul and Minneapolis. Beyond that, agricultural settlement, aided by the railroads, spread across the eastern margins of the Great Plains, supporting places like Kansas City and Omaha. By 1869, the year of the "golden spike," the iron rails linked up the old gold-field supply base of San Francisco with the nation's core, with such new nodes as Denver serving intermediate territory, including the mines of Colorado.

The Period 1880–1930

The pattern of expansion to 1930 was to add to the upper levels of the national urban system practically all the remaining cities that today constitute the apex of the hierarchy (fig. 15.1). In all, urban places expanded from 939 to 3,165, although the telling change occurred among towns with populations between 50,000 and 100,000, which rose from 15 in 1880 to 98 by the onset of the Great Depression.

Colonization of the Far West proceeded apace, but discontinuously, and challenged the declaration of the Census Bureau in 1890 that

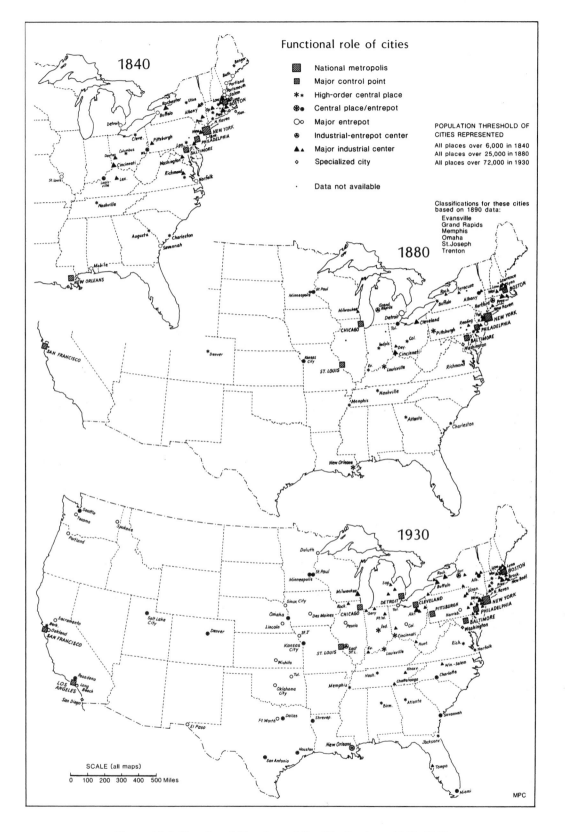

Figure 15.1 Functional Structure of the City System, 1840–1930

the American frontier had closed. Settlements grew in the Northwest based on timber exploitation and agriculture, and in California through agricultural and, later, limited industrial development. In addition to San Francisco, the major cities of Salt Lake City, Seattle, and Portland arose, and Los Angeles quadrupled in population from 319,000 to 1.2 million in the 20 years from 1910 to 1930. These centers developed truncated regional town networks around them, serving a dispersed population clustered in often isolated pockets of fertile—or not so fertile—settlement zones separated by vast distances (usually 400 miles or more) and rather extreme biophysical environments.

In the eastern third of the country much infilling of the urban pattern occurred throughout the South, now including Florida, and around the margins of the Appalachian Mountains. Less dramatic but equally significant was the rise of new and enlarged cities in the Northeast and Middle West as the regions matured. There were similarly important developments in the Great Plains states, where agricultural settlement pushed the Wheat Belt up against the ranching territory of the High Plains, and stimulated urban development in a broad north-south band from Minnesota and the Dakotas to Texas.

A Case Study of Railroad-Defined Urban Networks

Railroads became the heart, and perhaps the soul, of town development on the western margins of continuous agricultural settlement. As they penetrated the Plains in the 1880s and 1890s, the railroads not only stimulated cattle shipments from the vast ranches of the region but also provided the framework that enabled farmers to colonize the northern Plains and ranchers to move farther west. For their part, the railroads applied corporate lessons learned in more easterly settings (beginning with the Illinois Central Railroad in 1850) in matters of advertising, selling, and colonizing land; locating railroad lines and stations; and stimulating traffic and related commercial development. In effect the railroad companies not only coordinated the laying out of numerous town sites along their tracks but also defined the very network structure of the urban system that would serve the regions they plied.

In South Dakota, for example, of the 278 towns founded by 1889, 140 were railroad creations (fig. 15.2a). The uneven spatial pattern of town founding is easily explained. Farming settlement in the eastern half of the state fueled a wheat bonanza that attracted a dense pattern of railroad shipping points. Western areas were marked by rugged grasslands, mining activity in the Black Hills, and sparse development on former Indian reservations, supporting few towns at best. What distinguished these new urban networks from those in the settled East was the fluidity of town-site locations and the railroads' tactics in determining them, as well as their ability to influence subsequent growth.

On the Great Plains, the railroads were present at, or shortly after, the birth of most nucleated places and often would bypass young town sites by a mile or two to establish their own "town" and control urban development in that vicinity. In one stroke, the railroads could make or break new small towns, causing people and businesses to migrate to the rail connection and eliminating the investments of precocious town-site speculators "not in their confidence." Furthermore, the railroads had clear ideas about the appropriate spacing of towns along the tracks and even tried to set the level in the urban hierarchy that each new town should attain. They could do this through actively seeking colonists in eastern cities, advertising widely to encourage the establishment of specific businesses in particular places, netting would-be local bankers, and controlling through exclusive contracts which major shipping and supply firms (often those headquartered in Minneapolis) would set up facilities—elevators, lumberyards, and the like—in each town along the railroad.

The urban networks of the Plains were largely creatures of corporate strategy as the railroads became experienced "central place" planners in the West. It is ironic that these early-20th-century town systems, although strongly adjusted to a finely tuned collection and distribution machine—the railroad network—proved highly sensitive to external conditions. With the spread of the automobile and the rise of direct-mail-order houses with free rural postal delivery, business and shopping patterns changed at the expense of the small-town merchant, and many trade centers declined or even withered away after World War I. This was somewhat a national pattern, but its effects were

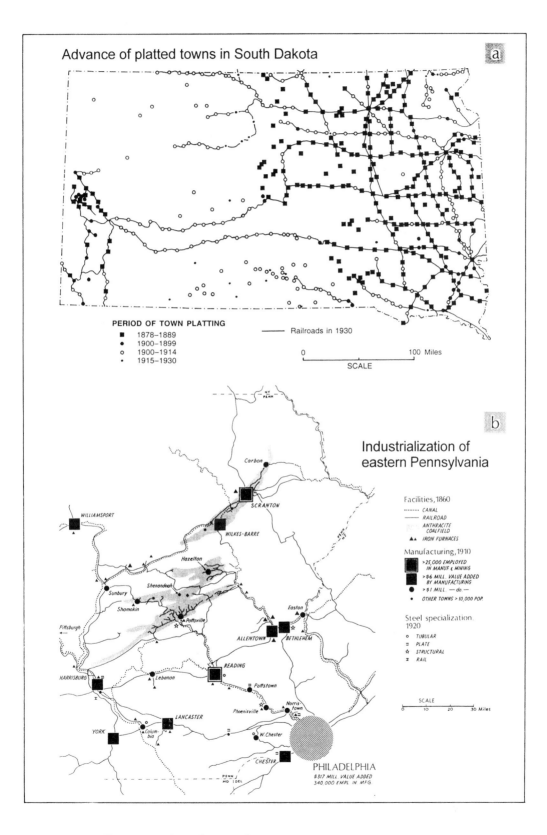

Figure 15.2 Case Studies: South Dakota and Eastern Pennsylvania

felt especially hard in areas of monoculture and extensive agriculture such as the Great Plains.

Differentiation: Growing Complementarity

The expansion of the urban network was accompanied and facilitated by changes in the roles that individual cities played in the national system, all driven by improvements in transportation, marketing, and manufactures. In earlier times the urban network consisted of numerous small central places tied to a few major seaboard entrepôts that shared the coast with small ports and fishing towns. By the mid-19th century, this "Atlantic" pattern necessarily changed to accommodate the tide of continental expansion and industrialization.

Commercial penetration of the interior required chains of *wholesaling centers* to collect and forward agricultural surpluses and other resources to the dense markets on the East Coast. The new western zones of exploitation attracted settlers who stimulated the development of local *central places* to provide administrative and retail services in the new areas. Such growth encouraged the concentration of high-order control functions—banking, investments, transport, export/import trade—in a few of the large cities, increasing their size and making them *major control points*. Local industrial activity emerged to reduce costly manufactured imports. While it flowered widely in districts of ready energy and raw materials, it prospered especially in eastern mercantile centers, reinforcing their dominant positions in the national urban system. With the dispersal of the national market, manufacturing emerged also in smaller and more concentrated *industrial centers* that could provide evident locational advantages with respect to one or more factors of production and distribution. Finally, other functions on occasion developed so singularly as to create *specialized cities,* such as seats of government. All these major functions—wholesaling, retailing, financial and legal services, transportation, industry, government, and social services—were present to some degree in most large and medium-sized cities across the country, but their proportions varied so widely as to create patently different urban roles with a distinct geography to them over time. The logic of this pattern and underlying process becomes somewhat clearer when viewed as a form of complementarity at the national scale.

In 1840 the spatial sorting of the city system was well under way. Still an Atlantic-oriented system, it hinged on the original "gateway" cities (New York, by then the undisputed economic capital, Philadelphia, Boston, and Baltimore) as the major control centers, secure within their immediate, fertile, mixed-farming, and industrious hinterlands with access to the continental interior (fig. 15.1). The planter South had more stunted gateways, principally New Orleans, and also Mobile, Savannah, Charleston, and Norfolk. What helped northeastern ports perpetuate their trading primacy was the extension of chains of wholesaling towns into the continental interior—the "spearheads" of the frontier—from New York through Albany and Buffalo to Detroit; or Philadelphia through Pittsburgh to Cincinnati and St. Louis. In the immediate hinterlands around the large Atlantic ports, many towns had grown into major regional service centers, creating local central-place networks of their own. Numerous towns emerged as small industrial places. In the West this pattern was being replicated, although St. Louis and Detroit acted very much as large outposts of the commercial system. New Orleans served clearly as a wholesaling center: 64 percent of all occupations were in commerce and navigation, compared with 44 percent for St. Louis. Its position controlling the Mississippi valley trade was so pivotal to the national urban system that it functioned as a major control point up to the Civil War.

Between 1840 and 1880 the rivers, canals, and then railroads of the Great Lakes and upper Mississippi region formed a transport system that initially fed the trade both south to New Orleans and east to New York, making St. Louis a national control point after 1850. But the increasing attraction of shipping via the Great Lakes route and the availability of direct rail links to the East, together with the blockages created by the Civil War, tipped the Middle West's commerce overwhelmingly eastward and subordinated St. Louis's growth to that of Chicago, so that in a mere 30 years Chicago developed into a major national control point (fig. 15.1). New Orleans never recovered from this fundamental reorientation of long-distance trade and slipped to the level of a mere "high-order," or regional-level, central place. Southern towns that grew large, such as Atlanta or Memphis, did so on the basis of central-place functions, a regionally homogeneous trend that reached as far north as Evansville and Indianapolis in Indiana.

The progress of the "mercantile" urban frontier was heralded at the margin of the Great Plains by the emergence of a distinct wholesale alignment running south from St. Paul through Omaha and St. Joseph to Kansas City, representing a new chain of gateways to the prairie Wheat Belt. Farther west, San Francisco surpassed 230,000 inhabitants by 1880; what New Orleans had been to the Mississippi basin before the Civil War, San Francisco became for the entire Pacific Coast region, a great entrepôt and regional capital.

Within the nation's expanded "core" region, now including the Great Lakes margin, the press of industrialization affected many old market towns well placed within this vast market. Worcester, Lawrence, Syracuse, and Reading, among others, prospered from industrialization. At the same time, the spread of commerce in the Middle West created larger markets for industrial products that combined with nearby resources and capital to foster a diversified pattern of industrial growth that benefited both small towns and large cities. Mercantile centers such as Milwaukee and Cleveland underwent heavy industrialization. Poised at the neck of this emerging "hourglass" manufacturing belt, Pittsburgh industrialized strongly but gained even more rapidly the diversified employment of a large regional metropolis (in 1880 the city had 21,204 people employed in mineral industries and manufacturing and 21,358 in the service sector). More specialized still was Washington, D.C., with a population of 178,000 (1880), in which almost two-thirds of those employed worked in service occupations.

Between 1880 and 1930, the growing specialization of urban roles became very clearly regionalized, as wholesaling and industry gained economic power over purely central-place functions. At the apex of the system, major new national control points emerged on the West Coast and in the heart of the Manufacturing Belt. Los Angeles profited from its climate, scenery, novel movie industry, and proximity to oil to claim economic control of southern California. Pittsburgh broke into the ranks of the nation's largest business centers, soon followed by Detroit and Cleveland—evidence of the power of the steel and automobile industries to concentrate allied corporate activities. Notwith-

standing these shifts, including Chicago's success in becoming the nation's second city, the ability of the four old eastern ports to remain atop the urban hierarchy underscores their sustained entrepreneurial dynamism and the geographical inertia it ultimately represents.

The most striking development was the growing importance and diffusion of wholesaling functions among American cities by 1930. A thick belt of wholesaling towns along the eastern margin of the Great Plains enlarged upon the base evident in 1880 and stretched from Duluth to San Antonio, while the remainder of the West was crisscrossed with mercantile chains (fig. 15.1). New wholesaling chains even emerged in the highly developed East along new axes, involving smaller-sized cities that represented "bypass" routes through the industrial heartland: the clearest of these included Jersey City, Harrisburg, Columbus, and East St. Louis.

The high-order central place was more widespread. Many of the large wholesale and industrial cities acted also as regional metropolises offering superior retail, professional, and other services for their regions. The upper echelon of this broad service hierarchy can be seen in 1930 in such cases as Cincinnati, Indianapolis, Louisville, Nashville, and Memphis, as well as in more mixed cases such as Minneapolis–St. Paul, Kansas City, Houston, Denver, Salt Lake City, and Seattle. The South experienced an urban renaissance during this period with the rise of regional centers such as Birmingham, Jacksonville, and Miami, based largely upon diversified service functions.

National industrial capacity between 1880 and 1930 became overwhelmingly urban in location, with many enterprises failing in small towns and rural areas, as economies of agglomeration and scale concentrated production. This favored established industrial towns, but it also helped medium-sized centers rise in the ranks of the national system. Examples include Waterbury, Schenectady, Erie, Youngstown, Lansing, South Bend, and Rockford. In addition, a new form of industrialization based on cheaper, nonunionized labor and greater proximity to raw materials was causing various industries to concentrate in the border South, favoring such towns as Knoxville, Chattanooga, and Winston-Salem.

Meanwhile, the urban subsystems of the West had come to vary considerably by the

1920s in historical development, resource base, and commercial articulation. Their archipelago-like network structure differed from the kinds of urban hierarchies evident in eastern zones of continuous settlement, and certain levels of local autonomy within the national system were much higher here than elsewhere. Manufacturing, for example, was often balanced and diverse in the cities of the Far West, including Los Angeles, because the intense division of labor developing among Manufacturing Belt cities could not be upheld in the West, where alternative sources of supply that might engender competition were so distant and costly.

A Case Study of Manufacturing Belt Synergy

The effect of heavy industrialization on urban systems in long-settled regions is well illustrated in eastern Pennsylvania. Since colonial days, the region boasted a network of country towns (such as Reading and Lancaster) serving the rich farmlands between the Delaware River and the front range of the Allegheny Mountains and the fertile valleys and iron furnaces within the ridge and valley districts. By 1860 turnpikes, two canals, and four railroads tied them to Philadelphia, already well launched upon an industrial path thanks to rich iron ore and anthracite coal deposits in the hills to the north and mercantile capital applied to industrial innovation (fig. 15.2b).

The industrialization of the region in the later 19th century depended, not on transport innovation, but rather on the agglomerating effects of proximity to raw materials and final markets. From 1860 to 1910, the region industrialized through coal mining and steelmaking that supplied a national market. Numerous mining towns sprang up, sprawling across mountainsides or tucked into narrow valleys. The largest—Scranton, Wilkes-Barre, Hazleton, Pottsville, and Shamokin—grew larger than their neighbors mainly because of the additional manufacturing they attracted, enterprises that came to the coal and thus saved the expense of haulage. Other towns concentrated on mining, and places like Shenandoah and Mount Carmel developed one-sided industrial profiles that oscillated widely with the fortunes of the Pennsylvania anthracite industry.

The ready availability of coal and limestone encouraged steel production near the mines, and

over time the trend toward larger and more integrated facilities encouraged the growth of a few urban places within the region (Pottsville, Scranton, and Harrisburg in particular), as well as towns with better access to Philadelphia and ocean outlets (Reading, South Bethlehem, Allentown, Columbia, Pottstown, Phoenixville, and Norristown). Tied to this heavy base of coal and steel came "next-stage, resource-using" industries such as foundry products and machinery, textile factories run on steam power, and construction materials (wire, nails, and the like). Here, location within the general region was sufficient to reap economies of agglomeration and scale, and of equal importance were factors such as transport, labor, and facility siting. Many industries of this type supported the growth of the largest cities in the area and of medium-sized towns like Williamsport, York, and Chester.

The hierarchy of industrial production gave substantial shape to the hierarchy of urban places by century's end, a fact that had not been true in 1860. Presiding over the region's transformation, and molding much of the early decision making through capital flows, the merchants and manufacturers of Philadelphia ensured that the port city remained the region's dominant economic focus. By 1910, the metropolis had 1.5 million inhabitants and contributed 70 percent ($317 million) of the value added by manufacture in eastern Pennsylvania. Far behind Philadelphia in industrial might was Reading in second place, with $21.3 million value-added, based largely on iron and steel, hosiery and knit goods, and foundry and machine goods. Reading had not yet surpassed 100,000 population in 1910, yet its well-rounded industrial base pushed it ahead of Scranton—which, with a population of 129,000, was second in overall population to Philadelphia—in manufacturing. While this region's industrialization was not typical of the Manufacturing Belt as a whole, it illustrates that industrialism brought a resifting of the urban hierarchy for those locations that would yield the best combination of least costs for the factors of production in key industries. Eastern Pennsylvania possessed superior natural resources close to the most highly developed rural and urban markets, and it industrialized massively late in the second half of the 19th century. This benefited Philadelphia greatly and brought the whole region to a level of urban expansion and specialization similar to that achieved in New England and in upstate New York.

Integration: Intercity and Hinterland Links

The division of labor implicit in urban network differentiation presupposes high levels of interdependence. The expansion and differentiation of the urban system could not have progressed so far in the 90 years from 1840 to 1930 without parallel developments in the technology and management of communications that would permit interaction among individual settlements in the far-flung system. Urban interdependence grew as new ways were devised to conquer distance. Sheer physical communication improved dramatically during this period through sequential connection by river, turnpike, canal, railroad, automobile, and air and through revolutions in electronic transmission of information. The effect of these changes was to redefine distance in terms of reduced cost and time, thus bringing urban places economically and psychologically closer together. Geographically, however, these improvements were severely biased in favor of some city and regional links rather than others. Even with the ultimate diffusion of some communication innovations throughout the city system, patterns of use were not uniform. The reasons lay not just in the variable routes used to reach resources and markets but also in the distinction between urban functions that controlled the physical movement of people and goods (transport control) and functions that controlled the terms of exchange (exchange control). The former could be shared among many nodal centers in the extended chains of communication; the latter required fewer hubs because of the greater scale economies realized, given that information transfer could eliminate intermediate processing points.

It is axiomatic that these improvements in exchange and movement tended to occur earliest between already favored places—favored, that is, with superior information and market potential—and that such initial advantage produced urban integration on terms favorable to established centers. The system nevertheless expanded on such a scale that new urban competitors with locational advantages could arise (and did, especially in the Middle West and Far West),

and territorial competition for hinterland trade and manufacturing capacity led to new forms of interdependence and spatial orderliness.

Within this context, various levels of autonomy existed as young settlements matured. In a city-system context, partial autonomy indicates the degree of control a center could exercise in effecting changes in the system that redounded to its benefit. From this perspective the most successful city throughout the period was New York, which managed to coordinate so much of the nation's trade as to remain the country's economic capital. While New York became eccentric to the westward gravitational shift of the domestic market—a shift that heavily favored Chicago after the Civil War—its entrepôt position facing the vital transatlantic markets in Europe assured its national mercantile dominance in the control of exchange, even after it had yielded much of its earlier control over physical movement. Other cities enjoyed much smaller measures of autonomy based on their regional location and "bridge" positions within the system.

An overview of national urban integration during the period can be gained from two sources. Neither is ideal, since no single index captures the complexity of the process, and systematic empirical evidence is hard to find on this topic. Nevertheless, the skeletal pattern of advancing urban interdependence with respect to the control of movement within the system can be glimpsed from the sequence by which cities engaging in long-distance commerce surpassed various thresholds of employment in transport and communications (fig. 15.3a). Clearly, there is a predictable association with the interregional expansion of the city system as a whole, particularly in the West. But many towns and cities in the Northeast, Middle West, and South gained significance only in later periods as transport nodes of major proportions (e.g., Atlanta), particularly where other functions such as manufacturing or retail servicing provided the main impetus to growth.

The more exclusive patterns in controlling exchange are revealed in the banking relations among large cities and between them and their trade hinterlands between 1880 and 1910. The "correspondent" system then used by America's individual banks to create a smoothly flowing financial-exchange network allows a reconstruction of its evolving geographical structure. Since

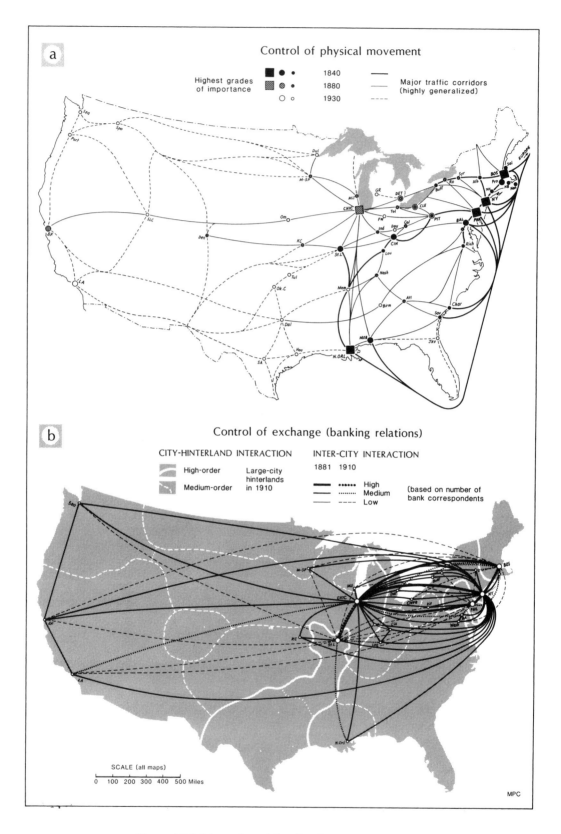

Figure 15.3 Integration of the City System, 1840–1930

early in the 19th century, the large eastern sea-ports had been active in developing financial ties with the interior, with New York in the lead. By 1880 a well-articulated pattern of high-level banking interdependency existed in which New York had strong reciprocal banking relations with Boston and Chicago and dominant influence over all other cities among the top 24 banking centers in the country (fig. 15.3b). Chicago appeared the next most integrated center on the basis of mutual banking exchange with New York, Boston, and Philadelphia and links with 20 among this group of cities. High-level integration was far less developed at the next lower stage, for Philadelphia and St. Louis could each boast major correspondent links with only 3 other places.

Thirty years later, however, banking integration had evolved considerably. The major lines of connectivity among these same cities had not changed substantially, but the pattern of cross-linkages with other cities and regional groupings had markedly intensified. Boston, Philadelphia, and St. Louis had been particularly successful in winning subsidiary channels of interaction from both larger and smaller centers (dashed lines in figure 15.3b). All three West Coast metropolises broadened their direct banking connections within the system. Numerous cities important in the control of physical movement, however, such as Dallas, Denver, and Salt Lake City, played no significant role in the high-level control of exchange during this long period.

The new spatial order showed also in the patterns of hinterland organization that emerged around large cities and in the "nesting" of hinterlands that resulted from hierarchical or nonhierarchical relationships among places. Because eastern cities had long fought for the limited backcountry near at hand, their mercantile interests were active throughout the 19th century in reaching out to the West for additional "tributary" territory, even if it had to be shared. In banking, antebellum New York had enjoyed virtual monopoly throughout the country regardless of distance or the remoteness of small-town banks. As late as 1876 New York banks had ties to 96 percent of all banks, but other centers began to give it competition in the 1880s. By 1910 patterns of territorial "partitioning" of the rest of the United States among the major centers were anything but regular

(fig. 15.3b), reflecting in part the inability of New York's correspondent network, with links to only 64 percent of all banks, to keep pace with bank proliferation nationwide. New York controlled much of the East outright, including all the Old South, keeping banking centers such as Cincinnati and Pittsburgh in very subordinate roles. Chicago, however, had organized practically the whole West except for a slender region of influence conceded to St. Louis. These patterns suggest the enormous strides made, particularly in the later 19th century, in forging the business integration of the urban system.

Implications

What does this review of the American urban network between 1860 and 1930 show? The constant expansion of the system meant that economic opportunity was always present, even if it meant migrating elsewhere and trying one's luck in a new place. The founding of new communities offered exceptional opportunities to those bringing entrepreneurial skills to new situations. Hence, social mobility often meant geographic mobility, and the urban network became a complex stage on which to test the proposition. Western cities were generally newer, less formed, and more open to new entrants. Specialization among cities meant new sources of wealth—spatially unrestricted opportunity. The mobility of capital ensured that geography could be exploited in concentrating resources at optimum locations for numerous purposes. In general, smaller towns boasted fewer economic functions and a narrower range of occupational classes, but such distinctions varied by region. Indeed, the regional differences in the timing and means of urbanization during this period were so distinct that one can only emphasize how greatly they matter in approaching questions about the general nature of urban change, both between and within cities.

THE TRANSFORMATION OF CITY SPACE

The evolving role of a particular city in the urban system during the later 19th century strongly influenced the shifting numbers of people, types of jobs, and nature of buildings and other facilities that concentrated at that location. Changing needs and opportunities in the expanding urban system, and each city's response to them, largely regulated the amount, periodicity, and kinds of new investments made, particularly whether established patterns would be simply extended or radically altered. Such changes translated into social and physical requirements that put variable pressure on the existing physical construction and spatial organization of the city. Because built forms are in themselves inert, the city's shifting needs led unceasingly to selective alteration of the built environment to keep up with new preferences. Yet while the morphology was changing, it was doing more than just passively catching up. The existing layout of landholdings, streets, and buildings powerfully influenced—and often controlled—the framework within which decisions were made about accommodating new buildings and land use.

The Dynamics of Physical Expansion

America's large cities faced immense problems in accommodating their exploding populations between the Civil War and the 1920s. They grew by extending the boundaries of their built-up areas far into the countryside and by increasing the density of the building stock within these areas, notably in and near the urban core. Citywide densities varied greatly; in 1880 New York averaged 46 people per acre, whereas Philadelphia then had a density of 10 (figures for other

major cities were Chicago 22, Boston 15, St. Louis 9, Baltimore 39, Cincinnati 16, and San Francisco 9 people per acre).

Chicago provides a good example of the changing connection between people, land, and buildings during the period. Chicago in 1890 contained a population of 1.1 million within a city composed of an estimated 171,000 buildings distributed over 53,117 acres of subdivided land. It is notable that in the 30 years before 1890, population rose at a steeper rate than subdivision activity and overall building construction (table 15.2). Building lots and housing had been in such supply that the ratio of people to land and buildings was very favorable through the 1880s. After 1890, subdividing slowed down relative to population and building construction because of the large surfeit of house lots. For example, the 3,827 single houses built in 1912 were exceeded by the 4,341 apartment buildings constructed that year, a trend sustained well into the World War I period. The high proportion of new buildings to new lots reflected the prior spatial dispersion of urban platting in the 19th century, the decline in the total number of new lots coming on the market, and the pressure—for locational reasons—to occupy available lots within the existing city area.

Urban growth through the outward extension of cities involved several processes. Landowners in the path of expansion responded sooner or later to increasing market prices and converted their land to urban, generally residential, use by subdividing it into streets, blocks, and lots for

Table 15.2 Indices of Chicago's Physical Growth, 1860–1930

	Population Index	Subdivision Index (1890 = 100)	Construction Index	Population per Subdivided Acre	Population per Building	Number of New Buildings per Newly Subdivided Acre[a]
Before 1860	11	27	24	8.2	2.9	2.9
1860–1870	28	45	57	12.9	3.2	5.8
1870–1880	50	75	75	13.9	4.3	1.9
1880–1890	100	100	100	20.9	6.5	3.3
1890–1900	153	119	149	26.8	6.7	8.1
1900–1910	196	125	195	32.8	6.6	24.8
1910–1920	243	144	247	35.4	6.4	9.1
1920–1930	303	158	314	40.2	6.3	14.8

[a]Last column applies to buildings erected during the indicated time period. All other columns apply to end date in each period.

individual sale. Characteristically, American urban land development in the mid-19th century largely separated the functions of selling house lots and building actual houses. Numerous entrepreneurs did build up whole streets at a time, but the scale of physical land planning was small, and in most cases new lot owners were expected to find their own means to erect their residences. Rectilinear street grids were nearly universal, lot densities varied widely within a small area, street systems did not always coordinate, and no inevitable logic applied to the sequence and timing by which the old land parcels of an area would be developed. As a result, many urban extensions were rigid in their microgeometry but haphazard in their gross patterns within the cityscape, although the extreme effects could be mitigated by either the informality of individually designed houses or the coherence of uniform buildings, particularly row houses. By the turn of the 20th century some changes were afoot, notably the growing popularity of curvilinear street layouts for better-class subdivisions, the rise of many integrated realtor-builder firms, and the advent of city planning, which introduced some rules concerning urban design.

Urban extension took many residents farther from their places of employment, and the growth of residential districts away from the urban core would have been inconceivable without new transport facilities. The advent of mass transit in the mid-19th century signaled the end of the completely "walking" city. Transport extension spanned several eras of technological innovation, from the horse-drawn omnibus introduced in New York in 1827, to the short-haul steam train, the horsecar, and, by the late 1880s, the cable car and electric streetcar. Each improvement saved time for the commuter and allowed ever more remote neighborhoods to enter the commuting field, while increased carrying capacity created operating efficiencies that resulted in lower travel costs as a proportion of income. This sequence of changes in intraurban travel permitted not only a greatly accelerated spatial expansion of the city but also the enhanced use of space as a means of separating formerly mixed urban activities of all kinds.

New York provides the most dramatic illustration. Contained within the lower one-third of the island of Manhattan and neighboring coastal Brooklyn in 1860, the urban built-up area almost tripled by 1900 (fig. 15.4). What had been tightly interdigitated areas of poor and better-off residential zones mixed with commercial and industrial uses south of 34th Street before the Civil War became well-defined poverty districts on the margins of a rapaciously northward-moving commercial-industrial core by century's end, as the building boom reached into Harlem and beyond, pulling the mansions of the elite and the tall, elegant row houses of the well-to-do around, and to the north of, Central Park. In Brooklyn, low-income areas proliferated in proximity to the daily work opportunities of the waterfront port facilities, while the middle and upper classes moved inland, especially along the streetcar lines of Fulton and Atlantic Streets.

Boston's "streetcar suburbs" have been better studied. The streetcar helped create residential districts of great physical variety, constructed mostly by small builders and businessmen, that offered a range of housing types and physical settings, all representative for their price levels of the new suburban ideal for superior living. On tree-shaded streets on sloping sites, new Queen Anne frame houses shared the quiet surroundings with late Italianate, Gothic Revival, or Richardsonian Romanesque detached homes, often of brick or stone. There were also Boston bowfronts, reproduced from the South End or Beacon Hill, and street after street of clapboard triple-deckers—a three-story, three-unit house type that was a marvelous stepladder to immigrant residential success.

Streetcars were not the only influence in the growth of these districts. The suburban movement was played out upon a landscape of colonial origin, fitting into a fairly dense network of existing roads connecting old village centers via established crossroads settlements, each road being more or less lined with former farmhouses, exurban residences, hotels, and taverns. To this settlement matrix was added, first, the steam railroad, which, in connecting the old village nodes with Boston, also contributed small knots of villas and occasional businesses in the vicinity of the railroad depots. These developments began about three miles from downtown Boston, and by the 1880s a railroad-based suburban culture and landscape were well established. In these respects, Boston mirrors general American processes of urban land development of the period, for the element of urban anticipation ensured that fringe development would be

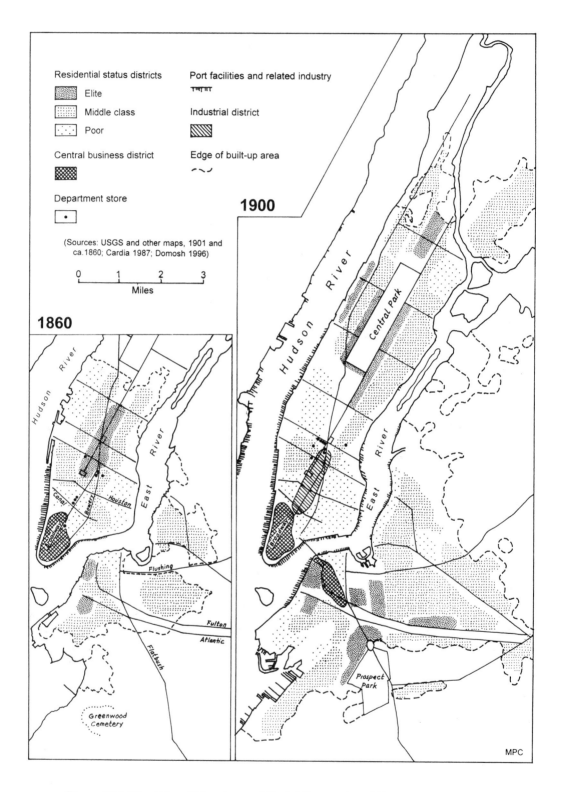

Residential status districts

- Elite
- Middle class
- Poor

Central business district

Department store

Port facilities and related industry

Industrial district

Edge of built-up area

(Sources: USGS and other maps, 1901 and ca.1860; Cardia 1987; Domosh 1996)

0   1   2   3
Miles

1860

1900

Hudson River

East River

Central Park

Canal

Bowery

Houston

Broadway

Flushing

Fulton

Atlantic

Flatbush

Greenwood Cemetery

Prospect Park

MPC

Figure 15.4 The Urban Extension and Social Geography of New York, 1860–1900

scattered. Thus, in an established region like Boston's, the streetcars responded to development as much as they stimulated it. By contrast, in the Los Angeles region, across the continent and in a slightly later period, the stimulative role of the streetcar was far more dominant.

House lots and streetcars were not the only prerequisites for urban extension. Utilities such as piped water, sewage drains, domestic gas and electric service, street lighting, and paving were all developed in time to be included on any list of necessary or desirable accoutrements of urban—and suburban—living. Major expenditures were required to supply most utilities to individual households because extensive networks of pipes or cable had to be installed above and below ground throughout the urban area. Patterns of wavelike service extension gradually moved outward from the business district, with master facilities sweeping along the major arterial streets to areas where the highest development densities would justify early connection. The issue of urban utilities often underlay the other concomitant process of urban extension: change in governmental jurisdiction. Spectacular physical expansion of urban areas became commonplace in America only after midcentury, and extension of cities' governmental authority followed almost naturally in the wake of significant numbers of urban workers' pioneering residence in the suburbs. By 1869 sufficient sentiment existed in Roxbury and Dorchester to win a vote for annexation to Boston. There was opposition from traditional quarters in these towns, but the central city was perceived as a great provider of modern urban services and an appropriate governmental form for the changing character of these formerly fringe towns.

Progressive Land Use Stratification

The term "metropolis" came into increasing favor during the middle of the 19th century to describe America's largest cities as a singular type of phenomenon, and it had gained common currency by the 1920s. This shift in terms denoted both the city's altered size and scale as well as its greater social and physical complexity. Geographically, these changes were expressed in the spatial separation of economic and social activities that had formerly coexisted in the same buildings and on the same streets. Although

New York, Boston, and Philadelphia had some specialized land use districts even in the late colonial period, the degree of functional separation, and indeed segregation, of activities in urban space was to emerge quite clearly after the 1850s and to become an immediate feature of newer cities.

The most striking developments were the rise of the central business district (CBD) as a highly specialized land use zone within the city; the gradual separation of industrial activity from the business core and its decentralization to industrial corridors and fringe belt zones that excluded most other land uses; the filtering of social and economic classes throughout the residential territory of the city so that particular districts and neighborhoods became socially, ethnically, and occupationally homogeneous; and the emergence of a hierarchically arranged network of subsidiary business centers in step with urban expansion. American cities before 1850 without doubt contained people and activities that varied in their concentration from one part to another, but urban size and changing social and economic forces combined after that date to reformulate spatially the large American city into clearly recognizable and often sharply bounded functional areas by the outbreak of World War I. Growing size and complexity encouraged a certain degree of spatial order for reasons of efficiency.

The business core of most large cities in the 1850s contained a great mixture of wholesale and retail traders, financiers, professionals, craftsmen and industrial concerns, haulers and handlers, messengers and cabbies, some government offices, and a motley array of residences, all competing for decent locations within what was already a very high-rent district. Between 1860 and 1920 the power of capital operated to sort out the winners and losers in this "bidding" contest: the economic growth of the metropolis demanded constant enlargement of the business district in terms of employment and space and pumped in the financial resources continuously to update and modernize its physical fabric. With each new business building, a nudge was given to land uses no longer in need of, or capable of retaining, central locations. With time, business not only came to dominate the downtown, to the virtual exclusion of residential functions, but also modernized its own pattern to the extent of evolving distinct subdistricts within the CBD in which types of businesses were heavily concentrated for convenient interaction and efficient supply. By the end of the period most major cities had separate downtown sectors for produce markets, wholesaling, retail shopping, finance, and government administration.

In the era of the walking city, the business core catered to practically the whole urban population; but as urban expansion progressed, many retail functions were replicated in newly developing neighborhoods at some distance from the center. Bakers, butchers, boot and shoe dealers, dry goods merchants, and the like spread across the city, clustering along major arteries and at key traffic nodes, to form subsidiary business centers. Over time, specialized retailers such as book and furniture stores, men's clothiers, and jewelers proliferated in the more important of these, representing a diffusion of more and more specialized retail services from the CBD down the hierarchy of shopping districts. As small operators were replaced in the CBD by large concerns, including after 1870 the new department stores and luxury goods merchants who sought trade among the commuters and hotel visitors (fig. 15.4), a great re-sorting of retail trade occurred whereby mundane and middle-level functions were increasingly offered by noncentral shopping districts at strategic locations within the expanded city.

Industry likewise began in the urban core in craft workshops located near commercial facilities such as waterpower sites, harbors, railroad stations, and other businesses. As the urban core became congested, land values rose, and many industrial processes became mechanized and larger scale, a dualism developed in industrial location patterns within large cities. Those industries that needed access to water or rail transport, such as the building trades or machinery production, or that depended on the business of the CBD, such as job printing or garment making, tended to stay within, or near the margins of, the business core. As that core expanded, such industry moved again but stayed within range of the downtown market. The development of Printers Row at the south end of Chicago's Loop in the 1880s illustrates this pattern. Other manufacturing that needed larger and cheaper space more than proximity to clients moved farther away, such as the Union Stockyards. By the 1890s, railroad com-

panies and land developers were creating specialized areas. such as the Central Manufacturing District in Chicago, at some distance from the city center, with integrated transport and power facilities and convenient labor pools in the ethnic neighborhoods that quickly coalesced around them.

In some cases these industrial belts encircled the city's growth rings of previous periods; in others they simply colonized the major waterway sites and railroad axes. Detroit's pattern was established early by the riverfront manufacturing belt and extended around the old city by belt railroads as the automotive and allied industries became established (fig. 15.5a).

Social Processes and
Residential Consequences

The social space of the midcentury walking city was comparatively heterogeneous. People of greatly differing income and social status often lived side-by-side in residential districts. Well-to-do neighborhoods, such as Society Hill in Philadelphia and Beacon Hill in Boston, were close to the bustling urban core, remnants of a passing era when the wealthy lived at the heart of the urban scene. Such areas were also near districts of very different character, such as the backside of Beacon Hill in Boston where a small community of blacks lived, or the North End with its artisans, shopkeepers, and longshoremen.

Immigrants arriving to live in eastern port cities after midcentury had little choice but to occupy cramped, rundown housing close to the work opportunities in and around the business core or wherever temporary jobs and squatting possibilities existed. In general, they formed a human wedge between the expanding commercial building stock and the traditional residents, who withdrew to better housing away from the CBD (fig. 15.4). This removal of the established social classes had begun earlier with the mounting commercial congestion of the inner city, the pioneering of more spacious residences at the edge of the city, and the appearance of public transport on major streets, but it unquestionably gained momentum with accelerated immigration.

Unprecedented urban growth created much new housing, which increasingly acclimatized people to change residential ownership more

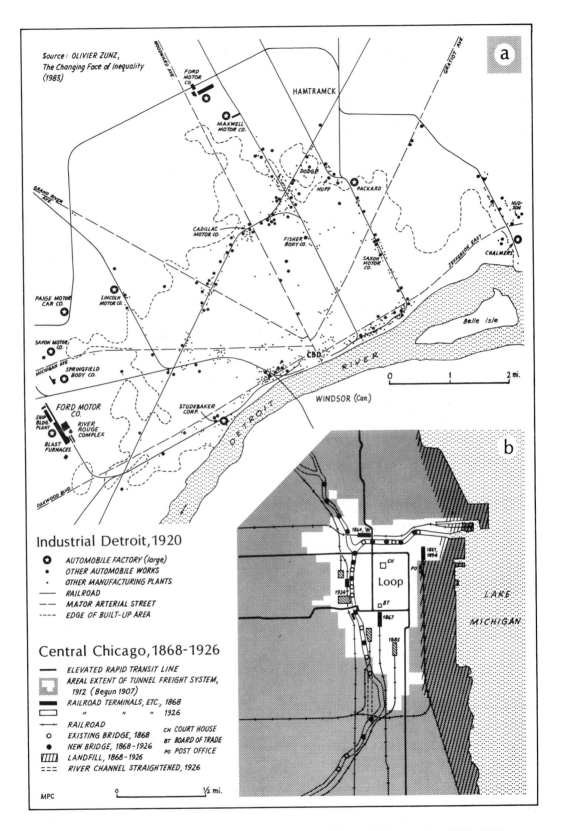

Figure 15.5 Industrial Detroit, 1920, and Relieving Chicago's Congestion, 1868–1926

frequently and thus to quicken the pace of residential "filtering." By this process the well-off gained the latest in housing styles, generally at the urban fringe; the middle classes took over the vacated homes of the former; and the working classes moved into houses disposed of by their former middle-class owners. Urban growth was generally so strong, however, that filtering needs to be seen in context: the supply of homes at particular prices rarely satisfied demand, so filtering was only a small part of the overall process by which housing was provided, new areas built up, and the city's social geography defined.

The social structure of American cities in the later 19th century grew at the extremes with consequences for residential patterns. Status differentials, whether denoted by occupation, income, or other measures, continued to rise as the propertied classes benefited from industrialization and general business growth and gained in wealth and numbers. This wealth was used to find residential seclusion from the "teeming masses," employing space to maintain social distinctions on a scale rarely seen before. The middle classes attempted a similar strategy, and the social mobility possible in late-19th-century urban America found supreme expression in residential mobility as a widespread familial experience. The poorer classes, full of immigrants, were consigned by low income to rent in slum and near slum conditions and to make frequent moves within confined districts; when family savings allowed escape, it was to areas remarkably uniform in general social composition. When substantial numbers of African Americans began migrating to industrial cities in the Northeast and Middle West after the turn of the century, they found themselves at the very bottom of the social hierarchy, with residential options reminiscent of those of the earliest immigrant groups.

The consequence of these social cleavages for residential patterns in most large cities was that social geography became spatially explicit. More and more, the wealthy disengaged residentially from the heart of the city and withdrew into secluded precincts, whose increasing homogeneity was protected by the financial barriers to ownership. This class, numerically small but financially significant as agents in the formation of the cityscape, generally created thin sectors of costly residential fabric, oriented to amenities such as lakeshores (Chicago's Gold Coast) or scenic hilly terrain (Washington's Mount Pleasant). The much larger middle class also moved centrifugally, although with less exclusivity, both absorbing genteel housing districts within the city where available and, more importantly, colonizing many new suburban areas. This opened the way for the even larger working class (including most immigrants) to expand into whatever existing housing opened up, often to double up in buildings converted for higher-density occupation (generally in the urban core), and also to absorb cheap housing in less desirable settings, such as floodplains, tidal flats, and awkward land parcels in the interstices between industrial plants and railroad facilities. Middle- and working-class districts proliferated widely, often arranged in sectors or discontinuous rings radiating from the urban core, depending on topographical barriers, timing of business cycles, and the location of industry. In the older eastern cities, the old neighborhoods of the urban core suffered various fates. Depending on location, they either succumbed to CBD expansion and were replaced by commercial buildings, or became rooming house districts or tenement quarters (in which, say, two-story housing was replaced by five- and six-story tenement blocks, as in Boston's North End), or simply deteriorated into slum conditions through overpopulation and financial disinvestment (slumlordism).

Social stratification by class, defined largely by income, may have determined the broad outlines of the large city's social geography, but that pattern was powerfully rewoven with ethnic thread. Immigrants who settled in cities often came to form ethnic "ghettos," districts overwhelmingly inhabited by nonnative people, either almost exclusively of one origin or of several in varying degrees. Common bonds and a common predicament held immigrants together in these usually dense neighborhoods until younger generations, more Americanized, would convert better incomes into residential relocation, perhaps even suburbanization. The ghetto model of ethnic enclaves, developed to describe the residential experience of some groups in some East Coast port cities such as New York and Boston, by no means fits all large American cities during the later 19th century. In Milwaukee, for example, Germans were proportionately numerous enough to settle districts of the city so extensive as to accommodate rich and poor alike within occupationally diverse neighborhoods that eased adjustment to American urban life far removed from the ghetto experience. In Detroit, a city late to industrialize, the period from 1880 to 1920 represented a major transformation from a social geography defined primarily by ethnic differences to one stratified clearly by class, and in which ethnic differences, although not absent, were not the guiding force in neighborhood reformation.

THE MOUNTING PROBLEMS OF URBANISM

The rapid growth, changing roles, and sharp internal transformations of large American cities from 1860 to 1930 placed enormous stress on their social and physical functions. Economic developments occurred in a generally laissez-faire ideological environment that enlarged the problems of providing adequate amenities such as infrastructure, housing, health, and governance. Responses to these problems took varied forms, ranging from franchises for private provision of public services to metropolitan jurisdictions for certain assets and, after the turn of the century, to the advent of comprehensive planning principles in a formal framework, signaled by the introduction in 1916 of land-use "zoning" in New York City. Some problems had very clear geographical dimensions.

Upgrading the Infrastructure

Commercial Improvements
The critical needs of commerce and industry in an urban context were (a) to keep abreast of technical improvements in transport facilities, and (b) to persuade the civic authorities whenever possible to subsidize their introduction, particularly where this involved costly rearrangement of the layout and fabric of the urban core. Improving harbors to accommodate ever larger ships, bridging waterways for better downtown access, and rationalizing freight interchange among railroad terminals were the key issues. Harbor commissioners demarcated new wharf lines, landfilling occurred, bridges were built at public and private expense, and rights-of-way were easily granted for belt rail-

ways and terminal consolidations. The changes these wrought in one burgeoning city can be seen in the case of Chicago (fig. 15.5b).

Building Fabric and Landfill
Most American cities were founded on flat, low-lying sites, and many encountered physical limits as building proceeded. Boston almost doubled its core area between 1860 and 1917 through extensive landfill on the surrounding tidal flats. Beginning in 1885, Chicago found it necessary to elevate its street system four feet above original grade to ensure drainage and functioning sewers. This enterprise required that all buildings in the city be built to the new level or raised up over fill to meet it. In working-class districts with little surplus cash for such modernization, many individual owners failed to comply or raised their cottages over a new basement and left the yards unfilled, creating undulating streetscapes with footbridges to some front doors that survive to this day. The urban fires that ravaged many cities mostly affected downtown areas. Chicago's 1871 fire was so extensive that building in wood was forbidden within subsequently established "fire limits," a requirement also disregarded and loosely policed in many localities, but which did result in the CBD's overnight conversion to brick and stone construction.

Congestion
By far the most common large-city problem was chronic downtown congestion, arising from the sharp increase in traffic within a business core that became denser year by year as ever taller buildings covered larger percentages of their ground lots. Hardest hit were northeastern cities like Boston and New York with narrow colonial streets. Street widening became common in Boston in the 1850s, sometimes robbing owners of the front 10 to 15 feet of their buildings when they could not be moved. By the 1890s, pedestrians, horse-drawn traffic, and electric streetcars confined to their tracks often created gridlock, and cities sought solutions in separating some of the traffic. Rapid transit made its appearance in New York with an elevated steam train in the 1870s, but electrification was to provide the real key to elevated and subway service. Elevated systems became popular in several cities, notably with the construction of Chicago's Loop in 1897 (fig. 15.5b), while

Boston began a subway system in the same year, followed by New York in 1904.

Amenities

The rising congestion of large cities after midcentury in both business and residential areas led to major movements to install urban parks as vital breathing spaces. Boston Common had long provided a model, but it was the application of new rural cemetery designs to New York's Central Park (begun in 1857) that started a trend, one that quickly became metropolitan in scale and systemic in concept (for example, the South and West Park system in Chicago, 1865–71). Provision for open space in really central locations did not fare well, as evidenced by the short life of the six-block public park set aside in Omaha's first plat of 1856, which succumbed to encroachment within a decade.

The difficulties encountered in developing a wide range of urban amenities in this period is reflected in what emerged through commercial enterprise, public initiative, and philanthropic gesture. Dance halls were common, and taverns ubiquitous but complex in their contribution to public well-being. More gracious were the beer gardens and private concert parks, often established by German interests, but they fell afoul of prohibition sentiment by the 1920s for their support of family drinking. Privately run amusement parks, racetracks, small museums, and exhibition halls proliferated, generally catering to popular taste. It was left to public effort and large-scale philanthropy to add major city libraries, museums, opera houses, and symphony orchestras to give leadership to the arts in the city. Occasional extravaganzas, like the 1876 Philadelphia Centennial Exposition or the World's Columbian Exposition in Chicago in 1893, played significant roles in spreading ideas and interest in new forms of living, technology, and urban design.

Housing, Health, and Social Adjustment

The free market in housing was unable to deflect the rise of urban slums in late-19th-century America. The tides of foreign immigration and rural influx propelled urban housing markets based on profit making to rely upon filtering to cope with redistribution. No profit could be made by housing the very poor in new single-family housing, as opposed to cramped quarters in inner-city locations in rundown buildings or in purpose-built tenement structures. The problems spurred "five-percent philanthropists" to experiment with subsidized housing for the poor, but generally such efforts were short-lived and foundered through mismanagement or tokenism. Native-born capitalists have often been blamed for slumlordism in this period. Boston's North End, however, while belonging to Yankee owners in the 1860s and 1870s during its Irish occupation, by 1917 had passed largely into Jewish and Italian ownership, by which time its residents were largely Italian. Better a slumlord in one's own image.

Overcrowding in districts with primitive household and street sanitation naturally encouraged epidemic outbreaks of disease, particularly cholera, which eventually led to reforms in water supply and public health services. In New York by the turn of the century, however, high mortality did not always coincide with the heaviest overcrowding and was sometimes variable among immigrant groups, with the Irish and Poles experiencing higher rates than Jews or Italians.

The concatenation of urban ills that built up in the largest cities over the decades after the Civil War drew forth a major effort at reform of everything from housing and health to crime, pollution, politics, and private morals. Reformers were convinced that the appalling state of the inner-city environment, and in particular the dilapidated and overcrowded housing, was the prime source of social deviance and that improving this environment would eliminate poverty as well as criminal and immoral behavior. Model tenements were constructed, model educational programs were instituted, and "settlement houses," such as Jane Addams's Hull House begun in Chicago in 1889, sought to improve the material circumstances and conduct of the poor family and to clean up the neighborhoods.

Collective efforts in this direction were not ineffective, for infant mortality was reduced, vocational training helped ghetto youths, kindergartens eased working mothers' daily problems and, above all, these initiatives focused a powerful spotlight on slum conditions. In failing to eradicate urban poverty, however, they raised the question whether the causes of poverty lay elsewhere than in the quality of the physical environment. The moral crusades to banish specific vice districts provided a clear lesson of this kind, since they were more successful in relocating than in eliminating prostitution and gambling, although the lessons were not always understood at the time.

Jurisdictional Conflicts:
Annexation, Suburban Incorporation,
and Metropolitanism

The period between 1870 and 1920 witnessed major shifts in urban governance. Cities modernized their charters and developed bureaucracies commensurate with their growing street-level workforces in an attempt to keep up with the increasing complexity of urban life. That mounting complexity was in some measure the result of enlarged scale, and cities, like corporations dedicated to self-perpetuation, generally attempted to expand their bounds through annexation. Boston's absorption of Roxbury and Dorchester in 1869 has been noted, Chicago's annexation of Lake and Hyde Park Townships in 1889 more than doubled the city's area in a single year, and New York expanded in 1898 through consolidation of Manhattan, the Bronx, Brooklyn, Queens, and Staten Island to form a metropolis of 3 million people. During most of the 19th century, the city was viewed as a paragon of urban services and efficient government.

As the century came to a close, however, that view changed among the suburbs. Outlying municipalities became disenchanted as city size bred inefficiency, indifference to local interests, higher taxes, and increasingly corrupt government. In most large metropolitan regions, annexations dwindled in size and frequency as suburban incorporations rose. Cambridge and Brookline refused union with Boston, but these entities had a long history of local government. More impressive was the wave of incorporations around such cities as Chicago, where comparatively new railroad commuter suburbs sought to forge their own destiny, even at the price of initially small-scale and limited development. By 1920 Chicago's expansion had run up against an almost continuous encircling wall of independent, incorporated "villages" and "cities."

Finally, large cities with major immigrant populations were experiencing a change in the distribution of power as ethnic leaders flexed their political muscle and "boss" government

became a reality. The traditional leaders sought, often with considerable success, to delay and dilute some of this transition by metropolitanizing urban governance. In Boston, the traditionally established Brahmins transferred as many functions as possible to the state legislature, the governor, and metropolitan commissions (for water, parks, and the like), and changed city councillors from ward to at-large representation, thus neatly diversifying power "to spread it around in little indistinct piles so the Irish would find it hard to gather."

REGIONAL DIFFERENCES AND SMALL TOWNS

No overview of this length can hope to do justice to the regional variations in American urban structure and form that emerged between the Civil War and the 1920s. Broad differences not considered here distinguished cities that were ethnically plural from those with few immigrants. What held in terms of class formation, residential accommodation, and industrialization for New York, Worcester, or Cincinnati would not have applied to Portland or Salt Lake City in the West. The effects of race on southern cities in this period must also be acknowledged, for the cleavages in ethnic relations in northern cities remained qualitatively different from the experience of a racial caste system that no Civil War could magically eradicate. Regions separated cities in terms of the channels of urban innovation to which they were tied, whether by the diffusion and timing of street railways or of building types. Further, regional variations reflected differences— whether of economic development or social character—between urbanization in so-called instant or shock cities of the West and those more easterly that arose more slowly through somewhat more organic evolution.

Similarly crucial is the caveat concerning urban scale. Much of the concern has been with large cities, because in them new trends emerged perhaps earliest or with greatest impact owing to their size. But there are valid questions to pose about urban thresholds for any and all urban phenomena: Did urban traits diffuse regionally, by proximal visitation, as it were, or hierarchically, because towns reached a size at which a characteristic would naturally emerge?

Was the small town in late-19th- and early-20th-century America merely an incipient metropolis, or was it a distinct type needing, in view of stagnant or stunted growth history, its own analysis? Certainly, small towns past their boom times and locked in at low levels of the urban hierarchy possessed a resignation to smallness that contrasted with the generally expansionist cultural milieu around them. Considering the cultural significance of the small town in American life, this lowly class of urbanism deserves proportionate recognition.

ADDITIONAL READING

Berry, B. J. L. 1991. "Long Waves in American Urban Evolution." In *Our Changing Cities,* ed. John Fraser Hart. Baltimore: Johns Hopkins University Press.

Borchert, J. R. 1967. "American Metropolitan Evolution." *Geographical Review* 57, no. 3: 301–32.

Colten, C. E. 1994. "Chicago's Waste Lands: Refuse Disposal and Urban Growth, 1840–1990." *Journal of Historical Geography* 20, no. 2: 124–42.

Conzen, M. P. 1981. "The American Urban System in the 19th Century." In *Geography and the Urban Environment: Research and Applications,* vol. 4, ed. David T. Herbert and Ronald J. Johnston. New York: Wiley & Sons.

Conzen, M. P., and K. N. Conzen. 1979. "Geographical Structure in 19th-Century Urban Retailing: Milwaukee, 1836–90." *Journal of Historical Geography* 5, no. 1: 45–66.

Cronon, W. J. 1991. *Nature's Metropolis: Chicago and the Great West.* New York: W. W. Norton.

Domosh, M. 1996. *Invented Cities: The Creation of Landscape in 19th-Century New York and Boston.* New Haven: Yale University Press.

Ford, L. R. 1994. *Cities and Buildings: Skyscrapers, Skidrows, and Suburbs.* Baltimore: Johns Hopkins University Press.

Groth, P. E. 1994. *Living Downtown: A History of Residential Hotels in the United States.* Berkeley and Los Angeles: University of California Press.

Groves, P. A., and E. K. Muller. 1975. "The Evolution of Black Residential Areas in Late 19th Century Cities." *Journal of Historical Geography* 1, no. 2: 169–92.

Hanchett, T. W. 1998. *Sorting Out the New South City: Race, Class, and Urban Development in Charlotte, 1875–1975.* Chapel Hill: University of North Carolina Press.

Hershberg, T., ed. 1981. *Philadelphia: Work, Space, Family and Group Experience in the 19th Century.* New York: Oxford University Press.

Hudson, J. C. 1985. *Plains Country Towns.* Minneapolis: University of Minnesota Press.

Jablonsky, T. J. 1993. *Pride in the Jungle: Community and Everyday Life in the Back of the Yards Chicago.* Baltimore: Johns Hopkins University Press.

LeBlanc, R. G. 1969. *Location of Manufacturing in New England in the 19th Century.* Dartmouth: Dartmouth College Publications in Geography.

Lemon, J. T. 1996. *Liberal Dreams and Nature's Limits: Great Cities of North America since 1600.* Toronto: Oxford University Press.

Lewis, P. F. 1972. "Small Town in Pennsylvania." *Annals of the Association of American Geographers* 62, no. 2: 323–51.

———. 1976. *New Orleans: The Making of an Urban Landscape.* Cambridge, Mass.: Ballinger.

Mayer, H. M., and R. C. Wade. 1969. *Chicago: Growth of a Metropolis.* Chicago: University of Chicago Press.

Meinig, D. W. 1972. "American Wests: Preface to a Geographical Introduction." *Annals of the Association of American Geographers* 62, no. 2: 159–84.

Meyer, D. R. 1980. "A Dynamic Model of the Integration of Frontier Urban Places into the United States System of Cities." *Economic Geography* 56, no. 2: 120–40.

Muller, E. K. 1996. "The Pittsburgh Survey and Greater Pittsburgh: A Muddled Metropolitan Geography." Pp. 69–87 in *Pittsburgh Surveyed: Social Science and Social Reform in the Early 20th Century,* ed. Maurine W. Greenwald and Margo J. Anderson. Pittsburgh: University of Pittsburgh Press.

Olson, S. H. 1981. *Baltimore: The Building of an American City.* Baltimore: Johns Hopkins University Press.

Pred, A. R. 1966. *The Spatial Dynamics of U.S. Urban Industrial Growth, 1800–1914.* Cambridge: Harvard University Press.

———. 1981. "Production, Family, and 'Free-time Projects': A Time-Geographic Perspective on the Individual and Societal Change in 19th-Century U.S. Cities." *Journal of Historical Geography* 7, no. 1: 3–36.

Radford, J. P. 1981. "The Social Geography of the 19th Century U.S. City." In *Geography and the Urban Environment: Research and Applications,* vol. 4, ed. D. T. Herbert and R. J. Johnston. New York: John Wiley & Sons.

Schneider, J. C. 1980. *Detroit and the Problem of Order, 1830–1880: A Geography of Crime, Riots, and Policing.* Lincoln: University of Nebraska Press.

Schreuder, Y. 1990. "The Impact of Labor Segmentation on the Ethnic Division of Labor and the Immigrant Residential Community: Polish Leather Workers in Wilmington, Delaware, in the Early 20th Century." *Journal of Historical Geography* 16, no. 4: 402–24.

Schuyler, D. 1986. *The New Urban Landscape: The Redefinition of City Form in 19th-Century America.* Baltimore: Johns Hopkins University Press.

Vill, M. J. 1986. "Building Enterprise in Late 19th-Century Baltimore." *Journal of Historical Geography* 12, no. 2: 162–81.

Walker, R., and R. D. Lewis. 2001. "Beyond the Crabgrass Frontier: Industry and the Spread of North American Cities, 1850–1950." *Journal of Historical Geography* 27, no. 1: 3–19.

Ward, D. 1989. *Poverty, Ethnicity, and the American City, 1840–1925: Changing Conceptions of the Slum and Ghetto.* New York: Cambridge University Press.

Warner, S. B., Jr. 1962. *Streetcar Suburbs: The Process of Growth in Boston 1870–1900.* Cambridge: Harvard University Press.

Winder, G. M. 1999. "The North American Manufacturing Belt in 1880: A Cluster of Regional Industrial Systems or One Large Industrial District?" *Economic Geography* 75, no. 1 (January): 71–92.

Zunz, O. 1982. *The Changing Face of Inequality: Urbanization, Industrial Development, and Immigrants in Detroit, 1880–1920.* Chicago: University of Chicago Press.

16

Realizing the Idea of Canada

GRAEME WYNN

Canada began as an idea. In the 1860s the prospect of building a country across the northern half of the continent was a bold vision indeed. Numbers were small, distances vast, and, perhaps most significant of all, Canada would have to be built across the north-south grain (the geography) of the continent.

From the outset the country was a mix of quite different elements, and with them a bundle of hopes and contradictions. Unlike nations that grew by the gradual extension of authority across space, Canada was a packaging of colonies created by decree, the British North America Act, in 1867. But politicians had differed in their opinions about how the new country should be organized. John A. Macdonald, who would become Canada's first prime minister, initially favored the creation of a strong unitary state. His counterpart from French Canada, George-Etienne Cartier, felt the distinctiveness of his people and preferred a structure that would allow local identities to flourish. The terms of Confederation recognized Cartier's concerns; citizens would not profess a common identity. Canadians felt few bonds of blood and belonging. Their sympathies and interests were more local: a cluster of distinct communities sharing some interests and sheltered under the umbrella of a federal structure that left room for the provinces to sustain difference. On this foundation, accommodating multiple identities and divided loyalties, Canadians sought to build a transcontinental country and secure a future separate from the United States. The challenges were hugely intensified by the success and vigor of that neighboring country. Despite the considerable achievements since 1867, they confront Canadians yet (fig. 16.1).

In 1866 British North America's population of approximately 3 million was scattered across an enormous area. The 2.5 million settlers of the St. Lawrence–Great Lakes lowland apart, these people occupied tiny, ill-connected fragments of territory. In the east, settlement clung to the shores and pushed inland only along a few fertile river valleys. A thousand miles of wild, rugged country separated the St. Lawrence settlements from a small enclave of Europeans at the Red River. The vast plains beyond were occupied by aboriginal peoples and a few thousand Métis (descendants of indigenous women and early fur traders). Europeans were confined, for the most part, to fur-trading posts because the interior was the domain of the Hudson's Bay Company and mission settlements. Across the Rocky Mountains aboriginal peoples outnumbered approximately 10,000 newcomers by perhaps 3 to 1. Even the Canadas East and West (approximately southern Quebec and southern Ontario today), which later historians would unite in the "commercial empire of the St. Lawrence," were divided by language, religion, and experience. Nowhere was the wilderness very distant, in space or time.

The fundamental pattern of European colonization in this northern realm was clear, and time would reveal its resilience. Primary resource industries were the basis of settlement. The fur trade, the fishery, the timber trade, agriculture, and (in the far west) the lure of gold had brought people to the wilderness and sustained them there. Each had generated its own distinctive settlement patterns and landscapes but all depended on lines of communication that facilitated trade, focused on towns, and connected local economies to others beyond North America. To a greater or lesser extent each had also generated markets for imported and locally produced foodstuffs and consumer goods. There were small clusters of industry in parts of Canada West and in Montreal, but in 1860 British North America was an overwhelmingly preindustrial, staple-producing cluster of predominantly rural and artisanal manufacturing communities linked through a handful of urban commercial centers to a transatlantic hearth. Political and economic consolidation would extend and ultimately transform, but not quite obliterate, this structure.

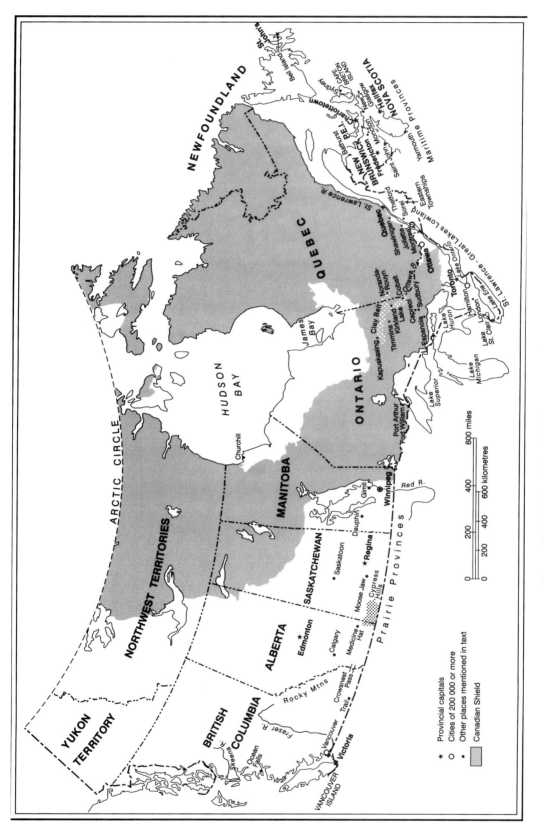

Figure 16.1 Modern Canada. Places named are cited in text.

MAKING SPACE

The essential territorial foundation of the new nation was established in less than a decade. The British North America Act, which created the Dominion of Canada on July 1, 1867, united Canada West and Canada East with New Brunswick and Nova Scotia. Three years later, Rupert's Land (the fur-trading territory draining into Hudson Bay) and the far northwest were transferred to the federal government for administration (fig. 16.2). Together they amounted to more than six times the area of the original provinces. From this extensive domain, a small area, centered on the early-19th-century Red River settlement, was established as the province of Manitoba. A year later, in 1871, the Crown colony of British Columbia entered Confederation, and Prince Edward Island became the seventh province in 1873. With the transfer of the Arctic islands from Britain to Canada in 1880, the late-19th- and early-20th-century limits of the Dominion were established.

Within this frame, internal boundary changes and shifting political jurisdictions reflected administrative requirements, the advance of settlement, and competing territorial ambitions. The district of Keewatin was created from the vast unorganized Northwest Territories and placed under the jurisdiction of Manitoba in 1876. In 1881 the boundaries of Manitoba were enlarged, and a year later the provisional districts of Alberta, Assiniboia, Athabaska, and Saskatchewan were set off from the Northwest Territories under their own lieutenant-governor. Renewing a long-standing claim to land north and west of its existing boundary, Ontario disputed the eastward extension of Manitoba; in 1889 resolution of the issue extended Ontario's territory to James Bay and contracted that of Manitoba. By 1898 Quebec's northern boundary was realigned to correspond with that of Ontario; Yukon was a separate territory, reflecting the discovery of gold in the Klondike; and three new districts had been erected in the remaining Northwest Territories. A growing population on the Prairies brought provincial status to Saskatchewan and Alberta in 1905, and in 1912 the boundaries of Quebec, Ontario, and Manitoba were extended to their present limits.

As the country expanded northwestward, a series of treaties, dated between 1871 and 1921, formalized in the eyes of the state the surrender of aboriginal claims to the land. In return indigenous peoples were granted reserves of at least 160 acres per family, small onetime monetary payments, and annuities. In British Columbia, where land appropriation had proceeded since 1864 without reference to the consent or wishes of the original occupants, aboriginal peoples were treated even more illiberally. Largely confined to reserves that were in some respects rural ghettos, the indigenous peoples of the west were displaced and disoriented by change. With their needs largely ignored, new diseases decimating their societies, and their traditional cultures eroding, Canada's indigenous population declined through the first decades of the 20th century. Proportionately, their numerical significance fell dramatically. They accounted for more than half of the population of British Columbia in 1881 but for less than one-eighth of the total in 1901.

By its acquisition of the Northwest Territories in 1870, the federal government both established the basis for a transcontinental nation and transformed the nature of Confederation. The original Dominion was a federation of equal provinces, each responsible for the administration of its Crown (or public) lands and entitled to revenues derived from them. In this respect Canada followed a British precedent quite distinct from the arrangements that made unappropriated lands in the United States the property of the federal government and established national jurisdiction over the public domain. Mindful of its nation-building task, however, the Canadian government retained direct control of Crown land in the western interior. All ungranted or waste lands in the Northwest Territories and the new province of Manitoba were declared a national endowment to be used "for the purposes of the Dominion." This provision was subsequently applied to Crown lands in the provinces of Alberta and Saskatchewan. Not until 1930 did these provinces gain control of their Crown lands and natural resources. This was long a source of grievance among Prairie dwellers, not least because British Columbia entered Confederation on the same basis as the original provinces.

With "one great country before it" the Dominion government implemented "one vast system of survey" across the western interior. Following the American pattern, the Prairie region was divided into a grid of farm holdings based

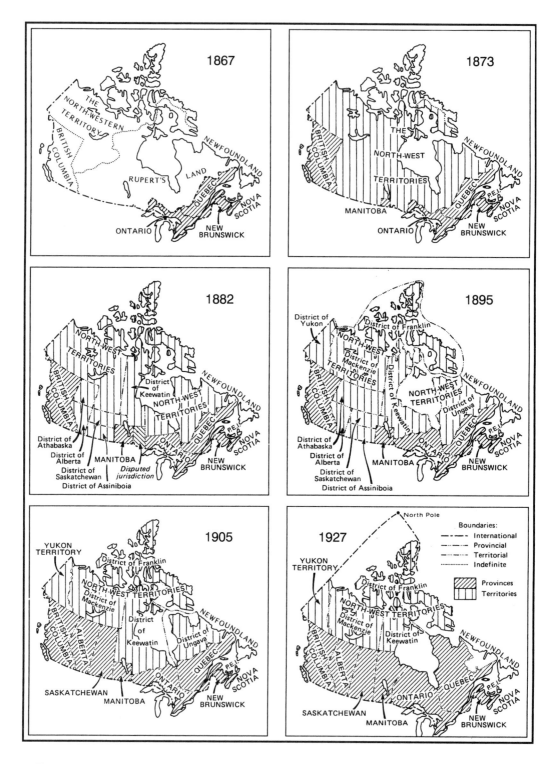

Figure 16.2 The Territorial Expansion of Canada (Adapted from the *National Atlas of Canada*)

on the 640-acre section and the 36-section township that marks the landscape, with scant regard for climate or local topography, from the Rio Grande to the Arctic Circle. Deviations from this pattern were rare. By the terms of the transfer of Rupert's Land, blocks of 50,000 acres or fewer were allowed the Hudson's Bay Company in the vicinity of their trading posts. River lots granted by the company were recognized, and the river-lot system was continued until 1884 for those residents, mostly Métis, who wanted it. In all, some 1.4 million acres were set aside by the Manitoba Act for Métis families. Special surveys were also implemented on certain irrigation lands in Alberta. Two sections of every surveyed township in the Dominion lands were set aside as an endowment for public schools; and south of the North Saskatchewan River, the Hudson's Bay Company received 1/20 of the surveyed land, a total of 6.6 million acres. By an act of 1872, provisions for the settlement of Dominion land were established. Homestead entries on quarter sections (160 acres) were registered for a $10 fee. Title to the property was granted after three years' residence and the completion of specified improvements.

BUILDING LINKS

Railroads were the arteries of national development (fig. 16.3). They tied the country together, east to west, and massively reduced the time and cost of overland movement within it. The British North America Act provided for the construction of an intercolonial line from the St. Lawrence to Halifax, and British Columbia entered Confederation on terms that included the completion of a transcontinental railway. And as though to emphasize the importance of improved communications in making the country, Prince Edward Island joined Canada on the promise of better links with the mainland. Railway building was a sustaining focus of early Canadian politics, and the results, in terms of track miles, were impressive. In 1867, Canada had 2,278 miles of operating track, most of it in Ontario. By 1875, 4,331 miles of first main track were in use; a decade later the figure topped 10,000, and by 1891 it was almost 14,000 miles. The Intercolonial (ICR) reached Halifax in 1876, and in November 1885 the

Canadian Pacific (CPR) line linked Vancouver to the St. Lawrence. Each followed routes more influenced by politics than by economics. Built and operated by the Dominion government, the ICR traced a circuitous path intended to reduce its vulnerability to American attack and ran through wilderness for much of its length. It failed to provide a return on capital invested. For the CPR, a southern route across the Prairies was favored over one through the fertile, dark-brown soils of the aspen parkland to reinforce Canadian interests in the border country. Construction of an all-Canadian line also meant building through the unproductive Canadian Shield north of Lake Huron and Lake Superior. Because the immediate prospects of private returns on costs were far lower than the social benefits of the railroad, the line was heavily subsidized by Dominion, provincial, and municipal governments. In all, the CPR received $25 million in cash and 25 million acres of land from the Dominion government, as well as tax and right-of-way concessions. Sizable sections of line built by government contractors west of Thunder Bay and in British Columbia were handed over to the company. Certain monopoly provisions were secured, and further land subsidies were negotiated in British Columbia. By agreement, preference, and the exercise of "indemnity selections," the CPR's land entitlement was heavily concentrated in the Prairie west. After surrendering some 6.8 million acres to retire debts in 1886, the company held approximately 2 million acres in Manitoba, 6 million in Saskatchewan, and 10 million in Alberta. Nor was the CPR the sole corporate recipient of Prairie land. Shorter "colonization railroads" proliferated during the 1880s. Ultimately, almost 3,000 miles of land-subsidized track were laid on the Prairies, and the CPR main line accounted for barely a third of this total. In the 1890s, almost half the agricultural land in the western interior was in railway hands. In all, railway land grants in the region amounted to some 32 million acres.

DEFINING EDEN

Vigorous efforts to encourage occupation of the western interior began with the annexation of the northwest. Suddenly, an area once considered an extension of the Great American Desert,

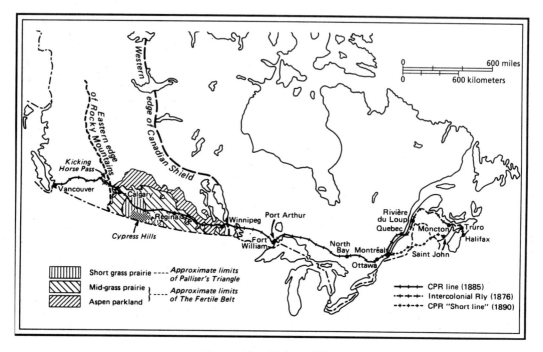

Figure 16.3 Railroad Ties

its soils dismissed as "sand and gravel with a slight intermixture of earth," was seen to offer the promise of Eden. Productive land seemed as boundless as the promoters' hopes, the climate as equable as their prose. The fertility of the Red River valley was rivaled only by the alluvium of the Nile; elsewhere the soil was said to drop "fatness" and hoard up wealth. Laudatory pamphlets appeared in enormous numbers from the pens of government, CPR, and local authors. Many of them were widely distributed. More than a million copies of the government's *Information for Intending Emigrants* were in circulation by 1873. In the scramble to boost the region, enthusiasm sometimes overwhelmed accuracy. One map, published in 1874, had the CPR crossing the plains, though it pointedly indicated which American lines were projected rather than completed. The "misdemeanors and scientific tricks" of John Macoun, one of the most ardent promoters of Manitoba and the northwest, were roundly denounced by an earlier surveyor, H. Y. Hind. But optimism was more characteristic than deliberate misrepresentation. Manitoba was sunny and fruitful. Farms were "free." Land was of the best. Advertisements for

2.75 million acres in the "Park Lands of the Fertile Belt" were alluring indeed. One Hudson's Bay Company advertisement of 1880 pointed out "The Land is Prairie, not Bush Land."

On the eastern flank of the Prairies, migrants from Ontario settled in small but increasing numbers after 1870, to grow wheat on a scale no longer practicable in their home counties. Several group settlements stemmed more directly from government encouragement. In the mid-1870s, 6,000 Mennonites from the Ukraine were given religious freedom, exemption from military service, and exclusive use of sizable blocks of land in southeastern Manitoba. Between 1874 and 1886 some 5,000 French Canadians from New England and Quebec established a dozen or so communities along the Red River and its tributaries. Icelanders and others also received group settlement lands in these years. Although many of the settlements were ethnically and linguistically distinct, traditional agricultural practices and settlement patterns rarely continued unaffected by the economic and environmental circumstances of the Prairies. By 1886, the agglomerated farm villages (*strassendorfer*) of the Mennonites were giving way to dispersed homesteads, and many Icelanders had left the Gimli region in search of better land.

Development also proceeded in the far western interior. Here pastoralism dominated. As the "beef bonanza" swept western North America, the small cattlemen who had begun ranching in the Alberta district during the 1870s were challenged by a growing number of large cattle companies. By 1886 there were 12,000 people (half of them Native), 100,000 cattle, and 25,000 sheep between the Cypress Hills and the Rockies; perhaps 80 percent of the beef stock was in herds of 400 or more. Four years later, with railroad connection to the St. Lawrence, beef from the Canadian cattle kingdom sold in British markets. In technique and economic character this industry bore many resemblances to its American counterpart. But those engaged in it—largely drawn from the Central Canadian middle class and the lesser landed gentry of Britain—were socially distinct from their American neighbors. Furthermore, the Canadian ranching frontier was set apart from the American tradition of squatter sovereignty on "free grass" land after 1881 by the introduction from Australia of a leasing system to control access to the rangeland. By offering as many as 100,000 acres for up to 21 years at a rental of one cent per acre, the Canadian government exercised more direct control over western development than did its American counterpart; perhaps incidentally, this involvement tended to minimize both the violence and the overstocking that marked the American rangelands.

Yet these were small gains from a frenzy of promotion. In 1886 the western interior had only 163,000 inhabitants. Some 60,000 of these were concentrated in the Manitoba lowlands, within 75 miles of Winnipeg, a city of 20,000. Most of the remainder were scattered across southwestern Manitoba and along the railroad in the Qu'Appelle River valley. Few had penetrated the semiarid area known as Palliser's Triangle, between Moose Jaw and Medicine Hat. The years between 1872 and 1885 accounted for only 8.8 percent of all Prairie homestead entries recorded before 1930. On average there were fewer than 3,000 entries a year between 1876 and 1896. If the western interior was no longer the "Great Lone Land" of the 1860s, it remained for much of the 19th century a region of few people and vast, undeveloped extent.

IMPLEMENTING A NATIONAL POLICY

Faced with the need to develop the west, the effects of a worldwide economic recession, the dumping of excess American industrial production in the Canadian market, and the emigration of unemployed Canadian workers to the United States, the Dominion government sought to expand domestic manufacturing and promote interregional trade in Canada. In 1879 a complex set of duties levied on imported commodities was cleverly designated "the National Policy." Import duties were not new, but now they were applied more systematically. A general levy of 20 percent was established on all items for which other rates of taxation were not specified. Rates on several designated commodities were established to make domestic products competitive with imports. In broad terms finished consumer goods incurred the heaviest tariffs. Such items as furniture and clothing bore charges of approximately 35 percent by value. Machinery, including farm implements, was taxed at some 25 percent; semifinished goods such as pig iron and rolled steel were charged 10 to 20 percent. Imported coal, charged 50 cents a ton in 1879, bore a 60-cent levy—over 20 percent—in the 1880s. The protection given to primary iron and steel in 1883 was raised with other tariffs in 1887. Together these fiscal policies offered something to every important economic interest in the country. Raising the cost of imports allowed Cape Breton coal into Montreal furnaces, Ontario flour into Maritime ovens, and central Canadian reapers onto Prairie farms. Domestic production was encouraged, new sinews of trade were created, and the regions of the new nation were bound together by commerce. According to John A. Macdonald, who led the Conservative Party to electoral victory in 1878 on the promise of the tariff, protection was a vital part of a wider national policy built upon territorial expansion, railway construction, and immigration. Together, proclaimed Macdonald, these initiatives would make of Canada "a union in interest, a union in trade, and a union in feeling." These hopes were slow to materialize, however. A quarter-century after these effusive claims another prime minister spoke of the need to "consolidate Confederation" and to "bring our people . . . gradually to become a nation." In 1900, Canada still bore the mark of 19th-century settlement more clearly

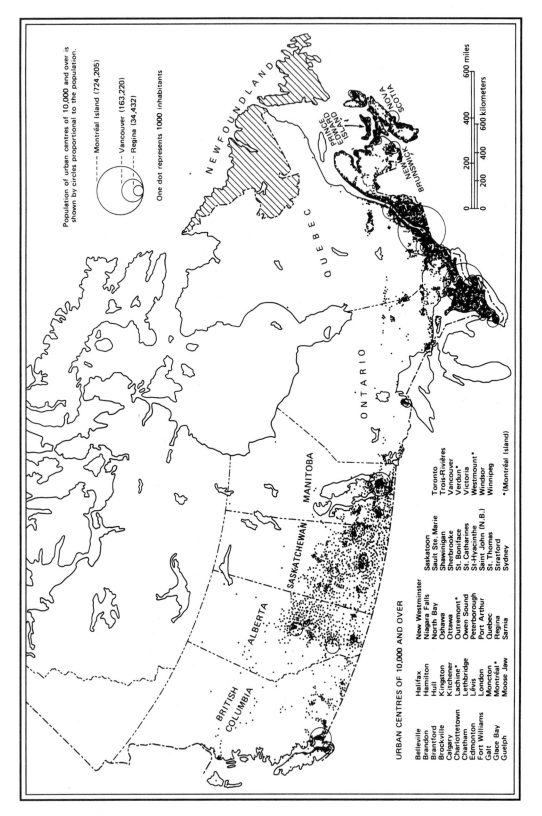

Figure 16.4 Canada's Population Distribution, 1921 (Adapted from *The National Atlas of Canada*)

than it reflected the ambitions of the National Policy.

A NEW ORDER

By 1930 a great transformation had occurred in the northern half of the continent. Some 10 million people called Canada home (fig. 16.4). Ontario had almost as many residents as the country of 1867. Growth, the watchword of the period, was evident on almost every front. New railroads, symbols of the national achievement, split the northern forest, wound through the mountains, and crisscrossed the plains. There was a mile of main track for every 237 Canadians. Wheat production was up almost 25-fold from its 1871 level. Prairie sod was still being broken, and deep in the Canadian Shield, new mines yielded gold and silver and nickel. Hydroelectric power, clean and inexhaustible, was being generated at dozens of remote dams. Pulp and paper mills turned northern trees into commercial products. Scientific surveys, transport improvements, and oil and mineral discoveries made the north a focus of commercial interest.

In the south, cities had grown at an astonishing rate. Montreal, a place of 100,000 people at Confederation, exceeded three-quarters of a million in the 1920s. Toronto grew almost tenfold in 50 years from its 1871 total of 56,000. By 1921, four other cities—Vancouver, Winnipeg, Ottawa, and Hamilton—had populations in excess of 100,000. An integrated network of urban places, linked by rail and, increasingly, by telephone, formed a national system. Manufacturing employment more than tripled (from 182,000 to 666,000) between 1870 and 1929, and value-added soared from $94 million to $1,713 million in the same period.

Population patterns provide the best single measure of geographical change during these years. Most striking was the sheer increase in numbers. Canada's population rose by 24 percent between 1881 and 1901, and by 64 percent in the 20 years that followed. In numerical terms this was an advance from 4.3 million to 5.3 million to 8.8 million, a doubling in 40 years. Equally significant were changes in the origins of immigrants and the westward shift of population in Canada. Some 6.15 million immigrants arrived in Canada between 1870 and 1930. Before 1900 they came, for the most part, from

Britain and northwestern Europe: Germany, France, and Scandinavia. Thereafter their number included an increasing proportion of central and eastern European peoples. The average annual inflow for the first half of the period (56,265) stood far below that for the second (152,886), when the Prairies attracted a greater proportion of immigrants than any other region of the country. Consequently, the original provinces accounted for a shrinking fraction of the nation's people between 1871 and 1931. Their growth in the last decades of the 19th century was less than the natural increase of their populations.

By 1931, Canadians were far more diverse than ever before. New waves of immigration had brought settlers from a great range of places. Those of German origin numbered 473,000, of Ukrainian 225,000; there were approximately 150,000 each of Polish, Jewish, and Dutch origin. Italians, Norwegians, Russians and Swedes were each 80,000 to 100,000 strong, and there were 46,500 Chinese and 23,000 Japanese among the 84,548 Canadians of Asiatic origin. Correspondingly, the proportion of British origin fell from 61 percent to 52 percent between 1871 and 1931. Canadians of French origin, 31 percent of the total in 1871, constituted only 28 percent 60 years later.

This varied population was also more heavily urban than that enumerated in earlier Canadian censuses. In broad terms, the country urbanized at a rate of 6 percent a decade between 1871 and 1901, 8 percent from 1901 to 1911, and 4 percent in the years 1911–21 and 1921–31. Urban dwellers, of whom an increasing fraction lived in large centers, increased from 19.6 percent to 53.7 percent. In 1881, Montreal, with 140,000 people, was the only city of 100,000 or more. By 1931, 2.3 million Canadians, a fifth of the total and fully 45 percent of those living in incorporated centers, resided in seven such places. The Maritimes (40 percent urban) and the Prairies (31 percent) were the only predominantly rural regions of Canada; almost two-thirds of Ontarians and 60 percent of Quebecers lived in urban places. British Columbia, the least urbanized of jurisdictions in 1871 (at 9 percent) was second only to Ontario in its proportion of urban residents by 1931; between 1891 and 1911 it was the most heavily urbanized province in the country. In Saskatchewan and Prince Edward Island only one inhabitant in five was urban in 1931; Alberta had crossed this threshold in 1904, and all other provinces in 1891 or earlier.

Together these changes reflected the economic transformation of Canada. Primary activity—agriculture and natural resource extraction—accounted for a shrinking proportion of national income. Real output per capita also grew more quickly than before. Gross national product (GNP) soared, increasing 3.7 times in real terms between 1890 and 1930. Rapid growth in the primary sector and rising exports of wheat, flour, minerals, and pulp and paper accounted for a substantial part of this quickening. But export expansion was paralleled by an increase in the specialization, diversification, and integration of the Canadian economy, predicated upon a massive extension of the country's transportation infrastructure and the development of its energy sources. The effects were immense, and evident in all sectors of economic life.

DIMENSIONS OF THE
GREAT TRANSFORMATION

New railroads were built at an astonishing rate. A dense network of branch lines, rarely more than 20 miles apart, was thrown across the western interior. Railways were built to encourage colonization in northern Ontario and Quebec. Mines in the Shield and the Cordillera required railroads to get their ore to markets; they were built. In 1901 and 1902, two new transcontinental railroads were initiated (fig. 16.5). The Grand Trunk Pacific, between Prince Rupert and Winnipeg, operated in conjunction with the National Transcontinental, built by the federal government from Winnipeg to Moncton, cutting through the heart of the Canadian Shield. The Canadian Northern, from Vancouver to Montreal via Edmonton, Dauphin (Manitoba), Capreol (Ontario), and Ottawa, grew initially by the amalgamation of local lines. Both systems received huge subsidies in cash and land from federal, provincial, and municipal governments. Construction costs on the National Transcontinental were enormous; critics of the Canadian Northern lamented the cheapness of its tracks.

Although neither of the new transcontinental lines was complete in 1914, railway mileage in operation had all but doubled since 1900. By 1915 there were 48,000 track miles in service. However, the impact of recession, war, and inflation upon an overbuilt railway network was disastrous. Between 1917 and 1923, the Grand Trunk Pacific, the Grand Trunk, and the Canadian Northern were taken over by the federal government and consolidated with other lines to form the government-owned Canadian National Railway system. Duplicate track was dismantled, a potential CPR monopoly was avoided, and Canada deepened its commitment to maintaining the framework of east-west integration.

Black Coal—and White

Coal was the fuel of the 19th century, and Canadian reserves were large; output rose steadily from 2 million tons in 1886 to approximately 15 million tons per year between 1913 and 1926. But Canada's coal lay on the flanks of the country: in Nova Scotia, in the Crowsnest Pass of the Rocky Mountains, and on Vancouver Island. Although mines in Nova Scotia shipped 2.4 million tons of coal to Quebec in 1914 and accounted for more than half of Canadian production, their main market was local. In the years before World War I, Canada—essentially central Canada—imported some 15 million tons of coal annually, approximately half of national requirements, from the United States. By 1921, however, coal met less than half of Canada's energy requirements.

Solutions to the problems of long-distance transmission late in the 19th century made possible the large-scale generation of electrical power at sites distant from consumers. This constituted a "Great Divide" in the economic development of the country. Contemporaries celebrated the potential of Canada's "white coal" and granted electricity almost magical qualities. Although much of this optimism was tempered by time, hydroelectricity development did allow the introduction of new industries and hastened the economic diversification of Canada. By 1904, the Shawinigan Power Company was transmitting electricity some 90 miles to Montreal and had encouraged power-intensive industries, such as aluminum processing, pulp and paper, and chemical manufacturing, to locate near its plant on the St. Maurice River. Fifteen years later transmission lines ran from Shawinigan to Quebec City and under the St. Lawrence to the asbestos deposit at Thetford Mines.

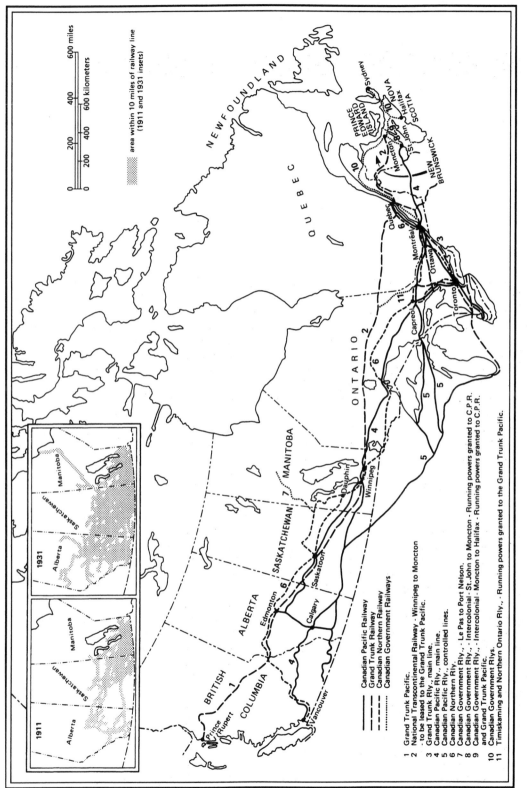

Figure 16.5 Transcontinental Railroads, 1915, showing areas within ten miles of a railroad in the Prairie Provinces, 1911 and 1931 (Adapted from Canada, Department of the Interior, 1915; and Warkentin 1968, 412).

Canadian Pacific Railway
Grand Trunk Railway
Canadian Northern Railway
Canadian Government Railways

1   Grand Trunk Pacific.
2   National Transcontinental Railway - Winnipeg to Moncton
    - to be leased to the Grand Trunk Pacific.
3   Grand Trunk Rly. - main line.
4   Canadian Pacific Rly. - main line.
5   Canadian Pacific Rly. - controlled lines.
6   Canadian Northern Rly.
7   Canadian Government Rly. - Le Pas to Port Nelson.
8   Canadian Government Rly. - Intercolonial - St.John to Moncton - Running powers granted to C.P.R.
9   Canadian Government Rly. - Intercolonial - Moncton to Halifax - Running powers granted to C.P.R.
10 and Grand Trunk Pacific.
    Canadian Government Rlys.
11 Timiskaming and Northern Ontario Rly. - Running powers granted to the Grand Trunk Pacific.

In Ontario, early development centered on Niagara Falls, which had the largest power plant in the world in the 1920s. Scale economies and public control of the resource (by the Ontario Hydro Electric Power Commission) brought Canadian energy costs below those in the United States, and considerable quantities of power were purchased by American firms before 1914. With Ontario Hydro's vigorous promotion of electricity for domestic manufacturing, electro-chemical firms crossed the border to take advantage of Canadian rates. Elsewhere, pulp and paper mills and ore refining plants depended on hydroelectricity. Electricity also drove the tramways and lit the streets of Canadian cities from Victoria to Saint John. Well might contemporaries have felt, with the prominent railroad engineer Thomas Keefer, that hydroelectricity development was the key to Canada's century, the harbinger of a new industrialization that would reduce the country's dependence on American coal and free it from its "hewer of wood" relationship to American industry.

Settling the "Last Best West"

Prairie settlement quickened remarkably at the turn of the century. More farms were established in this area between 1900 and 1904 than in the previous quarter-century. Almost two-thirds of all homestead entries before 1930 were made between 1900 and 1914. Some 75 million acres of farmland were taken up. The area of improved land quadrupled, and almost half of this was in wheat. Between 1901 and 1911 Canadian wheat production rose from 5.5 million to 23.0 million bushels. Ten years later Manitoba, Saskatchewan, and Alberta accounted for 280 million of Canada's 300 million bushels of output; in 1929 the country's wheat exports averaged a million bushels a day. As wheat went out—to the Lakehead at Prince Arthur and Fort William, to Hudson Bay at Churchill, or through the mountains to the west coast—so a massive traffic in goods and investments flowed back to the Prairies from British Columbia, central Canada, and beyond. The rate of capital formation in Canada quickened as each new homestead generated demand for buildings, farm machinery, and equipment. New farms stimulated railroad expansion and spawned hundreds of new grain-handling centers, each with its sidings, elevators, and loading platforms. New

families required consumer goods, ranging from clothing to hardware and home furnishings, and stores and warehouses sprang up to meet the demand. The east-west articulation of trade that the National Policy sought had begun to be realized.

Clifford Sifton, Canada's minister of the interior in the Liberal government of Wilfrid Laurier between 1896 and 1905 and vigorous advocate of Prairie settlement, has received much of the credit for these developments. The impact of his energy and talent upon the pattern and pace of immigration during these years cannot be denied. He streamlined his department, required railroads to choose their grant lands so that settlement could proceed without ambiguity, and encouraged the recruitment of agricultural immigrants from new, especially Slavic, areas of Europe. But structural factors were much more important determinants of change than Sifton's personality. Among those usually recognized are rising wheat prices in industrializing Europe and the United States; falling transport costs; declining interest rates; improvements in milling machinery, farm equipment, and grain varieties; and the closing of the American frontier. Each contributed, in the long run, to the settlement of the Canadian prairie. But neither singly nor together do they entirely account for the timing of agricultural expansion.

Western Canadian settlement was part of a wider North American process, and much of the prairie was at the margins of 19th-century cultivation. So long as subhumid land remained available in the United States, as it did in the 1880s, settlement gravitated there. Indeed, the northward shift of the extensive margin of cultivation rested in some degree on summer fallowing, newly developed in 1889. This technique, in which cropping occurred in alternate years, effectively stored moisture in the soil from one year to the next. This reduced the variability of yields and allowed farmers to settle semiarid areas with greater prospects of success than provided by an annual crop regime. Fortunately for Canadian prairie development, dry farming came into use just as wheat prices began to rise and the American frontier closed.

Change in the Older-Settled Countryside

Beyond the Prairies, agriculture responded to new circumstances created by mechanization, market shifts, and the growing integration of the Canadian economy. In Quebec, dairying and the cultivation of oats expanded in response to local and American urban demand in the 1850s. Twenty years later, depression encouraged technical improvements and specialization. Dairying came to dominate a mixed farming economy marked also by subsidiary patterns of regional specialization. Market gardening flourished near Montreal, and livestock in the Eastern Townships and along the south shore of the St. Lawrence below Quebec City. Farmers in the Beauce, the St. Maurice valley, and the Ottawa valley made hay for local lumber camps and exported some to New England camps as well. Others raised horses in Chambly County east of Montreal and grew tobacco in the Joliette area.

In Ontario, new machinery and new markets similarly recast agricultural patterns. Reapers, binders, and cream separators reduced the effort required by particular tasks and allowed farmers to improve production. The amount of improved land per farm increased by almost 30 percent. Farmers, said an agricultural newspaper of the day, had gone "from the rank[s] of a strenuous toiler[s] to the more complex status of . . . business proprietor[s]." As urban growth generated a demand for meat, dairy, and vegetable products and as British markets for butter, cheese, and stock expanded, mixed farming with an emphasis on livestock came to dominate much of southern Ontario. The province's contribution to the national wheat crop fell dramatically as prairie farming expanded. Between 1870 and 1900 the number of dairy cows in Ontario rose by 70 percent, and other cattle and swine numbers doubled. The quality of stock was also improved, and as farming became more differentiated, dual-purpose cattle—Ayrshires and Shorthorns—gave way to more specialized breeds, such as Jerseys for cream and Holsteins for milk.

Agricultural production was gradually adjusted to take advantage of regional differences in soil and climate. Circumstances broadly similar to those in Ontario affected agriculture in the Maritime Provinces, but in this marginal environment their impact was more detrimental. With the opening of the Canadian west, local production of cereal grains declined considerably. Competition from imported meat led to a decline in cattle (other than dairy cows) and sheep numbers after 1881. At the same time, re-

gional production of oats and roots, and butter output, increased considerably. To a significant degree these gains were attributable to improved farming practice. The development of apple orchards alleviated the consequences of an 1874 American duty that decimated potato farming in the Annapolis-Cornwallis valley, and new butter, egg, and bacon marketing cooperatives gave some farmers access to the expanding urban markets of New England; a short-lived fox-ranching industry made fortunes for a few Prince Edward Island families. But Maritime farmers increasingly concentrated on those crops least susceptible to outside competition or ran their holdings to provide the bulk of their own needs. Many left the land. Others joined the "harvest excursions" late each summer, taking the train west to assist with the Prairie wheat harvest and, perhaps, remaining to start new western lives.

Of Fishes and Forests

On both east and west coasts, concentration and consolidation marked the fishery. In the Maritime Provinces, new, expensive banks trawlers challenged the viability of the traditional dispersed inshore fishery by catching more fish with fewer men and serving a handful of large processing plants. At an intermediate scale, gasoline-powered boats allowed those who could afford them to range more widely in search of fish. And rail links gave certain harbors a great advantage, as cold storage facilities opened new markets in central Canada early in the 20th century. Both the capitalization and the productivity of the industry increased. But with a falling market for salt cod, there was hardship in the traditional economy. Despite diversification into lobster, salmon, haddock, and sardine fisheries, overall employment in the industry declined substantially between 1900 and 1930.

On the Pacific coast, similar trends marked a very different fishery. During the expansion of commercial salmon fishing in the late 19th century, canneries were built at the mouths of almost all of British Columbia's major rivers. Many of these were closed early in the 20th century with the introduction of larger motor-driven boats, able to bring their catches considerable distances to centralized processing plants located on the Fraser and Skeena Rivers. Here, too, there was consolidation of financial control, as numerous independent canneries either banded together under common leadership or were acquired by limited liability companies with economic roots in Britain and the United States. By 1928 the three largest canning companies accounted for 80 percent of production, up from about one-third ten years earlier and about 50 to 60 percent through the first decade of the century.

Patterns of forest exploitation were transformed between Confederation and the Great Depression. The traditional square-timber trade of eastern Canada declined rapidly in the late 19th century and had almost disappeared by 1912. Sawn lumber, increasingly for American markets, accounted for a growing proportion of Canadian wood production. In the east, new supply areas were opened by railroads that broke the industry's dependence on water for the movement of wood to markets. By 1886 the north shore produced one-third of the total cut of Georgian Bay, and there were a number of sawmills to the west, where the Canadian Pacific Railway crossed south-flowing rivers. Integrated systems of wood production, transportation, and marketing replaced the diffuse patterns and informal organization of the earlier timber trade. Mills grew in size and in capital cost as new saws, new machinery, and new power sources allowed a clear tenfold increase in daily output between 1850 and 1900.

On the Pacific coast, the impact of modern technology was even more decisive. Hand logging, by which the enormous trees of the coast were felled directly into the sea using only axes, jacks, and human effort, gave way to larger operations dependent upon steam donkey engines in the 1890s and logging railroads early in the new century. With these developments came locational concentration and the preeminence of a relatively small number of firms whose mills drew logs from sizable camps scattered over considerable distances. With the settlement of the Prairies, the major market for British Columbia lumber turned from the seaborne cargo trade to the western interior. By World War I, prefabricated buildings of British Columbia lumber, carried east on the CPR, dotted the landscape from the foothills of Alberta to the Clay Belt of Ontario.

Technological advances in paper manufacturing gave rise to a wood-pulp and paper industry in the late 19th century. From modest beginnings—there were 5 small mills in 1881—Canada's pulpwood production rivaled lumber output in value during the 1920s and exceeded it in the next decade. In 1923 almost $400 million was invested in the pulp industry. Some 25,000 people worked in approximately 100 mills, most of them in Quebec, Ontario, New Brunswick, and British Columbia. Wood-pulp output exceeded 2 million tons in 1922 and was valued at $85 million; paper production, mainly newsprint, was worth more than $100 million. Significantly, American capital and American corporate enterprise lay behind many of these new mills. With their strong ties to American markets and their often remote peripheral locations—Bathurst, Kapuskasing, Espanola, Ocean Falls, and other places—chosen for access to the resource, they had profoundly influenced patterns of trade and settlement in the country by 1929.

Minerals

Traditional patterns of Canadian mining—haphazard, ephemeral, small-scale, poorly capitalized—were radically transformed at the turn of the century. With the exception of the placer gold operations in the Yukon, which fired hopes of an Eldorado for small-scale, individual prospector-miners in 1897, Canadian mining after 1890 was capital intensive and largely dependent upon costly facilities for ore extraction, reduction, or smelting. A revolution in metallurgical technology generated enormous new demands for metallic minerals, and these accounted for over a third of Canadian output by 1910. Railway and geological surveys through distant wildernesses revealed new sources, and sites in the western mountains and the Laurentian Shield were quickly opened for exploitation. New mining towns dotted the landscape. In British Columbia many of these were little more than temporary camps. They grew almost overnight, provided work for a decade or two, then declined. Mountains and forests were despoiled, lives were lost, and impoverished villages were left in the valleys; fortunes, when they were made, generally accumulated elsewhere.

Not all mining towns were short-lived, however. Trail, British Columbia, was developed initially for the treatment of gold-bearing ore from Rossland; it evolved into a regional center of silver-lead smelting, subsequently expanded to produce zinc, and remains an important processing center today. Similarly, several mining sites in the Shield developed around costly chemical processing plants that operated for decades and endured to become sizable towns with a variety of functions. Ore roasting and smelting occurred in the 1890s at Copper Cliff, near Sudbury, a town that subsequently led the way in nickel extraction. Gold and silver discoveries between 1900 and 1912 gave rise to Timmins, Kirkland Lake, and Cobalt, and these places grew into service centers for the farming and pulpwood-cutting population of the surrounding Clay Belt. Copper and gold underpinned the development of the Noranda-Rouyn area of western Quebec in the 1920s.

AN INDUSTRIAL REVOLUTION

Technological advances, transport improvements, and free trade with the United States under the terms of the Reciprocity Treaty of 1854–66 "set agoing an industrial revolution" in the Canadas; by 1870 manufacturing contributed 19 percent to the country's GNP. This industry was heavily concentrated in the Montreal and Toronto-Hamilton regions. Perhaps three-quarters of Canadian manufacturing output came from Montreal in the 1870s, where both capital investment and productivity far exceeded Ontario levels. In Hamilton and Toronto slightly more than half of the city's workers toiled in establishments employing 50 or more, but generally traditional, small workplaces were the norm. In 1871, 88 percent of Toronto's industrial establishments had fewer than 30 workers; in Hamilton, the average was 17. Commercial functions remained significant in all three cities; beyond them, manufacturing was overwhelmingly small in scale and oriented to local or regional markets.

This base was made over in the half-century after 1879. With the exception of the 1890s, when growth slowed, Canadian manufacturing expanded decade by decade at a rate in advance of those achieved by most other industrializing countries. Between 1870 and 1915, the value of output rose at a compound annual average rate of 4.2 percent. During this period, the ratio of primary to secondary manufacturing changed little, but the leading industries of the 1870s— secondary iron and steel products, primary wood products, secondary leather products, and food and beverages (both primary and secondary)—accounted for a shrinking fraction of value-added as the range of Canadian manufacturing broadened.

Expansion and diversification were accompanied by an increasing concentration of capital and control. Industrial growth in the 1880s was led by a few hundred entrepreneurs, men of relatively small means who parlayed limited assets and their local market positions into considerable fortunes during the depression of the 1870s and the buoyant years that followed. Individualistic and aggressive, many of these people found themselves in vigorous competition as transport improvements broke down "natural" (local) monopolies and their businesses expanded into regional or national markets. Partnerships, mergers, and combines were the result, and they marked the drift toward oligopoly in Canadian manufacturing. Two examples from the early 1890s: the farm machinery works of Massey-Harris, formed from firms based in separate small towns in Ontario, and the organization of Dominion Cotton Mills, which attempted to bring all gray-cotton producers in Canada into a single company.

The pace of this movement increased enormously in the early 20th century. As expansion and integration proceeded, as new power sources and new production techniques were introduced, as new products were developed, and as competition intensified, personal and joint ownership of manufacturing plants gave way to more broadly based public financing of enterprises, generated by issuing of stocks and bonds. Only through corporate mergers and the floating of joint-stock companies could the costs of big business be borne. Between 1900 and 1913 there were 56 major industrial consolidations in Canada. Almost 3,500 joint-stock companies were chartered during this period; their capitalization stood at a staggering $2.2 billion. The consequences were dramatic. In 1870, some 39,000 Canadian manufacturing establishments employed 18,200 people; in 1890, 70,000 firms employed 351,000. Fifteen years later, an additional 31,000 Canadians worked in manufacturing, but they did so in a mere 15,200 plants. Although the number of establishments increased thereafter, the trend to larger enterprises continued. In 1929, 22,000 plants employed 666,000 Canadians.

Central Canada on the Rise

The regional impact of these developments was far from even. Under the shelter of the National Policy of 1879, countless small towns in Eastern Canada expanded their manufacturing sectors. Villages turned into hives of industry. In the Maritimes, cotton mills, sugar refineries, rope works, steel mills, and iron and steel manufacturing plants were established or expanded in a string of towns—Moncton, Amherst, Truro, New Glasgow, and Sydney, along the Intercolonial Railway—and in a scattering of coastal centers, including Halifax, Yarmouth, and St. Stephen. Most of them were the cooperative ventures of groups of local entrepreneurs. The Nova Scotia Steel and Coal Company, for example, developed from a modest partnership of two blacksmiths with the support of New Glasgow's leading merchant families in the 1880s. In Ontario, during the 1880s over half of all manufacturing occurred in places whose populations never exceeded 10,000.

There were dramatic increases in the value of manufacturing output during the 1880s: 66 percent in Nova Scotia, and 51 percent in each of Ontario and Quebec. This growth was most evident in the larger centers of these provinces. In Toronto, the major indices of manufacturing activity (output, value added, capital invested, and numbers employed) more than doubled between 1881 and 1891. Expansion in the production of food, beverages, and transport equipment gave Montreal almost 40 percent of national output in each of those sectors by 1891. Growth was less marked in Halifax, yet the value of industrial capital invested there more than doubled between 1880 and 1890, and at the latter date the value of the city's industrial output was 5.5 times that of its nearest provincial rival. Despite a slight decline in population in Saint John, New Brunswick, industrial capital investment and output from that city grew more rapidly than it did in Hamilton, a rising center of textile production and metal fabrication in Ontario. Winnipeg, alone on the Prairies, also showed the beginnings of railroad-related industry.

As industrial growth gained momentum, the centralizing tendencies of modern technology worked their effects on the geography of Canadian manufacturing. The growth of scale economies with new forms and means of production, the advantage of industrial linkages derived from locational concentration, and the capacity for spatial integration offered by the railroad all hastened change. In the late 19th century the consequences were perhaps most marked at the provincial scale and most evident in Ontario. In the 1860s, manufacturing had been widely dispersed; Toronto and Hamilton led the province in manufacturing employment, but there were significant concentrations to the west and eastward along the shore of Lake Ontario. Twenty-five years later most places had more manufacturing, but many had lost ground in relative terms. Secondary industry had concentrated in a narrow triangle with its apex near Lake St. Clair and its base on the western end of Lake Ontario. Six counties in this area accounted for half of the secondary manufacturing in Ontario and, in comparison with their population, had a disproportionately high share of the province's total. Toronto, Hamilton, the Grand River valley, and London stood out. Much primary manufacturing, tied to the location of its raw materials, remained scattered. Sawmilling, for example, was dispersed across the province in 1891, but most production centers were on the northern periphery of settled Ontario, bordering the Canadian Shield. On the other hand, the clay required for brick- and tile-making was available almost everywhere, and consolidation among these firms followed the pattern of secondary manufacturing.

The Maritimes Decline

By 1900 the influence of industrial and financial concentration in central Canada was being felt well beyond the St. Lawrence. In the Maritimes, a large number of the community-based, locally financed manufacturing concerns developed after 1879 were taken over by central Canadian companies. Only two of the region's cotton mills remained in local hands in 1893. By 1895 only confectionery production and manufacturing tied to the forest, fishing, and the iron and steel industries remained in local hands. Several of the region's textile, rope, sugar, glass, and paint plants were closed in the rationalization that followed consolidation.

With local supplies of coal and ready access to the rich Bell Island iron ore deposits of Newfoundland, the Maritime iron and steel industry remained competitive with its central Canadian counterparts through the early 20th century. Indeed, demand for rails, bridges, railcars, wire, nails, and stoves soared with the spread of settlement in Western Canada. Nova Scotia pig iron production increased some 13-fold between 1896 and 1912. By World War I, the Scotia Steel Company of Pictou County had some 6,000 employees engaged in mining coal and ore, producing pig iron and steel, and manufacturing a wide range of secondary metal products.

Nova Scotia's importance as an iron and steel producer began to decline in the 1910s. In 1912 the Canadian government eliminated the tariff protection afforded these products in the 19th century. Mill owners were slow to retool to meet changing product demands, and they suffered further from railway freight rates that more than doubled and in some cases tripled. The recession and price collapse that terminated spiraling postwar inflation in 1920 and 1921 dealt a crippling blow. Despite efforts to realize scale economies by mergers and consolidations—one of which saw Scotia Steel subsumed within the Montreal-based British Empire Steel Corporation that controlled the Cape Breton industry—the industrial base of the Maritimes was severely damaged. By 1925 the net value of regional manufacturing had fallen to less than half that of 1919. Nova Scotia's share of Canadian pig iron production fell from 43 to 30 percent between 1913 and 1929. Adjustments to tariffs and freight rates subsequently eased the worst problems, but the rise in manufacturing employment in 1928 and 1929 reflected a reorientation—to pulp and paper—rather than a recovery.

Decline in the Maritimes was evident in the tertiary sector too. Maritimes-based banks moved to, or were absorbed by, financial houses in Montreal and Toronto. By 1912, Toronto-based manufacturers such as Maple Leaf Milling, Massey-Harris, and Canadian General Electric, were establishing wholesale outlets in major Maritime cities. In the 1920s local retailers across the region felt the competition of brand-name goods offered by branches of national retail chains such as Tip Top Tailors. The introduction of catalog shopping by major department stores such as the T. Eaton Company of Toronto only exaggerated the shifts. Taken as a whole, the changes associated with the economic integration of Canadian space were striking indeed. In 1881, branch businesses based outside the Maritimes accounted for less than 10 percent of all businesses; by 1931 the figure ex-

ceeded 55 percent. In 50 years a high degree of regional autonomy in resource extraction, manufacturing, construction, transportation, trade, and services had given way to a considerable measure of dependence and the hegemony of Toronto and Montreal.

Economic Regions in the 1920s

By 1929, 82 percent of Canadian manufacturing output came from central Canada; Ontario alone accounted for 51 percent of the total. Production of the durable consumer goods that would lead manufacturing growth in the new age of electricity and the internal combustion engine was even more concentrated. At least 95 percent of Canadian automobiles, rubber tires, and agricultural implements came from Ontario, and the province also dominated in electrical goods (77 percent), machinery (72 percent), and hardware and tools (68 percent). Quebec's leadership was most evident in pulp and paper (54 percent of the national total) and the manufacture of railway rolling stock (53 percent) and in traditional slow-growth nondurable consumer goods such as cigars and cigarettes (86 percent), cotton textiles (75 percent), and boots and shoes, rubber footwear, and men's clothing (each 60–62 percent). The only sectors in which the rest of Canada held slightly more than their proportional share of national output were the generation of hydroelectric power, the manufacture of railway rolling stock, and the smelting of nonferrous metals.

Similar patterns were evident in the financial and commercial sectors. In the 1880s Canada had some 44 chartered banks based in 18 cities with approximately 300 branches; in the 1920s there were 11 banks with over 4,000 branches. All but one of them (a small Prairie establishment) had their headquarters in Montreal or Toronto. Insurance, trust, and loan activities grew, and an important mining stock exchange, founded in 1896–97, added further to the financial and managerial significance of Toronto. With over half of Canada's population concentrated in the St. Lawrence–Great Lakes lowland, Montreal and Toronto were also hubs of wholesale and retail trade. In 1929, Ontario and Quebec accounted for 62.5 percent of retail sales in the country. Sales in Ontario alone exceeded those of the Maritimes, the Prairies, and British Columbia combined, and the country's leading chain stores and department stores made their headquarters in Canada's two largest cities.

National integration yielded a clear pattern of regional specialization in Canada between 1850 and 1930. Cheaper communication, innovative technology, improved marketing systems, and modern managerial practices together undermined characteristic early-19th-century patterns of relatively unspecialized land use and economic organization and relatively high levels of local self-sufficiency. All sectors—agriculture, manufacturing, commerce, finance—felt the centralizing tendencies of such changes.

On the eve of the Great Depression, the nation's heartland, central Canada, provided capital, manufactures, and services to an extensive hinterland. Those regions reciprocated with resources—minerals, energy, food—and, particularly from the Maritimes and fringes of Ontario and Quebec, labor. The National Policy of 1879 had created the east-west trade that its proponents considered essential to the existence of a growing national economy. But economic integration failed to generate sentimental or emotional unity among Canadians. Rather, it fostered a strong drift toward regional inequality that emphasized the historical and geographical divisions of the country.

CHANGING CITIES

Canada's growing cities were also transformed between 1850 and 1930. At the beginning of this period, even the largest urban places were relatively undifferentiated spatially. Wharf and warehouse districts, retail zones, and fashionable streets might be distinguished, but none was entirely homogeneous. Rich people and poor, merchants and laborers may have occupied different streets, but they did so in most sections of the city. Segregation was at the level of the block rather than the neighborhood. Thus the urban fabric was an intricate mix of land uses, occupations, and housing types. Smaller places—busy commercial villages with a handful of mills and workshops, scattered across the settled countryside—were even more strikingly unsegregated. Differences in income and status set families and individuals apart, but in these modest-sized places across which people could readily move on foot , proximity reinforced perceptions of the community as a whole.

By the 1920s, paved streets with automobiles, rambling industrial sites, and blocks of look-alike tract housing were giving to both large towns and small the specialized, differentiated stamp of the modern urban place. Financial, managerial, and manufacturing activity concentrated disproportionately in heartland cities; trading and resource processing tended to be more dominant in those in the hinterland. But these differences were not always clear-cut. In Montreal and Toronto, as in such middle-order places as Hamilton and Saint John, sizable areas were devoted to manufacturing. In the dynamic western cities of Winnipeg and Vancouver, commercial uses dominated downtown areas; growing manufacturing zones were centered on resource processing plants such as abattoirs, flour mills, and sawmills but included enterprises producing construction materials and consumer goods.

In each of Canada's major cities, as to some degree in all urban places of 10,000 people or more, there was also a clear pattern of residential segregation. The rich occupied peripheral areas, their large dwellings remote from the bustle and dirt of the commercial and manufacturing sections of the city. The middle ranks of society—white-collar workers and some skilled tradesmen—concentrated in less grandiose inner suburbs. The poorer members of society occupied deteriorating houses on the fringes of the factory and commercial districts. Others built modest dwellings on small lots in newly developed workingmen's suburbs; in many cases these sites were poorly serviced. Such expressions as "the working-class part of town" and "the other side of the tracks" acquired meaningful currency, and the divisions they reflected were as marked in city landscapes as they were in the consciousness of the inhabitants.

UNCERTAINTY AND
THE IDEA OF CANADA

Sharp tensions stretched the fabric of social and economic life in Canada during the early 20th century. In countless, often subtle, ways, the traditional ethos—rural, conservative, individualistic, and optimistic—was challenged by urbanization, the rise of socialism, labor unions, and the stark reality of urban poverty. New organizations arose to represent emerging middle-class professions, and agriculture and industry struggled to secure their respective interests. French Canadian nationalism gained momentum, stirred first by Métis resistance to Protestant settlement in Manitoba in 1870 and given a symbol by the execution of the Métis leader Louis Riel in 1885. French Canadians resented the imperial fervor with which English Canadians sent troops to the Boer War in South Africa in 1899 and opposed military conscription in 1917. Those who had spread into eastern and northern Ontario were further annoyed by the decision of the provincial government to restrict French language instruction in schools after 1912.

Such sectionalism of interest, occupation, and language showed in the deeply divided national Parliament elected in 1921. Progressives, representing rural Canada, carried the Prairies and several Ontario constituencies; the Conservatives, authors of the National Policy in 1879, gained most of their seats in industrial Ontario; the Liberals, who opposed conscription, were the party of Quebec. Well might Canadians have concluded, in the words of their wartime prime minister, that the storms of World War I had moved the world from its accustomed anchorage, but those among them with a firm sense of history might also have recalled the concern shown for local identities expressed by George-Etienne Cartier 60 years before.

Canadian uncertainty owed not a little to the pattern of Canadian settlement. The country had been occupied piecemeal, in a zone bounded to the south by New England, the Great Lakes, and the 49th parallel and to the north by the Canadian Shield and the climatic limits of agriculture. Here, discrete pockets of land had been occupied over several centuries by successive waves of predominantly European migrants. In each instance, particular backgrounds and technologies, and economic and environmental circumstances had combined to yield a distinctive mix of people and place. As pockets of settlement became full, people left them, but their destinations lay to the south more often than to the west. Thus there was little spatial continuity to Canadian settlement. A broken ribbon of towns, farms, and camps lay strung out like islands—an archipelago—linked by networks of administration and communication, but their people shared too little history to feel strong emotional bonds. Common experience was local. For all

their economic importance, the railway and the telegraph had hardly had time, if indeed they had the capacity, to create a sense of national identity out of disparate settlements scattered across Canada's great east-west distances.

Here the contrast between Canadian and American experience was profound. Lacking the continuously unfolding agricultural frontier that sustained American economic growth for three centuries, Canadians hardly shared the westward replication of established cultural patterns that, for example, gave the appearance of New England to landscapes across the northern Midwest and imparted a sense of spatial continuity to the American experience. Nor was there much opportunity in Canada for the western blending of different eastern traditions to produce a distinctive, relatively homogeneous, national culture. Lacking these things, Canada also lacked the mythology associated with the ongoing American occupation of a bountiful land. Try as they might, Canadians would have difficulty seeing themselves in the way F. J. Turner envisaged his fellow Americans, as similar products of the frontier crucible; metaphorically, Canada was a mosaic rather than a melting pot. The pervasive belief in individual opportunity that underlay American liberalism could not flourish in Canada, where good land ran back so quickly into forest, swamp, and muskeg, and where the prospects of independent survival were so often limited by thin soils, an intractable climate, or resources that required large capital for their extraction.

Americans also possessed a firmer sense of their North American roots than did Canadians. The *Mayflower,* the "city upon a hill," Lexington, Manifest Destiny, and Reconstruction spoke, symbolically, to the foundation and continuous expansion of the American idea. The Declaration of Independence severed colonial ties to the mother country. By contrast, the Canadian past was short and fragmented, and the country's autonomy uncertain. Canada's longest-established European population, the French, looked back to their subjugation. They remembered the English conquest, the loss of a vast North American domain, and the financial dominance of an English and Scottish bourgeoisie. Acadians recalled their brutal expulsion from the Bay of Fundy, even as Nova Scotians developed a tourist trade on the popularity of *Evangeline,* H. W. Longfellow's epic poem about those events. English-speaking "Canada" was essentially a 19th-century phenomenon, and for much of this period, "Canadian" was little more than an administratively convenient term that referred to only a fraction of the people: those in the parts now called southern Ontario and Quebec, who entered Confederation in 1867. The Dominion retained its imperial allegiance. The achievement of a larger political Canada, coast to coast, came so suddenly, and so hard on the heels of the pioneer experience, that as the literary critic Northrop Frye put it, "to feel 'Canadian' was to feel part of a no-man's-land with huge rivers, lakes and islands that very few Canadians had ever seen."

Especially in those areas where familiar scales and patterns of local life were threatened by the continent-wide integration of space, the region came into focus as a more concrete and comprehensible locality than the somewhat abstract country. The homogenizing tendencies of modern metropolitan culture were likewise resisted, at least temporarily, by the invigoration of regional identities that matched closely the islands of Canadian settlement. In Quebec, for example, provincial entrepreneurs and industrial leaders who favored economic development and the doctrine of progress precipitated a significant backlash among many educated French Canadians. The latter sought to conserve the traditional values of their society through the publication of a nationalist journal *(L'Action Française),* the editorials of the Roman Catholic press (led by *Le Devoir* of Montreal), and such organizations as the Association Catholique de la Jeunesse Canadienne-française. In the 1920s, some among them dreamed of Quebec as a separate Laurentian republic, sheltered from the disrupting spirit of modern life, a society devoted to "things of the Spirit and scornful of wealth and economic development."

Similar cries for self-determination arose from the Maritimes. Residents of the three provinces were reminded of their distinctiveness and enjoined to "have old home weeks and stories and poetry and moving pictures and more local history in . . . [their] schools and colleges and anything else that . . . [would] bring the great fact of Maritime Canadianism home to . . . [their] hearths and bosoms as it never came before." And early in the 20th century there was a remarkable outpouring of Prairie fiction, much of which portrayed the distinctiveness of regional land and life while exploring the conflicting values of traditional community and materialistic society.

Nationalist concerns in the 1920s reflected the tension between achieving economic efficiency and maintaining community integrity. In some respects there were echoes of the differences that marked the Confederation debates here in the 1860s. Now, however, the very existence of a distinctive Canada appeared to be in question, given the insistent northward spread of American goods, attitudes, and values. American mass culture seemed certain to color Canadian attitudes with what the Vancouver *Star* described as "a reeking cloud of lower Americanisms." According to one article in the first issue of the *Canadian Historical Review,* the trickle had already become a flood by 1920. Canada was a vassal state; its economy, its society, and even its universities bore the strong imprint of the United States. Most Canadians would have considered such claims exaggerated, but there were over 300 American firms in southern Ontario by 1914. In Quebec, billboards and newspaper advertisements for Kellogg cereals, Chiclets gum, and Westinghouse appliances offered compelling evidence of American penetration of Canadian markets. By 1926, American investment in Canada exceeded British, and with American capital had come American union organizations. André Siegfried's conviction, developed just before World War I, that the Canadian dilemma was framed in the phrase "Moeurs américaines, loyalisme britannique" was amply confirmed in the 1920s. Even in government, it was observed at the end of the decade, "most of what is superimposed is British, but most of what works its way in from the bottom is American." Without resistance to the standardizing tendencies of modern American life, only time seemed to stand between Canadians and the erosion of such cultural and national autonomy as they had realized.

Old arguments affirming Canadian individuality by contrasting Canadian and American attitudes and institutions were advanced again in the 1920s. Some made tradition and heritage the cornerstones of their position by emphasizing the significance of Canada's British connection and by stretching to identify as unifying characteristics the "Norman blood" of its English and French populations, the tory tinge of its society, and so on. Others built their nationalist claims on "geographical" factors, especially land and location. These also seemed to set the country apart from the United States. Canada was the "True North" whose people were, in the environmentalist views of the time, necessarily strong and free. Travel accounts, explorers' reports, novels, and poetry developed northern imagery. Members of the Group of Seven—the country's dominant art movement in the 1920s, and ever since its most famous—embellished it with their bold, vivid paintings of the rocks and lakes and trees of the rugged Canadian Shield. In the folk geography of the late 1920s, concluded a contemporary, "Canada means the North." Through the following decade, historians searching for the nation's roots found them, variously, in the northern forest and in that northern entrance to the continent, the St. Lawrence–Great Lakes artery.

The leading social scientist of the day, Harold Innis, concluded from a monumental work on the fur trade, published in 1930, that Canada's boundaries reflected the northern fur traders' canoe routes. In this view the Canadian Pacific Railway and the National Policy simply reinforced patterns of early European commerce in the northern interior; Canada existed not in defiance of geography but because of it. Whatever credence this claim had, in 1930 few people questioned the idea of Canada as a transcontinental state despite the uncertainties, the challenges, and the tensions and despite vast differences between its regions and among its citizens. Over 75 years of sweeping change, the existence of a distinct, northern country had been realized, stretching from sea to sea to sea across the vast, and in many ways hostile, fringe of the American hemisphere.

Some of this distinctiveness rests on inherent ambiguity: a state thrown across the grain of the continent, held together by ribbons of steel rail and sinews of sheltered trade, its people less wedded to an overarching national concept than to various local identities. What a remarkable achievement! Future generations would continue to wrestle with Canada's reason for being, and their efforts would prove neither more nor less successful than those of their predecessors. Nor should Canadians be disappointed because the contradictions embedded in the very idea of Canada would seem to allow for a middle ground between acrimonious nationalism and the placeless life in an electronic global village as the new millennium opens.

ADDITIONAL READING

Acheson, T. W. 1972. "The National Policy and the Industrialization of the Maritimes." *Acadiensis* 1: 3–28.

Armour, L. 1981. *The Idea of Canada and the Crisis of Community.* Ottawa: Steel Rail Publishing.

Berger, C. 1971. *The Sense of Power: Studies in the Ideas of Canadian Imperialism, 1867–1914.* Toronto: University of Toronto Press.

Breen, D. H. 1983. *The Canadian Prairie West and the Ranching Frontier, 1874–1924.* Toronto: University of Toronto Press.

Brown, R. C., and R. Cook. 1976. *Canada 1896–1921: A Nation Transformed.* Toronto: McClelland & Stewart.

Canada. Department of Interior. 1915. *Atlas of Canada.* Ottawa: Department of Interior.

Carter, S. 1990. *Lost Harvests: Prairie Indian Reserve Farmers and Government Policy.* Montreal and Kingston: McGill-Queens University Press.

Conzen, M. P., T. A. Rumney, G. Wynn, eds. 1993. *A Scholar's Guide to Geographical Writing on the American and Canadian Past.* Chicago: University of Chicago Press.

Friesen, G. 1984. *The Canadian Prairies: A History.* Toronto: University of Toronto Press.

Frye, N. 1965. Conclusion to *Literary History of Canada: Canadian Literature in English,* ed. C. F. Klinck. Toronto: University of Toronto Press.

Grant, G. 1969. *Technology and Empire.* Toronto: Annasi.

Gentilcore, R. L., ed. 1993. *Historical Atlas of Canada.* Vol. 2, *The Land Transformed, 1800–1890.* Toronto and Montreal: University of Toronto Press / Les presses de l'université de Montréal.

Harris, R. C. 1997. *The Resettlement of British Columbia: Essays on Colonialism and Geographical Change.* Vancouver: University of British Columbia Press.

Kerr, D., and D. W. Holdsworth, eds. 1990. *Historical Atlas of Canada.* Vol. 3, *Addressing the 20th Century.* Toronto and Montreal: University of Toronto Press / Les presses de l'université de Montréal.

Linteau, P.-A., R. Durocher, J.-C. Robert. 1983. *Quebec: A History, 1867–1929.* Toronto: Lorimer.

McCann, L. D. 1983. "Metropolitanism and Branch Businesses in the Maritimes, 1881–1931." *Acadiensis* 13: 112–25.

McCann, L. D., and A. Gunn, eds. 1998. *Heartland and Hinterland*. Scarborough: Prentice-Hall Canada.

Norrie, K. H., and D. Owram. 1991. *A History of the Canadian Economy*. Toronto: Harcourt Brace Jovanovich.

Owram, D. 1980. *Promise of Eden: The Canadian Expansionist Movement and the Idea of the West*. Toronto: University of Toronto Press.

Palmer, B. D. 1983. *Working Class Experience*. Toronto: Butterworth.

Parr, J. 1990. *The Gender of Bread Winners: Women, Men, and Change in Two Industrial Towns, 1880–1950*. Toronto: University of Toronto Press.

Prentice, A., et al. 1988. *Canadian Women: A History*. Toronto: Harcourt Brace Jovanovich.

Smith, A. 1994. *Canada, an American Nation: Essays on Continentalism, Identity, and the Canadian Frame of Mind*. Montreal and Kingston: McGill-Queen's University Press.

Warkentin, J., ed. 1968. *Canada: A Geographical Interpretation*. Toronto: Methuen.

Zaslow, M. 1971. *The Opening of the Canadian North, 1870–1914*. Toronto: McClelland & Stewart.

PART V

REORGANIZATION

1930s AND ONWARD

Canada could have enjoyed:
English government,
French culture,
and American know-how.
Instead it ended up with:
English know-how,
French government,
and American culture.

> J. R. Colombo, *Oh Canada,* 1965

This monster of a land, this monster of a land, this mightiest of nations, this spawn of the future, turns out to be the macrocosm of microcosm me. . . . For all our enormous geographic range, for all our sectionalism, for all our interwoven breeds drawn from every part of the ethnic world, we are a nation, a new breed. . . . California Chinese, Boston Irish, Wisconsin German, yes, and Alabama Negroes, have more in common than they have apart. And this is the more remarkable because it happened so quickly.

> John Steinbeck, *Travels with Charley,* 1962

The remarkable thing is not that government costs so much, but that so many people of wealth have left. It's outrageous that the development of the metropolitan community has been organized with escape hatches that allow people to enjoy the proximity of the city while not paying their share of taxes. . . . Fiscal funkholes are what the suburbs are.

> John Kenneth Galbraith, *New York Times,* 1975

17

America between the Wars:
The Engineering of a New Geography

PEIRCE LEWIS

THE MELODRAMATIC YEARS

As the United States entered the 20th century, it was approaching a culminating moment in its national career. Ever since the beginning of the 1800s, the country had been converting itself from a collection of small rural settlements on the western margins of the Atlantic into an urban industrial power of continental scale. The momentum of change had been increasing rapidly, especially since the Civil War. By the time the United States entered World War I in 1917, America had become a fast-growing but still half-rural country, seen by many foreigners (and by some Americans) as a kind of political and economic adolescent—a country to be viewed warily but not altogether seriously by the world's great powers. Two years later, in the Hall of Mirrors at Versailles, America took its seat as a rather uneasy equal among those great powers. By 1945, at the end of World War II, there could be no further doubt; the United States had come of age economically, and it was unquestionably the most powerful nation on Earth. Looking back across the whole long period, America seemed to resemble a very large machine, driven by an enthusiastic but inexperienced driver, that has been accelerating erratically in second gear for a long time. In the period between World Wars I and II, amid great lurchings and grindings, that machine shifted into high gear.

Throughout the whole chaotic period, America's geography was undergoing profound and irreversible change, but that fact was far from obvious at the time. To be sure, some of the changes were subtle, and most people were too close to them to see overall patterns clearly. But it was also easy to be diverted by the procession of epic events between 1917 and 1945: World War I, the economic boom of the 1920s, the Great Depression of the 1930s, and finally a second world war. They were events of high drama, but that very drama tended to obscure basic changes that were already under way, quite independent of wars and economic convulsions.

The two wars were dreadful enough—ghastly international bloodlettings that left both winners and losers exhausted, impoverished, and embittered. But for many Americans, the wars were more exciting than terrible. The United States was a latecomer to both wars, and most of the fighting took place overseas, so that American territory largely escaped physical damage. In both wars, however, the power of American factories and armies ultimately tipped the balance of victory. By the end of World War II, historians had begun to call the 1900s "the American Century."

The two decades between the wars were just as dramatic, although at times they simply seemed demented. For many Americans (though by no means all) the Roaring Twenties were times of unprecedented prosperity, while at the same time, the whole national libido seemed to be spilling over in an orgy of hedonistic excess. To Americans of traditional mind, the country seemed to have come unhinged. Newspapers painted lurid pictures of sexual license and gang warfare, of bomb-throwing anarchists, and of courtroom trials to determine whether men had descended from monkeys. Bizarre creatures appeared from nowhere: flappers, Bolsheviks, rumrunners, hoodlums. And then, as a fitting climax to a crazy decade, the economy ballooned, then burst and crashed with paralyzing finality on Wall Street in October 1929, leaving the nation prostrate and sending shock waves around the world. Yet the crash was only the curtain-raiser for another epic drama, equally amenable to vivid caricature: a ruined nation, led by a charismatic president, struggling to reform its institutions and ultimately emerging chastened from the worst economic disaster in its history. Then just as things seemed to be getting better, a new and more frightful war broke out, and

America was dragged once more into the fighting. Altogether, it is hard to find three decades of American history as lurid and as packed with melodrama.

But the parade of colorful events obscures more subtle long-term happenings. During the interwar period, three major changes were taking place that would alter fundamentally the geography of the United States and with it the whole character of the country. One change was *technological,* involving nothing less than a total overhaul of the nation's system of transportation and communications, the whole machinery that held the country together. A second was *political,* as the federal government began to assume a much more active role in what had previously been regarded as private matters—the migration of people and the management of land and water. The third was *demographic:* the American people were migrating in unexpected numbers and in unexpected directions, leaving some parts of the country desolate and propelling others into positions of new importance.

BUILDING A NEW SYSTEM OF TRANSPORTATION AND COMMUNICATIONS

It is hard for those involved in them to recognize revolutions. So it was with the generation of young Americans who were growing up at the start of the 20th century. Very few realized that they were about to participate in a social and geographic upheaval, caused by the almost simultaneous adoption of four machines of transportation and communications. These were the automobile (and the road system it would require), the telephone, motion pictures, and the wireless radio. Any one of these devices by itself would have provoked major change. Arriving in combination, they brought on a cataclysm.

It was not the *invention* of the machines that made such an enormous difference in the fabric of American life. Actually, no single person "invented" any one of them. Each was a complicated device that had been evolving through a sequence of major and minor inventions spread over the last quarter of the 19th century. As of 1900, none had yet made any important impact on the fabric of American life; all were crude and expensive playthings for inventors or for

rich people in big cities, but they were not taken seriously in most of the country. What converted these gadgets into instruments of revolutionary change was *engineering*—the ingenious combination of machinery and corporate organization that would transform these curiosities into cheap, reliable, mass-produced necessities. That happened almost simultaneously in the short period between 1910 and 1925, when all four abruptly reached critical mass and were enthusiastically adopted by millions of Americans. By the end of the 1930s, almost nothing in America would be the same, including some of the country's most basic maps.

The airplane arrived at about the same time, of course, invented in 1903 and employed with spectacular effect in both world wars. Unlike the automobile, however, the airplane never came into common public use, partly because of cost, partly because it required great technical proficiency to fly. It was not until after World War II that airplanes came into widespread commercial use and began to affect the nation's transportation system on a grand scale.

The Coming of the Automobile

The automobile made the biggest difference. For the last half of the 19th century, the railroads had been the single dominant fact of America's transportation system—a centerpiece in the life of all Americans. If goods or people were moved any significant distance, they moved by railroad, or they did not move. Even ideas traveled by railroad, which handled most bulk deliveries of newspapers, magazines, and nearly all the nation's mail. To be located at any distance from a railroad was to be removed from the mainstream of the country—America's equivalent of Siberia. Altogether, it is hard to imagine a large country so totally dependent on a single technology.

By their very success, however, railroads had smothered competing modes of transportation. The nation's system of inland waterways had been allowed to fall into disrepair. It was even worse with rural roads; most of them were miserable tracks of mud and rubble, used mainly for short hauls of goods and mail between farms and the nearest railroad siding, and then only in good weather. There was nothing remotely approximating a national, or even a state, highway system.

While railroads provided mobility on a national scale, they were irksome things to many ordinary Americans. Privacy during travel was impossible; unless one owned a private railroad car, one traveled in the intimate company of strangers. Travelers were forced to conform to fixed rails and fixed schedules. If they had a long wait for a connecting train or simply had to stop overnight away from home, they had to stay in hotels near the railroad station, often disagreeable places in the noisiest and most crowded part of town.

The automobile promised freedom from all that—the promise of its name, *auto*-mobility. With a privately owned automobile, individuals could travel where and when they wanted, rapidly and cheaply over long distances. Such a thing had never happened before in human history, and the prospect was exhilarating. But two things were needed first: The price of automobiles had to drop to the point where ordinary people could afford them. And the country needed a system of decent long-distance roads. Both would require enormous expenditures of money and effort, but the rewards were too alluring to postpone. By 1910 both things had begun to happen; by 1920 America was in the process of retooling its whole basic transportation system. An elemental part of that process was the Model-T Ford, the most popular car ever built and, along with the cotton gin, the most influential machine ever manufactured in America.

Before the Model-T, most automobiles were toys for rich folk. Henry Ford changed that, not by any single invention, but by engineering a combination of previous inventions into a new form of industrial institution. In effect, he did three things that nobody had ever done before. First, he designed a car that was durable enough to stand up under the pounding of country roads yet simple enough to be repaired by any ingenious farm boy with reasonable access to spare parts and a bit of scrap metal or piano wire. Second, Ford designed a production line that reduced the act of assembling a complex machine to a large number of very simple steps. By so doing, he could hire factory workers with little mechanical experience, Americans fresh from the hills of Appalachia or European immigrants who could barely speak English, but who could turn out high-quality machines that would keep running for a long time. Third, and equally important, he designed and put into place the first large-scale system of automobile agencies. By 1927 there were 7,000 Ford agencies, ready to supply Ford owners with spare parts or to sell a new Ford to people who had never driven a car before and had never imagined they could own one. Now, at unbelievably low prices, the Model-T was within the reach of Everyman.

Ford introduced the Model-T in 1909, and it was an instant success. In 1915 his factories in Detroit turned out a million cars—the first time that ever happened. Ford continued building Model-Ts until 1929, when competition from Chevrolet finally forced him to begin producing the more sophisticated and comfortable closed sedan, the Model-A. By that time, however, he had produced some 29 million Model-Ts. It averaged out to an amazing figure: one Model-T for every four Americans.

The biggest change was in the lives of farmers. Before the Model-T, the word "farmer" was insultingly (but often correctly) used to describe a person who was isolated, ignorant, and crude. The Model-T started a process that would eventually make that definition obsolete in America. Ford's cheap little machine may not have looked like much, but it brought to a sudden end the mind-numbing rural isolation that had afflicted farmers since the beginning of history.

Like any huge, complicated enterprise, the auto industry soon came to be dominated by a few large, powerful companies. At the beginning of the century, a host of competitors had struggled to seize a corner of the mass market, or at least to carve out new niches in that market. Most of the new companies promptly went out of business, some because they were mismanaged, some because they misjudged the product or the market, but most because they were undersized and undercapitalized. The most successful of Ford's competitors imitated Ford's own techniques of mass manufacturing and mass marketing and operated at the same gigantic scale. By the 1930s the automobile industry had swelled to become the largest consumer of industrial raw materials in the United States, and its labor force was enormous. It was no place for corporate pygmies.

The immediate result was geographic concentration, as the biggest companies settled in a small number of urban places focused on southern Michigan. Detroit was the acknowledged capital, the location of Ford's main plants and the headquarters of Ford's chief competitors, the gigantic General Motors Corporation and the Chrysler Corporation. The city of Detroit exploded in consequence from a modest Great Lakes port to the nation's fourth-largest city. But similar things were happening throughout the Manufacturing Belt from southern Wisconsin to northern Ohio, and town after town became a booming city when the automobile industry moved in. The result was a region of large company towns, dependent on, and dominated by, one specific auto company. South Bend, Indiana, for example, became the creature of the Studebaker Corporation. Flint, Lansing, and Pontiac, Michigan, meant, respectively, Buick, Oldsmobile, and Pontiac. Furthermore, the scale of the automobile industry was so huge that mere suppliers of auto parts became industrial giants in their own right, and they too were concentrated in a few highly specialized places. Akron, Ohio, became a city of 250,000 people by supplying tires for the auto industry; Saginaw, Michigan, supplied General Motors with spark plugs and cast-iron motor blocks. All of these places took on much the same character: a boom-or-bust economy, depending on corporate whimsy or public taste for a particular model or brand. They underwent huge bursts of prosperity and immigration when plants were in production, and equal bursts of unemployment and outmigration when the plants were shut down for retooling, as most of them were each summer. Even worse, the auto industry was notoriously sensitive to economic fluctuations; if money was in short supply, cars were the first thing Americans stopped buying. As a result, the Great Depression struck the auto industry's undiversified towns with paralyzing force. It was no coincidence that those same cities saw the organization of America's biggest and most militant industrial labor unions during the 1930s, along with some of the country's bitterest and most violent strikes.

The explosive growth of the automobile industry during the 1910s and 1920s sent ripples, then tidal waves, across the face of the American economy. Nowhere was the effect felt more immediately than in the petroleum industry. Before the automobile, most of America's oil was refined into kerosene for use in oil lamps. Most of that oil had come from relatively small fields, like those of western Pennsylvania (where the world's first successful oil well had been drilled

in 1859) and southern California, and a few in Texas. In 1901, however, wildcatters brought in the most spectacular gusher the world had ever seen, at Spindletop near Beaumont in east Texas. The resulting oil rush revealed that Texas and Louisiana were sitting on top of not just one but several of the world's biggest oil and gas fields. Texas promptly became the nation's leading producer of oil and gas; and when subsequent discoveries were made in Oklahoma, they were more than matched by still newer discoveries in west Texas. By 1941, the American economy was so dependent on Texas, Oklahoma, and Louisiana oil that the federal government built a network of pipelines to the Northeast to carry the oil and gas and bypass the Nazi submarines that had been torpedoing tankers in the Atlantic.

The oil boom, in turn, produced its own effects, both immediate and distant. In the vicinity of the oil fields, by-products from refineries formed the basis for a sizable chemical industry along the Gulf Coast and lower Mississippi River. That industry was greatly stimulated by the discovery of ways to make synthetic rubber to replace natural rubber supplies from Southeast Asia, which had been seized by the Japanese during World War II. The boom in postwar plastics was another result of that episode.

Even more important was the simultaneous production of natural gas and cheap fuel oil for domestic heating. Most 19th-century Americans had heated their houses with wood- or coal-burning stoves. In most parts of the country, there was no shortage of either fuel. By the start of the 20th century, however, central heating had become a common fixture in most new houses, especially in the growing cities, and the fuel was almost always coal. Clean-burning anthracite was much favored over the oily and sulfurous bituminous coal, and northeastern Pennsylvania prospered mightily because it produced the bulk of the world's anthracite.

The discovery of Texas oil and gas and the building of a national pipeline system gave middle-income Americans the option of heating their houses with cheap, clean fuels that burned in furnaces that needed almost no tending. The conversion from coal to gas or oil was swift and joyful, as men and boys from coast to coast were freed from the daily chore of shoveling coal, hauling ashes, and breaking clinkers, and women were liberated from cleaning soot and coal dust from clothes, curtains, and furniture. By the end of World War II, coal furnaces were being converted as fast as American families could afford to do so. As they did, the Pennsylvania anthracite fields started to shut down, and thousands of miners were put out of work. It was not long before northeastern Pennsylvania fell into acute, permanent depression. Nor was it an isolated instance. The automobile and the machinery that went along with it set in motion chain reactions that reverberated back and forth across the economic map of the United States.

The huge new oil discoveries guaranteed America an unlimited supply of cheap gasoline at precisely the time that large numbers of middle-class Americans were first beginning to use cars. The increase in gasoline consumption, therefore, not only reflects the growth of a rich, new industry in Texas but also serves as an excellent measure of how much Americans were using their cars. During the 1920s, that increase was meteoric. In 1919 Americans consumed about 2.7 billion gallons of gasoline; by 1922 consumption had doubled. By 1926 it had doubled again and was on its way to doubling once more when the New York Stock Exchange collapsed in 1929. Thereafter, the data are curious and revealing. Even during the worst days of the depression, gasoline consumption declined only once (1931–32) and then only very slightly. From 1933 onward, consumption continued to increase, albeit not quite at the same frantic rate. The figures show that Americans had stopped buying many new automobiles but had not stopped driving the ones they already owned. And by 1941 there were almost 30 million cars and about 99 million people of driving age— one car for every 3.3 people. The automobile had become an entrenched institution in American life. Even an economic cataclysm could not dislodge it.

New Roads for New Cars

The explosion in auto production set off a simultaneous explosion in road building. Good roads, of course, made the ownership of automobiles increasingly attractive and symbiotically stimulated the sale of cars. Car owners, furthermore, tended to be fairly affluent and quickly came to constitute one of the most vocal and powerful voting blocs in the country. Politicians soon recognized that road building was a popular task for any government, irrespective of political party or ideological coloration.

It was one thing to build a good road here or there but quite another to build a national road system. The main question was how to pay for such a system; it was an expensive business to build highways that would stand up under heavy traffic and bad weather. A few experiments with toll roads in the New York metropolitan area were successful because New York was affluent and densely populated. But in most parts of the country, few roads could pay for themselves on a mile-by-mile basis. If a road system was to service the whole country, it would have to be a government enterprise, rather like running the post office or maintaining an army or navy. As early as the 1890s, several states had created highway departments, charged with designing roads to proper standards and letting bids to competent contractors. In 1916 Congress passed the Federal Aid Road Act, committing the federal government to support a national program of road improvement but leaving ultimate control of highway systems in the hands of individual states.

Meanwhile, engineers had been devising techniques of building cheaper roads that would stand up under heavy use. The greatest breakthrough came in 1920 with the discovery that eight inches of reinforced concrete, laid on a proper base of crushed rock, could withstand very heavy loads. Although concrete roads were initially costly, they required little maintenance. Before the end of the 1920s, concrete had become the material of choice in building any important road in the United States. More than incidentally, those concrete roads made possible the use of increasingly heavy trucks. Within 30 years, trucks had taken over the haulage of most general cargo in the United States and had driven many of the nation's railroads to the brink of bankruptcy.

Leaving control of roads in the hands of individual states had two unintended effects. First, since political support for road building came largely from farmers, states put a high priority on building light-weight, macadamized "farm-to-market" roads, in preference to heavy-duty interstate highways. In its initial stages, then, the building of good roads did not encourage long-distance traffic either of people or of goods; the railroads retained that business until the end of World War II. Instead, the new roads greatly stimulated short- and medium-distance travel—weekend excursions to grandmother's house a hundred miles away or a few days of camping alongside the road. Thus, while Americans were not yet in the habit of using cars for long-distance vacations, they were developing the institutions that would grow into a full-blown roadside tourist industry after World War II. What began as whimsical adventures in roadside tenting quickly produced new institutions. First, free, municipally financed campgrounds evolved into more elaborate campgrounds where a small fee was required; then to campgrounds with rude shelters; then to more permanent structures with running water and mattresses; then to "kozy kabins" with bedding, heating, and running water; and ultimately to "motels," a term reportedly used for the first time in San Luis Obispo, California, in 1927. Although nationwide motel chains would not emerge until after World War II, a New England restaurateur named Howard Johnson discovered in the 1930s that travelers could be taught to stop at a roadside establishment if it looked familiar and if it held out the promise of quick service and clean, unsurprising victuals. Howard Johnson's became the first of many fast-food chains to array their interchangeable logos and interchangeable food along the sides of America's newly democratic highways.

The second effect of state financing of roads was that only the richest states were able or willing to pay for elaborate road networks. Poor areas like the South were conspicuously lacking in good roads, and so was much of the West, where it was prohibitively expensive to build long-distance roads through sparsely populated areas.

Despite the gaps, a genuine national road system had begun to develop. By 1925, the network had grown so complicated that the American Association of State Highway Officials was impelled to devise a national highway numbering system, replacing the colorful but undependable practice of naming arterial highways. By that time, it had become possible to drive on uninterrupted paved roads to all the main population centers in the Northeast and along most of the well-traveled vacation routes between New York and Miami (fig. 17.1, top).

The 1930s saw rapid completion of the basic system, largely as a result of the depression. The New Deal undertook road building on an un-precedented scale, part of a massive public works program for relief of the unemployed. In the highly political business of road building, it is not surprising that special favor was bestowed on regions of the country that returned Democratic majorities and on the home districts of powerful congressmen. In effect, that meant the "Solid South," the 11 states of the old Confederacy that had been voting against Republicans since Reconstruction. During Franklin D. Roosevelt's first two terms of office, an area that had been almost roadless at the beginning of the depression gained an excellent system of concrete highways. By the end of the depression, it was possible to drive from coast to coast entirely on paved roads. Except in sparsely populated areas of the dry or mountainous West, most of America's rural country lay within easy reach of a paved road. All in all, it amounted to a national transformation (fig. 17.1, bottom).

Roads would not be used routinely for long-distance travel in most parts of the United States until well after World War II; driving was simply too slow. Highway engineers had not yet gotten into the habit of building bypasses around cities and towns, so long-distance drivers inevitably confronted a procession of urban traffic jams. In the country, a plethora of crossroads and driveways made driving both frustrating and dangerous. Commercial clutter alongside major highways made things even worse.

There was an obvious but expensive solution: build special arterial roads, where access was limited to a few carefully engineered intersections, and where commercial development was banned completely from the roadside. Typically, New York City provided the leadership in trying out the idea on a large scale. A few limited-access tollways had been built around the city to serve affluent suburbanites (the Bronx River Parkway, finished in 1923, was the first). But it was Robert Moses in the 1920s and the 1930s who used his extraordinary powers as director of the Port of New York Authority to finance and build an elaborate system of expressways and bridges, which would shortly tie the huge New York metropolitan area together and would ultimately extend its tentacles far into the surrounding countryside.

Long-distance driving, however, was still unusual. When it happened, as when New Yorkers drove to Miami on vacation, or when Okies migrated to California on Route 66, it was a cause for comment. During the late 1930s, two roads

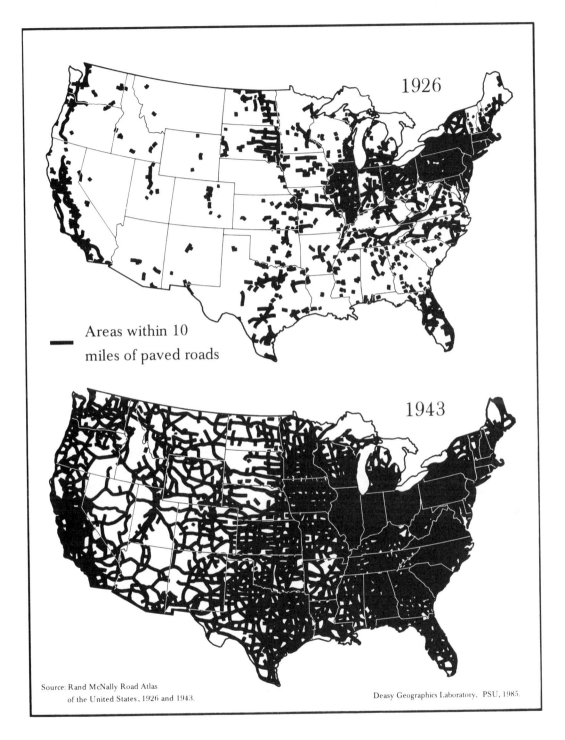

1926

Areas within 10
miles of paved roads

1943

Source: Rand McNally Road Atlas
   of the United States, 1926 and 1943.

Deasy Geographics Laboratory, PSU, 1985.

Figure 17.1 Paved Roads, 1926 and 1943

were built that would lay the groundwork for a massive change in American driving habits after World War II. One was the Pennsylvania Turnpike, a limited-access tollway that sliced smoothly across the Appalachian Mountains and reduced travel time between Pittsburgh and Harrisburg from two grueling days to an easy (and scenic) five hours. (Ironically, the turnpike was built atop the unfinished roadbed of a bankrupt railroad.) The other was the Arroyo Seco Parkway (now the Pasadena Freeway), a multi-lane, limited-access free highway between downtown Pasadena and Los Angeles. Each road proved an important point. The turnpike demonstrated that low-gradient, limited-access highways could be built for long distances, even over very difficult terrain, and still generate enough traffic to pay for themselves. The Arroyo Seco proved that Americans were willing to pay for extremely expensive roads through taxes, not by collecting special tolls. Both ideas were fundamental to democratizing American highways and to the thinking that created the interstate highway system of the 1950s and 1960s.

A NEW COMMUNICATIONS SYSTEM: TELEPHONES, MOVIES, AND RADIOS

Automobiles and roads were revolutionary devices because they made it easy and attractive to move goods and people in all sorts of directions in which they had never moved before. But there was a simultaneous revolution in the movement of ideas, sparked by powerful machines of communications: telephones, motion pictures, and wireless radios. All of these technologies did essentially the same thing: they allowed Americans in almost any part of the country to be plugged into the same national circuitry of ideas and tastes, to see faces and hear voices from the farthest corners of the earth. It was a highly democratic technology, available cheaply to huge numbers of people over vast expanses of territory. Before long, that technology had begun to blur some of America's sharpest geographic distinctions, the regional differences between North and South, between East and West, between city and country.

The effect of the telephone was felt first. At the turn of the century the telephone had been in commercial use for about two decades, but there were only about 1 million instruments in the whole country—primitive devices used mostly for short-distance, intraurban business conversations. The invention of the vacuum tube in 1906 made it possible to amplify telephone signals over long distances, and the first transcontinental commercial service was put in place by 1915, using only three relay stations. Still, long-distance calling was expensive; a three-minute call from New York to San Francisco cost $20.70. Short-distance service was much cheaper, however, and from 1900 to 1930, telephones were installed at an almost steady rate of about 600,000 instruments per year. By the time of the Wall Street crash in 1929, 40 percent of American households possessed a telephone, about 20 million in all.

The depression halted the telephone boom for a short time, but it did little to dampen American enthusiasm for the telephone. Just as with automobiles, few people had enough money to install a new instrument, but those who already had one continued to use it at an increasing rate. In 1930, Americans held 80 million phone conversations per day, and they kept talking throughout the depression. In 1940, with almost the same number of instruments, the number of conversations was up to 95 million a day. Well before the beginning of World War II, Americans had obviously acquired the telephone habit. They would never lose it.

To be sure, telephone service did not spread uniformly across the country. Cities received telephones first, just as later they acquired dial instruments and automatic switching equipment. The rough-and-ready quality of rural telephone exchanges was the butt of bad jokes until well after World War II. Poor parts of the country had very few phones, conspicuously in black areas of the South. But the cost of service continued to go down. The Bell Telephone Company, owner and operator of most American telephones, was applying the same principles of high-quality technology at very low prices that Henry Ford had used to democratize the Model-T. By 1945 the cost of that three-minute transcontinental call had dropped to $2.50, and local service was even cheaper by comparison. By the same time, an enormous proportion of the nation's social and commercial business was being transacted by telephone, and the majority of Americans had come to view telephone service as a kind of basic human necessity. To be without phone service was to be stranded in limbo.

Still, telephones were mainly instruments of two-way communication between individual persons. Radio and motion pictures stimulated a different kind of communication, for they operated en masse, and they operated one way, from producer to consumer, spreading mass culture almost instantaneously across the entire nation. Nothing like that had ever happened in a large modern country, and it is hardly surprising that Europe's intelligentsia were highly critical of American mass communications—especially movies, which were popular not only in America but all over the world. Their criticism did them little good. Once movies and radio came to town, nothing would ever be the same again.

The movies came first. Although they were widely available early in the century, they were hard to take seriously—flickering five-minute reels, designed for nickelodeons, showed simpleminded dramas, crudely staged and crudely acted. All that changed rapidly in the first decades of the 20th century. By 1912 D. W. Griffith had produced *The Birth of a Nation,* sometimes described as the first full-length feature film. It was instantly popular and hugely profitable. Other such films were quickly produced and in such numbers that any American town of any consequence boasted at least one movie house by the end of the decade. In 1927 Warner Brothers released Al Jolson's *Jazz Singer,* the first commercial film with coordinated sound track. By 1929 silent pictures were things of the past, as Hollywood went over to making "talkies." Meanwhile, box office receipts were booming. In 1922, the first year when data were available, American movie theaters were selling 40 million tickets per week. By 1930 the figure had risen to 90 million, and annual receipts totaled almost three-quarters of a *billion* dollars. Considering the scarcity of money at the time, this was an enormous sum.

American moviemaking had become big business, and it soon began to act like one. Just as automobile producers had achieved economies of scale by concentrating production in one small region, the movie industry settled down in southern California, taking advantage of the region's enormous environmental variety and year-round good weather for outdoor filming. Just as auto production put the horse and buggy out of business, the movie industry fairly well destroyed small-scale local entertainment in the United States—and a good deal of local

color in the process. Whether the critics liked it or not (and many did not), the movies opened a whole new world to millions of Americans. And it was the same world for everybody: people from farms and small towns saw exactly the same features and the same newsreels that big-city people were seeing. They laughed at the same jokes, wept at the same bathos, and thrilled to the same deeds of heroism. As a force of cultural convergence, there had never been anything like it.

But there shortly would be. In 1920, radio arrived like a thunderclap on the American scene and promptly began to do to the nation's culture the same thing that movies had been doing. As with telephones and movies, basic radio theory had been known since the late 19th century, and long-distance radio transmission by Morse code had become common before World War I. But not until 1915 had the technology accumulated to permit transmission of voice signals over long distances without gross distortion. Once that happened, commercial radio simply exploded. The first commercial radio station, KDKA in Pittsburgh, went on the air in November 1920, broadcasting the returns of the Harding-Cox presidential election. Three years later, there were 556 licensed stations in the United States, and a brand-new industry was manufacturing half a million radio sets per year. By 1929 more than 10 million American households were equipped with radios, and by the end of World War II they were virtually ubiquitous.

Unlike the movie and automobile industries, the radio industry could not tolerate unrestrained competition; there were, after all, a finite number of usable wavelengths, and the scramble to control those wavelengths threatened to reduce the airwaves to babbling chaos. In 1927 the government stepped in with the Federal Radio Act, creating what eventually became the Federal Communications Commission, armed with authority to grant licenses and to restrict the range and frequency of transmissions. Public control of radio waves, however, emphatically did not mean public broadcasting. Despite pleas from David Sarnoff of the Radio Corporation of America, the United States rejected the European model, where license fees supported publicly owned networks. American radio would be a commercial venture funded by advertising revenues, and those revenues soon grew very large indeed. As a result, there was a scramble to gain control of available wavelengths, and, after considerable litigation, 1926 saw the creation of the National Broadcasting Company, the first of several nationwide radio networks. It is hardly surprising that those networks came to be based in New York and Hollywood, where the nation's main entertainment industries were already well entrenched. There was, in consequence, much overlap in the ownership of radio networks and motion picture studios, with the result that radio broadcasts quickly grew increasingly homogeneous in content. By 1945 only a tiny fraction of the American population was beyond the range of a radio station affiliated with one of the four or five major national networks, all broadcasting essentially the same mix of news, drama, and popular music. Very few instruments in the history of technology have done so much so quickly to knock down the boundaries of geographic regionalism in the United States—or so much to promote the acceptance of homogeneous national culture, values, and tastes.

GOVERNMENT AS AGENT OF GEOGRAPHIC CHANGE

Few Americans at the turn of the century could have foreseen the profound impact of the new technology, but another change was coming that was just as difficult to predict, and geographically just as portentous. For the first time on a large scale, the federal government would undertake a permanent, active role in what had previously been regarded as private affairs—especially the movement of immigrants and the use of land and water. This move represented a major shift in political philosophy, and it cut raggedly across party lines.

Strong central government had been anathema to Americans since long before the Revolution. Most Americans agreed enthusiastically with Ralph Waldo Emerson's maxim: "The less government we have, the better—the fewer laws, and the less confided power." The Bill of Rights had been written to enforce that idea and had spelled out basic limits to federal power. But Americans held two other geographic rights to be equally fundamental: that people should be allowed to move when and where they pleased and that they should be permitted to do what they pleased with private property.

Toward the end of the 19th century, those attitudes had begun to change, especially as they affected private property rights. Populist farmers of the West and South had agitated successfully for government control over rates charged by private railroad companies. Theodore Roosevelt and his Progressive Republicans had extended that control by arguing that property rights were not absolute and that state and federal government possessed the power and moral authority to counterbalance the growing might of irresponsible corporations. Woodrow Wilson promoted similar arguments under Democratic auspices. The passage of the income tax amendment to the U.S. Constitution in 1913 laid the financial foundation for an enormous increase in federal power, but it was the logical culmination of a multipartisan process that had been gathering strength for several decades.

The federal intervention came in two sharply different areas, and from quite different political directions. The first occurred during the 1920s under the auspices of conservative Republican administrations and resulted in stringent controls over immigration. The second came in the 1930s under the New Deal in response to the depression, floods, and dust storms and resulted in massive new federal regulation of land and water. In both cases, the federal government took action that would have seemed outrageous at the turn of the century. And in both cases that government action changed the fundamental human and physical geography of the United States.

Immigration Controls

World War I greatly stimulated the growth of government activism and unprecedented interventions in what had traditionally been regarded as sacrosanct private affairs. Some of the wartime interventions were temporary; government seizure of the railroads, for example, came to a speedy end after the Armistice. But other "emergency" measures became permanent. Two in particular would quickly change the complexion of American life. One was national Prohibition; the other was the first set of comprehensive laws to limit foreign immigration. Within a very short time, Americans decided that Prohibition had been a mistake, and it was repealed by passage of the 21st Amendment in 1933. Stringent immigration controls, however, became a permanent institution.

The immigration laws represented a fundamental change in American policy and in attitudes. Throughout national history, free immigration had been an unquestioned cornerstone of national policy, and the idea of limiting the movement of European people into the country was generally viewed as un-American. (Excluding nonwhites was something else again. Immigrants from China had been completely barred since 1882 under provisions of the Chinese Exclusion Act, passed under pressure from the Knights of Labor and a coalition of frightened white Californians.) Two forces came together in 1918, however, to bring about a change in those basic attitudes. One was short-run disillusionment with the war and, by extension, with Europeans and other foreigners in general. The other was a growing fear that the country would be swamped with unassimilated immigrants.

A wide variety of Americans shared that fear. Some of the opposition to immigration came from nativists who simply did not like foreigners and what they considered foreign ideas. Some came from political reformers, progressives who had begun to doubt that immigrants from European tyrannies could be taught to understand America's democratic institutions. And labor unions almost unanimously feared and resented competition from immigrants who were willing to work for sweatshop wages.

Given the statistics, however, the fears were not ungrounded. As late as the 1890s, when immigration had averaged about 370,000 per year, the volume seemed tolerable. But in 1902, the numbers suddenly shot upward. In 1905, for the first time, the commissioner general of immigration counted more than a million new arrivals in a single year. That figure was coming to be normal, and there was no telling where it would go from there. Furthermore, a vast majority of immigrants had lately been coming from southern and eastern Europe, bringing languages and religions and customs that were unfamiliar and threatening to the native-born Americans of northwestern European ancestry who mainly owned and ran the country. Even more menacing to the old-line Americans, the areas of immigrant origin were spreading eastward and southward into yet stranger parts of the world—deep inside Russia and into the mountains and deserts of Asia Minor.

German submarines brought transatlantic passenger traffic to a temporary halt, but World War I also brought the first comprehensive legal restriction on immigration: a 1917 act, passed over President Wilson's veto, to impose literacy tests for new immigrants, a transparent effort to reduce the flow of people from southern and eastern Europe. Thereafter, legislation came thick and fast. In 1921, Congress established the first comprehensive quota system; in 1924, the law was tightened; and finally, the National Origins Act of 1929 reduced the total number of immigrants to a mere 150,000 per year, to be apportioned according to national origins of the U.S. population in 1920—that is, overwhelmingly northwestern European. Almost gratuitously, Congress also created a "barred zone" stretching across Asia from Japan to Persia, from which no immigrants of any kind would be admitted. (It is curious that no limits were imposed on immigration from Latin America.)

The geographic effect of the immigration laws was far reaching, but it was nowhere more immediately felt than in the nation's big industrial cities, and especially the gateway city of New York. Until World War I, non-English-speaking immigrants had sought refuge among their fellow nationals in large urban ghettos. More than incidentally, those ghettos had furnished urban America with a large pool of cheap labor for dirty work in heavy industry and marginal piecework in semilegal sweatshops and as domestic "help." Indeed, cheap foreign labor proved so useful that some of the large steel and auto companies routinely sent recruiters to Europe to collect men to work in the factories of Detroit, Buffalo, or Pittsburgh—a practice that naturally outraged both organized and nonorganized labor. The sudden stoppage of immigration forced employers to look elsewhere. From 1914 onward, after German submarines had put an abrupt end to transatlantic passenger traffic, recruiters headed south to seek out workers in the hills of Appalachia and the worn-out lands of the old Cotton Belt. The new migrants to the cities were no longer Poles, Italians, and Slovenes, but instead poor rural Americans, at first mainly white, but increasingly black as well.

Controlling the Use of Land and Water

Support for new immigration laws was widespread and had cut broadly across party and ideological lines. That was not true, however, when it came to a second major area of government activism, the array of issues loosely grouped under the heading of "conservation." Few issues so sharply divided "conservatives" from "progressives" as the question of the government's role in managing natural resources and in controlling the use of land and water.

The philosophical division was basic and strongly felt. Conservatives from both parties (but mostly Republican) held that private property was sacrosanct and that government had an obligation to stand aside when private citizens or companies wished to use the resources of land and water: grazing, mining, timbering, or hydroelectric development. Most progressives took the view that land and water were no longer inexhaustible and that public interest demanded that government take action to conserve, allocate, and, if necessary, develop natural resources. While conservatives feared the tyranny of government power, progressives feared and resented the growing power of corporate wealth, which, they believed, was bent on plundering the public domain for private profit.

To progressives, government support of conservation was an urgent necessity; to conservatives, government supervision of land and water was a first step toward despotism. The conservation movement had won major successes under the progressive administrations of Theodore Roosevelt and Woodrow Wilson, but it had been hamstrung under the conservative presidencies of Harding, Coolidge, and Hoover. The election of 1932 changed all that, as Franklin D. Roosevelt's New Deal embarked on the most comprehensive and vigorous program of land-use and water control in American history. If the 1920s were bad times for American conservation, the 1930s were correspondingly good and permanently entrenched the conservation movement in the seats of national power.

The bitterest battle was fought over the generation and distribution of electric power. That fight lasted several decades and epitomized the political chasm between conservatives and progressives over land and water policy, as well as a wide range of economic, social, and even aesthetic issues. As recently as the beginning of the 20th century, electricity was not a major issue in the Untied States; total national production was only about 6 billion kilowatt hours—a paltry 60 kilowatt hours per capita per year—with much of the power used to run municipal streetcars.

But by 1929 production had risen to 117 billion kilowatt hours, and in much of the country electricity had become a basic domestic necessity. Most farms, however, were still without electricity and the comforts that went with it: lighting and proper refrigeration, not to mention the well pumps, washing machines, and milking machines that could have reduced the backbreaking work of running a farm. Nor was there much chance for a farmer to obtain electric power as long as it was generated and distributed by privately owned utilities, which saw little profit in (and therefore little reason for) extending power lines into sparsely populated rural country. Progressive senators from farm states, led by George Norris of Nebraska, repeatedly denounced the private power trusts and urged the use of public funds to create public power companies and to build hydroelectric dams, but the Republican administrations of the 1920s pronounced such enterprises to be "sheer socialism" (in Herbert Hoover's words), and therefore anathema. Indeed, the Coolidge administration almost succeeded in selling the government's Wilson Dam at Muscle Shoals on the Tennessee River to a private holding company. The dam had been authorized during World War I to generate power to make nitrates for munitions, but the conservatives wanted no truck with such schemes in peacetime.

Occasionally, conservatives agreed to use federal funds for large public works projects, but only when they were seen as necessary to protect or enhance private property. Thus, after the Mississippi River went on an epic rampage in 1927, the U.S. Army Corps of Engineers was given permanent authority over flood control throughout the whole Mississippi basin. In 1928, Congress authorized the building of Boulder (later Hoover) Dam on the lower Colorado River. But power generation was only part of the dam's purpose; the project was also designed to furnish irrigation water to corporate agriculture in the Coachella and Imperial Valleys of southern California. It was clearly understood that the power generated at Boulder Dam would be sold to private utilities.

The New Deal changed all that. Roosevelt, elected with a clear mandate to reverse the conservative policies of the 1920s, had a special (and personal) commitment to conservation of land and water and to federal support for such efforts. Many of his policy advisers were social

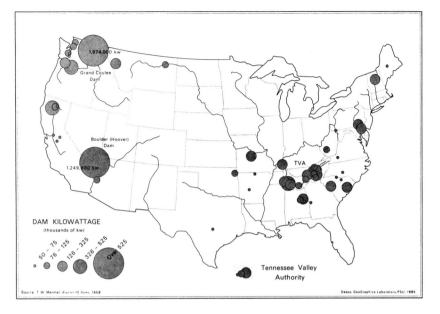

Figure 17.2 Hydroelectric Dam Building, 1925–1945

activists, eager to prove that a democratic government could do more than simply react to emergencies and could act as a positive force for regional economic and social reform, in sharp contrast with what they saw as the selfish and scandal-ridden record of their conservative predecessors.

An early augury of Roosevelt's ambitions came less than a month after the inauguration, as the president sent to Congress a proposal to establish the Tennessee Valley Authority (TVA). At first blush, TVA seemed merely an expensive scheme to build dams on the Tennessee and Cumberland Rivers to produce fertilizer and public power. In fact, it was much more than that. TVA was aimed at nothing less than changing the basic geography of a huge, poverty-stricken region that sprawled over much of the southwestern Appalachians and upper South. It would be a showcase, demonstrating what comprehensive planning by a benevolent democratic government could do.

The backbone of TVA was a system of more than 20 large dams (fig. 17.2) that would generate power cheap enough for mountain people to afford and entice industry and employment to the remote rural area. In addition, the dams would control floods on the evil-tempered rivers and create 652 miles of nine-foot channel navi-

gable by heavy barges from Knoxville in eastern Tennessee to Paducah on the Ohio River. As an added attraction, the convoluted shores of TVA's many lakes would be available for recreation and as a tourist attraction.

But that was only the beginning. A small army of government planners was dispatched to the valley to teach farmers how to control soil erosion and reforest denuded slopes. Others arrived to help local people create self-supporting, home-owned industries and build new model towns. In all, TVA was designed to help people of the Tennessee Valley build a self-reliant society, free of privation and domination by outsiders—a utopian dream come true. Ultimately, TVA lost much of its luster through administrative and ideological wrangling, and as things turned out, none of its utopian social goals came close to realization. But its physical results were genuinely impressive; much of the valley's most damaged land was restored to productive use, and the abundance of cheap power did attract new industry to the region. It became known all over the world as one of the New Deal's most visible and glamorous achievements.

The New Deal undertook other large hydroelectric projects, although none with quite the panache and sweeping social ambitions of TVA. Boulder Dam was finished by the mid-1930s, and its cheap power and water quickly stimulated economic growth in the desert oases of Arizona, Nevada, and southern California (fig. 17.2). Even more ambitious was a system of extremely large dams on the Columbia River, which, because of its large volume, steady flow, and deep dammable canyons, possessed the largest hydroelectric potential of any American river. The linchpin of the Columbia system was the colossal Grand Coulee Dam—when it was finished, the largest human-made structure on Earth. Before the end of the 1940s, the Columbia was converted from a wild river into a staircase of placid lakes, and Washington, Oregon, and Idaho were wallowing in an abundance of cheap electric power and irrigation water. The Columbia dam system received much less publicity than TVA, but it stimulated vigorous agricultural development in the middle Columbia valley. Even more important in the long run, hydroelectric power from the Columbia became the basis for a major concentration of power-consuming industries during World War II, notably aluminum, aircraft, and plutonium refining. Only much later would questions be raised about the environmental consequences of these enormous dams.

The New Deal also undertook a massive program to provide farmers with electric power. Under the aegis of the 1935 Rural Electrification Administration (REA), low-interest loans were made available to string power lines into remote rural areas. By 1941, four out of ten American farms had electric service; by 1950, nine out of ten. The combination of electricity with new rural roads made a quiet revolution in the countryside, for it brought a sudden end to the numbing isolation of American farmers and to the drudgery that had made farm life burdensome since time immemorial. Arthur Schlesinger Jr. remarked: "No single event, save perhaps for the invention of the automobile, so effectively diminished the aching resentment of the farmers and so swiftly closed the gap between country and city. No single public agency [as REA] ever so enriched and brightened the quality of rural living."

No amount of rural electrification, however, would cure the general economic misery that plagued American farmers since the end of World War I. Two facts lay at the root of the matter: First, low and undependable prices of farm products kept many farmers in a state of chronic debt and prevented many from making a decent living. Second, many farmers were trying to eke a living from marginal land. The problem of credit was nationwide, but the land problem was especially grievous in two sorely afflicted regions: the old Cotton Belt of the Deep South, and the wheat and rangeland of the western Great Plains.

Conditions in the rural South were bad at best, especially in the old cotton country where the infamous sharecropping system kept millions of African Americans and whites in a semifeudal servitude of poverty, malnutrition, and ignorance, which was in some ways worse than pre–Civil War slavery. Decades of single-crop farming had completely destroyed the best soils in the South, but the ultimate catastrophe was the boll weevil, an insect that had entered the United States from Mexico in the 1890s and, by the 1920s, had become epidemic throughout the whole Cotton Belt, where it regularly destroyed a large part of the cotton crop (fig. 17.3). The agricultural depression of the 1920s was the straw that broke the camel's back, and by the 1930s much of the traditional Cotton Belt was disappearing, as huge areas of cropland were abandoned to grow back into piney woods.

In the western Plains, nature had visited a different kind of calamity. In a broad swath of territory from Montana and the Dakotas south to west Texas, farmers and ranchers had incautiously settled on land with highly unpredictable rainfall. Much of the settlement had occurred in years when farm prices and rainfall both were abnormally high, notably during World War I. But after the war, disaster struck. Prices failed in the 1920s and brought economic depression. In the early 1930s rainfall failed, bringing massive crop failures, blinding dust storms, and economic ruin (fig. 17.3). Unlike the South, where depression was endemic and easy to overlook or take for granted, disaster on the Plains struck suddenly and visibly. In 1934 winds blew topsoil off the dry, plowed fields in vast dramatic clouds, and farmers by the thousands began to abandon the devastated land for greener pastures, most conspicuously California (figs. 17.4 and 17.5). Even doctrinaire conservatives admitted that something had to be done.

With customary energy, the New Dealers attacked the agricultural crisis on a broad front, passing laws that would become permanent fixtures in American agriculture. After decades of

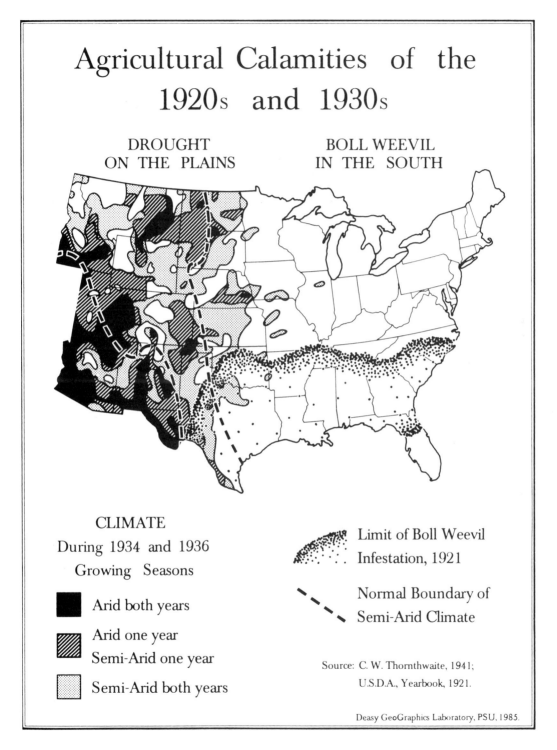

Figure 17.3 Agricultural Calamities of the 1920s and 1930s

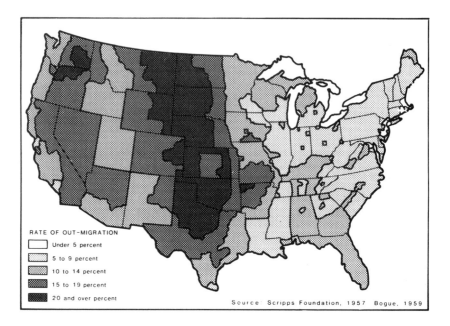

Figure 17.4 Out-Migration, 1935–1940

squabbling over range rights, Congress passed the Taylor Grazing Act in 1934, sharply curtailing the density of grazing on government-owned land. In 1935, during the worst of the dust bowl times, the Soil Conservation Service (SCS) was created as an agency of the Department of Agriculture. The SCS left permanent marks on the landscape by promoting contour plowing and techniques of dry farming, where strips of land were left fallow in alternate years to conserve and gather moisture. Just as far-reaching, the government undertook to raise farm prices by regulating both supply and demand. As for demand, the government set about to create it when necessary by guaranteeing to purchase and store a variety of basic (and not-so-basic) commodities at fixed prices. In return for guaranteed prices, farmers were required to curtail production by a complicated system of limits on planting and harvesting. The system eventually turned the federal government into a major force in determining who would grow what, where, and how much. By the end of the 1930s, the invisible hand of the free market no longer designed the nation's agricultural landscape; the federal government did.

In addition, the New Deal undertook massive programs intended to repair and restore damaged land. Government land acquisitions were hugely increased so that in the first three years of the New Deal alone, the government purchased twice as much forest land as had been bought in the entire previous history of the national forest system. One of Roosevelt's favorite programs was the Civilian Conservation Corps (CCC), in which unemployed young men could submit to quasi-military discipline and go out into the wilds to plant trees, fight fires, and build campgrounds, trails, and fire towers, in return for food, shelter, and nominal pay. By the time of World War II, some 2.5 million young men had served in the CCC. Although its life span was short, the impact of the CCC was profound, especially in reforestation. It has been calculated that of all the trees ever planted in the United States, the CCC was responsible for planting more than half.

But public works projects and congressional legislation could not solve the main problems of marginal land. In much of the United States, the only really satisfactory answer was to reduce agricultural population on those lands. Throughout the interwar period a steady stream of defeated farmers packed their families and possessions into automobiles and departed permanently. As Will Rogers remarked, America was the only nation in the world to go to the poorhouse in an automobile. Ironically, very lit-

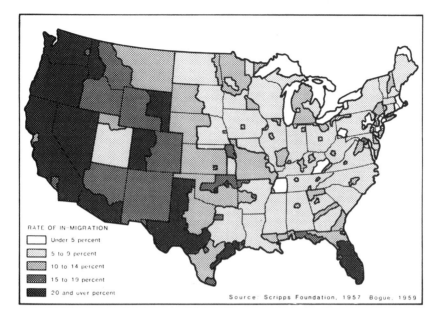

RATE OF IN-MIGRATION

	Under 5 percent
	5 to 9 percent
	10 to 14 percent
	15 to 19 percent
	20 and over percent

Source: Scripps Foundation, 1957　Bogue, 1959

Figure 17.5 In-Migration, 1935–1940

tle land was actually retired from agriculture during the 1930s, and in the stricken regions of the western Plains, farm acreage actually increased (figs. 17.6 and 17.7). The net effect was to increase the *size* of individual farms and ranches, which reduced pressure on the land and eventually encouraged conservation. That long-run benefit, however, was of little comfort to the farmers who continued to flee. As the decade of the 1930s wore on, the whole nation seemed to be moving.

PEOPLE MOVING

Mobility has always seemed an especially American trait. Mobile people settled the country in the first place, and geographic mobility had always been the key to economic and social betterment. In some ways, then, the mobility of the interwar period was merely a continuation of something that had been going on for a long time. But in other ways, the incessant movement of whole populations seemed more feverish than anything that had gone before. For one thing, the wild fluctuations of the economy—the boom of the 1920s, the depression of the 1930s—alternately pulled and pushed people from place to place with unprecedented force, often under

dramatic and heart-rending circumstances. For another, increasing numbers of people were moving to new places, not so much for traditional economic reasons, but simply for pleasure. For yet another, the newly democratized automobile allowed people to move to places that would have been unreachable by railroad in previous times, with the result that new patterns of population began to emerge on the American map. But, just as important, movements of people to and fro across the country had begun to attract attention from the radio and motion picture industries and from popular novelists, so that internal migration was now taking place in the unremitting glare of publicity.

Although the movement of people during the 1920s and the 1930s sometimes seemed frantic and confused, rather as if someone had kicked over an anthill, in fact most of the migration fell into one of three major streams: from rural to urban areas, from central cities to the suburbs, or from cold climates toward sunshine and balmy temperatures.

Rural Losses, Urban Gains

Rural-urban migration, of course, was nothing new to the United States; urbanization had long been one of the basic demographic hallmarks of

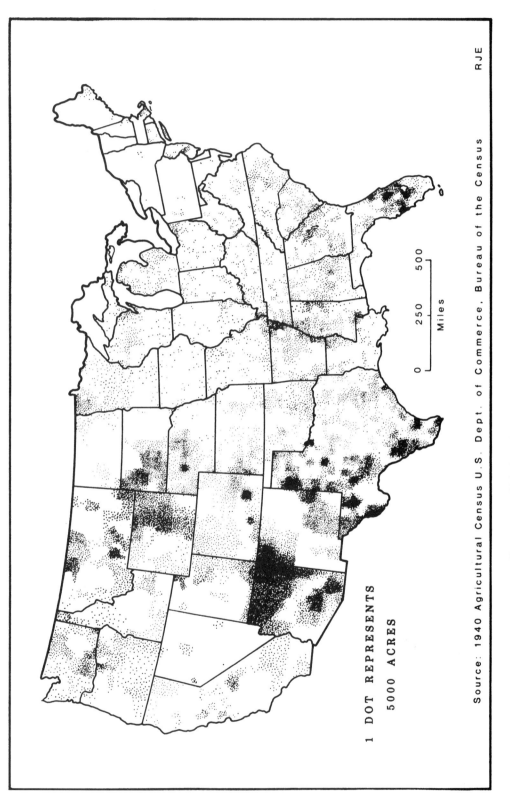

1 DOT REPRESENTS

5000 ACRES

Source: 1940 Agricultural Census U.S. Dept. of Commerce, Bureau of the Census   RJE

Figure 17.6 U.S. Farmland Acreage Increase, 1930–1940

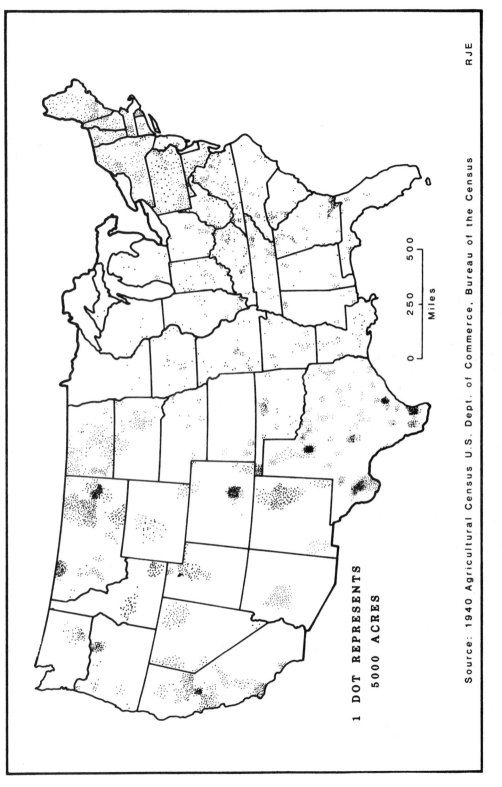

1 DOT REPRESENTS
5000 ACRES

Source: 1940 Agricultural Census U.S. Dept. of Commerce, Bureau of the Census   RJE

Figure 17.7 U.S. Farmland Acreage Decrease, 1930–1940

industrializing nations throughout the world. But 1920 marked a tipping point in the shifting balance of population: for the first time in American history, the census reported that more people lived in urban areas than in rural areas.

That aggregate statistic, however, tells only part of the story. There was no absolute decline in rural population, at least as the census defined the word "rural." Indeed, during the worst years of the early depression, rural areas reported a sharp surge in population, as people who had moved to the city to find jobs in the 1920s went home again to escape urban breadlines. But despite boom and bust, national population was increasing, and the increase was almost entirely urban. That urban growth was greatly stimulated by World War II and the explosive growth of defense industries, especially in the Northeast and on the West Coast. But unlike after World War I, this trend continued unabated through the 1940s and 1950s, and so did migration to urban areas.

Within the rural areas, moreover, enormous changes were afoot. The population on farms, and in the villages and towns that depended on farms, had been dropping by fits and starts. Meanwhile, other areas were growing rapidly, especially the unincorporated fringes of large cities—suburban territory that the census defined as "rural" but that in fact was rural in name only.

Although farm population varied only slightly between 1910 and 1940, hovering between 32.5 million and 30.5 million, World War II brought a sudden change, and between 1940 and 1945 the nation's farm population dropped by more than 6 million people. Taken as a proportion of the national total, the decline was even more dramatic. At the beginning of World War I, about one-third of the American population lived on farms. At the end of World War II, the proportion had declined to about one-sixth. That age-old institution, the family farm, was evaporating.

Strong national and regional forces were at work to dislodge farmers from the land. Part of the trouble went back to World War I, when the United States had taken on the job of feeding, clothing, and supplying both its own armies and those of its allies—not to mention a sizable part of the Allied civilian population as well. The price of food shot up dramatically as a result: staples like meat and milk roughly doubled in price from 1914 to 1920, and the price of potatoes and flour tripled. Farmers rushed out to buy new land and machinery at inflated prices but could not pay for them when the boom ended after the Armistice because prices dropped as European farmers reentered the international market. The 1920s, therefore, saw not only a depression in American farm prices but also a terrible episode of mortgage foreclosures and farm abandonments that was especially cruel in poor and marginal parts of the countryside. If farm conditions seemed to improve slightly after the Wall Street crash, it was only because the depression in the cities was so grim. Even without cash income, most farmers could at least feed their families from local produce, which was more than could be said for the men selling pencils on the streets of Akron or Sacramento.

Against the background of general depression, the added burden of crop failure was more than many farmers could take, especially in the dust bowl and in the weevil-ravaged country of the Deep South. In both areas, farmers fled the land that once had been among the most productive in the United States (fig. 17.4). The exodus from the dust bowl received especially wide publicity and shocked the national conscience. The dust itself was dismayingly visible; in March 1934 dust clouds blackened the skies over much of the Middle West and then drifted eastward to deposit a layer of grit as far away as New York and Washington. The dust eventually settled, but the human tragedy went on and on. The whole episode seemed a cosmic indictment of ecological carelessness and indifference to human pain. Epochal films were made about the subject, notably *The Plow That Broke the Plains* (1936), a documentary made by the federal government to warn against the tragic consequences of thoughtless agricultural practices, but which also won widespread acclaim as a chronicle of human tragedy and waste. Its companion piece, *The River,* recounted the destruction wrought by uncontrolled floods on the Mississippi. The two films were powerful propaganda for federal conservation efforts and not-so-subtle attacks on laissez-faire economics. The best-known and most influential account of the dust bowl exodus, however, was John Steinbeck's *Grapes of Wrath* (1939), which recounted the tragic flight of the Okies from their ravaged farms on the High Plains westward across the deserts to a hostile reception in the not-so-green Eden of

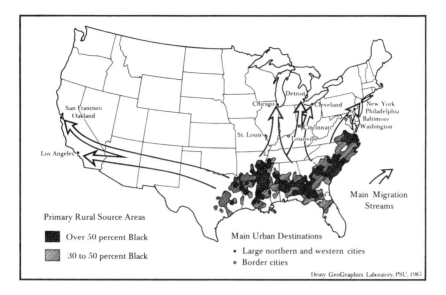

Figure 17.8 African American Migration, World War I through World War II

southern California. Few American migrations had ever received such unfavorable publicity.

In the long run, however, it was the movement of people from the old rural South to the new urban North that would make the greatest difference to the future of America. Northward migration had been going on ever since the Civil War, but it was greatly stimulated by World War I, which created a large number of industrial jobs in northern cities, where most of America's armaments were being made. Before the war, many of the jobs (especially menial ones) had been filled by newly arrived immigrants. But the war halted European emigration, and to make up the slack, employers began to fill the jobs with refugees from rural poverty—and in 1917 that meant southerners. Some were whites from the Appalachian hills, and there was nothing unusual about that. But others were African Americans, and that was something new; racism in the United States was deeply embedded in law and custom, and African Americans were routinely barred from most industrial jobs. Now with the wartime shortage of labor, some northern employers began to hire a few African Americans—not many and seldom in skilled jobs. But it was a start, especially important in the gigantic auto plants of Michigan and the steel mills of Ohio and Illinois. New jobs did not mean new social attitudes, howev-

er, and African Americans were excluded from desirable housing and were greeted with hostility by white workers who perceived African Americans as menacing to their jobs. But despite wretched housing and threats of violence, the ghettos of Detroit and Chicago provided African Americans with better housing and a better living (not to mention better health and education) than the guarantee of poverty, illiteracy, and malnutrition as sharecroppers in Alabama or Mississippi. Thus, while African Americans continued to be the last hired and the first fired in the steel mills of Baltimore and the automobile factories of Flint and Lansing, they continued to come.

Except during the depression, nearly all African American migration was from country to city, but certain cities were much favored over others. A few African Americans drifted into southern cities, if only because they were nearby, but they were rarely seen as havens of opportunity, much less tolerance. The typical African American migrant headed north—usually as directly as possible by way of main-line railroads (fig. 17.8). Thus, African Americans from the Carolinas and Florida mainly ended up in East Coast cities; those from Alabama and the middle South usually went to Ohio or Michigan; those from the Mississippi valley headed due north, straight up the Illinois Central Railroad's main line from New Orleans to Chicago. The favored destinations were the largest cities— New York, Philadelphia, Chicago, and Detroit; medium-sized cities like Fort Wayne and Syracuse were much less popular. Genuine small towns were almost completely shunned. Sheer distance evidently had a considerable influence on the destination of migrants, and many African Americans simply stopped in the first big nonsouthern city they came to: the "border" cities of St. Louis, Louisville, Cincinnati, Baltimore, and Washington. Conversely, very few went beyond the broad belt of favored cities between Chicago and New York. Distant places like Boston, Minneapolis, Seattle, and Portland, Oregon, received only small numbers of African Americans. Starting around World War II, that rule would be broken too, as sizable numbers of African Americans joined the general westward migration to Los Angeles and the San Francisco Bay area. Few African Americans went to Canada, however, despite the ease of crossing the border and Canada's long-standing reputation for racial tolerance.

For many African Americans, the move from unsophisticated regions of the rural South with abundant supplies of personal space to the bowels of crowded cosmopolitan cities was shocking and unsettling, damaging to individuals, and destructive of family life. The ghettos of northern cities, it turned out, were functioning quite differently for African Americans than they previously had for immigrant whites. That difference was crucial in the history of American racial relations. In earlier times, white immigrant ghettos had acted as way stations from Europe to America, as buffers against culture shock in a new land. Thus, in spite of poor, expensive, and crowded housing, the ghettos had performed a useful function; and besides, their residents knew that eventually they could move out geographically and up socially. The African American ghetto was different. Surrounded by hostile whites, an African American, however talented, had no easy way to escape. To make matters worse, the perpetual shortage of ghetto housing raised rents to extortionate rates, a fact that was especially galling in decrepit buildings owned by absentee white landlords. Meanwhile, ghetto schools and infrastructure deteriorated with the departure of politically influential whites, while young African Americans found themselves caught between two cultures—no

longer rural South, and not yet urban North. The arbitrary confines of the ghetto created pressure cookers for acute social frustration.

In spite of white hostility, African American ghettos continued to grow inexorably, commonly forming wedge-shaped sectors that fanned out from the oldest African American neighborhoods near downtown railroad stations. Chicago's huge South Side ghetto was typical, spreading from an apex on the edge of the Loop to include the 63rd Street Station (the main Illinois Central Railroad port of entry for African Americans from the Mississippi valley), thence southward to the Indiana state line and beyond. Similar patterns emerged on Chicago's west side and in several sectors of Detroit, Philadelphia, Cleveland, and elsewhere. In most instances, those wedges of African American population advanced most rapidly into areas of low-value housing that had previously been the homes of older white immigrant groups, and racial anger erupted into open violence—between African Americans on the one hand and Jews, Poles, and Appalachian whites on the other. Chicago saw a major race riot in 1919, as did Detroit in 1943.

Flight to the Suburbs

Despite the volume of African American migration to northern cities, the growth of those cities slackened significantly during the 1920s and 1930s. Although the depression was immediately responsible for the slowdown in the early 1930s, there was a second, more permanent reason: the quickening movement of middle- and upper-income whites to the suburbs. Census enumerations showed that many of the new suburbanites had moved out from the inner city, and that was no surprise. But the census also revealed that an equal number were new migrants from distant places who moved directly to the suburbs—newcomers who wanted the economic benefits of living in a metropolitan area but had no wish to live in the crowded city. From the 1920s onward, suburbs would be the fastest-growing segment of America's human landscape.

Suburbs were nothing new in the American experience. Even in the late 18th century, affluent New Yorkers lived on the bosky bluffs of Brooklyn Heights and commuted by ferryboat to Manhattan. But the great suburban revolution erupted only in the late 19th century with the building of electric streetcar systems. By 1910, on the eve of the automotive age, all American cities of any consequence had attracted a spattering of suburbs beyond their city limits, strung like beads along commuter railroads and electric trolley lines.

From 1910 onward, however, suburbs were increasingly being designed for people with automobiles. And just as the automobile changed almost everything it touched, it changed the shape and behavior of suburbs too. It allowed suburbs to grow faster than ever before, made their shapes more amorphous, and encouraged sparser densities than were usual in the relatively compact streetcar suburbs.

The geographic pattern of these new suburbs would have important political consequences. By the 1930s, most big northern cities had discovered to their dismay that further territorial expansion had been choked off by a noose of incorporated suburbs, each of which made its own laws, collected its own taxes, and defied annexation by the city that had spawned it. A kind of siege mentality resulted, with the city pitted against its encircling suburbs in a state of permanent political hostility, which made comprehensive metropolitan planning extremely difficult. In addition, the duplication of municipal services turned out to be very expensive, especially to the parent city, which had to maintain aging infrastructure with a diminishing tax base. The arrangement was racially ominous, too, because many suburbs had learned to use a combination of zoning ordinances and real estate covenants to bar settlement by African Americans. Although such restrictions were declared in 1948 to be unconstitutional and thus unenforceable, they had been deeply entrenched during the 1920s, when the inner rings of automobile suburbs were taking on permanent form. Thus, the inner city grew blacker and poorer, while the suburbs remained almost lily-white and, inevitably, much more affluent than the city. So, while the law ultimately changed, the geographic patterns scarcely changed at all. As in so many ways, human geography turned out to be a very conservative thing.

As often happens in geographic matters, West Coast suburbs looked different from those of the East—and the difference led to widespread misunderstanding about what was happening to American cities. In the Northeast, most big cities had grown up during the 19th century around clearly defined nucleated cores focused on railroad junctions. In the West, however, notably on the Los Angeles plain and around the fringes of San Francisco Bay, the automobile had begun to produce a host of scattered settlements that looked like suburbs but failed to cluster tightly around any single dominant core. As those settlements grew inexorably together in the 1910s and 1920s, a new kind of urban fabric began to emerge—not a ring of suburbs around a city, but instead a conurbation of nuclei that together *were* the city. Supercilious northeasterners described Los Angeles as "fifty suburbs in search of a city" and persuaded themselves that Los Angeles's urban morphology was somehow peculiar to California, and therefore perverse. They failed to comprehend that the use of automobiles discouraged the creation of *any* new cities with nucleated cores. So, while eastern cities retained such centers from earlier times and would continue to use them, it was different in the new cities of the South and West, where clearly defined nuclei were small or nonexistent. As factories and shopping centers moved out gradually to the country in pursuit of the affluent residents, suburbanites increasingly found it unnecessary to commute downtown for shopping and work, because they found jobs and did their shopping nearby. On a map, this new urban morphology looked like a galaxy of stars and planets, held together by mutual gravitational attraction but with large empty spaces between. This "galactic city," it turned out, was not some Californian peculiarity but an altogether new kind of city that would burst into full bloom after World War II wherever new cities were under construction. This happened first and most conspicuously in the South and West, and these cities were increasingly visible on the extended fringes of the old northern cities. From 1940 onward, the process was epidemic, but it was not new. The skeletal structure of that galactic city was already in place in Los Angeles by the end of the 1920s.

The suburbs of the interwar period were architecturally distinctive as well, and today they are easy to recognize because they contrast so sharply with the look of what came before and after. Through the 19th century and well into the 20th, fashions in American domestic architecture had been changing with some regularity, so that whole neighborhoods were often dominated by whatever style happened to be in vogue at the time: neo-Gothic, neo-Italianate, neo-Romanesque, all culminating with the decorated enthusiasm of the Queen Anne mode of the 1880s and 1890s, which combined a variety of styles *tutti frutti* on the same building. By World War I, fashions had become calmer but no less eclectic. Settlers in the new suburbs could choose from a large fixed menu of styles, collectively termed "period houses of the 1920s."

All period houses did not look alike, but all of them evoked the supposed architectural spirit of some far-off place or time from the vaguely historic but always picturesque past. One set of styles came putatively from American tradition, bearing such names as "Colonial," "Federal," "Cape Cod," or "Williamsburg." Another set of styles evoked picturesque Europe: neo-Tudor with imitation half-timbering and imitation leaded windows, Dutch Colonial with gambrel roofs, and a variety of "Hispanic" or Mission-style houses whose popularity was stimulated by America's sudden discovery of Florida's and California's supposed Iberian roots. Of greatest long-run significance, however, was the California bungalow, the first vernacular American house to come from the West Coast and not the East.

Since period houses and bungalows both came in various forms, they could be set down next to one another in any of innumerable combinations. The result was no single style but rather a special mixture of styles that distinguished the automobile suburb of the 1920s. But as with so many other things, the Great Depression ended it all. After the Wall Street crash, very few people had money to build houses of any kind, and the moratorium continued through World War II, with shortages of labor and building material. When building resumed after the war, almost 20 years had elapsed, and it was as if the country had emerged from a period of architectural amnesia. All that remained of the rich predepression variety was a small selection of neo-Colonial styles, much beloved of postwar real estate developers, and built by the square mile for returning veterans.

Migration to the Sun

Of all the migration streams of the interwar period, the migration to the sun seems best to capture the zeitgeist of the 1920s and 1930s. The migration itself was not new; people had been moving to Florida and California in significant numbers since the mid-19th century, so that each state had grown consistently at rates well in excess of the national average. Nor was the motivation new. Migrants to both states had been lured by hyperbolic advertising, descriptions of lotus lands where ordinary people could escape from the corrupted environments of the North and East, where human cares would evaporate under sunny skies and balmy breezes, and where easy fortunes were made on every side—in gold mining, in real estate, or in cultivating exotic fruit. Moving to California or Florida was a promise of better health, greater wealth, and a plenitude of happiness, in an environment that was distant and exotic enough to be interesting but not so exotic as to be uncomfortable. In the American experience it was a new kind of migration, where people moved less for economic improvement or religious principle than for reasons that were largely hedonistic. While hedonism had not yet become quite respectable, the migration was receiving enormous national publicity from radio and motion pictures. There was good reason for the publicity. Between 1920 and 1940, Florida and California were far and away the fastest-growing states in the Union, and the population of both states doubled (fig. 17.5).

Ever since the gold rush, California had enjoyed a special niche in America's geographic imagination. Among other things, the state had been promoted as a place of great agricultural opportunity, where a host of environments would permit almost anything to grow, and where failed farmers from the East could not help but succeed. The facts, alas, were otherwise, and few of the migrants ended up as farmers. The reasons were simple and powerful. Most of California's best land was owned by a few large corporations, notoriously the Southern Pacific Railroad, the state's largest private landowner, which had run much of southern California like a feudal fiefdom. Furthermore, for most of California to yield up its promised bounty, irrigation was necessary with water brought in from great depths or great distances, and that was expensive, far beyond the means of the ordinary dirt farmer. Then, too, California's most profitable agricultural products were not ordinary marketables like wheat or cattle (although California raised plenty of both) but exotics that could be grown nowhere else in the United States and thus enjoyed a national monopoly. But national distribution of exotic, high-priced crops like winter lettuce or artichokes was not a job for small-time amateurs, even when cooperatives like Sunkist (oranges) and Calavo (avocados) were formed to help keep quality and prices high. Most of the market was halfway across the continent, and that market could be reached only with mass planning and major capital investment. California agriculture, in short, was big business—"factories in the field," to borrow the title from Carey McWilliams's 1939 book on the subject. Except for migrant farm laborers, most newcomers to California ended up living in cities, rarely on farms or in small towns. The small market town of the midwestern sort was a rare species in most of California. For most migrants, a new beginning meant the San Francisco Bay area or the Los Angeles plain.

Meanwhile, California had gradually ceased to act merely as a receptacle for people and ideas from the East and was rapidly becoming an innovator and arbiter of national fashions. During the 19th century, Californians had done everything possible to escape the stigma of being a frontier outpost. Cultural artifacts of every kind were slavishly and self-consciously designed to look "eastern." Buildings and monuments were copied from eastern architects; eastern biota were planted in gardens and arboreta; towns were laid out to look as much like Missouri or Ohio as possible. By the turn of the century the trend had begun to reverse, and a few Californian innovations began to flow eastward. The watershed date was 1915, when the state held two major world's fairs simultaneously: the Panama-Pacific Exposition in San Francisco and the California-Pacific Exposition in San Diego. The San Francisco fair was the more dignified, partly a celebration of the city's recovery from the 1906 earthquake, partly a reminder that "America's Mediterranean" was an important place in its own right. The San Diego exposition was far more eye-catching, designed as a monument to California's Hispanic heritage and notifying the world that California was now mature enough to possess its own history. Within a short time California architecture had suddenly become a national vogue with California bungalows and "Mission-style" cosmetics erupting all across the country.

Thus, for all of the easterners' snide remarks that California was becoming a kind of cloud-cuckoo-land, where exotic plants and exotic people grew in the eternal glare of Hollywood klieg lights, California was in fact becoming a super-American place. If America was affluent and mobile, urban and comfortable, California was all of those things, and more so. (It seemed only natural that Californians would own more cars per capita than the people of any other state.) If America's cities were growing bigger and spreading over larger areas, California would have some of the biggest and most sprawling cities in the country. And despite the sniping from eastern highbrows, many footloose people seemed enchanted by California's combination of super-Americanism and benevolent environment. When, in World War II, California served as America's main port of embarkation for the Pacific theater of war, thousands of young servicemen saw California for the first time and liked what they saw. When they returned from the war, many of them returned not to Keokuk or Schenectady but to the suburbs of San Francisco and Los Angeles, there to raise families and live happily ever after. Twenty years later California had become the most populous state in the Union.

Florida, however, was a different matter, although at first glance it seemed to have a good deal in common with California, at least as seen from a distance by potential migrants. Both states were insular places, made attractive by their climate but removed from the main centers of American population, to be reached only by long journeys across uninviting territory—the driest parts of the arid West, the poorest parts of the poverty-stricken South. Both were exotic to their respective regions; if California was the least western of western states, Florida was the least southern state in the South. And both states boomed in the 1920s and the 1930s, growing at similar rates and for many of the same reasons. Nevertheless, there were crucial differences, largely explained by Florida's eccentric history and geography.

Until the 1890s, most Floridians lived in a ragged fringe of isolated rural country just south of the Alabama and Georgia state lines. That concentration had dictated the location of the state capital in Tallahassee, sited in limbo at the midpoint between the two old Spanish settlements of St. Augustine on the Atlantic coast and Pensacola on the Gulf of Mexico. Elsewhere, the state's population was scattered in a desultory array of small fishing villages and nascent fruit and vegetable farms along the Indian River. The slave economy of the South had never penetrated much of Florida, which remained largely empty—outside both the southern mainstream and the national mainstream.

The change began in 1883 when Henry Flagler, a major shareholder in Standard Oil, brought his ailing wife to an isolated health resort on the lower St. Johns River. He concluded that Florida's climatic charms were salable to northerners if only there were hotels to house the visitors and a railroad to bring them there. Flagler built his Florida headquarters at the palatial Ponce de Leon Hotel in St. Augustine; by the early 1900s, his Florida East Coast Railroad was finished to Key West with hotels strung along the rail line at several intermediate locations. Almost at the same time, another Yankee tycoon, Henry Plant, built a similar system to attract tourists to the Gulf coast, anchored by a rail line to Tampa, where he built the flamboyantly Moorish-style Tampa Bay Hotel. Flagler and Plant promptly started to advertise the virtues of Florida, in a crescendo of ballyhoo that set the tone for much of Florida's later growth.

There was a permanent quality of impermanence to that growth, in sharp contrast with that of California. Florida's lack of natural resources, in combination with the state's eccentric location, had discouraged the growth of permanent manufacturing industries. Even Florida agriculture tended to be a chancy kind of thing. Its chief products were citrus fruits and winter vegetables, both highly sensitive to winter frosts and to perturbations in northern commodity prices. Florida's growth, therefore, tended to come in flashes and to depend inordinately on sandy beaches and balmy winters. Even climate was a mixed blessing. Florida summers were hot, steamy, and seemingly eternal. Until the arrival of air-conditioning, a tourist might come to enjoy the winter weather; but summer was a time to sit in the shade and do as little as possible or, better yet, to flee the state entirely. Many people came to Florida, therefore, as seasonal visitors, with no intention of remaining as permanent residents. (The main exception was St. Petersburg, which by the 1920s had become a retirement place for the elderly, and America's largest geriatric city.) All this was in sharp contrast with California, where sheer distance made temporary visits from the Northeast and Middle West both difficult and expensive. Thus, Florida

clearly won over California in attracting the rich trade in winter tourists. People went to California to put down roots; Florida was a place to escape the cares of the world, to unwind, relax, and enjoy oneself.

The difference profoundly affected the kinds of places that California and Florida would ultimately become. Migrants to California, knowing themselves to be permanent settlers, took fierce interest in purifying the state's political apparatus, in creating a first-class public university system, and in protecting California's handsome mountains and coasts from commercial despoliation. It was natural that California would give birth to institutions like the Sierra Club and that much of its coastline and wild lands would be reserved for public enjoyment. Environmentalists found hard going in Florida, where state parks were virtually unknown. There most land was simply viewed as real estate; state parks seemed a waste of private land and the chance to make a profit. Much of the state was up for sale to the highest bidder.

By the early 1920s, the bidding had grown very shrill indeed, as the greatest of all Florida real estate booms rolled into high gear. Frederick Lewis Allen called it "the most delicious fever of real estate speculation which had attacked the United States in ninety years." Suddenly towns and cities were springing up where Flagler had built lonely hotels. Land was subdivided, sold, bought, and resold; bridges and roads were thrown across sand dunes and mangrove swamps; residential streets were carved into the quivering muck. Prices went up and up again, in a dizzying spiral of speculation, profit taking, and fraud. The most frenzied speculation and the most extravagant swindles occurred in Miami, whose population leaped from 30,000 in 1920 to 75,000 at the peak of the boom in 1925, but nearly all of Florida's east coast was caught up in the rampage. Subdivisions, hotels, and new cities were springing up from Jacksonville to Key West, and if the Gulf coast was spared the worst excesses, it was only because much of that coast remained inaccessible.

The bubble had to burst, and it did. In early 1926 the bottom dropped out of the real estate market, and Florida investors received a financial preview of what the whole nation would behold on Wall Street three years later. Then in September, as if nature itself had been waiting to administer the coup de grace, the most ferocious hurricane in living memory struck Miami and the adjacent "Gold Coast." The storm killed 400 people outright, injured 6,300, and left 50,000 people without homes. It ruined the city of Miami and its promising suburb of Miami Beach, and it left the real estate market prostrate.

But only for a while. Despite human frailty and natural disaster, people still came to Florida, and they kept coming even during the depression. By 1940 it was obvious that Florida was a state that would have to be taken seriously. No longer was it an outpost on the tattered fringe of the nation's poorest region; it was rapidly becoming one of America's most populous and influential states. As retirement ages dropped and Americans were finding more leisure time at their disposal, Florida would receive more winter tourists and more elderly retirees as permanent residents. And as America grew more affluent and more demanding, Florida's subtropical agriculture would become big business, greatly encouraged by new methods of freezing vegetables and (of all things) concentrated orange juice. In a way, Florida's growth was a metaphor for America at large. Only a very large and very affluent country could afford to create and support a whole state whose main income derived from orange juice, sunbathing, and profits from the sale of real estate. Florida had become big and exotic because America had become big and rich.

ENGINEERING A NEW AMERICAN GEOGRAPHY

The first half of the 20th century was a pageant of dramatic events and colorful personalities. But if we look beyond the details and the dazzle, it becomes clear that the period was a watershed between an older geographic order of the late 19th century and a new, streamlined order of the 20th. While few Americans suspected it at the time, for better or for worse, they were engineering a new world.

The full shape of that new world would not become evident until well after World War II, but the basic structure was clearly visible by the late 1930s. The structure had been set in place with the greatest innocence. The business of technology was typical. In the 40 years between 1900 and 1940 the United States installed a whole new basic network of transportation and communications, but it would not dawn on most Americans until the 1950s and 1960s that automobiles, telephones, movies, and radios were more than simple devices that would bring them more comfortable lives but were like Hindu gods, capable of destroying and creating worlds. With similar unconcern about long-term consequences, Americans had invoked the power of government to regulate the flow of immigrants and to control the use of water and land; only much later would they discover that such things as immigration controls, crop subsidies, and flood-control projects would take on lives of their own and create whole new landscapes. In much the same way, migrant Americans had begun to move in new directions and for unfamiliar reasons, but it would not become apparent until after World War II that the sum of these migrations would yield an entirely new geography. And whether Americans liked it or not, they would have to live with that new geography. There would be no turning back.

ADDITIONAL READING

Allen, F. L. 1931. *Only Yesterday: An Informal History of the 1920s.* New York: Harper & Bros.

———. 1939. *Since Yesterday: The 1930s in America.* New York: Harper & Bros.

———. 1952. *The Big Change: American Transforms Itself, 1900–1950.* New York: Harper & Bros.

Belasco, W. J. 1980. *Americans on the Road: From Autocamp to Motel, 1910–1945.* Cambridge: MIT Press.

Bogue, D. J. 1959. *The Population of the United States.* Glencoe, Ill.: Free Press.

Caro, R. 1974. *The Power Broker: Robert Moses and the Fall of New York.* New York: Alfred A. Knopf.

Derr, M. 1989. *Some Kind of Paradise: A Chronicle of Man and the Land in Florida.* New York: William Morrow.

Freidel, F. 1990. *Franklin D. Roosevelt: A Rendezvous with Destiny.* Boston: Little, Brown.

Goldman, E. 1953. *Rendezvous with Destiny: A History of Modern American Reform.* New York: Alfred A. Knopf.

Hugill, P. J. 1982. "Good Roads and the Automobile in the United States, 1880–1929." *Geographical Review* 72: 327–49.

Manners, G. 1974. "The Office in Metropolis: An Opportunity for Shaping Metropolitan America." *Economic Geography* 50: 93–110.

McWilliams, C. 1973. *Southern California Country: An Island on the Land.* New York: Duell, Sloan & Pearce, 1946. Reprint, Santa Barbara: Peregrine Smith.

Morgan N. 1969. *The California Syndrome.* Englewood Cliffs, N.J.: Prentice-Hall.

Nelson, H. J. 1959. "The Spread of an Artificial Landscape over Southern California." *Annals of the Association of American Geographers* 49: 80–99.

Schlesinger, A., Jr. 1957. *The Crisis of the Old Order: 1919–1933.* Boston: Houghton Mifflin.

———. 1958. *The Coming of the New Deal.* Boston: Houghton Mifflin.

———. 1960. *The Politics of Upheaval.* Boston: Houghton Mifflin.

U.S. Census Bureau. 1975. *Historical Statistics of the United States, Colonial Times to 1970.* Washington: Government Printing Office.

18

The Other America:
Changes in Rural America during the 20th Century

JOHN C. HUDSON

The "other" America is rural America. It is the more important segment of the nation if land area is taken as the measure of significance but much less important if one regards population numbers as the criterion. Geographers recognize that both population and geographical area must be taken into account in order to understand a people's occupation of their national territory. This chapter focuses on some of the major transformations of rural America that have taken place during the 20th century.

While the proper definition of "rural" has long been debated, the Bureau of the Census defines rural population simply as that portion of the total population that is not urban, meaning all people residing outside of places of 2,500 or more inhabitants or outside the densely built-up portions of urbanized areas. The rural population consists of the residents of farms and small towns and of open-country residential settings that are nonagricultural. By the year 2000, only about 7 percent of rural residents lived on farms. Nearly half of all rural residents live in metropolitan areas (which, in census terms, means a county containing a city of at least 50,000 people). The rural population thus contains a substantial number of urban fringe dwellers.

Cities and other population clusters have always been so important in the United States that the familiar generalization claiming that Americans were once "a nation of farmers" has never been strictly true. But prior to 1920, when the census revealed that for the first time more than half of the population resided in urban areas, the United States was predominantly a nation of small towns and farms. Since 1920 the rural population has grown by roughly 30 percent, while the urban population has grown more than 230 percent. Today, the United States is not only predominantly urban (73 percent), it is even more strongly metropolitan: 78 percent of the total population lives in metropolitan areas.

Broad, general statistics such as these mask some important underlying geographical differences between different parts of the country. The West, where more than 80 percent of all people live in cities, has the highest urban percentage, but it also contains by far the largest share of counties with low population densities (fig. 18.1). Large areas of the West have low population densities because their environments were not attractive to agricultural settlement. People there have always tended to live either in cities or in more densely settled, irrigated agricultural areas where the land is used intensively.

In contrast, the South's population is only about 65 percent urban today, and the region contains three of every seven U.S. rural residents. Historically speaking, cities have been less important in the South's settlement history. Even though the region's farm population has fallen drastically in the past several decades, there remains a strong tendency for southerners to live outside of population clusters.

In yet another sense, the Middle West is the nation's most rural region because it contains the largest number of farm residents. Nearly half of all U.S. farm residents live in the midwestern states, and the concentration is growing. Agriculture has remained an important economic activity in the Middle West, while it has declined in both the Northeast and parts of the South during the past five decades. Although half of the Middle West's farm residents moved off their farms between 1965 and the end of the century, the rate of decline was even more rapid in other sections of the country. Even as its farm population dwindles, the Middle West's share of the farm population grows.

Depending on the criterion one chooses, then, the West, the South, or the Middle West might be considered the most rural portion of the United States. The West is the most sparsely settled, the South is the most rural, and the Middle West is the most agricultural. Only the Northeast, which contains barely a quarter of a

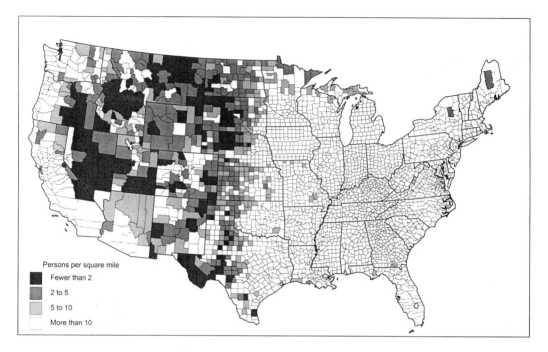

Figure 18.1 Population Density, 1990

million farm residents today, ranks low in terms of all three definitions. Apart from rugged upland areas and the northern Maine woods, the Northeast contains no sparsely settled territory.

An examination of rural America over the 20th century reveals some important dimensions of settlement formation that have produced the patterns in evidence today. During this period the agricultural frontier came to a close, small towns underwent a radical transformation in their structure and function, and agriculture became more mechanized as well as less dependent on a large population to support it.

THE LAST AGRICULTURAL FRONTIERS

When the superintendent of the census noted in 1890 that the unoccupied portion of the country had become so broken up by isolated bodies of settlement that there no longer existed a line marking the frontier, the limit of settlement at a density of two persons per square mile coincided roughly with the 100th meridian of longitude, a line joining central North Dakota with the middle of Texas. Nearly all of the counties

with fewer than two persons per square mile lie west of this line today as well, even though there has been a steady shift of the national population westward (and slightly southward) during the 11 decades that have elapsed since the frontier supposedly closed. Nearly all of the counties that are sparsely settled at the start of the 21st century were in the same category a century ago. Many that were in the "fewer than two persons per square mile" category in 1890 have become much more densely settled since that time, especially in urbanized sections of the West.

The last agricultural frontiers in the West were settled between 1890 and 1920. This was a period when farming replaced ranching in the drier counties of the western Great Plains and in scattered areas between the Rocky Mountains and the Cascades and Sierra Nevada ranges. More precisely, this last agricultural frontier also represented a final push of Euro-American settlement into the grasslands. It coincided with two upswings in nationwide economic prosperity: the first decade of the 20th century and a second boom during World War I. An increase in demand for grain cereals on the world market was mainly responsible. Portions of the Texas

Panhandle, western Kansas, eastern Colorado, the western Dakotas, and eastern Montana became specialized wheat-raising areas during these two periods.

Droughts had caused a retreat of agriculture from the western fringes of these same areas during the 1890s, but they were subsequently resettled. Farms grew both in number and in size with the adoption of new methods for farming dry lands, which were introduced around 1900. The most widely used of these techniques was a group of practices known as "dry farming," which made it possible to extend wheat production into areas where it had been marginal under the technology in use prior to that time. Dry farming involves the alternate use of parallel strips of land for crops one year and as fallow the next. The fallow strips are kept bare of vegetation by cultivating to remove weeds that would otherwise take up the precious soil moisture. Two years of precipitation thus are used to grow one year of crop by alternating the cropped and fallow strips year after year.

Another hallmark of the dryland agricultural frontier was its heavy reliance on mechanization. Large-scale farming became feasible with the introduction of heavy farm tractors, large harvesting machines (grain combines), and other implements that were far larger than any that had been in use during the era of animal-powered cultivation. As a result, labor requirements were kept low per acre of cropland, a condition that was also a necessity given the sparse populations in these areas. This last agricultural frontier was a mechanized one that utilized lands of somewhat marginal quality, farming them less intensively via the annual process of land rotation.

Congress responded to the new push west in the 20th century by liberalizing the land laws to enable homesteaders to acquire larger tracts of land for only a small fee. The Enlarged Homestead Act of 1909 doubled the previous size of homesteads to 320 acres in drier portions of the grasslands. The size doubled again under provisions of the Stock Raising Homestead Act of 1916, which awarded 640-acre (square mile) tracts in areas where the land was suitable primarily for grazing rather than for crops. Although both of these enlargements recognized that more land was needed in areas of lower precipitation, no system of land classification existed to avoid plowing lands that were unfit for crop farming because of other environmental limits such as poor soils or rugged topography.

Some lands that were first settled by farmers during the first decades of the 20th century became stable, long-term producers of wheat and other small grains. These districts include portions of the Missouri Plateau in Montana and the Dakotas where soils are of good quality despite low rainfall, as well as portions of western Nebraska, Kansas, Oklahoma, and Texas that are included in the same category. But in other areas, especially where soils are sandy and prone to erosion if the soil surface is left bare, agriculture could not be sustained. The most dramatic display of agriculture's overextension in the western Plains came during the dust bowl years of the 1930s, when a sequence of much-drier-than-normal years led to total crop failure and widespread blowing-soil conditions. This resulted in yet another episode of settlement abandonment.

Another version of a "last frontier" for agriculture involved the introduction of irrigation. In 1902 Congress passed the Newlands Act (Reclamation Act of 1902), which established the procedure for organizing and financing irrigation districts in the western states. Although irrigation itself is an ancient system of farming, it became more widely adopted through the various irrigation projects that were established following passage of federal legislation. Many irrigation schemes were small in scale and involved diversion of water from a flowing stream through small tracts of floodplain land where crops like sugar beets, onions, potatoes, and dry edible beans were grown.

New zones of irrigated agriculture continued to appear in the western intermontane basins into the 1940s. The arid Columbia Basin of central Washington State was developed during this period, following construction of Grand Coulee Dam on the Columbia River. While some dry-farmed crops had been grown here previously, the intent was to create more than a million acres of land that could be farmed intensively by more than 15,000 farm families. Irrigation on such a scale proved costly, however, and the number of farms that would benefit fell short of expectations. While such massive transformations of the environment were technologically possible, the need for them declined as the number of persons employed in agriculture continued its downward trend. Introduction of new irrigation schemes had to be balanced against the possibility that the same crops could be grown more cheaply elsewhere. Small irrigation farms, like other small-scale farming operations, did not fare well in competition without a subsidy. Even large-scale irrigation farming was sheltered from competition through the low price of water charged to users.

These last frontiers of American agriculture have remained controversial because their development took place largely after the main period of agricultural expansion in the nation had ended. The dust bowl era gave rise to the notion that crop farming was unsuited to the drier, western grasslands. Conservation tillage practices, the use of land rotation to conserve soil moisture, and the gradual acceptance of agricultural practices that disturb the soil cover as little as possible have proven that grain farming is a sustainable form of agriculture in much of the western Great Plains. Dryland agriculture cannot be as intensive here as once believed, however, and parts of the Great Plains region have declined in their land-use intensity during the past several decades.

Irrigation has been even more controversial than dryland agriculture in many parts of the West. Schemes to divert surface waters for agricultural purposes have had to compete with other water uses, especially those associated with increased residential water demands for cities. Underground aquifers, such as the Ogallala formation that underlies most of the High Plains, have been exploited to transform the whole surface environment into a zone of grain production to support livestock feeding. Applications of agricultural chemicals to support this system have led to contamination of groundwater supplies. In practical terms, the economics of water use imposed the real limits to agricultural settlement. Popular opposition to technologies introduced to overcome environmental limits has included calls to return to a land-use system similar to that which prevailed before agricultural colonization took place.

GROWTH AND DECLINE OF SMALL TOWNS

Of the two most familiar types of rural settlement in the United States, farms and small towns, the latter have been the more difficult for geographers to categorize. Urban geographers have viewed small towns primarily as service centers for the local, rural population, an interpretation that traces back to German central-place theorists such as Christaller and Lösch. Many historical geographers, notably Vance, have interpreted towns as playing a more active role in organizing trade relations between distant markets and local producers of staple exports. No single, satisfactory theory of town formation exists, and thus there is little agreement in the literature as to the reasons for town growth or decline.

Small towns experienced a series of economic and social transformations as America grew more complex. Changes in transportation technology often are responsible for producing responses in settlement systems, and this has been especially true for the network of trade-center towns. Transportation technology shaped the evolution of towns as individual entities by setting the pattern for interaction with other places.

The shift from wagon to riverboat transportation characterized the first half of the 19th century just as the shift from rivers to railways characterized the second half. The towns of rural America were at their peak of influence in the early decades of the 20th century. Still unchallenged by new transport innovations, America's small towns were spaced like beads on a string along the railway lines connecting them to the distant metropolis (fig. 18.2). Competing railways laid lines of track that crisscrossed one another, giving the impression of a network in which towns were equally accessible in all directions.

In fact, however, such perfect access was rarely the case, nor was it a necessary aspect of the system. Towns "down the track" were always more accessible to larger, distant cities than they were to much closer communities to which they lacked direct rail connection. Small-town America in the early 20th century was strongly hierarchical, with well-defined levels of importance for towns based on their frequency of access to outlying centers.

The distribution of mail was just one reflection of this hierarchy. In the case of southwestern Minnesota, most mail flowed through Minneapolis and St. Paul as it passed between outlying centers and the rest of the nation, although some railroad lines even in Minnesota were more directly connected to Chicago. There was no town without a post office, and very few post offices were without daily-except-Sunday mail service via the railroad. Sacks of mail were transferred between trains at numerous outlying junctions.

The density of towns was uniform in an agricultural area like southwestern Minnesota because of the constancy of the resource base from place to place. Towns were regularly spaced at the railroads' insistence, because that was the optimal way to capture traffic in agricultural produce (mainly wheat and other small grains in Minnesota at that time). A single company never owned closely parallel lines of track because that only divided the business. New lines were laid halfway between existing competitors' lines because that was the best way to capture traffic.

Geographers typically regard towns such as these as having been demanded into existence by rural producer-consumers. In areas such as this one, however, railroads founded nearly all towns (except those few dating before 1870) for the purpose of capturing and organizing the traffic coming to their lines. Railroads preferred to locate and plat their own towns, building through existing population centers only when

necessary to protect a transportation monopoly. One railroad-created town is Almora, (located north of Alexandria in figure 18.2), which was established in 1905 when the Soo Line Railroad constructed a new line of track (fig. 18.3). Almora's small six-block plat indicates that the railroad company realized there was limited growth potential there, although it reserved lands for future platting into residential blocks on the north side of the town.

The railroad depot was the focal point of the community, and the main business street (Aldrich Avenue), which began at the depot, was about two blocks long. Each block face was divided, in typical railroad fashion, into ten business lots each 25 feet wide. When the map was published, Almora's physical existence was nothing but rows of stakes driven into the ground. But those who wished to start a business in Almora knew they needed to purchase one of the 25-foot lots on Aldrich Avenue, erect a store building, and prepare themselves for whatever trade came their way. Grain elevators and lumber dealers typically leased the larger lots along the railroad track. Banks often were

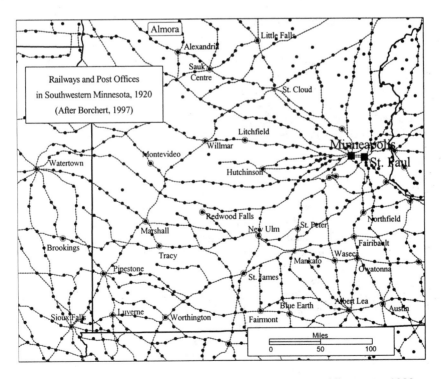

Figure 18.2 Railways and Post Offices in Southwestern Minnesota, 1920

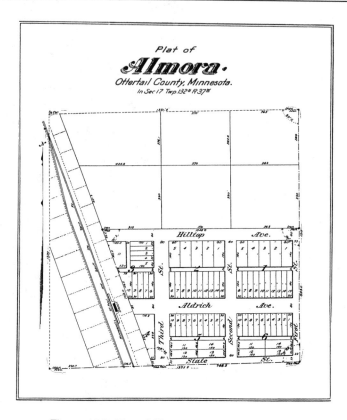

Figure 18.3 Plat of Almora, Early 20th Century

located on corner lots in business districts, and dry goods, hardware, grocery, and other stores filled in the other spaces, depending on the town's ability to attract merchant-residents.

Like many other such communities, Almora was not much of a success. In 1907 the railroad advertised that a "drug store, doctor, feed mill, cheese factory, creamery, blacksmith, and bank" were needed. This short list of retail and small-scale manufacturing businesses indicates the railroad's realistic view of the town's potential and its assessment that the town's location, on the prairie-woodland fringe, made it about equally likely that Almora's trade area would specialize in grain farming or in dairy farming. But only nine of the business lots had been sold by 1907, and only one grain elevator was in operation. The lack of a bank signaled that the town was not going to grow rapidly, since, without a bank, farmers were unlikely to make Almora their primary trade center. The presence of only a single grain elevator meant that farmers had no choice of buyer when selling their crops and thus that they would be forced to sell at whatever price the grain company set.

At a more abstract level towns like Almora can be viewed as part of a complex network of economic production and exchange. The network of economic transactions defined the town's purpose and place in the system. The farmer needed credit in the form of a loan from a local banker in order to purchase machinery to harvest his crop. He obtained the loan by offering his crop or land and buildings as collateral. The banker obtained the money to loan the farmer by borrowing from a bank in a larger city. The farmer's obligation was sold "up" through the hierarchy of cities in the markets for farm mortgages. The machinery needed to harvest the crop was manufactured in a larger, regional city and shipped down the line to the farmer, who harvested his crop and shipped it to market up the same line.

The railroad financed its line by selling bonds to investors through the New York, Boston, London, and Paris financial markets and paid interest on the bonds primarily from the revenue it collected hauling crops to market. Transportation charges were subtracted from the amount the grain buyer paid the farmer for his crop before it was shipped. The bushel price the farmer received for the crop was determined in advance of the harvest through the futures market, in which obligations to deliver a quantity of some crop were offered for sale, usually in a distant city.

All of the transactions—involving commodities, durable goods, money, infrastructure, information, or obligations—flowed up and down, from farm to metropolis, through the hierarchy of towns. In fact, small trade-center towns like Almora were scaled-down copies of the metropolis. Almora's plat consisted of only six city blocks, each 300 feet on a side, but these blocks, including their division into building lots and residential lots, exactly imitated the geometry of real estate in the metropolis. Each town performed, in every transaction, its own small fraction of the total work done by the economic system. The tempo of transactions was enhanced by upswings in worldwide economic cycles and dampened by downturns. Crop failures propagated a series of adjustments beginning at the lower end of the hierarchy. Depressions, wars, and other dislocations made their impact felt from the upper end.

The shift from railway to highway networks that connected small towns to one another and to the rest of the nation began in the 1920s, but it did not have a major impact until the 1960s, when the quality of roads began to improve markedly. Hauling a crop to market in a horse-drawn wagon required a large expenditure of time; a motorized truck made it possible to reach trade centers that had been too distant before. The adoption of automobiles and trucks expanded the trading radius of the small town, and rural dwellers discovered they now had a choice of trade centers. Smaller towns, in general, were at a disadvantage to larger ones; larger trade centers offered a wider variety of goods and services, and they often charged lower prices. Rural schools were once necessary because of the same limits imposed by transportation technology, but they too underwent consolidation into districts based on fewer, more widely spaced schools when local road-transportation access improved.

Trade-center towns declined in population to the extent that they became redundant in the new transportation era. Between the late 1920s and the 1960s these changes were felt primarily in the towns' retail functions and school systems. Economic decline also meant population decline, although the retired farmers who moved to nearby towns replaced part of the population loss. As long as a town's railroad and grain elevator remained, however, its initial purpose was maintained.

A second wave of changes in transportation infrastructure and grain-marketing technology was felt beginning in the 1970s. Having long lost their monopoly on transportation, railroads became specialized haulers of just a few bulk commodities and were no longer central to the community. Changes in the economics of grain marketing favored much larger grain elevators, located in towns four or five times as far apart, which made many railway lines redundant. Small-town elevators were closed, tracks were ripped up, and the final blow to many towns was thereby inflicted. Almora still has a railroad, but it is no longer functional in the grain-collection system. The town's population, which peaked at approximately 150, has now declined to only a few residents.

CHANGING PATTERNS OF AGRICULTURE

At the national scale, regions of agricultural growth and decline can be identified with respect to changes in land, labor, and capital inputs that have accompanied the evolution of agriculture (fig. 18.4). A general proxy for the broad category "agricultural change" is available by examining the changing ratio of capital and labor inputs to land inputs in an area. At a given level of technology, the greater the amounts of capital and labor employed per unit area, the greater is the intensity of agriculture. If technology remains constant, agriculture becomes more intensive if more labor and more capital, in some combination, are employed to farm a given amount of land.

All systems of agricultural production modernized to some extent over the course of the 20th century. Almost as pervasive has been the tendency to employ less labor per unit of output in all forms of agricultural production. These two trends are related because technological

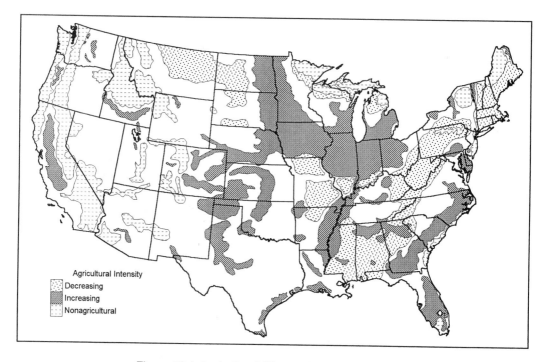

Figure 18.4 Agricultural Change in the 20th Century

change has meant that labor has had to become more productive (less labor used for a given ratio of capital-to-land inputs). Capital typically flows into agriculture from other sectors of the economy during periods when new agricultural production techniques are being developed.

The adoption of new technology by individual farmers, in contrast, is possible only by achieving greater efficiencies in the use of capital and labor inputs. This practically limits the adoption of new technology to areas where such efficiencies can be achieved, meaning that new technology is most often applied to land that is already the most productive. Contrasts within agricultural regions, such as the Corn and Cotton Belts, have been enhanced as a result of the adoption of new technology, with a retreat of production from some areas at the same time that it has intensified in others.

From the beginnings of American agriculture until 1920, most production increases resulted from increasing the number of acres in production. This remained an option only as long as unused or lightly used land was waiting to be brought into production. Many agricultural innovations were made prior to the 1920s, and they were often put to fullest use on the latest frontier where land was underutilized in terms of resource availability. When new lands for expansion were no longer available, the only option to meet increased demand for agricultural products was to innovate—to invest in new production technologies. This, in turn, meant that those lands that received added investment increased in value. Farmers who stood to profit from making such investments had to adopt the innovations. Farmers in less favored areas stood to profit much less from adopting new technologies and therefore could not afford to make the change. In the latter case, they either switched to some other combination of crop-livestock enterprise or left agriculture altogether.

Geographically, the result of these processes has been to force production of a given agricultural system into core areas where it is most suitable from an economic perspective. The rapid adoption of hybrid corn in the Middle West during the 1940s is one such example. Hybrid seed corn was expensive because seed had to be purchased each year rather than saved from the previous year's crop. Hybrid corn was adopted rapidly in Illinois and Iowa, the heart of the Corn Belt, but was adopted slowly on the region's periphery, where soils were not as productive, the growing season was too short, or market infrastructure was lacking. The hybrid-seed-corn revolution intensified corn production on the best lands of the Corn Belt in the 1940s. Continued improvement in corn hybrids produced more intensification on the best lands in later years as well.

Introduction of mechanized cotton pickers had a similar impact in the South. Areas marginal for cotton generally declined after mechanical pickers were introduced in the 1940s. In contrast, cotton production intensified in the coastal plain, the Texas High Plains, and the Central Valley of California as a result of adopting the new technology. Decreasing agricultural intensity characterized large areas of the old Cotton Belt. Some farmers shifted into poultry (broiler) production, especially in areas of rolling to hilly land unsuited to large, mechanized equipment. Because poultry production came to be organized mainly by companies involved in packing and marketing the product, areas outside the sphere of operation of the poultry processors did not have this option. Many portions of the old Cotton Belt reverted to pine woods and became part of the forestry economy more than of agriculture.

Technological change also can portend the rapid shift out of an established region of production into a new one where all of the resources are available but where they remained underutilized. Increased consumer demand for red meat during the 1960s pushed beef prices upward, but production costs were comparatively high in the Middle West, which had long been the traditional area for corn fattening of cattle. Beginning in the late 1960s, cattle feeding and meatpacking shifted out of the Middle West and into the Great Plains, where production costs were lower but where feed-grain production had been limited in former times because of insufficient rainfall to grow feed crops such as corn. Introduction of new irrigation devices, such as the center-pivot machine, made it possible to raise corn on lands that until recently had been marginal even for wheat. As a result, by the 1980s more than half of the beef industry of the United States was located in areas of aquifer-based irrigation in the High Plains of Kansas, Nebraska, Colorado, and Texas.

The movement of cattle feeding to the Great Plains did not produce agricultural deintensification in the Middle West, however, because farmers there shifted from feeding their crops to livestock to selling their crops of corn and soybeans for cash. This, in turn, was made possible by a large increase in the world's demand for feed grains and by new industrial as well as food uses for both corn and soybeans. Farmers plowed old cattle pastures under to provide new corn and soybean acreages during the 1970s. The flow of export grain began to move to market via barges on the Mississippi River linking the Middle West with New Orleans, which became the nation's largest grain-shipping port.

Intensification generally accompanies the shift from a lower-value to a higher-value crop. The shift from oats to soybeans during the 1940s is an example. Introduction of tractors and other self-propelled machinery on farms led to a rapid decline in the use of horses for power. Oats, which had been grown primarily as a feed crop for on-farm use, were no longer required. The rapid adoption of soybeans beginning in the 1940s was made possible in part because of the acreage that had been freed through the discontinuation of oats. Because soybeans were a valuable crop when sold for cash (they can also be used as a forage crop for cattle), they were often planted on expensive land, such as land that had undergone the expense of drainage for agricultural purposes. The expansion of soybean crops accompanied the expansion of drainage activities in the delta wetlands of both Mississippi and Arkansas. Soybeans contributed substantially to the agricultural intensification of the lower Mississippi valley, as did expansion there of the rice and cotton crops.

A somewhat similar sequence of events has taken place on the inner coastal plain, from eastern North Carolina to southwestern Georgia. Apart from the alluvial Mississippi valley, the inner coastal plain is now the most important area of crop production in the South. Coastal plain soils are not especially fertile in comparison with those of the Middle West or even most of the Great Plains, but they produce abundant crops when sufficient mineral fertilizers are applied. Tobacco, corn, cotton, peanuts, and soybeans are all produced in large quantities in this region today, often on lands that were in a heavy forest cover until only recently. Forests are cut, land is cleared, drainage ditches are dug, and the land is leveled—all activities that require substantial capital investment—in anticipation of the substantial production that can be achieved on such lands. Sale of feed grains to the southern poultry industry (which otherwise has to import grain from the Middle West) has been one stimulus for the round of activities necessary to bring coastal plain land into production.

All of these examples of increased agricultural intensity were accompanied by a continued reduction in the farm population and, in some instances, continued decline within the rural population generally. Increased operating efficiencies in larger farm units have led to farm consolidation and therefore to an increase in off-farm migration. The more technological innovations are substituted for labor on the farm, the fewer are the demands on infrastructure to support the farm population. While technology has increased the demand for skilled labor, relatively few people are required to perform skilled tasks. The shift toward a more complex agricultural intensity thus decreases the support for trade-center towns originally designed to serve the farm population.

In many cases small towns in agricultural areas have shifted away from a dependence on agriculture and invested in schemes to promote local manufacturing industries that, although they are sometimes agriculture-related as well, are likely to be industries that could equally well locate elsewhere. There has been a growing trend for small towns to develop economies far less related to the nature of agricultural production in their vicinity than was true formerly.

A general deintensification of agriculture has taken place in the hillier lands of the eastern United States for much of the 20th century. Hilly lands generally are unsuited to mechanized agricultural production, and they often produce soils of inferior quality as well. Because no form of agricultural production is available that can simultaneously thrive under these conditions and also sustain a high level of agricultural intensity, these areas have shifted out of agriculture. New England began to experience such conditions even in the 19th century, when new lands opened to settlement in the West put New England farmers at a disadvantage. New England's dairy industry has declined over time, whereas dairying has been responsible for agricultural intensification in parts of Wisconsin, Minnesota, and the Central Valley of California.

Commodities that are typically produced in greater quantities than markets can absorb have been regulated by production quotas since the 1940s. The means of achieving desired production levels for crops has been to set limits on the crop's total acreage. Federal programs have generally sought to achieve these targets by making it attractive for farmers to retire their less productive or erosion-prone croplands. The northern Great Plains wheat zone is one where substantial amounts of land have been removed from production by placing lands in a conservation reserve (or "soil bank," as it was formerly known). The northern Plains became an area of decreased agricultural intensity with the introduction of dry-farming methods that employ fewer inputs per acre of land in crops. Rural depopulation has been drastic in some of the dry-farmed wheat areas of the northern Great Plains during the past two decades.

While wheat production has reintensified in the better lands of eastern North Dakota, western Minnesota, and central Kansas, it has declined in parts of Montana and the western Dakotas. Thus far, at least, no crop has emerged that can replace wheat, and thus a significant amount of land has been idled, completing another step in agricultural deintensification. Farmers are paid to withhold marginal lands from production, but trade-center towns are not compensated for the reduction in activity level that necessarily results from using the land less intensively. Population loss is thereby accelerated.

WHO LIVES ON THE FARM?

Demographic changes accompanying the evolution of American agriculture have not been limited to just a decline in the number of farmers. As recently as the 1920s, there were more than 5 million persons of African descent living on farms in the United States. They were concentrated in plantation districts of the South but lived in other southern and western regions as well. In 1920, just prior to the massive migrations to northern industrial cities, almost half of the African American population of the United States still lived on farms. Many were tenants and sharecroppers and experienced a standard of living well below that of African American urban residents of that era. The attraction of jobs in the North, the experience of white violence against African Americans in the South, and the declining need for labor force on plantations all contributed to the exodus.

In 1990 only 69,000 African Americans lived on farms anywhere in the United States. This reduction, which amounts to more than 98 percent of the 1920 African American farm population, is one of the largest rural demographic shifts of the 20th century, although one that has drawn comparatively little attention. While the decline of sharecropping and share-tenancy can be seen as a positive development, an unintended result of the many changes affecting agriculture has been to almost eradicate the African American farmer.

African Americans have been affected negatively by most of the technology-driven changes in American agriculture. Undercapitalized from the beginning, African American farmers struggled unsuccessfully to compete in an environment that brought increasing returns to the scale of farm operations. There are successful African American farm operators in the alluvial counties of Mississippi, Arkansas, and Louisiana, as well as in isolated cotton and tobacco districts of the Atlantic coastal plain today, but African Americans have almost totally disappeared from the agricultural scene elsewhere. The loss of African American farm families accounts for about one-third of the total loss in farm population within the South during the 1920–90 period.

Hispanic farm residents have increased in numbers during this same period. Just as the presence of African Americans in American agriculture is historically rooted in the patterns of slavery in the South, the appearance of Hispanics after 1900 was associated with seasonal migratory labor in the West (and, to a lesser extent, Florida). Migration from Mexico established a large Hispanic agricultural population in southern Texas by 1930. Migration resumed after the 1930s, when the migratory workforce became increasingly dominated by persons of Mexican ancestry living in the United States. Even by the late 1920s Hispanics accounted for between 75 percent and 90 percent of the seasonal work force of the U.S. sugar beet industry, which was concentrated in irrigated oases of the West, especially in Colorado, Wyoming, and Idaho.

Numerous seasonal migrations eventually produced small resident Hispanic populations in all of the western states, concentrated almost exclusively within zones of irrigation farming. Eventually seasonal farmworkers became farm managers and then farm owners, a development that began in California and spread to other states. Hispanic farm operators are concentrated in the older irrigated areas, such as the Rio Grande valley of Texas, the San Joaquin valley of California, and the Colorado piedmont north of Denver. Less than 1 percent of the U.S. Hispanic population lives on farms, but their onfarm presence is not declining in numerical or percentage terms.

With a white population percentage of 97.5 in 1990, farming has become one of the whitest occupations in the United States. The European ethnicities associated with farming in most areas of agricultural success within the nation are as noticeable today as they were a century ago. In fact, the persistence of ethnic patterns can be related to population decline (or very slow growth) within rural areas. Places that grow receive a mix of new people through inmigration from various origins, whereas places that decline rely mainly on keeping a fraction of the natural increase in the local population to achieve what growth they can.

Notably endogamous groups, such as the German-Russian wheat farmers of the Great Plains, still maintain ethnic dominance in the communities where their ancestors first settled in the 1870s and 1890s. The same is true for other rural regions of special ethnic and cultural character, such as the sugarcane parishes of Louisiana (French Acadian); the irrigation, dry farming, and ranching districts of the Utah and Idaho mountains (Mormon); and the dairy farming regions of central Wisconsin and Minnesota (German or Scandinavian). Rural cultural patterns have changed slowly in these areas because of the lack of developments, such as significant urbanization, that would have overturned what was already established.

Historically, farm families were larger than nonfarm families. The need for farm labor is often cited as an explanation for the difference, but the discrepancy was also due in part to inertia. Rural populations also are more traditional, and family-size expectations declined more slowly in the farming population than they did in others. Completed family size for farm-resident women today is roughly 2.5 children, compared with 2.0 children for nonfarm women; in

1910 these values equaled 5.6 and 3.6, respectively. Stated in another way, completed family size was 55 percent larger on the farm than in the city in 1910 but only 25 percent larger in 1990. In this respect, as in many others, the rural population is becoming less distinct.

The large decrease in family size on the farm is reflected in many other trends, including changes in the work performed by farm women. Sixty percent of farm men now list agriculture as their primary employment (that is, 40 percent work mainly off the farm), whereas almost 80 percent of employed farm women work primarily off the farm. Farm women have their largest employment concentration in technical, sales, and administrative-support occupations. Nonetheless, farm women perform a variety of on-farm tasks and are an important part of the farm workforce. Along with men, they have become heavy-equipment operators, driving grain combines and grain trucks at harvest time, and operating tractors pulling seeding equipment as well as fertilizer and herbicide applicators during spring planting and cultivation.

CONCLUSION

Rural America experienced massive changes during the 20th century. The last agricultural frontiers were still awaiting occupation at the beginning of the century, and the business of founding new towns was a field of activity, especially for western railroads, that still saw new lines of track extended into recently developed farming districts. Apart from irrigation developments, which continue to reshape agricultural regions even today, the last of the expansion booms took place during World War I, when favorable conditions for agricultural colonization revived for a brief period.

Technological changes are foremost among those that have affected life on the farm and in small towns. Agricultural trade centers were at their peak of influence in the early decades of the 20th century, before the shift from rail to highway networks began to reshape the economies of small towns. Another series of adjustments came after the 1960s, when highway improvements and changes in marketing procedures for bulk commodities such as grain made numerous small towns redundant in the role that they had been created to perform.

The map of American agriculture has been altered at several scales over the past several decades. New technology has driven many changes that have drastically reduced the need for farm labor and that have made the economical size of farm operating units several times larger than it was in the 1940s. The rural landscape has become depopulated as a consequence. Many small towns that once relied on agriculture for their support have shifted into manufacturing and have grown as a result. "Rural" no longer carries the connotation that it once did, now that more than half of all rural dwellers live within the limits of metropolitan areas.

At the national scale agricultural regions have expanded, contracted, and, in some cases, leapfrogged into new areas in response to technological changes that have magnified differences in resource endowments between regions. Some environmental factors (such as precipitation deficiency) mean much less than they did in the 19th century, whereas others (smoothness of topography) have acquired greater significance. The challenges posed by environmental limits will continue into the future as debates about agricultural sustainability and the wise use of land resources are projected over an ever more urbanized landscape.

ADDITIONAL READING

Aiken, C. S. 1998. *The Cotton Plantation South since the Civil War.* Baltimore: Johns Hopkins University Press.

Beale, C. L. 1956. *Characteristics of Farm-Operator Households by Number of Young Children.* U.S. Department of Agriculture, Agricultural Marketing Service, AMS 118. Washington, D.C.: U.S. Government Printing Office.

Borchert, J. R. 1997. "The Heyday of the Railway Post Office in Minnesota." *Minnegazette* (Winter): 18–34.

———. 1972. "America's Changing Metropolitan Regions." *Annals of the Association of American Geographers* 62: 352–73.

Christaller, W. 1966. *Central Places in Southern Ger-

many. Translated by C. W. Basin. Englewood Cliffs, N.J.: Prentice-Hall.

Dahman, D. C., and L. T. Dacquel. 1992. *Residents of Farms and Rural Areas: 1990.* U.S. Bureau of the Census, Current Population Reports, Series P-20, No. 457, Washington: U.S. Government Printing Office.

Hart, J. F. 1991. *The Land That Feeds Us.* New York: W. W. Norton.

———. 1998. *The Rural Landscape.* Baltimore: Johns Hopkins University Press.

Hudson, J. C. 1985. *Plains Country Towns.* Minneapolis: University of Minnesota Press.

———. 1991. "New Grain Networks in an Old Urban System." In *Our Changing Cities,* ed. J. F. Hart. Baltimore: Johns Hopkins University Press.

———. 1994. *Making the Corn Belt. A Geographical History of Midwestern Agriculture.* Bloomington: Indiana University Press..

Lösch, A. 1954. *The Economics of Location.* Translated by W. F. Woglom with the assistance of W. F. Stolper. New Haven: Yale University Press.

Metzler, W. H., and F. O. Sargent. 1960. *Migratory Farmworkers in the Midcontinent Streams.* U.S. Department of Agriculture, Agricultural Research Service, Production Research Report 41. Washington, D.C.: U.S. Government Printing Office.

Soo Line Railroad. 1907. *Dozens of New Towns.* Minneapolis: n.p.

Vance, J. E., Jr. 1970. *The Merchant's World: The Geography of Wholesaling.* Englewood Cliffs, N.J.: Prentice-Hall.

———. 1995. *The North American Railroad: Its Origin, Evolution, and Geography.* Baltimore: Johns Hopkins University Press.

19

The 20th-Century American City

EDWARD K. MULLER

The geography of the American industrial metropolis had taken shape by the beginning of World War I. At its center was downtown, signified by the cluster of skyscrapers heralding the power of corporate capital. Masses of people entered downtown each day through grand railroad stations or on electric streetcars, hurrying to work, attracted to glittering department stores, or entertained in elegant hotels and amusement districts. Wholesaling, manufacturing, and wharving activities concentrated in older 19th-century built landscapes adjacent to downtown. These areas were, in turn, embedded in a sea of immigrant and African American neighborhoods, varying from impoverished and unhealthy slums to overcrowded, but viable, working-class communities. Suburban residential communities sorted by class and sometimes ethnicity, railroad corridors of large mass-production factories, and small industrial satellite towns extended beyond the densely settled central neighborhoods for 10 to 30 miles. Commuter railroads, mass transit, telephones, telegraphy, and freight-hauling firms tied these diverse areas of city and suburb together into metropolitan industrial regions, formally recognized by the U.S. Census in 1910 as Metropolitan Districts.

Unplanned rapid development, unprecedented immigration, and general faith in the efficacy of the private sector had spawned intractable environmental and social problems, despite the wealth generated by industrialization. Charities, civic organizations, and the new social work profession addressed the social and health issues arising from poverty, overcrowded low-income housing, smoke-filled skies, and inadequate sanitation. Engineers, landscape architects, and urban planners wrestled with severe traffic congestion, inappropriately mixed land uses, and overwhelmed infrastructure. In spite of notable public works successes, the creation of enduring public and voluntary civic institutions, and some governmental interventions from the 1880s to the 1910s,

more than 30 years of progressive reforms had failed to solve the industrial metropolis's daunting problems.

Politicians and civic leaders confronted the governmental fragmentation of sprawling metropolitan regions. The consolidation of the five boroughs of Brooklyn, Manhattan, Queens, the Bronx, and Staten Island into a single municipal entity of New York City in 1898 had optimistically signaled the arrival of the efficient, rational ordering of urban America, which progressive reformers believed would make cities better places to live in the 20th century. The metropolitan amalgamation of local governmental jurisdictions and infrastructure, such as the Boston-area water and parks authorities, held out the promise of eradicating inefficiencies exacerbated by the extreme governmental fragmentation of industrial metropolises. By 1910, however, suburban municipalities across America actively resisted annexation. They wished to maintain their autonomy over the development, taxation, and administration of their municipalities. This suspicion of metropolitan government lasted throughout the 20th century. Although in 1998 New York City officially celebrated the centennial of its consolidation, many New Yorkers questioned the wisdom of the earlier act, and most metropolitan areas remained as governmentally fragmented as ever.

The persistent jurisdictional complexity of metropolitan areas throughout the 20th century reflected fundamental American values, social characteristics, and institutions. Rising national income supported a long-term increase in the standard of living and for many Americans heightened the emphasis on consumption and leisure activities. Of course, not all Americans participated in this prosperity, as economic inequality persisted. Most, however, believed in the superiority of capitalism and distrusted government. They embraced the right of individuals and private enterprise to function with a minimum of governmental interference. Thus, capital was free to move about the nation, and within the constraints of income, most people could also move freely, develop and use private property as they wished, and live amid people of similar social characteristics and outlook. This freedom allowed these Americans to seek out new regions of the country, develop the urban periphery for residential and commercial purposes, compete with the central city for business, and attempt to control the social composition of their areas. New technologies of transportation and communication enhanced mobility and greatly enlarged locational opportunities of both individuals and businesses. Democratic politics meant that Americans could organize to have government at all levels promote their goals and interests, while limiting government regulation, control over development, and redistribution of income. Concomitantly, people without adequate income, disadvantaged by race or sexual orientation, and unable to influence government did not enjoy such freedoms and governmental support. The story line of 20th-century urban geography is, therefore, the differential growth of cities resulting from the shift of capital and people from the North and Midwest to the South and West, the centrifugal movement of individuals and businesses from the central city to the suburbs, the growing independence of the suburbs from the central city, and the continued separation of people by class, race, and lifestyle in central cities or older suburban neighborhoods.

THE INTERWAR DECADES

Visions

After World War I accelerating metropolitan decentralization, especially with the public's embrace of the new automobile; continued growth of retailing, offices, and entertainment in downtowns; and the influx of impoverished rural migrants threatened to exacerbate the city's difficulties. While most urban planners in the 1920s struggled daily with retrofitting 19th-century street plans to the automobile, implementing land use zoning, and preparing comprehensive plans in hope of bringing some order to development, a few critical observers tried to envision more dramatic spatial solutions for organizing the 20th-century metropo-

lis. In 1922 a handful of planning visionaries created the Regional Planning Association of America (RPAA) and met throughout the decade to advocate a more balanced vision of the metropolitan region, one inspired by Ebenezer Howard's *Garden Cities of Tomorrow*. Their most prominent member, Lewis Mumford, decried the consequences of minimally restrained development and urged the planning of both individual communities and whole metropolitan regions. The RPAA projected the construction of self-contained communities of 50,000 residents in the metropolitan periphery, buffered from each other and the central city by open space and specialized in function with respect to each other. Following Clarence Perry's communitarian precepts, housing within these communities would be organized in planned neighborhoods centered around the school, with housing, recreation, and shopping clustered in "superblocks" and pedestrian circulation separated from vehicular traffic. The successful completion of the self-contained communities of Sunnyside Gardens (1924) and Radburn (1928) in the New York metropolitan region, designed by RPAA members Clarence Stein and Henry Wright, suggested the advantages of community planning. However, the RPAA's regional vision required massive state intervention in private markets and accordingly never seriously challenged prevailing development practices and free-market philosophies, although it would inspire some post–World War II projects like Reston, Virginia, and Columbia, Maryland.

In 1930 architect Frank Lloyd Wright proposed another regional configuration, which took contemporary trends of increasing individual mobility to the extreme. In his plan, entitled Broadacre City, Wright arranged homes, work, and services linearly along highways. This dispersed settlement scheme emphasized individual accessibility at the expense of community coherence. Although impractical in the face of rapid urban growth and land consumption and anathema to progressive planning tenets, Wright's plan nonetheless recognized the popularity of personal mobility and household autonomy, which would shape urban form throughout the century.

Although far less visionary, civic leaders and planners in New York City and Los Angeles proposed two other solutions for managing metropolitan expansion, which did become models after the mid-20th century. During most of the 1920s Thomas Adams coordinated a team of planners that surveyed the New York metropolitan region and produced a report entitled the *Regional Plan of New York and Its Environs*. Adams's plan reinforced New York City as the dominant central city of the region, assigned new industry to the periphery, and emphasized improved circulation of people and goods within the region by rail and road, including tunnels, bridges, and hundreds of miles of circumferential highways. Greater efficiency of movement, it was argued, would preserve Manhattan's viability for commuters, shoppers, and businesses, while simultaneously facilitating the relentless growth of residential communities and industrial satellites in the region. Adams's scheme accepted the premise of continued metropolitan growth and prevailing trends in development, but it broke new ground in its regional scope of planning.

Across the continent, rapidly growing Los Angeles was also experiencing debilitating traffic congestion from an electric streetcar and interurban system focused on the city center and the explosion of automobile ownership. At the behest of the Automobile Club of Southern California civic leaders also adopted a transportation solution, but in contrast to Adams's New York plan, they projected a low-density landscape of residential communities and local commercial centers. They envisioned a network of highways that would deemphasize the dominance of the central city and link together the sprawling single-family subdivisions sprouting up in the southern California desert. Unlike the discarded visions of reorganized regional settlement propounded by Mumford, Wright, and other communitarians, transportation elements of the New York and Los Angeles plans were implemented in the 1930s and subsequent decades.

If Wright's Broadacre City was impractical and the RPAA's regional city too radical for civic leaders, then the more conventional solutions of New York City and Los Angeles foreshadowed the city's future. Although the communitarians remained prominent in the 1930s with the federal government's support of planning, the prosaic prescriptions of lightly regulated regional growth and more efficient transportation merged comfortably with the predilections of the development industry and civic boosters. In so doing, urban processes familiar to the first third of the century—unfettered decentralization, escalating traffic volumes, selective centralization of some activities, and sorting out of social groups by class, ethnicity, and race in tedious subdivisions—continued to shape urban form, checked only by the dampened real estate market and neglect of infrastructure during the Great Depression and World War II. Urban problems associated with rapid suburban growth, racial and immigrant concentration, and central-city congestion worsened over the years. By 1945, the geographical outlines of the American city still closely resembled the industrial metropolis of the early 20th century.

The Twenties

No innovation affected the city in the 1920s more than the automobile. Fed up with mass transit's poor service, financial corruption, mismanagement, and democratic patronage, middle-class urbanites opted for the privacy, speed, and flexibility of the automobile. With Henry Ford's assembly line leading the way in decreasing prices, even working-class Americans could consider buying cars. Car owners and their automobile associations demanded improved roads. In 1916 and 1921 the federal government passed legislation to assist states in building paved highways. States embarked on massive highway construction programs, and cities similarly improved their streets. As it would prove to be true for the rest of the century, rather than solving traffic problems, bigger and better highways only encouraged increased use.

Better roads promoted more suburban development. The development industry adapted its residential subdivisions to this new means of transportation. Freed from the locational constraints of pedestrian access to railroad and trolley stops, developers built suburbs in the interstices between rail lines as well as farther into the countryside. They lowered densities with larger lot sizes; lowered house heights with California bungalow, prairie, and similarly small, flexible-floor-plan styles; and built garages often attached to houses. When not lowering house heights, builders put up period-revival-style houses harkening back to earlier American traditions (e.g., Federal or Cape Cod) or evoking European traditions (e.g., Dutch Colonial, Spanish Colonial, or English Tudor styles). Without question, however, the bungalow held the most significance for future suburban styles. Suburban subdivisions were aimed at middle-class buyers; most working-class Americans could not afford to buy homes in speculatively built, residential suburbs. At best, they located in industrial suburbs or built their own homes in unincorporated districts over the course of several years.

Retailers began to adjust to the changing locus of their customers. Major department stores had already begun to build branches in subregional commercial centers of the central city. As traffic worsened in nearby villages patronized by suburban residents, retailers experimented with arterial shopping corridors and large, stand-alone stores. A few pre–World War I shopping complexes provided precedents for planned suburban shopping districts, but J. C. Nichols's 1923 Country Club Plaza in suburban Kansas City is usually considered the first shopping center with coordinated design and ample off-street parking for cars. A few other suburban developers mimicked Nichols's concept, though most of the growth of peripheral retailing was lodged in arterial strips. Overall, while downtowns still dominated retailing, the convenience of the automobile for shopping elsewhere in the metropolitan region was being established in the 1920s.

While villages wrestled with the crush of suburban shoppers using cars, downtowns also felt imperiled by the flood of motor vehicles. Older streets and bridges were too narrow, especially with trolleys claiming rights-of-way. Parking was inadequate, and even major arteries of ingress and egress were ill equipped for the traffic volume. Civic leaders heard the motorists' complaints, watched retailers eye the mushrooming suburban market, and feared for the long-term health of downtown. Planning and public works departments strove to relieve the congestion with improved, new highways, but congestion only grew more fearsome by the decade's end. Planners struggled with the torrent of requests for zoning variations and nuisance complaints resulting from the development of gasoline stations, home owners' garages, automobile dealerships, and repair shops throughout the central city. A new wave of skyscrapers, movie palaces, and nearby baseball parks in the 1920s maintained the dominance downtown of offices, retailing, and entertainment, but rapid residential suburbanization, new suburban retail districts, and traffic congestion challenged civic leaders to find ways to retain downtown's centrality in the future. Indeed, Thomas Adams's plan for New York was explicitly designed to preserve Manhattan's prominence within its burgeoning metropolitan region.

If the 1920s' embrace of the automobile anticipated the contours of lifestyles and spatial form prevalent in the second half of the century, then the urban migration of rural Americans, especially African Americans, foreshadowed the social dilemma that would grip central cities for decades to come. The sharp decline of European immigration with the outbreak of World War I and legislation restricting immigration in the early 1920s produced a demand for labor in the growing industrial cities of the Northeast, Midwest, and West Coast. Poor farmers from the South and Great Plains fled the hardships of working the land to seek these opportunities. Even Hispanic populations crossed the border, the vanguard of a later massive movement. By the beginning of the Great Depression, African Americans numbered in the tens of thousands in northern cities, and Hispanics formed noticeable minorities in cities like New York, Miami, and Los Angeles.

The migrants, like European immigrants before them, crowded into housing of older central-city neighborhoods adjacent or easily accessible to the vast array of unskilled jobs in the central business district. Originally they shared these areas with European immigrants. However, as successful immigrants or their progeny left for better neighborhoods, African Americans claimed the housing and began to build their own community institutions. With the more visible presence of African Americans, residential discrimination by whites sharply increased, and racial ghettos formed. Under the sustained pressure of migrants coming throughout the 1920s, ghettos became more densely inhabited and expanded into adjacent white residential neighborhoods, from which some former white residents had fled, selling their homes. These racial ghettos, like the South Side of Chicago and Harlem in upper Manhattan, became lively centers of African American urban culture. African American businesses, arts, sports, and social services flourished alongside numbers running, illegal speakeasies, and other vice activities (fig. 19.1). While they engaged in segregated but traditional American music societies and literary clubs, often with individual popular success, African Americans also evolved culturally significant new art forms such as jazz. They fiercely debated the wisdom of pursuing a strategy of trying to assimilate with the larger white society or of maintaining a separate life.

By discriminating against African Americans at every level, the white majority gave assimilationists little encouragement. Occupational segmentation kept men and women in low-paying and insecure unskilled factory, service, and do-

mestic jobs. The ensuing impoverishment of the minority migrant population, along with residential instability and implacable segregation, led to severely overcrowded housing conditions, atrocious sanitation, and difficult social problems. Families, kinfolk, boarders, and neighbors helped each other through tough times, but social critics were concerned about the African American ghettos, just as they had worried about European immigrant conditions a generation earlier.

Unsavory residential conditions were not confined to racial ghettos. Although many immigrant families and their American-born children enjoyed greater prosperity in the 1920s and moved out to lower-density city neighborhoods and older streetcar suburbs, others remained

Figure 19.1 Harlem, Art Workshop
(Courtesy National Archives and Records Administration)

trapped in deteriorating neighborhoods with all of the associated housing problems. Vibrant ethnic social institutions, businesses, and churches flourished in the improving economic and political niches that ethnic groups carved out. But they could not mask the persistent American urban dilemma of inadequate housing for low-income households. Housing reformers continued to address the issue with model multiple-family projects and pleas for public enforcement of housing codes, but they experienced the same limited success as earlier reformers had. The slim profit margins of erecting decent low-income housing did not attract substantial private investment. Accordingly, low-income residents remained dependent on either run-down, heavily subdivided buildings often owned by absentee landlords or cheaply constructed houses thrown together by speculative builders or corporations. Despite suburban

growth, greater prosperity, and the curtailment of immigration, the city's social geography remained sharply divided by class, race, and ethnicity.

The Thirties

The stock market crash in 1929 and the ensuing decade of depression in the 1930s finally brought urban problems to the nation's attention. The economy crumbled, unemployment rose, banks failed, the real estate market collapsed, and city home owners increasingly defaulted on mortgage payments as well as local tax obligations. The burden of relief overwhelmed the resources of private charities and then fell upon local governments just as their tax revenues declined (fig. 19.2). In the face of this economic debacle, the long-standing urban problems of traffic congestion, deteriorating in-

Figure 19.2 Depression Soup Kitchen, Chicago, 1931
(Courtesy National Archives and Records Administration)

frastructure, and decaying central neighborhoods worsened because relief and other social priorities prevailed.

With the election of Franklin D. Roosevelt as president in 1932 and the establishment of Democrats in political power, the federal government pursued programs to create jobs and pump up the economy. These programs simultaneously addressed some of the city's public works needs and instituted significant new urban initiatives. Two New Deal administrations, the Civil Works Administration (CWA, 1933–34) and the Works Progress Administration (WPA, 1935–43), addressed the employment problem by putting people to work designing and constructing roads, schools, libraries, playgrounds, parks, and public buildings. Federal funds also supported planners in surveying city housing, land-use, and income patterns. The data that they gathered underscored the widespread distribution of poverty and substandard housing in cities. Like the CWA and the WPA, the Public Works Administration (PWA, 1933–39) created employment through grants and loans for the construction of infrastructure, more than half of which was spent in urban areas. The PWA built bigger projects like bridges, tunnels, rapid transit lines, expressways, sewage and water facilities, and power plants. The PWA also funded a few slum clearance and public housing projects.

Some housing reformers and planners had long advocated more radical solutions to the housing and slum problems of American cities than the model projects and housing code proscriptions. In the early 1930s national housing conferences recommended slum clearance and public housing measures. Created at the end of 1933, the Federal Emergency Housing Corporation (FEHC) tore down some slum housing in nearly three dozen cities and replaced it with nearly 22,000 rental units in public housing projects carefully designed by some of the nation's best architects. Private industry opposed governmental intervention in private enterprise's domain as socialistic. The U.S. Circuit of Appeals stopped FEHC in 1935 on the grounds that the federal government could not exercise eminent domain for local housing, since housing was not a federal purpose.

In 1937 Congress circumvented the court's ruling and created the U.S. Housing Authority (USHA) to finance and oversee the erection by local municipal housing authorities of "safe and sanitary" low-income public housing in slum areas. The initial projects, built before the mid-1940s, involved low-rise buildings, careful site planning, and solid construction. Although white and minority families occupied public housing, most projects were racially segregated. USHA developed more than 150,000 new units; unfortunately, estimates of substandard houses ranged as high as 10 million units across the country.

While the New Deal pursued this unprecedented foray into low-income housing, it also vigorously supported private home ownership as a means to stem mortgage foreclosures, prop up real estate markets, and revive the homebuilding industry. The Home Owners Loan Corporation (HOLC, 1933) refinanced one-sixth of the nation's private mortgage debt, while the Federal Housing Administration (FHA, 1936) provided governmental security for mortgages, lowered down payments, extended the life of loans, and therefore lowered monthly repayment schedules. In this manner, these agencies stimulated an increase in debt-financed home ownership, especially among lower-middle- and working-class families. These programs favored investment in new homes over older ones and increased segregation. As securers of local bank loans, HOLC and FHA were anxious that the loans were safe. With the advice of local banking and real estate officials, they drew up maps that divided metropolitan areas into neighborhoods that were safe, problematic, and unsafe for investment. This system undervalued older, poor, and often nonwhite communities, making it difficult for them to obtain federally secured loans. In particular, FHA policy viewed racial mixing as deleterious for neighborhood stability and investment. Accordingly, a high percentage of the loans went to white middle-class families and for new homes mostly in suburban neighborhoods, rather than for the resale of older homes in poorer city areas.

Together, New Deal urban policies reinforced current urban geographical trends. Improved highways and federal mortgage programs fostered further urban decentralization and continued slow investment or disinvestment in older city neighborhoods. Although slum clearance and public housing addressed inner-city deterioration, public housing and mortgage policies also attenuated the economic and social segregation of metropolitan communities. Even the most radical New Deal program for altering traditional development patterns emphasized suburban growth and social exclusion. In its brief two-year existence the Suburban Settlement Division of the Resettlement Administration promulgated a program to improve working-class housing conditions by building entire towns on the urban periphery. These towns followed the best communitarian planning tenets demonstrated in planned communities such as Sunnyside Gardens. Three new Greenbelt towns, outside Washington, Cincinnati, and Milwaukee, included open green buffer zones, land for individual gardens, superblock organization, separation of pedestrian and vehicular traffic, recreational facilities, complete infrastructure, and mixed housing accommodations. However, the three towns lacked employment opportunities, were restricted to white residents, and functioned mostly as well-planned suburban dormitories.

Despite some new infrastructure, slum clearance, and public housing, the primary urban vision of the New Deal was a suburban one. Older inner cities fared badly during the depression in both the media and popular culture. Reformers and planners met regularly to discuss urban issues and advocated comprehensive, metropolitan-wide planning. However, few could envision restricting suburban growth and private property prerogatives in order to redirect investment from greener suburban pastures to aging central cities.

THE IMPACT OF WORLD WAR II

The years of war in the first half of the 1940s accelerated many trends evident in the 1920s. Within metropolitan areas, Defense Department demands for expanded and modern plants accelerated the move of manufacturing to the urban periphery, especially in the aviation and electronics industries. Huge airplane plants on Los Angeles's periphery and electronic firms outside of Boston, for example, extended metropolitan boundaries. At the same time, the conscious dispersal of military bases and defense industries to the South and West for strategic and political reasons quickened the shift of regional economic growth from the Manufacturing Belt to the emerging Sunbelt. The widespread economic growth resulting from wartime mobilization temporarily masked this regional restructuring. Depression-riddled cities like Detroit and Pittsburgh felt relieved at the rejuvenation of their massive industrial complex, while cities from Norfolk to Houston and San Diego to Seattle struggled to cope with the growing pains caused by new economic activities. Differential regional growth became pronounced after the war and continued for decades. Southern congressional power continued the flow of defense spending to the South and West during the Cold War years and tilted other federal programs to the advantage of these regions as well. Air-conditioning made year-round living in these hot-weather areas acceptable, even preferable to many people, while lower tax policies, antiunion sentiment, and aggressive local economic development strategies created a favorable business climate. Metropolitan population growth rates of the South and West consistently exceeded those of northern and midwestern cities. Whereas nine of the ten largest metropolitan areas in 1920 and 1950 were in the North and Midwest, half were in the Sunbelt by 1980.

Industrial growth and armed-service mobilization rejuvenated the rural-to-urban migrations of predepression decades. White and African American men and women moved to the factory jobs and military positions concentrating in and around urban areas. Although wartime migration was temporary by nature, the eye-opening exposure to urban life changed the horizons of many migrants for a lifetime. Along with economic opportunity, however, came an enormous demand for housing, which, following years of minimal new construction due to the depression, public housing and defense housing construction were unable to fulfill. Moreover, the surge of African Americans into this tight real estate market further overcrowded already inadequate housing conditions in the ghettos and worsened racial tensions so that violence sometimes erupted. Thus, war pulled the cities out of depression and restarted economic and population growth, but wartime priorities left unaddressed long-standing problems of deteriorating infrastructure, inadequate housing, declining inner-city neighborhoods, and festering racial inequalities.

Civic leaders, urban planners, and politicians extended their depression-era discussions of urban problems throughout the war in preparation for the postwar years, during which (they aptly recognized) cities would have to find solutions. Master planning, slum clearance, public housing, redevelopment, well-designed suburban communities, and limited-access expressways were all accepted as part of the urban future. The plans of urban experts, however, ran headlong into the pent-up demand of middle-class Americans for single-family homes and a modern (read suburban) lifestyle, the power of the development industry to resume business as free from governmental control as possible, and the changing parameters of postwar economic and social conditions.

POSTWAR CITIES

In the 1920s, middle-class Americans dreamed of moving to their own homes in the suburbs, and many achieved their goals before the onset of the Great Depression. In the decades following World War II, a broader proportion of the population set about achieving this American dream. Postwar prosperity, government policies, success of the labor movement, the development industry's power, economic restructuring, the baby boom, and the new generation's desire to assimilate more fully into American life all facilitated the massive expansion of the suburbs. However, white middle America's realization of their dream came, in part, at the expense of African Americans' fulfilling their hopes of a better life in the cities. The rapid development of the urban periphery both reflected and caused disinvestment in the center city. While traditional class lines seemed to blur, racism exacerbated this unhealthy relationship between city and suburb. By the end of the postwar period in the middle 1960s, it was no longer clear that many metropolitan communities were subordinated to the central city. The word "suburb" did not reflect adequately their function or form.

The New Suburbs

By 1946 American families itched to leave the crowded and aging housing of their cities for single-family homes that they could call their own. Fifteen years of depression and war had severely curtailed discretionary income, birthrates, and the construction of new houses.

The new adult generation was native-born, fresh from the assimilating and sobering experience of military service or defense work, and eager to start families. White Americans put the hard times behind them; postwar prosperity underwrote desires for raising children, owning homes, enjoying modern conveniences, and leaving behind their immigrant roots in the city. As soon as the war ended, the 20-year baby boom began. Both advertising and the media heralded the middle-class lifestyle of the suburbs. The success of the union movement, spurred on by the 1935 Wagner Act that guaranteed the right to organize, provided blue-collar workers the income, leisure time, and security to raise aspirations and join the middle class in the years to come.

The development industry just as eagerly sought to accommodate these young families, and government policy subsidized the construction of new housing on the urban periphery. Both large corporate developers and small, traditional speculative builders saw the opportunity to expand the dream to families formerly priced out of the suburban market. By designing small standardized houses and adopting mass-production, prefabrication techniques, William Levitt on the East Coast and Henry Kaiser on the West Coast built massive communities of inexpensive detached homes on the edges of New York, Philadelphia, Los Angeles, San Francisco, and Portland. Levitt erected in four years 17,000 nearly identical 800-square-foot Cape Cod and ranch-style houses at the new Long Island community of Levittown. Priced 15 percent or more below typical market prices, these homes appealed to veterans and their families living in cramped apartments or doubled up with relatives. Kaiser Community Homes similarly found its late-1940s venture into massive housing development at Panorama City in the San Fernando Valley in great demand and financially successful. Although large community developments cropped up in most metropolitan areas, small builders continued to put up large numbers of new homes, with increased efficiency.

Government policy fueled this rapid development of postwar suburbs. The Federal Housing Administration, which had revolutionized the average American's access to home ownership in the 1930s, was now buttressed by the Veterans Housing Administration (VHA), which extended similar mortgage terms to veterans. Congress further tipped the scales toward home ownership by making real estate taxes and mortgage interest both income tax deductions. Federal and state subsidies, especially after the 1956 National Interstate and Defense Highway Act, underwrote highway construction to the urban periphery. The combination of these supply-side subsidies and housing innovations with pent-up, media-enhanced consumer demand drove the rate of home ownership from less than half of all households in 1945 to nearly two-thirds in 1970.

Massive residential suburbanization transformed the metropolitan landscape. The automobile suburbs of the 1920s had foreshadowed the contours of this new environment. The new subdivisions were loosely tethered to major highways and had greatly enlarged lot sizes and community boundaries. The consumption of space awed urban observers. Community builders sometimes tried to incorporate the principles of green spaces or village centers prescribed by earlier planning reformers, but profit goals and the targeting of low-end markets frequently rendered such features expensive embellishments. Inexperienced and compliant local governments gave developers free rein to build subdivisions. Without comprehensive planning, monotonous geometrically patterned subdivisions sprawled across the landscape and blended together into a sea of single-family detached homes tied to a hierarchy of roads and highways. The large tracts of homes with only a few stylistic options for buyers emphasized ranch, contemporary, and split-level styles that did away with porches, parlors, and entry halls and featured informal open floor plans with more direct access to the outdoors. Most new suburbs did not have civic centers or parks. Pedestrian access to community facilities and institutions remained a city artifact.

The postwar suburb's detached homes and dependence on the auto neatly expressed middle-class cultural imperatives, emphasizing individual success, the nuclear family, privacy, mobility, and social homogeneity. The single-family home on its own lot, outfitted with modern floor plans and appliances, signaled one's rising economic status and material success. It reflected the choice to move away from the old, dense, ethnic neighborhood of city row houses and apartments and, perhaps, the growing African American population. Residential covenants in

deeds until 1948, exclusive zoning laws, and real estate practices kept out unwanted social groups. The original Levittown contracts, for example, forbade sale to non-Caucasians. Largely white, the new suburbs were mainly sorted out socially by class through the housing prices of subdivisions.

As in earlier eras, postwar suburbanization was more than a residential movement. Industrial development of greenfields in the urban periphery continued to occur. Federal highway subsidies as well as Defense Department support of Cold War industries encouraged new suburban plants. Industrial restructuring, often attributed to the last third of the 20th century, began soon after the war. The central cities' complex of older companies and manufacturing plants suffered a long, steady process of deindustrialization, while both Sunbelt metropolises and the suburbs benefited from the changes. Ironically, the growing success of the labor movement partially drove the restructuring process. Some industries such as textiles and garmentmaking, which had begun moving South for cheaper, nonunion labor in the early 20th century, found new sources of even cheaper labor overseas. While New England cities suffered from the first movement, Middle Atlantic cities, especially Philadelphia, lost out in this second phase of relocation and closures. Other older industries like steel, chemicals, and rubber downsized or shuttered older central-city plants, while they further automated production and built new facilities in the suburbs or near growing Sunbelt markets. Newer automobile manufacturers, airplane fabricators, and electronics firms also sought the cheap land, tax breaks, and parklike environment of suburban greenfields and attracted the labor force and housing developers to them.

Suburban industrial parks married motor-vehicle accessibility with the aesthetics of modernism. Limited-access and landscaped expressways appeared long before World War II as solutions to city traffic congestion. As axial routes, however, they failed to solve the intercity traveler's dilemma of getting through cities. Bypass highways around cities, built with federal subsidies for military strategical reasons justified by World War II and the Cold War, aided intercity traffic but also offered better access among suburbs and to specific points in the city. Interstate highway money extended bypasses into circumferential beltways that encircled cities. Intersections of beltways and radial arteries became magnets for industrial and wholesaling development. Sleek, unadorned, and one-story commercial buildings with landscaped grounds and on-site surface parking deliberately contrasted with the soot-covered, multistory, dirty-windowed, brick and reinforced concrete factories jammed together on lots along city streets and railroad sidings. They appealed to the middle-class image of a modern postwar America.

If the industrial park attracted its workers to the suburbs as much as it followed them, the regional shopping center clearly followed its consumers. Few residential developers concerned themselves with the provision of goods and services for new suburbanites. By the early 1950s the corridors of shops along arterial highways were becoming congested, as the older village centers had before the war. New, small, linear shopping centers with a narrow strip of off-street parking offered convenience for nearby residents, although suburbanites still relied on downtown and city regional districts for other kinds of goods. Large merchandisers recognized the potential of this new, relatively affluent market. Having already opened branch stores in the city outside of downtown, they logically envisioned building new ones in the suburbs. Without extant suburban civic centers, commercial developers invented their own destination points by assembling land near expressway or interstate intersections, providing ample parking, and managing the environment for the many stores that leased space.

At first the development of regional shopping centers proceeded slowly across metropolitan America. Less than two dozen had been constructed by the mid-1950s. Congressional passage of an accelerated depreciation deduction for new building in the 1954 Internal Revenue Code stimulated investment in shopping centers as tax shelters. Nearly 250 centers were constructed in the next decade.

By containing branch department stores and a large variety of specialty shops, the new regional shopping centers competed with city retail districts, especially downtown. Because these centers were privately managed properties, developers could eradicate the dirt, noise, chaos, ethnic diversity, and perceived danger of downtown. In 1956 the first climate-controlled, indoor mall opened near Minneapolis. Private ownership not only controlled the environment but also regulated the social character of what masqueraded as public space. Mall security could keep out undesirables like vagrants or panhandlers, and as a series of court cases confirmed, shopping-center owners could also limit the exercise of free speech by banning protests. Developers sometimes provided community meeting facilities for acceptable functions. Thus, the regional shopping center through its commercial and community functions filled, albeit inadequately, the void of civic centers in the suburbs. Suburban towns could preserve the class and racial composition of both neighborhoods and commercial spaces, which appealed to middle-class white residents.

Older Central Cities

The economic restructuring, government policies, and demographic trends, all of which favored rapid suburban growth, challenged the viability of central cities. Manufacturers and wholesalers eager to expand into modern horizontal plants found few adequate undeveloped sites in the city and bridled under the growing traffic congestion that frustrated their shift from rail to truck transportation. Suburban industrial parks offered attractive solutions to these problems. Downsized and closed plants diminished the cities' manufacturing employment. By the early 1960s Detroit had lost more than 100,000 manufacturing jobs. Philadelphia's manufacturing employment skidded by 25 percent as metal, textile, garment, and chemical industries reduced their workforces or left the city. Civic leaders scrambled to retain factories with land and tax incentives as well as improved highways, but they could not reverse the decline.

While older industrial corridors and districts, often adjacent to central business districts, deteriorated, downtowns also underwent a transition that diminished their preeminent positions in metropolitan areas. Merchants faced pressures similar to those that confronted manufacturers: older buildings, traffic congestion, high taxes, and suburban competition. As downtown retail sales plummeted, many stores, even some department stores once hallmarks of downtown, closed or downsized by the 1970s. Further, the marked increase in travel by airplane and automobile at the expense of railroad passenger service, coupled with the rise of national motel chains such as Holiday Inn along interstate highways, undermined the vitality of elegant hotels and grand central train stations. In turn, downtown entertainment venues were hurt by the declining numbers of shoppers and intercity travelers, as well as by competition from new suburban movie theaters. Closed department stores and movie theaters along with underused railroad terminals and hotels gave downtowns a tawdry appearance.

But not all the news was bad for downtowns. The long-term shift in the American economy from blue-collar employment to white-collar administrative and professional services and government jobs generated increased demand for offices. The heightened importance of the exchange of information in the economy kept many office activities concentrated in downtowns, where face-to-face communications and prestigious addresses were available. These functions kept alive "deal-making" venues like businessmen's clubs and restaurants. Although few skyscrapers were built in the first decade after the war, favorable tax policies, urban redevelopment, and the corporate penchant for advertising their prestige spawned a new generation of shining towers after the mid-1950s. Eschewing the ornamentation of skyscrapers built before the war, architects embraced the minimalist, functional style of modernism. By the end of the 1960s simple, modestly tall glass and metal boxes populated most downtowns alongside the ornate masonry behemoths of earlier eras. Despite this redevelopment, the narrowing function of downtown toward offices, which resulted in diminishing street life in the evenings and on weekends, and the unmistakable signs of disinvestment aggravated the central city's sense of embattlement in the 1960s.

In spite of the shift in growth from the urban core to the periphery, the rural migration to central cities, which had resumed with wartime industrial production, continued unabated for 20 years after the war, furthering the reorganization of the metropolitan social geography begun decades earlier. White Appalachian families sought the factory jobs of the midwestern cities, while Puerto Ricans moved to New York, Philadelphia, and Chicago (fig. 19.3). Mexicans and Cubans created substantial communities in southern California cities and Miami, respectively. As was true earlier in the century, African Americans made up the largest proportion of this migration. The more than 5 million African Americans who migrated between 1940 and 1970 hoped to enjoy high-paying industrial work, improved housing, and better civil rights than they experienced in the South. As a result of this migration and the suburban relocation of many white families, the African American proportion of central-city populations rose markedly. African Americans formed a majority of the population of Newark, Atlanta, and Washington by 1970 and approached half of the populations of Detroit, Baltimore, St. Louis, Richmond, Birmingham, and New Orleans.

The adopted cities of these migrants rarely lived up to their expectations. African Americans arrived as the transformation of the urban economy, especially disinvestment in manufacturing in the central city, diminished the number of well-paying, secure jobs and increased the resolve of white, often union, workers to defend their industrial niches. Discrimination by employers further constrained the employment opportunities of African Americans. Many states and cities passed fair-employment legislation, but inadequate penalties and enforcement rendered them ineffective.

If the deteriorating employment situation stifled economic aspirations, housing conditions clearly delineated for many African Americans the racial inequalities of American cities. Despite the filtering down of housing sold by white families moving to the suburbs, the long-standing substandard conditions of low-income housing worsened under the burden of too many poor migrants. Moreover, residential segregation hemmed African Americans and other minority newcomers into specific neighborhoods, which only expanded beyond their informal racial perimeters at rates unable to accommodate the influx.

Real estate brokers, loan providers, federal housing officials, and white residents all tried to preserve the racial composition of neighborhoods. In 1948 the Supreme Court ended restrictive covenants on deeds prohibiting the sale of houses to specific social groups. However, this decision proved to be a hollow victory for integrationists. The continuation of discriminatory redlining policies by the FHA and local

Figure 19.3 Overcrowded Poor White Housing, Chicago
(Courtesy National Archives and Records Administration)

banks limited African Americans' access to credit and discouraged builders from operating in minority sections of the city. Zoning restrictions for many neighborhoods set minimum lot sizes and architectural standards out of the reach of minorities or prohibited multifamily occupancy. White real estate agents refused African American brokers access to listings in white areas and would not show houses in these communities to minority buyers. White neighborhood protective associations, sometimes backed by racial hate groups like the Ku Klux Klan, vigilantly guarded against incursions by unwanted groups.

The dynamics of the real estate market would not, however, allow racially determined residential patterns to remained fixed. White resistance to African American newcomers in their neighborhoods faced the problems of demographic change and white flight's downward pressures on housing values. Young families departing for the suburbs left behind aging and often poorer residents, sapping the vitality of many ethnic neighborhoods and, in white residents' view, diminishing their ability to hold off African American buyers. Other families fled their old neighborhoods because of federally mandated school integration or the first sign of racial change, anticipating declining property values. Absentee owners of slum housing and real estate agencies profited handsomely from racial change, often with the cooperation of public officials. In the practice known as blockbusting, unscrupulous real estate agents induced white flight and racial change by spreading fear of African American buyers, buying cheaply houses that were put on the market in a panic and selling them at higher prices to new, minority owners, to whom they extended mortgage money. Thus, African American demand, the suburban lure, white fear, and the real estate industry fostered expansion of African American residential areas.

White residents contested racial transition. Political and physical conflicts frequently erupted at minority penetration of neighborhood frontiers. Some white communities with modest residential turnover and substantial political power withstood racial pressure. However, others failed to keep out minorities, and the second ghetto emerged in most cities, larger than the prewar African American ghettos but still overcrowded and poor. Residential discrimination remained so virulent that middle-class minorities who escaped poor residential areas still resided in racially segregated communities.

Public policy was also deeply implicated in the emergence of the second ghetto during the postwar era. In the face of disinvestment and racial change, civic leaders, with the support of the federal government, dusted off redevelopment ideas hatched during the 1930s and 1940s and set about renewing their cities' economies and physical environments. Businessmen and politicians agreed that slum clearance would stop the spread of urban disinvestment or blight and create undeveloped acreage, which, along with new expressways, would allow central cities to compete with suburbs. Redevelopment would follow. Pro-growth coalitions of civic leaders targeted for renewal the deteriorating sections of central business districts and adjacent older neighborhoods usually occupied by poor ethnic and African American communities. Demolition in these central locations, it was believed, would remove the blight that created negative perceptions of downtown, diminish congestion that prevented adequate accessibility and parking, and open up land for new businesses, entertainment venues, and middle-class housing. The fate of former residents was only a secondary concern, for they were viewed as part of the problem.

Many states passed enabling legislation for urban renewal during the 1940s, which encouraged a few cities, such as Pittsburgh and St. Louis, to begin redevelopment. Congress's passage of the 1949 Housing Act made federal financial resources available to local redevelopment authorities, which assembled land parcels, cleared them, and resold them to developers primarily for residential construction. This legislation stimulated little redevelopment because local leaders were more interested in enhancing downtowns than in solving housing problems.

By shifting the emphasis from housing to commercial redevelopment, the Housing Act of 1954 and an amendment in 1959 released the enormous energies for redeveloping central business areas, which had been gathering for more than two decades. Within ten years, hundreds of urban renewal projects bulldozed innumerable old buildings, clearing thousands of acres of land. With great fanfare Baltimore, Boston, Atlanta, Cleveland, and other cities unveiled plans for luxury apartments, skyscrapers, stores, hotels, parking garages, and cultural and sports facilities on formerly obsolete waterfronts or in adjacent rundown manufacturing areas and neighborhoods. Moreover, cities used funds authorized under the 1956 federal Interstate Highway Act to build expressways into and around downtowns (fig. 19.4). High-speed access for automobiles to downtown, modernistic glass skyscrapers, expansive landscaped streetscapes, and new amenities all projected an image that older central cities had regained the vitality they had had at the century's beginning.

Although federal support mostly underwrote downtown redevelopment, low-income housing was not entirely neglected. Cities took advantage of public housing funding to erect thousands of public housing units. Working under modernistic strictures and striving to contain costs, housing authorities built austere apartment blocks and towers set in expansive open spaces, which were set apart from surrounding neighborhood stores and services (fig. 19.5). The Pruitt-Igoe complex in St. Louis, for example, contained 33 11-story apartment buildings. The scale, verticality, and isolation of such housing projects made them worlds unto themselves apart from the larger community.

In public housing's early years, before the mid-1950s, housing managers emphasized the selection of married couples with children who could pay the subsidized rents. They enforced rules for appropriate behavior and maintained the grounds. Residents felt lucky to have escaped the city's slums, and communities formed within the projects. Reformers' aspirations for public housing seemed achievable for a time. Freed from the private market, public housing provided safe and sanitary, though spare, shelter

Figure 19.4 Expressway Cutting through Downtown Miami
(Courtesy National Archives and Records Administration)

that offered a way station for families to husband their resources in a positive environment before moving on to better housing.

By the mid-1950s, however, housing reformers were beginning to despair for the future of public housing. Political priorities undermined their goal of rejuvenating neighborhoods with large, well-designed projects. Local officials often used public housing to keep African American populations segregated. City housing authorities, operating under the auspices of the U.S. Housing Authority, retained responsibility for the location and design of public housing projects. Since white home owners often resisted placement of public housing projects in their neighborhoods, municipal officials found it politically acceptable to concentrate housing projects in minority neighborhoods and other areas where white communities were not threatened. Moreover, by using public housing as a means to make urban renewal palatable in targeted neighborhoods, politicians sacrificed community rebuilding for expeditious and inexpensive housing. Renewal-site residents, including those in dysfunctional households, gained precedence for occupancy over working families. Housing managers were also pressured to enforce maximum income limits, removing successful families. The proportion of residents on welfare markedly increased. Accordingly, public housing lost the way-station function for low-income working families and became warehouses for the poorest residents. By the 1960s, many public housing projects were underfunded, poorly maintained, dangerous, and unhealthy.

These hard-won public policies for urban reform—slum clearance, redevelopment, public housing, and new expressways—were ushered in with high expectations and implemented on a large scale, but they did not inoculate the cities against either serious social and economic problems or the suburban challenge. Governmental programs may have slowed down the decay of the central business district, but they also exacerbated the sores of class and race, which were embedded in the inequalities of American urban life. Urban renewal and expressway construction demolished vast swaths of poor inner-city neighborhoods under the banner of eradicating blight. Although some white neighborhoods also experienced demolition, the devastation of African American communities was so exten-

sive that critics referred to urban renewal as "negro removal." In some instances, civic leaders deliberately used slum clearance as a means to relocate ghettos, not simply as a way to assemble developable sites. Expressways sliced communities into two parts, isolating them from each other as well as from other areas of the city. Some renewal sites remained underdeveloped for years and accelerated disinvestment in the neighborhoods. Public housing, promised to those dislocated by slum clearance, was either unable to accommodate all of those removed or was completed too late for the residents' use. In short, federally subsidized redevelopment often destroyed the social fabric of communities, hastened disinvestment, and forced already burgeoning African American populations to expand ghetto boundaries into resistant neighborhoods.

In the 1960s, white and African American communities increasingly protested urban renewal proposals for demolition of their neighborhoods. Neighborhood associations demanded participation in the planning process. Critics such as Jane Jacobs detested the sterile, modernistic streetscapes and pointed out that the

Figure 19.5 Stateway Gardens High-Rise Public Housing Project, Chicago
(Courtesy National Archives and Records Administration)

loss of pedestrian-friendly public spaces and small businesses robbed cities of their vitality. White working-class and minority groups objected to top-down planning that favored corporate and commercial interests over neighborhood communities.

The inequalities of income and power were vividly reflected in postwar planning. By the mid-1960s, white working-class city communities felt embattled by liberals promoting integration and pro-growth coalitions focused on downtown redevelopment. African Americans were exasperated by discrimination in employment, education, and housing as well as by the glaring disparities between thriving white suburbs and their deteriorating city neighborhoods. Intensified by the national civil rights movement, these frustrations erupted in violent protests, the burning of African American neighborhoods, and massive looting. The charred remains of many inner-city neighborhoods starkly testified to the 20th century's persistent, growing inequalities between whites and African Americans expressed in the uneven spatial development of metropolitan areas.

THE POSTINDUSTRIAL METROPOLIS

The urban riots of the 1960s spurred the federal government to act. The dramatic images of violence, looting, and burning on television rallied political support for antipoverty and antiracism programs designed to raise the incomes of poor families; remove racial barriers to housing, employment, education, and political rights; invest in people's education and occupational skills; and rebuild the inner cities. These social welfare and civil rights programs effected some positive results, if not the satisfactory solutions that political rhetoric trumpeted. Federal programs that replaced urban renewal—Model Cities and 1970s block grants—underwrote many infrastructure and redevelopment projects, but they failed to reverse the central city's general decline in retailing, manufacturing, and even the proportion of offices. In fact, with rising political power in the 1970s, the suburbs attracted the thrust of federal policy at the expense of central cities.

Economic and social trends long at work and continued governmental subsidies for suburbanization heightened the rapid development of ur-

ban peripheries and continued to erode the central city's vitality in the last third of the century. Persistent deindustrialization in northern cities shuttered the remaining "smokestack" factories, which had once dominated waterfronts and railroad corridors of the city and older inner suburbs, and with them went their well-paying union jobs. While mass-production plants did not disappear entirely from the urban economy, smaller flexible, batch-oriented operators became more prevalent. The new manufacturing industries emphasized a dual labor force of highly skilled occupations and unskilled, routinized jobs. Service industries such as business and financial services, entertainment, retailing, personal services, education, and health care, which grew rapidly, also employed a dual workforce. Further, large corporations broke the tradition of long-term secure employment and eliminated thousands of jobs in management and labor as a result of mergers, new communication and computing technologies, and shareholder demands to produce greater profits. Thus, the urban economy was becoming more polarized between upper- and lower-income occupations with diminishing proportions of secure blue- and white-collar, lower-middle-income positions, particularly for those with limited education.

New social patterns both affected and responded to these economic changes. Households diminished in size as people married later, separated more frequently, and had fewer children. Contributing to this phenomenon were rising numbers of working women; the elderly, who were living longer on average; and persons choosing alternative lifestyles to the traditional nuclear family. Moreover, as the postwar baby boomers obtained positions of power and responsibility, they heartily embraced consumption and leisure while turning away from the family-centered ethnic and religious central-city communities or postwar suburban neighborhoods of their parents' generation. These young urban professionals splurged their new wealth on huge homes, fancy cars, exclusive vacations, and upscale entertainment. At the same time, immigration resumed, notably among Hispanic and Asian peoples. By the 1980s, American cities, with the exception of some older Rustbelt ones such as Buffalo and Pittsburgh, once again experienced large numbers of non-English-speaking newcomers crowding older residential areas, filling low-paying jobs, and tackling small-scale entrepreneurial ventures. Paradoxically, African American populations, which were finally achieving some political power, including mayoralty offices, and expecting the associated economic rewards, faced competition from immigrants for jobs, housing, and power. Finally, the political ascendancy of conservatism at the end of the 1970s renewed an emphasis on individualism and the perceived efficiencies of the private market and thus challenged the legitimacy of large government and the social welfare state.

The spatial outcomes of these social and economic trends extended long-standing geographical patterns and worked new developments altogether. Most familiar was the continued development of single-family, detached housing in suburban subdivisions. However, both suburban populations and the landscape became more diverse as singles, minorities, the elderly, and even some new immigrants sought residences there. These groups new to suburbia generally melded into the residential landscape, but dense town-house developments and large retirement complexes also arose to accommodate limited budgets and smaller households. Once isolated in exclusive residential areas positioned well beyond easy access from the city or industrial suburbs, wealthy families perceived a loss of security in this automobile age and sought refuge in gated communities. Walls and security guards created protective cocoons around expensive housing developments, which often included golf courses or marinas.

The more diverse suburban landscape did not remedy the paucity of tight-knit social communities. Postmodern society's emphasis on individualism and materialism, along with increased numbers of working women, exacerbated the community-less character of subdivision designs, automobile orientation, and dependence on new communications technologies. By the 1980s increasing traffic congestion; crime, especially among adolescents; and endless sprawl led to political pressure for recreational facilities and parks, preservation of wooded and open lands, and control over development. These demands revived long-standing conflicts between private market and communitarian impulses. Appalled by suburbia's deteriorating quality of life and sensing opportunity, some planners and developers proposed new

designs that derived inspiration from past communities such as Riverside (Illinois), Radburn, and Columbia. Nostalgically referencing selected features of 19th-century small towns, these new community builders, sometimes called "new urbanists," planned town centers, accommodated pedestrians, slowed down motor vehicles, provided for outdoor recreation, and controlled development. Generally serving higher-income households, requiring changes in entrenched zoning codes that facilitated suburban sprawl, and needing considerable capital, these new urban communities are still few in number and not yet clearly capable of replacing sprawling suburbs.

The growth of commercial activities greatly intensified at high-access intersections of circumferential beltways and primary radial arteries and interstate highways. While the distinction between suburban office and industrial parks blurred as both activities located in the same campuslike settings, the amount of office space mushroomed and challenged the total square footage in the downtowns of older cities, while surpassing it in the newer Sunbelt metropolises. Corporate headquarters and professional business services joined routine, back-office functions, which had gravitated in previous years to the suburbs for lower costs and access to female labor. Some corporations built offices on spacious landscaped grounds, but other firms located in clusters of office buildings amid parking lots, public transit, and services common to downtowns. With airlines capturing nearly all intercity and international travel, airports became locational magnets for office functions, cargo-handling firms, and some kinds of manufacturers. Highway corridors between downtowns and airports as well as intersections with good access to airports were particularly popular locations for businesses. As a result of this suburban office growth, the flow of commuters from suburb to suburb after the 1970s often exceeded the traditional suburb-to-central-city movement.

With most metropolitan growth in employment and population occurring beyond the central city and older suburbs, retailers increased their commitment to shopping malls, high-access nodes, and arterial corridors in the outer ring of suburbs. The number of shopping centers and malls tripled between the mid-1960s and the mid-1980s. Mall sizes increased as well.

Specialty, "big-box" retailers of appliances, furniture, linens, hardware, and office supplies built huge stores outside the malls, while restaurants, movie complexes, and hotels deepened the suburban market. Together, the sprawling retail complexes, office clusters, and entertainment activities, including professional sports arenas and stadiums, set amid a sea of housing subdivisions and condominium developments created virtual cities in their own right, where people lived, worked, and recreated without going to central cities. This new suburban landscape at the end of the 20th century extended over several counties of a metropolitan area and had multiple centers of employment and activity, dubbed "edge cities" by Joel Garreau, linked together by a network of expressways.

The flood of investment to the suburbs magnified the plight of central cities. The urban riots of the 1960s, deteriorating public schools, and declining economic bases spurred more white flight. Central-city populations fell across the nation, tax bases eroded, and public services deteriorated. Civil rights legislation in the 1960s, opening up employment and housing, allowed some middle-income minorities to join the exodus to the suburbs.

The African American population remaining in the city was generally poor and, with the collapse of manufacturing, less able to obtain secure, reasonably paid work. Mass transit failed to provide access to suburban jobs. Inadequate educational attainment left many inner-city residents ill equipped for the postindustrial, technologically advanced economy. Poor minority populations became isolated from the urban mainstream because they were increasingly dependent on low-paying, dead-end service jobs or welfare; had lost middle-class leaders, who were moving to the suburbs; and were concentrated in public housing projects or older slum housing. Rising numbers of single-female-headed households placed children in extreme poverty. Homeless people and street beggars proliferated. This inner-city underclass was vulnerable to drugs and prone to crime, which intensified the burden of welfare and white America's fear. Crime and the media's exploitation of it widened the gap between city and suburb.

Some people, however, disliked the suburban environment or would not conform to its social constraints. Despite its drawbacks, the city still had advantages in cultural institutions, high-quality older houses, and pedestrian neighborhoods. Neighborhood associations and development councils worked tirelessly to nourish their communities, although city officials stubbornly maintained their focus on downtown areas. Wealthy neighborhoods had the financial resources and political clout to fend off blight. Designating buildings and districts as historically significant was a favorite defensive strategy for neighborhood conservation. Young, often childless professionals, artistic folks, and gays and lesbians rehabilitated neglected row houses and lofts of former commercial buildings in unfashionable neighborhoods. In a process called "gentrification," individuals or developers rehabilitated run-down buildings and either resided in them or sold them for handsome profits. Gentrification not only displaced building occupants but also drove away elderly and poorer residents who could not afford rising property taxes. City officials encouraged this change in neighborhood social composition as the price of retaining or attracting middle-income taxpayers. These elite professional and alternative neighborhoods mirrored in their contrast to underclass ghettos the polarization of the city's economy.

Hispanic and Asian immigrants reclaimed central neighborhoods or moved to older suburbs in many cities. Like European immigrants a century earlier, they overcrowded residences and opened neighborhood shops. In cities like New York and Los Angeles the immigrants, sometimes illegally in the country, often toiled in sweatshops. The neighborhoods took on specific immigrant cultural identities, so that the presence of ethnic restaurants, street vendors, and diverse languages enriched the city landscape and attractions.

In the late 1970s, downtown interests shifted their redevelopment strategies. Continued corporate preference for prestigious locations underwrote a new wave of office towers, this time sporting playful ornamentation inspired by earlier-20th-century skyscrapers. Federal grant programs supported these new offices, but tax incentives for restoring historic commercial buildings also leveraged private capital for more redevelopment. Historic rehabilitation recognized the significance of pedestrian-friendly, visually diverse, and energetic environments. City hall and downtown business associations

Figure 19.6 Chess Game, Fountain Square, Downtown Cincinnati
(Courtesy National Archives and Records Administration)

worked to enliven the stark modernist, postwar landscape with street furnishings, sidewalk vendors, outdoor dining, and refurbished park spaces (fig. 19.6). Finally, a few cities even turned to new or expanded subway and light-rail mass transit systems.

Civic leaders believed they had a competitive advantage over suburbs in entertainment for the metropolitan population and tourists. Partnerships between city government and private developers converted old central waterfronts into festive complexes of stadiums, convention centers, hotels, shops, and cultural institutions such as aquariums and historical museums. They included upscale apartments, waterfront trails, marinas (if feasible), and landscaped parks (fig. 19.7). A few cities bet on casinos to generate development. City partnerships with nonprofit organizations staged grand celebrations for New Year's Eve or the Fourth of July and programmed attractions such as regattas and arts festivals all year long. These new developments gave older downtowns a distinctive metropolitan function once again and reinvigorated central business areas. Critics doubted that the low-paying service jobs produced by tourist services

and entertainment represented the best use of huge public investments as a solution to inner-city income disparities. For many cities of the Sunbelt, such as Phoenix and Charlotte, which experienced most of their growth since the 1950s, downtowns remained only modest commercial complexes, despite concerted public investment, one among others in the metropolitan area.

CONCLUSION

At the end of the 20th century, new technologies of transportation and communication, deep-rooted preferences for single detached homes on private lots, governmental policies favoring new greenfield construction, and the persistent divisions by class, race, and the ethnicity of new immigrants have created a sprawling metropolitan landscape of such overwhelming dimensions that even the "visionaries" of the 1920s, who worried about the implications of unchecked suburban growth, could not have imagined it. While elements of the earlier industrial metropolis remain visible in the landscapes of older cities, the newer cities of the Sunbelt South and West seemed to be different geographical entities. The older cities retain vestiges of having once been centered and hierarchical in spatial organization, but these newer cities that experienced their growth primarily in the second half of the 20th century are polycentric and unbounded, in the words of Carl Abbott. They are a collection of independent suburban realms sewn together by expressways into a metropolitan quilt. The suburban peripheries of older cities have increasingly taken on a similar composition.

Much like those who wrote about the problems of unplanned metropolitan growth in the 1920s, contemporary critics derogatorily define the new urban form as suburban sprawl with unacceptable economic, social, and environmental costs. The enormous land consumption, dependence on the automobile, air pollution, high service costs, related disinvestment in older built-up areas, especially in the central cities, and the subsequent isolation of the poor are, in this view, not sustainable over the long term. Even some suburbanites have become alarmed

at the deterioration of their quality of life and lack of a sense of community. Young professionals and older families whose children have grown up look to the central city or specially designed new towns for convenient cultural amenities; a more pedestrian lifestyle; greater facilities for outdoor recreation, such as bike trails; and in some instances a more diverse social composition. Those seeking an alternative to suburban sprawl propose urban-growth boundaries, greenways, increased use of light-rail transit, higher-density housing, and pedestrian-friendly designs that promote a sense of community among neighbors. Portland, Oregon, is seen as a model of a city instituting regional planning to attain these goals, while new towns like Seaside and Celebration, both in Florida, are models for building from scratch. Just as the new automobile-oriented suburbs and retail facilities of the 1920s, along with inner-city racial ghettos, signaled emerging urban forms that would transform the industrial metropolis, these contemporary alternatives to suburban sprawl may foreshadow the changing urban geography of the 21st century.

Figure 19.7 Inner Harbor Redevelopment Area, Downtown Baltimore
(Courtesy National Archives and Records Administration)

ADDITIONAL READING

Abbott, C. 1993. *The Metropolitan Frontier: Cities in the Modern American West.* Tucson: University of Arizona Press.

Bauman, J. F. 1987. *Public Housing, Race, and Renewal: Urban Planning in Philadelphia, 1920–1974.* Philadelphia: Temple University Press.

Bernard, R. M., and B. R. Rice. 1983. *Sunbelt Cities: Politics and Growth since World War II.* Austin: University of Texas Press.

Bottles, S. L. 1987. *Los Angeles and the Automobile: The Making of the Modern City.* Berkeley and Los Angeles: University of California Press.

Fishman, R. 1977. *Urban Utopias in the 20th Century: Ebenezer Howard, Frank Lloyd Wright, and Le Corbusier.* New York: Basic Books.

Ford, L. R. 1994. *Cities and Buildings: Skyscrapers, Skid Rows, and Suburbs.* Baltimore: Johns Hopkins University Press..

Garreau, J. 1991. *Edge City: Life on the New Frontier.* New York: Doubleday.

Harris, R. 1996. *Unplanned Suburbs: Toronto's American Tragedy, 1900–1950.* Baltimore: Johns Hopkins University Press.

Harvey, D. 1989. *The Condition of Postmodernity: An Enquiry into the Origins of Cultural Change.* London: Basil Blackwell.

Hirsch, A. R. 1983. *Making the Second Ghetto: Race and Housing in Chicago, 1940–1960.* London: Cambridge University Press.

Hise, G. 1997. *Magnetic Los Angeles: Planning the 20th-Century Metropolis.* Baltimore: Johns Hopkins University Press.

Jackson, K. T. 1985. *Crabgrass Frontier: The Suburbanization of the United States.* New York: Oxford University Press.

Jacobs, J. 1961. *The Death and Life of Great American Cities.* New York: Random House.

Kunstler, J. H. 1993. *The Geography of Nowhere: The Rise and Decline of America's Man-Made Landscape.* New York: Simon & Schuster.

Lemann, N. 1991. *The Promised Land: The Great Black Migration and How It Changed America.* New York: Alfred A. Knopf.

Lemon, J. T. 1996. *Liberal Dreams and Nature's Limits: Great Cities of North America since 1600.* New York: Oxford University Press.

Lubove, R. 1963. *Community Planning in the 1920s: The Contribution of the Regional Planning Association of America.* Pittsburgh: University of Pittsburgh Press.

Longstreth, R. 1997. *City Center to Regional Mall: Architecture, the Automobile, and Retailing in Los Angeles, 1920–1950.* Cambridge: MIT Press.

Massey, D. S., and N. A. Denton. 1993. *American Apartheid: Segregation and the Making of the Underclass.* Cambridge: Harvard University Press.

Relph, E. 1987. *The Modern Urban Landscape.* Baltimore: Johns Hopkins University Press.

Scott, M. 1969. *American City Planning since 1890.* Berkeley and Los Angeles: University of California Press.

Teaford, J. C. 1990. *The Rough Road to Renaissance: Urban Revitalization in America, 1940–1985.* Baltimore: Johns Hopkins University Press.

20

Canadian Cities in a North American Context

RICHARD S. HARRIS

Americans think very little about Canada, and even less about Canadian cities. On April 10, 1997, Prime Minister Jean Chrétien visited Washington, D.C. This was headline news only in Canada. Indeed, commenting on news coverage south of the border, the front page of the Toronto Sun in effect asked "Jean Who?" Lakes, mountains, and snow loom large in Americans' composite image of Canada, while cities lie, at best, in the middle distance. As a result, the great majority of Americans who have written about U.S. cities—their history, growth, character, plight, and prospects—have hardly ever thought to use the Canadian experience as a point of reference. In contrast, exposed daily to American media and products, Canadians are obsessed by their southern neighbors. English Canadians define their culture in relation (and in opposition) to that of the United States. (Quebecers are another story.) Those who have written about Canadian cities have found it natural to conceptualize Canadian cities in terms of American models, notably those developed by Burgess, Hoyt, Harris, and Ullman. Some have found it useful to compare and contrast the two national experiences, and recently James Lemon has suggested that this can throw light not only on the Canadian experience but also on the American. This comparative perspective, which this chapter seeks to develop, can be fruitful.

One reason for making comparisons is that, when brought into the open, they may be found wanting. For example, when levels of home ownership and residential densities are compared, it turns out that the experience of U.S., Canadian, and Australian cities is very similar. Indeed, responding to the suggestion of Kenneth Jackson, a prominent American urban historian, that the United States was the first suburban nation, the Australian historian Graeme Davison has argued that that dubious honor belongs more properly to Australia. Similar questions may be raised about the interpretation of urban ethnicity. Americans have thought of their nation as the land of opportunity for the huddled masses of Europe and, more recently, Latin America and Asia. They have treated the ethnic neighborhood as a prominent and distinctive element of the urban scene. But immigration has figured at least as prominently in the history of Canada, Australia, and New Zealand (fig. 20.1). Relative to its population, Canada now takes in twice as many immigrants as the United States. In several important respects, then, American cities and suburbs have not been so unique after all. Even when explicit comparisons do not overthrow established assumptions, they can at least qualify and clarify them. Stereotypically, Americans have thought of their cities as melting pots, while Canadians (at least in recent years) have preferred to speak of theirs as urban mosaics. Comparative research has not dismissed these stereotypes altogether, but it has certainly modified them considerably. In adopting a comparative frame of reference, then, I try to illuminate not only the Canadian urban experience but also the American.

The obvious procedure for comparing Canadian and U.S. cities is to review similarities and differences in turn, as these have evolved over time. As it happens, the several alternative interpretations of urban development in Canada that scholars have offered have tended to emphasize these respective dimensions. Most notably, a "continental" view has assumed and emphasized national similarities; a "nationalist" perspective, the differences. A third, less coherent, "regional" interpretation has raised questions about whether continent or nation are appropriate frames of reference. A fourth, which I label "convergence," is more historical in character and reconciles the other three, in part by reconstructing them. Each of these interpretations is incomplete. Even the convergent view leaves some matters unresolved. Collectively, however, they refer to all major aspects of urban development in Canada. After sketching a framework for considering these aspects, I examine them through a discussion of these four interpretative frameworks.

Figure 20.1 British immigrants arriving in Toronto, 1912. (Courtesy City of Toronto Archives)

A FRAMEWORK

In order to make comparisons, one needs a framework. Historical urban geographers tend to see cities through the prism of landscape and morphology, understanding that the built environment and the geographical patterning of urban areas reflect a combination of economic, social, political, and cultural forces. The relative weight attached to these forces has shifted over time. A recent resurgence of interest in cultural issues has focused new attention on the issues of gender, race, sexual orientation, and cultural identity. Even so, most writers agree that in understanding the growth and form of cities in Canada, as elsewhere, economic forces are fundamental.

The growth of cities depends upon jobs and investment. Toronto has grown at the expense of Montreal for much of the 20th century because more companies have found it advantageous to locate there. Within any metropolitan area, where job growth occurs—downtown, at the fringe, in clusters, or in a scattered fashion—depends upon what types of jobs are being created (or lost). Companies have usually found that for manufacturing, as opposed to office functions, a suburban location is the most profitable. In cities like Hamilton (Ontario) and Pittsburgh, dominated by capital-intensive manufacturing industry, jobs decentralized quite early (fig. 20.2). In cities like Toronto and New York, with a good deal of employment in labor-intensive industries (notably garments), as well as in public administration, finance, and other head offices, employment for many decades remained more centralized.

Economic processes determine not only a city's growth and form, but also its social geography. Where jobs go, people follow. Workers concentrated close to their workplaces, and this was especially true before World War II, when most people commuted on foot or by transit. In cities as large as Montreal and Toronto this was even true for centrally located workplaces, accessible by transit from large parts of the urban area. Clustered labor sheds were especially apparent in industrial suburbs and satellite towns, which were inaccessible from further afield. Society and culture influence such economic processes, sometimes powerfully. In particular, ethnicity, race, and gender help to form the city's social geography. First-generation immigrants have usually preferred to cluster with

Figure 20.2 The New Suburban Works of the Montreal Locomotive and Machine Company, 1905
(From E. Chambers, *The Book of Canada,* 1905, p. 69)

others who share the same language, religion, and tastes. This clustering was true even for those who differed only in minor ways from the host society. Until the middle of the 20th century, most immigrants to Canada came from the British Isles. Given the strong British influence on Canadian culture—in terms of language, food, mores, religion, and political institutions—"Brits" differed only in subtle ways from their hosts. Even so, and for at least a decade or so after arrival, many clustered in specific districts, often at the suburban fringe. In Toronto they soon moved beyond city limits to parts of York Township that became known as "Little Britain," "Picadilly," and "Earlscourt." In Winnipeg, while eastern European immigrants clustered in the North End, many of the British made their home in Elmwood. On the west coast they helped to make South Vancouver an immigrant workers' suburb.

Segregation, of course, has not always been a matter of choice alone. Even British immigrants to Canada faced some discrimination in the early decades of the 20th century. This was especially true of the English, who were resented for their superior attitude toward "colonials." Taking its cue from a job advertisement seen in a Toronto store window, a book published in London in 1909 cautioned prospective immigrants with the title *No English Need Apply.* Other immigrants faced more severe racism. The Chinese, in particular, were for some decades treated as barely human. In Toronto they were the only ethnic group that the makers of the annual city directory did not deign to list. In Vancouver, where they were relatively numerous, they were compelled to concentrate in a "Chinatown" and subjected to various humiliations. Other groups—Jews, Italians, and, in the interwar years, eastern Europeans—clustered voluntarily but also as a means of defense. For many the veneer of voluntariness was thin indeed. Until the practice was declared illegal in the late 1940s, restrictive covenants shaped many residential areas. The Westdale area of Hamilton, Ontario, developed during the interwar years as a middle-income suburb, included covenants that excluded a long list of nationalities, among them "Negroes, Asiatics, Bulgarians, Austrians, Russians, Serbs, Rumanians, Turks, Armenians, whether British subjects or not." Such deed restrictions were probably quite common, at least in the "better" subdivisions.

Where immigrant groups concentrated in specific types of work, the location of the industry determined where the group would cluster. The best-documented example was the concentration of Toronto's Jewish population on either side of Spadina Avenue. After 1900, Jews rapidly made their way into the garment trade. This was Toronto's largest single industry, concentrated just west of the downtown, and Jews settled close by. In Winnipeg, eastern European immigrants swept into the city's North End, close to the rail yards where many worked. If cultural differences encouraged segregation, economic considerations helped to determine exactly where clustering occurred.

In ways that are only now being understood, the culture of gender has also shaped the social and economic geography of the city. We tend to think that only in recent years have large numbers of women entered the labor force. In fact, women commonly worked for pay in the 19th century, and in the first half of the 20th century young women worked until they married. Some immigrant districts, and small towns, relied upon women's paid labor. In such cases, gender roles and relations had to be adjusted, underlining their importance in daily life. When families moved to the suburbs, a more and more marked gender division of labor developed. Some women, usually employed daughters living at home, faced increasingly long commutes. For this reason, in the early part of the 20th century the journey to work of employed women rose more rapidly than that for employed men, many of whom walked to nearby jobs in newly decentralized factories. Most married women, however, were fully occupied keeping house and raising children, especially in unserviced suburbs where they worked hard to maintain basic standards of cleanliness. From the 1920s to the 1950s, suburban women did not usually have access to automobiles, and, where transit was meager, their "urban" experience was one of isolation. As the labor force participation rate of women increased steadily after 1945, however, a wider range of jobs became available to them in the suburbs. In some cases, companies set up in the suburbs to gain access to the new, and comparatively cheap, female labor pool. In this manner gender relations reflected and shaped the changing geography of Canadian urban areas. The character of Canada's urban experience can be understood within this loose framework of pattern and process, the economic influences of employment and transportation, and the cultural importance of class, ethnicity, and gender.

INTERPRETATIONS OF CANADIAN CITIES

Over the last quarter of the 20th century, Canadian scholars have tried to make sense of the nation's urban experience by comparing it with that of the United States. Some interpretations have been clearly articulated, while others have remained more fragmented. Taking some at face value and constructing others from a more dispersed literature, I discuss four views of the Canadian urban experience in the 20th century. The first of these has been labeled "continentalism." Three others I label "nationalist," "regionalist," and "convergent."

Continentalism

To outside observers, and especially to Europeans, Canadian and U.S. cities look very similar. To a degree that is still unusual in most of Europe, skyscrapers dominate all major North American cities. Beyond the central area, however, and especially in the postwar suburbs, densities are low. Land uses are segregated and are linked mainly by cars and trucks. Residential land use is clearly separated from commercial and industrial; further, each type of residential development is separated from the others, single-family homes from town houses and apartments, with still finer gradations among single-family dwellings in terms of lot size, service quality, and hence price. Moreover, the routine ownership of automobiles and quite large, single-family homes underlines the common affluence of these societies.

One of the more distinctive features of North American cities has been their ethnic diversity and the presence of ethnic enclaves. The latter usually took the form of the city neighborhood, although immigrant settlement at the fringe has always occurred. Recently, immigrant concentrations in suburbs have again become common, creating friction and attracting attention both in Canada and in the United States. The influx of Asian immigrants into American suburbs like Monterey Park, outside Los Angeles, has Canadian parallels in Markham, north of Toronto,

and Richmond, south of Vancouver. Along with Australia and New Zealand, Canada and the United States are two of the few countries that have a policy of actively attracting immigrants. Although there were periods in the 20th century of tightly controlled immigration to both countries, notably during the interwar years, in general immigrants have helped to make cities distinctive in their ethnic diversity.

Arguably, behind these similarities of pattern are comparable processes of settlement. Most importantly, and with few exceptions, land has long been regarded as a commodity to be bought and used by the highest bidder. The notion of inherited or common rights, legacies of feudalism in many European countries, has been alien. The economic logic of capitalism, manifested in the requirements of industry and commerce, has never been seriously challenged. Many writers have argued that, by European standards, land use planning is weak in both Canada and the United States. Certainly, no federal or local government has taken significant initiatives for urban development along the lines of Stockholm's land banking or Britain's postwar new-towns policy. In neither country has public, or publicly sponsored, co-op housing been seriously promoted as anything but a residual policy for the urban poor. The most spectacular examples of planned suburbs or towns have been private initiatives: Pullman, south of Chicago, for example, or the postwar suburb of Don Mills, outside Toronto. In other respects, the argument that both Canadian and American cities are unplanned can be misleading. The landscape and layout of postwar fringe development has been governed by precise and elaborate guidelines regarding such things as street widths, house setbacks from the street, and parking-to-floor-space ratios. More important than any supposed weakness of regulation in recent years has been the purpose that it has been designed to serve. Economic efficiency has been paramount. Planners and politicians have given in to the commercial logic of planned shopping centers, malls, and lately of "big box" retailing, regardless of the consequences for older commercial districts and especially inner cities. In the 1990s a groundswell of resistance to this logic coalesced under the rubric of the "new urbanism." Its advocates argue for a return to "traditional" forms of urban development: the street grid, high densities, tight controls over the automobile, a mixture of land uses, and development controls that stress size of structure rather than current use. It is not yet clear how influential this movement might become, but it seems to face equivalent challenges on both sides of the border. Late in the 1990s, one of the larger new urbanist projects on the continent is being planned for a suburb of Toronto. As its local proponents have emphasized, this project represents just as much a break with recent precedent in the Toronto area as it would in the suburbs of New York or Detroit.

These arguments represent the core of a continentalist interpretation of Canadian cities, which gained favor during the 1960s. It was implied in the use of American research and texts to illuminate the Canadian urban experience and was then made explicit in the early editions of Yeates and Garner's book *The North American City*. The authors drew examples of urban patterns and processes unequally, but indifferently, from north and south of the 49th parallel. They wrote of a weakly regulated, free land market that continent-wide was producing a low density of development and segregated land uses, together with class, ethnic, and racial segregation.

As long as the continentalist viewpoint remained implicit, it tended to assume that which in fact needed to be shown: that Canadian and U.S. cities were essentially similar. It also had to gloss over some obvious differences, the most notable being the unimportance of race as a factor in the social structure and geography of Canadian cities. As a result, it soon encountered critics.

The Nationalist View: Continentalism Challenged

During the 1960s there was a resurgence of English Canadian nationalism that defined itself in opposition to the United States. There was popular criticism of America's global role, notably in Vietnam, and also of the growing reach of American multinational corporations. Canadians had reason to be sensitive on this issue. Ever since the Canadian government established tariff barriers under the National Policy after 1879, American manufacturing companies had been establishing branch plants in Canada. In the Toronto and Hamilton region of southern On-

tario, companies like Kodak, Goodyear, Ford, Willys-Overland, Westinghouse, and Procter and Gamble had become major employers by the 1920s. These companies provided jobs, but the key investment decisions were made elsewhere. The 1920s was a crucial transitional decade. In 1922 the United States overtook Britain as Canada's main source of foreign investment and was soon the main destination of Canadian exports. After World War II, the British influence on Canadian life steadily waned, while the United States loomed larger. By 1961, almost 60 percent of all investment in manufacturing was not of Canadian origin; 44 percent was from the United States alone.

Both cultural and economic influences of the United States caused concern. The magnitude of U.S. investment was the immediate source of anxiety. Responding to popular pressure on the economic front, in 1971 the federal government established the Canada Development Corporation to promote investments by Canadians in Canadian companies, and two years later it created the Foreign Investment Review Agency to screen new foreign investment. Cultural imperialism also aroused opposition as American network television, as well as retail and fast food chains, made its presence felt. When African Americans rioted and American cities burned, Canadians looked on with growing concern. More and more Canadians felt that their country was being drawn into the American empire and a way of life about which growing numbers of Americans themselves felt uneasy.

From this groundswell of English Canadian nationalism, and as both the quantity and quality of research on Canadian cities developed during the 1970s and 1980s, there emerged an alternative to the continentalist view. Michael Goldberg and John Mercer spelled it out most fully in *The Myth of the North American City*. These writers—both of whom were immigrants, one from New York and the other from Glasgow—commented that in the 1960s the fashion had been "for Canadian urban policy analysts, of which there were painfully few back then, to think of Canadian cities and urban issues in American terms." This had struck them as "ludicrous" since "our initial travels around Canada and its cities failed to reveal urban dilemmas on any scale whatsoever that would begin to approximate the urban problems each of us had just left." Relying upon published surveys and statistics, they set out to demonstrate that Canadian cities were different.

Mercer and Goldberg accumulated quite impressive evidence. They showed that, on the average, Canadian cities were denser and that their residents relied more upon public transit while owning and using fewer cars. At the time that they wrote, inner-city poverty and the associated problems of crime and fiscal viability were not major issues in Canada, and indeed city-suburban income differences were minor. They pointed out that the ethnic and racial composition of Canadian cities had been very different from that of U.S. cities. Historically, the British numerically dominated until after World War II. In later decades, not only had there been many fewer Hispanics and blacks than in the United States, but most of the latter were recent immigrants from the Caribbean (fig. 20.3). On the average, Caribbean immigrants differed in terms of education and culture from African Americans, while slavery affected race relations in

Canada in only minor or indirect ways. The absence of census data on race made it impossible for Mercer and Goldberg to document racial segregation, but recent research has confirmed that, as expected, it is much less marked than in the United States. Most important of all, although the issue of race is at the heart of most debates about cities and urban policy in the United States, it is only one among many considerations in Canada and is rarely the most prominent.

Mercer and Goldberg also showed that Canadian cities were differently, and arguably better, governed. The proliferation of municipal governments and special-purpose service districts had become a notable feature of American metropolitan areas over the course of the 20th century. To some extent, the same trend had been apparent in Canada. For example when, after 1913, the City of Toronto stopped annexing new territory, a series of suburbs formed. Here, however, as elsewhere, the process did not proceed

Figure 20.3 Africville, in Halifax, Nova Scotia, just before it was cleared in the 1960s. (Courtesy Formac Publishing)

as rapidly or go as far as it has around many U.S. cities. Moreover, it has been fitfully countered by provincial efforts to create metropolitan institutions. Perhaps the best-known initiative was Ontario's 1954 establishment of metropolitan government for Toronto. This was widely credited for not only the efficient provision of services but also the equalization of resources among member municipalities. Important metro-level structures have been created for other major Canadian cities, including Ottawa, Montreal, Hamilton, Vancouver, and, most dramatically, Winnipeg's "Unicity," a single-level government for the whole metropolitan area. These initiatives have depended upon the fact that Canadian municipalities have no constitutional status and can readily be made, restructured, and unmade at the behest of provincial legislatures.

Some of the national contrasts in local government and city-suburban differences may have increased since Goldberg and Mercer first wrote. The Ontario provincial government has amalgamated local municipalities in the Toronto and Hamilton areas, despite strong local opposition. Because local governments have constitutional powers in the United States, states are not in a position to take such a high-handed approach. Indeed, in the United States the major trend of the past decade has been the increasing fragmentation of public powers through the formation of so-called shadow governments, whereby home owner associations manage planned subdivisions and circumvent the established structures of government. Many of these are associated with the emergence of gated communities. One of the more significant consequences of this trend has been to render even more difficult the transfer of funds from one district to another, exacerbating the fiscal problems of many inner cities, as well as poorer fringe areas. No equivalent trend has yet emerged in Canada.

On the issue of city-suburban differences it is too soon to say whether the Canadian advantage will grow, or even persist. One of the most widely discussed urban trends of the past three decades has been the gentrification of many inner-city neighborhoods. For some time gentrification seemed to have a relatively large impact on Canadian cities, most notably in Vancouver and Toronto, but also in Montreal, Halifax, and Calgary (fig. 20.4). Although a good deal has

been written on the subject, Larry Bourne in the 1990s introduced a cautionary note. He has emphasized that suburbanization is still the dominant trend in Canada, that Toronto and Vancouver are by no means typical, and that even in Toronto gentrification has done little more than stabilize average city incomes vis-à-vis the suburbs. The most recent evidence reported by John Mercer and Kim England suggests that Bourne may have a point. It indicates that, as recently as the 1980s, central cities in Canada were faring better in relation to their suburbs than their U.S. counterparts. In the early 1990s, however, this pattern was reversed.

Those who have acknowledged the cumulative weight of these Canadian-U.S. differences have generally preferred some sort of cultural explanation. Mercer and Goldberg themselves report survey evidence that apparently shows that Canadians are less competitive, more deferential, and more cautious and place a higher value on peace, order, and good government than do Americans. Like many others, they see this as part of Canada's British cultural and political legacy. Historical geographer James Lemon has developed this line of argument. In *Liberal Dreams and Nature's Limits: Great Cities of North America since 1600,* he takes the nationalist interpretation to a logical conclusion. As he points out, since the 1960s some Americans have looked to Canadian cities, especially Toronto, as a model of how American cities should be run. They have praised Toronto's safety and cleanliness, the efficiency and viability of its transit system, and the health of its inner city. Lemon argues that the virtues of Toronto are those of Canadian cities as a whole, reflecting more activist and socially conscious governments. Instead of assuming that Canadian policy should mirror American, Lemon argues that the way forward is for American cities to follow Canada. The wheel has turned full circle. Arguably, from being dependent upon American ideas about cities, Canada is now in a position to export its own urban culture and experience.

The nationalist interpretation has highlighted the differences that exist, on the average, between Canadian and U.S. cities. In the process, arguably, it gives these differences more weight than they deserve. The experience of racialized minorities and the extent of racial segregation in the two countries are obviously different, but in terms of immigrant ethnicity, class, and gender,

Figure 20.4 The cover of Jon Caulfield's book *City Form and Everyday Life* (1994) shows an example of the gabled row house, a type that characterized late-19th-century Toronto. (Reproduced with the permission of the University of Toronto Press)

the similarities are striking. How do we weigh the importance of one against the other? One's answer depends to a considerable extent upon the relative weight that one attaches to gender or class issues, as opposed to race. Marxists and feminists are likely to see a continental experience; those who are more attuned to cultural issues, and especially the processes by which racial identities are defined and labeled, will see things differently.

Most of the debate about how best to interpret Canadian cities has been framed in terms of nation and continent, as if these are the only alternatives. Although never expressed as cogently, another interpretation rejects these categories and instead emphasizes that there are other ways of identifying significant regions.

Regionalism I: Many Nations

Any geographical unit may be thought of as a region. A nation is a region defined on the basis of citizenship and, in varying degrees, culture. A continent is a region that is defined, above all, by its physiography. Neither criterion is necessarily very important in shaping the form and character of cities. Arguably, other factors and hence other regional categories are needed in order to comprehend what we normally refer to as Canadian cities.

From a regionalist point of view it can be argued that national averages for Canadian (and also U.S.) cities are largely meaningless. To locals, as to most visitors, Halifax, Montreal, Toronto, Winnipeg, Calgary, and Vancouver look and feel like very different places, as do Boston, New Orleans, Peoria, and Los Angeles. In this view, they reflect cultures and processes of city building, which are regional rather than national in character. Geographers and others have identified regions in different ways. One of the stronger regional traditions within Canada has been to identify heartlands and hinterlands, regions that are distinguished in part by their relative prosperity and also in terms of economic power. In Canada, as in most countries, economic control has been exerted from a hierarchy of metropolitan centers located in specific regions. At the beginning of the 20th century Montreal was clearly on top of the domestic urban hierarchy, but Toronto has usurped its role. Networks of economic control and investment, however, do not necessarily correspond to the sorts of cultural regions that most people would identify. To this day, it is the physiography of the country, coupled with the historical pattern of settlement, that defines such regions. The resulting archipelago of regions often has closer connections with adjacent parts of the United States than with other parts of Canada.

In recent years the journalist Joel Garreau has popularized the idea that the national border between the United States and Canada may not matter as much as other regional boundaries. He has argued that in cultural terms there are not two nations in North America north of the Rio Grande but nine. One ("Dixie") lies wholly within the United States, and one (Quebec) within Canada. One, "Mexamerica," straddles the border between the United States and Mexico, and another, "The Islands," encompasses part of the United States and the Caribbean. Canada and the United States share the remaining five: New England, the prairie "Breadbasket," the western "Empty Quarter," a west coast "Ecotopia," and the midwestern "Foundry." Since most of these regions straddle the national border, each major Canadian city (except Montreal) shares more with its counterpart in the United States than with other Canadian cities: Halifax with Boston, Winnipeg with Omaha, Calgary with Denver, Vancouver with Seattle, and, less plausibly, Toronto with Cleveland

or Pittsburgh.

Garreau says little about processes of city building, but it is not difficult to identify elements that are distinctive to at least some of these cities. Most obviously, since the mid-19th century Montreal has stood out in terms of its linguistic mix of French and English. The proportional share of Anglophones declined steadily for most of the 20th century but is still about a quarter. As a result, the ethnic geography of the city, with its extensive French- and English-speaking districts crosscut by varied nationalities, has been wholly unique. What has also set Montreal apart has been a distinctive housing stock and pattern of property ownership. Since the third quarter of the 19th century, Montreal has had a large number of low-rise apartments and "plexes," that is to say dwelling units that are stacked on one another but which retain separate entrances to the street (fig. 20.5). Visually this still stands in contrast to the gabled row housing of Toronto. As a result, and before the development of condominium tenure, Montreal's home ownership rate was for many decades exceptionally low, even dipping below that of New York City in the early part of the 20th century. French Canadian and English Canadian scholars alike used to believe that this unusual situation reflected the city's ethnic makeup. They assumed that French Canadians attached less value to owning their own homes. This never made much sense, since home ownership levels in other Quebec cities were as high as in English Canada, even in places like Quebec City that are overwhelmingly francophone. Recent research has shown that ownership levels were at least as high among French-speaking Montrealers as among the English. Scholars have suggested that the patterns and processes of land development in Montreal have been unique to the place, not to an ethnic culture. Either way, Montreal has visibly stood out from other Canadian cities.

Out on the west coast, patterns of urbanism were very different. Vancouver never developed the sort of dense row housing that characterized Halifax, Montreal, and Toronto. By the 1920s, variations on the California bungalow defined the residential landscape, and levels of home ownership were high, in part because many workers acquired homes by building their own. In the early 20th century, owner construction of modest single-family homes was common

Figure 20.5 "Plexes" in Montreal each have a front entrance to the street with access by an external staircase. (Courtesy Marc Choko)

around Toronto and other Ontario cities. Still, however, there was an important difference. Around Toronto, detached homes were a new addition to a Victorian city of gabled row housing, but in Vancouver they defined the urban landscape from the beginning.

The contrast of Vancouver with Toronto suggests that the most important regional distinctions are to be made on the basis of age. In particular, those places that grew up as walking cities, or where streetcars determined the shape of early suburban settlement, were once relatively dense. For this reason they have tended to support more viable transit systems to this day. Those that grew up with the automobile look and function differently. Since European settlement in both Canada and the United States proceeded westwards, simplifying the more complex categories of Garreau and other writers,

one may therefore argue for a basic distinction between eastern and western cities. Here again, however, the border is not important.

Regionalism II: No Nations

There is no reason why the regionalist line of argument should be confined to the North American continent. The "metropolitan" interpretation of Canadian history identifies heartlands and hinterlands within the country and recognizes the importance of American sources of investment. Since the 1950s when he first elaborated this interpretation, however, historian Maurice Careless has also recognized the earlier influence of Britain, and specifically London. More recently, the Pacific Rim nations have made their influence felt. The effect of the recent migration of people and capital from Hong Kong is just one example. During the 1980s and 1990s, Chinese Canadians grew rapidly in number and now make up the largest minority populations in Vancouver and Toronto. A majority of the undergraduate population of the University of Toronto—the country's largest university—are of Asian origin (mostly Chinese). The Hong Kong Bank of Canada is now the country's fastest-growing bank; and a Hong Kong investor now controls much of Niagara-on-the-Lake, home of the Shaw Festival and one of the nation's symbolic cultural centers.

Although Canadian cities have obviously been channels for the international flow of people and capital, few urban historical scholars have attempted to set the continental urban experience in a wider international context. The Australian urban historian Lionel Frost, however, has shown that many of the key features of Canadian and U.S. cities—low densities, high levels of home and car ownership, the norm of the single-family home, the segregation of land use—have long been shared by cities in other countries, notably Australia and New Zealand. This should not be surprising. The circumstances and forces that have shaped cities in all of these countries are essentially the same. Among the more important of these, over the past century and a half, have been relatively abundant land, high incomes, cheap wood, and similar building technologies. The balloon frame, for example, has helped to make housing affordable not just because it reduces construction costs but also because it enables many amateurs to build their own homes. Patterns and processes in all of these settler colonies have a generic quality. Within this framework, Frost suggests that age of settlement, coupled with institutional factors such as transit, provide a common basis for regional distinctiveness. Sydney may be grouped with Montreal and Philadelphia, while to the group of newer cities, which includes Vancouver and Seattle, he would add a place like Perth. In this perspective neither Canada nor North America is the important point of reference.

Cultural as well as economic criteria complicate the picture further. Among the settler societies, many important cultural details were also shared. For example, all have generally welcomed immigrants. This fact reflects, and has implications for, their attitudes toward ethnic diversity and ethnic neighborhoods. Racism and discrimination against ethnic minorities have played an unfortunately large role in each of these countries. In Canada, for example, the treatment of Chinese and Jewish immigrants in the early 20th century was sometimes shameful, and for a number of years after World War II attitudes toward southern European immigrants were, at best, patronizing. Nevertheless, and especially in recent years, ethnic diversity has been not only tolerated but indeed, sometimes rather naïvely, celebrated. The idea of "multiculturalism" has gained an influence that it lacks in Europe. Toronto, like Melbourne and San Francisco, prides itself on its ethnic neighborhoods in a way that Berlin, Marseilles, and Birmingham, England, do not.

Moreover, as the major sources of immigrants have changed, so too have the ethnic makeup and character of cities in all of these countries. In the 19th century the major source for all of these countries was the British Isles and, more generally, northwestern Europe. By the turn of the 20th century the mixture had shifted toward eastern Europe and then dropped off (in part due to immigration controls) during the interwar years. After World War II, the United States began to receive large numbers of Hispanics, chiefly from Puerto Rico and Mexico. The migration of these groups has had a major effect on a few cities, notably New York and Los Angeles, in ways that have no parallels in Canada or Australia. Other migrant streams have affected each of these countries in similar ways. Large numbers relocated from southern Europe (Italy, Greece, and then Portugal), followed by the Caribbean in the 1960s, and subsequently a mixture of Asian countries from the late 1970s onward. National differences in immigration policy and in the preferences of specific immigrant groups have had some effect. Canada, for example, was shamefully slow to accept Jewish immigrants during the 1930s and 1940s. Like Australia, however, it welcomed Italians during the 1940s and 1950s and in recent decades has accepted many Asians, including Hong Kong Chinese. Because of shared British colonial backgrounds, Caribbean immigrants traveled in much larger numbers to Canada and Australia than to the United States. For reasons that are less clear, Greek immigrants preferred Australia to Canada, but for the Portuguese the priorities were reversed. The results are variations on essentially the same theme. Thus, for example, Toronto and Melbourne, cities of a similar age and size, have a similar feel and, excepting the Greeks and Portuguese, contain a remarkably similar ethnic mix. Although their densities differ, in cultural terms they have more in common with one another than they do with their western counterparts, Vancouver and Perth. This pattern, then, implies a different sort of regionalism, one that is international in its points of reference.

The main problem with the regionalist view is that it seems more relevant to the past than to the present. In Canada, as in the United States, local and regional patterns of urban development were much more distinctive in the 19th century than they are today. Housing illustrates the point. In terms of the appearance and ownership of its housing stock, Montreal was most distinctive in the late 19th and early 20th centuries. Since the World War II it has steadily become more similar to Toronto, and indeed to other North American (and even Australian) cities. Most new housing has taken the form of single-family dwellings, not plexes, and levels of home ownership have risen steadily. Architectural styles remain somewhat distinctive, but not as much as in the past. Elsewhere in Canada, from the 1950s until the 1980s, similar sorts of housing at much the same densities were built at the fringe of cities all across the country. It is true that the recent revival of historical architectural styles has restored some of the appearance of local and regional identity. Thus, the suburbs of Toronto now boast gabled row housing in polychromatic brick veneer, a local tradition, while more bungalows in Vancouver again sport cedar shakes (a type of roofing). This is not a trivial development. Quite apart from its increasing association with "new urbanist" subdivision planning, the revival of past architectural styles is affecting the suburban landscape. But it does not mark the reappearance of regional urbanism. New housing is, mostly, for owner occupancy, often in the form of condominium tenure, and is built by developers who, although they do typically confine their activities to the local or (at most) regional scale, operate in essentially the same ways everywhere. The financing for land development, construction, and house purchase is provided on the same terms and, indeed, usually by the same lending institutions across the country. (The partial exception is Quebec, where local *caisses populaires*—a type of credit union—still play a significant role.) Thus, the suburbs of Toronto do not make

it different from Montreal or Vancouver but rather from those sections of the metropolitan area that were developed before World War II. Old Toronto has gabled row houses, old Montreal has its plexes, and Vancouver its California bungalows. Regional urbanism is not dead, but it is clearly on the wane.

The decline of regional urbanism suggests that the continental or nationalist interpretations of Canadian cities might have been gaining force. In fact, by introducing a historical perspective in a more systematic way, it is possible to reconstruct these alternatives under what might be termed the convergence view.

Convergence

According to the convergence view, Canadian cities were once distinctive but are ceasing to be so. The possibility of convergence, construed as a threat, is a powerful influence upon many of those who have articulated a nationalist view. A writer like James Lemon is keenly aware of the forces of Americanization, forces that he is striving to halt, and even reverse. What distinguishes the convergence view from the fears of nationalists, however, is the assumption that even if this trend has not completely run its course, it eventually, and inevitably, will.

There is substantial evidence in support of this interpretation. Many aspects of Canadian urban development were more distinctive before World War II than after. One of the more important of these was the process of land development, house construction, and financing. Over the course of the 20th century, land development has increasingly been taken over by vertically integrated developers who are involved in all stages of the process from land subdivision through design, construction, marketing, and even consumer financing. Financial institutions now monopolize the provision of financing, which is standardized by the universal adoption of the long-term amortized mortgage. In a more halting fashion, large professional builders have come to dominate house building.

These trends have brought urban development practices in Canada and the United States into closer alignment. In the United States institutional lenders, led by the savings and loans, dominated the mortgage market throughout the 20th century. In Canada, however, as late as the 1950s, private individuals held the majority of residential mortgages. Since savings and loan associations pioneered amortization, while individual lenders in both countries preferred to invest in shorter-term "balloon-type" mortgages that were associated with higher down payments, Canadians made less use of mortgage credit until well into the postwar era. There were also differences in the way that homes were actually built. Vertically integrated land developers appeared on the Canadian scene later than in the United States. Encouraged by favorable tax policy, they then grew with exceptional rapidity after World War II. Developers themselves did not at first undertake house construction and typically sold lots singly or in small groups to builders. Until the Great Depression, a large minority of these builders seem to have been amateurs, building for their own use. I have estimated that around Toronto owner-builders accounted for as much as two-fifths of all homes built in the first two decades of the 20th century, and the proportion was just as high in western cities. It seems that in the United States these amateurs played a smaller role, although they did stage a major, but temporary, comeback in the years immediately after World War II. Overall, then, the postwar growth of commercial builders, land developers, and mortgage lending institutions has been especially rapid in Canada, bringing it more closely in line with American practice.

Trends toward convergence in the private land development process have been paralleled and encouraged by Canadian federal and local governments. In the United States the federal government's first permanent housing initiative was the establishment of the Federal Housing Administration in 1933. The FHA's purpose was to revive the construction industry by encouraging efficiency in construction and in the provision of financing. It introduced mortgage insurance and used this lever to promote the amortized mortgage. With much the same purposes in mind, in 1935 the Canadian government passed the Dominion Housing Act (DHA). At first the DHA and its successor National Housing Act (NHA) of 1938 made provision for loans to be made jointly by the federal government and approved lending institutions. Since at that time banks were prohibited from mortgage lending, and because the Canadian equivalents of the American savings and loans were not very effective, most of the approved mortgage

lenders were insurance companies. In 1954, however, a shortage of mortgage funds compelled the government to bring banks into the picture. At the same time, the joint-loan scheme was abandoned, and FHA-style insured mortgages became the norm. In stages, then, over a period of two decades, the Canadian government helped to bring a very important part of the land development process into alignment with that in the United States.

At the local and provincial levels the picture is more complex. Proponents of the nationalist view have argued that Canadian metropolitan regions are better governed and more closely planned. This is consistent with the assumption that Canadians place greater value upon good government and less upon individual freedom of action. In fact, however, metropolitan planning only emerged after World War II. In the early part of the 20th century the suburbs of most Canadian cities were weakly regulated and largely unplanned. Certainly this was true of Toronto, the Canadian city that has most frequently been held up as a model of good planning. By U.S. standards, the City of Toronto was efficiently run. Civic corruption was minimal, building regulations and health standards were strictly enforced. However, beyond city limits, almost anything went. Until the Village of Forest Hill was formed in 1924, none of Toronto's suburbs fit the image of the planned, middle-class suburb about which so many American scholars have written. The absence of suburban regulation discouraged commercial builders and created possibilities for the amateur. The same contrast between civic efficiency and suburban freedom prevailed elsewhere in Ontario and to the west. In the first half of the 20th century, then, the contrasts in civic government and planning were greater in Canada than in the United States. It has only been in the postwar era that the regulation of many suburban areas has caught up with, and then surpassed, the situation in U.S. suburbs. The net effect has been to support the convergence in development practices noted earlier.

A convergence is apparent not only in the processes but also in the patterns of urban growth. The postwar suburbs of Toronto, Montreal, and Vancouver have not only looked increasingly like each other but also more like those of Cleveland or Seattle. The point has been made many times, and nowhere more effectively than by Joel Garreau. Having made the case for nine North American nations, he has more recently described the new type of clustered suburban development, or "edge city," that, he argues, has been taking shape in much the same way everywhere. In this context he suggests that "Canada is a particularly interesting place to watch Edge Cities flourish, because it is, in many ways, the control experiment for America." Overstating certain contrasts in order to underline his point, he continues, "[D]espite draconian government controls, ... despite an emphasis on mass transit and a relative lack of freeways, despite vibrant and bustling and safe urban centers, despite a relative lack of racial problems ... downtown Toronto has only 46 percent of its area's (retail) market. Almost a dozen Edge Cities are growing up around it."

What Garreau is inclined to celebrate, many Canadians and Americans have learned to deplore. In Canada, as in the United States, the formation of large new suburban retail centers is affecting the viability of downtowns. Toronto's is still thriving, but many others are not. In Montreal, a city that in economic terms has stagnated for three decades, many of the city's stores are vacant. The West Edmonton Mall, for some years the largest in the world, sucked business out of the nearby downtown of Edmonton. In the smaller urban centers, central retail districts have suffered their steepest decline. In southern Ontario, for example, which has the largest concentration of small and medium-sized urban centers in the country, the downtowns of places like Hamilton, St. Catharines, and Brantford are beleaguered by vacant buildings and lots reminiscent of neighboring Buffalo. In this context Toronto and Vancouver look like exceptions, with most Canadian centers moving along a path that many American cities have already traversed.

Suburbanization and gentrification have affected different cities in different degrees. As local variations have become more obvious, it is difficult to generalize about city-suburban differences in Canada. Since the same trend seems to have been occurring in the United States, we may say that in this regard the growth of local diversity has also contributed to a convergence of experience in the two countries.

It does not greatly matter whether this convergence is part of the continuing Americanization of Canada or whether it is simply part of a process of homogenization produced by economic forces that are international in scope. Either way, the net effect is that residual Canadian differences, inherited from earlier phases of urban development, are steadily being eroded and enveloped.

The convergence thesis is arguably the most persuasive of all interpretations of Canadian cities. It can incorporate, by reconstructing, most aspects of the other three. From this point of view, a nationally distinct form of urbanism is being transformed into something that is continental, indeed international, in character. Logically, that which remains is mostly a legacy. But what is the nature of that legacy, and how is it important? In order to answer this question, we need to revisit and reconsider the framework that was outlined earlier. In particular, we need to look more closely at the relationship between social process and spatial form.

Process, Form, and Unintended Consequences

Although geographical patterns reflect economic, social, and cultural forces, once these have been created and embodied in the built environment, they acquire a significance and an inertia of their own. As a result, past, and perhaps very distinctive, processes can have an enduring effect on the appearance and functioning of a city. Unless such effects are recognized, they can cause us to make misleading inferences about the relationship between process and form.

An example illustrates the significance of the historical legacy and also the way in which this legacy can confuse our understanding of the distinctive nature of Canadian urbanism. The case in question is Toronto, which to many American and Canadian observers is the exemplary Canadian city. Toronto has been praised for comparatively high densities and transit usage and for a central city that has remained healthy in economic, social, and political terms. Nationalists like to attribute these features to metropolitan government, well-supported public transit, and good planning. The implication, or suggestion, is that the health of Toronto reflects the Canadian virtues of good government.

In contrast, it can be argued that much of the postwar health of Toronto is attributable to an earlier phase of development, as this was embodied in the built environment. From 1891 until 1921 the Toronto Railway Company (TRC) held a licensed monopoly on streetcar service in Toronto. The TRC interpreted its mandate as that of providing service only within the city limits that had existed in 1891. It moved slowly to service areas that the city annexed after the turn of the century and refused to extend its lines into any suburb. Unlike their counterparts in the United States, transit companies in other Canadian cities seem to have followed a similar strategy. The result was that development, both within and beyond city limits, occurred at high densities. Thirty-, 25-, and even 20-foot lots were the norm during the boom in land subdivision that occurred in the years leading up to World War I. This boom was so large that many lots created at that time remained undeveloped for years, in some cases until the late 1940s. Even after the TRC franchise was revoked in 1921 and the newly created Toronto Transportation Commission began to build suburban lines, development continued to occur at relatively high densities (fig. 20.6).

In conjunction with other factors, the TRC's policy also affected the social geography of the city. Industrial decentralization encouraged workers to settle at the fringe. Since many workers were British immigrants who had the sorts of skills the new suburban factories demanded, immigrant enclaves emerged there. The absence, or lax enforcement, of building regulations facilitated this trend. This situation enabled workers to build their own very modest homes and discouraged commercial builders from erecting more substantial homes for the middle class. By the start of the 20th century the middle class had come to expect new homes to have basic services, and builders who catered to this market confined their activities to the city. The result was the growth and consolidation of middle-class neighborhoods like Rosedale, the Annex, and a good deal of North Toronto.

The pattern of urban development that occurred in Toronto in the first three decades of the 20th century left a significant legacy. It created dense residential settlement in the city and throughout much of the prewar suburbs. This provided a favorable context for the expansion of public transit into the postwar decades. It also confirmed the attractiveness of the city to the middle class, while establishing the workaday character of many of the prewar suburbs. Gentrification often expands from beachheads of middle-class settlement, and if in Toronto these have been comparatively numerous, it is because of the decisions that developers, builders, and middle-class home buyers made before the depression. It may be true that Toronto is well managed—although some doubts have recently

Figure 20.6 The opening of a new streetcar line in an already developed area of suburban Toronto, 1925. (Courtesy Toronto Transit Commission Archives)

been expressed on that score—and it may also be true that this exemplifies a continuing difference between U.S. and Canadian cities. It is clear, however, that a great deal is owed to the past. To some degree urban Canadians are living on borrowed time.

IMPLICATIONS

Canadian nationalists like to think that their cities are different from, and in many respects better than, those of their American cousins. They also like to believe that they can take some credit for this situation: that lower crime rates reflect a more tolerant and less unequal society; that healthy cities reflect more efficient government, better planning, and a more socially conscious electorate. The implication might be that Americans have something to learn from their Canadian cousins. Is this true?

There is probably some truth to the notion that Canadian cities work better, in part because of peculiarly Canadian virtues, but the point can easily be overstated. A case in point is the issue of racism. The history of racism in Canada is long and discreditable. Racial conflict has admittedly played a smaller part in Canadian than in American life and has had only a minor effect on the geography of Canadian cities. In large part, however, this is because racialized minorities have made up a smaller part of the population. Public recognition of racial conflict has also been minimized in recent years by an official veneer of multiculturalism. Even so, however, racial and ethnic stereotyping is still common. In cities where such minorities are numerous, as Native Canadians are in Winnipeg and blacks are in Toronto, local tensions can run high. Similarly, if Canadians continue to rely more upon public transit, that is, in part, because

real incomes have been somewhat lower than in the United States. Especially in the first half of the 20th century, levels of auto ownership were appreciably lower. Moreover, denser patterns of settlement, which were established in that era, have continued to provide a favorable environment for transit even after multiple-car ownership has become the household norm. In other words, many of the more important differences in the urban experience of Canadians and Americans can be explained by subtly contrasting circumstances, and not by differences in national values.

If it is true that circumstances, not values or policies, have been of critical importance, it may seem that Americans and Canadians do not have much to learn from one another. Americans of whatever color must deal with the fact that racialized groups make up a significant minority in many U.S. cities. Likewise they must manage urban environments that are already low in density and must deal with cities that in many cases are in serious difficulty. It is unhelpful to exhort them to copy Toronto. The lessons are not quite of this kind. Rather, I believe that a comparative frame of reference underlines the extent to which we are traveling down the same road. If, as I have suggested, the forms of urbanism in Canada and the United States are converging, urban residents in both countries must ask whether this is what they want. One of the virtues of the comparative point of view is that it broadens our appreciation for urban possibilities, especially if it is extended to include other countries that are experiencing similar trends. Detroit cannot be made to look like Toronto, still less like Montreal. Understood in their particular contexts and times, however, such cities may yet provide clues and inspiration to those who are engaged in designing new communities and remodeling old.

ADDITIONAL READING

Anderson, K. J. 1991. *Vancouver's Chinatown: Racial Discourse in Canada, 1875–1980.* Montreal and Kingston: McGill-Queen's University Press.

Bourne, L. S. 1993. "Close Together and Worlds Apart: An Analysis of Changes in the Ecology of Income in Canadian Cities." *Urban Studies* 30: 1293–1317.

Careless, J. M. S. 1989. *Frontier and Metropolis: Regions, Cities, and Identities in Canada before 1914.* Toronto: University of Toronto Press.

Cullingworth, J. B. 1993. *The Political Culture of Planning: American Land Use Planning in Comparative Perspective.* New York: Routledge.

Davison, G. 1995. "Australia: The First Suburban Nation?" *Journal of Urban History* 22: 40–74.

Fong, E. 1996. "A Comparative Perspective on Racial Residential Segregation: American and Canadian Experiences." *The Sociological Quarterly* 37: 199–226.

Frost, L. 1991. *The New Urban Frontier: Urbanization and City-Building in Australasia and the American West.* Sydney: University of New South Wales Press.

Gad, G., and M. Matthew. 1999. "Central and Suburban Downtowns." In *Canadian Cities in Transition. The 21st Century,* ed. T. Bunting and P. Filion. London: Arnold.

Garreau, J. 1981. *The Nine Nations of North America.* Boston: Houghton Mifflin.

———. 1991. *Edge City: Life on the New Urban Frontier.* New York: Doubleday.

Goldberg, M. A., and J. Mercer. 1986. *The Myth of the North American City: Continentalism Challenged.* Vancouver: University of British Columbia Press.

Harris, R. 1996. *Unplanned Suburbs: Toronto's American Tragedy, 1900–1950.* Baltimore: Johns Hopkins University Press.

———. 2000. "More American than the United States: Housing in Urban Canada in the 20th Century." *Journal of Urban History* 26: 456–78.

Harris, R., and R. Lewis. 2001. "The Geography of North American Cities and Suburbs, 1900–1950: A New Synthesis." *Journal of Urban History* 27: 262–92.

Jackson, K. T. 1985. *Crabgrass Frontier: The Suburbanization of the United States.* New York: Oxford University Press.

Kerr, D., and D. W. Holdsworth. 1990. *Historical Atlas of Canada.* Vol. 3, *Addressing the 20th Century.* Toronto: University of Toronto Press.

Lemon, J. T. 1996. *Liberal Dreams and Nature's Limits. Great Cities of North America since 1600.* Toronto: Oxford University Press.

Lewis, R. 2000. *Manufacturing Montreal: The Making of an Industrial Landscape, 1850–1930.* Baltimore: Johns Hopkins University Press.

Ley, D. 1996. *The New Middle Class and the Remaking of the Central City.* Toronto: Oxford University Press.

McCann, L. 1999. "Suburbs of Desire: The Suburban Landscape of Canadian Cities, 1900–1950." In *Changing Suburbs: Foundation, Form, and Function,* ed. R. Harris and P. J. Larkham. London: E & FN Spon.

McCann, L., and A. Gunn. 1998. *Heartland and Hinterland: A Regional Geography of Canada.* Scarborough, Ont.: Prentice-Hall.

Mercer, J., and K. England. 1999. "Canadian Cities in a Continental Context: Global and Continental Perspectives on Canadian Urban Development." In *Canadian Cities in Transition: The 21st Century,* ed. T. Bunting and P. Filion. London: Arnold.

Relph, E. 1986. *The Modern Urban Landscape.* Baltimore: Johns Hopkins University Press.

Sewell, J. 1993. *The Shape of the City: Toronto Struggles with Modern Planning.* Toronto: University of Toronto Press.

Stelter, G. 1977. "A Sense of Time and Place: The Historian's Approach to Canada's Urban Past." In *The Canadian City,* ed. G. A. Stelter and A. F. J. Artibise. Toronto: McClelland & Stewart.

Strong-Boag, V. 1991. "Home Dreams: Women and the Suburban Experiment in Canada, 1945–60." *Canadian Historical Review* 72: 471–504.

Urban History Review. Contents of this journal of Canadian urban history may be searched on the Web at www.science.mcmaster.ca/Geography/urbanhis.html.

Yeates, M., and B. Garner. 1976. *The North American City.* New York: Harper & Row.

PART VI

CONCLUSION

21

Afterword: Historical Geography since 1987

ANNE KELLY KNOWLES

Empire, nation, culture, region, and other terms related to them do not refer to fixed and readily defined entities. Such words are an essential, generalized shorthand for elusive formations that are continuously under construction and alteration. I have tried to use them with care. Indeed, a major purpose of this project is to help us understand them a little more clearly in their special application to America and Americans."

Donald W. Meinig, *Continental America, 1800–1867*

I take as a starting point the fact that we live in a world defined by continuous culture wars. . . . [M]y primary goal has been to show how 'culture' is never any thing, but is rather a struggled-over set of social relations, relations shot through with structures of power, structures of dominance and subordination. . . . [N]o decent cultural analysis (geographic or otherwise) can draw on culture itself as a source of explanation; rather culture is always something to be explained as it is socially produced through myriad struggles over and in spaces, scales, and landscapes.

Don Mitchell, *Cultural Geography: A Critical Introduction*

The years following publication of Mitchell and Groves's *North America: The Historical Geography of a Changing Continent* have been remarkable for the field we call historical geography. In no other academic generation have so many landmark publications appeared or so many books by younger scholars. Paul Starrs, editor of the *Geographical Review,* declared in 2000 that "the last decade [was] the best time ever to be an historical geographer." At the same time, historical geography has been challenged by the growing hegemony of social theory in academic discourse. The rapid emergence of new cultural geography, the most influential movement in human geography since the early 1980s, brought the challenge close to home. As the epigrams above indicate, striking differences in style and substance characterize what many have seen as a divide separating empirically driven historical geography from theoretically driven "critical" geography. In this chapter I will try to summarize those differences while highlighting work that demonstrates the strength of framing detailed empirical research in the context of theoretical or historiographic debates. Space limitations allow me scant room to do justice to the outpouring of scholarship in recent years. I can only point to a few outstanding examples in hopes that they will induce readers to explore much more widely on their own.

THE CHALLENGE OF SOCIAL THEORY

In his introduction to the first edition (reprinted here, chapter 1), Robert Mitchell described a fairly benign contrast "between studies that use the past as the distinctive focus to be examined on its own terms¶ and those that use the past selectively to explore the historical validity of current theories of human behavior" (10). While this distinction continues to hold true, it misses the depth of difference between much of the historical geography produced before about 1990 and the highly theoretical, linguistically sensitive, politically charged treatment of the past inspired by social theory—an ideological approach that challenges virtually all of the assumptions upon which history "on its own terms" is based.

First, geography anchored in social theory is often avowedly political, whereas many historical geographers from Andrew Clark to Donald Meinig have not made politics an explicit part of their scholarship. Marxist scholars working in cultural geography see culture as the product of ongoing struggles for power (Don Mitchell's "culture wars") whose analysis should inform political action. Geographers who employ theories of discourse rightly apply the theories' critique of objectivity to their own work, declaring their theoretical and sometimes personal political position as part of their intellectual argument. Feminist theory, which has entered geography mainly through studies of gender identity and its complex relationship to landscape, has focused scholars' attention on the politics of daily experience. Political consciousness distinguishes these interwoven veins of scholarship from much historical geography.

Second, the relativism of current social theory holds that every situation has multiple and equally valid meanings. Denying authoritative interpretation, historical studies in new cultural geography often take as their object a historical singularity—one document, one building, one confrontation, even a gesture—whose various meanings emerge in the course of theoretically informed analysis. The aim of giving voice to nonelite meanings has turned geographers' attention to a plethora of new subjects related to identity among historically powerless or marginalized people. Like scholarship in sociology, anthropology, and cultural studies, recent geographical studies treat race, class, sexuality, ethnicity, nationalism, and transiency versus rootedness as mental constructs with concrete spatial outcomes, the latter being governed by those with the power and resources to build their vision of society. The challenge here comes not from the idea that the powerful command landscapes that the powerless build and inhabit—an old idea in historical geography—but from the focus on resistance to power as expressed in overt political struggle and the ways individuals and groups interpret their place, using that word in all its rich metaphorical meanings.

Third, the view that all knowledge and representation are subjective has inspired critical geographers to challenge historical geographers' regard of landscape. *Social Formation and Symbolic Landscape,* by Denis Cosgrove, and *The Iconography of Landscape,* edited by Cosgrove and Stephen Daniels, initiated a flood of studies that analyze the symbolic and conflicting meanings of landscape paintings, photographs, spectacle, and public versus private spaces in built landscapes. To the extent that this body of work acknowledges historical geography, it too often pillories the field's least sophisticated morphological work and studies of vernacular architecture, which were written in the 1950s and 1960s (see, for example, Don Mitchell's *Cultural Geography: A Critical Introduction* [2000], especially pages 35 and 293). The positive challenge of theoretical landscape analysis comes from the overarching argument that landscape is an extremely complex social formation whose physicality lends remarkable force to the meanings people give to it. Landscape has become the text on which social meaning is inscribed; the palimpsest of power; the site of resistance; the scrim that alternately conceals the workings of capitalist society and reveals our projected identities.

Paradoxically, postmodern and poststructuralist analyses of landscape and its representation in maps have inculcated a distrust of all things visual among some critical geographers. Derek Gregory and J. Brian Harley set the tone. This unacknowledged privileging of word over images helps explain the striking absence of maps, particularly maps presenting research findings, in much of the theoretically oriented cultural geography published since 1987. Restricting cartography to the very limited role of locating places is consistent with the ideological position that one's interpretation of the past should not privilege a single view. It is also consistent with the argument that maps were historically the product of elite and oppressive worldviews and that making maps continues to be an exercise of power that obscures itself behind aesthetics, just as the silent solidity of landscapes obscures the exploitative struggles that produced them.

THEORY, HISTORIOGRAPHY, AND EMPIRICISM IN HISTORICAL GEOGRAPHY

I entered graduate school to study historical geography the same year (1987) that Mitchell and Groves's first edition of *North America* was published, just as social theory was gaining momentum as a new stimulus to geographical thought. In the intervening years, social theory has clearly had a tonic effect on the subdiscipline. It has awakened historical geographers to the value of acknowledging and studying power—or rather inequalities of power—as perhaps *the* fundamental quality of social relations, and it has made them more self-conscious about their work, which in the long run is a good thing. At the same time, theory has proven inadequate to explain historical and geographical contingency, that is, why things happened as they did, where and when they did. The best scholarship in historical geography has always addressed matters of broad historical significance through detailed empirical research. The difference now is that for many historical geographers, matters of significance also include how one's empirical findings bear on theoretical issues.

In the remainder of this chapter, I will touch on several veins of scholarship that represent both the great variety of recent historical geography and the varying degrees to which geographers who focus on the past have incorporated social theory in their work.

But before doing that I must explain the artificial dichotomy that I have suggested in contrasting critical geography, based in social theory, against empirical historical geography. Although I have spoken of "social theory" as if it were a single perspective, the term in fact refers to a catalog of philosophical and epistemological perspectives, including postmodernism, poststructuralism, and various strains of Marxist thought. These approaches to understanding society and reality seem more similar than they are when one sets up their critique of objectivity in opposition to the empirical view that reality can be ascertained objectively by experience, observation, or experiment without recourse to theory. The truth is that all historical geographers use both theory and empirical data. Yet for many of us during the past 14 years the gulf between those who embraced social theory and those who practiced "traditional," empirical geography seemed real and worrying. I hope what follows will show that historical geography is emerging from a divisive period with new vigor and promise.

Marxist-inspired approaches to historical geography are best represented by three very different writers: David Harvey, Don Mitchell, and Peter Hugill. Harvey has been one of the leading thinkers in critical geography for many years, more for the originality and clarity of his writing than for his direct influence as a teacher. Beginning with *The Limits to Capital*, Harvey has de-

veloped a sustained argument for a Marxist geography, or what he calls historical-geographical materialism. His prescient critique of postmodernism in *The Condition of Postmodernity* convinced many cultural geographers of the need to acknowledge the politics implicit in all social structures, whether fabricated in bricks and mortar or in the social imaginary. In addition to producing book-length theoretical arguments, Harvey has produced a number of case studies that set a high standard for theoretically informed, empirically grounded historical geography, notably a widely cited study of the Basilica of Sacré-Coeur in his 1989 book *The Urban Experience*.

Don Mitchell is in many ways Harvey's intellectual heir. In his study of California's agricultural labor system, *The Lie of the Land*, Mitchell demonstrates the explanatory power of materialist Marxist analysis when applied to landscapes that were shaped by decades of brute exploitation. His research is central to an emerging body of work on the historical geography of American labor and capital, other examples of which include Andrew Herod's collection, *Organizing the Landscape*, and George Henderson's *California and the Fictions of Capital*. Mitchell's textbook, *Cultural Geography: A Critical Introduction*, is an exceptionally accessible summary of new cultural geography as well as a sharp critique of its tendencies toward solipsism. A very different offshoot of Marxist thought, Immanuel Wallerstein's world systems theory, provides the frame for Peter Hugill's technological histories of world trade (1993) and communications (1999), which set North American developments in the context of changing global core-periphery relations.

Marx did not say much explicitly about geography. Historical geographers have more readily found inspiration and guiding ideas in the highly geographical sensibility of French social theorists, particularly Michel Foucault's writings on the exercise of power through control of space and spatial form. The idea of landscape as an expression of power is now basic to many historical geographers' approach to past places. Matthew Hannah applies Foucault's notion of governmentality to the policy and practice of the U.S. Census under the leadership of Francis Walker. Hannah argues that Walker strove to make the census a serviceable arm of government, particularly through the conceptual and physical mastery of territory. The spatial exercise of governmental power is also the driving theme of R. Cole Harris's *Making Native Space* (2001). In this monograph Harris builds on his earlier consideration of Canadian imperialism, *The Resettlement of British Columbia* (1997), here examining the colonial strategies by which Native people were dispossessed of their land, their resistance to such treatment, and the impact of minuscule reserves on Native lives and livelihoods. The new field of legal geography follows a similar trend in dealing with landscape as the terrain of legal contest and the consequence of legal discourse (Delaney 1998; Forest 2000).

One of the dominant ideas in theoretically focused historical geography is that individuals and groups continuously negotiate their identity (the meaning they give themselves) while moving through, and responding to, the landscapes in which they live. Discourse theory developed by Foucault and many others gives geographers tools to analyze, for example, the ways urban architecture has reflexively shaped gender and class relations (Domosh 1996; Mattingly 1998). Steven Hoelscher's study (1998) of a Swiss American town casts the ethnic festival as a means by which immigrants and their descendants negotiated distinctive identities through changing historical circumstances.

Few historical geographers work at a further remove from social theory than Donald Meinig, and yet the crowning publication of his career takes as its main theme the creative destruction wreaked by American imperialism, one of the favorite themes of critical geography. Meinig is writing the fourth and final volume of *The Shaping of America: A Geographical Perspective on 500 Years of History* as this book goes to press. American history in Meinig's telling is a tale of territorial conquest, subjugation of conquered peoples, consensus-building in the interest of expansion, and the development of institutions and infrastructure to stabilize and extend territorial control. Although criticized for failing to acknowledge the theoretical (or, perhaps more accurately, the philosophical) underpinnings of his work, Meinig explicitly models the imperial organization of national and regional space in spatial diagrams. The impulse behind his project is to tell the geographical stories that other historians miss. His arguments engage historiographic issues, such as the causes of the Civil War,

rather than theoretical debates.

Historiography is the business of revising our understanding of history in light of new evidence, the reinterpretation of existing evidence, new methods, or theoretical models that reframe old questions. A great deal of historical geography over the past 25 years has addressed historiographic debates. Carville Earle has most consistently followed this approach. His essays contend, for example, that regional differences between agricultural labor markets fueled sectional conflict before the Civil War and that 19th-century southern farmers did not mine the soil as historians have argued. My study of Welsh immigrants' engagement with 19th-century American capitalism, *Calvinists Incorporated: Welsh Immigrants on Ohio's Industrial Frontier* (1997), bridges the historiographic divide between social history's emphasis on the persistence of immigrant culture and economic history's emphasis on market assimilation, arguing that core cultural values had profound but unpredictable effects on economic behavior. In *The Cotton Plantation South since the Civil War* (1998), Charles Aiken debunks long-standing myths about the role of plantations in southern society by documenting the changing details of their uniquely American landscapes—details that lay unnoticed or unremarked by generations of southern historians. Aiken's revisionist history links geographical change to community formation, attitudes toward race and class, political struggle, and ultimately the civil rights movement. Like Harvey, Aiken uses historical evidence to strip away layers of mystification that obscure the original meanings embedded in historical landscapes. In both men's work the force of argument comes from highly contextualized, clearly articulated empirical research.

Historical geographers have made particularly strong contributions to the historiography of the American West in recent years, in regional studies of culture formation and environmental change. To the extent that these studies treat the identity of regions as a composite of physical landscape, settlement processes, and contact and conflict between resident peoples, they bear a resemblance to Carl Sauer's approach to historical landscapes. They differ fundamentally from Sauer's approach, however, by examining the ongoing process of landscape transformation rather than celebrating the characteristic landscape of a defining epoch (Wyckoff 1998). Historical geographers now bring a healthy skepticism to any claim of landscape tradition. For example, Joseph Wood, building on the notion of invented tradition (Hobsbawm and Ranger 1983; Bowden 1992), argues that what we think of as the classic New England village, the historical landscape home of American democracy and tranquil community, was created by mid-19th-century elites to counter the impression of regional decline.

The most dynamic aspect of landscape transformation in North America has often been the tremendous environmental damage and reshaping done by resource exploitation. Historical geographers have produced outstanding environmental histories. Exemplary studies include Michael Williams's *Americans and Their Forests,* John Wright's *Rocky Mountain Divide,* Paul Starrs's *Let the Cowboy Ride,* and the essays collected in Christopher Boone's *City and the Environment.* One must also mention David Lowenthal's rewritten biography of George Perkins Marsh (2000), a key figure in the history of American conservation, and historian William Cronon's influential study of Chicago and its hinterland, *Nature's Metropolis.* The most powerful environmental studies by geographers, such as Hugh Prince's *Wetlands of the American Midwest* and Blake Gumprecht's *Los Angeles River,* draw on a tremendous range of empirical sources to reconstruct the phases of a landscape's physical alteration, the economic and political forces behind it, and the impact of changing attitudes on land policy.

The past 14 years have also witnessed remarkable change in the history of cartography,

close kin to historical geography. Two multivolume publishing projects deserve special notice. *The History of Cartography* (Woodward and Harley 1987–98) and *Historical Atlas of Canada* (1987–93) are towering achievements. These projects have codified major fields of study, stimulated a wealth of new research, and incorporated theoretical perspectives that are transforming scholars' regard for maps as historical artifacts and means of communicating geographical knowledge. I expect that historical geography will become even more visual in coming years, as scholars develop more rigorous techniques for applying geographic information systems (GIS) to their historical questions and analytical methods (Knowles 2000). Other modes of geographic visualization, such as virtual reality, will soon become tools of historical representation as well.

In conclusion, historical geography has found new voices between the first and second editions of this volume. Differences of language, intellectual reference, and method have at times created strain and incomprehension between self-styled historical geographers and critical geographers. Alienation is always a pity, for it leads to scholars' missing what is valuable and constructively provocative in one another's work. Whatever we call ourselves, the elements common to geographers' best historical work since 1987 would have been familiar to Carl Sauer: empirical research that digs for answers to historical questions, critical examination of landscape, and a desire to understand how the material world has been shaped by human action and ideas.

ADDITIONAL READING

Aiken, C. 1998. *The Cotton Plantation South since the Civil War.* Baltimore: Johns Hopkins University Press.

Boone, C. G., ed. 1997. *City and the Environment. Historical Geography* 25, special issue.

Bowden, M. J. 1992. "The Invention of Tradition in America." *Journal of Historical Geography* 18: 3–26.

Cosgrove, D. 1984. *Social Formation and Symbolic Landscape.* London: Croom Helm.

Cosgrove, D., and S. Daniels, eds. 1988. *The Iconography of Landscape: Essays on the Symbolic Representation, Design, and Use of Past Environments.* Cambridge: Cambridge University Press.

Cronon, W. 1991. *Nature's Metropolis: Chicago and the Great West.* New York: Norton.

Delaney, D. 1998. *Race, Place, and the Law, 1836–1948.* Austin: University of Texas Press.

Domosh, M. 1996. *Invented Cities: The Creation of Landscape in 19th-Century New York and Boston.* New Haven: Yale University Press.

Earle, C. 1992. *Geographical Inquiry and American Historical Problems.* Stanford: Stanford University Press.

Forest, B., ed. 2000. *Geography, Law, and Legal Geographies. Historical Geography* 28, special issue.

Gregory, D. 1994. "Geography and the Cartographic

Anxiety." Pp. 70–205 in *Geographical Imaginations*. Cambridge, Mass.: Blackwell.

Gumprecht, B. 1999. *The Los Angeles River: Its Life, Death, and Possible Rebirth*. Baltimore: Johns Hopkins University Press.

Hannah, M. G. 2000. *Governmentality and the Mastery of Territory in 19th-Century America*. Cambridge: Cambridge University Press.

Harley, J. B. 1988. "Maps, Knowledge, and Power." Pp. 277–312 in *The Iconography of Landscape*, ed. D. Cosgrove and S. Daniels. Cambridge: Cambridge University Press.

Harris, R. C. 1997. *The Resettlement of British Columbia: Essays on Colonialism and Geographical Change*. Vancouver: University of British Columbia Press.

———. 2001. *Making Native Space: Colonialism, Resistance, and Reserves in British Columbia*. Vancouver: University of British Columbia Press.

Harvey, D. 1989a. *The Condition of Postmodernity*. Oxford: Basil Blackwell.

———. 1989b. *The Limits to Capital*. Oxford: Blackwell, 1982. Reprint, Chicago: University of Chicago Press, Midway Reprint.

———. 1989c. *The Urban Experience*. Baltimore: Johns Hopkins University Press.

———. 1996. *Justice, Nature, and the Geography of Difference*. London: Basil Blackwell.

Henderson, G. L. 1999. *California and the Fictions of Capital*. New York: Oxford University Press.

Herod, A., ed. 1998. *Organizing the Landscape: Geographical Perspectives on Labor Unionism*. Minneapolis: University of Minnesota Press.

Historical Atlas of Canada. 1987–93. Geoffrey Matthews, cartographic ed. Vol. 1, *From the Beginning to 1800*, ed. by R. C. Harris (1987); vol. 2, *The Land Transformed, 1800–1891*, ed. by R. L. Gentilcore (1993); vol. 3, *Addressing the 20th Century*, ed. by D. P. Kerr and D. W. Holdsworth (1990). Toronto and Montreal: University of Toronto Press/Les presses de l'université de Montréal.

Hobsbawm, E., and T. Ranger. eds. 1983. *The Invention of Tradition*. New York: Cambridge University Press.

Hoelscher, S. D. 1998. *Ethnicity on Stage: The Invention of Ethnic Place in America's Little Switzerland*. Madison: University of Wisconsin Press.

Hugill, P. J. 1993. *World Trade since 1431: Geography, Technology, and Capitalism*. Baltimore: Johns Hopkins University Press.

———. 1999. *Global Communications since 1844: Geopolitics and Technology*. Baltimore: Johns Hopkins University Press.

Knowles, A. K. 1997. *Calvinists Incorporated: Welsh Immigrants on Ohio's Industrial Frontier*. Chicago: University of Chicago Press.

———, ed. 2000. *Historical GIS: The Spatial Turn in Social Science History*. Social Science History 24, special issue.

Lowenthal, D. 2000. *George Perkins Marsh: Prophet of Conservation*. Seattle: University of Washington Press.

Mattingly, D. J., ed. 1998. *Gender and the City*. Historical Geography 26, special issue.

Meinig, D. W. 1986–98. *The Shaping of America: A Geographical Perspective on 500 Years of History*. Vol. 1, *Atlantic America, 1492–1800* (1986); vol. 2, *Continental America, 1800–1867* (1993); vol. 3, *Transcontinental America, 1850–1915* (1998). New Haven: Yale University Press.

Mitchell, D. 1996. *The Lie of the Land: Migrant Workers and the California Landscape*. Minneapolis: University of Minnesota Press.

———. 2000. *Cultural Geography: A Critical Introduction*. Oxford: Blackwell.

Prince, H. 1998. *Wetlands of the American Midwest: A Historical Geography of Changing Attitudes*. Chicago: University of Chicago Press.

Starrs, P. F. 1998. *Let the Cowboy Ride: Cattle Ranching in the American West*. Baltimore: Johns Hopkins University Press.

———. 2000. Review of *Creating Colorado*, by W. Wyckoff. *Historical Geography* 28: 293.

Wallerstein, I. 1974–89. *The Modern World-System*. Vol. 1, *Capitalist Agriculture and the Origins of the European World-Economy in the 16th Century* (1974); vol. 2, *Mercantilism and the Consolidation of the European World-Economy, 1600–1750* (1980);·vol. 3, *The Second Era of Great Expansion of the Capitalist World-Economy, 1730–1840s* (1989). San Diego: Academic Press.

Williams, M. 1989. *Americans and Their Forests: A Historical Geography*. Cambridge: Cambridge University Press.

Wood, J. S. 1997. *The New England Village*. Baltimore: Johns Hopkins University Press.

Woodward, D., and J. B. Harley, eds. 1987–98. *The History of Cartography*. Vol. 1, *Cartography in Prehistoric, Ancient, and Medieval Europe and the Mediterranean* (1987); vol. 2, bk. 1, *Cartography in the Traditional Islamic and South Asian Societies* (1992); vol. 2, bk. 2, *Cartography in the Traditional East and Southeast Asian Societies* (1994); Woodward and G. M. Lewis, eds., vol. 2, bk. 3, *Cartography in the Traditional African, American, Arctic, Australian, and Pacific Societies* (1998). Chicago: University of Chicago Press.

Wright, J. B. 1993. *Rocky Mountain Divide: Selling and Saving the West*. Austin: University of Texas Press.

22

Sources for Recreating the North American Past

RONALD E. GRIM, THOMAS A. RUMNEY,

AND THOMAS F. McILWRAITH

Science fiction writers commonly use time machines to go back into history, but historical geographers can only fantasize about such inventions. They do not have the luxury of exploring, observing, and recording past geographic landscapes in person. Rather, they conduct most of their primary research or fieldwork in archival and manuscript repositories. In this chapter we touch on a range of materials to which readers of this book might turn for the next step in their discovery of the historical geography of North America. Bibliographies, footnotes, and historical documents are their most widely used research tools. During the past 35 or 40 years, the basis of historical geographers' research in America has been the discovery of data and its spatial distribution through critical analysis of sources contemporary to the period being studied. Although many kinds of primary sources are potentially useful, historical geographers have used some types of documents, both textual and graphic, more successfully than others.

Textual documents, whether in manuscript or printed format, provide the basic source for most qualitative and quantitative information. Exploration accounts and travel diaries have been useful in documenting the growth of geographical knowledge or the initial perception of frontier regions. Governmental archives at the national, regional (state or province), and local levels normally document matters of a political or legal nature, but they often contain information relevant to geographical issues as well. For example, numerous records pertain to the establishment and survey of boundaries, the regulation and monitoring of commerce and trade, the founding and planning of cities and towns, the utilization and preservation of natural resources, and the financing and construction of transportation systems. Population counts and demographic statistics can be derived from censuses, tax rolls, or militia lists at all three levels of government; information on real and mov-

able property can be found, primarily at the local level, in such records as land patents, deeds, wills, and estate inventories. Business records, such as merchant and plantation accounts, and company archives document the economic activity of individual enterprises, while newspaper advertisements and business directories are useful for studying a wide range of economic activity.

Graphic sources—including maps, photographs (aerials too), and landscape sketches—provide both a spatial and a visual perspective for many historical studies. Although often used casually as illustrative elements of a study, many such documents, when critically appraised for their respective biases, can stand alone as primary sources. Maps, at all scales, certainly may be used in this way.

The quantity and quality of primary source materials that are available for any particular historical geographical problem will depend on the time period in which the information was recorded, the record-keeping practices of the government bodies and individuals involved, and the archival practices of the successive holders of the documents. It is clearly impossible in an introductory essay to identify and evaluate all the potential documents and repositories that may be useful for historical geographers, so this survey will focus on some of the basic primary sources that researchers have successfully employed to re-create past geographies of North America.

THE UNITED STATES

Archival sources form the basis of current research in the historical geography of the United States, yet few practitioners have written book-length studies or compiled comprehensive surveys of pertinent sources. Since these vary from one region to another, the best strategy for the beginning student is to survey the bibliographies and footnotes found in the historical literature for specific topics or areas. We suggest three comprehensive guides as a start: McManis 1965, an updating to 1980 by Grim (1982) that includes numerous entries and comments pertaining to textual and cartographic resources, and Conzen, Rumney, and Wynn 1993, the most recent and the most comprehensive bibliographic survey, although it does not place as much emphasis on sources.

General Guides and Directories

The National Historical Publications and Records Commission (NHPRC 1988) provides the most comprehensive directory of archival and historical manuscript collections in the United States. It describes over 4,000 repositories: federal agencies, state and local archives and historical societies, museums, and the archives of corporations, universities, and other organizations. Besides giving the address, hours of opening, and user services, each entry includes a summary statement of holdings and bibliographical references to guides and finding aids. This directory also includes cross-references to entries in the *National Union Catalog of Manuscript Collections* (1959–93), a multivolume, thoroughly indexed publication of the Library of Congress that includes descriptions of approximately 72,300 individual manuscript collections in 1,406 repositories throughout the United States. There is no intention of publishing further volumes, but the program continues, and entries added since 1986 can be searched on-line through the catalog home page (http://lcweb. loc.gov/coll/nucmc/) or through "Archives USA" (http://archives.chadwyck.com), a commercial subscription service.

Sites outside the United States also contain source materials relating to the nation's historical and geographical development, particularly for the colonial period. Raimo 1979 provides the most recent guide to British and Irish manuscript collections. A significant body of American material in Spanish archives has been photocopied and deposited in American libraries (Jiménez Codinach 1994). Canadian sites are given explicit attention later in this chapter.

The NHPRC has a particularly successful program for making significant collections of manuscripts widely available, encompassing over 200 letterpress and microfilm publications (NHPRC 1976).

Although most of these projects pertain to the papers of prominent American political figures or corporate bodies, several are of individuals of geographical interest; among them are Charles C. Fremont, Benjamin Latrobe, Stephen H. Long, Frederick Law Olmsted, Zebulon Pike, Henry R. Schoolcraft, and Isaac I. Stevens. Hale's guide (1961) has listings for most states and provinces; it includes censuses; government records at national, county, and local levels; and also church, personal, and business records. Microfilm copies of many of the county and local records are available through the Genealogical Society Library, Salt Lake City, Utah (Wimmer and Pope 1975; Gerlach and Nichols 1975).

Cartographic resources are most typically found in state archives, libraries, and historical societies, but public libraries in the largest cities and the libraries of universities with major geography departments are also sources. The current guide to map collections (Cobb 1990) lists staff, opening hours, description of holdings, and publications. Ehrenberg's directory (1987) of the Washington area is particularly useful, detailing many repositories and mapping agencies of national scope.

During the 1990s many institutions began to scan and digitize key documents in their collections, making primary texts and images available on the Internet. The travel savings could be enormous. The number of potentially useful websites is growing daily, but because of the expense of converting documents to digital images, institutions can anticipate putting only a very small percentage of their holdings on-line. The few sites that are noted in this essay demonstrate the potential of this medium.

Guides and Inventories to Specific Collections

The National Archives and Records Administration (NARA), the official repository for the noncurrent records of the various agencies of the U.S. government, consists of 3 facilities in Washington, 12 regional archives, and 10 presidential libraries. Viola 1984 gives a general overview of the National Archives, and Matchette et al. 1995 gives a comprehensive description of the records from over 500 agencies, bureaus, and commissions that had been

accessioned as of September 1, 1994, plus a listing of the published finding aids and microfilm
publications. The National Archives home page
(www.nara.gov/) provides a directory of the various research facilities, a list of publications,
and limited search capabilities.

Besides the numerous preliminary inventories, special lists, and reference information papers, which describe various segments of these
records, the National Archives has sponsored a
number of conferences designed to acquaint
specific academic groups with the research potential of its holdings. The proceedings of the
conference for historical geographers (Ehrenberg 1975) includes a list of finding aids that
cover such topics as exploration and settlement,
population, agriculture, trade and commerce,
manufacturing and industry, transportation, urban development, and natural resources.

The Library of Congress, also located in
Washington, D.C., serves as the national library.
With a collection of over 100 million items, including 17 million cataloged books, 47 million
manuscripts, 4.5 million maps, almost 60,000
atlases, and 12.5 million prints and photographs,
as well as resources in numerous other formats,
it is the largest and most comprehensive library
in the country. No single publication lists all the
library's holdings, but Goodrum 1980 and Virga
1997 give good overviews, and Melville 1980
discusses special collections. The library's
home page (www.loc.gov) provides access to a
number of research services, including the capability to search the library's on-line catalog
(http://lcweb.loc.gov/catalog/) and its American
Memory website (http://memory.loc.gov),
which reproduces a large selection of the library's holdings and is being continually expanded. The American Memory website also includes a Learning Page (http://memory.loc.gov/
ammem/ndlpedu/index.html), which provides
links to related Internet resources, both historical and geographical, and ideas for lessons.
During the 1990s the special collection divisions within the library prepared illustrated
guides to their holdings, including maps (Ehrenberg et al. 1996). Thematic guides that contain
major cartographic or geographic components
include discovery and exploration (De Vorsey
1992), African Americans (Ham 1993), and Native Americans (Frazier 1996).

Federal government publications are widely
available and richly useful. Of particular interest
to geographers are congressional reports, annual reports of the executive departments and bureaus, and explorers' accounts; all can be traced
through Schmeckebier and Eastin 1969. One especially important body of government documents, available on microfiche, is the U.S. Congressional Serial Set (C.I.S. 1975–79), an
ongoing collection that includes the *American
State Papers*, congressional journals, and the annual reports of federal executive agencies. Within the Congressional Serial Set are more than
50,000 maps, indexed by Koepp (1995–97).

Archives and Manuscripts

Travel and Exploration Accounts
Historical geographers have traditionally
used the descriptions found in travelers' diaries
and explorers' reports for reconstructing physical landscapes, settlement patterns, economic
activity, and, more recently, environmental perception. Matthews 1974 lists over 5,000 manuscript diaries in 350 collections, and Matthews
1945 identifies published diaries dating from
before 1861; both are fairly comprehensive.
Several bibliographies also list diaries and travel accounts by broad regions or individual
states. For example, over 2,700 diaries pertaining to the southeastern United States are identified in a six-volume set published by the University of Oklahoma Press (Coulter 1948; Clark,
1956–59, 1962); Hubach 1961 lists travel literature pertaining to the midwestern states.

A significant subset of travel literature includes the reports prepared by government-
sponsored exploring expeditions during the
19th century. Although these sources have their
own inherent biases—military reconnaissance
and economic exploitation, for instance—they
have the potential for presenting a more balanced representation than private accounts,
which may suffer from exaggeration, untruth,
or literary license. Many were issued as part of
the Congressional Serial Set (Hasse 1899;
Schmeckebier 1971). Schubert 1980 describes
the records of the Army Topographical Engineers. Considerable attention has also been devoted to the maps created by these expeditions
(Wheat 1957–63); Ehrenberg 1973b and Ladd
1962 detail two major map collections in Washington. The bicentennial celebration of the
Lewis and Clark expedition has prompted the
appearance of numerous Internet sites; one of

the more substantial ones integrates excerpts from the expedition's journals with maps ("Discovering Lewis and Clark," www.lewisclark .org).

Population Records

The most familiar and probably most useful source of population information is the federal government's published census. Every ten years, beginning in 1790, the government has enumerated the population for the purpose of determining representation in Congress. The information gathered in the first census was brief (name of head of household and number of free and non-free members), but subsequent enumerations collected much more. For example, the 1850 census started listing names of family members as well as age, sex, occupation, and birthplace. Published censuses have always been available in hard copy (U.S. Bureau of the Census 1909, 1974, 1975) and are now on the Internet (http://fisher.lib.virginia.edu/census/). Also of interest to geographers are the statistical atlases that accompanied the censuses from 1870 to 1920 (Cappon 1979); those for 1870, 1880, and 1890 are available on the Internet (http://memory.loc.gov/ammem/gmdhtml/setlhome.html).

The manuscript census schedules on which the field data were recorded have proven indispensable for microstudies. Currently, schedules from 1790 to 1920 are available on microfilm and open to general research, and the National Archives has issued several useful publications pertaining to their use, such as that by Delle Donne (1973). For a discussion of the content of each census schedule and a union list, see the compilation by Franklin (1986). Manuscript census schedules are arranged according to the area canvassed by each enumerator, and several cartographic tools allow researchers to display their information spatially. The Census Bureau has compiled enumeration-district boundary descriptions from 1840 to 1970, and many county and city maps since about 1900 show these features (Rhoads and Ashby 1958). Shelley 1975, Long 1984, and Thorndale and Dollarhide 1987 are useful for identifying boundaries and their changes in the 19th century, before the Census Bureau started compiling such details.

Population data for the colonial period are not as readily available or as systematic and comprehensive in coverage as data in the federal censuses. Various levels of colonial administration made population counts and compiled tax and militia lists, but with no regularity or uniformity. Greene and Harrington 1932 and Wells 1975 continue to be the standard references. Herman Friis (1968), a historical geographer, has constructed ten remarkable dot maps that show the changing population distribution along the Atlantic seaboard from 1625 to 1790.

Property Records

The process of surveying and disposing of the public domain in the United States has generated a wealth of records that are useful to historical geographers. Land-survey records, which consist of field notes and survey plats, have a primary legal value for establishing the boundaries of a parcel of land, as well as a secondary value for reconstructing vegetation patterns from witness trees and related comments recorded in the notes. Land-disposal records—patents or deeds, land-entry papers, and tract books—document the sale and resale of the land and are useful for reconstructing the landownership process.

A distinction must be made between the public-land states—those in which the federal government was the original owner of the land—and those without public lands. These latter included the original 13 states plus Maine, Vermont, West Virginia, Kentucky, Tennessee, and Texas, in which the original ownership was vested in the colonial or state government. Records from the public-land states, including surveys and initial transactions, are housed either with the National Archives or the Bureau of Land Management (successor to the original General Land Office). Records of original surveys and transactions in those states without public lands are in the custody of the respective state land offices or state archives. For all states, subsequent land sales or transfers were handled locally, usually at the county level, and normally have been maintained in a county clerk's office. They have suffered the ravages of fire and war, and in recent years the older portions of many of these records have been centralized in state archives. Kirkham (1963), a genealogist, provides the only comprehensive guide to land records at all government levels.

No comprehensive guide exists for public-land records. Summary overviews report such matters as instructions, plats, and field notes

(Pattison 1956; Bouman 1976; Grim 1990a), and others discuss land-entry papers, tract books, monthly abstracts, patents, and township plats (Yoshpe and Brower 1949; Maxwell 1973; and Smith 1975). Abstracts and full images of the land patents issued by the federal government between 1820 and 1908 are available through the Bureau of Land Management's website (http://glorecords.blm.gov/). These records can be used to reconstruct original landownership by township within the public-land states, but to carry on the story after initial sale out of the public domain can be most tedious. Rent rolls or assessment lists, when available, can be helpful, as can the commercially published county landownership maps and plat books. These were quite prevalent during the last half of the 19th century and the early 20th century, and the largest collection in the country today is in the Library of Congress (Stephenson 1967; LeGear 1950). Conzen (1990) and Thrower (1961) are among those historical geographers who have discussed the research potential of these sources.

Other Textual Records

Merrens 1963 discusses various types of primary sources that are available for reconstructing the historical geography of the original 13 colonies; Merrens 1977 concentrates on South Carolina. These sources include tax lists, customs statistics, merchant records, family letters, newspapers, estate inventories, land surveys, local court minutes, travel accounts, ecclesiastical reports and maps. Merrens (1969, 1978) shows the value of promotional literature, official reports, travel and natural history accounts, and settlers' statements in reconstructing the physical environment and settlers' perceptions of it.

The U.S. Census Bureau's census of manufactures is a major source of 19th-century industrial statistics (Fishbein 1973). Walsh (1970, 1971) discusses the value and accuracy of this information. The Society of American Archivists has published a directory (1980) of the archival holdings of over 200 individual industries and private businesses. Note particularly the business and industrial archives of the Eleutherian Mills Historical Library near Wilmington, Delaware (Riggs 1970), and, for the colonial period, those of the research library at Colonial Williamsburg (McGregor 1969).

Newspapers have been used widely to study the development of political and public opinion, but they offer great potential also for geographical studies (Wacker 1974; Farrell 1977; Preston 1977) and are widely accessible on microfilm. Advertisements, specialized newspapers, and circulation statistics provide useful spatial information about commerce, manufacturing, and agriculture. Brigham (1976), Gregory (1937), and the Library of Congress catalog (1984) offer useful bibliographies. Ristow (1957) and Monmonier (1989) focus on newspaper maps; Bosse (1993a, 1993b) has done specialized work on newspaper maps of the Civil War era.

City residential and business directories provide a useful complement to the manuscript census schedules for studies of population mobility and social or economic characteristics. Spear 1978 lists over 1,600 directories, most of which are available in the American Antiquarian Society Library. Kirkham 1974 lists directories for the 300 largest American cities. Conzen 1972 and Knights 1969 provide useful analyses of the content, biases, and research potential of city directories.

Maps

A wide range of cartographic materials is available for historical geographical research. The essays edited by Buisseret (1990) demonstrate the possibilities, focusing on such diverse topics as exploration and military maps, land and topographic surveys, landscape views, urban maps and panoramas, fire insurance maps, and aerial imagery. Each chapter provides an extensive annotated bibliography. No current comprehensive listing of map bibliographies for the United States exists, but several older reference tools are still useful (Library of Congress 1973, 1980; Ristow 1973). Ristow 1985 and Schwartz and Ehrenberg (1980) provide a selection of illustrations that highlight American map production. Burden (1996), LeGear (1950), and Hargett (1971) provide compilations in three specialized areas of interest to historical geographers among many that could be mentioned. Regional map bibliographies cover, for example, the Southeast (Cumming 1998), the West (Wheat 1957–63), and the Midwest (Newberry Library, 1980); others focus on individual states or cities, as well as on particular time periods and distinctive topics.

With the introduction of large flatbed scanners and data-compression software, it is possible to scan large maps at very high resolutions and make them readily available on the Internet. The Geography and Map Division of the Library of Congress has been a pioneer in applying these technologies to cartographic collections. Images available on the Library's American Memory site (http://memory.loc.gov/ammem/gmdhtml/gmd home.html) date from 1544 to the present and are organized into six broad thematic categories: discovery and exploration, conservation and environment, cultural landscape, transportation and communication, cities and towns, and military battles and campaigns. Another website displays a significant private collection (www.davidrumsey.com).

Topographic Maps

For historical geographers reconstructing past physical landscapes, the absence of a systematic program of topographic mapping in the United States prior to the end of the 19th century has sent them exploring individual localities. One of the best sources is the topographic surveys of major battle sites in the American Revolution and the Civil War. For the Revolutionary War era see McLaughlin 1975 and Sellers and Van Ee 1981. Other useful Revolutionary War map bibliographies, all of which are well illustrated, include Nebenzahl 1975, Marshall and Peckham 1976, and Rice and Brown 1972. There is also an outstanding historical atlas for this time period (Cappon, Petchenik, and Long 1976). The National Archives and Records Administration 1986 and Stephenson 1989 offer the largest collections of Civil War maps. Look for more and more of this material appearing on the Library's American Memory website (http://memory.loc.gov/ammem/gmd html/milhome.html).

In the 1880s, when the U.S. Geological Survey (USGS) was established, a systematic and comprehensive topographic mapping program began. Moffat 1986 provides a checklist of topographic maps published before 1940, and Thompson 1981 an inventory of the current range of USGS products. Aerial photography was introduced in the 1930s as a major innovation in gathering geographic information, and Taylor and Spurr (1973) describe one of the largest and earliest collections, including material from the Geological Survey, the U.S. Forest Service, and the Department of Agriculture.

Urban Maps.

Ehrenberg (1973a) reviews city and townsite plans, census enumeration-district maps, real property surveys, and aerial photographs, all of which contribute to our understanding of the origins, growth, and internal structure of cities, particularly during the 19th and 20th centuries. Reps (1965, 1972, 1979) has focused on original town plans in a number of well-illustrated and comprehensive regional studies.

One of the most valuable research tools for historical urban studies is fire insurance maps, of which the D. A. Sanborn Company of New York was the major publisher. Prepared primarily for underwriters seeking to determine the risk of insuring properties, these maps provide block-by-block inventories of individual buildings in approximately 12,000 cities and towns in the United States and Canada from the late 19th century to the middle of the 20th. They may effectively be used in conjunction with city directories and manuscript census schedules. The guide to the large collection in the Geography and Map Division of the Library of Congress (1981) includes an introductory essay describing the development and intended use of these maps. Rees and Hoeber (1973) describe another large collection in California, and Hoehn (1976–77) provides a union listing covering both the United States and Canada.

The panoramic view is another type of urban map useful for determining the internal spatial structure of cities. Drawn in perspective from an elevation of 2,000 to 3,000 feet, these commercially published bird's-eye views show a town's street pattern as well as individual buildings. The drawings provide reasonably accurate portrayals of the major towns and cities in the United States and Canada from the middle of the 19th century through the first quarter of the 20th century, although users should be on the watch for exaggerations; commonly city fathers commissioned these views to promote the business, commercial, or industrial virtues of their respective cities. Reps 1984 offers a union list of available plans and includes introductory chapters discussing the creation and reliability of the drawings. The largest collection of panoramic views, consisting of almost 1,700 images, is in the Library of Congress (Hébert and Dempsey 1984), and now available at the website http://memo ry.loc.gov/ammem/gmdhtml/cithome.html, un- der the category "Cities and Towns."

CANADA

It would seem tedious to go through a similar listing for the Canadian scene, and, furthermore, it would be substantially repetitious. Instead, we draw attention to three thoroughly modern sources and invite readers to use them—and particularly their extensive referencing—as starting points on their own journeys of discov- ery. These are the *Historical Atlas of Canada,* the *Dictionary of Canadian Biography,* and a television documentary, *Canada, a People's History,* which has a parallel published version (Gillmore and Turgeon 2000). Each opens up a myriad of questions, and all are supported by detailed bibliographies of primary and sec- ondary sources. Sections headed "Further Read- ing" or the credit lines at the end of a videotape are not just for people preparing doctoral disser- tations or writing books. These three sources are ideal starting points for undergraduate students seeking references firmly seated in a historical geography of North America (and not just Cana- da) that they may yet understand only imper- fectly.

The *Historical Atlas of Canada* (HAC) (Gen- tilcore 1993; Harris 1987; Kerr and Holdsworth 1990) is an award-winning series and the fore- most resource currently available for studying the historical geography of Canada. In its wide- ranging celebration of spatial relations and processes, it is distinctively a geographers' piece. The maps are detailed and numerous, the narrative informative and balanced, and the art- work beautiful. Each of the nearly 200 plates has been authored by one or more scholars from research fields that range well beyond geogra- phy and functions as an essay on a particular as- pect of Canadian geographical change. A de- tailed listing of primary and secondary sources accompanies each plate, inviting further re- search. Both in its production and in its subse- quent use, HAC has been the focus for a gener- ation of Canadian research, and the echoes continue through to younger scholars who are becoming acquainted with it and seeing the op- portunities to go further.

Consider, as an example, "Prehistoric Trade"

(vol. 1, plate 14). Three maps, composed by an archeologist and an anthropologist, fill a large- format double-spread. The main map extends northward from about 38° N latitude to include Alaska, the Canadian Arctic, and western Greenland. This map shows the centers from which prehistoric trade goods—copper, obsidi- an, silica, shells, and even amber from Ellesmere Island— diffused and traces hypothe- sized lines of diffusion. It is a spectacular com- pilation of decades of fragmentary detail, brought together in a single image of an era when the Canadian-American boundary did not exist. Plate 14 gives priority to such unfamiliar places as Knife Ridge (in the upper Missouri), Edziza (interior of British Columbia), Batza Tena (central Alaska), and Albanel (southeast of James Bay). Case-study maps of the Pacific ob- sidian trade and the Adena burial cult in the Great Lakes region add to our understanding of the spatial dynamics of a distant era.

The HAC on-line project opens up interac- tive and read-only opportunities and is steadily expanding (www.mercator.geog.utoronto.ca/ hacddp.page1.htm). The portrayal of mapped information for different dates, or different parts of the country, is becoming possible, and new scholarly questions—on feminism, Native rights, housing, substance abuse, high-tech in- dustry, and more—can be asked in the context of work already done. The HAC is an avenue for continuing historical geographical research. Li- braries across Canada, and many in the United States, have it. For a compressed glimpse in hard copy, try the *Concise Historical Atlas of Canada* (Dean et. al. 1998), which includes es- says especially composed for this new edition.

The *Dictionary of Canadian Biography* (DCB) is 14 volumes long, and growing, and fills some 10,000 pages. It contains the life sto- ries of thousands of ordinary people doing ordi- nary things across the land, from the era of New France and before through to the early 20th cen- tury. Consider just one individual at random: John Seabury Pearce (1842–1909), described by his biographer (Baeyer 1994) as "merchant, seedsman, author, and office holder." Pearce de- veloped a wholesale seed business in Ontario late in the 19th century, railed against the forces contributing to rural depopulation, and ended up as a champion of the educational value of land- scape gardening and the City Beautiful move- ment. What a geographical career, and how very transnational too. As with each DCB entry, Pearce's concludes with a thorough bibliography of primary and secondary sources, naming their repositories across Canada and often in the United States and elsewhere. In an effective, if seemingly primitive, version of hot-linked texts, DCB cross-referencing among the biographies allows readers to follow thematic leads. A CD-ROM version of the DCB, prepared in 2000, provides linkages from earlier volumes (back to 1966) to more recent ones. The DCB is a truly living source and outstandingly important for historical geographers.

Canada, a People's History is a remarkable television documentary prepared by the Canadian Broadcasting Corporation and first shown in 2000. It is designed to rekindle in the minds of Canadians the belief that indeed the country has a lively and absorbing history. Many citizens have been doubtful for a good many years, so this presentation is timely, and it uses a popular medium that gives geography a central role. The producers choose to engage the views and opinions of uncelebrated participants in the great events: a nun enduring the siege of Quebec, a snowbound trapper, a soldier at Lundy's Lane in the War of 1812, even Benjamin Franklin as a newspaperman in Montreal, before he was famous. These and others take their places, and so does the land. What was the angle of the rising sun striking the Plains of Abraham on that fateful September day in 1759? What did livestock in Niagara look like? How many children and incapacitated people might have been on the streets of Halifax? Is a roof of slate or shingle? The interplay of space and place challenged researchers as seldom before, and the list of credits reports a wide range of museums, galleries, libraries, and archives that participated in the production. Historical geographers everywhere have much to gain from the visual media that can be scrutinized carefully for questions that may be pursued in more traditional forms of archival research and presented in text, or possibly in future documentary films or on-line presentations.

TRANSNATIONAL OPPORTUNITIES

For a bibliographic essay to be divided along national boundaries is a reflection of the strength of government-based sources of information and also of the nationalistic nature of sources of financial support. Or is it? True, census bureaus in Canada and the United States each compile their own information, and states or provinces or municipalities do not go beyond their own jurisdictions. But, refreshingly often, national agencies—the National Science Foundation in the United States, the Social Sciences and Humanities Research Council in Canada—support research that crosses old lines, yielding researchers, and their bibliographies, that do so too. Add in such international funding programs as the Fulbright, Guggenheim, and others; supportive journals—the *American Review of Canadian Studies* and the *Canadian Review of American Studies*, to give but two with symmetrical titles—and consciously international compilations such as Conzen, Rumney, and Wynn 1993, and the line between the United States and Canada becomes more and more blurred.

The *Atlas of Early American History* (Cappon, Petchenik, and Long 1976) is one instance of a reference in the American section of this chapter that covers material also relevant to Canada. Map collections serve interests in both countries (Dahl 1986). So too do the Society of American Archivists' business records (1980) and Preston's compilation on newspapers (1977). Many citations of American material are reminders to readers to seek their Canadian equivalents, for everything from censuses to fire insurance atlases (Buchanan and Gad 1994) and photographs (Schwartz 1996). Land records in Canada are, as in the United States, held partially at the federal level and partially at the provincial level. The common use of the English language is a great facilitator, of course, but the French influence in New England and the Spanish along the lower British Columbia coast yield cross-border references too. Some leads suggested for U.S. inquiry will open up large categories in Canada, including those to do with Acadia, the Atlantic fisheries, and the Inuit and First Nations. Others steer one on into British colonial records and, quite possibly from there, back into the 13 colonies. For all this searching, the National Archives and the National Library in Ottawa provide the same website tracking services as their equivalent American institutions (www.archives.ca). See also the website of the Association of Canadian Map Libraries (www.sscl.uno.ca/assoc/acmla

/html). In the emerging vernacular of Web-based information, "Log on and follow the prompts." Discover how much the records of the two nations are, like their historical geographies, interwoven.

The Hudson's Bay Company (www.gov.mb.ca/chc/archives/hbca/index.html) and the Canadian Pacific Railway (www.cpr.ca/internet/content/corporate/history/history.asp) hold a special place in Canadian historical geography, as do the Dupont Corporation (www.hagley.lib.de.us/catalog.html) and the railroad Union Pacific Corporation (www.uprr.com/upr/ffh/history/) in American. Yet each of them has contributed to the broader North American story, as their corporate records attest. Canadian readers who peruse only the Canadian section of this chapter are missing much of both substance and critical evaluation, as are Americans who read only the American parts. Nor should geographers in either camp assume exclusive rights to materials outlined here; indeed, mutual, cross-disciplinary sleuthing is a taproot into further understanding of America. The authors of the chapters in this book value the richness of a manuscript census, a traveler's diary, a small-town newspaper, a ledger, and a picture collection. These are the stuff of inquiry, open to novice and old hand alike and irrespective of the nation that claims them. They are the building blocks for historical geographies of North America yet to be.

ADDITIONAL READING

Note the following abbreviations for sources in the United States. GPO: Government Printing Office. LC: Library of Congress. NARA: National Archives and Records Administration. NARS: National Archives and Records Service. NHPRC: National Historical Publications and Records Commission.

Baeyer, E. von. 1994. "John Seabury Pearce." *Dictionary of Canadian Biography* 13: 821–22.

Bosse, D. 1993a. *Civil War Maps: A Cartobibliography of the Northern Daily Press.* Westport, Conn.: Greenwood Press.

———. 1993b. *Civil War Newspaper Maps: A Historical Atlas.* Baltimore: Johns Hopkins University Press.

Bouman, L. J. 1976. "The Survey Records of the General Land Office ..." Pp. 263–72 in *American Congress on Surveying and Mapping Proceedings of 36th Annual Meeting.* Falls Church, Va.: American Congress on Surveying and Mapping.

Brigham, C. S., comp. 1976. *History and Bibliography of American Newspapers, 1690–1820.* Worcester, Mass.: American Antiquarian Society, 1947. Reprint, Westport, Conn.: Greenwood Press.

Buchanan, E., and G. H. K. Gad. 1994. "Charles Edward Goad." *Dictionary of Canadian Biography* 13: 384–86.

Buisseret, D., ed. 1990. *From Sea Charts to Satellite Images: Interpreting North American History through Maps.* Chicago: University of Chicago Press.

Burden, P. D. 1996. *The Mapping of North America.* Rickmansworth, England: Raleigh Publications.

Cappon, L. J. 1979. "The Historical Map in American Atlases." *Annals of the Association of American Geographers* 69: 622–34.

Cappon, L. J., B. B. Petchenik, and J. H. Long, eds. 1976. *Atlas of Early American History: The Revolutionary Era, 1760–1790.* Princeton: Princeton University Press.

CIS (Congressional Information Service). 1975–79. *U.S. Serial Set Index, 1789–1969.* 36 vols. Bethesda, Md.: Congressional Information Service.

Clark, T. D., ed. 1956–59. *Travels in the Old South: A Bibliography.* 3 vols. Norman: University of Oklahoma Press.

———. 1962. *Travels in the New South: A Bibliography.* 2 vols. Norman: University of Oklahoma Press.

Cobb, D., comp. 1990. *Guide to U.S. Map Resources.* 2d ed. Chicago: American Libraries Association.

Conzen, M. P. 1972. "State Business Directories in Historical and Geographical Research." *Historical Geography Newsletter* 2: 1–14.

———. 1990. "North American County Maps and Atlases." Pp. 186–211 in *From Sea Charts to Satellite Images,* ed. D. Buisseret. Chicago: University of Chicago Press.

Conzen, M. P., T. A. Rumney, and G. Wynn, eds. 1993. *A Scholar's Guide to Geographical Writing on the American and Canadian Past.* Chicago: University of Chicago Press.

Coulter, E. M., ed. 1948. *Travels in the Confederate States: A Bibliography.* Norman: University of Oklahoma Press.

Cumming, W. P. 1998. *The Southeast in Early Maps.* 3d ed. Chapel Hill: University of North Carolina.

Dahl, E. H. 1986. *Historical Maps of Canada, Folios 1–3.* Ottawa: Association of Canadian Map Libraries.

Dean, W. G., C. E. Heidenreich, T. F. McIlwraith, and

J. Warkentin, eds. 1998. *Concise Historical Atlas of Canada.* Toronto: University of Toronto Press.

Delle Donne, C. R. 1973. *Federal Census Schedules, 1850–1880: Primary Sources for Historical Research.* Washington: NARS.

De Vorsey, L. 1992. *Keys to the Encounter: A Library of Congress Resource Guide for the Study of the Age of Discovery.* Washington: LC.

Dictionary of Canadian Biography. 1966–2000. 14 vols. Toronto: University of Toronto Press.

Ehrenberg, R. E. 1973a. *Cartographic Records in the National Archives for Urban Studies.* Washington: NARS.

———. 1973b. *Geographic Exploration and Mapping in the 19th Century: A Survey of the Records in the National Archives.* Washington: NARS.

———. 1987. *Scholar's Guide to Washington, D.C., for Cartography and Remote Sensing.* Washington: Smithsonian Institute.

———, ed. 1975. *Pattern and Process: Research in Historical Geography.* Washington: Howard University Press.

Ehrenberg, R. E., et. al., comps. 1996. *Library of Congress Geography and Maps: An Illustrated Guide.* Washington: LC.

Farrell, R. T. 1977. "Advice to Farmers: The Content of Agricultural Newspapers, 1860–1910." *Agricultural History* 51: 209–17.

Fishbein, M. H. 1973. *The Censuses of Manufactures, 1810–1890.* Washington: NARS.

Franklin, W. N., comp. 1986. *Federal Population and Mortality Census Schedules, 1790–1890.* Rev. ed. Washington: NARS.

Frazier, P., ed. 1996. *Many Nations: A Library of Congress Resource Guide for the Study of ... Native Peoples.* Washington: LC.

Friis, H. R. 1968. *A Series of Population Maps of the Colonies and the United States, 1625–1790.* Rev. ed. New York: American Geographical Society.

Gentilcore, R. L., ed. 1993. *Historical Atlas of Canada.* Vol. 2, *The Land Transformed, 1800–1890.* Toronto and Montreal: University of Toronto Press / Les presses de l'université de Montréal.

Gerlach, L. R., and M. L. Nichols. 1975. "The Mormon Genealogical Society and Research Opportunities in Early American History." *William and Mary Quarterly,* 3d ser., 32: 625–29.

Gillmor, D., and P. Turgeon. 2000. *Canada: A People's History.* Toronto: McClelland & Stewart.

Goodrum, C. A. 1980. *Treasures of the Library of Congress.* New York: Abrams.

Greene, E. B., and V. B. Harrington. 1932. *American Population before the Federal Census of 1790.* New York: Columbia University Press.

Gregory, W. 1937. *American Newspapers, 1821–1936: A Union List of Files Available in the United States and Canada.* New York: Wilson.

Grim, R. E. 1982. *Historical Geography of the United States: A Guide to Information Sources.* Detroit: Gale Research.

———. 1990a. "Maps of the Township and Range System." Pp. 89–109 in *From Sea Charts to Satellite Images,* ed. D. Buisseret. Chicago: University of Chicago Press.

———. 1990b. "Sources of General Land Office Maps." Pp. 311–15 in *From Sea Charts to Satellite Images,* ed. D. Buisseret. Chicago: University of Chicago Press.

Hale, R. W., ed. 1961. *Guide to Photocopied Historical Materials in the United States and Canada.* Ithaca: Cornell University Press.

Ham, D. N., ed. 1993. *The African-American Mosaic: A Library of Congress Guide for the Study of Black History and Culture.* Washington: LC.

Hargett, J. 1971. *List of Selected Maps of States and Territories.* Washington: NARS.

Harris, R. C., ed. 1987. *Historical Atlas of Canada.* Vol. 1, *From the Beginning to 1800.* Toronto and Montreal: University of Toronto Press / Les presses de l'université de Montréal.

Hasse, A. R. 1899. *Reports of Explorations Printed in the Documents of the United States Government.* Washington: GPO.

Hébert, J. R., and P. Dempsey. 1984. *Panoramic Maps of Cities in the United States and Canada: A Checklist of Maps ... in the Library of Congress.* 2d ed. Washington: LC.

Hoehn, R. P., et al. 1976–77. *Union List of Sanborn Fire Insurance Maps Held by Institutions in the United States and Canada.* 2 vols. Santa Cruz, Calif.: Western Association of Map Libraries.

Hubach, R. R. 1961. *Early Midwestern Travel Narratives: An Annotated Bibliography, 1634–1850.* Detroit: Wayne State University Press.

Jiménez Codinach, E. G. 1994. *The Hispanic World, 1492–1898: A Guide to Photoreproduced Manuscripts from Spain in ... the United States, Guam, and Puerto Rico.* Washington: LC.

Kerr, D., and D. W. Holdsworth, eds. 1990. *Historical Atlas of Canada.* Vol. 3, *Addressing the 20th Century.* Toronto and Montreal: University of Toronto Press / Les presses de l'université de Montréal.

Kirkham, E. K. 1974. *A Handy Guide to Record-Searching in the Larger Cities of the United States.* Logan, Utah: Everton Publishers.

———. 1963. *The Land Records of America and Their Genealogical Value.* Washington: E. K. Kirkham.

Knights, P. R. 1969. "City Directories as Aids to Ante-Bellum Urban Studies: A Research Note." *Historical Methods Newsletter* 2: 1–10.

Koepp, D. P., ed. 1995–97. *Index and Carto-Bibliography of Maps, 1789–1969.* 16 vols. Bethesda, Md.: Congressional Information Service.

Ladd, R. S. 1962. *Maps Showing Explorers' Routes,*

Trails, and Early Roads in the United States: An Annotated List. Washington: LC.

LeGear, C. E. 1950. *United States Atlases: A List of National, State, County, City, and Regional Atlases in the Library of Congress.* Washington: LC.

Library of Congress. 1959–93. *National Union Catalog of Manuscript Collections.* 29 vols. Hamden, Conn.: Shoe String Press.

———. 1973. *The Bibliography of Cartography.* 5 vols. Boston: G. K. Hall, 1973; first supp, 2 vols., 1980.

———. 1981. *Fire Insurance Maps in the Library of Congress: Plans of North American Cities and Towns Produced by the Sanborn Map Company.* Washington: LC.

———. 1984. *Newspapers in Microfilm: United States, 1948–83.* 2 vols. Washington: LC.

Long, J. H. 1984. *Historical Atlas and Chronology of County Boundaries, 1788–1980.* 5 vols. Boston: G. K. Hall.

Marshall, D. W., and H. H. Peckham. 1976. *Campaigns of the American Revolution: An Atlas of Manuscript Maps.* Ann Arbor: University of Michigan Press.

Matchette, R. B., et al., comps. 1995. *Guide to Federal Records in the National Archives of the United States.* 3 vols. Washington: NARA.

Matthews, W. 1945. *American Diaries: An Annotated Bibliography of Diaries Written Prior to 1861.* Berkeley and Los Angeles: University of California Press.

———. 1974. *American Diaries in Manuscript, 1580–1954: A Descriptive Bibliography.* Athens: University of Georgia Press.

Maxwell, R. S. 1973. *Public Land Records of the Federal Government, 1800–1950, and Their Statistical Significance.* Washington: NARS.

McGregor, M. G. 1969. *Guide to the Manuscript Collections of Colonial Williamsburg.* 2d ed. Williamsburg, Va.: Colonial Williamsburg.

McLaughlin, P. D., comp. 1975. *Pre-Federal Maps in the National Archives: An Annotated List.* Rev. ed. Washington: NARS.

McManis, D. R. 1965. *Historical Geography of the United States: A Bibliography.* Ypsilanti: Eastern Michigan University.

Melville, A., comp. 1980. *Special Collections in the Library of Congress: A Selective Guide.* Washington: LC.

Merrens, H. R. 1963. "Source Materials for the Geography of Colonial America." *Professional Geographer* 15: 8–11.

———. 1969. "The Physical Environment of Early America: Images and Image Makers in Colonial South Carolina." *Geographical Review* 59: 530–56.

———. 1977. *The Colonial South Carolina Scene: Contemporary Views, 1697–1774.* Columbia: University of South Carolina Press.

———. 1978. "Praxis and Theory in the Writing of American Historical Geography." *Journal of Historical Geography* 4: 277–90.

Moffat, R. M. 1986. *Map Index to Topographic Quadrangles of the United States, 1882–1940.* Santa Cruz, Calif.: Western Association of Map Libraries.

Monmonier, M. 1989. *Maps with the News: The Development of American Journalistic Cartography.* Chicago: University of Chicago Press.

———. 1986. *A Guide to Civil War Maps in the National Archives.* Washington: NARA.

———. 1988. *Directory of Archives and Manuscript Repositories in the United States.* 2d ed. Phoenix: Oryx Press.

Nebenzahl, K. 1975. *A Bibliography of Printed Battle Plans of the American Revolution, 1775–1795.* Chicago: University of Chicago Press.

Newberry Library. 1980. *Checklist of Printed Maps of the Middle West to 1900.* 11 vols. Boston: G. K. Hall.

NHPRC (National Historical Publications and Records Commission). 1976. *Publications Catalog.* Washington: NARS.

Pattison, W. D. 1956. "Use of the U.S. Public Land Survey Plats and Notes as Descriptive Sources." *Professional Geographer* 8: 10–14.

Preston, R. E. 1977. "Audit Bureau of Circulation Daily Newspaper Records as a Source in Studies of Post-1915 Settlement Patterns in the United States and Canada." *Historical Geography Newsletter* 7: 1–12.

Raimo, J. W., ed. 1979. *A Guide to Manuscripts Relating to America in Great Britain and Ireland.* Rev. ed. Westport, Conn.: Meckler Books.

Rees, G., and M. Hoeber. 1973. *A Catalogue of Sanborn Atlases at California State University, Northridge.* Santa Cruz, Calif.: Western Association of Map Libraries.

Reps, J. W. 1965. *Making of Urban America: A History of City Planning.* Princeton: Princeton University Press.

———. 1972. *Tidewater Towns: City Planning in Colonial Virginia and Maryland.* Charlottesville: University Press of Virginia.

———. 1979. *Cities of the American West: A History of Frontier Urban Planning.* Princeton: Princeton University Press.

———. 1984. *Views and Viewmakers of Urban America: Lithographs of Towns and Cities in the United States and Canada ... 1825–1925.* Columbia: University of Missouri Press.

Rhoads, J. B., and C. M. Ashby, comps. 1958. *Preliminary Inventory of the Cartographic Records of the Bureau of the Census.* Washington: NARS.

Rice, H. C., Jr., and A. S. K. Brown, eds. and trans.

1972. *The American Campaigns of Rochambeau's Army, 1780–83.* Vol. 2, *Itineraries, Maps, and Views.* Princeton: Princeton University Press.

Riggs, J. B. 1970. *A Guide to the Manuscripts in the Eleutherian Mills Historical Library ... through 1965.* Greenville, Del.: Eleutherian Mills Historical Library.

Ristow, W. W. 1957. "Journalistic Cartography." *Surveying and Mapping* 17: 369–90.

———. 1973. *Guide to the History of Cartography: An Annotated List of References ... .* Washington: LC.

———. 1985. *American Maps and Mapmakers: Commercial Cartography in the 19th Century.* Detroit: Wayne State University Press.

Schmeckebier, L. F. 1971. *Catalogue and Index of the Publications of the Hayden, King, Powell, and Wheeler Surveys.* Washington: GPO, 1904. Reprint, New York: Da Capo Press.

Schmeckebier, L. F., and R. B. Eastin. 1969. *Government Publications and Their Use.* 2d rev. ed. Washington: Brookings Institution.

Schubert, F. N. 1980. "Legacy of Topographical Engineers: Textual and Cartographic Records of Western Exploration, 1819–1860." *Government Publications Review* 7A: 111–16.

Schwartz, J. M. 1996. "Some Major Canadian Collections." *History of Photography* 20: 166–85.

Schwartz, S. I., and R. E. Ehrenberg. 1980. *The Mapping of America.* New York: Abrams.

Sellers, J. R., and P. M. Van Ee. 1981. *Maps and Charts of North America and the West Indies, 1750–1789: A Guide to the Collections in the Library of Congress.* Washington: LC.

Shelley, M. H., comp. 1975. *Ward Maps of United States Cities: A Selective Checklist of Pre-1900 Maps in the Library of Congress.* Washington: LC.

Smith, J. 1975. "Settlement of the Public Domain as Reflected in Federal Records: Suggested Research Approaches." In *Pattern and Process,* ed. R. E. Ehrenberg. Washington: Howard University Press.

Society of American Archivists. 1980. *Directory of Business Archives in the United States and Canada.* Chicago: Society of American Archivists.

Spear, D. N. 1978. *Bibliography of American Directories through 1860.* Worcester, Mass.: American Antiquarian Society, 1961. Reprint, Westport, Conn.: Greenwood Press.

Stephenson, R. W., comp. 1967. *Land Ownership Maps: A Checklist of 19th-Century United States County Maps in the Library of Congress.* Washington: LC.

———. 1989. *Civil War Maps: An Annotated List of Maps and Atlases in the Library of Congress.* Washington: LC.

Taylor, C. E., and R. E. Spurr, comps. 1973. *Aerial Photographs in the National Archives.* Rev. ed. Washington: NARS.

Thompson, M. M. 1981. *Maps for America: The Cartographic Products of the U.S. Geological Survey and Others.* 2d ed. Reston, Va.: U.S. Geological Survey.

Thorndale, W., and W. Dollarhide. 1987. *Map Guide to the U.S. Federal Censuses, 1790–1920.* Baltimore: Genealogical Publishing.

Thrower, N. W. J. 1961. "The County Atlas of the United States." *Surveying and Mapping* 21: 365–73.

U.S. Bureau of the Census. 1909. *A Century of Population Growth from the First Census ... .to the Twelfth, 1790–1900.* Washington: GPO.

———. 1974. *Catalog of Publications, 1790–1972.* Washington: GPO.

———. 1975. *Historical Statistics of the United States, Colonial Times to 1970.* 3d ed. Washington: GPO.

Viola, H. J. 1984. *The National Archives of the United States.* New York: Abrams.

Virga, V., et al. 1997. *Eyes of the Nation: A Visual History of the United States.* New York: Alfred A. Knopf.

Wacker, P. O. 1974. "Historical Geographers, Newspaper Advertisements, and the Bicentennial Celebration." *Professional Geographer* 26: 12–18.

Walsh, M. 1970. "The Census as an Accurate Source of Information: The Value of Mid-19th-Century Manufacturing Returns." *Historical Methods Newsletter* 3: 3–13.

———. 1971. "The Value of Mid-19th-Century Manufacturing Returns: The Printed Census and Manuscript Compilations Compared." *Historical Methods Newsletter* 4: 43–51.

Wells, R. V. 1975. *The Population of the British Colonies in America before 1776: A Survey of Census Data.* Princeton: Princeton University Press.

Wheat, C. I. 1957–63. *Mapping the Trans-Mississippi West, 1540–1861.* 5 vols. San Francisco: Institute of Historical Cartography.

Wimmer, L. T., and C. Pope. 1975. "The Genealogical Society Library of Salt Lake City: A Source of Data for Economic and Social Historians." *Historical Methods Newsletter* 8: 51–88.

Yoshpe, H. P., and P. P. Brower, comps. 1949. *Preliminary Inventory of the Land-Entry Papers of the General Land Office.* Washington: National Archives.

Index

central business district (CBD), 347–48

Chaleur Bay (Newfoundland), 40

Champlain, Samuel de, 41, 69–70

Charlesfort (S.C.), 43, 131

chemical industry, 384

Cherokees, 122, 150

Chesapeake area: Anglo-American colonization of, 102–6; capitals and, 128; counties of, 126; population of, 120; urbanization of, 131

Chicago (Ill.): banking and links of, 343; congestion of, 349; districts of, 348; growth of, 174, 176, 344; South Side ghetto of, 401; urban problems of, 351; wheat farming and, 181

Chickasaws, 85–86

Chinese Exclusion Act, 391

Chinese immigrants, 279, 292, 447, 455

Chrétien, Jean, 445

Christianity: in 18th century, 123; Columbus and, 35; Greenland and, 29; Native Americans and, 95–96, 263. *See also* churches; missions; religion

Chrysler Corporation, 384

churches, 123, 127, 129

Cimarron County (Okla.), 258

cities, Canadian, 445–61: change of, 374; continentalism and, 449–50; convergence view and, 456–59; form of, 459–61; framework for comparison with U.S. cities, 446–49; nationalist view and, 450–53; regionalism and, 453–56

cities, U.S.: city space, transformation of, 343–51; Civil War and, 333; in Far West, 273–75; ghettos and, 298–303, 350, 436, 441; growth of, 173–74; historical geography and, 14–15; immigrants and, 296–98; impact of World War II on, 429–31; industrialization and, 198–203; interwar, 424–29; manufacturing specialization of, 328; mercantile, 197–98; migrants in, 287; population of, *189, 190, 191, 194;* postwar, 431–39; regional differences, 353–54; relationship to suburbs, 401–2; shaping of national city system, 333–43; study of, 13–15; trans-Appalachian, 175; and urbanism, problems of, 351–53

city planning, 345–47, 424, 426

Civilian Conservation Corps (CCC), 396

Civil War (U.S.), 19, 219, 308, 333

Civil Works Administration (CWA), 427

Clark, Andrew H., 7–9

class, 116, 138, 452–53. *See also* society

climate: agricultural specialization and, 312, 317–18; Corn Belt and, 178; cotton and, 176–77; of Dakota, 243; English pioneers and, 93; of Far West, 261–62; of Florida, 404–5; of Great Plains, 237; of trans-Appalachia, 186

coal mining, 320, 340, 366, 384–85

Cochran, Thomas, 204

cod fisheries, 65–67, 78, 213. *See also* fisheries

coke, 327

Collier, John, 26

colonies, American, in 18th century: agriculture and

rural industry in, 131–35; capitalist nature of, 138; ethnicity, race, and religion and, 122–23; independence and, 138; local government of, 126–30; population growth of, 119–22; settlement patterns, 123–26; trade and, 135–38; urbanization, 130–31

colonization: aboriginal landscape, 25–27; America, naming of, 37–38; Atlantic outlook, 31–33; Columbian exchange, 27–28; eastern seaboard exploration, 38–45; exploration theory and, 30–31; New World, disclosure of, 35–37; pre-Columbian contact, 28–30. *See also* Anglo-American colonization; France in North America; Spanish Borderlands

Colorado, 254, 255, 320–21

Columbia Basin (Wash.), 411–12

Columbian exchange, 27–28

Columbian Exchange, The (Crosby), 27

Columbia Plateau, 271

Columbus, Christopher: Columbian exchange and, 27; as explorer, 3, 30; John Cabot and, 38; quincentenary of, 47; western sea route hypothesis of, 32–33; worldview of, 34–35

commerce: Canadian, 373–74; farming patterns and, 172–76; Native American, 211; Northeastern, 191–94; urban networks and, 338–40. *See also* trade

commodity flows, 166

communication: and economic integration, 311–12; telegraph, 192–93; telephones, movies, and radios, 388–90

community, 108, 127, 374

community planning, 424, 440, 449

Company of New France, 72

Condition of Postmodernity, The (Harvey), 467

condominiums, 456

Confederation of New England, 107

congestion, urban, 349, 351–52, 425, 426

Congress (U.S.): first session of, 143; land sales and, 160, 162–63; prejudice and, 279; railroads and, 308

Connecticut, 107–10, 130

conservation, 391–97, 411–12, 418

Constitution (U.S.), 143, 160

Constitution Act (Canada), 221

consumption, mass, 205

Continental America (Meinig), 465

continentalism, 449–50

copper mining, 273

corn: farming areas for, 132; labor and, 184–86; leading states for, *316;* specialization of, 312–13; in trans-Appalachian region, 171; in western Great Plains, 254

Corn Belt: in Great Plains, 255; hybrid corn and, 416; of Indiana and Illinois, 176; rise of, 317; settlement in, 180–84, 186; slavery and, 184–86; of trans-Appalachian region, 178

Corn Laws (Britain), 223